A Toy Train Story

The Remarkable History Of M.T.H. Electric Trains

Jacqueline Chaverini Allen

Research Editor
John Hubbard

Produced And Published By
M.T.H. Electric Trains

Columbia, Maryland

Special thanks to Tony Lash, Lou Caponi, Rudy Paulovich, Frank Rash, and Jack Rash for their assistance in providing samples and information. Most importantly, special thanks goes to all the M.T.H. employees who helped build the company into the force it is today.

ISBN 0-615-11526-8

M.T.H. Electric Trains® is a leading producer of a wide range of tinplate and scale railroad models, for both O and standard gauges. For current catalogs of the firm's products, write to the company's headquarters or visit your nearest hobby shop.

M.T.H. Electric Trains
7020 Columbia Gateway Drive
Columbia, MD 21046-1532
Fax number: 410-381-6122
www.mth-railking.com

A Toy Train Story

The
Remarkable History
Of
M.T.H. Electric Trains

DEDICATION

Doris and Paul Wolf are the sort of people that someone would choose as parents, if that were somehow possible, which is perhaps all that needs to be said about them. To meet them is to admire them and enjoy the occasion.

If it were up to the rest of the employees at M.T.H. Electric Trains, they might ask that the book also be dedicated to all of you who purchase, operate, and enjoy M.T.H. trains, who are vital to the continuing success of their company.

A Toy Train Story

Table of Contents

Chapter I

Chapter II

Chapter III

Chapter IV

Chapter V

Chapter VI

INTRODUCTION

This is a true story . . . a true Toy Train Story about a phenomenally successful model railroading company that in just twenty short years went from a small home-based operation, to become a top competitor in the business. Within these pages unfolds the tale of how a small idea grew into a gigantic operation and a sizeable firm that now employs more than 100 people in the U.S., offers hobbyists more than 2400 products, and claims 800 authorized dealers. This toy train story chronicles how a one-time cottage industry, with humble beginnings and almost no resources, has quickly advanced to the cutting edge because of its use of technology and innovative ideas.

However, A Toy Train Story is also about the youthful individual force who generated the early development of this company, and who today stands strong with a regiment of toy train revolutionaries to energize and direct this thriving organization. This Story intertwines the life and times of the company's founder with the growth and expansion of the firm itself.

This narrative describes the adventures of a young boy who discovered the joy and excitement of model railroading early in his life. This real life drama details how a bright and animated youngster took his love for this hobby and swiftly turned it into a full-time successful career, achieving heights of which he once dreamed. This toy train story is about Mike Wolf and how in a very short time he created M.T.H. Electric Trains® and made it a recognized leader in the model train business today.

As you explore and enjoy the history of M.T.H. as it is presented in the pages of this first edition of A Toy Train Story, you can anticipate the sequels that will follow. This is a true story with no visible conclusion in sight.

So stay tuned as the adventures go on . . . and on . . . and on!

M.T.H.
THE FIRST TWENTY YEARS

I

MTH
N.Y.C
NEW YORK CENTRAL
M.T.H.

THE MAIN YARD

The Headquarters of M.T.H. Electric Trains

As you round the curve on the eastern stretch of tree-lined Columbia Gateway Drive in Columbia, Maryland, your eyes are drawn to a sprawling adobe-red brick structure, which stands out from all the rest of the surrounding contemporary office buildings. The unusual brickwork that runs around the whole top of the edifice distinguishes it. From a distance that brick work looks like railroad tracks. As you draw closer, you discover that the special masonry design does indeed represent a railroad track! A turn into the parking lot of this intriguing building places you on the distinctive doorstep of Mike's Train House, or as it's professionally known in the trade, M.T.H. Electric Trains.

The company logo, which includes an illustration of the Blue Comet Locomotive, is etched into the large window that is prominently displayed above the grand glass portals to M.T.H. Once you pass through this impressive entrance to the headquarters of M.T.H. Electric Trains, you are immediately enveloped by the railroad ambiance permeating the building.

Straight ahead is an imposing reception desk, which looks like an old railroad ticket counter. With its rich, dark-stained wood paneling and its magnificent matching columns, it stands to welcome visitors with the old train station appearance of the past.

Directly above the reception desk is the five-foot round, colorful M.T.H. logo. One look at this prominent insignia, which represents one of America's leaders in the model train industry, assures the visitor that he or she is in a place where professionalism, quality and customer satisfaction are priorities.

To the right is a replica of a Pennsylvania Railroad Club Car that serves as a conference room. To the left is what appears to be the storefront of an old-fashioned hobby shop. It consists of an expansive wall of wood-framed windows with a glass double door entry.

Adorning the windows of the "hobby shop" is an extraordinary sampling of model train locomotives, which are well known to most railroad fans. The muffled sounds of engine whistles and horns emanate from within the "shop." Instinctively, you peer through the framed glass panes to discover what treasures lie beyond the window displays. Then as the open doors beckon you, and you cross the threshold of this magical room, you are instantly transported to an enchanted world of model railroading where the realities of time and place vanish for a while.

In this splendid and very special corner of M.T.H., on any given day you might find a smiling young man in his late thirties who is neatly dressed in casual attire, entrenched at the controls of a most amazing train display. That man is Mike Wolf, the "keeper of the keys," the founder and President of M.T.H. Electric Trains.

Mike often surveys this display of a railroad kingdom, like a benevolent giant towering above a miniature world of mountains, hills and valleys, adorned with diminutive replicas of people from many walks of life. This amazingly life-like model railroad demonstrates incredible attention to details, like several species from the animal world; a variety of industrial, urban, and agricultural structures; a few criss-crossing highways and byways; and of course, an extensive network of train tracks with switches and crossings for freight and passenger locomotives. The 15 ½ feet by 15 ½ feet platform sprawled before Mike reveals an authentic scene of Americana. With six trains running simultaneously, Mike only needs to touch a button or move the transformer control to direct his empire as he wishes.

However, glass, bricks, mortar, and model railroad layouts are not the reality of M.T.H. Electric Trains. What is not immediately seen by the casual visitor upon first crossing the threshold of M.T.H. Electric Trains, is the dynamic organization - the talented and dedicated M.T.H. staff, currently numbering more than one hundred. Most visitors never get to observe the vigorous activity of the expanding workforce, led by a core group of exceptional management executives, many of whom are long-time friends and associates of Mike Wolf. Together the organization has labored to raise M.T.H. to a level of excellence rivaled by few in this industry.

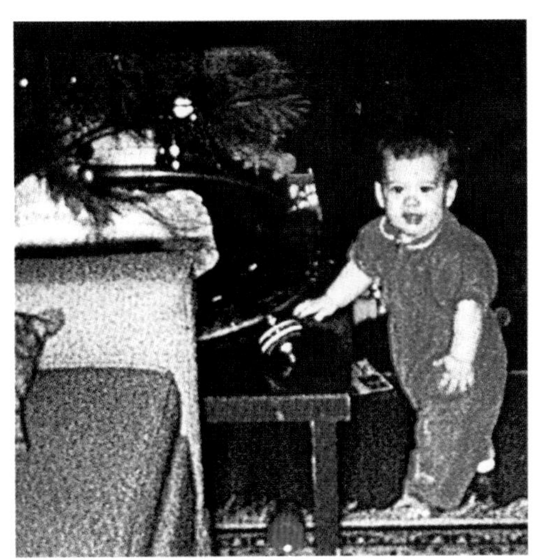

Owner Mike Wolf at age 1.

How did it come to this? How did Mike's Train House become M.T.H. Electric Trains, a more than $50 million a year company that manufactures and distributes the highest quality and most diverse model railroad products in the trade? How did it all start?

Perhaps M.T.H. was born some 39 years ago in the mind of Mike Wolf, the small child whose subconscious vision of a future M.T.H. may have been captured for a brief moment in one Christmas photograph. In that photo, Mike gleefully gazes at the chugging train that encircles the family Christmas tree. You can see the sparkle in his eyes. You can almost hear the uninhibited chuckle, and the clapping little hands. That photo may well have been a telling look into the future of Mike Wolf, now the owner and President of M.T.H. Electric Trains.

As you turn the pages, and read this toy train story, you will take a ride on the fast track of M.T.H.'s history to-date. You will discover how Mike Wolf turned what started out as Mike's Train House (often referred to as M.T.H. and literally run out of Mike's home when it first started), into the thriving entrepreneurial entity now recognized as M.T.H. Electric Trains.

You will also see that there is new track being laid ahead, for M.T.H. still has many miles to travel. And for those model railroaders who hop aboard the M.T.H. Express there are many more exciting adventures just around the next curve.

TRACK PLANNING FOR M.T.H. ELECTRIC TRAINS

The Emerging Entrepreneurial Spirit

While the seeds of model railroading were subconsciously rooted in the mind of the young Mike Wolf, it was his developing interest in entrepreneurial ventures that was the driving force behind his current phenomenal success. From a very early age, Mike was a hard working young man with business savvy. Almost from the beginning, he cultivated a business philosophy based on hard work and making something that the buying public really wants or needs, but offering it to customers better and cheaper than competitors.

The young Mike Wolf frequently sought out opportunities to earn his own income. Like most young kids, Mike set up Kool-Aid Stands, and sponsored yard sales where he and his friends could cash in on some of their old toys that had lost their fancy. Then at the tender age of ten, Mike took some preliminary steps toward becoming a movie mogul. He scripted an "Evil Knievel" type movie titled "Daring Motorcycle Feats." He then cast a friend who was skilled in performing some stunts on his Yamaha in the starring role of a dazzling motor bike dare-devil. He used an 8-mm movie camera to film. When production on the film was completed, Mike first tried to get

Yamaha to buy it for use as a promotional tool. Not surprisingly, Yamaha rejected Mike's offer, stating that the company did not want to encourage the use of their bikes for such dangerous stunts.

So Mike created a small movie theater, promoted the film to neighborhood kids, and then charged admission to the excited crowds who came to see the movie. His movie patrons were thrilled. He offered his movie-going customers good entertainment at a cheaper price than the local movie theaters charged. For all intents and purposes, this miniscule, but rather significant, neighborhood business venture was a grand childhood success for Mike Wolf.

In February 1973 when Mike was twelve, he took another turn in the road of entrepreneurial adventure, which would ultimately lead him to the secret of his own success. Mike entered the world of model train building.

The original home of Williams Electric Trains 1973.

TRAINING WITH WILLIAMS REPRODUCTIONS LIMITED

Learning the Toy Train Business

In Mike Wolf's neighborhood in Howard County, Maryland, there was a man named Jerry Williams who turned his hobby of collecting toy trains into a business of manufacturing toy trains. In 1970, Jerry Williams established Williams Reproductions Limited in the basement of his home, where he employed a toy train assembly staff, which consisted of some neighborhood teenagers and eventually some women who lived in the area. Jeff Strank (now a Vice President at M.T.H.), who was a good friend of Mike Wolf's, worked for Williams Reproductions, and he recruited Mike to work for them also.

When Mike began his employment at Williams Reproductions, he spent almost every Saturday working with other recruited school friends who assembled sheet-metal trains. They sat at long tables in Jerry Williams' basement and diligently constructed the reproductions of trains already on the market, which were more expensive than the ones being produced by Williams Reproductions.

Mike's first job at Williams was assembling latch couplers for reproductions of prewar Lionel trains. This involved positioning the coupler shank, latch, and rivet properly, then flattening the rivet with a hammer, then doing the same thing again and again and again. It was tedious work, but there was plenty of idle banter among the group of young workers to make it interesting. Within a few years, some of the assemblers were girls, and in the teen-age years it was a pretty big deal to work side by side with those of the opposite sex! Lunch often became a social event. At least it was as much of a social event as many teenagers of that time experienced. Regardless, having the girls working there made the repetitive work endurable for Mike and his buddies.

If the Williams workers' accumulated hourly wages earned came to $17.50, Jerry paid them $20.00. If they had worked enough hours to earn $18.50 he still paid them $20.00. Although they were good workers, they did learn how to use this to their advantage, working just enough hours to get the extra pay.

The pay was $1.50 per hour, which at that time was fifteen cents over the minimum wage. The assemblers all had official time cards to record the hours they worked. However, there was a very special added benefit in working for Williams Reproductions: Jerry usually added something extra to the paychecks. For those kids, that little extra became a real incentive bonus.

Mike and the others really savored the financial freedom they now enjoyed because of their employment at Williams Reproductions. The newly acquired ability to go out and buy things with their train pay was great! Furthermore, these kids were earning enough money to make some pretty significant purchases. For example, Mike was excited because he was able to buy a brand new radio for his room. Jeff purchased a bike that he had wanted for some time.

The whole idea of working hard certainly proved to have its rewards. The rewards were enticing enough to be something Mike wanted to keep earning. Obviously Mike developed a strong work ethic at a young age, and it became the foundation and strength for building M.T.H. Electric Trains.

These youthful employees of Williams Reproductions Limited often worked extended hours because there were always tight production schedules to meet. Most of these youngsters (Mike included) did not get to participate much in team sports, and a lot of the other fun things that kids that age enjoy. However, they are the first to admit they made a conscious decision to do this because they really liked having a job and earning money, and a few like Mike wanted to learn more about the business of model railroading.

Jeff Strank Vice President of Product Support

MINI-BIO: JEFF STRANK

Jeff Strank has been friends with Mike Wolf since they were young boys. Like Mike, Jeff graduated from Atholton High School. Jeff started with Williams even before Mike, back in 1972, when the pay was only $1.35 per hour. His first job was assembling brass pantographs for No. 9 locomotives. He worked for Williams Reproductions from 1972 until 1983.

Jeff graduated from the University of Maryland, College Park in 1983, with a degree in Chemical Engineering. He then accepted a job with Lockheed-Martin, where he was responsible for advance manufacturing technology, materials engineering and process development for thrust reversers used on commercial jet aircraft. Jeff's last assignment at Lockheed-Martin included a one-year stay in Thailand as a technical field representative.

Jeff always maintained contact with Mike Wolf. In fact, he even helped him sell train parts at the York TCA meet nearly every year, although he was employed elsewhere. In 1996 Mike asked him to join M.T.H. Electric Trains, and Jeff is now Vice President of Product Support, responsible for the Service and Parts Departments. He also assumes responsibility for special projects as they arise.

Mike worked many evenings during the school week, and as a result his schoolwork, which was not one of his favorite things to do, began to slip. Mike's Dad was legitimately concerned, and he presented his son with an ultimatum: "The schoolwork must improve, Mike, or you will have to stop working for Williams!" Mike knew he had to find a way to get his schoolwork done because he really did not want to give up his job at Williams Reproductions. Mike thought about his different school subjects. He was doing fine in math, primarily because he liked it, and he was good at it. He wasn't too worried about most of his other subjects because he had invested just enough energy and time into most of them to get his work done, and to get passing grades. However, his English was threatening to do him in! He didn't see the value of it as a youngster, and he really did not like it, but he realized he was going to have to do something to make it better.

Mike painfully spelled out his dilemma to his boss, Jerry Williams, whose immediate concern was losing a really good employee. Jerry quickly devised a plan for solving the schoolwork problem. After a quick consultation with his wife, Sally, he told Mike not to worry. It seems Sally was an English "whiz," and as she was always willing to help out with her husband's business, she agreed to become Mike's personal English tutor. Sally worked diligently with Mike to try to help him with his learning, but she soon realized that Mike wasn't slipping because he could not do the work. The truth was that Mike hated English and he just did not want to do the work! Mike's mind was on train work, not schoolwork! He was concerned about production schedules, assembling trains and earning money, not about writing short stories, understanding grammar, and reading classic literature!

Before long, Sally found that she wasn't doing much teaching of English. Instead, she was pushing and pulling Mike along just to get through his assignments. Perhaps giving away the answers and sometimes dictating the short story lines, and occasionally almost writing the paragraphs herself is a more accurate account of how Sally helped Mike. The bottom line was that she did not want Williams Reproductions to lose one of their best employees, and she also did not want Mike to have problems in school, so she did everything she possibly could to get Mike's English assignments completed.

The results of this surreptitious approach to the study of English were remarkable. According to school records Mike's homework improved so much and so rapidly that he was transferred to an Honors class. Although Mike's in-class tests remained a problem, he was able to do well enough to bring his grades up to a level that was acceptable to his Dad. That was what really mattered to Mike at the time!

In the grand scheme of things, it turned out just fine for everyone. Jerry Williams was pleased, because one of his hardest workers could continue to work the many hours needed per week to meet production schedules. Mike's teacher was probably pleased, believing that one of her young students had suddenly experienced a miraculous burst of motivational energy to do better in her English Class. Mike's father was pleased to know that his son took him seriously, and that he actually listened to what his Dad said. Sally Williams must have been pleased to a certain extent. Her dedicated attempts to tutor Mike played a part in keeping her husband's business on the road to success. However, it's pretty certain that she would have preferred a little more genuine teaching of English. Of course, Mike was the most pleased of all because he did not have to give up his job at Williams Reproductions. In addition, he was eagerly learning about a fascinating business from the ground up, and he was formulating ways to increase his earning power.

Although Mike and many of the other Williams workers did not have much time for organized sports or other extra-curricular activities, Mike did wrestle while he was in school. He credits wrestling with teaching him discipline and commitment and thanks his coaches, Ed Boxwell and Earl Lauer, for helping him to learn these important lessons.

Despite Mike's tremendous success in the model railroad industry, he realizes that his writing skills are not one of his strengths, and obviously that has to do with the way he got around English. Furthermore, he strongly encourages youngsters to learn as much as they can, as best they can, while they can!

In 1978, when Mike graduated from Atholton High School, in Columbia, Maryland, he was making $7.50 per hour working at Williams Reproductions. Although he had not received a salary increase in three years, Mike really looked forward to going to his job each day because he thrived in the entrepreneurial environment of Williams Reproductions. Mike was like a sponge soaking up experience and collecting knowledge of the whole model train industry because he knew that one day he would be doing this on his own.

At seventeen, Mike began to formulate his plans for a career, and going to college was not originally a part of Mike's plan. By that time, Mike really did know a lot about the manufacture and sale of model trains, and he knew he could earn some decent money in this business. If he had gotten his way, he would not have continued his formal education. However, Mike's parents strongly believed in the importance of getting a college education, and Mike respected their authority.

Because he wanted to please his parents, and because he valued his father's guidance, Mike enrolled at the University of Maryland. He also continued to work his job at Williams Reproductions. Unfortunately, Mike registered for too many credit hours at Maryland. Between attending classes, trying to get class assignments done, and traveling back and forth between the Maryland campus and Williams Reproductions in Columbia, Mike was overwhelmed. Naturally something had to give. Not surprisingly, his academic standing went into a tailspin, and he failed one course and wound up with a D in two others.

Both Mike and his folks recognized that this wasn't going to work. Something had to change. So Mike left the University of Maryland and enrolled at Howard Community College, which is conveniently located close to Mike's home and Williams Reproductions. The reduction in travel between school, work, and home was significant. Plus, this time Mike carried a manageable load of coursework. After two years Mike graduated with an AA degree in Marketing and Personnel Management. His academic standing was good enough to permit him to transfer to Towson State University in Baltimore, where he majored in Business Administration.

Throughout Mike's college years, he took on more and more responsibilities at Williams Reproductions. Soon he was second in command, as the assembly foreman. Mike's responsibilities also included managing shipping operations, serving as the chief repairman, and getting everything else done that he was given to do. It was a lot for one person, but Mike did it well because he wanted every opportunity to gain more knowledge and experience. Mike was grooming himself for the day when he could go out on his own.

SCRATCHBUILDING THE INITIAL STATION

Opening the Doors to Mike's House of Trains

That day got a little closer when in July 1980 he started his own model train business, Mike's Train House. (Mike was still a full time employee of Williams Reproductions, Ltd. He set up his own business as a sideline/night time venture.) This was truly an appropriate name for the business because Mike ran his operation for selling Williams' Trains, directly out of his own home. With all of the merchandise Mike stored in his home, it often felt to those who lived there, like it was, in fact, "Mike's House of Trains."

Mike kept quite a bit of stock at home. His second floor bedroom took on the characteristics of a warehouse filled to the brim with trains. Mike's father was rightfully concerned about the 2400 pound load straining the floor of Mike's room. (The stock items consisted mostly of rugged and heavy die-cast GG-1 locomotives.) So the Senior Wolf worked some quick math and calculated, with a sigh of relief, that the extra and unusual load would not do permanent damage to the house. Obviously he was correct, for the structure still stands soundly today.

Almost from the moment Mike ventured out on his own sideline business, he was in tune with model railroaders' desire for variety. As a result, Mike began offering custom painted versions of various Williams products, specializing in sets of passenger cars. The customized paint work was done by Lenny Carparelli, who used his parents' basement as a workshop.

One popular product was a set of Southern Railway coaches painted green and white, with a matching Trainmaster locomotive. The

The original home of "Mike's Train House".

cars were decorated with a plastic strip that was painted white. All of the painting on the cars was of acceptable quality except for that paint on the plastic strips, which showed a tendency to flake or peel off. Mike sold five sets of the cars and locomotives to Lou Caponi, a well-known tinplate train dealer in Homes, Pennsylvania. Shortly after this sale, when Mike and Lou attended the same train show, Lou came up to Mike and put his strong heavy arm around Mike's shoulders and in a deep voice he slowly told him, "Mike . . . we have a problem . . . the paint on the stripes of the cars you sold me . . . is coming off!"

Lou showed Mike the cars with the peeling stripes and Mike was obviously embarrassed. It was critically important for him to build a good reputation in this business as he was starting out if his dreams of success were to be realized. He knew he had to come up with a quick plan of restitution for this important model train dealer. Fortunately Mike had enough cash in his pocket to offer to buy back the defective cars from Mr. Caponi. The dealer appreciated Mike's fast response and he decided to keep the locomotives that were a part of the original sale. This embarrassing incident was a crucial lesson that Mike has never forgotten.

Furthermore, the way Mike handled the problem with Lou Caponi resulted in Mike gaining a relationship with the dealer that proved quite valuable. This was especially true in 1984, when Mike was planning to reproduce Lionel's 214R refrigerator car. At that time, Mike bought a disassembled car at a Cherry Hill, NJ, train meet for $1,500 to use as a toolmaker's sample. A man from nearby Philadelphia who was also at the meet and knew of Mike's intentions, approached him, claiming that he knew an Italian firm that would quote a good price to make the car. Mike took the man's name, address and phone number and then trustingly gave him the car parts.

Months passed with little word from "the man from Philadelphia." Mike phoned him repeatedly, but there was not even a hint of progress. To make matters worse, when Mike requested that the parts be returned, the man totally ignored him. Mike was very concerned that he was "out" the $1500 investment he made, plus who knew whether or not this guy had run off with the materials to make his own reproduction!

One day when Mike was talking to Lou Caponi he mentioned what had happened. Lou was upset to hear that this person had done this to Mike. He offered to see if he could help resolve this problem, and Mike agreed appreciatively. Lou is a man of great stature with an impressive demeanor, that can cause someone to sit up and take notice if Lou so desires! Initially, Lou used the phone to contact the man. When he finally made contact he calmly stated, "You stole a model railroad car from Mike Wolf. Return it or I'm coming over to see you." Unfortunately, the Philadelphian did not take this warning seriously. So Lou decided he needed to see the guy in person to make his point. Armed with the address from Mike's original encounter with this fellow, Lou drove to the man's house in the dark of night. The man was not at home when Lou arrived, so he quietly parked in front of the house and patiently waited for the man from Philadelphia to show up.

The man did finally appear, and as soon as he saw him, Lou got out of his car, told him who he was and in no uncertain terms, what he wanted. Definitely surprised and perhaps a little frightened by Lou's size and confrontational approach, the man asked no questions. He immediately opened the trunk of his car and turned the car parts over to Lou Caponi. Lou quickly sent the $1500 worth of parts back to Mike who was very grateful for `Big Lou' Caponi's intervention. Mike later sent the car parts to Samhongsa, the Korean contractor who eventually manufactured them for M.T.H.

Originally, Mike's conservative parents did not encourage him to go into business for himself. Mike's Mom tried to point out how difficult running your own business can be. She emphasized how much more important good health and a solid family life are. However, Mike believed he could enjoy good health and eventually his own family, despite the hard work required to have a successful model train business.

Before long, Mike went on to become one of Williams' biggest and most successful dealers. In spite of their initial reservations, Mike's parents were fully behind him by then, and they have remained very strong supporters of his chosen career. Whether by deliberate choice or the total lack thereof (based on the fact that Mike ran his business directly out of the family home), Mike's parents, Doris and Paul Wolf, provided positive reinforcement as Mike's fledgling business developed tractive force. In truth, they actually provided some fuel power by helping Mike when he needed it. In 1983, Paul Wolf made a strategic loan to his son, which enabled Mike to enter into the actual business of model train manufacturing.

Doris Wolf was also a big help to Mike's business, particularly in the mid-1980s when she diligently covered the phones, assembled cars, and helped out with mailing and United Parcel Service (UPS) deliveries. Although at that time she didn't quite understand the driving force behind Mike's determination to be a successful entrepreneur, she was willing to do whatever she could to help him realize his dreams.

At that time, Mike's dreams were nearly single-focused and fitting for that point of his life. He knew full well from accumulated experience that if he worked hard and smart he could earn a fairly lucrative income in the model railroading industry. He also wanted his folks to understand that he did not intend to become obsessed with his model train business. Mike wanted his parents to see that this business was not going to control his life at the expense of his health and well-being. So he tried to convince his folks that he only wanted to work as hard as necessary to become economically independent enough to afford a season ticket to see his all-time favorite professional football team, the Miami Dolphins . . . and of course attend every home game!

Mike's mail order business quickly increased to the point where there were daily UPS pickups at his house for the packaged trains ordered by model railroad enthusiasts. Making sure that someone was there for the UPS pickups soon became a problem, because at that time Mike worked with a skeleton crew, and there were just so many things each of them could do. Not surprisingly, Mike devised an inventive plan that eliminated the need for anyone to be present when UPS made its pickups. He presented his plan to the UPS driver and before long the procedure became routine.

Every evening, Mike and his meager staff would package and address all the model train shipments that were ready to go out that day. Then they would load them carefully into an unlocked, battered 1965 red Ford Falcon that was always parked at the same spot in front of his parents' home. Then to indicate that there was in fact a shipment for pickup, Mike would knot a big red rag high up on the antenna of the car as a secret signal to the driver to pick up his parcels for that day. This was a rather trusting scheme that probably would not work as well today. Considering the value of model train products and the potential for some conniving thief to catch on to the scheme, there might be many shipments that just disappeared! Still and all, the system worked for quite a while, and Mike was able to build his business without the expense of hiring additional employees.

THE CONSIST BEGINS TO GROW

Putting the Parts Together

It's well known among railroaders and model train fans alike that there is much more to the train experience than meets the eye. The beauty and performance power of a classic locomotive and its trailing consist come about only as the result of careful design and construction. Every part used to create a rugged locomotive and its freight or passenger cars is essential. In fact, a train cannot run without all of its working components, and railroaders always need replacement parts!

Mike Wolf was fortunate enough to have a pointed learning experience in the replacement parts trade early in his developing model railroad career. In the fall of 1975, Jerry Williams began taking Mike to the twice annual TCA (Train Collectors Association) York Train Show in Pennsylvania, to give him some help in greeting customers while manning the Williams Reproductions model train booth, and setting out train replacement parts to sell. Jerry needed enough free time to talk to his existing and valued train customers, and to build relationships with new ones. The largest train show in the world provided the best opportunity for Mike to learn a great deal about this business, and he was happy to be able to attend for the years he did so with Williams.

In 1977, to provide some incentive for Mike, Jerry offered for the first time to pay him ten percent of whatever he sold at the big show. What happened was incredible and probably another one of those signs of what Mike's future was going to be in the model train business. Jerry Williams had recently expanded his product line, and thus had a much wider assortment of replacement/repair parts available at the York Train Meet. Train collectors soon spotted the new, formerly unavailable parts for sale. Once the word was out, a long line of customers started to form. Although the faces in the line changed, the line itself remained long throughout the meet.

Mike Wolf was selling replacement parts for tinplate reproductions almost faster than he could collect the money from the happy model railroaders. When it was all said and done, the seventeen-year old Mike Wolf was exhausted but thrilled with his new-found success. Furthermore, he knew once he totaled the amount of sales he had on replacement parts, that the number was going to be big! With a ten percent commission promised to him by Jerry Williams, he could hardly contain his excitement. In the final analysis, Mike sold $150,000 worth of parts in those two days, and earned a cool fifteen thousand dollars! The budding entrepreneur was on his way to developing into a full-fledged winner in the model railroad industry.

Jerry Williams eventually reduced Mike's commission to five percent of the total sold, and the backlog of demand for many tinplate parts soon dissipated, so there were no repeat windfalls for Mike. Still, his long-time involvement in the tinplate parts business provided him with many valuable business contacts and names of prospective M.T.H. customers. It also gave Mike some additional ongoing income, which he could use to increase his inventory of Williams trains for Mike's Train House to sell.

Perhaps the most crucial thing Mike learned from his high stakes experience at the York Train Meet was that replacement parts in model railroading are very important. Train parts obviously do not last forever. Whether it is a model railroad, or the main line of a major railroad company, train parts wear out and break down. The replacement parts aspect of railroading is critical.

As a result of this lesson, when Jerry Williams was ready to sell his replacement parts business, Mike moved quickly to buy it. This was in 1982, and Mike had just graduated from Towson State University with a degree in Business Administration. Mike's formal education, along with the fact that he had been selling the Williams Reproductions replacement parts at train shows for over seven years, helped to shape him into an astute businessman who knew he needed to expand his capabilities. The timing was perfect to do just that. Mike worked out a contract whereby he purchased the inventory and the rights to use Williams tooling and dies. This cost Mike $40,000, which was paid over one year. Ultimately, Mike purchased the tooling outright.

In twenty short years Mike Wolf has helped reshape the face of model railroading.

INCREASING TRACTIVE FORCE FOR M.T.H.

Moving M.T.H. up the Grade

Early in 1983 Jerry Williams grew weary of the intense pace of running his toy train business. At that time he also was getting involved in real estate development, and he needed cash to pursue this venture. These two issues, along with his belief that the market for reproductions of standard gauge trains was fairly well exhausted, led him to decide to sell all of his standard gauge tooling. The tooling equipment included the stamping dies and tools accumulated by Williams from 1970 through 1983.

When Mike realized Jerry Williams was going to sell all of this equipment, he immediately recognized an opportunity to further increase the size and strength of his own business by purchasing it. Mike knew almost from the beginning of his involvement in the model train business that providing customers with a variety of products was essential for success. He also knew that a model train manufacturer couldn't provide customers with variety without having substantial tooling. Mike Wolf has always believed it is necessary to invest in needed tooling to meet customer demands. In addition, Mike had a different vision of the model railroad business, and he believed there was still a solid demand for reproductions of these toy trains. Besides, Mike had always treasured the standard gauge trains from the twenties and thirties, and he was determined to see their continued availability on the market.

There was one hurdle to get over before Mike could buy the tooling equipment from Jerry Williams: a pretty big investment of cash, of which Mike only had a portion. Because Jerry Williams knew that Mike did not have the immediate means to buy all of the tooling equipment, he was reluctant at first to make a deal with him. To complicate things further, Jerry Williams had another person interested in buying the equipment. Jerry suggested Mike talk to this other person and explore the possibility of some kind of partnership purchase of the tooling equipment. Mike followed the suggestion but soon discovered that this other potential buyer was not interested in a partnership. He worked alone and he intended to buy the equipment by himself. This did not deter Mike, who knew he would purchase the tooling equipment one way or another, but he had to move fast; the other buyer had the money and wanted to make the purchase right then. Williams knew how badly Mike wanted to buy the equipment. Even though Jerry needed the money quickly to get on with his real estate development project, he waited for Mike to come up with it. Mike is very grateful to Jerry Williams for doing this.

This simple black and white presentation represented the first M.T.H. catalog in 1983.

As it turned out, Mike's Father came to his rescue. Paul Wolf had already recognized that his son was going to be a successful businessman. His hard work and determination to succeed were evident in everything he did concerning his interests in model railroading. Knowing this and having complete trust in Mike's judgment, Paul Wolf took a gigantic leap of faith. He withdrew the entire contents of his retirement savings fund and gave it to Mike to purchase the tooling equipment. This sum, along with Mike's own cash, provided the necessary down payment of $50,000. Mike was counting on paying Jerry the unpaid balance of $100,000 out of income generated by selling products made from the tooling.

Mike learned early in his model railroading career that many model railroad products are sold through catalog presentation. Sometimes that is all potential customers have to go on when they are deciding whether or not they want to make a purchase. There was only one minor problem. Mike had a very limited budget for advertising. He could not afford to produce what he wanted at that time. So he did the best he could. He published a black and white brochure with photos of his products, shot by a professional photographer in Baltimore.

Mike's first brochure advertised a production run of 125 each of the No. 9, No. 381, and No. 408 locomotives, and one thousand transmission towers. The locomotives were painted to match the Lionel colors for these engines, which were made in the 1930s. Mike knew through instinct and experience that these items were popular in the toy train community. Furthermore, these were some of Mike's favorite pieces and his enthusiasm would help to sell everything. Mike also chose these particular items because he calculated that if he sold them, these products would generate enough cash for him to pay off his debts for the tooling equipment.

MINI-BIO: MARK HIPP

M.T.H.'s Second in command Vice President Mark Hipp.

Mark Hipp graduated from Atholton High in 1979, where he and Mike first became good friends. Unlike Mike and some of his other friends, Mark only got involved with the model train business after he finished high school. It was then that he started working with Williams Reproductions. Mark was affiliated with Williams from 1979-1982. From 1983 to 1987, Mark was under subcontract to M.T.H. to do spray painting for their train parts.

Mark graduated from Howard Community College in 1982, with a degree in Electronics Technology. He became a full-time employee at M.T.H. in 1990, when he became a project manager for M.T.H.'s Lionel Classics products. Mark is now the Vice President of Production at M.T.H. Electric Trains.

Mike Wolf has always viewed Mark as an exceptionally hard-working and valuable team member, and this was Mike's perception long before Mark married Barbara Wolf, Mike's sister. Mark and Barbara have three children, Vincent, Chelsey and David.

He distributed this brochure to potential customers he met when he attended the thirty-plus train shows held on the weekends throughout the year. The way Mike tells the story, it was his continual presence and ability to sell the products in hand at the shows he attended that resulted in his sales success then. The brochure was a necessary detail but it wasn't what sold his products.

It was July 1983 when Mike started to receive shipments from Minnesota of sheet metal parts that had been produced on the newly purchased tooling equipment. When the raw parts arrived in boxes, Mike would transport them to a local plater in Baltimore where a military-specified primer would be applied before they were painted. In addition, some of the parts needed some sub-assembly and others needed to be nickel-plated. As more and more parts began arriving from Minnesota, Mike had to inventory and store them. "Where was this storage going to be?" was the next logical question. Of course the answer was obvious! Mike stored them at home along with everything else that was a part of his growing business in the world of model trains. Mike's Train House was beginning to bulge at the seams.

Hipp Enterprises had an excellent reputation for doing high quality work. Mark developed this outstanding reputation by striving for zero defects in all the work he performed, and in delivering finished products to customers on time. However, this was not always an easy thing to accomplish.

For example, in 1991 Mark received a sample body of a Lackawanna MU car from Samhongsa, the manufacturer in Korea, just two days before Lionel Trains needed a painted sample of it for the Toy Fair. Mark was responsible for the spray painting, but when he finished the job, he decided to repaint some details on the roof, because he was not quite satisfied with the car's appearance. He applied the paint, and was speeding the drying with a heat gun, when he was called away to the telephone. Because he was in a hurry, he forgot to redirect the heat away from the plastic car body, and by the time he returned, the work was ruined. Mark immediately made an emergency call to Samhongsa in Korea and requested another MU car. Samhongsa shipped off another one by priority air freight, and Mark was able to deliver the Lackawanna MU car to the Toy Fair just in time.

The next issue Mike needed to address was getting the sheet metal parts painted. He contracted for the painting with Mark Hipp, a high school friend who owned Hipp Enterprises. Mark was someone he knew well, and someone he knew would give him the quality and production effort he required. Furthermore, Mark had experience painting model trains because Hipp Enterprises was already under contract to do similar work for Williams reproductions. Mark Hipp did all the spray painting in the garage of his parents' home. In fact, he had quite an area in which to work because his father had just built a new three-car garage, which he willingly gave up so that Mark could have the space for Hipp Enterprises spray painting operation.

The engines and other items were assembled in the basement of Mike Wolf's parents' home. Clearly this would have been much harder to do without the cooperation and support of Mike's parents. Their willingness to sacrifice the routine of daily living within the family household was essential to getting Mike's business off the ground, without Mike incurring the national debt in start-up costs.

In the fall of 1983, Mike gathered up his newly produced brochures and headed off to a train meet in Pikesville, Maryland. This meet was sponsored by the TCA, and Mike felt this was a good time and place to start testing the market. Mike was apprehensive. He was acutely aware that he had invested the entirety of his own very small private fortune, as well as his Mom and Dad's retirement future into a venture of somewhat uncertain outcome. What would happen if he could not sell his model train products? This was a major risk! Nonetheless, Mike went forward and in his own words, "I did a lot of praying." Mike's praying and his strong faith are what sustained him through these very stressful times, and as he says, "I and my business are truly blessed . . . M.T.H. belongs to God. There's no way I would have all of this without Him!"

When Mike finally trekked off to the meet in Pikesville he had tempered his anxiety and fear with a degree of excitement and some positive expectations. These feelings were soon intensified because Mike sold the first products of Mike's Train House. Mike's customers came from all walks of life. There were many professionals - doctors, lawyers, etc. - and there were many everyday, hard working folks. The one thing that can be said about all of the customers was that every single one had a passion for this hobby of model railroading and toy trains.

Mike did sell everything he intended to, but in the final analysis he was left with no money! Between payments to Jerry Williams and his Dad and the cost of printing his brochure, his pockets were empty. However, he would soon be free of debt and that fueled his energy for moving forward.

Mike was able to deliver all of the engines and cars ordered by his customers within four to six months. Moreover, he discovered that customers wanted other products for which he now had the tooling. He soon began to re-run the tooling equipment in Minnesota for the 418/428 passenger cars to go with the engines sold. The sales made at the meet in Pikesville, along with all of Mike's efforts to that point, made it possible for him to finish repaying his father's generous and timely loan. Then even though he was still a little worried, he started to develop new ideas on how to expand his model railroad business venture.

Perhaps in the annals of history, the biographies of most entrepreneurs reveal the same type of anxiety and fear that Mike felt as he actually took the big plunge at the TCA Meet in 1983. However, these negative feelings eventually gave way to optimism and a visionary approach to the future, because to make a dream come true it takes confidence, belief in the dream, determination and often times, a lot of guts just to plow ahead. Undoubtedly Mike Wolf is blessed with all of those traits, and with an outstanding business intuition!

Mike cherishes the memory of his very first customer who bought an M.T.H. locomotive. The purchase took place during the fall 1983 train meet, in Pikesville, Maryland, when Bill Hanson, a TCA Member, told Mike that he wanted to order one of the No. 9 locomotives offered. Young Mike responded with near-disbelief. "Really? You really want to buy one? You realize you have to pay for it in advance? You understand they're not built yet?"

"Yes, I understand that," said Mr. Hanson. With that response, Mr. Hanson became the first purchaser of an M.T.H. locomotive, and Mike has always remembered him with gratitude. In fact, often when Mike got to see Mr. Hanson and then introduce him to other folks, he would say proudly, "This is Bill Hanson, my very first M.T.H. customer!" (Regrettably, Mr. Hanson has since passed away.)

KITBASHING

Building the Business Mike's Way

Mike Wolf had his own ideas about how he wanted to build his business almost from the very beginning. As stated earlier, these ideas were not always fully understood by the folks around him who were his strongest supporters, but they trusted his judgment based on what he had accomplished so far. Who could really challenge his ongoing enthusiasm!

Many of Mike's most successful ventures were achieved by determining what toy train products were not on the market, but were on the wish lists of the majority of hobbyists. Then Mike would make plans to produce those items, knowing there was a strong market for them. For example, one day in 1985 when Mike was at a train meet, he purchased a black Lionel 400 E locomotive with brass trim for $1,500. The engine was an original collector's piece made in the 1930s. Mike brought the 400E home and carefully placed it on the mantelpiece in the living room. Because the paint on the engine was chipped and it showed other major signs of wear and tear, Mike's Mom was not thrilled to see it displayed on her mantel. She was further dismayed when she found out that Mike paid fifteen hundred dollars for it. She asked, "Why, is that ugly old dilapidated engine on our beautiful mantel, Mike, and why did you pay so much for it?" He replied, "Mom, you can not see it just yet, but one day that locomotive will make me rich!"

The 400E locomotive was such a significant engine because it was the largest and most desirable piece that Lionel had ever produced. However, many hobbyists could not afford to pay fifteen hundred dollars for a collector's original, which could not even be operated because running them on tracks supposedly decreases the value. Purchasing a reproduction of this engine was impossible because no train manufacturers, including

Mike's second catalog promoting the 400E is symbolic of the many firsts in the model train industry.

Williams, were making it. Mike's plans to reproduce it with every detail exactly the same as the original would give the buying public an engine that, because it was a reproduction, could be operated on a layout. This whole project had the potential for being very successful not only because this engine was in demand, but also because there would be a substantial after-market parts business.

Yet Mike had to take a big risk. The tooling investment required was very high because the engine was going to be built with a die-cast frame, exactly like the original locomotive made back in the 1930s. Producing die-cast products requires some very expensive tooling equipment. To manage a decent return on the investment, there must be a substantial number of products produced and sold.

Nevertheless, the project got underway. Before long, that 400 E locomotive was indeed one of the key items that helped to raise Mike's model train career to the next level of success and became the main part of the M.T.H. logo.

In 1985, while working at Williams Reproductions, Mike Wolf had the opportunity to make a key contact with a man by the name of Mr. Se Yong Lee, who represented Samhongsa Company, Ltd., a Korean model train manufacturer. Mr. Lee had scheduled a visit to Williams Reproductions, which was intended to develop a working relationship with Jerry Williams and his train company. Williams Reproductions was using another Korean manufacturer at that time, and Mr. Lee wanted to see if he could convince Jerry Williams to give his company a try. Jerry confided in Mike that he was going to meet with Mr. Lee and listen to what he had to say, but that he (Jerry) had already made up his mind that he was not going to start doing business with Samhongsa. Mike then asked Jerry Williams if he would mind if he talked to Mr. Lee about getting Samhongsa to build trains for him. Jerry Williams told Mike that it was fine to go ahead with that, and so Mike did. Jerry Williams felt no threat of competition from Mike because of an agreement which Mike and Jerry established while Mike still worked for Williams. As long as Mike continued in Jerry Williams's employ, Mike could build standard gauge trains on his own, but he worked for Williams Reproductions in the "O" gauge market.

Mike met Mr. Lee briefly on his visit to Williams. He explained what he was looking for in an overseas supplier of standard gauge trains for M.T.H. Then he gave Mr. Lee his card and told him he would be in touch with him. Now that Mike had received the 214R refrigerator cars parts that Lou Caponi had retrieved from the man

The Standard Gauge 200 Series Box Car was among the first items produced for M.T.H. by Samhongsa.

Mike was elated when he opened the shipment of 200-series car reproductions from Samhongsa. As he tells the story, "I put the cars down on the garage floor and hooked up the couplers and then I got down on my hands and knees to act as the engine for this train, and then I just pulled them around on the concrete floor! I was so excited . . . I was like a kid with a new toy! I just couldn't believe what I was seeing. These great quality cars were finally made for me, and I could afford to buy them, and I knew I could sell them. I was jumping for joy! It was a great moment in my business!"

from Philadelphia, Mike decided to ask Mr. Lee if his company could do the work. Mr. Lee asked Mike to send him the car. Mike felt a quick sense of déjà vu since he had almost lost his fifteen hundred dollar 214R refrigerator car once under similar circumstances. Understandably, Mike was hesitant to go through this again, but he also knew that if he wanted to find overseas suppliers to build trains for him at a cost he could afford, he was going to have to take the risk of losing his 214R refrigerator car. So he agreed. In fact, he not only sent the 214 R, but he also purchased and sent the 200 series box and cattle cars.

The 200 series freight cars were the first M.T.H. tinplate reproduction rolling stock that would be produced using tooling made in Korea. The Samhongsa organization wanted very much to build trains for M.T.H., so they created all the tooling for the first three 200 series cars at their own expense. The Samhongsa Company then built these first three cars and shipped them off to an anxiously waiting Mike Wolf.

Mike remembers how excited he was on that early summer day, when the large box arrived from Korea. As he quickly tore off the packaging, he uncovered some remarkable toy train cars. His treasure included a boxcar, refrigerator car and cattle car, all fully assembled but unpainted. He could almost hear the "clickety-clack" of the car wheels on train tracks as he examined each one. Mike turned each piece over as he very carefully inspected the parts and assembly. He realized he was holding an accurate and high quality reproduction.

These freight cars would sell easily to toy train enthusiasts. Furthermore, Samhongsa had offered an agreeable price quotation, which meant Mike could make some money too. He knew immediately that he would contract with the Korean firm to manufacture the parts to build them. This was the beginning of a long-standing work-

Mike Wolf and Samhongsa President Se Yong Lee

While reminiscing about his company's history, Mike remembers the various means of communicating with his overseas colleagues:

"In 1985, we corresponded via routine mail. First class mail traveled overseas by air, and if waiting for a quick response . . . well, that could be expected in a week or so. Telephone calls were expensive and inconvenient, because of the time difference between the U.S. and Korea. After a few years we began to communicate via Telex. Messages were short, because you paid per word, but it only took about three days to get a reply. After a year or so, Se Yong Lee suggested that they correspond using fax machines. This seemed the ultimate in speed and convenience. You could send almost any form of message, and receive an answer in an hour. Naturally we have stayed abreast of the latest technology and we use it to our advantage. In fact, technology like the Internet has revolutionized our ability to communicate effectively almost instantly and of course very efficiently!"

ing relationship between Mike and Samhongsa that has an unshakable foundation built on sincere trust and friendship.

Although Mike was getting closer and closer to becoming a totally independent operation in the model train business, for the time being he continued as one of the nation's largest dealers of Williams trains. Mike explains, "I stayed on with Williams for as long as I could. You see, for anyone to set up their own business involves a lot of risk and numerous unknowns. Hard as it may be to believe, I had difficulty giving up a weekly salary upon which I knew I could depend . . . even though it was still only $7.50 per hour, and I was now making more money selling M.T.H. products! However, I was taking every penny I brought in to M.T.H. and reinvesting it in the company, so I did not have much if anything in the way of cash reserves. I just needed to keep the Williams job for as long as possible!"

At that time, Mike was selling a major percentage of the brass O gauge models then being manufactured for Williams by Tae Hwa, another Korean firm, as well as Williams' other products. Therefore, Williams was happy to have him working for him. Finally in the spring of 1985, Mike decided to move forward into the model train business with full force. At the age of 25, Mike left Williams Reproductions to concentrate on his own business. He still sold Williams products, but more importantly, he focused on selling his own model railroading stock.

MANEUVERING THROUGH A SWITCH

Mike Uncouples

With all that was going on in the way of increased business activity and parts shipments coming in, Mike needed to find additional working space outside his home. Neither the business nor the family could survive much more co-mingling! Mike especially needed a facility where he could assemble his various train products.

Jerry Williams's business had grown so much that he had moved his operation out of his house some seven years earlier. Williams Reproductions, Ltd., was now located at 6560 Dobbin Road, Columbia, Maryland, which was part of an expanding industrial/office park. The company had acquired more office/assembly/warehouse space than they needed. Mike approached Williams and asked him if he could have some of the unused space in Williams's facility to store parts and to assemble some twelve hundred 200-series standard gauge freight cars. Williams agreed to let Mike use the space for storage, and he designated certain sections for Mike to use for assembly during night hours.

While most M.T.H. activity still took place in Mike's family home, the 200 series cars were assembled in the new quarters of Williams Reproductions. Mike continued to use his home address as that of his business. About a year later Williams Reproductions moved to a new building in Columbia, Maryland, and Mike's Train House went with them.

M.T.H. now leased a 4,000 square foot subdivision in Williams's new complex, located at 6660 B Dobbin Road. The M.T.H. spray painting operation moved from the Hipp family garage to the new building. The new location for the business is also where the assembly of several reproductions took place. These reproductions included the No. 400E locomotives, more 200 series freight cars, and Blue Comet passenger cars.

Mike, Mark Hipp and Ryan Iseman (M.T.H.'s first official employee) were busy painting and assembling trains during the week, and selling them at train shows on weekends. Mike went to these shows with Mark and/or Ryan, and they sold the existing inventories of Williams Reproductions and M.T.H. Trains.

At that time, Mike did not have much money so he did not have a significant inventory. His income was mostly generated by the M.T.H. orders taken for products in the catalogs, which then would be manufactured.

During this period Mike attended as many as thirty train shows a year, often having to drive long distances. Because Mike had a lot of merchandise and marketing materials to transport to these events, he needed a reliable and large vehicle to accomplish this. To keep his operating costs down he opted for the purchase of a very used van that only cost $100. Mike responded to an ad in the paper, and the original owner was undoubtedly pleased to unload it. Given the price of the van, one can only imagine how very used it actually was.

Making the van somewhat reliable required a number of repairs. Fortunately, at that point, Mike's leisure hobby was drag racing, and he knew a lot about repairing old cars. Mike had learned a great deal about auto mechanics and repair from his Dad, and this knowledge and experience came in very handy at a time when he needed to keep his costs way down. Mike did all the repairs on the van himself.

Mike was able to get the van up and running, but not without frequent and massive infusions of motor oil. One round trip from Columbia, Maryland, to the Norristown, Pennsylvania, train meet (a distance of about 240 miles) required four gallons of oil. That averaged about sixty miles per gallon of oil! Because the vehicle's need

M.T.H.'s first company vehicle is typical of the struggles of a young company.

MINI-BIO: RYAN ISEMAN

M.T.H.'s first "official" employee Vice President of Operations Ryan Iseman.

Ryan Iseman is among that special group of Mike's close childhood friends who have become loyal and hard-working employees of M.T.H. In fact, Ryan and Mike have been friends since they were only five or six years old. Ryan graduated from Atholton High School in 1980.

Among Ryan's distinguishing characteristics are his persistence and determination. Mike recalls that when he was working for Williams, Ryan wanted desperately to work there too. Ryan would make weekly visits to the Williams headquarters, which at that time was the Williams basement, to ask for a job. Jerry Williams got so tired of seeing him at the door, that he finally gave in and told Mike to go ahead and hire Ryan.

Ryan worked as an assembler for Williams Reproductions from 1975 to 1981. He then worked for the U. S. National Security Agency from 1981 until 1986, which is when he came to work for M.T.H. Ryan is currently Vice President of Operations, in charge of shipping, receiving, and the everyday in-house operations of the M.T.H. building.

Not only is Ryan a dedicated M.T.H. employee, but both of his parents also became part of the M.T.H. Family. Ryan's mother Sally worked for M.T.H. handling phone calls and spare parts orders. Ryan's father, Bob, is now retired and also works part-time at M.T.H. Bob deals with special product handling and with maintenance and repair problems.

for oil became so great, Mike would collect and save used motor oil from his parents, neighbors, and anyone else, to reduce the cost of running the van.

This pitiful vehicle also had several problems that did not warrant the expense of repair, considering Mike's rigid operating budget. For example, the door and window gaskets were all gone, the heater did not work, and the van had a number of cracks and openings in the body. On cold days, a trip in that excuse for a vehicle was pure torture. As it turned out, a particular trip to a Norristown meet was one of those days. In fact, it was freezing and the snow was falling and blowing. It got so unbearably frigid inside the van that Mike and Mark Hipp, who was traveling with him, stopped on the side of the road and used duct tape to try to cover up all the many cracks around the doors and windows from the inside.

Just as they were completing the patch-up work, a car with familiar flashing red and blue lights on top of it pulled up directly behind them on the shoulder of the road. The policeman got out of the car very deliberately and headed straight for the van with a rather quick stride. Mike feared the worst. He had visions of his operating budget taking a big hit for the traffic ticket he anticipated. He thought the ticket could even be a violation of some law concerning driving such a decrepit vehicle out on the road. Nonetheless, he was so cold, and because he and Mark had just sealed up the windows and doors he yelled to the officer through the glass, "Please don't make us open the window," and then he loudly explained their situation. It's hard to imagine what that officer was thinking - or how hard he must have laughed about their predicament later - but as it happened the policeman had only stopped to ask if they needed roadside assistance. When he turned around and walked back to his squad car, Mike breathed a sigh of relief.

From 1983 through 1988, Mark Hipp spray painted nearly all the train parts, while Mike and Ryan Iseman completed most of the assembly. Things worked out very well with this arrangement. However, there came a point when Mark broke his hand and he was temporarily unable to spray paint. Someone within the limited organization had to take over these duties because the operating budget would not allow for the added expense of another employee, even though it was just temporary. As a result, Mike took over the spray painting even though he really hated doing the work. He did a respectable job of spray painting, but he was not as vigilant as Mark. Mark was meticulous with his paint work, and he had a standing rule that painted parts could not be handled for at least twenty-four hours after they were sprayed; when a part that wasn't completely dry was taken too soon, it sometimes got damaged. When that happened, Mark would have to strip the paint from the part and start the process all over. Occasionally, this requirement created some problems because Mike or Ryan would upset Mark by sneaking a part they needed out of the drying area before its time to speed up the production process. Mike simply wanted to get the trains assembled and delivered to customers as soon as possible so he could maintain a healthy cash flow for M.T.H.

Work at M.T.H. was not always routine. Throughout the growth of M.T.H., there were some scary moments. For instance, one day after Mark swept out the spray painting booth and poured the accumulated paint dust into a cardboard box, a perilous fire broke out in the work area. The accumulated paint dust was in that container just long enough to ignite spontaneously. The ensuing fire, which broke out around 4:00 a.m., damaged a significant number of completed train products, like the 392 locomotives. A number of the metal engines just melted from the intensity of the heat from the fire. Plus the fire destroyed one complete order of 35 engines for M.T.H. dealer Frank's Roundhouse. There was considerable damage not only from the fire, but also from the water from the sprinkler system. The building's dry wall and most of the boxed trains and parts were almost totally destroyed. The total damage assessment for the inventory amounted to $25,000. Perhaps the greatest loss was the time and energy needed to get everything cleaned up and back on track. The event could have been a full-blown disaster, destroying both M.T.H.'s and Williams' facilities. As it was, the fire was reasonably well contained, and the damage was covered by insurance.

6560 Gerwig Lane building.

M.T.H. MEETS GRADE RESISTANCE

Waiting at the Lionel Crossing Gate

All the while Mike Wolf continued to plan and develop more and more Lionel tinplate items for reproduction. Between 1969 and 1986, when Lionel products were manufactured by General Mills, MPC-Fundimensions and Kenner-Parker, not much was done to discourage businesses like M.T.H. from reproducing earlier Lionel products. The only clearly stated demand and legal mandate referred to the fact that reproductions could not be sold with any sort of Lionel markings or logos on them. However, with the competition increasing, it was inevitable that the firms producing Lionel trains would at some point try to restrict, control or prevent M.T.H. and others from continuing to make and sell reproductions of Lionel's pre-World War II trains and accessories.

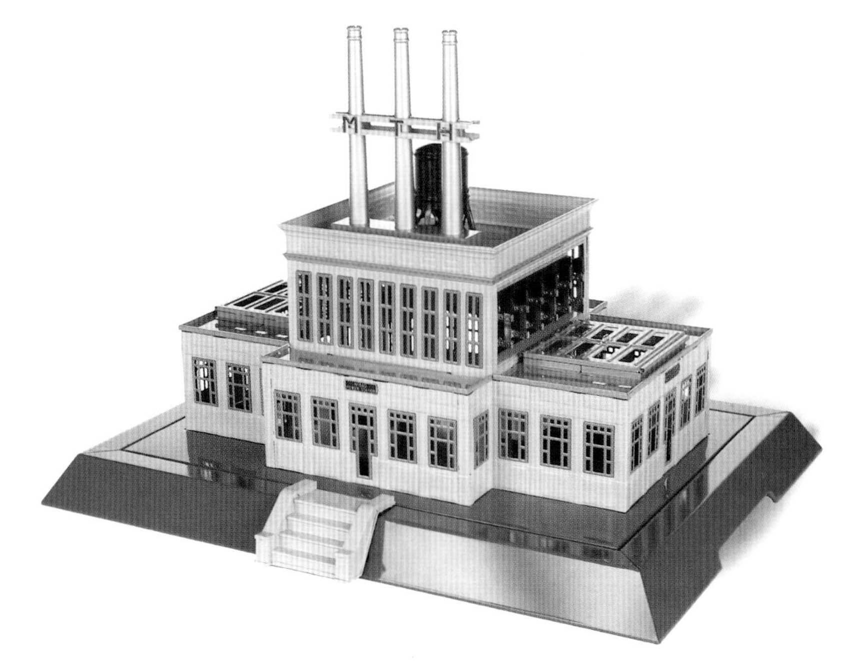

The M.T.H. reproduction of an 840 Powerhouse.

In 1986 the Lionel name and tooling equipment were purchased by Richard Kughn, a train collector who was a real estate developer by trade. Now that Lionel Trains, Inc. was under new management and ownership, they began to exert legal pressure to prevent certain firms that were making and selling reproductions of Lionel products and/or related spare parts, from continuing to do so.

One such business, T-Reproductions, of Johnson City, Tennessee, was served with a ominous legal suit requiring that they totally cease the reproduction of Lionel items, regardless of what logos or marks were on them. Norman Thomas, Jr., owner of the business, sent a letter explaining what had happened and what he intended to do as a result, to tinplate hobbyists. The relevant part of the text of that letter follows here:

"Dear Customer: September 1, 1987
Lionel Inc. of Mt. Clemens, Michigan has filed suit in federal court against T-Reproductions for the reproduction of prestige pre-war accessories. The lawsuit alleges that T-R has infringed upon the "trade marks" of Lionel including "exact colors", numbers #300, #840, etc.

As of this date and to our knowledge, T-R is the only company or individual that has actually been sued. This action forces T-R to sell off its inventory, and we will no longer be allowed to manufacture our products. The defense of this suit, whether we are right or wrong, over months or years, and carried to its conclusion, will cost $100,000 to $200,000. These legal costs far exceed the financial ability of our little company to continue making these products. When the current inventory (which is very small) is exhausted, there will be no more..."

Thomas went on to list his remaining inventory which he was selling. He thanked his customers for their support, and that marked the end of T-Reproductions making copies of old Lionel items. The reality was that this incident pretty much put T-Reproductions out of business then. (Norman Thomas is back in business today making reproductions of old Buddy-L Trains.)

Lionel came to an agreement with other businesses allowing them to obtain licenses from Lionel Trains, Inc., in order to continue to make and sell certain products. Some of these products were considered to be novelty items like tee shirts, key chains, etc. Lionel did not want anyone else to make their trains with the Lionel name on it.

M.T.H.'s attorney held the opinion that Lionel's case had no legal merit because any copyright protection on the trains that M.T.H. was making was outdated, and Lionel was not making any of these particular trains at that time. Therefore, M.T.H. was not overly concerned. Furthermore, Mike's Train House was never formally threatened with legal action, as was T-Reproductions. Everyone found this to be very curious because M.T.H. continued to develop new Lionel reproductions throughout 1986 and most of 1987. In fact, M.T.H. eventually produced more total goods, and generated more income from these products, than all other firms making such reproductions, combined. Exactly why Lionel Trains, Inc. did not threaten M.T.H. with legal action, however well or poorly supported by law, remains a mystery. There is some speculation regarding this, and it may relate to where and how M.T.H. was having their trains and parts manufactured.

In October 1986 Dan Cooney, a Vice President and Chief Operating Officer for Lionel Trains Inc., contacted Samhongsa to propose that the Korean firm begin to produce model train products for Lionel as a direct contractor. Lionel wanted to work with Samhongsa because they knew the quality of the train products the Korean company produced. Lionel also knew that M.T.H. was enjoying great success in the model train business in part because of the quality of the products they were selling, which of course was credited to Samhongsa. Therefore, the logical assumption is that Lionel was looking for ways to knock M.T.H. out of the competition.

Korean manufacturer, Samhongsa, who made most of the parts for M.T.H., had a remarkable sense of loyalty to M.T.H. Their desire to maintain the on-going positive relationship with M.T.H. made it impossible for Lionel to negotiate a contract with them, no matter how hard they tried. Lionel apparently did very much want to contract with them, perhaps to eventually push M.T.H. out of their relationship with Samhongsa. Samhongsa remained supportive of M.T.H., with whom they had a trusting and long-term relationship, and the Korean firm made that clear to Lionel. In the end, Samhongsa's director, Se Yong Lee, declined Lionel's offer, stating that they (Samhongsa) preferred to continue to work through M.T.H., whom they knew well and trusted fully. Mr. Lee told Mike what had transpired with Lionel, and he encouraged Mike to contact them.

When Mike heard what had happened, he decided to turn this into an opportunity instead of seeing it as a threat. He contacted Dan Cooney, who was a major decision maker at Lionel Trains, to present him with a proposal for a three-party business relationship involving M.T.H., Samhongsa and Lionel. Dan Cooney turned down the proposal. After all, Lionel was attempting to eliminate the competition and that was not going to happen if they worked with the competition.

M.T.H. produced an extraordinary variety of model railroad train reproductions in just four years time. To illustrate the point, there follows a list of the various reproductions offered by M.T.H. through the fall of 1987:

9 Locomotive
381 Locomotive
408 Locomotive
94 Transmission Tower
428 Series of Passenger Cars
213 Stock Car
214 Boxcar
214R Refrigerator Car
400E Locomotive
215 Tank Car
216 Hopper Car
217 Caboose
420 Series of Blue Comet Cars
840 Power House
208 Tool Box Set
211 Flat Car
220 Searchlight Car
212 Gondola
92 Floodlight Tower
205 Container Set
155 Freight Shed
163 Station Cart Set
300 Hell Gate Bridge
392E Locomotive
424 Series of Stephen Girard Cars
385E Locomotive
1766 Ives Transition Cars
435 Small Power Station
436 Medium Sized Power Station
218 Dump Car
438 Signal Tower
437 Tower
550 Station Figures
263E Locomotive
613 Series of Passenger Cars
214R 1987 TCA Convention Car

Early in 1987 Lionel tried to persuade Samhongsa to reconsider their subcontracting offer. Lee gave him the same response. The Korean train builder was not going to contract directly with Lionel. After Lee told him about this second contact, Mike again got in touch with Lionel Trains, at Se Yong Lee's suggestion. Once more Cooney turned Mike away, indicating no interest in working with M.T.H. to obtain Samhongsa production.

At just about the time that all of this was taking place, Mike Wolf entered into a rather substantial real estate transaction. Always the rising entrepreneur, he wisely purchased ten of the twenty units in a newly constructed building in an office/industrial condominium complex, located at 9693 Gerwig Lane, Columbia, Maryland. Mike chose six of the units to be identified under one address, 9693A, to lease back to Mike's Train House. He then arranged for other occupants to rent the rest of the units. In the new headquarters of Mike's Train House, Mike continued to develop plans for growing his model train business. Mike generated ideas for projects and prepared cost estimates for other tinplate items that he planned to reproduce.

"*The Thursday Night Club*"

Mike celebrated the opening of the new M.T.H. building on Gerwig Lane by having a special Open House. He invited a number of people including an array of train collectors as well as non-train folks. The event was so successful and was enjoyed by so many participants that Mike decided to make it a regular occurrence. This gave birth to the Thursday Night Club.

Occasionally Mike would invite a guest speaker from Lionel or some of the other train lines M.T.H. sold. One time when Lionel President Nick DeGrazia was featured, the crowd was so big it was difficult to get inside.

The Thursday Night Club continued until the closing of M.T.H.'s retail store in September of 1993, and after the termination of M.T.H.'s status as a Lionel dealer. However, the Thursday Night Club drew many people into the hobby, and several of the participants became M.T.H. dealers.

In July of 1987, Mike received an unexpected phone call from Dan Cooney of Lionel Trains. Cooney called to ask Mike to fly up to Mount Clemens, Michigan, Lionel's headquarters, so they could open discussions on how they might work together. A meeting was scheduled for one month from the day of the phone call. Mike was determined that this trip to Michigan to meet with Lionel was not going to be wasted time. So he immediately contacted his Philadelphia-based attorney, Charlie Bloom, who happened to be not only an excellent lawyer, but also an avid train collector.

During the month before the scheduled meeting in Michigan, Charlie and Mike worked together to develop a contract that among other things stated: "M.T.H. would step out of the competition with Lionel in terms of tinplate reproductions . . . by giving up the manufacture of any tinplate reproductions under the M.T.H. name for five years. . . if Lionel would agree to permitting M.T.H. to manufacture Lionel Tinplate Trains, with the Lionel name on it, and exclusively for Lionel, during those five years. . . and that Lionel would guarantee M.T.H. minimum purchasing amounts of those trains during the five years." The contract further stated, "M.T.H. would maintain the parts business, but change the name of that business to the Lionel Classic Service Center. . . which would handle all the warranty issues and sell replacement parts."

Also during that month leading up to the Michigan meeting, Mike purchased an original Lionel O gauge Hiawatha train set that was very popular among hobbyists. His intent was to convince Lionel to let him re-manufacture this train set for them. In fact, within the month, Mike took the Hiawatha set to Korea for a meeting with Samhongsa. After convincing Samhongsa that the proposed new arrangement with Lionel, if they accepted the contract, would be a win/win result for all parties, Mike asked Samhongsa to quote a price for making the Hiawatha set. Mike took the price and scheduling quote from Samhongsa and developed a formal proposal for Lionel and then packaged it with the contract Charlie and he had prepared.

A month after that phone call from Cooney in July 1987, Mike made the trip to Michigan and there he met with Cooney and Art Peisner, the President of Lionel. The events that unfolded at the meeting are described in Mike's own words:

The Lionel folks told me that they had invited me up there to see if there was any way the two sides, M.T.H. and Lionel, could work together, if at all possible. They told me that they felt I was violating their trademark by making reproductions and that, if at all possible, maybe we could come to some kind of an arrangement. That's how the meeting began, so I opened my briefcase and handed them a copy of the draft of the contract and the quote for the Hiawatha, which was a product that I was offering to make (for them). They looked at it and reviewed it but didn't read the whole contract. They told me they wanted some time to review it . . . and then they would get back with me. They also said they were a little surprised that I had taken the time and made the effort to have all those documents prepared. [Lionel had not yet learned that Mike was not only energetic and deliberate in business matters, but he was also savvy!] Lionel admitted it was too much for them to absorb that fast.

However, within three months Lionel Trains and M.T.H. negotiated the terms of the contract, and they approved the Hiawatha project with M.T.H. as a contractor to Lionel. This agreement provided Mike and M.T.H. with a guaranteed income for five years, and it allowed Mike to focus his energy on seeding and feeding his own business.

Mike made one of his units at the Gerwig Lane building into a delicatessen. It was run by his partner in the deli venture, who happened to be a native of Thailand. She hired another young Thai woman to work in the deli. As it was located next door to M.T.H. and because he owned it, Mike naturally often picked up his lunch there. He immediately noticed the attractive new worker, whose name was Rasamee. After a number of pleasant conversations, Mike and Rasamee got to know each other. Before long, they realized their relationship was developing into more than a friendship - they were falling in love!

Rasamee became Mrs. Wolf in the spring of 1993. Two years later, Mike and Rasamee Wolf adopted a daughter, Melissa, now five years old.

The Lionel Classic Logo was commonplace at train shows.

The first Lionel release produced by M.T.H., the 1987 O Gauge Hiawatha set.

SIGNAL CONTROL

Keeping the Passengers Informed

Mike wanted to make sure that all of his valued customers clearly understood what had taken place. To that end, he composed and distributed a letter explaining the new arrangement with Lionel, to personally notify each of his customers. A copy of that letter appears below.

MIKE'S TRAIN HOUSE
9396 A Gerwig Lane
Columbia, Maryland 21046
(301) 381-2580

Dear Friends,

It is with great pleasure that I inform you that Mike's Train House (MTH) recently signed an agreement with Lionel Trains, Inc. contracting MTH to manufacture '0' gauge and standard gauge tinplate reproductions from the original Lionel line. I want to reassure all my customers that MTH was not coerced into this deal but readily agreed to the contract. We feel that Lionel's participation in this market will attract new customers into the hobby and allow us to manufacture the many different items you, our customers, have been asking for.

As a result of this agreement, we will no longer manufacture '0' gauge or standard gauge tinplate reproductions under the MTH name. However, we will become a full-service Lionel distributor carrying the complete Lionel '0' gauge Collector and Traditional Lines, the Lionel Large Gauge Line, and of course, the "Lionel Classics" Line. In addition, we will add the 1 Gauge Line from the Railway Express Agency and of course, continue to carry the complete product line from Williams' Electric Trains. In addition to the already mentioned product lines, we also have a limited number of hardback books on the history of Williams' Electric Trains, detailing their inception in 1972 to their rise as one of Lionel's chief competitors in the late '70's and '80's.

Besides manufacturing the "Classics" tinplate items for Lionel, MTH will also manufacture replacement '0' and standard gauge tinplate parts for all Lionel Service Stations. The parts will also be available directly from our Lionel Classics Service Center, of which we have enclosed a complimentary parts catalog, for your ordering convenience.

Our customers are very valued to us and we want to pledge our continued support for you with good, friendly service and a wide and exciting product line to choose from. As I am sure you are aware, quantities are very limited, so please don't hesitate to place your order early to avoid any disappointment in the future. If you have any questions please feel to call or write.

Thank you for your continued support over the years.

Sincerely yours,

Mike Wolf

As time went on, Mike continued to nurture the working relationship with Lionel. Around the beginning of 1988 Mike presented Lionel Trains, Inc. with additional proposals for more tinplate products, also to be manufactured by Samhongsa. These were the 390E locomotive, the 300 series passenger cars, and the 115 station. Lionel quickly approved these items for inclusion in their Classics line, and they were advertised in flyers and the 1988 Lionel catalog.

Meanwhile, M.T.H. had become one of Lionel's biggest dealers . In fact, M.T.H. sales had reached the point that Mike needed some additional expert help to manage and operate this aspect of the company. This is when Mike hired Rich Foster, M.T.H.'s current Vice President of Sales, to assume responsibility for sales and distribution of Lionel and Williams products.

STREAMLINING

Keeping up with Technology

Early in 1988 the products M.T.H. built for Lionel Trains, Inc. were painted at M.T.H.'s Gerwig Lane headquarters. However, Mike had other ideas about how to make this part of the operation more efficient, and in the long-term, more cost effective. Mike has always been a supporter of using the latest and greatest technology to make it easier to work smarter instead of harder. Therefore, he was always investigating what was new in the model train manufacturing industry.

After researching the options, M.T.H. purchased the latest American-made spray painting equipment in an attempt to stay current with the industry and to make this part of the production process faster and better. After getting Samhongsa to agree, Mike directed that the new spray painting equipment be shipped to Samhongsa. Mike and Mark Hipp made the twenty hour flight to Seoul, Korea, to help Samhongsa with the installation and break-in of the new equipment, as well as to assist their staff in learning how to use the new spray painter. Mike and Mark stayed in Korea for a month.

To save Mike the cost of staying in an expensive hotel, Se Yong Lee arranged for them to live in his father's home while they were in Korea. Mike and Mark found the arrangement to be very pleasant. Their accommodations were comfortable and the environment was very clean and cordial. Mike remembers that he was especially intrigued by the floor heating system in the home, which was noticeably efficient and effective. In fact, he liked it so much that he had the same kind of system installed in the home he had built for himself in 1993 and later in M.T.H.'s current headquarters.

Once the spray painting equipment was in place and fully operational, and the Samhongsa employees trained in how to use it, the spray painting part of the train production process moved along much faster, and it was definitely the best way to operate. Once this occurred, Lionel Classics' products were almost always painted and completely assembled in Korea.

The high visibility Hiawatha Project was in full swing by then. Because it was going to be the first product produced in this new arrangement that M.T.H. had with Lionel, everything had to be near perfect. This was especially clear to Samhongsa.

As a way of employing an unbiased system of checks and balances, Lionel contracted with the Korean branch of SGS Testing, to perform a final inspection of the Hiawatha sets, just before shipping them to the U.S. The firm examined the sets using a series of product quality gradations. They decided to pass the lot even though they uncovered a few minor paint blemishes or scratches that were mostly cosmetic imperfections. The sets had already been loaded into a shipping container when word came to Se Yong Lee that the material had

MINI-BIO: RICH FOSTER

Vice President of Sales Rich Foster

Rich Foster graduated from Atholton High School in 1980, in the same class as Andy Edleman and Ryan Iseman. He then graduated from the University of Maryland, College Park in 1984. Later, Rich went back to college and received a marketing degree from the University of Maryland, University College.

Unlike the other Vice Presidents at M.T.H., Rich did not work for Williams Reproductions. However, Rich and Mike Wolf knew each other in high school. Throughout the years that Rich was pursuing a career in management and sales in the landscaping business, he and Mike often ran into each other. Mike knew of Rich's sales expertise and felt he would be an asset to M.T.H. So Mike offered him a job. It took some time for Rich to make a decision. He was hesitant because he did not know much about the model train business when Mike offered him the job.

Nevertheless, Rich decided to try it, thinking that it might be a short term venture for him. Some twelve years later, Rich, as the Vice President of Sales, is beginning to think this might be a long-term commitment!

Rich is now an expert in the sales and marketing area of the model railroad industry, and he works closely with Andy Edleman, the Vice President of Marketing at M.T.H., as well as Mike Wolf. He also loves being in this business because as he claims, "The folks involved in this hobby are really good people. They are honest, fun-loving individuals who are truly passionate about this hobby!"

State-of-the-art spray painting equipment is one of the many reasons M.T.H. is a market leader today.

passed Lionel's inspection criteria, but that some minor defects were found. Lee reacted immediately by ordering all the sets removed from the container and thoroughly inspected, then reworked as required. Only after this final effort were the Hiawatha sets reloaded into the container and shipped to Lionel Trains, Inc. This is a prime example of how Samhongsa has earned their reputation for producing high-quality products, and why M.T.H. has built such a lasting relationship with the company.

CONSTRUCTING BRANCH LINES

Product Development

Around this time, Art Peisner and Dan Cooney requested something from Mike Wolf that set him on another track involving an expansion for M.T.H. For quite some time, Richard Kughn, the Chairman of the Board for Lionel Trains, Inc. had been an avid collector of Lionel trains and of railroad memorabilia. In fact, around 1988 he purchased a real-life Reading T-1 4-8-4 steam locomotive. This was the real thing, built to a scale of 1:1. Kughn kept the engine in a roundhouse in Western Maryland.

Because he owned the real locomotive, Kughn wanted his company to make the T-1 for its Collector Line. However, Lionel was too busy with other work to handle this project. Not surprisingly, Art and Dan asked Mike if he was interested in producing a die-cast version of the locomotive, as a contractor. One of the things a smart entrepreneur learns immediately is that if you want to be successful, when a customer or client asks you to do something, you always say "Yes!" You worry about how you are going to do it after you close the deal! Naturally Mike said, "Yes!" and as a result the T-1 became the first of the Collector Line items to be manufactured through M.T.H. This 4-8-4 locomotive made its first appearance in Lionel's 1989 catalog.

The Korean-produced Lionel Classics and Collector Line items were successful and profitable for both Lionel Trains, Inc. and M.T.H. Nonetheless, the ongoing relationship between the two organizations was showing signs of strain because of some strong differences of opinion. Those differences included Mike's concern about Lionel's plan for production quantities. He believed that the numbers of certain items Lionel proposed to manufacture were too large. Producing too much of any product usually means that inventory begins to pile up and ultimately it becomes difficult, if not impossible, to sell. Obviously this is not a good way to run a business.

Mike argued that the numbers projected for several projects, including the Hiawatha set, and specific items in the Classic Lines, such as the 384 locomotive and its cars, the 115 and 126 stations, and 440 signal bridge, were higher than what the market would bear. In the Collector line, Mike was worried that Lionel planned to overproduce just about all of the items. Mike's substantial and proven experience in developing and selling his own M.T.H. reproductions had clearly demonstrated to him what kind of demand there was for these kinds of products. (Mike has always kept his ear to the ground to stay on top of what customers really wanted.) He repeatedly tried to convince the Lionel decision-makers not to overproduce. Unfortunately, his warnings went unheeded more often than not.

Other incidents strained the relationship between M.T.H. and Lionel. For example, Mike believed Lionel's decision to paint the 384E locomotive in a creamy gray color with red trim was a major mistake. After all, as Mike explained, "Most railroad hobbyists want to create or collect exact replicas of the real thing. They want their displays or collections to be as close to real life as possible." With certainty Mike knew that nearly all collectors wanted this locomotive in its authentic black enamel finish, and he told his Lionel colleagues. Lionel once again chose to ignore his advice.

Mike was well aware that he was considered an outsider at Lionel Trains. Furthermore, it became clear that some key Lionel people did not like Mike's attempts to influence the choice of new products and matters relating to marketing and sales policies. Undoubtedly Mike was working under difficult circumstances. Still, because Mike loved the old Lionel trains, he worked hard to develop new projects and to provide Lionel Trains, Inc. with the highest quality reproductions M.T.H. could supply.

One of the projects Mike proposed to Lionel was a revival of their Girls' Set produced in 1958, and coveted by serious Lionel collectors. Lionel's management objected to the idea, pointing out that a competitor, MDK, Inc. had already offered their own K-Line Girls' set, which was generally similar in color and style to the original Lionel product. Mike continued to argue his point, emphasizing that when a competitor introduces a new product or reinvents an old one, that is the perfect time to jump into the race with the competition. Mike's long-standing philosophy dictated that creating and introducing the exact same product, albeit much better and perhaps less expensive, was the key to success. Eventually Lionel's people decided to follow Mike's advice. They did indeed reproduce their own 1958 Girl's Set, which was favorably received on the market.

Mike continued to propose new Classics and Collector Line products to Lionel's management, and to advise them on such matters as proposed production quantities. M.T.H. arranged for the following items to be manufactured for Lionel, and they were advertised in the 1989 Catalog:

Classics Line:

1-384E	*Locomotive*
1-500	*500 Series Freight Car Set*
1-440	*Signal Bridge And Switch Panel*
1-44	*Electric Freight Set, O Gauge*
1-200	*Trolley*
1-201	*Trolley*
1-381E	*Locomotive, Green*
1-400 Series	*Green State Cars*
1-126	*Station*
1-390	*Black Locomotive*
1-300	*Series Passenger car Set*
1-1989	*Standard Gauge Christmas Boxcar*

Collector Line:

	Reading T-1

Lionel's 1990 Catalog was filled with the following products produced under subcontract by M.T.H.:

Classics Line:

1-318E	*Freight Set, With 500 Series Freight Cars*
1-43	*Clockwork Boat, Runabout*
7	*Old Steam Locomotive in Brass*
	Passenger Cars in Brass
1-400E	*Locomotive Blue Comet Cars, Standard Gauge*
1990	*Standard Gauge Christmas Boxcar*
437	*Switch Tower*
390	*Fireball Express with 300 Series Cars*
	Green Illinois State Car

Collector Line:

L3A	*NYC Mohawk*
	Rail Chief Cars

At Mike Wolf's urging, Lionel re-released the Girl's Train though production ultimately took place in Michigan.

DERAILMENT OF THE LOCAL LIMITED

M.T.H. Clears the Wreckage

During the first couple of years of the working arrangement between Lionel and M.T.H., Mike Wolf continued to be an important dealer for Williams Reproductions, Limited. However, the relationship between M.T.H. and Williams was destined to head off the tracks.

In 1986, about a year after M.T.H. had contracted with Samhongsa to manufacture tinplate trains, Williams changed their mind and also contracted with the Korean firm. This was so that Williams could produce a prestige line of O scale brass, two- and three-rail locomotives, which were to be known as the Crown Edition Line. The Crown Edition Line brass steam locomotives were built ¼ inch to a foot scale. They were bigger than any of the traditional Lionel engines. These products quickly and deservedly earned the approval of train collectors because they were new and different from anything else on the market at that time.

In 1990 Samhongsa built another locomotive for Williams Reproductions: the enormous articulated Southern Pacific Cab Forward Steam Engine. M.T.H. received an allocation of the product and started selling it to their customers, at the advertised price of $1,300. However, very soon after, Williams decided to sell his remaining Cab Forwards directly to the public at a retail price of $750. This created a major problem for M.T.H. and the other dealers selling this product because they had a number of these new locomotives still remaining in their inventory. Furthermore, they had been selling the Cab Forward to other customers at a much higher price than for what Williams was now quoting. This was certainly not good business in the eyes of those model train lovers who had purchased the Cab Forward at the higher price!

As expected, Mike Wolf was upset by this rather unethical action. Therefore, Mike requested that Williams rectify the situation by offering some sort of compensation to M.T.H. so that they in turn could offer a rebate to the customers who had already purchased the Cab Forward.

Mike's request was refused by Williams. As a result, Mike felt he had no choice but to stop selling Williams' trains. It was a sad day when that happened because Mike had been the Williams dealer with the most sales for many years. After many years, the Williams-M.T.H. pairing had uncoupled.

At about this time an incident involving one of Williams's key employees, Andy Edleman, deepened the tension between Wolf and Williams. In 1980 Mike Wolf had recruited Andy Edleman, to work for Williams. After Mike left Williams in 1985, Andy replaced him as General Manager. Unfortunately, by 1990 there was a strain in the relationship between Edleman and Williams. This strain was the outgrowth of numerous disagreements between Williams and Edleman, but the breaking point came when Williams told Andy that he wanted Andy to close his parts business, which Williams had previously authorized. In effect, Williams wanted to lower Andy's Income!

This ultimately led to Andy tendering his resignation. Mike offered Andy a job at M.T.H. after he found out about the rift with Williams. Mike knew Andy had a good background in the model train business, and he also respected his talents and strong work ethic. This major shift in key staff took place in September of 1990. At that time, Andy became the Project Manager overseeing the work for the various trains being made for Lionel.

Late in 1990 the relationship between Williams Reproductions, Ltd. and Samhongsa Co., Ltd. came to an end because of some disagreements. This left the Korean firm with unfinished products, reduced prospects for future work, and a skilled workforce for which there was now insufficient work. Before ending the relationship with Samhongsa, Williams had placed orders for two more Crown Edition locomotives, which they now refused to purchase. These projects were under way so M.T.H. agreed to take on the financing for them. The Crown Edition locomotives being produced were the Pennsylvania T-1 Duplex and the GG-1 Electric.

Meanwhile back in the States, Mike Wolf wanted and needed another line of products to replace Williams' Crown Edition Line, which he was no longer selling. Because Samhongsa was suffering as a result of the terminated working contract between them and Williams, Mike felt he could help himself and Samhongsa at the same

MINI-BIO: ANDY EDLEMAN

Vice President of Marketing Andy Edleman

ANDY EDLEMAN GRADUATED FROM ATHOLTON HIGH SCHOOL IN 1980, AND FROM THE UNIVERSITY OF MARYLAND, COLLEGE PARK IN 1986, WITH A DEGREE IN JOURNALISM, AND A MINOR IN MARKETING. MIKE WOLF HIRED ANDY AS AN ASSEMBLER FOR WILLIAMS REPRODUCTIONS IN THE SUMMER OF 1980.

UPON MIKE'S 1985 DEPARTURE ANDY BECAME GENERAL MANAGER FOR WILLIAMS. FROM 1988 TO 1990, ANDY HELPED TO STEER WILLIAMS' CROWN EDITION LINE TO MARKET PROMINENCE. HE ALSO OWNED A TOY TRAIN PARTS BUSINESS GEARED TO SUPPLY ITEMS FOR WILLIAMS' PRODUCTS. ANDY JOINED M.T.H. IN SEPTEMBER OF 1990, AND BEFORE LONG HE BECAME THE PROJECT MANAGER FOR THE WEAVER BRASS LOCOMOTIVES, WHICH INCLUDED THE PREPARATION OF BEAUTIFULLY PHOTOGRAPHED GOLD EDITION CATALOGS.

ANDY HAS BEEN INSTRUMENTAL IN LEADING THE M.T.H. MARKETING EFFORT IN TERMS OF PACKAGING, PRESENTATION AND THE USE OF MULTIMEDIA AND INTERNET TOOLS. AS VICE PRESIDENT OF MARKETING, HE HAS EXPERTLY MOVED M.T.H. ALONG IN ADVERTISING AND PROMOTIONAL CAMPAIGNS, TO A LEVEL WHERE M.T.H. IS RECOGNIZED NATIONALLY AS A TOP COMPETITOR IN THE HOBBY INDUSTRY.

IN A RECENT INTERVIEW, ANDY NOTED THAT THERE ARE STILL "PEOPLE OUT THERE" IN THE MARKETPLACE WHO FEEL THAT M.T.H.'S YOUNG MANAGEMENT IS LACKING IN INDUSTRIAL KNOW-HOW. TO REFUTE THAT NOTION, ANDY POINTED OUT THAT, AMONG HIS COLLEAGUES, THERE ARE OVER ONE HUNDRED YEARS EXPERIENCE IN PRODUCING AND SELLING THREE-RAIL TRAINS.

MARRIED IN 1989, ANDY AND LISA EDLEMAN HAVE A DAUGHTER, JORDAN, AND A SON, TROY.

time. He just needed to tie up a few loose ends before proposing his plan to Samhongsa.

As luck would have it, he had already paved the way for his new venture when he had talked with Frank and Jack Rash of Frank's Roundhouse. Frank and Jack knew Bob Weaver, of Quality Craft Models/Weaver Trains, very well and had collaborated with him on model train projects. He was well respected in the trade, so Frank and Jack spoke to him on Mike's behalf. They asked him if he was interested in having O scale brass locomotives made in Korea. Weaver responded with interest but said he was unable to finance new projects of this size.

Mike planned to create some new business relationships not only with Weaver, but also with Frank Rash. Mike presented Weaver and Rash with some business proposals. To begin with, Mike proposed that M.T.H. would finance the manufacture of the Weaver Line of Gold Edition locomotives for several years. Mike suggested that other models, which he would select, should be built too, and Mike further assured them that he would handle the quality control for everything produced. Furthermore, Mike and Andy took full responsibility for producing the Catalogs for these items, as well as designing the Weaver Logo for these Gold Edition products. In addition, M.T.H. agreed to absorb fifty percent of each production run of Gold Edition items, while Weaver would be responsible for twenty five percent, and Frank Rash, trading as Frank's Roundhouse, would take the remaining twenty five percent.

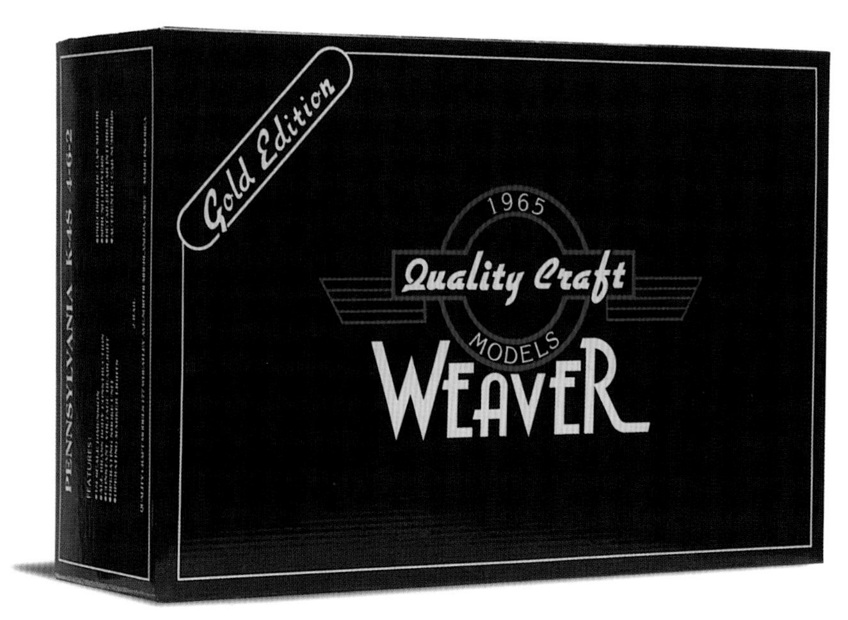

M.T.H. controlled all marketing aspects of the Weaver Gold Edition Line, including packaging.

The former Williams Crown Edition Pennsylvania T-1 Duplex and GG-1 Electric that M.T.H. had agreed to finance when Williams and Samhongsa went different ways became projects number five and six in Weaver's Gold Edition Line. They were available for sale a year later, at the end of 1991 or soon after.

Not long after this, M.T.H. bought back all of the tooling for making non-brass Weaver locomotives, from Frank Rash and Bob Weaver.

Weaver-M.T.H. Gold Edition Products

The Weaver-M.T.H. cooperative relationship continued until 1996, resulting in the following Gold Edition products, in the order of their release:

Pennsy M-1A Mountain	*September*	*1990*
Union Pacific FEF-3 4-8-4	*February*	*1991*
EMD E-8 AA Diesel	*February*	*1991*
Nickel Plate Berkshire 2-8-4	*April*	*1991*
EMD E-8 B Unit	*October*	*1991*
Great Northern R-2 2-8-8-2	*October*	*1991*
Pennsy T-1 4-4-4-4	*December*	*1991*
Pennsy GG-1 electric, scale	*February*	*1992*
Pennsylvania G-5 4-6-0	*April*	*1992*
Alco C-630 Diesel	*Summer*	*1992*
New York Central USRA 0-6-0	*June*	*1992*
NYC J-3 Dreyfuss Hudson	*September*	*1992*
NYC Empire State Express	*October*	*1992*
Pennsylvania H-10 2-8-0	*April*	*1993*
Southern Pacific GS-2	*July*	*1993*
Pennsylvania K-4s Pacific	*August*	*1993*
Baldwin Sharknose Diesel AB	*Fall*	*1993*
Pennsylvania L-1 Mikado	*November*	*1993*
Canadian Pacific H-1e 4-6-4	*January*	*1994*
Pennsylvania A-5s 0-4-0	*Spring*	*1994*
Alco C-628 Diesel	*Spring*	*1994*
Santa Fe Blue Goose 4-6-4	*Spring*	*1994*
Pennsylvania Torpedo 4-6-4	*Spring*	*1994*
Lehigh Valley John Wilkes 4-6-4	*Spring*	*1995*
B & O Cincinnatian 4-6-2	*Spring*	*1995*
Milwaukee Hiawatha 4-4-2	*Spring*	*1995*
Southern Tennessean 4-6-2	*Spring*	*1996*

The Gold Edition line also included sets of scale length passenger cars, decorated in various railroad colors and heralds.

The following tooling for making non-brass Weaver locomotives was eventually solely owned by M.T.H.:

EMD E8 A Diesel
EMD E8 B Unit
Scale Pennsylvania GG-1 Electric
Alco C 630 Diesel
Baldwin Sharknose AB Diesel
Alco C 628 Diesel
SD 40-2 Diesel

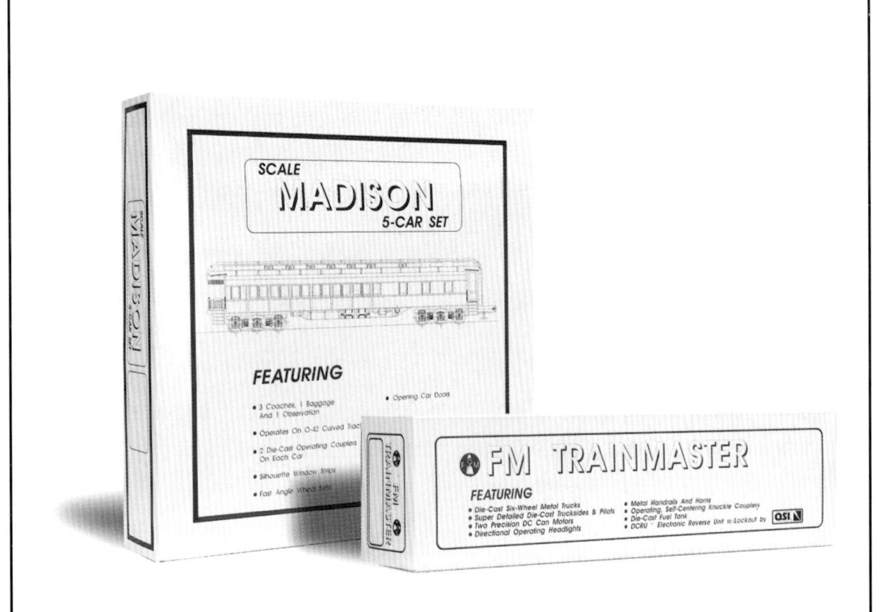

Some Korean-made train products labeled as 'Custom Trains' showed up briefly, in 1992. Around 1990 Williams Reproductions planned a production run of FM Trainmaster locomotives. They had the plastic body shells molded in the United States, and ordered the floor/motor truck assemblies from Samhongsa. Frank Rash, the owner of Frank's Roundhouse, bought the bodies from Williams, expecting to sell them as replacement parts, then learned about the floor assemblies available in Korea. M.T.H. advanced the money to buy the parts from Samhongsa and to complete the assembly of the Trainmasters. There were also scale length heavyweight passenger cars that became Custom Trains products. These were cars ordered by Williams and completely assembled by Samhongsa, but not shipped to the U.S. M.T.H. also advanced the money for the cars, and advertised both Custom Trains items in a 1992 flyer/catalog.

MIKE OBSERVES THE RED EYE SIGNAL AHEAD

M.T.H. Proceeds with Caution, Then Stops on the Lionel Tracks

The contract between M.T.H. and Lionel Trains, Inc. continued through 1991 and 1992. As might be expected, their disagreements continued as well. Over time, Lionel ordered fewer and fewer products from M.T.H. This obviously had a negative impact on M.T.H.'s and Samhongsa's income. Mike became concerned because the terms of the 1987 agreement between Lionel and M.T.H. required that Lionel pay M.T.H. amounts that were a percentage of the total cost of Lionel Classic train products delivered to Lionel. Therefore, if less was ordered and produced, then logically M.T.H.'s compensation was reduced, too. A minimum purchase provision in the contract had guaranteed a certain level of income to M.T.H., but this part of the contract was eliminated from their agreement in 1990, after a long discussion Mike had with Richard Kughn. Mike was forced to make some compromises for the sake of fulfilling his long-term plans for the O Gauge market, so he agreed to the elimination of this clause from the contract. Lionel appeared ready to cut back on orders for Collector Line items as well, for which M.T.H. was compensated on a per-product basis. Mike Wolf began to plan ways to recover the anticipated loss of corporate income.

In 1992 Mike had proposed to Lionel that he spearhead a project for manufacturing the Dash 8 Diesel Locomotive in Korea. Lionel was not interested. Early in 1993 Mike reactivated this project, planning to have the locomotive manufactured in Korea, but selling it as an M.T.H. product.

M.T.H. printed a brochure showing the various products the company intended to produce, including an assortment of lithographed toys and the proposed Dash 8 Engine in both 8-wheel and 12-wheel versions. M.T.H. first presented the brochures at the York Train Meet in April, 1993. When Richard Kughn from Lionel stopped by the booth, he picked up the M.T.H. brochure with the Dash 8 Locomotive pictured. When Kughn asked Mike to confirm that M.T.H. planned to manufacture this engine on their own, Mike said that was what he planned to do.

The Lionel-M.T.H.-Samhongsa items for 1991 were as follows:

Classics Line: *1-408E Locomotive (brown)*
State Car Set (brown)
44 Clockwork Boat Racer
1991 Standard Gauge Christmas Boxcar
Extra "Barnard" Blue Comet Car
Racing Automobile Set
Gray Nickel 400E and 1-217 Caboose
"O" Gauge Blue Comet Set

Collector Line: *Lift Bridge*
Semi Scale Freight Cars (Hopper/Box/Tank/Caboose)
Lackawanna MU cars, powered & unpowered
Pennsylvania S2 Turbine Locomotive
Pennsylvania N8 Caboose
Chessie T-1 locomotive

1992 production included:

Classics Line: *American Flyer Presidential Special Set*
Extra Brown State Car 'Illinois'
1-214 Box Car
1-215 Tank Car

Collector Line: *Southern Mikado Locomotive*
Lackawanna MU Cars, both unpowered
Pennsy MU Cars, powered & unpowered
Denver and Rio Grande PA-1 ABA Diesel
Western Maryland Shay Locomotive
Pennsylvania Silver/Red GG-1
Semi Scale Reefer and Stock Car

In early 1993 M.T.H.-Samhongsa made two other products for Lionel Trains, Inc. They were the Pennsylvania MU cars, both unpowered, the Lackawanna PA-1 diesel, and the Non-Cataloged Special Frisco Mikado.

The die used to mold the Lionel Collector Line silver and red GG-1 is the same tool used to make the Williams Crown Edition locomotive. The die became the property of Samhongsa when Williams and Samhongsa went their separate ways. M.T.H./Lionel Trains, Inc. used the die after making some modifications on both the inside and outside of the tool thus differentiating the Williams and Lionel Versions.

Obviously displeased, Kughn then asked him to meet him in his van to talk about this. When they met, Kughn said he didn't like the idea of M.T.H. bringing out this product in competition with Lionel Trains, Inc. He stated that it certainly seemed like there was a conflict of interest in M.T.H. taking this action. Kughn was clearly upset when he said he had to look after the best interests of his company. Mike responded with, "I also have to look out for the best interests of M.T.H.!" As the discussion grew in intensity, Kughn declared that if M.T.H. persisted in selling the Dash 8 Engine and other competitive products, Kughn would consider terminating M.T.H. as an authorized Lionel dealer. Mike reminded Kughn that M.T.H. had orders for $750,000 of 1993 Lionel trains that he could not fill if Kughn terminated his Lionel dealership status.

However, within a few days Lionel Trains officially notified Mike that they were dissolving their relationship, and they also terminated M.T.H.'s dealership contract. Richard Kughn had made good on his threat, and the immediate cause of Lionel's action was M.T.H.'s announcement of the Dash 8 locomotive.

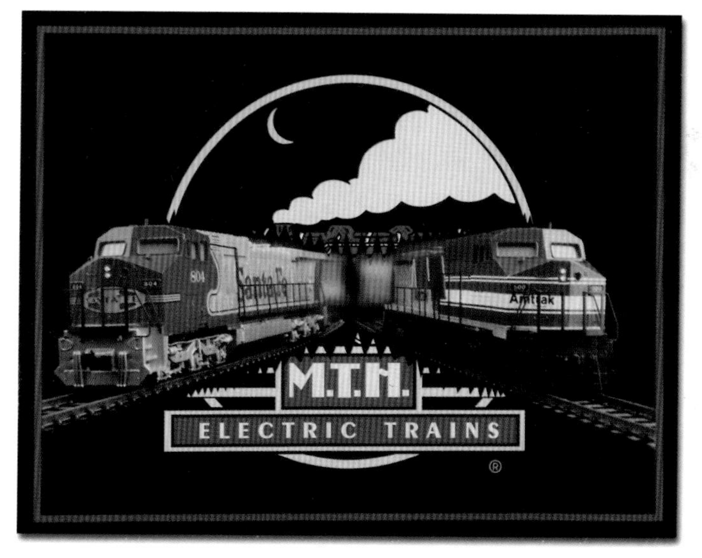

The first M.T.H. catalog, which led to the split from Lionel Trains Incorporated.

The impact on M.T.H. was significant. Lionel's decision to terminate the dealership agreement naturally resulted in a huge loss of income for M.T.H. M.T.H. had no choice but to take legal action against Lionel Trains, Inc. for damages. They filed an anti-trust law suit, claiming that by canceling M.T.H.'s dealer agreement with

Lionel, Lionel was attempting to put M.T.H. out of business. Lionel Trains, Inc. answered with a countersuit claiming that M.T.H. was trading off the Lionel name. The legal battle lasted for three long years as the case dragged through the legal proceedings. However, Mike was tenacious and he had great confidence in his team of lawyers. In addition, he knew he was right and as long as he continued to speak the truth he believed he would come out on top. Lionel finally agreed to settle the case. It cost both M.T.H. and Lionel a great deal in time and legal fees, but Mike feels justified by the fact that Lionel did ultimately have to pay him. The amount of the settlement can not be disclosed.

With the tumultuous end of the relationship with Lionel Trains, Inc. in 1993, there was no longer any reason why M.T.H. should not return to the way the business operated in the years 1983-1987. Therefore, M.T.H. went back to manufacturing three-rail trains under the M.T.H. logo.

M.T.H. DESIGNATES MILE POSTS

The Pace of M.T.H. Growth and Development Picks Up Speed

With the termination of the contract with Lionel, M.T.H. took the opportunity to take stock of the business and to determine in which direction they now wanted to head. After several frustrating years trying unsuccessfully to persuade Lionel to make a wider variety of locomotives never before seen in O Gauge, Mike was finally free to exercise his vision. And he did so with a passion. M.T.H.'s philosophy is that model railroaders should have the opportunity to buy the high-quality products they want, in the roadnames they want, for a reasonable price. It is this focus on the customer that would lead M.T.H. in the following years to add new product lines and to produce more different locomotives than any of the company's competitors had in their lifetimes.

Mike started to think about some past projects that he was unable to get Lionel to accept. He recalled that in 1992, Lionel had rejected as too expensive his proposal that M.T.H.-Samhongsa build a die-cast scale model of the Union Pacific Challenger. The Challenger, which was a huge model, would be the first die-cast articulated engine ever produced in O Gauge. Mike never forgot the idea, and now it seemed like a good time to reconsider it. In fact, the Union Pacific Challenger Project pointed M.T.H. in a critically important direction that led to the successful development of what would come to be known as M.T.H.'s distinguished Premier Line of steam locomotives. By mid-1993 Mike set the project in full motion.

In the meantime, M.T.H. was very concerned that Lionel might somehow find out about their production plans and then develop a similar product, which would weaken the sales prospects for M.T.H.'s own expensive die-cast locomotive. Almost as a self-fulfilling prophecy, Lionel did attempt to obtain knowledge of M.T.H.'s activities concerning production of any new engines.

This occurred initially during Mike's first deposition in the legal action against Lionel. The time was July, 1993, and during the deposition, Lionel's attorney made a deliberate effort to learn the details of the project which was to follow M.T.H.'s production of the Dash 8 diesel. He asked Mike direct questions concerning his plans. Mike declined to answer. Fortunately, the judge ruled in Mike's favor stating, "Identification of the specific projects M.T.H. is planning has no relevance to the case at hand."

This information could have been very helpful for Lionel if they had obtained it, because M.T.H. had already begun planning three more locomotives to follow the Challenger. However, Mike was able to keep all of this information close to his vest, and with the work of his skillful attorney he was able to maintain his right to business secrecy. Throughout the course of the legal proceedings, M.T.H. retained this right, and the subsequent products-in-planning were thereafter referred to only as projects X, Y, and Z.

The decision to move forward with the manufacture of the scale die-cast Challenger was one of the most difficult ever made by M.T.H. The critical issue was to determine if the locomotive should be made of sheet brass or die-cast.

There was little risk in producing another brass locomotive. M.T.H. had already successfully helped to develop and sell Williams Crown Edition products and had also arranged for the production and marketing of an impressive series of brass engines for Weaver Trains. The first-hand experience of accomplishing this ensured that M.T.H.

could certainly sell its own brass locomotive. However, production runs for brass products were small, especially for expensive ones, and M.T.H.'s product planners were looking to generate major increases in the company's gross income and market share.

Die-cast products had the advantage of being heavy, sturdy engines, like those from the forties and fifties. However, die-cast tooling is expensive and would represent a major investment and major risk for a company just regaining its independence. The decision to go die-cast could successfully propel M.T.H. into a whole new area of toy train production or it could mean a discouraging setback.

Key M.T.H. staff met to discuss strategy and to reach a consensus. Initially, the direction of the pivotal planning meeting tended toward caution and the lower risk of producing the Challenger in brass. That was until Ryan Iseman voiced his opinion with confidence and a clear vision of the great future ahead for M.T.H. He stated, "It must be die-cast, if we're to move ahead."

Until then, only Lionel was producing die-cast products. Ryan knew that if M.T.H. could jump into the model train market with die-cast products, they could be a formidable competitor. His comment caused the rest of the group in the meeting to analyze their thinking. Even though they were heading into uncharted waters, there promised to be great rewards for the company if they could sell the die-cast Challenger successfully. After a lively discussion of the pros and cons of producing a die-cast Challenger versus a brass one, opinion began to sway toward a die-cast product. After all, if M.T.H. wanted to challenge the competition, there was no better way than with the Challenger locomotive! In the final analysis, the group opted for traveling the risky route. There was considerable anxiety. Tooling costs would run to nearly half a million dollars, and failure of the project could set M.T.H.'s plans back for years, perhaps even bring down the company. There was a long list of "what ifs," but once the decision was made, everyone got behind it and did their best to make it a successful business venture.

When the Challenger was first announced, the pre-orders for it were pretty scarce, because potential buyers did not really know what the quality of this articulated die-cast steamer would be. However, once production models became available in early 1994, customers saw that this die-cast steamer was of a higher quality than anything that had been available in O Gauge for years and offered a return to the hey day of model railroading. The orders began pouring in. M.T.H. started delivery of these engines in January and February of 1994.

M.T.H.'s decision to produce the Challenger as a die-cast locomotive was definitely the right one. The Premier Steamers have been a resounding success. The prospects for the future looked excellent. In fact, shortly afterward, M.T.H. pretty much had the market cornered for die-cast ¼" scale steam engines, because M.T.H. now had the very valuable design ability, production knowledge, and capacity to produce these engines profitably. At the same time, Lionel did not proceed immediately to make similar products.

M.T.H.'s dealer network began to grow from a solid base of a couple hundred. Once M.T.H. started manufacturing products under the M.T.H. logo, they stopped selling other lines of model train items. This encouraged new dealers to sign on with M.T.H. because the threat of competition diminished.

With the number of M.T.H. dealers increasing daily, along with the circulation of catalogs and M.T.H.'s presence at train shows, M.T.H. brand recognition started to expand rapidly among avid model train collectors. Until this point, it was primarily the tinplate train collectors who were familiar with M.T.H. products because of the letters "M.T.H." stamped on the steel floors of reproductions. Now M.T.H. was offering an ever-growing selection of scale and near-scale model trains, which they diligently marketed to modern-era train enthusiasts. In addition, M.T.H. offered not only a variety of new locomotives, but they also produced a mounting assortment of freight and passenger cars. Variety, quality, and affordability were fast becoming associated with the now widely-recognized M.T.H. name.

M.T.H. was leading a revolution in the toy train business. Because Samhongsa's manufacturing capabilities were excellent, M.T.H. developed new products at a pace never before known in the three-rail train industry.

M.T.H. has always been highly sensitive to any trends that surfaced among model railroaders. By way of observation, talking to a significant number of hobbyists and dealers, and of course keeping an eye on sales numbers, Mike quickly realized that quality sound systems were absolutely essential for his new locomotives. If given a choice, most model train buyers opted for engines with sound, whether they were built-in or retrofitted. Knowing this, M.T.H. wanted to be sure they could offer this option to customers, but they did not have this capability in-house. So M.T.H. established a solid working relationship with QSI, Inc. of Beaverton, Oregon, a company that specializes in developing and producing toy train sound systems.

The die-cast Challenger (1994) was the first M.T.H. product advertised as incorporating M.T.H.'s Proto-Sound® system. For this particular item, QSI created a new design, 2-board system. M.T.H. hardwired this system into the locomotive tender. Prior to the Challenger, M.T.H. met customer demand for train sound systems on an as-needed basis. The company routinely purchased what they determined to be a sufficient supply of QSI components to be installed as an aftermarket add-on on locomotives sold.

As time went on, and M.T.H. grew, the company recognized the need to secure its supply, because M.T.H. was not yet ready to develop and produce its own sound systems. In 1996 M.T.H. signed a contract with QSI, paying them an annual royalty, with the agreement that M.T.H. would be the only manufacturer offering locomotives with built-in QSI sound systems. The contract also stipulated that every locomotive so equipped would be identified in M.T.H.'s catalogs, with the QSI logo prominently displayed. Thus began a long-term mutually rewarding business alliance.

M.T.H. rapidly developed a wide range of products with appealing equipment options. For example, early in the effort to produce the Gold Edition locomotives for Weaver Trains/Quality Craft Models, QSI licensed its semi-conductor reversing unit, the DCRU, to Weaver. M.T.H. requested permission to build the reversing unit at no charge to QSI. Soon after receiving permission from QSI, M.T.H. began retrofitting QSI's sound systems into Weaver locomotives for those purchasers who wanted this option. A similar adaptation was arranged for M.T.H.'s own Dash 8-40 locomotive, introduced in 1993.

Mike also remembered the pre-war collectors and returned to his first love - the tinplate reproductions. Although M.T.H. did not make tinplate trains again until 1996, they continued their homage to Mike's beloved prewar tinplate by introducing the Hell Gate Bridge in 1994 and two Powerhouses in 1995. At the same time, M.T.H. also undertook the reproduction of a series of lithographed toys appealing to a specific group of toy collectors. These included the Amos 'n Andy Car, Hi-Way Henry, Mr. Atomic Robot, Robby Space Patrol, and the Kingsbury Firehouse.

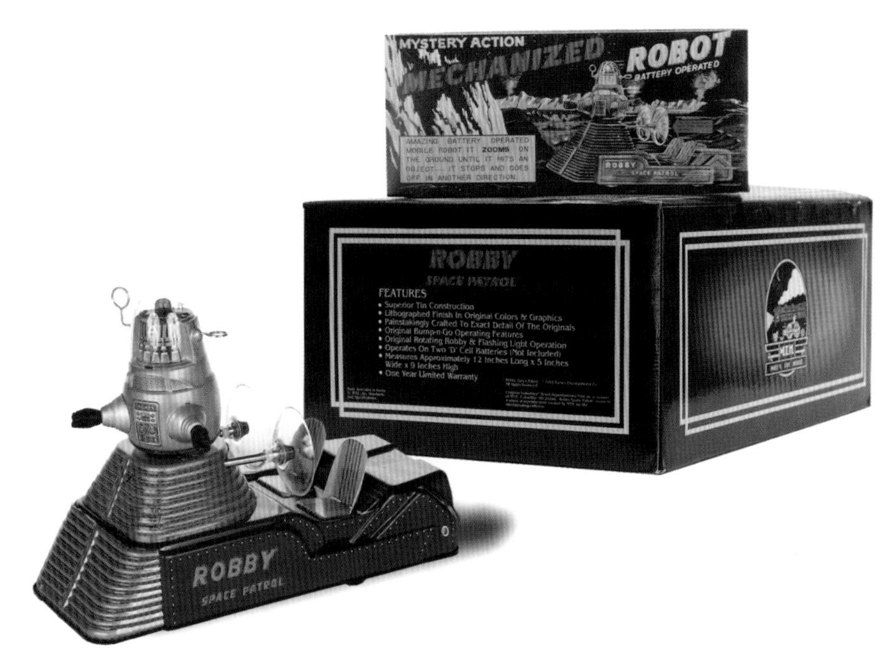

"ROBBY SPACE PATROL" headlined M.T.H.'s foray into the toy collecting market.

Although it was an interesting direction in which to move, this venture was not cost-effective when compared to development and production expenses and the market demand. In addition, those purchasers interested in antique toy collecting were not that easy to reach or target as a market. The media for advertising in that area was very limited and it did not provide for focusing on particular items like robots. The products eventually sold out, but this project was terminated.

Nevertheless, that stage of M.T.H.'s history had some memorable moments. For example, in 1993 Mike was at a York Train Meet, with his brochure advertising his Dash 8-40 diesel and several of his lithographed reproduction toys. Noticing the brochure with the special toys, a man stepped up to Mike and asked if he was interested in buying a like-new Mr. Atomic Robot. Mr. Atomic Robot was about 9 ½ inches tall, about 6 inches wide, and was a very popular antique toy. The robot was one of very few originals produced only in 1962, and it was sold through the Sears Catalog. Therefore, it was a valuable collector's piece.

Of course Mike was interested, but not as a collector. After a brief discussion related to how much the transaction would cost and how soon Mike could have the robot, the two made a verbal deal. An agreement was reached for Mike to purchase the robot for $22,000. The owner of the toy immediately set off for his New York home to retrieve Mr. Atomic Robot, agreeing to meet Mike back at York that evening. Meanwhile, Mike called Mark Hipp in Columbia, Maryland, and asked him to get $22,000 cash (the seller only wanted cash) from the bank, and then bring it to York. Mark responded quickly and before long he delivered the money to Mike in York.

As agreed, Mike, Ryan, and Rich Foster met with the man that night in the Holiday Inn bar in York. Mr. Atomic arrived in his soft-lined cushioned carrying case. The man carefully removed the robot from its case, and ever so gently set him down on the tabletop. Mike examined every inch of the robot very thoroughly. Satisfied that he was getting what was promised, he handed over the "king's ransom" of $22,000, and then began to test out Mr. Atomic Robot. Mike placed the battery-operated robot on the bar table where they were sitting. He then started to put the toy through its paces. The M.T.H. team members who were sitting at the table put up their hands around the table to prevent the robot from falling off. Mr. Atomic Robot shuffled all around the table top, changing direction when it bumped into a pair of protective hands.

The Cragstan "Mr. Atomic" was painstakingly reproduced from a $22,000.00 1962 original.

The former owner was mortified, as he anxiously asked Mike, "What are you doing? That's a collector's item! You don't play with a collector's item!" Mike calmly explained that the Robot as he had known it would soon cease to exist, because Mike's plan called for it to be taken apart. This man just stood there with his mouth hanging open, while Mike further explained that each of the pieces that had been assembled to make this wonderful robot would eventually have their outsides flattened for measurement and study by Samhongsa.

Mike's scheme involved the Korean firm creating accurate lithographic plates and other components, so that the robot could be reproduced. This specific Mr. Atomic would no longer be shuffling around, blinking his robot lights and doing his robot thing. However, he would be the model from which his yet-to-be seen clones would be created.

M.T.H. produced 500 silver and 500 blue Mr. Atomic Robots. Each reproduction included a certificate in the packaging that documented the serial number of the piece and where in the line of production it was made (e.g., 1 of 500, 5 of 500, etc.). All of them eventually sold, and M.T.H. did make some money on them. Several model train customers bought them just so they could own a collector's piece.

MOVING FROM THE BRANCH LINE TO THE MAIN LINE

M.T.H. Develops into a Class by Itself

1995, M.T.H.'s fifteenth anniversary year, proved a banner year for the company. That fall, M.T.H. expanded in still another direction. After introducing about fifteen new styles of locomotives and many rolling stock items, M.T.H. announced an entirely new line of products: the RailKing® Line. Railking® is the smaller (O-31 and O-27) line of locomotives and cars, somewhat less detailed than the Premier line (as the original scale line came to be named), but with the same sturdy construction and quality performance. The first Railking® products were the New York Central and Santa Fe 4-8-2 L-3 Mohawk, the Pennsylvania GG-1, and several freight cars.

Because Railking® items operate on smaller radius track than most scale products and generally cost significantly less than their larger

Initial RailKing packaging sported the traditional purple and yellow colors of M.T.H.

counterparts, they are the ideal medium for model railroaders who have space limitations and are on a budget. M.T.H. introduced the line for just that reason. Before the RailKing roll-out, M.T.H. was doing business primarily in the high-end market. There was no way for entry-level or casual hobbyists to enjoy M.T.H. products. Part of the M.T.H. mission is for the company to help spread a wholesome hobby the entire family could enjoy together to new markets. The RailKing line allowed them to do just that.

M.T.H. also believed that the RailKing line would fill a major gap in the O Gauge market. When M.T.H. was a large Lionel distributor, people came to M.T.H.'s Gerwig Lane store looking for a train set to go around their Christmas tree. They frequently recalled the big, heavy, black steam engines from their youth and wanted a set like that. These customers often found the Lionel offerings far less substantial than what they wanted, but they could not afford the high prices of the more substantial engines that were available. Mike remembered those customers in 1995 when he introduced the RailKing line, knowing that he was providing the heavy engines people craved for a price they could afford. That same year, M.T.H. sold their first packaged train sets. The sets did not yet come complete with track and transformer and all the extras that make Ready-To-Run™ sets today such a great value. But they did provide that high quality steam engine and sturdy trains customers had been yearning for.

Initially the RailKing Line was limited to a relatively small assortment of items, and it was positioned for several years at the end of M.T.H.'s sleek catalogs, which are published three times annually. Eventually, though, this new line gained in popularity among model train enthusiasts. In fact, it became so successful that in the Volume One 1998 Catalog, RailKing products were placed first, before the Premier and Tinplate Traditions Lines. In Volume One of the Year 2000 Millennium Catalogs, RailKing has its own separate catalog filled with new items and long-time favorites!

1995 also saw several other significant additions to the operating and sound features of M.T.H.'s product lines. In that year, the first smoking diesel was introduced, the first cab chatter was included in Proto-Sound®, and the first operating ditch lights were installed into locomotives. M.T.H. continued to raise the bar for the competition by bringing innovative ideas to model railroading.

Eventually RailKing established its own bright and colorful identity within the M.T.H. product line.

Sometimes just plain good luck figures prominently into the way things work out for a business. For example, in 1995 when M.T.H. began to develop the RailKing Line, Lionel and other competitors were already having much of their product manufactured in the Peoples Republic of China. M.T.H. wanted to do the same thing to reduce their production costs, but doing so required the expertise of someone who knew how to do business in that area of the world. M.T.H. did not have that expertise in-house.

However, when Mike was working with Lionel, he had made the acquaintance of Dave Krebiehl, who was an engineer there. Dave had a significant amount of experience doing business in China. Dave and Mike had frequently traveled overseas together for Lionel, and had become good friends. Mike says, "Dave is one of the most practical engineers I have ever met. I have always had great respect for his engineering abilities as well as his good common sense. We became friends and even though he ultimately came to work for me, we have been able to maintain a wonderful friendship over the years."

Just when M.T.H. needed someone to build relationships with manufacturers in China, Mike found out that Krebiehl had left Lionel.

Mike recruited him, and before long Dave was sent directly from Michigan, where he lived, to China. Dave's mission was to locate firms which could produce model train products for a price and quality, acceptable to M.T.H.

Krebiehl knew of a company in China that fit these requirements. So he went over to China specifically wanting to meet with that firm, even though he planned to investigate other possibilities too, while he was there. Unfortunately, his initial attempts to find the company he was looking for proved futile, and after a week or so of diligent searching, he was beginning to get discouraged. In the meantime, he had investigated a few other companies, but he was not satisfied with the quality of their work, and he knew M.T.H. would not be either.

One day he was meeting another manufacturer's representative in the lobby of a Hong Kong hotel. Dave mentioned Mike Wolf's name

MINI-BIO: DAVE KREBIEHL

Dave Krebiehl is one of the key M.T.H. employees who did not know Mike as a youngster, working for Williams. He grew up in Michigan, and attended Oakland University in Rochester, Michigan where he studied systems engineering.

His early professional experience involved moving up through the ranks in quality management in several companies. In 1989, Dave was hired by Lionel as the Director of Quality Improvement. This is when he came to know and work with Mike Wolf, a sub-contractor for Lionel at the time. Dave was directed by the president of Lionel to develop a business relationship with Mike and serve as the liaison between the two companies. Through working together, the relationship between Mike and Dave evolved into personal friendship.

In 1995, when Mike learned that Dave was leaving Lionel, he quickly offered him a job with M.T.H. in Maryland. Dave moved his family to Maryland in May, 1995, to begin working at M.T.H. headquarters. After two years, and incredible growth of M.T.H., the Krebiehls decided they were too far from family. Dave made "the most difficult professional decision of my life" and left M.T.H. to return home with his family.

Because Mike knew that Dave's a valuable team member, he arranged to create a separate Research and Development office in Michigan and re-hired him in 1998. Dave is currently the Vice President of Research and Development, and he has orchestrated the development of products including the Z-4000 Remote Control System, Proto-Sound 2.0 with DCS, Loco-Sound IR Remote Control, and more.

Dave and his wife Sue have been married for fifteen years. They have two children: Josh, 11 and Alicia, 9.

Dave Krebiehl, Vice President of Research and Development

in the course of their initial conversation. Another man nearby overheard Mike's name and he immediately came over to the pair of businessmen and introduced himself as Mr. K. K. Ku. Mr. Ku asked some questions to verify where Dave was from. Dave responded, choosing his words carefully, because Dave was waiting for a severance check from Lionel, and he did not want to say or do anything that might get back to Lionel and jeopardize getting the payment. After exchanging pleasantries, Krebiehl explained his mission while mentioning his inability to locate the Chinese firm. Ku said, "I know them. I'll take you there."

Mike Wolf with Mr. Lee and Mr. Thong, the owners of Waytechson.

Shortly after that, a meeting was arranged for Dave, and once it took place, it proved to be most successful. Before Mike ultimately met with the company he learned that the firm was manufacturing products for Lionel. However, very soon after Mike met with the owners of Waytechson, a solid long-term relationship was established. Mike became good friends with the owners. This, coupled with a number of frustrations they were experiencing with Lionel, resulted in the company ending the Lionel relationship. In fact, Waytechson now produces all M.T.H. freight cars, RailKing passenger cars, operating and non-operating accessories, and small trackside accessory items as well. Moreover, the firm now has an exclusive relationship, producing model train products only for M.T.H. Electric Trains.

M.T.H.'s unprecedented growth has continued in the past several years. As the company's growth has gathered momentum, they have introduced more new-tooled products and provided a wider variety of options for O Gauge railroaders.

The most significant event of 1996 was the announcement of the first ever RailKing articulated steamer. The design came about almost by chance-as if it were destined to happen. Mike was in Korea in one of the M.T.H. design areas, when he saw an engineer looking at CAD drawings for the Challenger. The design team was demonstrating a new software program that could tell what size an engine would be to run on what size of track, so Mike asked, just out of curiosity, to see a Challenger that would run on O-31 track. The original result wasn't quite right, but Mike and the design engineer worked together to tweak the design until they came up with a plan for a Challenger that looked like a Challenger and would run on regular O-31 track. It was serendipity. M.T.H. would certainly have made a RailKing articulated steamer and developed that product line at some point, but they know it would have happened later than it did if Mike had not happened by the engineer's desk just as he was looking at those drawings.

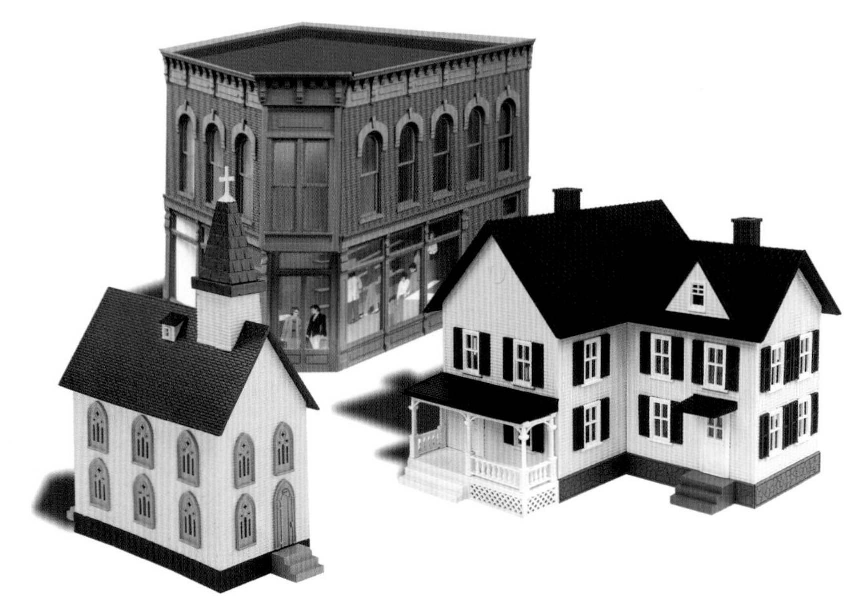

M.T.H. recognizes the value and simplicity of pre-assembled, ready to use accessories.

In 1996, M.T.H. also offered its first painted and fully assembled RailTown™ buildings. These buildings included the Church, Farm House, and Country House, and they have been followed by many more buildings, including factories, a bank, and other buildings that bring a layout to life. M.T.H. was now beginning to set the pace for creating those special items every model railroader desired to make displays more authentic and lifelike.

Tinplate reproductions reappeared in the M.T.H. line during the mid 1990s as Tinplate Traditions.

This was also the year that M.T.H. returned to production of tinplate trains, with the 408E Electric and the #613 4-car passenger set. Mike had always loved these beautiful trains and was glad to make affordable versions available to model railroaders again. This line was named Tinplate Traditions™, and it completed M.T.H.'s range of product lines.

In 1996, M.T.H. also introduced the first passenger station and freight yard announcements into the Proto-Sound package. These are favorite features of many M.T.H. customers and one that, at the time this book went to press, no competitor had ever duplicated.

With the 1997 Volume One catalog, M.T.H. decided to expand even farther into the entry-level market than they had in 1995 by developing the RailKing Ready-To-Run™ sets. These starter sets, as they are commonly known, included track and a transformer for the first time. Manufacturing complete sets requires a significant additional investment in production tooling and facilities, particularly with regard to producing sufficient quantities of track. Therefore, when M.T.H. made the decision to go ahead and package these starter sets, it was a bold move.

With the advent of the Ready-To-Run sets, M.T.H.'s vision of opening the hobby of model railroading to all manner of enthusiasts was becoming more of a reality. These complete sets are ideal for first-time buyers because they are affordable and very easy to assemble and run. In addition, the Ready-to-Run sets eliminate concerns about what kind of transformer is needed and how much track one must buy. The simplicity of the packaged sets encourages newcomers to explore the hobby. In the years since, the Ready-To-Run sets have grown to include an interactive CD ROM containing track planning software, a choice of digital sound systems, and a wireless infrared remote control, making true their motto: The Complete Solution.

Furthermore, the company perceived the starter sets as an effective means of advertising, as a sort of business card, in Mike's words. Their quality, versatility, and simplicity are good "hooks." M.T.H. was certain that the equipment included in the sets (the sturdy, detailed locomotives; the durable, colorful cars; the powerful transformer; and the easy-to-assemble track system) would give model railroaders a positive experience. M.T.H. believed that once a customer bought the high quality Ready-To-Run sets, the sets would bring these customers back for more products.

It all played out just as M.T.H. thought it would. In fact, the debut and successful run of the Ready-To-Run sets have significantly contributed to the tremendous growth of the O Gauge market in the past

RailKing Ready-To-Run train sets contain features unmatched by any other railroading manufacturer.

few years. In fact, the O Gauge railroading market has actually doubled in the seven years since M.T.H. split from Lionel and began making and promoting their own products.

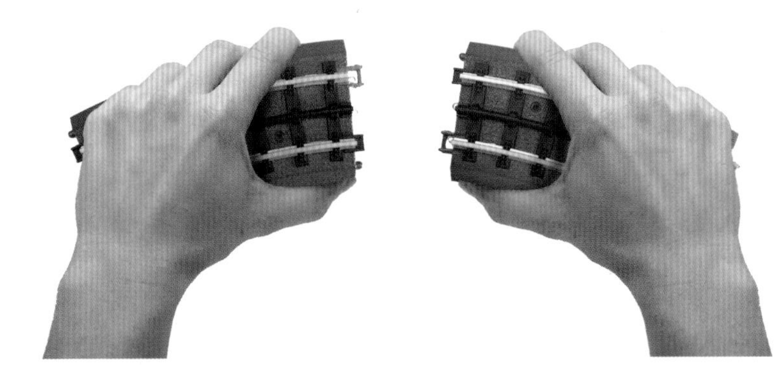

RealTrax is the only O Gauge track system to feature a built-in roadbed and simple, easy assembly.

All this work developing sets and thinking about putting them under Christmas trees had brought about another big development in the M.T.H. product line: the RealTrax™ snap-together track system with a roadbed. Because Mike was the one who insisted his family have a train around the tree every Christmas, his wife insisted that he be the one who clean up the oily mess the track left on the carpet afterward. There had to be a better plan! One common option was to put a sheet of plywood under the tree and track, but that wasn't very appealing; Mike didn't want to mar his Christmas image with a big piece of wood in the middle of the festivities. And so M.T.H. went to work. They developed a revolutionary track system that included a roadbed under the track. It was easy to set up - it just snapped together with no pins to lose or break - and it went anywhere. The roadbed eliminated the problem of oil and grease dripping onto the carpet beneath. It is the perfect track system for people who prefer not to keep a permanent layout. M.T.H. had learned from customer feedback that a bad track system had served as a barrier to the sale of starter sets for some of M.T.H.'s competitors. The 1997 roll-out of RealTrax™ solved the problem. As of the printing of this book, no other competitor has made a track system with the roadbed built in.

In the beginning, RealTrax was called RiteTrax. However, the Atlas Model Railroad Company, Inc. claimed ownership of the name based on their motto: "You're on the Right Track . . . with Atlas." Although Mike maintains that M.T.H. would have won a legal battle over the trademark (with the expression "on the right track" being a cliché and with the different spelling of the words), he voluntarily changed the name of the new track system and put his energy into competing with Atlas in the marketplace, not in the courts.

The 1997 M.T.H. catalogs heralded the appearance of some other important new items from the company. For example, the Gas Station made its first appearance as one of M.T.H.'s first operating accessories. Its outstanding success led the company to offer other equally popular operating pieces, such as a fire station and car wash.

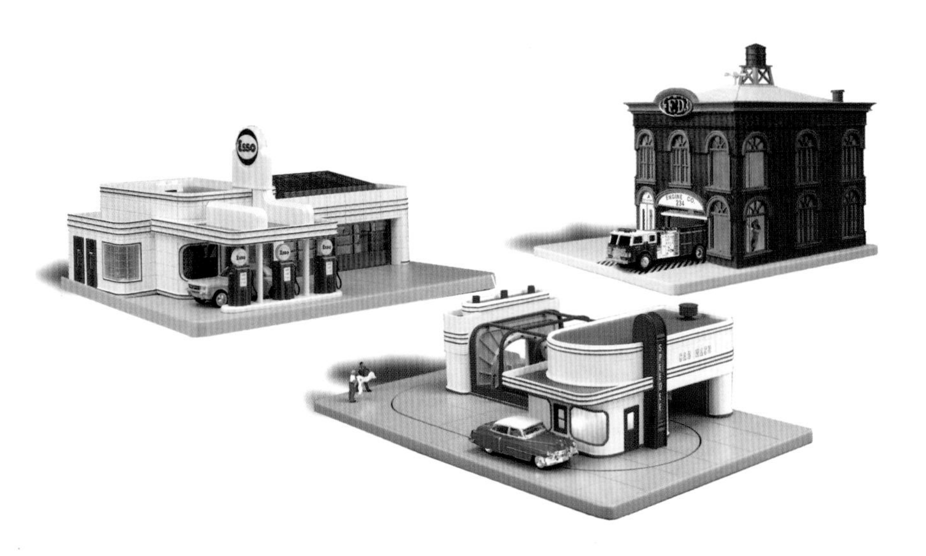

RailKing operating accessories feature state-of-the-art synchronized operation and movement.

The 1997 catalogs also advertised the Big Boy, the largest steamer ever produced in the railroad industry. When M.T.H. created this classic engine it was the first time it was ever available in O Gauge.

In the Spring 1997 catalog, M.T.H. also presented the Z-2000 transformer. Mike personally spearheaded the project to create this new device. The Z-2000 took on so many modifications and enhancements that it eventually evolved into the Z-4000®. This was O Gauge's first ever UL-approved high-powered transformer, and it proved to be a landmark in M.T.H.'s technical development.

The 1997 Volume Two catalog featured Mike's favorite locomotive, the tinplate 400E, offered for the first time in both contemporary and traditional versions. The contemporary version is for the model rail-

The M.T.H. Big Boy is the largest die-cast O Gauge steam engine ever produced, weighing 18 pounds and measuring nearly three feet long.

roader who likes the old look and the metal trains but who wants modern operational features, such as a Pittman motor, sound system, and smoke unit. The traditional version is equipped with the same kind of AC wound motor and mechanical whistle found in the original, and it does not have a smoke unit. It is almost identical to the early Standard Gauge trains.

Mike anticipated that the traditional trains would far outsell the contemporary models, while Rich Foster (V.P of Sales) and Andy Edleman (V.P. of Marketing) persisted in promoting the contemporary ones. Rich and Andy believed the contemporary design would be more popular. Mike is grateful for Rich and Andy's intuition and persistence, which proved to be right on the mark in this case. As it turned out, the tinplate models with the modern operating features outsell the traditional version by two to one. Nevertheless, Mike continues to offer the old-fashioned version for the traditionalists out there, and Mike admits that's the one he prefers.

In 1998, M.T.H. presented another dynamic locomotive - the largest diesel ever to thunder along the rails - the DD40X Centennial.

This was also the year M.T.H. offered their own line of switches. Mike's experience from his days as a distributor for other companies taught him that model railroad switches could be a problem. This is because the switches on the market then often failed to operate properly. As a result, this product was frequently returned to the store where it was purchased. Knowing this, M.T.H. invested a great deal of time and effort into developing reliable switches that could meet the built-up demand in the market. The resulting M.T.H. switches have been a welcome success.

Like its fellow UP alumnus the DD40X takes the O Gauge crown as the largest diesel ever produced.

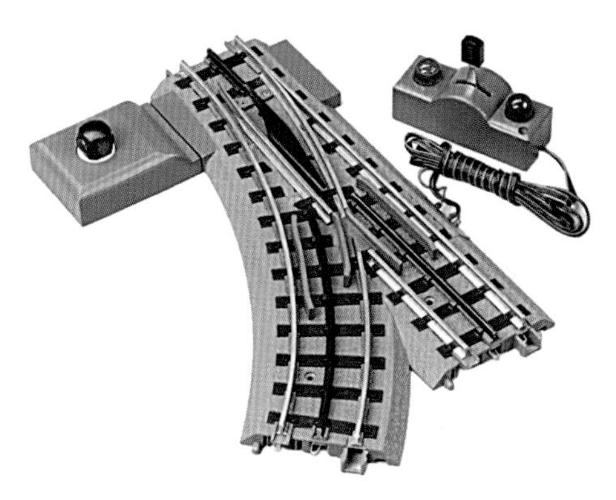
The RealTrax switch design objective was clear - they must work!

The third major development of 1998 involved not a product but a great new service. This is the year M.T.H. established the M.T.H. Railroaders Club℠ (MTHRRC). This club provides a forum for M.T.H. fans to collect and share information, as well as to stay current on M.T.H. products and services. Becoming a member in the Club also provides an opportunity to purchase special promotional items before the general public and at reduced costs.

The first year of the club's existence members were offered a special edition RailKing box car and other benefits, as part of the membership fee. The Club and its benefits have expanded significantly over the years and now all three lines are represented. When members join, they can specify which Club Line they prefer - RailKing, Premier, or Tinplate Traditions. Club members receive a bi-monthly newsletter, The CrossingGate®, which offers announcements about upcoming products, shipping schedules, service tips, and many other features of interest to model railroaders. In addition, Club Members now have a special section of the M.T.H. website dedicated to their use. The website additionally affords Club Members space on the M.T.H. server to design and publish their own web pages.

Ever since Mike first introduced RealTrax, the model railroaders who frequent the Ready To Roll hobby shop in Miami, Florida, had been pushing him to produce a track system especially well suited for a permanent scale layout. In the 1999 Volume Two Catalog, M.T.H. responded to the challenge by announcing ScaleTrax™. To be as near scale as possible, M.T.H. had to sacrifice compatibility with other track systems. Before ScaleTrax, O Gauge three-rail track systems had maintained very similar profiles to the standard that Lionel set decades before. ScaleTrax has a profile much lower than previous three-rail track systems, so it is much closer to actual scale than any others which were produced before. Because there is a trend toward increasing numbers of scale operators building more scale layouts, it is becoming clear that ScaleTrax has very large market potential.

In 1999, M.T.H. became the first model railroad manufacturer to offer train sets with a CD ROM that included track layout software, a video, and other important information for the first time buyer. The packaging of this product was perceived as critical to its success. Therefore, M.T.H. worked closely with an experienced marketing consultant to develop its look. The CD ROM package, which is titled RailWare™, was advertised with a photograph of a grandfather sitting behind his grandson, who is at the computer intently demonstrating how the software works for the older gentleman. The implied message is that model railroading can bring together different generations of a family. The idea is that after the grandson helps use the software, the grandfather can share his knowledge of railroads and modeling experience. As each person shares the wisdom and know-how of his or her own age group, everyone enjoys this wonderful hobby together. M.T.H. believes the CD ROM is a valuable tool that enhances the excellence of their train sets. Furthermore, as M.T.H. continues to expand efforts to promote this hobby to upcoming generations, there will continue to be an endorsement of family values and time spent together in model railroading.

The year 2000 began with a flourish at M.T.H. For starters, as the 2000 Volume One Catalog was coming together, there were so many products to display that the catalog had to be split into two distinct books for the very first time. The two books are the Premier and Tinplate Traditions Catalog, and the RailKing Catalog.

M.T.H. Railroaders Club Members receive a variety of benefits including specially marked cars, bi-monthly newsletters, interactive CD Roms , and even their own web pages.

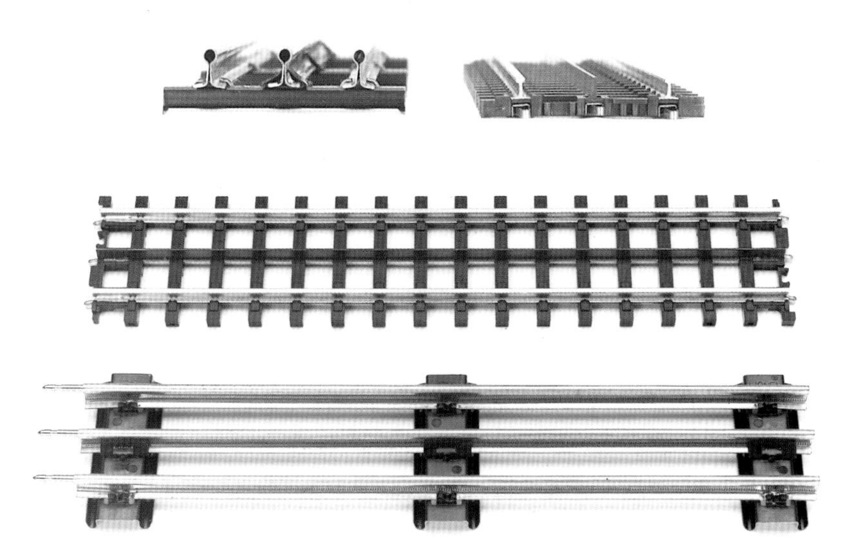

ScaleTrax is the perfect solution for modelers looking for realism. The track features the lowest rail profile available.

M.T.H. saluted the coming of the new millennium with their special gold- and platinum-plated Millennium Edition engines and cars. These exclusive products are sure to be valuable collectors' items.

The Premier and Tinplate Traditions Catalog includes the Westinghouse Schnabel car, which is the largest freight car ever made. This monster of a model measures more than two feet in length.

The 2000 Volume Two catalog introduces a catenary system, which has been a frequent request from a substantial group of M.T.H. fans. This new product will enable model railroaders who strive for an authentic look to achieve it. Their electric trains will become more prototypical when pantographs are connected to the catenary system.

The process for developing and producing any M.T.H. product is rather interesting. First of all, M.T.H. receives considerable correspondence from model railroaders who are hoping for certain models to be made. They often send the company photos or drawings and quite a bit of additional information for certain requests. All of this is kept on file, and when it comes time to develop new products, Mike and his key staff review this information and often select an idea for a project from the files. M.T.H. also collects information from the Warranty Cards sent in to the headquarters by folks purchasing M.T.H. products. These cards provide survey data related to new products consumers might want. This data is also considered when deciding on the development and production of a new M.T.H. model. In addition, M.T.H. subscribes to several railroad publications. The marketing and product development staff reviews these resources to discover new and unusual engines and cars that are part of a railroad's past or current rosters.

All of these sources for identifying a new product are most valuable. Furthermore, the input arouses creativity and enhances M.T.H.'s ability to produce a diverse number of models. As Mike says, "We have made some odd engines, but this helps to increase the variety and uniqueness of what we can offer consumers. In turn, I believe that this stimulates our growth."

Once a new product is identified for development and production, an intense research process is initiated. A trained and experienced staff dedicated entirely to research operates full-time at M.T.H. Historical drawings, similar models, and technical specifications are carefully reviewed before the design and production teams develop a model. M.T.H. has always believed in using the latest technology available, such as CAD drawings and rapid prototype equipment, to ensure an efficient and exact design process. Once the piece is designed, a pre-production sample is produced. Then the tooling is made and samples are tested repeatedly. After all of the "bugs" have been eliminated, the parts are made and the engine is built.

M.T.H. marked the new millennium celebration with several unique offerings including this 18 karat gold- and platinum-plated NYC Hudson.

In this catalog, M.T.H. also offers some entertaining Americana in the form of licensed McDonald's products: a Ready-To-Run freight set and a replica of a vintage McDonald's Restaurant.

As exciting as all these developments were, perhaps the biggest announcement in M.T.H. history is in the 2000 Volume Two catalog. This is where M.T.H. introduced Proto-Sound 2.0 with a Digital Command System (DCS) and Loco-Sound™. Loco-Sound brings full locomotive sound to even the inexpensive train sets. And Proto-Sound 2.0 provides not only richer and more realistic sound than has been available before but also a vast array of new operational features, such as speed control in one mph increments, controllable smoke output, and the ability to command each locomotive individually. DCS is also the first fully compatible command system in O Gauge railroading. It can operate a Lionel train in command mode, a M.T.H. train in DCS command mode and a conventional locomotive on the same track at the same time.

In a recent conversation (1999) between Mike Wolf and Dick Christianson, of Classic Toy Trains magazine, Christianson admitted to being amazed at the number of new products involving all-new tooling that M.T.H. has introduced in recent years. M.T.H. provided some impressive numbers:

Since 1993 M.T.H. has introduced the following all-new tooled products:

62 Steam Engines
77 Diesel, Turbine, and Electric Locomotives
91 Different Kinds of Freight Cars
24 Different Kinds of Passenger Cars

This list, which developed in only seven years, represents more new-tooled products than M.T.H.'s chief competitor has made in nearly one hundred years.

M.T.H. - A PRIME MOVER

Facilities Expansion

By 1995, The enthusiastic acceptance of this vast array of M.T.H.'s new model railroad products and the resulting rapid increase in the volume of products arriving from overseas caused an urgent need for expanded office and warehouse space. Not surprisingly, M.T.H. had reached a point where deliveries to the Gerwig Lane location needed to be carefully scheduled.

Because there was no room in the building for the new items coming in from overseas, all unloading and shifting of boxes had to take place on the parking lot behind the building. The trucking companies delivering the containers were notified that they had to arrive early in the day. When the shipment arrived, it was loaded on to pallets just outside the building. Tarpaulins to cover the new arrivals were kept readily accessible in case of inclement weather.

M.T.H. thinks that the second volume of the Year 2000 Catalog displays the best assemblage of Ready-to-Run sets ever produced. Among those are:

Pennsylvania Turbine Sets
(includes both freight and passenger sets)
Southern Pacific Daylight Passenger Set
Santa Fe Super Chief Passenger Set
Norfolk & Western J Passenger Set
McDonald's Freight Set
Christmas Set (plays Christmas music)

The process for moving these newly shipped items in and out of the M.T.H. offices was well choreographed and quick. The goal was to rapidly unpack the new shipment, inspect the merchandise, and then determine what items went to which dealers. Then the items ordered by each dealer were immediately but carefully repackaged, addressed to the appropriate dealers, and then picked up by the parcel delivery service before the end of the day. This was an efficient operation but one with tight deadlines and significant pressure.

Anything not already on order was then considered an in-stock item that needed to be stored until it was sold. Because space was so limited, this often required crowding boxes into offices and every other imaginable nook and cranny in the existing space. It also meant that everyone had to help to find storage space as well as assist in moving and stacking the new in-stock items. No one employed at M.T.H., including all corporate officers, was exempt from this often exhausting task. Like the other officers, Mike was part of the crew who got the products unloaded when shipments came in. He recalls, "Once when we got a big shipment of scale Hudsons in I was helping to unload and line them up on the skids. One of the big stacks accidentally fell over on me and knocked me over. I got a nasty injury on my wrist which to this day hurts when I move it a certain way!"

In 1996, the lack of adequate office and warehouse space at the Gerwig Lane location reached a breaking point. M.T.H. had to find a new facility. Mike really did not want to lease any more space because he believed that paying rent was just throwing money away. So, he started looking for a piece of land to buy and build a structure of his own. Initially he considered the parcel of land beside where his offices were located at that time. The real estate person who was helping him to locate a piece of property discouraged him from this purchase, leading him instead to a much more upscale and valuable parcel of land in the Columbia Gateway complex. As Mike was told, "The long term value on the Columbia Gateway property would increase much more than the land next to his Gerwig Lane facility." Mike agreed and made the purchase.

Plans were developed and approved, and construction began on a new forty-five thousand square foot building. In September, 1997, the new facility was completed and ready for occupancy. On November 6, 1997, M.T.H. celebrated the Official Grand Opening of its new headquarters, at 7020 Columbia Gateway Drive, and it was a memorable occasion.

In attendance were representatives of the local Howard County Government, members of the press, and representatives of the firms that financed and built the structure. Se Yong Lee and his wife also flew over from Korea just for this momentous occasion. There were guided tours, interviews by the press, and lots and lots of photographs taken.

One of the more meaningful photos was shot by a photographer from O Gauge Railroading magazine. The picture shows Mike and his lovely wife Rasamee standing with his proud parents, Doris and Paul Wolf, in the spectacular lobby of the new headquarters. This photo was enlarged and presented to Mike by O Gauge Railroading.

M.T.H.'s new building measures 125,000 square feet, housing all domestic operations.

Today it hangs on a wall near Mike's office. In the photo Mike and his family are positioned in front of the grand M.T.H. Electric Trains logo strategically mounted on the wall of the lobby.

The M.T.H. logo is a cherished gift made just for the Grand Opening by Mr. Lee and Mr. Thong of Waytechson. The huge logo is made of cast aluminum and is bolted not only into the wall but also into the ceiling beams.

Despite the inauguration of the expansive new facility that M.T.H. claimed as its own, the storage and office space issues did not disappear. Fortunately, M.T.H. had enough foresight to anticipate continuous growth and thus plan for future facility expansion. It was a good thing that they did because an escalating volume of products was processed through the facility. Very soon after the move into the new facility construction work commenced on an 80,000 square foot addition to the new building, to be used for additional warehousing and space for repackaging of products arriving as bulk shipments. This

Mike Wolf with his wife Rasamee and his parents, Doris and Paul Wolf.

addition was completed in 1998 and immediately put to use. To someone not familiar with the rapid increase of the M.T.H. product lines, this expansion of M.T.H.'s building might look like an over-extension or overly optimistic sales expectations. Such is not the case! There was a genuine need for more space. The fact that in 1997, only 101 sea-going containers of model train products were received by M.T.H. (82 at the Gerwig Lane site and 19 at the new building), yet one year later the total had grown to 178, thoroughly justified the need. In 1999, the number of containers totaled 187. M.T.H. anticipates that of this impressive rate of growth will continue and has purchased an additional six acre lot for any needed expansion. The next twenty years should be even better than the first!

STATION STOP . . . BUT NOT THE END OF THE LINE

It's Been Quite a Journey So Far!

In 2000 M.T.H. is in its twenty-first year of operation. Although young in years, Mike and his corporation have come a long way, and there are a lot of memories. Some of those memories focus on Mike's first impressions of railroading and people close to him who were a part of that industry. For example, Mike remembers his maternal Grandfather, William Reismeier, a machinist in the mechanical department of the Pennsylvania Railroad. He proudly put in more than 49-years of service, and he is listed in the railroad's Roll of Honor. Then there is Mike's father, Paul, who just after high school worked for the Pennsylvania Railroad as well, setting rivets in the roofs of Madison-type cars. There had to be a lot of stories told by Mike's Father and Grandfather that influenced Mike's interest in trains.

Mike remembers his years working for Williams Reproductions, and appreciates the experience and opportunities that came his way there. He recalls the risk taken by his father, when Mike borrowed so much of his parents' money to buy Williams's tooling. He still laughs when he remembers opening that surprise box from Samhongsa, with the 200 series cars inside. He recalls the relationship with Lionel, with some good recollections, and some not so good. He looks back at the many difficult decisions that had to be made concerning new products and high tool costs, most of which were the right decisions. He fondly recollects the many bonds of friendship developed throughout his company's twenty-one-year history. Having made over sixty trips to Asia, he has come to know, trust and appreciate the skill and commitment of his Korean and Chinese colleagues.

The M.T.H. journey to date has been quite a ride on the rails! Mike Wolf and M.T.H. have accomplished much, and have substantial reason for pride. For instance, M.T.H. is proud to have received two Model Railroader Readers' Choice Awards. One award was for the 2-rail Big Boy locomotive and one was for the Operating Gas Station, which won the Accessory Of The Year Award. This is a very big mark of distinction in the model railroading industry, and M.T.H is pleased to have been rewarded with two of them.

M.T.H. also takes pride in the fact that they are the only O Gauge manufacturer that has made die-cast steam engines in the 2-rail version. (The company has also done some 2-rail diesels.) The typical runs for two-rail items are small; M.T.H. often makes only 50 pieces of any given model in 2-rail. This is because the 2-rail O Gauge market is very small. Nonetheless, M.T.H. is proud to have served this constituency.

From 1993 to the present day, M.T.H. has generated a revolution in the toy train industry with its innovation, creativity, determination, and measured confidence. Consider that M.T.H. has developed and produced an amazing number of new products that have been heralded by model railroaders. In the first catalog, in 1993, M.T.H. promoted only 15 separate items. Only seven years later, in just the first two of three year 2000 catalogs, M.T.H. promoted 550 separate items. This is phenomenal growth for such a short period of time. At the same time, M.T.H. has expanded its dealer and customer services to ensure complete satisfaction.

M.T.H. has made more newly-tooled motive power than any other manufacturer in O Gauge railroading, including Lionel, who has been doing this for 100 years. M.T.H. spent $32 million in tooling and millions more in research and development in this seven year period. This commitment to variety and continuous improvement in M.T.H. products will continue.

M.T.H. also firmly believes in utilizing the most current and best technology. State-of-the-art is not just a catch phrase at this company! The wise use of technology can be the deciding factor between success and failure in this industry. To emphasize this point, Mike says, "I picked up the Asian business philosophy in the years of doing business overseas. 'Invest for the future,' is a good way to run a business!" In simple terms that means all investments made today should be based on what they will do for you in the future, over the long-term. Investing to earn an immediate return is not always smart. This is why M.T.H. has always invested so heavily in new tooling and technology; technology is the future.

Using the most current technology in this business is valuable not only for its impact on the quality and variety of trains, but also for the way it enhances capabilities on the web site, the point-of-sale systems, and the computers and software in the M.T.H. facilities. One key example of this is the online Product Locator Service, a database that allows customers to locate specific items at retailers around the country. The Point-of-Sale system that will be in stores in late 2000 is another good example. This system allows users to view all M.T.H. products in a particular retailer's inventory. The system will also automatically update a dealer's inventory in the Product Locator system found on M.T.H.'s web site. The Product Locator and Point-of-Sale system also demonstrate M.T.H.'s dedication to working continuously to strengthen relationships with dealers and to provide marketing and sales support. The success of every dealer in the ever-growing network of Authorized M.T.H. Train Merchants is vital to M.T.H.'s success.

M.T.H. believes that for retailers to succeed in the changing economy, they will have to combine the traditional brick and mortar retail services with the effectiveness and far-reaching capabilities of the internet. This is one of the reasons that M.T.H. willingly invested company funds to develop the Product Locator and Point-of-Sale System.

M.T.H. has established a standard of excellence and responsiveness that revolutionizes the toy train industry and challenges even the oldest of competitors. Competition in the O Gauge market has been growing rapidly since M.T.H. entered the market. All of M.T.H.'s variety and new tooling has forced others to make new tooling.

Maryland's Entrepreneur of the Year for 1998

In 1998 Mike Wolf was nominated by M.T.H.'s Maryland bank as a candidate for the Maryland Entrepreneur of the Year Award, in the Retail Products Category. The competition was sponsored by Ernst and Young, USA Today, NASDAQ, and other Maryland corporations. Businesses were judged on the basis of profitable operation, good management, and for having an active role in the community. Mike won the Maryland State award, from among over seven hundred nominees. The competition for the national award was held in Palm Springs, California, where Mike lost out to Papa John's Pizza, but he was proud that M.T.H. Electric Trains achieved some national recognition and publicity.

Fortunately M.T.H. has experienced remarkable success, particularly in recent years. Mike very much appreciates that good fortune, and fully realizes the importance of sharing this.

To begin with, Mike is highly sensitive to the fact that M.T.H.'s success is in part a result of the quality and dedication of the company's employees. In recognizing this fact, Mike is committed to sustaining the well being of the company not just for himself, but also for more than 100 employees.

What's more, over the years, Mike Wolf learned that responsibility and caring for others goes far beyond our immediate circle of family and friends. Because of this realization, he developed a strong sense of purpose to make the world a better place to live, especially when it comes to children. To that end, for some time now, Mike has routinely and generously shared his success through significant gifts to charities.

Since the late eighties M.T.H. has demonstrated its corporate commitment to help improve community life. At first the company contributed to the operation of a home for pregnant women, sponsored by Catholic Charities. However, Mike developed a special interest in helping abused children, which led him to Saint Vincent's Orphanage, in Timonium, Maryland. M.T.H. built the orphanage a swimming pool and remodeled the living quarters for the youngsters living there. M.T.H. also built a computer lab and a technical center at St. Vincent's, where the children can learn a variety of technical skills. Office job training and learning how to work in a restaurant are additional instructional programs offered to the young people there. Furthermore, M.T.H. delivers a number of Christmas presents to St. Vincent's each year.

Mike's life-long love for the Miami Dolphins led Mike to support children's needs in South Florida by pledging to contribute $1,000 for each touchdown pass Marino completed, with the money to go to the Dan Marino Foundation, a charitable organization active within the National Football League.

In 1998 M.T.H. pledged to support abused children by contributing ten dollars for each packaged train set marked with the corporation's pledge. This commitment raised $140,000 which was given to the Ed Block Courage Award program, a foundation sponsored with the aid of the national Football League, to help find new homes for abused children. A similar program was developed in 1999 for the Dan Marino Foundation, resulting in a $200,000 donation.

Last year the M.T.H. Electric Trains foundation provided half a million dollars, much of which went to support the Young Life Movement, which is a Christian high school organization that is designed to involve students in worthwhile after school activities. Mike belonged to this organization in high school, and is pleased to support its work in schools throughout the country

M.T.H. believes this competition is good for the consumers who enjoy the benefits of more variety, innovation, and higher quality.

M.T.H. was the first manufacturer in O Gauge to put a factory-installed digital sound system into trains, and Lionel had to answer. M.T.H. was the first to put an operating smoke system into diesel engines, so Lionel needed to meet that challenge. M.T.H. was the first to make a die-cast articulated steam engine, and Lionel needed to do that too.

The competition doesn't work just one way. For example, K-Line was the first manufacturer to put fully detailed interiors into cabooses, and M.T.H. had to rise to that occasion. K-Line offered separately painted handrails on locomotives, and M.T.H. followed suit. So competition is not just forcing others to raise the level of quality. Competition also demands that M.T.H. perform to its highest potential. Meanwhile, the consumer wins all the way around as a result. This is why so many people from other gauges have moved into O Gauge and fueled such tremendous growth in the last few years. Some of the other gauges have become stagnant because of lack of competition, which is the outcome of those manufacturers agreeing not to compete head-to-head. The problem with this is that with no pressure to compete and improve, there are no innovations in those markets.

Despite pressure from some quarters to make non-competition agreements within O Gauge, M.T.H. promises its customers they will not do that. Mike Wolf believes in the capitalistic system, in competition, and in the American Dream. Mike sums it up when he says, "Competition drives creativity and R&D [Research and Development]." The kind of R&D that comes from competition can be used to develop better products in O Gauge railroading but it can also be used in different marketplaces. The O Gauge Market has never been healthier than it is right now. Given their phenomenal success at rejuvenating O Gauge railroading, M.T.H. is also interested in exploring opportunities to penetrate the markets for different model railroad gauges in the future, while positioning itself to explore marketing other hobby lines.

Perhaps the most challenging aspect of the M.T.H. experience over the last seven years has been managing the company's skyrocketing growth, which sometimes involved a few growing pains. Maintaining adequate and comfortable work space, recruiting qualified staff, ensuring responsive service, and investing in the most efficient state-of-the-art equipment are some of the issues of concern that need vigilant monitoring. However, these are also factors that, if dealt with effectively, will contribute to the continued growth and success of M.T.H.

Mike Wolf and M.T.H. especially thank the dealers and customers who have been so patient and loyal throughout the years. Mike is anxious to take the firm into the 21st Century with many new projects and artfully managed expansion. Mike's admittedly ambitious long-term goal for M.T.H. is to have a train set around every Christmas tree in the country. However, as Mike states, "We've only scratched the surface of what we're capable of doing in this area, but we plan to dig deeper and keep this exciting and revolutionary business going as we blaze new trails in the industry."

PENNSYLVANIA
COLUMBIA
M.T.H.
ELECTRIC TRAINS®

TINPLATE

The Commander
4689

TINPLATE TRADITIONS LINE
INTRODUCTION

Although tinplate reproductions were around at the birth of Mike's Train House, Tinplate Traditions® was the last M.T.H. product line to receive its own name, in 1996. As its name suggests, this line includes reproductions of what collectors call tinplate trains, made chiefly of stamped sheet die-cast metal, with a less realistic appearance than models in the Premier or RailKing® lines. The original tinplate items that M.T.H. duplicates were produced predominantly between the two world wars and are generally referred to as "pre-war" items. M.T.H. has made reproductions of Standard and O Gauge tinplate products.

Tinplate Traditions reproductions can generally be distinguished from earlier M.T.H. reproductions (1983-88) by their being marked with the new corporate name, M.T.H. Electric Trains, rather than the older name, Mike's Train House. The locomotives in this newer line generally come with a choice of Traditional equipment, which includes an AC motor and mechanical E-unit, or Contemporary equipment, which includes flywheel-equipped motors and Proto-Sound®. Beginning with the 2000 volume two catalog, Contemporary equipment includes Proto-Sound® 2.0 with DCS.

Tinplate Traditions items are distinguished by the "10-" prefix to their four-digit item numbers. The suffixes indicate the following:
10-1130-0 Traditional Equipment
10-1130-1 Contemporary Equipment

The Tinplate Traditions line also includes several accessories, such as the Hell Gate Bridge, a Power House, and a Roundhouse. Some of the O Gauge accessories are included in the RailKing line, so when seeking a particular accessory in this book, see the RailKing as well as the Tinplate Traditions listings.

The models in this section are arranged by item type, then by item description, catalog, and delivery date. You can also refer to the indexes which are organized in the same order as the book's pictures. The indexes also include information on operation (i.e. Standard or O Gauge, etc.). The item page layouts provide complete information on each item: item type, roadname, the first catalog the item was offered in, the date the item was delivered, item number, and equipment available.

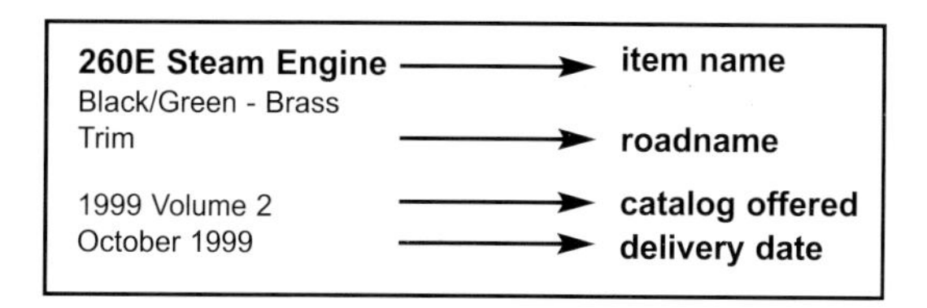

TINPLATE TRADITIONS LINE
STEAM LOCOMOTIVES

Tinplate Traditions® steamers evoke memories of the glory days of model railroading. M.T.H. has made these reproductions of classic tinplate steam engines in Standard and O Gauges. They have made five different engines, each an exact reproduction of an original pre-war model, in a variety of paint schemes. Each has a stamped metal body and brightly painted enamel, and many have brass or nickel trim. Many tinplate steam engines come with a choice of contemporary or traditional equipment. Contemporary engines have flywheel-equipped motors and Proto-Sound, while traditional steamers have an AC motor and mechanical E-unit similar to those in the original models. M.T.H. president Mike Wolf favors the artistry of tinplate trains and enjoys making them for those model railroaders who also prefer their nostalgic look.

O GAUGE

260E Steam Engine
Black/Green - Brass Trim

1999 Volume 2
October 1999

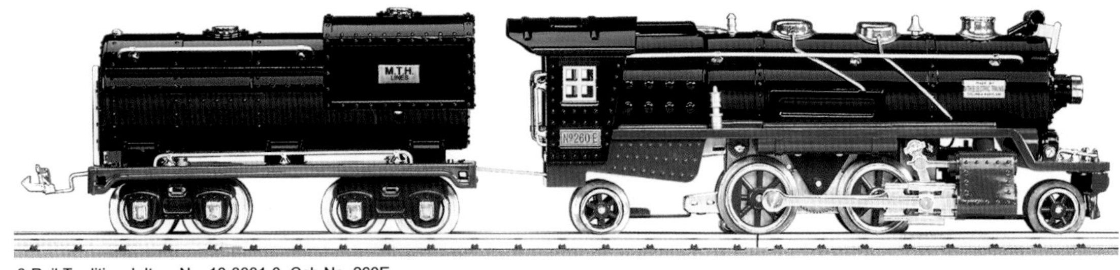

3-Rail Traditional, Item No. 10-3001-0, Cab No. 260E
3-Rail Contemporary with Proto-Sound®, Item No. 10-3001-1, Cab No. 260E

260E Steam Engine
Black/Cream - Brass Trim

1999 Volume 2
October 1999

3-Rail Traditional, Item No. 10-3002-0, Cab No. 260E
3-Rail Contemporary with Proto-Sound®, Item No. 10-3002-1, Cab No. 260E

263 Tinplate Loco & Tender
Gray/Nickel

1998 Volume 1
May 1998

3-Rail Traditional, Item No. 10-1063-0, Cab No. 263
3-Rail Contemporary with Proto-Sound®, Item No. 10-1063-1, Cab No. 263

263 Tinplate Loco & Tender
Blue Comet Blue

1998 Volume 1
May 1998

3-Rail Traditional, Item No. 10-1062-0, Cab No. 263
3-Rail Contemporary with Proto-Sound®, Item No. 10-1062-1, Cab No. 263

STANDARD GAUGE

#1134 Ives Steamer
Black

2000 Volume 1
July 2000

3-Rail Traditional, Item No. 10-1123-0, Cab No.1134
3-Rail Contemporary with Proto-Sound® 2.0, Item No. 10-1123-1, Cab No. 1134

392E Steam Engine & Tender
Black/Brass Trim

1998 Volume 3
December 1998

3-Rail Traditional, Item No. 10-1092-0, Cab No. 392E
3-Rail Contemporary with Proto-Sound®, Item No. 10-1092-1, Cab No. 392E

392E Steam Engine & Tender
Gray/Nickel Trim

1998 Volume 3
December 1998

3-Rail Traditional, Item No. 10-1091-0, Cab No. 392E
3-Rail Contemporary with Proto-Sound®, Item No. 10-1091-1, Cab No. 392E

400E Tinplate Steam Engine
Black/Brass Trim

1997 Volume 2
February 1998

3-Rail Traditional, Item No. 10-1061, Cab No. 400E
3-Rail Contemporary with Proto-Sound®, Item No. 10-1060, Cab No. 400E

400E Tinplate Steam Engine
Grey/Nickel Trim

1997 Volume 2
February 1998

3-Rail Traditional, Item No. 10-1059, Cab No. 400E
3-Rail Contemporary with Proto-Sound®, Item No. 10-1058, Cab No. 400E

400E Tinplate Steam Engine
Blue/Brass Trim

1999 Volume 2
December 1999

3-Rail Traditional, Item No. 10-1112-0, Cab No. 400E
3-Rail Contemporary with Proto-Sound®, Item No. 10-1112-1, Cab No. 400E

400E Tinplate Steam Engine
Crackle Black/Brass Trim

1999 Volume 2
December 1999

3-Rail Traditional, Item No. 10-1113-0, Cab No. 400E
3-Rail Contemporary with Proto-Sound®, Item No. 10-1113-1, Cab No. 400E

TINPLATE TRADITIONS LINE
Electric Locomotives

Colorful Tinplate Traditions® Standard Gauge electric engines feature stamped metal bodies, brightly painted enamel, metal latch couplers, operating headlights, and metal wheels and axles. These locomotives are exact replicas of the tinplate pieces first produced between the two world wars. To date, M.T.H. has reproduced three different kinds of electric engines in several different paint schemes. Most are available in a choice of contemporary or traditional equipment. Traditional engines come equipped with AC motors and mechanical E-units similar to those found in the originals, while Contemporary models have with flywheel-equipped motors and Proto-Sound to allow for more modern operation. These beautiful reproductions are sure to please anyone who loves the romance of the pre-war period of model railroading.

381E Locomotive
State Green

1998 Volume 2
April 1998

3-Rail Traditional, Item No. 10-1077-0, Cab No. 381E
3-Rail Contemporary with Proto-Sound®, Item No. 10-1077-1, Cab No. 381E

408E Tinplate Electric Engine
Apple Green

Spring 1996
May 1996

3-Rail Traditional, Item No. 10-1022, Cab No. 408E

408E Tinplate Electric Engine
Two-Tone Brown

Spring 1996
May 1996

3-Rail Traditional, Item No. 10-1023, Cab No. 408E
3-Rail Contemporary with Proto-Sound® 2.0, Item No. 10-1132-1, Cab No. 408E
3-Rail Traditional, Item No. 10-1132-0, Cab No. 408E

408E Tinplate Electric Engine
Dark Green

2000 Volume 2
October 2000

3-Rail Traditional, Item No. 10-1131-0, Cab No. 408E
3-Rail Contemporary with Proto-Sound® 2.0, Item No. 10-1131-1, Cab No. 408E

#9E Locomotive
Two-Tone Green

1998 Volume 1
November 1997

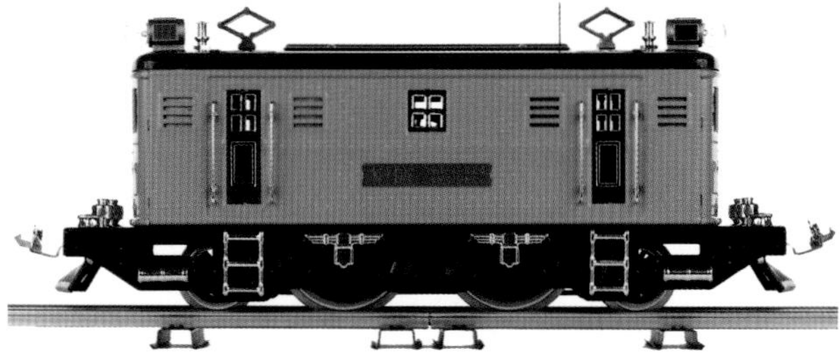

3-Rail Traditional, Item No. 10-1066-0, Cab No. 9E
3-Rail Contemporary with Proto-Sound®, Item No. 10-1066-1, Cab No. 9E

#9E Locomotive
Gray/Nickel

1998 Volume 1
November 1997

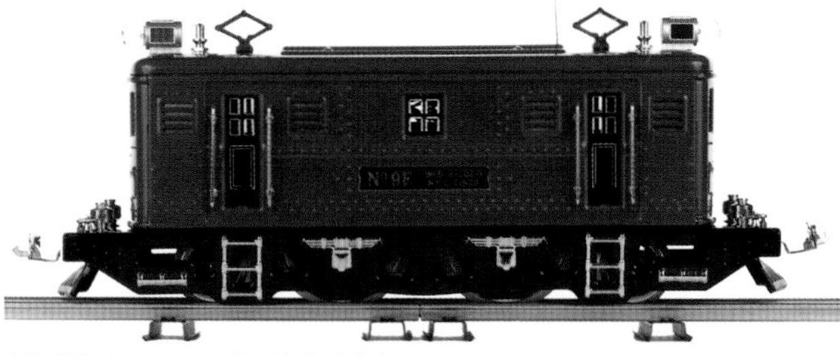

3-Rail Traditional, Item No. 10-1067-0, Cab No. 9E
3-Rail Contemporary with Proto-Sound®, Item No. 10-1067-1, Cab No. 9E

#9E Locomotive
Orange

1999 Volume 1
May 1999

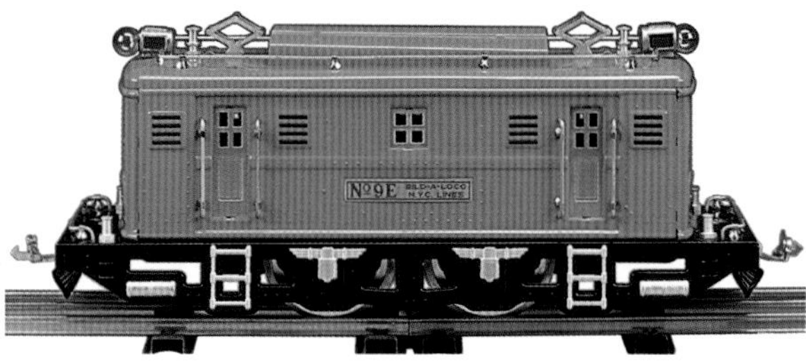

3-Rail Traditional, Item No. 10-1104-0, Cab No. 9E
3-Rail Contemporary with Proto-Sound®, Item No. 10-1104-1, Cab No. 9E

#9E Locomotive
Dark Green

1999 Volume 1
May 1999

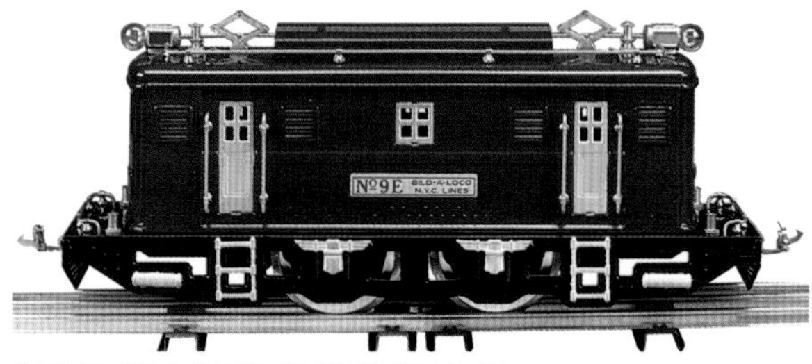

3-Rail Traditional, Item No. 10-1105-0, Cab No. 9E
3-Rail Contemporary with Proto-Sound®, Item No. 10-1105-1, Cab No. 9E

TINPLATE TRADITIONS LINE
ROLLING STOCK

The Tinplate Traditions® line features rolling stock from three different tinplate series: the 200 and slightly smaller 500 series in Standard Gauge, and the 800 series in O Gauge. Each freight car is constructed of stamped metal components, with a brightly painted enamel finish. Most boast brass or nickel trim, and all models feature black oxide trucks, metal journal boxes, and sprung latch couplers. While most Tinplate Traditions freight cars are reproductions of earlier cars, M.T.H. has introduced a few new cars, such as the 200 and 500 series Standard Gauge ore cars advertised in the 2000 volume two catalog. These colorful and varied cars are the perfect accompaniment to M.T.H.'s tinplate locomotives. As this book goes to press, M.T.H. has promoted or produced twenty-seven different pieces of tinplate rolling stock from the three series.

200 Series Std. Gauge Box Car
Yellow/Brown with Nickel Trim
Item No. 10-201, Car No. 214

Fall/Winter 1996
June 1996

200 Series Std. Gauge Box Car
Cream/Orange with Brass Trim
Item No. 10-202, Car No. 214

Fall/Winter 1996
June 1996

200 Series Std. Gauge Box Car
MTHRRC - 1999
Item No. 10-1109, Car No. 214

1999 Volume 2
October 1999

200 Series Std. Gauge Caboose
Red/Red
Item No. 10-1054, Car No. 217

Spring 1997
December 1997

200 Series Std. Gauge Caboose
Peacock/Red
Item No. 10-1055, Car No. 217

Spring 1997
December 1997

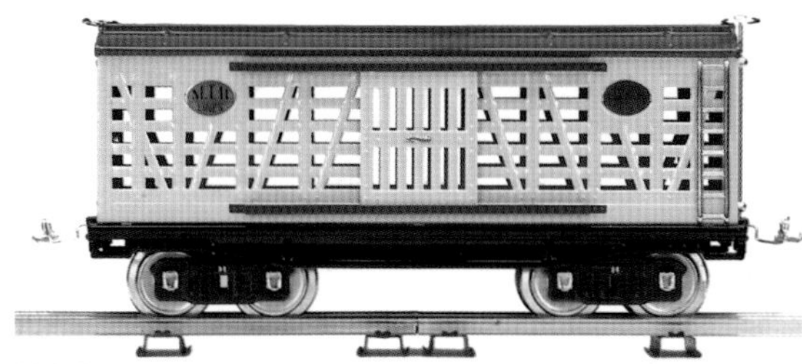

200 Series Std. Gauge Cattle Car
Cream/Maroon with Nickel Trim
Item No. 10-204, Car No. 213

Fall/Winter 1996
June 1996

200 Series Std. Gauge Cattle Car
Terra Cotta/Green with Brass Trim
Item No. 10-203, Car No. 213

Fall/Winter 1996
June 1996

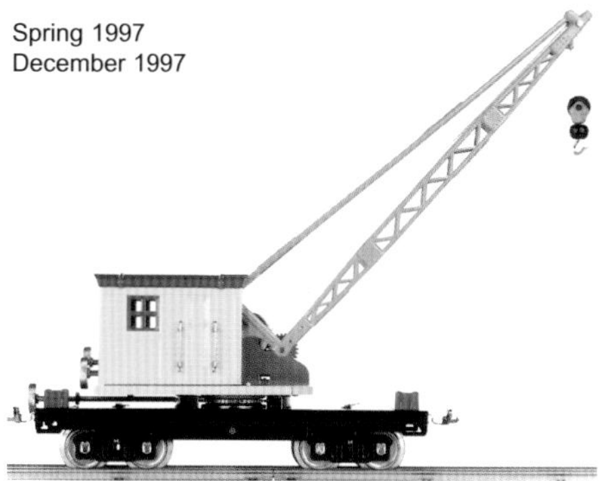

200 Series Std. Gauge Crane Car
Yellow with Nickel Trim
Item No. 10-1081, Car No. 219

1998 Volume 3
October 1998

200 Series Std. Gauge Crane Car
Peacock with Brass Trim
Item No. 10-1082, Car No. 219

1998 Volume 3
October 1998

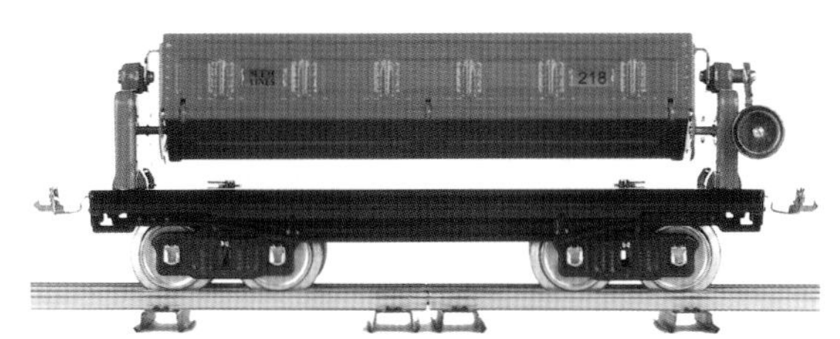

200 Series Std. Gauge Dump Car
Mojave with Nickel Trim
Item No. 10-1083, Car No. 218

1998 Volume 3
October 1998

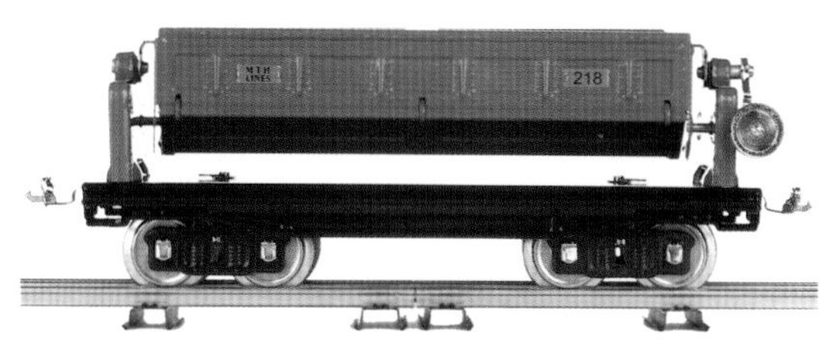

200 Series Std. Gauge Dump Car
Mojave with Brass Trim
Item No. 10-1084, Car No. 218

1998 Volume 3
October 1998

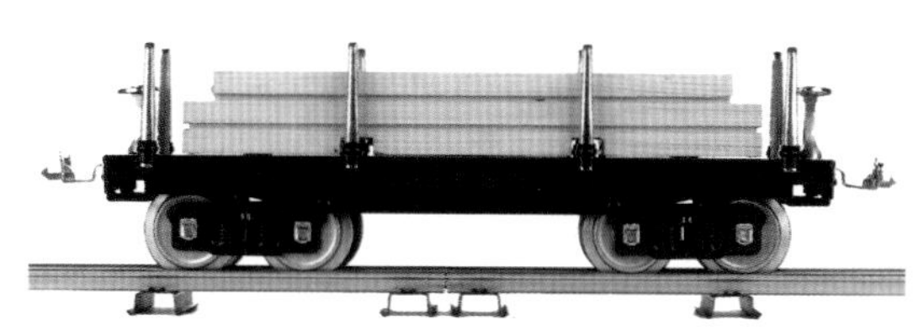

200 Series Std. Gauge Flat Car
Black with Nickel Trim
Item No. 10-1071, Car No. 211

1998 Volume 2
April 1998

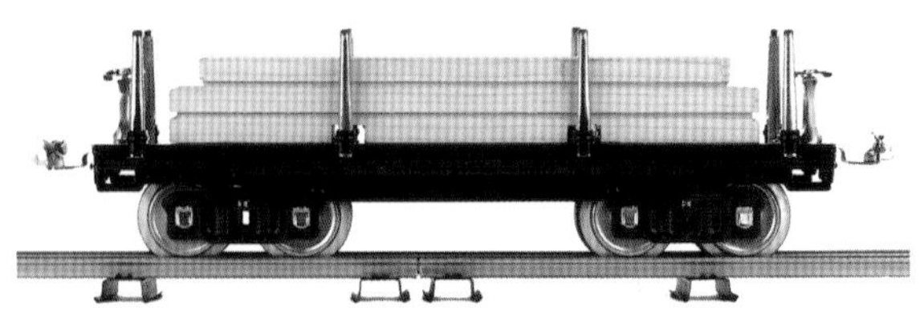

200 Series Std. Gauge Flat Car
Black with Brass Trim
Item No. 10-1072, Car No. 211

1998 Volume 2
April 1998

200 Series Std. Gauge Gondola Car
Maroon with Brass Trim
Item No. 10-1073, Car No. 212

1998 Volume 2
April 1998

200 Series Std. Gauge Gondola Car
Green with Nickel Trim
Item No. 10-1074, Car No. 212

1998 Volume 2
November 1998

200 Series Std. Gauge Hopper Car
Green with Nickel Trim
Item No. 10-1052, Car No. 216

Spring 1997
December 1997

200 Series Std. Gauge Hopper Car
Green with Brass Trim
Item No. 10-1053, Car No. 216

Spring 1997
December 1997

200 Series Std. Gauge Ore Car
Maroon with Brass Trim
3-Rail, Item No. 10-1130, Car No. 212

2000 Volume 2
May 2000

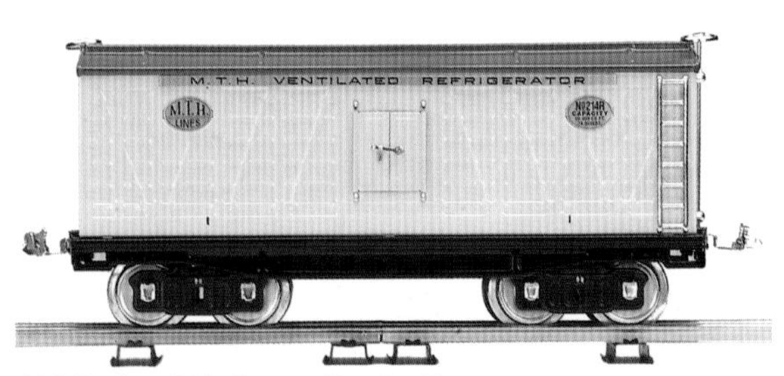

200 Series Std. Gauge Reefer Car
Ivory/Peacock with Brass Trim
Item No. 10-205, Car No. 205

Fall/Winter 1996
June 1996

200 Series Std. Gauge Reefer Car
White/Blue with Nickel Trim
Item No. 10-206, Car No. 214R

Fall/Winter 1996
June 1996

200 Series Std. Gauge Searchlight Car
Terra Cotta with Brass Trim
Item No. 10-1075, Car No. 220

1998 Volume 2
April 1998

200 Series Std. Gauge Searchlight Car
Green with Nickel Trim
Item No. 10-1076, Car No. 220

1998 Volume 2
April 1998

200 Series Std. Gauge Tank Car
Orange with Nickel Trim
Item No. 10-1050, Car No. 215

Spring 1997
December 1997

200 Series Std. Gauge Tank Car
Green with Brass Trim
Item No. 10-1051, Car No. 215

Spring 1997
December 1997

200 Series Std. Gauge Tank Car
MTHRRC - 2000
Item No. 10-1127, Car No. 241

2000 Volume 2
May 2000

500 Series Std. Gauge Box Car
Yellow with Nickel Trim
Item No. 10-1085, Car No. 514

1998 Volume 3
November 1998

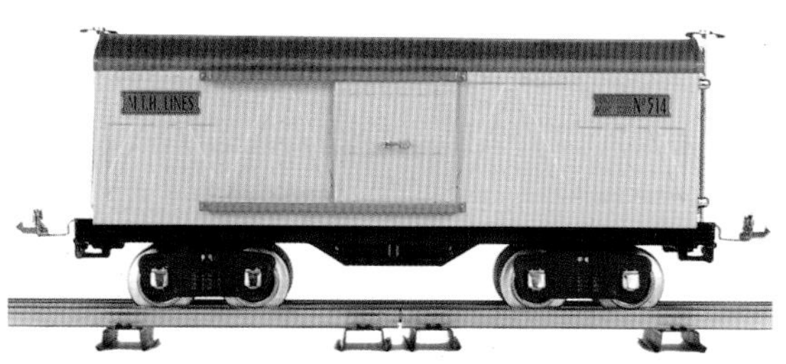

500 Series Std. Gauge Box Car
Cream with Brass Trim
Item No. 10-1086, Car No. 514

1998 Volume 3
November 1998

500 Series Std. Gauge Caboose
Red with Nickel Trim
Item No. 10-1099, Car No.517

1999 Volume 1
April 1999

500 Series Std. Gauge Caboose
Green/Red with Brass Trim
Item No. 10-1098, Car No. 517

1999 Volume 1
April 1999

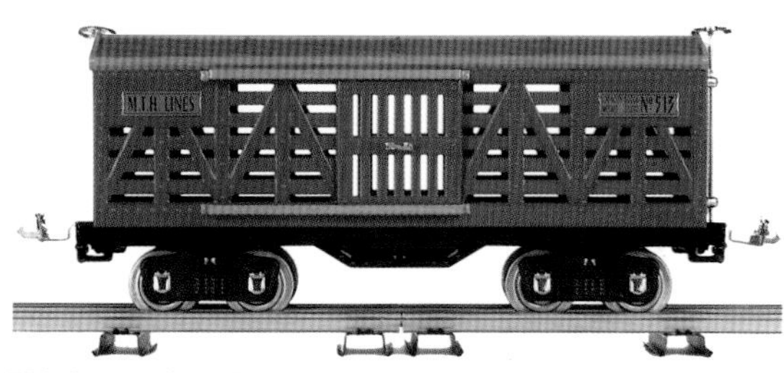

500 Series Std. Gauge Cattle Car
Green/Orange with Brass Trim
Item No. 10-1087, Car No. 513

1998 Volume 3
November 1998

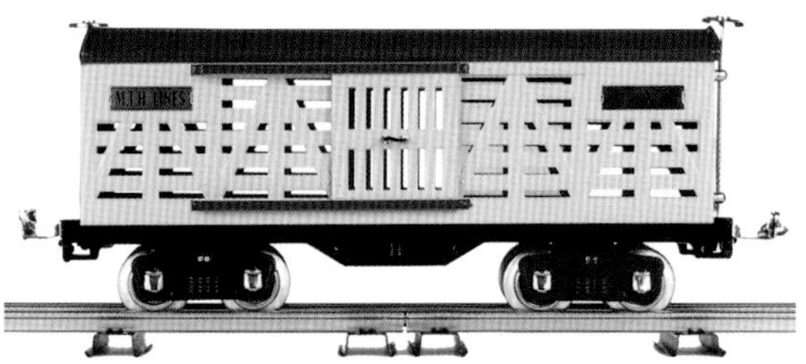

500 Series Std. Gauge Cattle Car
Cream/Maroon with Nickel Trim
Item No. 10-1088, Car No. 513

1998 Volume 3
November 1998

500 Series Std. Gauge Flat Car
Dark Green with Brass Trim
Item No. 10-1117, Car No. 511

1999 Volume 3
February 2000

500 Series Std. Gauge Flat Car
Light Green with Nickel Trim
Item No. 10-1118, Car No. 511

1999 Volume 3
February 2000

500 Series Std. Gauge Gondola Car
Peacock with Brass Trim
Item No. 10-1119, Car No. 512

1999 Volume 3
February 2000

500 Series Std. Gauge Gondola Car
Green with Nickel Trim
Item No. 10-1120, Car No. 512

1999 Volume 3
February 2000

500 Series Std. Gauge Hopper Car
Red with Brass Trim
Item No. 10-1101, Car No. 516

1999 Volume 1
April 1999

500 Series Std. Gauge Hopper Car
Red with Nickel Trim
Item No. 10-1100, Car No. 516

1999 Volume 1
April 1999

500 Series Std. Gauge Ore Car
Green with Brass Trim
Item No. 10-1129, Car No. 516

2000 Volume 2
May 2000

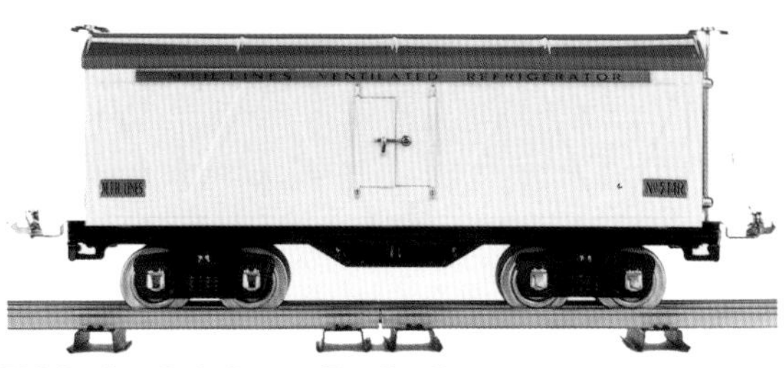

500 Series Std. Gauge Reefer Car
White/Blue with Nickel Trim
Item No. 10-1089, Car No. 514R

1998 Volume 3
November 1998

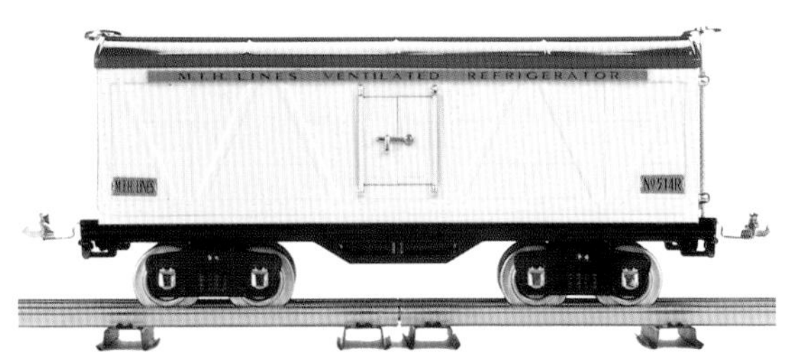

500 Series Std. Gauge Reefer Car
Ivory/Peacock with Brass Trim
Item No. 10-1090, Car No. 514R

1998 Volume 3
November 1998

500 Series Std. Gauge Searchlight Car
Black/Terra Cotta with Brass Trim
Item No. 10-1115, Car No. 520

1999 Volume 3
February 2000

500 Series Std. Gauge Searchlight Car
Black/Green with Nickel Trim
Item No. 10-1116, Car No. 520

1999 Volume 3
February 2000

500 Series Std. Gauge Tank Car
Orange Shell with Nickel Trim
Item No. 10-1102, Car No. 515

1999 Volume 1
April 1999

500 Series Std. Gauge Tank Car
Silver Sunoco with Brass Trim
Item No. 10-1103, Car No. 515

1999 Volume 1
April 1999

800 Series O Gauge Box Car
Orange with Brown
Item No. 10-3003, Car No. 814

1999 Volume 2
October 1999

800 Series O Gauge Caboose
Red with Brown
Item No. 10-3004, Car No. 817

1999 Volume 2
October 1999

800 Series O Gauge Cattle Car
Tuscan with Nickel Trim
Item No. 10-3005, Car No. 813

1999 Volume 2
October 1999

800 Series O Gauge Gondola Car
Orange with Black
Item No. 10-3006, Car No. 812

1999 Volume 2
October 1999

800 Series O Gauge Hopper Car
Black with Nickel Trim
Item No. 10-3007, Car No. 816

1999 Volume 2
October 1999

800 Series O Gauge Reefer Car
White with Brown
Item No. 10-3008, Car No. 814R

1999 Volume 2
October 1999

200 Series Std. Gauge Caboose
Train Collector's Association
Item No. 10-2001, Car No. 1999

Uncataloged Item
June 1999

TINPLATE TRADITIONS LINE
Specialty Sets

M.T.H. has produced four different Tinplate Traditions® specialty sets, as this book goes to press. There is an O Gauge 800 series 4-car freight set, which is sure to look handsome behind an O Gauge tinplate steamer. The most exciting specialty sets, however, are the Presidential passenger set, which includes an electric engine and 4 passenger cars, and the Ives Circus set. These two sets include minute details and precisely matched paint that make them exact replicas of the prized originals from the 1920s and '30s. There is also an 18K gold-plated Presidential passenger set especially created to celebrate the dawning of the new millennium. Each specialty set includes the high quality construction and attention to detail that make Tinplate Traditions reproductions valued additions to any pre-war collection.

#800 Series 4-Car Freight Set

Fall/Winter 1996
December 1997

Item No. 10-1042 Car Nos. 812 Green Gondola, 814 Brown/Yellow Box Car, 816 Black Hopper, 817 Red/Peacock Caboose

Std. Gauge Presidential Locomotive Passenger Set
Two-Tone Blue

2000 Volume 1
March 2000

3-Rail Traditional, Item No. 10-1122-0 Car Nos. 4390 Club "Academy" , 4391 Pullman "Academy" , 4392 Observation "Army-Navy" , 4392 Diner "West Point" . Engine No. 4689
3-Rail Contemporary with Proto-Sound® 2.0, Item No. 10-1122-1, Car Nos. see above

Ives 6-Car Circus Set
Circus

2000 Volume 1
July 2000

Item No. 10-1125 Car Nos. Flat Car with Cages-196C (3 cars), Circus Animal Car 193C, Circus Performers Car 185, Circus Equipment Car 192C

Std. Gauge Presidential Locomotive Passenger Set
Millennium Special

2000 Volume 1
March 2000

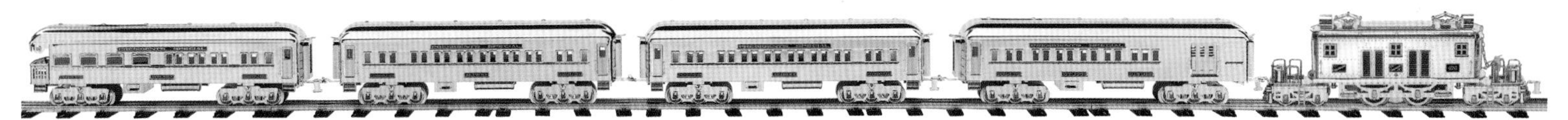

3-Rail Traditional, Item No. 10-1126-0 Car Nos. 4391 Pullman "J.Lionel Cowen, 4390 Club "Harry C. Ives", 4393 Diner "Louis Marx", 4392 Observation "A.C. Gilbert". Engine No. 4689
3-Rail Contemporary with Proto-Sound® 2.0, Item No. 10-1126-1, Car Nos. see above

TINPLATE TRADITIONS LINE
Passenger Sets

Brightly colored passenger cars in Standard and O Gauges complement the steam and electric engines in the Tinplate Traditions® line. At press time, M.T.H. has produced five different four-car passenger sets, including faithful reproductions of the famous Blue Comet and celebrated State Car sets. The three kinds of individual cars were produced, including the solarium car, created by long-time train enthusiast Bill Thomas and named "Maryland" in honor of the company's home state, the Halley Standard Gauge Blue Comet car, and the Philadelphia Girard car. Standard Gauge passenger cars feature stamped metal bodies, metal latch couplers, illuminated interiors, detailed seat interiors, and metal wheels and axles. The 613 series O Gauge passenger sets feature stamped sheet metal bodies, floors, and trucks, pre-war box couplers, metal wheels and axles, stamped metal trucks, sliding baggage doors, and a removable roof. They are available in several colors.

4-Car Std. Gauge 418 Set
Orange

1999 Volume 1
May 1999

Item No. 10-1106, Car Names Observation, Dining Car, Parlor Car (Coach), Parlor Car (Baggage)

4-Car Std. Gauge 418 Set
Dark Green

1999 Volume 1
May 1999

Item No. 10-1107, Car Names Observation, Dining Car, Parlor Car (Coach), Parlor Car (Baggage)

4-Car Std. Gauge Blue Comet Set
Two-Tone Blue with Brass Trim

1999 Volume 2
December 1999

Item No. 10-1114, Car Names 420 Faye Pullman, 421 Westphal Pullman, 423 Halley Pullman, 422 Tempel Observation

4-Car Std. Gauge State Set
Two-Tone State Green

998 Volume 2
April 1999

Item No. 10-1078, Car Names 416 New York Observation, 415 Maryland Solarium, 413 Colorado Pullman, 412 California Pullman

4-Car Std. Gauge State Set
Two-Tone Brown

2000 Volume 2
October 2000

Item No. 10-1135, Car Names 2416 New York Observation, 2412 California Pullman, 2413 Colorado Pullman, 415 Maryland Solarium

4-Car Std. Gauge Stephen Girard Set
Two-Tone Green

1998 Volume 1
November 1997

Item No. 10-1068, Car Nos. 426 Coral Isle Observation, 427 Philadelphia Coach, 425 Stephen Girard Coach, 424 Liberty Bell Coach

#613 4-Car O Gauge Passenger Set
Green

Spring 1996
February 1996

Item No. 10-1024, Car Nos. 614 Observation, 613 Pullman, 612 Pullman, 615 Baggage

#613 4-Car O Gauge Passenger Set
Terra Cotta

Spring 1996
January 1996

Item No. 10-1025, Car Nos. 614 Observation, 613 Pullman, 612 Pullman, 615 Baggage

#613 4-Car O Gauge Passenger Set
Blue Comet Blue

1998 Volume 1
May 1998

Item No. 10-1064, Car Nos. 614 Observation, 613 Pullman, 612 Pullman, 615 Baggage

#613 4-Car O Gauge Passenger Set
Red/Silver

1998 Volume 1
May 1998

Item No. 10-1065, Car Nos. 614 Observation, 613 Pullman, 612 Pullman, 615 Baggage

Std. Gauge Solarium State Car
Two-Tone Brown

2000 Volume 2
October 2000

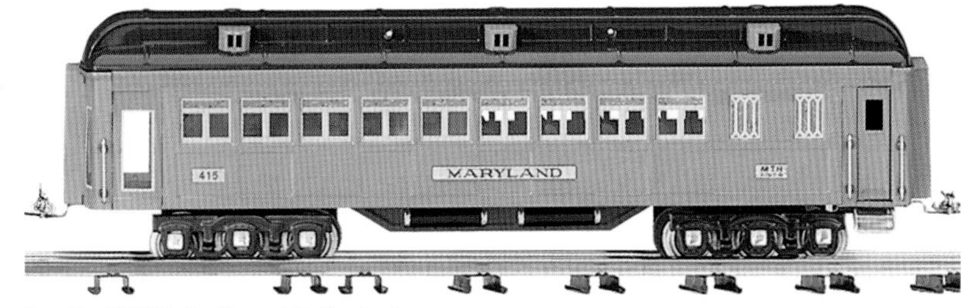

Item No. 10-1137, Car Name 415 Maryland

Std. Gauge Solarium State Car
Two-Tone Green

2000 Volume 2
October 2000

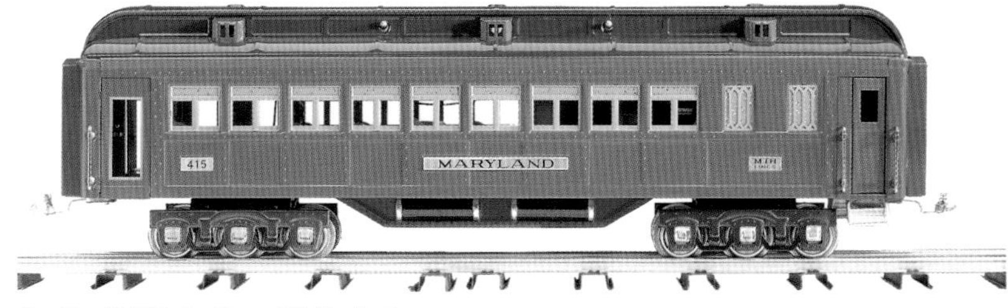

Item No. 10-1138, Car Name 415 Maryland

Std. Gauge State Car
Two-Tone State Green

1998 Volume 2
January 1999

Item No. 10-1079, Car Name 414 Illinois

Std. Gauge State Car
Two-Tone Brown

2000 Volume 2
October 2000

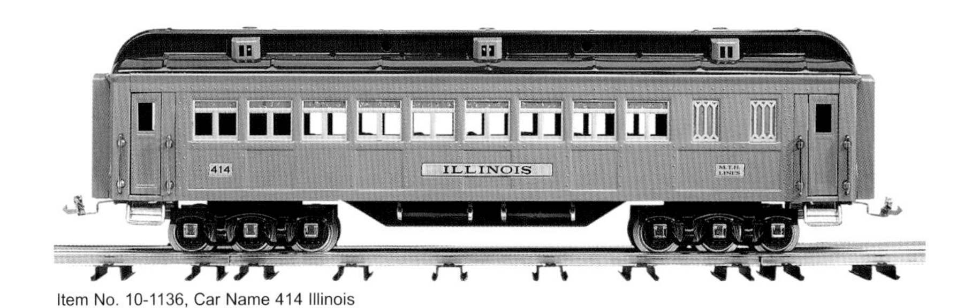

Item No. 10-1136, Car Name 414 Illinois

TINPLATE TRADITIONS LINE
Accessories

M.T.H. has produced twenty-nine different Tinplate Traditions® accessories, including a roundhouse, several kinds of towers and railroad signals, and the famous Hell Gate Bridge. The toys, like Mr. Atomic, that the company produced in its early years are also considered part of this category. Some have die-cast components, such as signal poles, but many are of stamped metal construction and boast tinplate's signature bright enamel paint finish. Each tinplate accessory is an accurate reproduction of an earlier piece, including die-cast construction where it is used. M.T.H. has improved the operating mechanism in some of the operating accessories, but that has not altered the appearance. M.T.H.'s Standard Gauge track is the same kind of tubular track that will be familiar to model railroaders, but it has an improved switch mechanism. These accessories and track are sure to bring any Standard Gauge layout to life.

116 Passenger Station
White/Red
Item No. 10-1070

1998 Volume 2
April 1998

#155 Freight Shed
Terra Cotta/Cream
Item No. 10-1057

1997 Volume 2
February 1998

192 Villa Set

Item No. 10-1110

1999 Volume 2
August 1999

436 Powerhouse
Terra Cotta
Item No. 10-1080

1998 Volume 3
July 1998

#437 Switch Tower
Terra Cotta
Item No. 10-1121

1999 Volume 3
March 2000

#438 Tinplate Signal Tower
Red/White
Item No. 10-1049

Spring 1997
February 1998

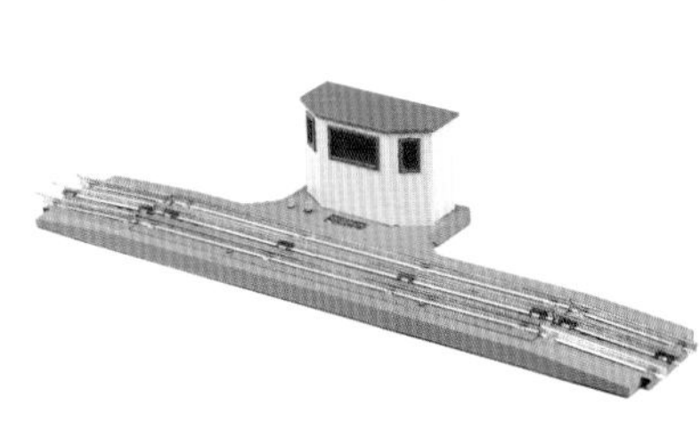
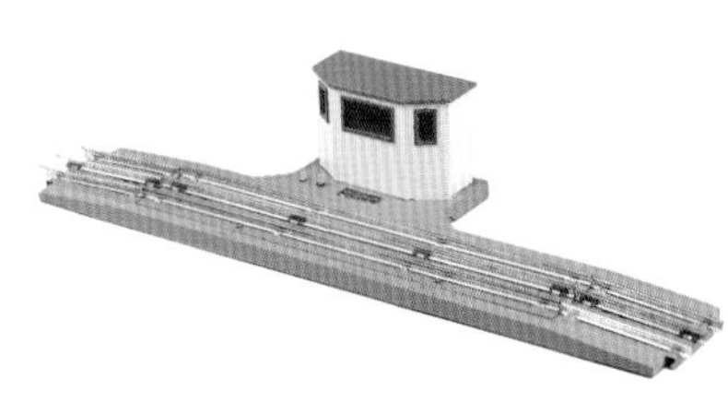

 # 441 Weigh Scale
Terra Cotta/Cream
Item No. 10-1069

1998 Volume 2
April 1998

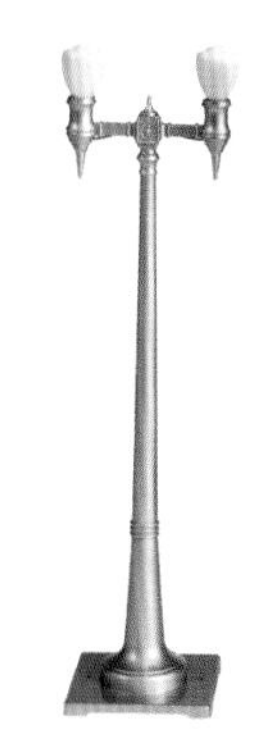

#63 Lamp Post Set
Aluminum
Item No. 10-1108

1999 Volume 1
February 1999

#67 Lamp Post Set
Dark Green
Item No. 10-1095

1999 Volume 1
February 1999

#71 Telegraph Post Set
Peacock/Red
Item No. 10-1094

1999 Volume 1
February 1999

#71 Telegraph Post Set
Gray/Red
Item No. 10-1093

1999 Volume 1
February 1999

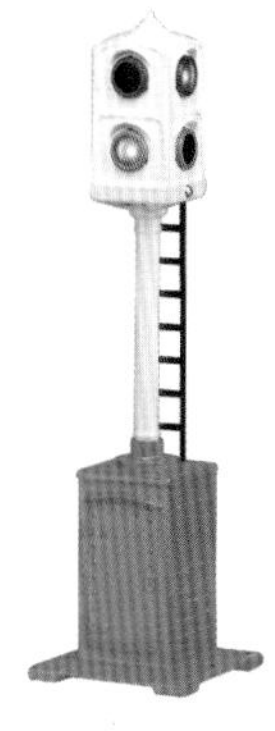

#78 Std. Gauge Block Signal
Orange/Cream
Item No. 10-1097

1999 Volume 3
November 1999

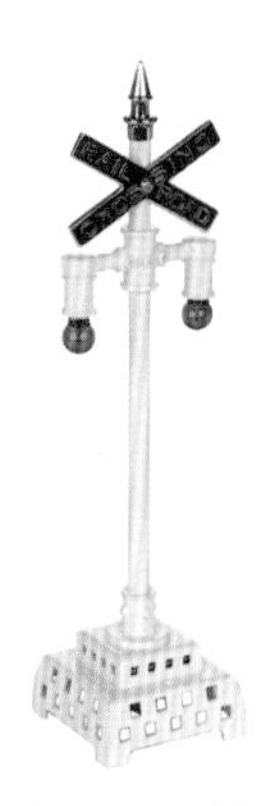

#79 Operating Crossing Signal
White
Item No. 10-1046

Spring 1997
February 1998

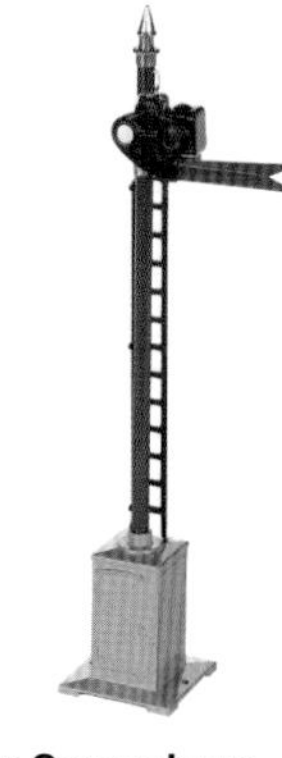

#80 Operating Semaphore
Orange/Black
Item No. 10-1047

Spring 1997
February 1998

#87 Railroad Crossing Signal
Dark Green/White
Item No. 10-1096

1999 Volume 1
February 1999

#92 Floodlight Tower Set
Terra Cotta/Green
Item No. 10-1044

Fall/Winter 1996
October 1997

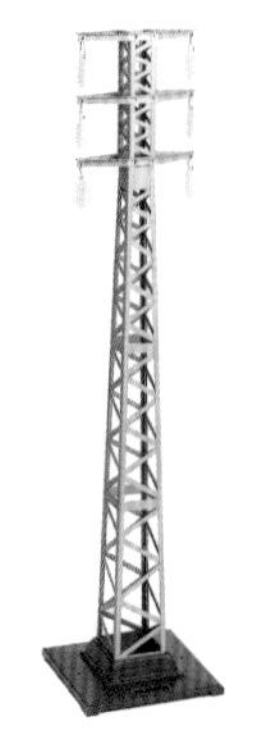

#94 High Tension Tower Set
Red/Silver
Item No. 10-1043

Fall/Winter 1996
October 1997

#99 Operating Block Signal
Cream/Red
Item No. 10-1048

Spring 1997
February 1998

Amos & Andy Operating Tin Toy

Item No. 10-1002

Fall 1993
December 1995

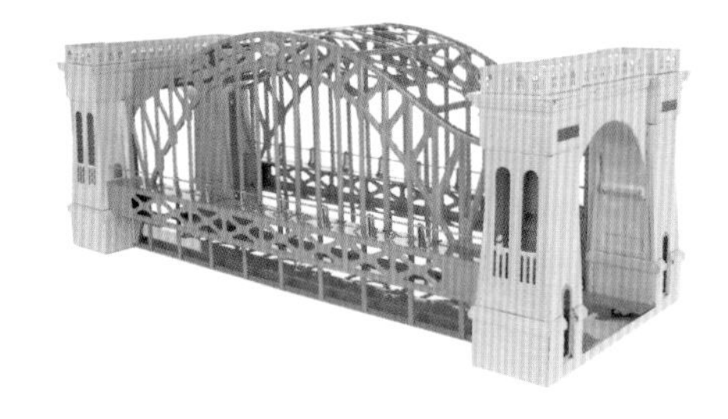

Hell Gate Bridge
Cream/Green
Item No. 10-1015

Winter 1994
November 1998

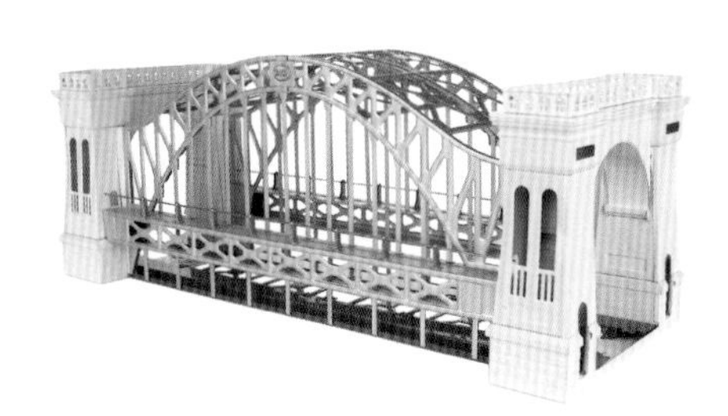

Hell Gate Bridge
White/Silver/Red
Item No. 10-1016

Winter 1994
November 1998

Hi-way Henry Operating Tin Toy

Item No. 10-1001

Fall 1993
December 1993

Kingsbury Fire House & Pumper

Item No. 10-1003

Fall 1993
August 1993

Mr. Atomic Tinplate Toy
Silver
Item No. 10-1010

Fall 1993
December 1995

Mr. Atomic Tinplate Toy
Blue
Item No. 10-1014

Fall 1993
April 1994

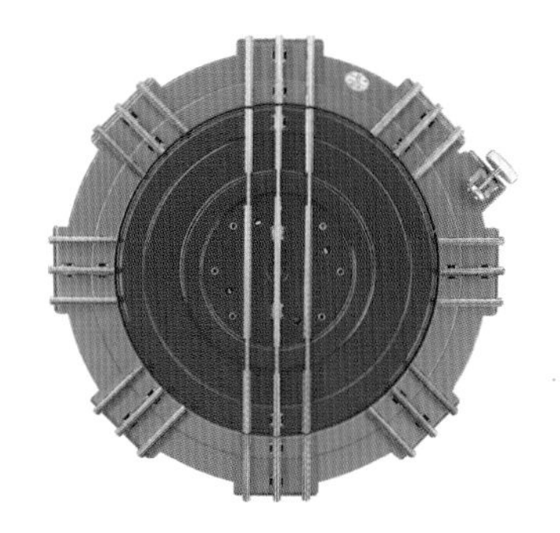

No. 200 Turntable

Item No. 10-200

1999 Volume 2
November 1999

No. 444 Roundhouse Section
Brown/Cream
Item No. 10-1111

1999 Volume 2
November 1999

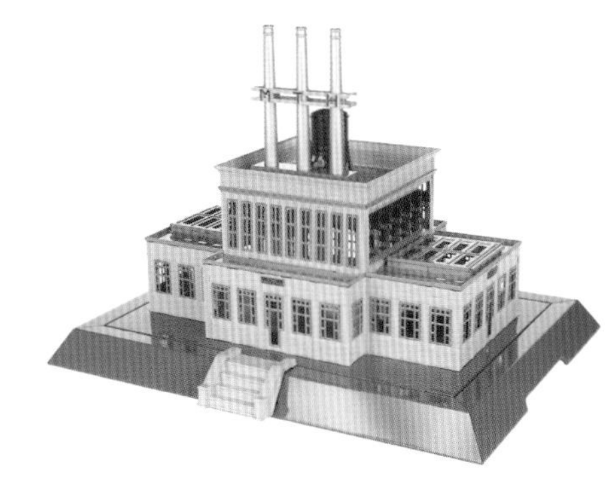

Powerhouse
Cream/Orange
Item No. 10-1017

Fall 1995
June 1995

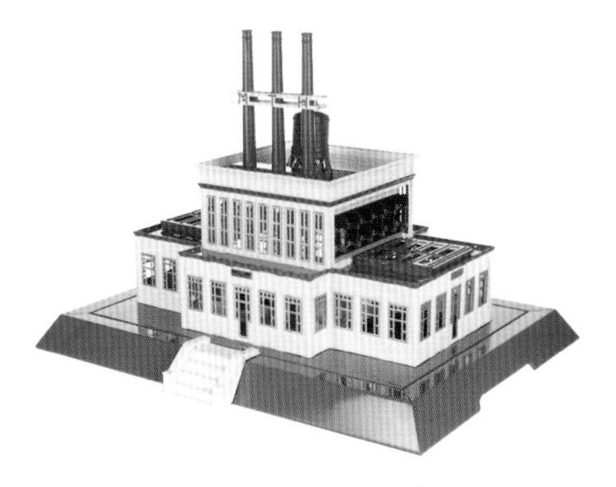

Powerhouse
White/Red
Item No. 10-1018

Fall 1995
June 1995

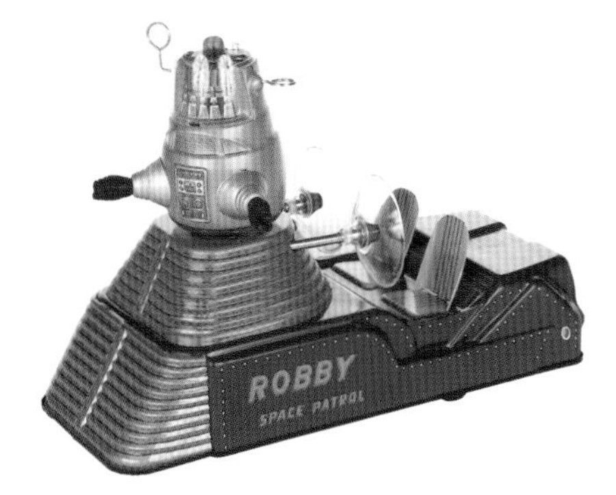

Robby Space Patrol Operating Robot

Item No. 10-1004

Fall 1993
November 1993

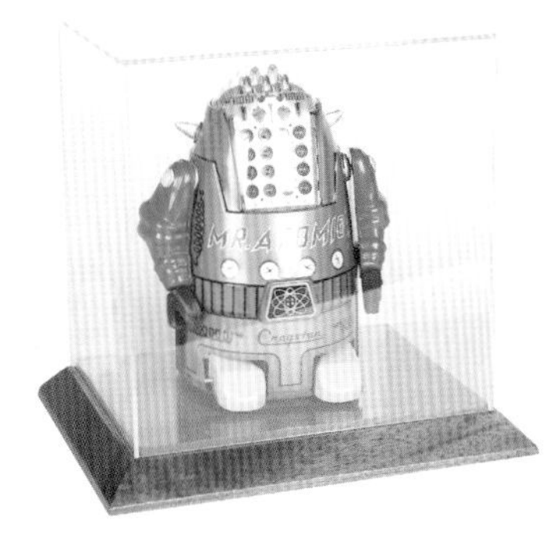

Show Case Mr. Atomic
Blue
Item No. 10-1011

Uncataloged Item
April 1994

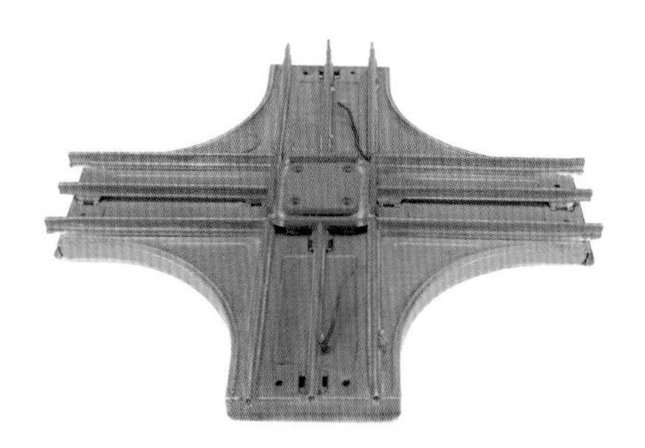

Std. Gauge 90* Crossover

Item No. 10-4006

2000 Volume 2
May 2000

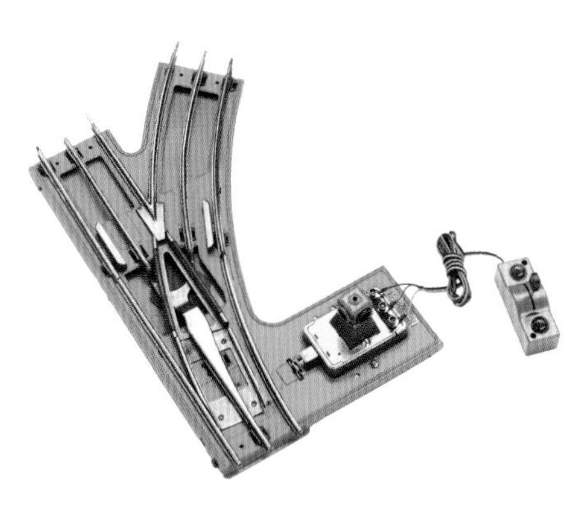

Std. Gauge Switch - Right Hand

Item No. 10-4001

1999 Volume 3
June 2000

Std. Gauge Switch Tower
Brown/Cream
Item No. 10-1124

2000 Volume 1
May 2000

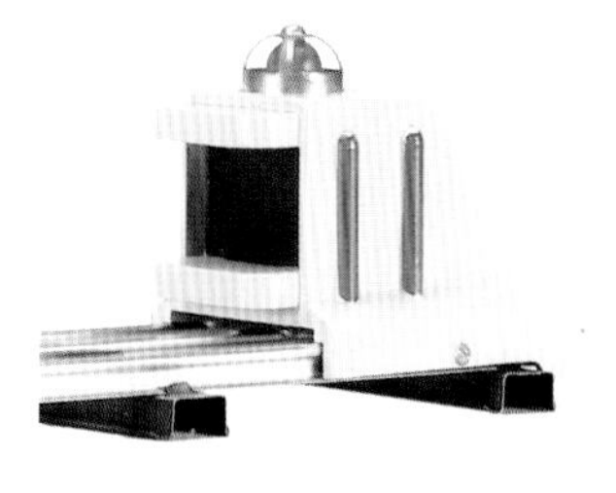

Std. Gauge Track Bumpers
Cream/Red
Item No. 10-4005

2000 Volume 2
June 2000

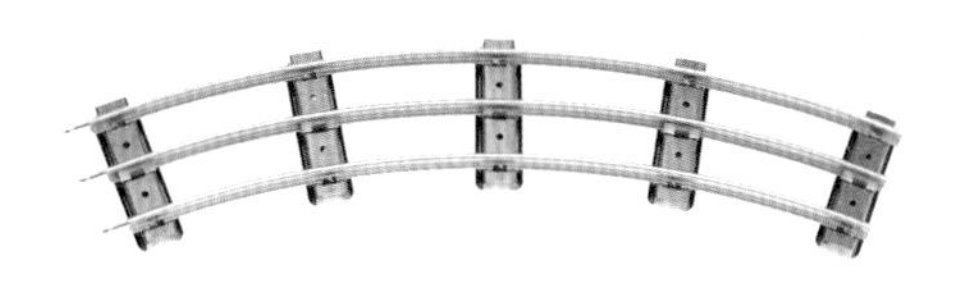

Std. Gauge Track - Reg. Curved

Item No. 10-1039

Summer 1996
March 1997

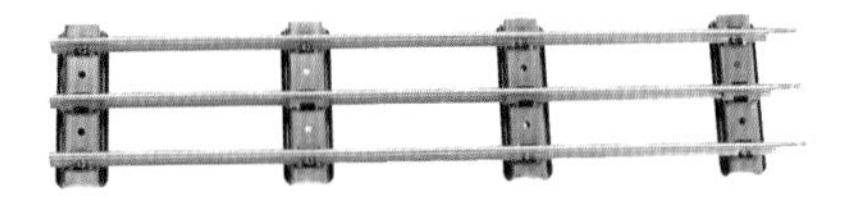

Std. Gauge Track - Reg. Straight

Item No. 10-1038

Summer 1996
March 1997

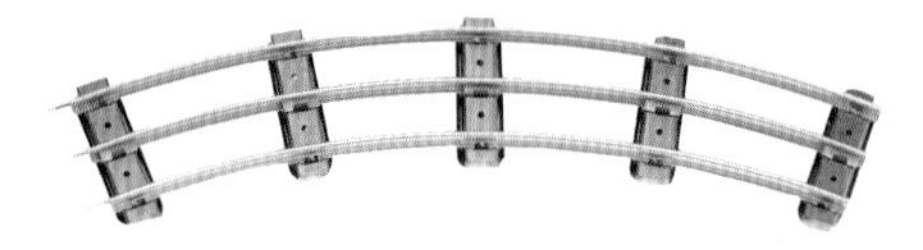

Std. Gauge Track - Wide Radius Curve

Item No. 10-1041

Summer 1996
March 1997

Std. Gauge Track - Wide Radius Straight

Item No. 10-1040

Summer 1996
March 1997

Std. Gauge Switch (Wide Radius) Left Hand *(photo not available)*
Item No. 10-4004

1999 Volume 3
June 2000

Std. Gauge Switch - Left Hand *(photo not available)*

Item No. 10-4002

1999 Volume 3
June 2000

Std. Gauge Switch (Wide Radius) Right Hand *(photo not available)*
Item No. 10-4003

1999 Volume 3
June 2000

M.T.H. TINPLATE LINE 1983 - 1987

The M.T.H. line consists of those products the company made in its early days, from 1983-87. These items are all faithful reproductions of pre-war tinplate favorites. In the early 1980s, when M.T.H. began making these reproductions, the collectors' market was booming, and early tinplate models were extremely expensive. M.T.H. president Mike Wolf saw a demand for more inexpensive versions of these beautiful collectors' pieces, and the M.T.H. line was born. This early line includes a full range of tinplate products: steam and electric engines, the Hell Gate Bridge, switch towers, floodlight towers, and other towers, freight and passenger cars, a roundhouse, power houses, and many others. Each is of high quality sheet metal or die-cast construction and features the characteristic bright paint that distinguishes the original pre-war tinplate trains. This section includes photographs only of the tinplate items that M.T.H. has not re-run since 1993. The other items listed without photographs have been re-run (though sometimes with different colors); photographs of them can be found in the Tinplate Traditions® section of the book.

#385E Standard Gauge Locomotive
Black with Brass

1987
April 1987

3-Rail, Item No. NONE, Cab No. 385E

#1766 Ives Std. Gauge 3-Car Passenger Set
Terra Cotta with Maroon

1987
May 1987

Item No. NONE, Car Nos. 1766, 1767, 1768

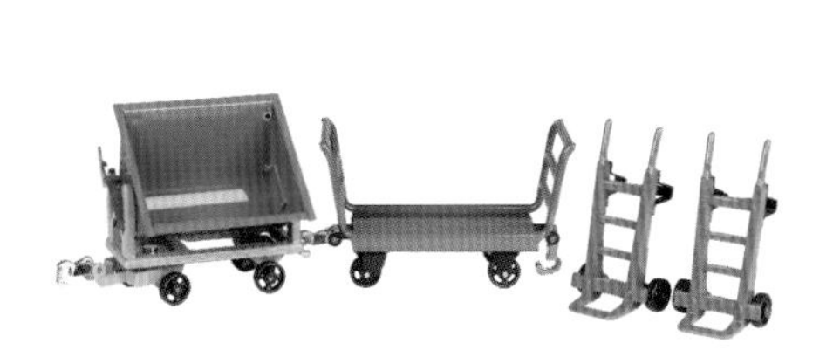

#163 Freight Cart Set
Red/Blue/Green
Item No. NONE

1986
June 1986

#208 Tool Box & Tools
Silver
Item No. NONE

1986
June 1986

#550 Railroad Figure Set
6 People
Item No. NONE

1987
June 1987

#435 Small Powerhouse
Ivory/Brown
Item No. NONE

1987
June 1987

STEAM LOCOMOTIVES

#260 O Gauge Locomotive
Black/Green
3-Rail with 8-Wheel Tender, Item No. NONE, Cab No. 260

1987
June 1987

#260 O Gauge Locomotive
Black/Green
3-Rail with 12-Wheel Tender, Item No. NONE, Cab No. 260

1987
June 1987

#260 O Gauge Locomotive
Gunmetal
3-Rail with 12-Wheel Tender, Item No. NONE, Cab No. 260

1987
June 1987

#260 O Gauge Locomotive
Black/Black
3-Rail with 8-Wheel Tender, Item No. NONE, Cab No. 260

1987
June 1987

#260 O Gauge Locomotive
Black/Black
3-Rail with 8-Wheel Tender, Item No. NONE, Cab No. 260

1987
June 1987

#263 O Gauge Locomotive
Gunmetal
3-Rail, Item No. NONE, Cab No. 263

1987
June 1987

#263 O Gauge Locomotive
Black
3-Rail, Item No. NONE, Cab No. 263

1987
June 1987

#263 O Gauge Locomotive
Two-Tone Blue
3-Rail, Item No. NONE, Cab No. 263

1987
June 1987

#385 Standard Gauge Locomotive
Black with Nickel
3-Rail, Item No. NONE, Cab No. 385

1987
April 1987

#385 Standard Gauge Locomotive
Gunmetal with Brass
3-Rail, Item No. NONE, Cab No. 385

1987
April 1987

#385 Standard Gauge Locomotive
Gunmetal with Nickel
3-Rail, Item No. NONE, Cab No..385

1987
April 1987

#385 Standard Gauge Locomotive
Crackle Black with Nickel
3-Rail, Item No. NONE, Cab No. 385

1987
April 1987

#392 Standard Gauge Locomotive
Black with Brass
3-Rail, Item No. NONE, Cab No. 392

1987
February 1987

#392 Standard Gauge Locomotive
Black with Nickel
3-Rail, Item No. NONE, Cab No. 392

1987
February 1987

#392 Standard Gauge Locomotive
Gunmetal with Brass
3-Rail, Item No. NONE, Cab No. 392

1987
February 1987

#392 Standard Gauge Locomotive
Gunmetal with Nickel
3-Rail, Item No. NONE, Cab No. 392

1987
February 1987

#392 Standard Gauge Locomotive
Two-Tone Blue with Brass
3-Rail, Item No. NONE, Cab No. 392

1987
February 1987

#392 Standard Gauge Locomotive
Two-Tone Blue with /Nickel
3-Rail, Item No. NONE, Cab No. 392

1987
February 1987

#392 Standard Gauge Locomotive
Crackle Black with Brass
3-Rail, Item No. NONE, Cab No. 392

1987
June 1987

#392 Standard Gauge Locomotive
Crackle Black with Nickel
3-Rail, Item No. NONE, Cab No. 392

1987
June 1987

#400 E Standard Gauge Locomotive
Two-Tone Blue with Nickel
3-Rail, Item No. NONE, Cab No. 400E

1985
Fall 1985

#400 E Standard Gauge Locomotive
Two-Tone Blue with Brass
3-Rail, Item No. NONE, Cab No. 400E

1985
Fall 1985

#400 E Standard Gauge Locomotive
Black with Brass
3-Rail, Item No. NONE, Cab No. 400E

1985
Fall 1985

#400 E Standard Gauge Locomotive
Grey with Nickel
3-Rail, Item No. NONE, Cab No. 400E

1985
Fall 1985

#400 E Standard Gauge Locomotive
Gunmetal with Brass
3-Rail, Item No. NONE, Cab No. 400E

1985
Fall 1985

#400 E Standard Gauge Locomotive
Crackle Black with Brass
3-Rail, Item No. NONE, Cab No. 400E

1985
Fall 1985

#400 E Standard Gauge Locomotive
TT Brown with Brass
3-Rail, Item No. NONE, Cab No. 400E

1986
Mid-1986

#400 E Standard Gauge Locomotive
State Green with Brass
3-Rail, Item No. NONE, Cab No. 400E

1986
Mid-1986

#400 E Standard Gauge Locomotive
Black with Nickel
3-Rail, Item No. NONE, Cab No. 400E

1986
Mid-1986

#400 E Std. Gauge Locomotive Kit
Kit, no motor
3-Rail, Item No. 80-062, Cab No. 400E

1985
Fall 1985

ELECTRIC LOCOMOTIVES

#381 Std. Gauge Locomotive
State Green
3-Rail, Item No. NONE, Cab No. 381

1983
Fall 1983

#408 Std. Gauge Locomotive
Two-Tone Brown
3-Rail, Item No. NONE, Cab No. 408

1983
Fall 1983

#408 Std. Gauge Locomotive
Apple Green
3-Rail, Item No. NONE, Cab No. 408

1983
Fall 1983

#408 Std. Gauge Locomotive
Dark Green
3-Rail, Item No. NONE, Cab No. 408

1983
Fall 1983

#408 Std. Gauge Locomotive
Mojave
3-Rail, Item No. NONE, Cab No. 408

1983
Fall 1983

#9E Std. Gauge Locomotive
Gunmetal Gray with Nickel Trim
3-Rail, Item No. NONE, Cab No. 9E

1983
Fall 1983

#9E Std. Gauge Locomotive
Two-Tone Green with Brass Trim
3-Rail, Item No. NONE, Cab No. 9E

1983
Fall 1983

#9E Std. Gauge Locomotive
Dark Green with Brass Trim
3-Rail, Item No. NONE, Cab No. 9E

1983
Fall 1983

#9E Std. Gauge Locomotive
Orange with Brass Trim
3-Rail, Item No. NONE, Cab No. 9E

1983
Fall 1983

#9E Std. Gauge Locomotive Kit
Undecorated
3-Rail, Item No. NONE, Cab No. 9E

1983
Fall 1983

ROLLING STOCK

#211 Flat Car Standard Gauge
Black with Brass
Item No. NONE, Car No. 211

1986
Late 1986

#211 Flat Car Standard Gauge
Black with Nickel
Item No. NONE, Car No. 211

1986
Late 1986

#212 Gondola Standard Gauge
Grey with Brass
Item No. NONE, Car No. 212

1986
Late 1986

#212 Gondola Standard Gauge
Maroon with Brass
Item No. NONE, Car No. 212

1986
Fall 1986

#212 Gondola Standard Gauge
Medium Green with Nickel
Item No. NONE, Car No. 212

1986
Fall 1986

#212 Gondola Standard Gauge
Dark Green with Brass
Item No. NONE, Car No. 212

1986
Late 1986

#213 Cattle Car Standard Gauge
Cream/Maroon with Nickel
Item No. NONE, Car No. 213

1985
March 1985

#213 Cattle Car Standard Gauge
Terra Cotta/Green with Brass
Item No. NONE, Car No. 213

1985
March 1985

#213 Cattle Car Standard Gauge
Terra Cotta/Maroon with Brass
Item No. NONE, Car No. 213

1985
March 1985

#213 Cattle Car Standard Gauge
Mojave/Maroon with Brass
Item No. NONE, Car No. 213

1985
March 1985

#213 Cattle Car - TCA
Dark Blue with Gold
Item No. 80-085, Car No. 213

1987
June 1987

#214 Box Car Standard Gauge
Cream/Orange with Brass
Item No. NONE, Car No. 214

1985
March 1985

#214 Box Car Standard Gauge
Terra Cotta, Dark Green with Brass
Item No. NONE, Car No. 214

1985
March 1985

#214 Box Car Standard Gauge
Yellow/Brown with Nickel
Item No. NONE, Car No. 214

1985
March 1985

#214 Box Car Standard Gauge
Yellow/Brown with Brass
Item No. NONE, Car No. 214

1985
March 1985

#214 R Refrig. Car Standard Gauge
Ivory/Peacock with Brass
Item No. NONE, Car No. 214

1985
March 1985

#214 R Refrig. Car Standard Gauge
White/Light Blue with Nickel
Item No. NONE, Car No. 214

1985
March 1985

#214 R TCA Car
Red/Cream
Item No. NONE, Car No. 214

1987
June 1987

#215 Tank Car Standard Gauge
Pea Green with Brass
Item No. NONE, Car No. 215

1986
Mid-1986

#215 Tank Car Standard Gauge
Ivory with Brass
Item No. NONE, Car No. 215

1986
Mid-1986

#215 Tank Car Standard Gauge
Aluminum with Nickel
Item No. NONE, Car No. 215

1986
Mid-1986

#215 Tank Car Standard Gauge
Aluminum with Brass
Item No. NONE, Car No. 215

1986
Mid-1986

#215 Tank Car Standard Gauge
Orange with Brass
Item No. NONE, Car No. 215

1986
Mid-1986

#216 Hopper Standard Gauge
Dark Green with Brass
Item No. NONE, Cab No. 216

1986
Mid-1986

#216 Hopper Standard Gauge
Dark Green with Nickel
Item No. NONE, Car No. 216

1986
Mid-1986

#216 Hopper Standard Gauge
Red with Brass
Item No. NONE, Car No. 216

1986
Mid-1986

#216 Hopper Standard Gauge
Red with Nickel
Item No. NONE, Car No. 216

1986
Mid-1986

#217 Caboose Standard Gauge
Orange/Maroon, Green
Item No. NONE, Car No. 217

1986
Mid-1986

#217 Caboose Standard Gauge
Red/Peacock with Brass
Item No. NONE, Car No. 217

1986
Mid-1986

#217 Caboose Standard Gauge
Red/Red with Nickel
Item No. NONE, Car No. 217

1986
Mid-1986

#217 Caboose Standard Gauge
Pea Green/Red with Brass
Item No. NONE, Car No. 217

1986
Mid-1986

#218 Dump Car Standard Gauge
Mojave with Brass
Item No. NONE, Car No. 218

1987
August 1987

#218 Dump Car Standard Gauge
Mojave with Nickel
Item No. NONE, Car No. 218

1987
August 1987

#218 Dump Car Standard Gauge
Dark Green with Brass
Item No. NONE, Car No. 218

1987
August 1987

#218 Dump Car Standard Gauge
Dark Green with Nickel
Item No. NONE, Car No. 218

1987
August 1987

#219 Crane Car Standard Gauge
Peacock with Brass
Item No. NONE, Car No. 219

1987
August 1987

#219 Crane Car Standard Gauge
White with Brass
Item No. NONE, Car No. 219

1987
August 1987

#219 Crane Car Standard Gauge
Yellow with Nickel
Item No. NONE, Car No. 219

1987
August 1987

#219 Crane Car Standard Gauge
Cream with Nickel
Item No. NONE, Car No. 219

1987
August 1987

#219 Crane Car Standard Gauge
Ivory with Nickel
Item No. NONE, Car No. 219

1987
August 1987

#220 Searchlight Car Standard Gauge
Terra Cotta with Brass
Item No. NONE, Car No. 220

1986
Late 1986

#220 Searchlight Car Standard Gauge
Green with Nickel
Item No. NONE, Car No. 220

1986
Late 1986

PASSENGER CARS

#1766 Ives Std. Gauge 3-Car Passenger Set
Terra Cotta/Maroon
Item No. NONE, Car Nos. 1766, 1767, 1768

1987
May 1987

#1766 Ives Std. Gauge 4-Car Passenger Set
Red/Maroon
Item No. NONE, Car Nos. 1766(2), 1767, 1768

1987
May 1987

#1766 Ives Std. Gauge 4-Car Passenger Set
Terra Cotta/Maroon
Item No. NONE, Car Nos. 1766(2), 1767, 1768

1987
May 1987

#1766 Ives/Lionel Std. Gauge Coach
Red/Maroon
Item No. NONE, Car No. 1766

1987
May 1987

#1766 Ives/Lionel Std. Gauge Coach
Terra Cotta/Maroon
Item No. NONE, Car No. 1766

1987
May 1987

3-Car Standard Gauge Blue Comet Passenger Set
Light Two-Tone Blue
Item No. NONE, Car Nos. 420 Faye, 421 Westphal, 422 Tempel

1986
July 1986

3-Car Standard Gauge Blue Comet Passenger Set
Dark Two-Tone Blue
Item No. NONE, Car Nos. 420 Faye , 421 Westphal , 422 Tempel

1986
July 1986

4-Car Std. Gauge 418 Set with 4-Wheel Trucks
Orange
Item No. NONE, Car Nos. 427 Diner , 428 Pullman , 429 Combine , 490 Observation

1984
June 1984

4-Car Std. Gauge 418 Set with 4-Wheel Trucks
Dark Green
Item No. NONE, Car Nos. 427 Diner , 428 Pullman , 429 Combine , 490 Observation

1984
June 1984

4-Car Std. Gauge 418 Set with 4-Wheel Trucks
Apple Green
Item No. NONE, Car Nos. 427 Diner , 428 Pullman , 429 Combine , 490 Observation

1984
June 1984

4-Car Std. Gauge 418 Set with 4-Wheel Trucks
Mojave
Item No. NONE, Car Nos. 427 Diner, 428 Pullman, 429 Combine, 490 Observation

1984
June 1984

4-Car Std. Gauge 418 Set with 4-Wheel Trucks
Two-Tone Brown
Item No. NONE, Car Nos. 427 Diner, 428 Pullman, 429 Combine, 490 Observation

1984
June 1984

4-Car Std. Gauge 418 Set with 4-Wheel Trucks
State Green
Item No. NONE, Car Nos. 427 Diner, 428 Pullman, 429 Combine, 490 Observation

1984
June 1984

4-Car Std. Gauge 418 Set with 6-Wheel Trucks
Orange
Item No. NONE, Car Nos. 427 Diner, 428 Pullman, 429 Combine, 490 Observation

1984
June 1984

4-Car Std. Gauge 418 Set with 6-Wheel Trucks
Dark Green
Item No. NONE, Car Nos. 427 Diner, 428 Pullman, 429 Combine, 490 Observation

1984
June 1984

4-Car Std. Gauge 418 Set with 6-Wheel Trucks
Apple Green
Item No. NONE, Car Nos. 427 Diner , 428 Pullman , 429 Combine , 490 Observation

1984
June 1984

4-Car Std. Gauge 418 Set with 6-Wheel Trucks
Mojave
Item No. NONE, Car Nos. 427 Diner , 428 Pullman , 429 Combine , 490 Observation

1984
June 1984

4-Car Std. Gauge 418 Set with 6-Wheel Trucks
Two-Tone Brown
Item No. NONE, Car Nos. 427 Diner , 428 Pullman , 429 Combine , 490 Observation

1984
June 1984

4-Car Std. Gauge 418 Set with 6-Wheel Trucks
State Green
Item No. NONE, Car Nos. 427 Diner , 428 Pullman , 429 Combine , 490 Observation

1984
June 1984

#423 Halley Pullman Standard Gauge
Dark Two-Tone Blue
Item No. NONE, Car No. 423 Halley

1986
July 1986

#423 Halley Pullman Standard Gauge
Light Two-Tone Blue
Item No. NONE, Car No. 423 Halley

1986
July 1986

#427 Philadelphia Stephen Girard Standard Gauge Car
Two-Tone Green with Brass
Item No. NONE, Car No. 427 Philadelphia

1987
Early 1987

#427 Philadelphia Stephen Girard Standard Gauge Car
Two-Tone Green with Nickel
Item No. NONE, Car No. 427 Philadelphia

1987
Early 1987

#427 Philadelphia Stephen Girard Standard Gauge Car
Two-Tone Blue/Brass
Item No. NONE, Car No. 427 Philadelphia

1987
February 1987

#427 Philadelphia Stephen Girard Standard Gauge Car
Two-Tone Blue with Nickel
Item No. NONE, Car No. 427 Philadelphia

1987
February 1987

600 Series O Gauge 4-Car Passenger Set
Terra Cotta/Maroon
Item No. NONE, Car Nos. 615 Baggage , 612 Pullman , 613 Pullman , 614 Observation

1987
Fall 1987

600 Series O Gauge 4-Car Passenger Set
Lt. Red with Aluminum
Item No. NONE, Car Nos. 615 Baggage , 612 Pullman , 613 Pullman , 614 Observation

1987
Fall 1987

600 Series O Gauge 4-Car Passenger Set
State Green
Item No. NONE, Car Nos. 615 Baggage , 612 Pullman , 613 Pullman , 614 Observation

1987
Fall 1987

600 Series O Gauge 4-Car Passenger Set
Two-Tone Blue
Item No. NONE, Car Nos. 615 Baggage , 612 Pullman , 613 Pullman , 614 Observation

1987
Fall 1987

#616 Pullman Extra Coach
Terra Cotta/Maroon
Item No. NONE, Car No. 616 Pullman

1987
Fall 1987

#616 Pullman Extra Coach
Red with Aluminum
Item No. NONE, Car No. 616 Pullman

1987
Fall 1987

#616 Pullman Extra Coach
Two-Tone Green
Item No. NONE, Car No. 616 Pullman

1987
Fall 1987

#616 Pullman Extra Coach
Two-Tone Blue
Item No. NONE, Car No. 616 Pullman

1987
Fall 1987

Stephen Girard Standard Gauge 3-Car Passenger Set
Two-Tone Green with Brass
Item No. NONE, Car Nos. 424 Liberty Bell , 425 Stephen Girard , 426 Coral Isle

1987
Early 1987

Stephen Girard Standard Gauge 3-Car Passenger Set
Two-Tone Green with Nickel
Item No. NONE, Car Nos. 424 Liberty Bell , 425 Stephen Girard , 426 Coral Isle

1987
Early1987

Stephen Girard Standard Gauge 3-Car Passenger Set
Two-Tone Blue with Nickel
Item No. NONE, Car Nos. 424 Liberty Bell , 425 Stephen Girard , 426 Coral Isle

1987
Early1987

Stephen Girard Standard Gauge 3-Car Passenger Set
Two-Tone Blue with Brass
Item No. NONE, Car Nos. 424 Liberty Bell , 425 Stephen Girard , 426 Coral Isle

1987
June 1987

ACCESSORIES

#155 Freight Shed
Yellow/Maroon
Item No. NONE

1986
June 1986

#155 Freight Shed
White/Grey
Item No. NONE

1986
June 1986

#163 Freight Cart Set
Red/Green/Orange
Item No. NONE

1986
June 1986

#200 Turntable
Green
Item No. NONE

1987
June 1987

#205 Container Set
Dark Green with Brass
Item No. NONE

1986
June 1905

#205 Container Set
Black with Nickel
Item No. NONE

1986
June 1905

#208 Tool Box & Tools
Grey
Item No. NONE

1986
June 1986

#300 Hell Gate Bridge
White/Silver
Item No. NONE

1987
June 1987

#300 Hell Gate Bridge
Apple Green/Cream
Item No. NONE

1987
June 1987

#435 Small Powerhouse
Terra Cotta/Cream
Item No. NONE

1987
June 1987

#435 Small Powerhouse
Cream/Brown
Item No. NONE

1987
June 1987

#436 Medium Powerhouse
Terra Cotta/Yellow
Item No. NONE

1987
June 1987

#436 Medium Powerhouse
Orange/Cream
Item No. NONE

1987
June 1987

#436 Medium Powerhouse
Cream/Mustard
Item No. NONE

1987
June 1987

#437 Switch Tower
Orange/Pea Green
Item No. NONE

1987
June 1987

#437 Switch Tower
Cream/Peacock
Item No. NONE

1987
June 1987

#437 Switch Tower
Yellow/Orange
Item No. NONE

1987
May 1987

#438 Switch Tower
Orange/Pea Green
Item No. NONE

1987
June 1987

#438 Switch Tower
Mojave/Orange
Item No. NONE

1987
June 1987

#438 Switch Tower
Grey/Ivory
Item No. NONE

1987
June 1987

#444 Roundhouse Section

Item No. NONE

1987
June 1987

#840 Powerhouse
Cream/Orange
Item No. NONE

1986
June 1986

#840 Powerhouse
White/Red
Item No. NONE

1986
June 1986

#92 Floodlight Tower
Red/Silver
Item No. NONE

1986
June 1986

#92 Floodlight Tower
Orange/Green
Item No. NONE

1986
June 1986

#94 High Tension Tower Set (3)
Red/Silver
Item No. NONE

1983
June 1983

#94 High Tension Tower Set (3)
Terra Cotta/Green
Item No. NONE

1986
June 1986

PREMIER LINE

460
5344

PREMIER LINE

INTRODUCTION

M.T.H.'s Premier line includes ¼" Scale locomotives, freight cars, passenger cars, ScaleTrax track system, and high-end electronic equipment such as the Z-4000 transformer and remote system and the DCS Remote Control System. Premier products are made for the serious O Gauge model railroader, to whom prototypical detail and scale proportions are important.

The line began in 1993 with the Dash 8-40 diesel, and the die-cast Challenger followed soon after. It was not until the Spring 1996 catalog, issued in October, 1995, that the Premier line was given its name. The name was necessitated by the introduction of the RailKing line, so customers and dealers would have an easy way to differentiate between the two lines.

Premier items were initially identified with a four-digit number. When sound systems became optional in Premier locomotives, M.T.H. added suffix letters to distinguish locomotives with different equipment, as follows:

2010 L	three-rail, no sound
2010 LP	three rail, with Proto-Sound®
2010 S	two-rail, no sound

In 1996 the prefix MT was added to the front of Premier line product numbers, as a means of distinguishing between Premier and RailKing products. Prefix and suffix letters were dropped when the current numbering system was adopted. Premier line items now have a "20-" prefix, and suffix numbers are as follows:

20-2167-1	three-rail
20-2167-2	two-rail
20-2167-3	B-unit

Sound systems are now standard equipment in all Premier three-rail locomotives; the first Premier locomotives with the new Proto-Sound® 2.0 system are currently scheduled for July 2000. However, two-rail version of Premier locomotives omit the sound system.

The models in this section are arranged by item type (i.e. F-3 AA sets are all together), item name then by catalog introductory date. The delivery date is also included. You can also see an index which is organized in the same order as the book's pictures. The indexes also include information on operation (i.e. O-31, O-72, etc.) The item page layouts provide complete information on each item: item type, roadname, the first catalog the item was offered in, the date the item was delivered, item number, and equipment available.

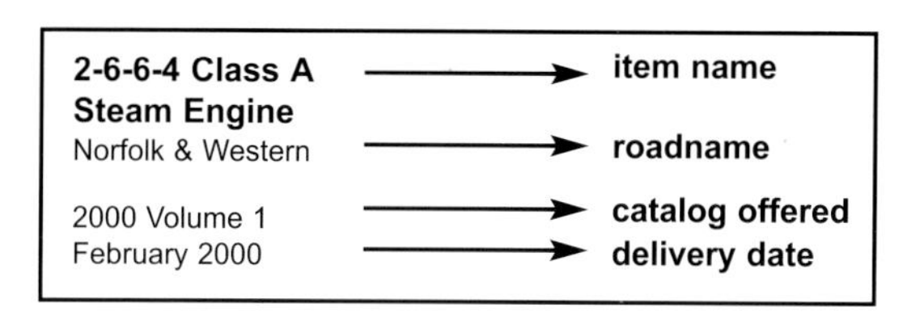

PREMIER LINE
Steam Locomotives

Premier steam engines are the gold standard in O Gauge railroading. These beautifully detailed 1:48 scale locomotives display the highest quality craftsmanship, realistic detail, and solid construction that provide smooth, powerful performance. Each Premier steamer offers die-cast boiler and tender construction, flywheel-equipped power, billowing smoke from the ProtoSmoke® system, and many other top-of-the-line qualities that make for the most realistic and reliable engines on the O Gauge market. And each Premier steam locomotive commands impressive power that allows it to pull long, realistic consists, making for incredibly authentic layouts. Premier steam locomotives were introduced to fulfill the needs of established model railroaders, operators, and collectors for whom accuracy, quality, and detail are essential. And while the authenticity of detail is designed to please the most discriminating model railroader, most of the locomotives are designed to run on the 3-rail track that most O Gauge railroaders prefer. At the time this book goes to press, M.T.H. has produced or promoted twenty-eight distinctly different varieties of steam engines and three auxiliary water tenders.

2-6-6-4 Class A Steam Engine
Norfolk & Western

2000 Volume 1
February 2000

3-Rail with Proto-Sound®, Item No. 20-3036-1, Cab No. 1218
2-Rail, Item No. 20-3036-2, Cab No. 1218

2-6-6-6 Allegheny Steam Engine
Chesapeake & Ohio

Spring 1996
April 1996

3-Rail with Proto-Sound®, Item No. 20-3017-1, Cab No. 1604
2-Rail, Item No. 20-3017-2, Cab No. 1604

2-8-0, C-9, S.P. Gauge 1
Southern Pacific

Winter 1994
Cancelled

Electric Version, Item No. 20-5001
Live Steam Version, Item No. 20-5002
Live Steam Kit Version, Item No. 20-5003

2-8-4 Berkshire Steam Engine
Nickel Plate Road

1999 Volume 2
August 1999

3-Rail with Proto-Sound®, Item No. 20-3032-1, Cab No. 765
2-Rail, Item No. 20-3032-2, Cab No. 765

2-8-8-2 Y3 Steam Engine
Baltimore & Ohio

15th Anniversary
February 1995

3-Rail with Proto-Sound®, Item No. 20-3010-1, Cab No. 7032

2-8-8-2 Y3
Steam Engine
Pennsylvania

15th Anniversary
February 1995

3-Rail with Proto-Sound®, Item No. 20-3011-1, Cab No. 374

2-8-8-2 Y3
Steam Engine
Union Pacific

15th Anniversary
February 1995

3-Rail with Proto-Sound®, Item No. 20-3012-1, Cab No. 3670

2-8-8-2 Y6b
Steam Engine
Norfolk & Western

15th Anniversary
February 1995

3-Rail with Proto-Sound®, Item No. 20-3009-1, Cab No. 2197
2-Rail, Item No. 20-3009-2, Cab No. 2197

2-8-8-4 Yellowstone
Steam Engine
Duluth Missabe & Iron Range

1999 Volume 1
February 1999

3-Rail with Proto-Sound®, Item No. 20-3030-1, Cab No. 227
2-Rail, Item No. 20-3030-2, Cab No. 227

4-4-2 Atlantic
Steam Engine
Pennsylvania

2000 Volume 1
August 2000

3-Rail with Proto-Sound® 2.0, Item No. 20-3038-1, Cab No. 1600
2-Rail, Item No. 20-3038-2, Cab No. 1600

4-4-4-4 T-1 Duplex
Steam Engine
Pennsylvania

2000 Volume 1
June 2000

3-Rail with Proto-Sound®, Item No. 20-3043-1, Cab No. 5505
2-Rail, Item No. 20-3043-2, Cab No. 5505

4-6-0 G-5
Steam Engine
Pennsylvania

1999 Volume 1
January 1999

3-Rail with Proto-Sound®, Item No. 20-3031-1, Cab No. 5740
2-Rail, Item No. 20-2031-2, Cab No. 5740

4-6-2 Blue Comet
Steam Engine
Jersey Central

1998 Volume 2
September 1998

3-Rail with Proto-Sound®, Item No. 20-3028-1, Cab No. 833
2-Rail, Item No. 20-3028-2, Cab No. 833

4-6-2 K-4s Pacific
Steam Engine
Pennsylvania

Summer 1996
September 1996

3-Rail with Proto-Sound®, Item No. 20-3018-1, Cab No. 5400
2-Rail, Item No. 20-3018-2, Cab No. 5400
3-Rail with Proto-Sound®, Item No. 20-3019-1, Cab No. 5495
2-Rail, Item No. 20-3019-2, Cab No. 5495

4-6-2 Ps-4
Steam Engine
Southern

Fall 1994
September 1994

3-Rail with Proto-Sound®, Item No. 20-3005-1, Cab No. 1396
3-Rail with Proto-Sound®, Item No. 20-3006-1, Cab No. 1401

4-6-2 USRA Heavy Pacific Steam Engine
New York Central

Fall 1994
September 1994

3-Rail with Proto-Sound®, Item No. 20-3007-1, Cab No. 4912

4-6-2 USRA Heavy Pacific Steam Engine
Santa Fe

Fall 1994
September 1994

3-Rail with Proto-Sound®, Item No. 20-3008-1, Cab No. 3421

4-6-4 Dreyfuss Steam Engine
New York Central

2000 Volume 2
October 2000

3-Rail with Proto-Sound® 2.0, Item No. 20-3045-1, Cab No. 5450

4-6-4 E-4 Hudson Steam Engine
Chicago NorthWestern

1999 Volume 3
December 1999

3-Rail with Proto-Sound®, Item No. 20-3034-1, Cab No. 4008
2-Rail, Item No. 20-3034-2, Cab No. 4008

4-6-4 Empire State Express Steam Engine
New York Central

Winter 1995
January 1996

3-Rail with Proto-Sound®, Item No. 20-3016-1, Cab Nos. 5426, 5429
2-Rail, Item No. 20-3016-2, Cab Nos. 5426, 5429

4-6-4 J-1e Hudson Steam Engine
New York Central

Fall/Winter 1996
December 1996

3-Rail with Proto-Sound®, Item No. 20-3020-1, Cab No. 5344
2-Rail, Item No. 20-3020-2, Cab No. 5344

4-6-4 J-1e Hudson Steam Engine
New York Central

2000 Volume 1
May 2000

3-Rail with Proto-Sound®, Item No. 20-3040-1, Cab No. 2000

4-6-6-4, Challenger Steam Engine
Union Pacific

Spring 1994
March 1994

3-Rail with Proto-Sound®, Item No. 20-3000-1, Cab No. 3982

4-6-6-4, Challenger Steam Engine
Union Pacific

Spring 1994
March 1994

3-Rail with Proto-Sound®, Item No. 20-3001-1, Cab No. 3977

4-6-6-4 Challenger Steam Engine
Union Pacific

Spring 1994
March 1994

3-Rail with Proto-Sound®, Item No. 20-3002-1, Cab No. 3985

4-6-6-4 Challenger Steam Engine
Denver & Rio Grande

Spring 1994
March 1994

3-Rail with Proto-Sound®, Item No. 20-3003-1, Cab No. 3800

4-6-6-4 Challenger Steam Engine
Clinchfield

Spring 1994
March 1994

3-Rail with Proto-Sound®, Item No. 20-3004-1, Cab No. 670

4-8-4 Greenbrier Steam Engine
Chesapeake & Ohio

1999 Volume 3
December 1999

3-Rail with Proto-Sound®, Item No. 20-3035-1, Cab No. 614
2-Rail, Item No. 20-3035-2, Cab No. 614

4-8-4 Gs-4 Steam Engine
Southern Pacific

1998 Volume 3
January 1999

3-Rail with Proto-Sound®, Item No. 20-3029-1, Cab No. 4449
2-Rail, Item No. 20-3029-2, Cab No. 4449

4-8-4 J Steam Locomotive
Norfolk & Western

1997 Volume 2
January 1998

3-Rail with Proto-Sound®, Item No. 20-3024-1, Cab No. 611
2-Rail, Item No. 20-3024-2, Cab No. 611

4-8-4 Northern Steam Engine
Santa Fe

Fall 1995
September 1995

3-Rail with Proto-Sound®, Item No. 20-3013-1, Cab No. 2903
2-Rail, Item No. 20-3013-2, Cab No. 2903
3-Rail with Proto-Sound®, Item No. 20-3014-1, Cab No. 2912
2-Rail, Item No. 20-3014-2, Cab No. 2912

3-Rail with Proto-Sound®, Item No. 20-3015-1, Cab No. 2921
2-Rail, Item No. 20-3015-2, Cab No. 2921

4-8-8-2 Cab Forward Steam Engine
Southern Pacific

1998 Volume 1
February 1998

3-Rail with Proto-Sound®, Item No. 20-3125-1, Cab No. 4128
2-Rail, Item No. 20-3125-2, Cab No. 4128

4-8-8-4 Big Boy Steam Engine
Union Pacific

Spring 1997
February 1997

3-Rail with Proto-Sound®, Item No. 20-3021-1, Cab No. 4012
2-Rail, Item No. 20-3021-2, Cab No. 4012
3-Rail with Proto-Sound®, Item No. 20-80001a (1999 DAP), Cab No. 4018

4-Truck Shay Steam Engine
West Virginia Pulp & Paper

1997 Volume 1
May 1997

3-Rail with Proto-Sound®, Item No. 20-3023-1, Cab No. 2903
2-Rail, Item No. 20-3023-2, Cab No. 2903

Auxiliary Water Tender
Union Pacific

Spring 1997 February 1997

3-Rail, Item No. 20-3022, Cab No. NONE

Auxiliary Water Tender
Norfolk & Western

1998 Volume 1
March 1998

3-Rail, Item No. 20-3027, Cab No. NONE
3-Rail, Item No. 20-3046, Cab No. NONE

Auxiliary Water Tender
Southern Pacific

2000 Volume 1
March 2000

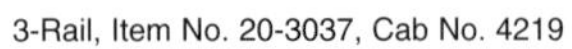
3-Rail, Item No. 20-3037, Cab No. 4219

Auxiliary Water Tender
Norfolk & Western

1998 Volume 1
March 1998

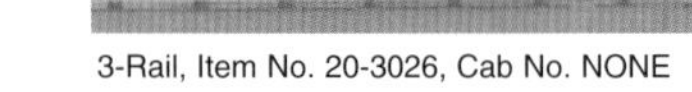
3-Rail, Item No. 20-3026, Cab No. NONE

Climax Logging Locomotive
Hillcrest Lumber Company

2000 Volume 2
September 2000

3-Rail with Proto-Sound® 2.0, Item No. 20-3039-1, Cab No. 10
2-Rail, Item No. 20-3039-2, Cab No. 10

FEF 4-8-4 Northern Steam Engine
Union Pacific

2000 Volume 2
August 2000

3-Rail with Proto-Sound® 2.0, Item No. 20-3044-1, Cab No. 844

Premier Line
Diesel, Turbine, and Electric Locomotives

M.T.H. Premier diesel and electric engines are in a class by themselves. Each of these scale locomotives offers outstanding workmanship and an impressive level of detail that makes them a prize to own. Many Premier diesels feature metal grill details, and additional operating features such as spinning roof fans, operating marker lights, and illuminated number boards. Premier electric engines provide realistic details such as operating metal pantographs, metal handrails, and decorative horn. Each item features a precisely designed body and a crisp, detailed paint scheme modeled closely on the original. This careful attention to detail does not stop with the appearance of the models. Each Premier locomotive is of the highest-quality construction to ensure their consistent, powerful performance. They feature durable ABS plastic or die-cast metal construction and precision flywheel-equipped motors that ensure the engines long lives pulling long trains, some with more than fifty cars. As this book goes to press, M.T.H. has promoted or produced forty-eight different Premier diesel turbine and electric engines or configurations.

#80 Coal Turbine Locomotive
Union Pacific

1999 Volume 3
March 2000

3-Rail with Proto-Sound®, Item No. 20-2214-1, Cab No. 80
2-Rail, Item No. 20-2214-2, Cab No. 80

AEM-7 Electric Locomotive
Amtrak

1999 Volume 2
June 1999

3-Rail with Proto-Sound®, Item No. 20-5505-1, Cab Nos. 906, 924, 938

AEM-7 Electric Locomotive
SEPTA

1999 Volume 2
June 1999

3-Rail with Proto-Sound®, Item No. 20-5506-1, Cab Nos. 2303, 2305, 2307

Alco PA AA Diesel Set
New York Central

Spring 1994
June 1994

3-Rail with Electronic Horn, Item No. 20-2018-0, Cab Nos. 4200, 4204
3-Rail with Proto-Sound®, Item No. 20-2018-1, Cab Nos. 4200, 4204
2-Rail, Item No. 20-2018-2, Cab Nos. 4200, 4204

Alco PA AA Diesel Set
Pennsylvania

Spring 1994
June 1994

3-Rail with Electronic Horn, Item No. 20-2019-0, Cab Nos. 5757A, 5759A
3-Rail with Proto-Sound®, Item No. 20-2019-1, Cab Nos. 5757A, 5759A
2-Rail, Item No. 20-2019-2, Cab Nos. 5757A, 5759A

Alco PA AA Diesel Set
Southern

Spring 1994
June 1994

3-Rail with Electronic Horn, Item No. 20-2020-0, Cab Nos. 6900, 6902
3-Rail with Proto-Sound®, Item No. 20-2020-1, Cab Nos. 6900, 6902
2-Rail, Item No. 20-2020-2, Cab Nos. 6900, 6902

Alco PA AA Diesel Set
Union Pacific

Spring 1994
June 1994

3-Rail with Electronic Horn, Item No. 20-2021-0, Cab Nos. 600A, 603A
3-Rail with Proto-Sound®, Item No. 20-2021-1, Cab Nos. 600A, 603A
2-Rail, Item No. 20-2021-2, Cab Nos. 600A, 603A

Alco PA AA Diesel Set
Southern Pacific

Spring 1994
June 1994

3-Rail with Electronic Horn, Item No. 20-2022-0, Cab Nos. 6019, 6020
3-Rail with Proto-Sound®, Item No. 20-2022-1, Cab Nos. 6019, 6020
2-Rail, Item No. 20-2022-2, Cab Nos. 6019, 6020

Alco PA AA Diesel Set
Wabash

Spring 1994
June 1994

3-Rail with Electronic Horn, Item No. 20-2023-0, Cab Nos. 1020-A, 1021-A
3-Rail with Proto-Sound®, Item No. 20-2023-1, Cab Nos. 1020-A, 1021-A
2-Rail, Item No. 20-2023-2, Cab Nos. 1020-A, 1021-A

Alco PA AA Diesel Set
Santa Fe

Spring 1994
June 1994

3-Rail with Electronic Horn, Item No. 20-2024-0, Cab Nos. 51, 53
3-Rail with Proto-Sound®, Item No. 20-2024-1, Cab Nos. 51, 53
2-Rail, Item No. 20-2024-2, Cab Nos. 51, 53

Alco PA ABA Diesel Set
Nickel Plate Road

1999 Volume 1
May 1999

3-Rail with Proto-Sound®, Item No. 20-2192-1, Cab Nos. 185, 190

Alco PA ABA Diesel Set
Lehigh Valley

1999 Volume 1
May 1999

3-Rail with Proto-Sound®, Item No. 20-2193-1, Cab Nos. 609, 610

Alco PA ABA Diesel Set
Missouri - Kansas- Texas (MKT)

1999 Volume 1
May 1999

3-Rail with Proto-Sound®, Item No. 20-2194-1, Cab Nos. 151C, 153A (A units)

Alco PA B Unit
New York Central

Spring 1994
June 1994

3-Rail, Item No. 20-2025-0, Cab No. 4302
2-Rail, Item No. 20-2025-2, Cab No. 4302
3-Rail Powered, Item No. 20-2025-3, Cab No. 4303
2-Rail Powered, Item No. 20-2025-5, Cab No. 4303

Alco PA B Unit
Pennsylvania

Spring 1994
June 1994

3-Rail, Item No. 20-2026-0, Cab No. 5758B
2-Rail, Item No. 20-2026-2, Cab No. 5758B
3-Rail Powered, Item No. 20-2026-3, Cab No. 5749B
2-Rail Powered, Item No. 20-2026-5, Cab No. 5749B

Alco PA B Unit
Southern

Spring 1994
June 1994

3-Rail, Item No. 20-2027-0, Cab No. 6901
2-Rail, Item No. 20-2027-2, Cab No. 6901
3-Rail Powered, Item No. 20-2027-3, Cab No. 6902
2-Rail Powered, Item No. 20-2027-5, Cab No. 6902

Alco PA B Unit
Union Pacific

Spring 1994
June 1994

3-Rail, Item No. 20-2028-0, Cab No. 601B
2-Rail, Item No. 20-2028-2, Cab No. 601B
3-Rail Powered, Item No. 20-2028-3, Cab No. 603B
2-Rail Powered, Item No. 20-2028-5, Cab No. 603B

Alco PA B Unit
Southern Pacific

Spring 1994
June 1994

3-Rail, Item No. 20-2029-0, Cab No. 5918
2-Rail, Item No. 20-2029-2, Cab No. 5918
3-Rail Powered, Item No. 20-2029-3, Cab No. 5919
2-Rail Powered, Item No. 20-2029-5, Cab No. 5919

Alco PA B Unit
Wabash

Spring 1994
June 1994

3-Rail, Item No. 20-2030-0, Cab No. 1020B
2-Rail, Item No. 20-2030-2, Cab No. 1020B
3-Rail Powered, Item No. 20-2030-3, Cab No. 1021B
2-Rail Powered, Item No. 20-2030-5, Cab No. 1021B

Alco PA B Unit
Santa Fe

Spring 1994
June 1994

3-Rail, Item No. 20-2031-0, Cab No. NONE
2-Rail, Item No. 20-2031-2, Cab No. NONE
3-Rail Powered, Item No. 20-2031-3, Cab No. NONE
2-Rail Powered, Item No. 20-2031-5, Cab No. NONE

Alco PA B Unit
Erie Lackawanna

Fall 1994
June 1994

3-Rail, Item No. 20-2032-0, Cab No. 858B

AS-616 Diesel
Pennsylvania

Summer 1996
October 1996

3-Rail with Electronic Horn, Item No. 20-2133-0, Cab Nos. 8111, 8112, 8115
3-Rail with Proto-Sound®, Item No. 20-2133-1, Cab Nos. 8111, 8112, 8115
2-Rail, Item No. 20-2133-2, Cab Nos. 8111, 8112, 8115

AS-616 Diesel
Bessemer & Lake Erie

Summer 1996
October 1996

3-Rail with Electronic Horn, Item No. 20-2134-0, Cab Nos. 408, 409, 411
3-Rail with Proto-Sound®, Item No. 20-2134-1, Cab Nos. 408, 409, 411
2-Rail, Item No. 20-2134-2, Cab Nos. 408, 409, 411

AS-616 Diesel
Soo Line

Summer 1996
October 1996

3-Rail with Electronic Horn, Item No. 20-2135-0, Cab Nos. 390, 392, 395
3-Rail with Proto-Sound®, Item No. 20-2135-1, Cab Nos. 390, 392, 395
2-Rail, Item No. 20-2135-2, Cab Nos. 390, 392, 395

AS-616 Diesel
Chicago NorthWestern

Summer 1996
October 1996

3-Rail with Electronic Horn, Item No. 20-2136-0, Cab Nos. 8029, 8032, 8035
3-Rail with Proto-Sound®, Item No. 20-2136-1, Cab Nos. 8029, 8032, 8035
2-Rail, Item No. 20-2136-2, Cab Nos. 8029, 8032, 8035

AS-616 Diesel
Southern Pacific

Summer 1996
October 1996

3-Rail with Electronic Horn, Item No. 20-2137-0, Cab Nos. 5232, 5235, 5239
3-Rail with Proto-Sound®, Item No. 20-2137-1, Cab Nos. 5232, 5235, 5239
2-Rail, Item No. 20-2137-2, Cab Nos. 5232, 5235, 5239

AS-616 Diesel
Union Pacific

Summer 1996
October 1996

3-Rail with Electronic Horn, Item No. 20-2138-0, Cab Nos. 1260, 1263, 1265
3-Rail with Proto-Sound®, Item No. 20-2138-1, Cab Nos. 1260, 1263, 1265
2-Rail, Item No. 20-2138-2, Cab Nos. 1260, 1263, 1265

BL-2 Diesel Engine
Western Maryland

Summer 1996
August 1996

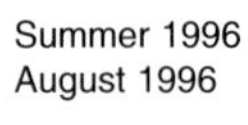

3-Rail with Electronic Horn, Item No. 20-2129-0, Cab Nos. 1260, 1263, 1265
3-Rail with Proto-Sound®, Item No. 20-2129-1, Cab Nos. 1260, 1263, 1265
2-Rail, Item No. 20-2129-2, Cab Nos. 1260, 1263, 1265

BL-2 Diesel Engine
Florida East Coast

Summer 1996
August 1996

3-Rail with Electronic Horn, Item No. 20-2130-0, Cab Nos. 601, 604, 606
3-Rail with Proto-Sound®, Item No. 20-2130-1, Cab Nos. 601, 604, 606
2-Rail, Item No. 20-2130-2, Cab Nos. 601, 604, 606

BL-2 Diesel Engine
Monon

Summer 1996
August 1996

3-Rail with Electronic Horn, Item No. 20-2131-0, Cab Nos. 30, 33, 36
3-Rail with Proto-Sound®, Item No. 20-2131-1, Cab Nos. 30, 33, 36
2-Rail, Item No. 20-2131-2, Cab Nos. 30, 33, 36

BL-2 Diesel Engine
Electro Motive Division

Summer 1996
August 1996

3-Rail with Electronic Horn, Item No. 20-2132-0, Cab Nos. 497, 499, 503
3-Rail with Proto-Sound®, Item No. 20-2132-1, Cab Nos. 497, 499, 503
2-Rail, Item No. 20-2132-2, Cab Nos. 497, 499, 503

C30-7 Diesel Engine
Burlington Northern

Spring 1994
April 1994

3-Rail with Electronic Horn, Item No. 20-2010-0, Cab Nos. 5000, 5005, 5010
3-Rail with Proto-Sound®, Item No. 20-2010-1, Cab Nos. 5000, 5005, 5010
2-Rail, Item No. 20-2010-2, Cab Nos. 5000, 5005, 5010

C30-7 Diesel Engine
Conrail

Spring 1994
April 1994

3-Rail with Electronic Horn, Item No. 20-2011-0, Cab Nos. 6600, 6605, 6609
3-Rail with Proto-Sound®, Item No. 20-2011-1, Cab Nos. 6600, 6605, 6609
2-Rail, Item No. 20-2011-2, Cab Nos. 6600, 6605, 6609

C30-7 Diesel Engine
CSX

Spring 1994
April 1994

3-Rail with Electronic Horn, Item No. 20-2012-0, Cab Nos. 7000, 7009, 7015
3-Rail with Proto-Sound®, Item No. 20-2012-1, Cab Nos. 7000, 7009, 7015
2-Rail, Item No. 20-2012-2, Cab Nos. 7000, 7009, 7015

C30-7 Diesel Engine
Norfolk & Western

Spring 1994
April 1994

3-Rail with Electronic Horn, Item No. 20-2014-0, Cab Nos. 8003, 8012, 8026
3-Rail with Proto-Sound®, Item No. 20-2014-1, Cab Nos. 8003, 8012, 8026
2-Rail, Item No. 20-2014-2, Cab Nos. 8003, 8012, 8026

C30-7 Diesel Engine
Santa Fe

Spring 1994
April 1994

3-Rail with Electronic Horn, Item No. 20-2015-0, Cab Nos. 8123, 8140, 8152
3-Rail with Proto-Sound®, Item No. 20-2015-1, Cab Nos. 8123, 8140, 8152
2-Rail, Item No. 20-2015-2, Cab Nos. 8123, 8140, 8152

C30-7 Diesel Engine
Louisville & Nashville - Family Lines

Spring 1994
April 1994

3-Rail with Electronic Horn, Item No. 20-2016-0, Cab Nos. 7070, 7080, 7090
3-Rail with Proto-Sound®, Item No. 20-2016-1, Cab Nos. 7070, 7080, 7090
2-Rail, Item No. 20-2016-2, Cab Nos. 7070, 7080, 7090

C30-7 Diesel Engine
Union Pacific

Spring 1994
April 1994

3-Rail with Electronic Horn, Item No. 20-2017-0, Cab Nos. 2460, 2472, 2486
3-Rail with Proto-Sound®, Item No. 20-2017-1, Cab Nos. 2460, 2472, 2486
2-Rail, Item No. 20-2017-2, Cab Nos. 2460, 2472, 2486

C30-7 Diesel Engine
Norfolk Southern

Spring 1994
April 1994

3-Rail with Electronic Horn, Item No. 20-2013-0, Cab Nos. 8050, 8064, 8073
3-Rail with Proto-Sound®, Item No. 20-2013-1, Cab Nos. 8050, 8064, 8073
2-Rail, Item No. 20-2013-2, Cab Nos. 8050, 8064, 8073

Centipede AA Diesel Set
Pennsylvania

1999 Volume 2
October 1999

3-Rail with Proto-Sound®, Item No. 20-2200-1, Cab No. 5823
2-Rail, Item No. 20-2200-2, Cab No. 5823

Dash-8 Diesel Engine
Union Pacific

Fall 1993
October 1993

3-Rail with Electronic Horn, Item No. 20-2001-0, Cab Nos. 9359, 9355, 9401
3-Rail with Proto-Sound®, Item No. 20-2001-1, Cab Nos. 9359, 9355, 9401
2-Rail, Item No. 20-2001-2, Cab Nos. 9359, 9355, 9401

Dash-8 Diesel Engine
Norfolk Southern

Fall 1993
October 1993

3-Rail with Electronic Horn, Item No. 20-2002-0, Cab Nos. 8691, 8699, 8705
3-Rail with Proto-Sound®, Item No. 20-2002-1, Cab Nos. 8691, 8699, 8705
2-Rail, Item No. 20-2002-2, Cab Nos. 8691, 8699, 8705

Dash-8 Diesel Engine
Conrail

Fall 1993
October 1993

3-Rail with Electronic Horn, Item No. 20-2004-0, Cab Nos. 6050, 6055, 6059
3-Rail with Proto-Sound®, Item No. 20-2004-1, Cab Nos. 6050, 6055, 6059
2-Rail, Item No. 20-2004-2, Cab Nos. 6050, 6055, 6059

Dash-8 Diesel Engine
Chicago NorthWestern

Fall 1993
October 1993

3-Rail with Electronic Horn, Item No. 20-2005-0, Cab Nos. 8545, 8505, 8538
3-Rail with Proto-Sound®, Item No. 20-2005-1, Cab Nos. 8545, 8505, 8538
2-Rail, Item No. 20-2005-2, Cab Nos. 8545, 8505, 8538

Dash-8 Diesel Engine
Amtrak

Fall 1993
October 1993

3-Rail with Electronic Horn, Item No. 20-2007-0, Cab Nos. 500, 510, 512
3-Rail with Proto-Sound®, Item No. 20-2007-1, Cab Nos. 500, 510, 512
2-Rail, Item No. 20-2007-2, Cab Nos. 500, 510, 512
3-Rail with Proto-Sound®, Item No. 20-2171-1, Cab Nos. 501, 502, 509

Dash-8 Diesel Engine
Santa Fe

Fall 1993
October 1993

3-Rail with Electronic Horn, Item No. 20-2008-0, Cab No. 500
3-Rail with Proto-Sound®, Item No. 20-2008-1, Cab No. 500
2-Rail, Item No. 20-2008-2, Cab No. 500

Dash-8 Diesel Engine
Burlington

Fall 1993
October 1993

3-Rail with Electronic Horn, Item No. 20-2003-0, Cab Nos. 9243, 9244, 9245
3-Rail with Proto-Sound®, Item No. 20-2003-1, Cab Nos. 9243, 9244, 9245
2-Rail, Item No. 20-2003-2, Cab Nos. 9243, 9244, 9245

Dash-8 Diesel Engine
CSX

Fall 1993
October 1993

3-Rail with Electronic Horn, Item No. 20-2006-0, Cab Nos. 7599, 7653, 7753
3-Rail with Proto-Sound®, Item No. 20-2006-1, Cab Nos. 7599, 7653, 7753
2-Rail, Item No. 20-2006-2, Cab Nos. 7599, 7653, 7753

Dash-9 Diesel Engine
Chicago NorthWestern

1997 Volume 1
November 1997

3-Rail with Proto-Sound®, Item No. 20-2159-1, Cab Nos. 8602, 8636, 8730
2-Rail, Item No. 20-2159-2, Cab Nos. 8602, 8636, 8730

Dash-9 Diesel Engine
G.E. Demonstrator

1997 Volume 1
November 1997

3-Rail with Proto-Sound®, Item No. 20-2160-1, Cab Nos. 2000, 2001, 2002
2-Rail, Item No. 20-2160-2, Cab Nos. 2000, 2001, 2002

Dash-9 Diesel Engine
BNSF

1998 Volume 1
May 1998

3-Rail with Proto-Sound®, Item No. 20-2172-1, Cab Nos. 972, 966
2-Rail, Item No. 20-2172-2, Cab Nos. 972, 966
All sets included 4 Husky Stack Cars, number 20-95006 thru 20-95009.

DC-3 Rail Inspection Car
Union Pacific

2000 Volume 2
August 2000

3-Rail with Proto-Sound® 2.0, Item No. 20-2242-1, Cab No. DC-3

DD40AX Diesel Engine
Union Pacific

1998 Volume 1
May 1998

3-Rail with Proto-Sound®, Item No. 20-2178-1, Cab Nos. 6900, 6922

DL-109 Diesel Engine
Milwaukee Road

2000 Volume 1
February 2000

3-Rail with Proto-Sound®, Item No. 20-2222-1, Cab No. 14

DL-109 Diesel Engine
Santa Fe

2000 Volume 1
February 2000

3-Rail with Proto-Sound®, Item No. 20-2223-1, Cab No. 50

DL-110 Powered B Unit Diesel Engine
Milwaukee Road

2000 Volume 2
July 2000

3-Rail, Item No. 20-2222-3, Cab No. 14B

DL-110 Powered B Unit Diesel Engine
Santa Fe

2000 Volume 2
July 2000

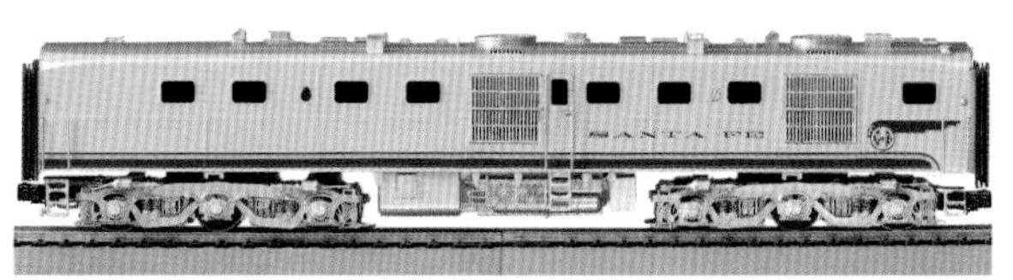

3-Rail, Item No. 20-2223-3, Cab No. 51

E-2 Bi-Polar Electric
Milwaukee Road

2000 Volume 2
October 2000

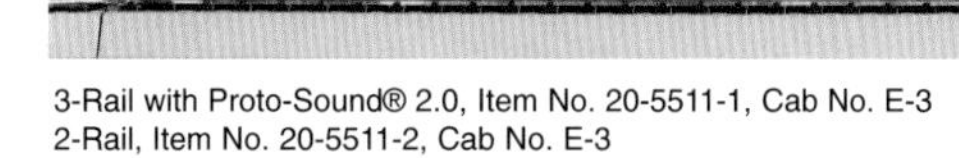

3-Rail with Proto-Sound® 2.0, Item No. 20-5511-1, Cab No. E-3
2-Rail, Item No. 20-5511-2, Cab No. E-3

E-33 Rectifier Electric
New Haven

2000 Volume 1
April 2000

3-Rail with Proto-Sound®, Item No. 20-5508-1, Cab Nos. 302, 303, 308

E-33 Rectifier Electric
Conrail

2000 Volume 1
April 2000

3-Rail with Proto-Sound®, Item No. 20-5509-1, Cab Nos. 4604, 4605, 4608

E-8 ABA Diesel Engine Set
Seaboard

1997 Volume 2
January 1998

3-Rail with Proto-Sound®, Item No. 20-2168-1, Cab Nos. 3049, 3050

E-8 ABA Diesel Engine Set
Rock Island

1997 Volume 2
January 1998

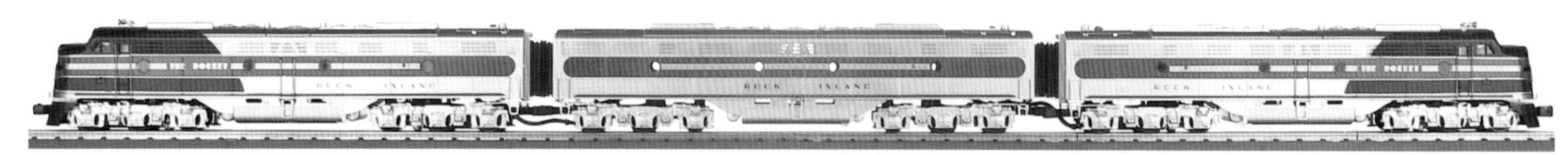

3-Rail with Proto-Sound®, Item No. 20-2169-1, Cab Nos. 643, 646

E-8 ABA Diesel Engine Set
Baltimore & Ohio

1997 Volume 2
January 1998

3-Rail with Proto-Sound®, Item No. 20-2170-1, Cab Nos. 1441, 1440

E-8 ABA Diesel Engine Set
Pere Marquette

1999 Volume 3
December 1999

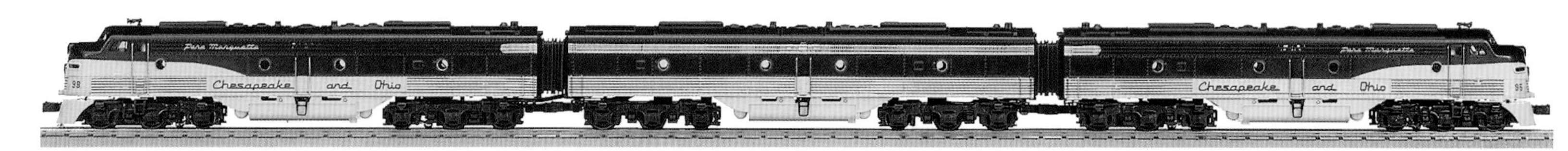

3-Rail with Proto-Sound®, Item No. 20-2205-1, Cab Nos. 95, 98

E-8 ABA Diesel Engine Set
Electro Motive Division

1999 Volume 3
December 1999

3-Rail with Proto-Sound®, Item No. 20-2206-1, Cab Nos. 1,2,3

E-8 ABA Diesel Engine Set
Kansas City Southern

1999 Volume 3
December 1999

3-Rail with Proto-Sound®, Item No. 20-2207-1, Cab Nos. 26, 28

E-8 ABA Diesel Engine Set
Union Pacific

1999 Volume 3
December 1999

3-Rail with Proto-Sound®, Item No. 20-2208-1, Cab Nos. 951, 963, 949

E-8 ABA Diesel Engine Set
Santa Fe

2000 Volume 2
August 2000

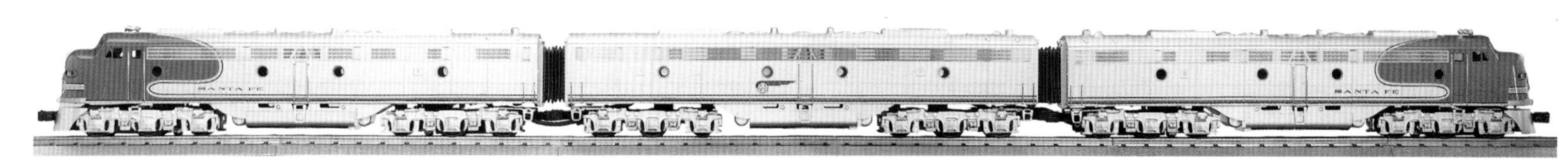

3-Rail with Proto-Sound® 2.0, Item No. 20-2234-1, Cab Nos. 83, 84

E-8 ABA Diesel Engine Set
Illinois Central

2000 Volume 2
August 2000

3-Rail with Proto-Sound® 2.0, Item No. 20-2235-1, Cab Nos. 4025, 4104, 4024

E-8 ABA Diesel Engine Set
Erie

2000 Volume 2
August 2000

3-Rail with Proto-Sound® 2.0, Item No. 20-2236-1, Cab Nos. 833, 833B, 832

E-8 ABA Diesel Engine Set
Chicago NorthWestern

2000 Volume 2
August 2000

3-Rail with Proto-Sound® 2.0, Item No. 20-2237-1, Cab Nos. 5029A, 5029B, 5030A

EP-5 Electric Engine
New Haven

1999 Volume 1
March 1999

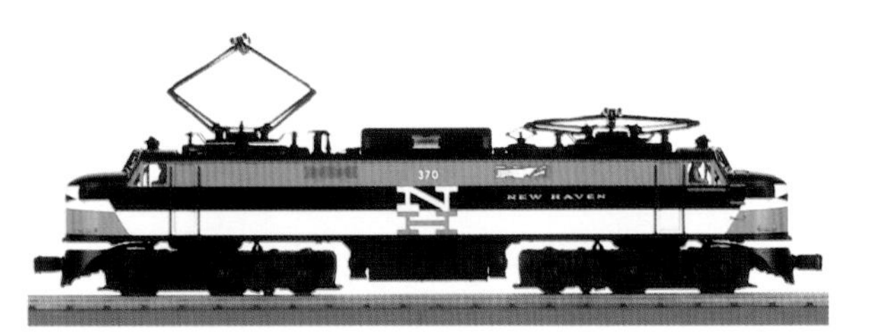

3-Rail with Proto-Sound®, Item No. 20-2195-1, Cab Nos. 370, 375

EP-5 Electric Engine
Great Northern

1999 Volume 1
March 1999

3-Rail with Proto-Sound®, Item No. 20-2196-1, Cab Nos. 2357, 2358, 2359

F-3 AA Diesel Set
Baltimore & Ohio

Winter 1994
January 1995

3-Rail with Electronic Horn, Item No. 20-2050-0, Cab Nos. 86, 86A
3-Rail with Proto-Sound®, Item No. 20-2050-1, Cab Nos. 86, 86A
2-Rail, Item No. 20-2050-2, Cab Nos. 86, 86A

F-3 AA Diesel Set
Denver & Rio Grande

Winter 1994
January 1995

3-Rail with Electronic Horn, Item No. 20-2051-0, Cab Nos. 5521, 5524
3-Rail with Proto-Sound®, Item No. 20-2051-1, Cab Nos. 5521, 5524
2-Rail, Item No. 20-2051-2, Cab Nos. 5521, 5524

F-3 AA Diesel Set
Florida East Coast

Winter 1994
January 1995

3-Rail with Electronic Horn, Item No. 20-2052-0, Cab Nos. 501, 503
3-Rail with Proto-Sound®, Item No. 20-2052-1, Cab Nos. 501, 503
2-Rail, Item No. 20-2052-2, Cab Nos. 501, 503

F-3 AA Diesel Set
Jersey Central

Winter 1994
January 1995

3-Rail with Electronic Horn, Item No. 20-2053-0, Cab Nos. 56D57 (both units)
3-Rail with Proto-Sound®, Item No. 20-2053-1, Cab Nos. 56D57 (both units)
2-Rail, Item No. 20-2053-2, Cab Nos. 56D57 (both units)

F-3 AA Diesel Set
Pennsylvania

Winter 1994
January 1995

3-Rail with Electronic Horn, Item No. 20-2054-0, Cab Nos. 9500A, 9502A
3-Rail with Proto-Sound®, Item No. 20-2054-1, Cab Nos. 9500A, 9502A
2-Rail, Item No. 20-2054-2, Cab Nos. 9500A, 9502A

F-3 AA Diesel Set
Union Pacific

Winter 1994
January 1995

3-Rail with Electronic Horn, Item No. 20-2055-0, Cab Nos. 1447, 1449
3-Rail with Proto-Sound®, Item No. 20-2055-1, Cab Nos. 1447, 1449
2-Rail, Item No. 20-2055-2, Cab Nos. 1447, 1449

F-3 AA Diesel Set
Western Pacific

Winter 1994
January 1995

3-Rail with Electronic Horn, Item No. 20-2056-0, Cab Nos. 801, 803
3-Rail with Proto-Sound®, Item No. 20-2056-1, Cab Nos. 801, 803
2-Rail, Item No. 20-2056-2, Cab Nos. 801, 803

F-3 AA Diesel Set
Canadian Pacific

Winter 1994
January 1995

3-Rail with Electronic Horn, Item No. 20-2057-0, Cab Nos. 4001, 4002
3-Rail with Proto-Sound®, Item No. 20-2057-1, Cab Nos. 4001, 4002
2-Rail, Item No. 20-2057-2, Cab Nos. 4001, 4002

F-3 AA Diesel Set
Western Maryland

Fall 1995
July 1995

3-Rail with Electronic Horn, Item No. 20-2083-0, Cab Nos. 51, 52
3-Rail with Proto-Sound®, Item No. 20-2083-1, Cab Nos. 51, 52
2-Rail, Item No. 20-2083-2, Cab Nos. 51, 52

F-3 AA Diesel Set
Texas Special

Fall 1995
July 1995

3-Rail with Electronic Horn, Item No. 20-2084-0, Cab Nos. 201A, 201C
3-Rail with Proto-Sound®, Item No. 20-2084-1, Cab Nos. 201A, 201C
2-Rail, Item No. 20-2084-2, Cab Nos. 201A, 201C

F-3 AA Diesel Set
Burlington

Fall 1995
July 1995

3-Rail with Electronic Horn, Item No. 20-2085-0, Cab Nos. 9960A, 9960C
3-Rail with Proto-Sound®, Item No. 20-2085-1, Cab Nos. 9960A, 9960C
2-Rail, Item No. 20-2085-2, Cab Nos. 9960A, 9960C

F-3 AA Diesel Set
Lehigh Valley

Fall 1995
July 1995

3-Rail with Electronic Horn, Item No. 20-2086-0, Cab Nos. 510, 512 (A units), 511 for B unit
3-Rail with Proto-Sound®, Item No. 20-2086-1, Cab Nos. 510, 512 (A units), 511 for B unit
2-Rail, Item No. 20-2086-2, Cab Nos. 510, 512 (A units), 511 for B unit

F-3 AA Diesel Set
Northern Pacific

Fall 1995
July 1995

3-Rail with Electronic Horn, Item No. 20-2087-0, Cab Nos. 6506A, 6506D (A units), 6506B for B unit
3-Rail with Proto-Sound®, Item No. 20-2087-1, Cab Nos. 6506A, 6506D (A units), 6506B for B unit
2-Rail, Item No. 20-2087-2, Cab Nos. 6506A, 6506D (A units), 6506B for B uni

F-3 AA Diesel Set
Atlantic Coast Line

Fall 1995
July 1995

3-Rail with Electronic Horn, Item No. 20-2088-0, Cab Nos. 341, 342 (A units), 341-B for B unit
3-Rail with Proto-Sound®, Item No. 20-2088-1, Cab Nos. 341, 342 (A units), 341-B for B unit
2-Rail, Item No. 20-2088-2, Cab Nos. 341, 342 (A units), 341-B for B unit

F-3 AA Diesel Set
New Haven

Fall 1995
July 1995

3-Rail with Electronic Horn, Item No. 20-2089-0, Cab Nos. 1197, 1199 (A units), 1198 for B unit
3-Rail with Proto-Sound®, Item No. 20-2089-1, Cab Nos. 1197, 1199 (A units), 1198 for B unit
2-Rail, Item No. 20-2089-2, Cab Nos. 1197, 1199 (A units), 1198 for B unit

F-3 AA Diesel Set
Electro Motive Division

Fall 1995
July 1995

3-Rail with Electronic Horn, Item No. 20-2090-0, Cab Nos. 752, 754
3-Rail with Proto-Sound®, Item No. 20-2090-1, Cab Nos. 752, 754
2-Rail, Item No. 20-2090-2, Cab Nos. 752, 754

F-3 AA Diesel Set
Chesapeake & Ohio

Summer 1996
July 1996

3-Rail with Electronic Horn, Item No. 20-2125-0, Cab Nos. 8010, 8011
3-Rail with Proto-Sound®, Item No. 20-2125-1, Cab Nos. 8010, 8011
2-Rail, Item No. 20-2125-2, Cab Nos. 8010, 8011

F-3 AA Diesel Set
Boston & Maine

Summer 1996
July 1996

3-Rail with Electronic Horn, Item No. 20-2126-0, Cab Nos. 4227, 4228
3-Rail with Proto-Sound®, Item No. 20-2126-1, Cab Nos. 4227, 4228
2-Rail, Item No. 20-2126-2, Cab Nos. 4227, 4228

F-3 AA Diesel Set
Rock Island

Summer 1996
July 1996

3-Rail with Electronic Horn, Item No. 20-2127-0, Cab Nos. 51, 52
3-Rail with Proto-Sound®, Item No. 20-2127-1, Cab Nos. 51, 52
2-Rail, Item No. 20-2127-2, Cab Nos. 51, 52

F-3 AA Diesel Set
Alaska

Summer 1996
July 1996

3-Rail with Electronic Horn, Item No. 20-2128-0, Cab Nos. 1516, 1518 (A units), 1517 for B unit
3-Rail with Proto-Sound®, Item No. 20-2128-1, Cab Nos. 1516, 1518 (A units), 1517 for B unit
2-Rail, Item No. 20-2128-2, Cab Nos. Cab Nos. 1516, 1518 (A units), 1517 for B unit

F-3 AA Diesel Set
Santa Fe

Spring 1997
June 1997

3-Rail with Proto-Sound®, Item No. 20-2151-1, Cab Nos. 20, 21

F-3 AA Diesel Set
Louisville & Nashville

Spring 1997
July 1997

3-Rail with Proto-Sound®, Item No. 20-2152-1, Cab Nos. 800, 801

F-3 AA Diesel Set
Canadian Pacific

Uncataloged Item
August 1999

3-Rail with Proto-Sound®, Item No. 20-80001b1 (1999 DAP), Cab No. 2373

F-3 ABA Diesel Set
New York Central

1998 Volume 1
March 1998

3-Rail with Proto-Sound®, Item No. 20-2176-1, Cab Nos. 1608, 2414, 1630

F-3 ABA Diesel Set
Southern

1998 Volume 1
March 1998

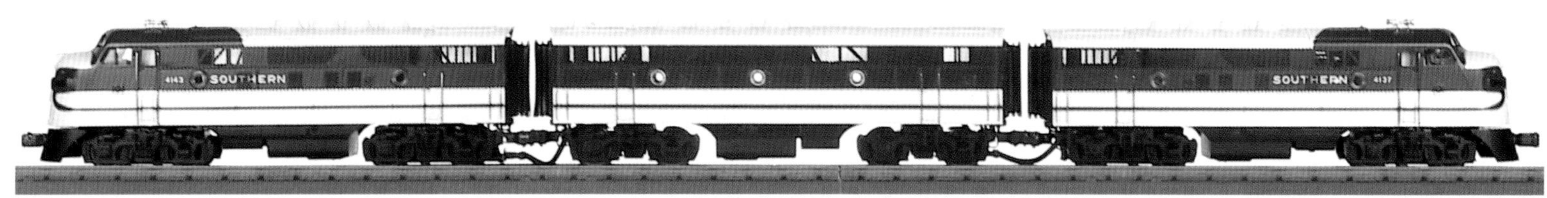

3-Rail with Proto-Sound®, Item No. 20-2177-1, Cab Nos. 4137, 4350, 4200

F-3 ABA Diesel Set
Reading

1999 Volume 1
June 1999

3-Rail with Proto-Sound®, Item No. 20-2198-1, Cab Nos. 276, 279

F-3 ABA Diesel Set
Southern Pacific

1999 Volume 1
June 1999

3-Rail with Proto-Sound®, Item No. 20-2199-1, Cab Nos. 6180, 6181 (A units), 8080 for B unit.

F-3 ABA Diesel Set
Santa Fe

2000 Volume 1
July 2000

3-Rail with Proto-Sound®, Item No. 20-2219-1, Cab Nos. 100, 101 (A Units), 102 (B Unit)

F-3 ABA Diesel Set
Pennsylvania

2000 Volume 1
July 2000

3-Rail with Proto-Sound®, Item No. 20-2218-1, Cab Nos. 9785(A), 9781(B), 9791(A)

F-3 ABA Diesel Set
Great Northern

2000 Volume 1
July 2000

3-Rail with Proto-Sound®, Item No. 20-2220-1, Cab Nos. 352(A), 352(B), 352(A)

F-3 ABA Diesel Set
Santa Fe - Clear Body

Uncataloged Item
June 2000

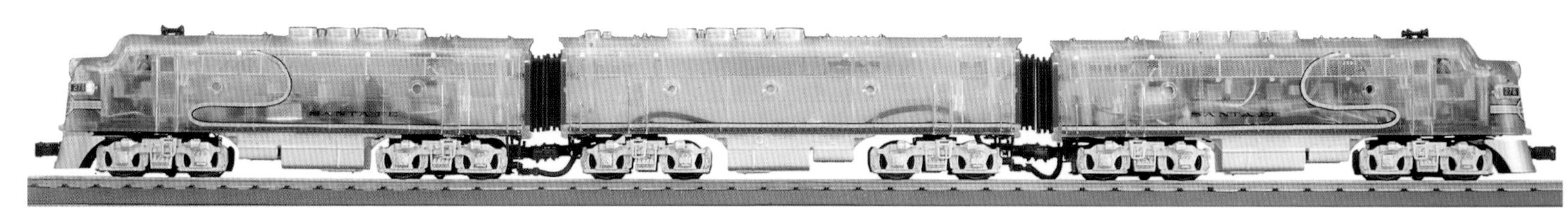

3-Rail with Proto-Sound® 2.0, Item No. 20-80002a (2000 DAP), Cab Nos. 276, 278 (A Units), NONE (B Unit)

F-3 B Unit
Baltimore & Ohio

Winter 1994
January 1995

3-Rail Non-Powered, Item No. 20-2058-3, Cab No. NONE
3-Rail Powered, Item No. 20-2050-3, Cab No. NONE
2-Rail, Item No. 20-2058-2, Cab No. NONE

F-3 B Unit
Denver & Rio Grande

Winter 1994
January 1995

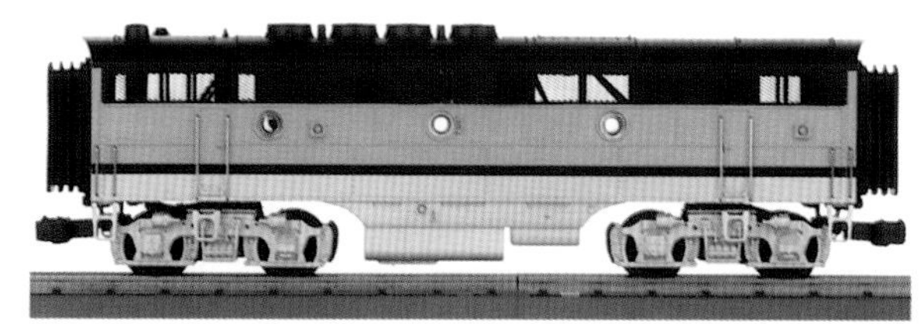

3-Rail Non-Powered, Item No. 20-2059-3, Cab No. NONE
3-Rail Powered, Item No. 20-2051-3, Cab No. NONE
2-Rail, Item No. 20-2059-2, Cab No. NONE

F-3 B Unit
Florida East Coast

Winter 1994
January 1995

3-Rail Non-Powered, Item No. 20-2060-3, Cab No. 551
3-Rail Powered, Item No. 20-2052-3, Cab No. 551
2-Rail, Item No. 20-2060-3S, Cab No. 551

F-3 B Unit
Jersey Central

Winter 1994
January 1995

3-Rail Non-Powered, Item No. 20-2061-3, Cab No. D CRP
3-Rail Powered, Item No. 20-2053-3, Cab No.D CRP
2-Rail, Item No. 20-2061-3S, Cab No. D CRP

F-3 B Unit
Union Pacific

Winter 1994
January 1995

3-Rail Non-Powered, Item No. 20-2063-3, Cab No. 1448
3-Rail Powered, Item No. 20-2055-3, Cab No. 1448
2-Rail, Item No. 20-2063-3S, Cab No. 1448

F-3 B Unit
Western Pacific

Winter 1994
January 1995

3-Rail Non-Powered, Item No. 20-2064-3, Cab No. NONE
3-Rail Powered, Item No. 20-2056-3, Cab No. NONE
2-Rail, Item No. 20-2064-3S, Cab No. NONE

F-3 B Unit
Canadian Pacific

Winter 1994
January 1995

3-Rail Non-Powered, Item No. 20-2065-3, Cab No. 4400
3-Rail Powered, Item No. 20-2057-3, Cab No. 4400
2-Rail, Item No. 20-2065-3S, Cab No. 4400

F-3 B Unit
Western Maryland

Fall 1995
June 1995

3-Rail Non-Powered, Item No. 20-2091-3, Cab No. 406
3-Rail Powered, Item No. 20-2083-3, Cab No. 409
2-Rail, Item No. 20-2091-3S, Cab No. 406

F-3 B Unit
Texas Special

Fall 1995
July 1995

3-Rail Non-Powered, Item No. 20-2092-3, Cab No. NONE
3-Rail Powered, Item No. 20-2084-3, Cab No. NONE
2-Rail, Item No. 20-2092-3S, Cab No. NONE

F-3 B Unit
Burlington

Fall 1995
July 1995

3-Rail Non-Powered, Item No. 20-2093-3, Cab No. NONE
3-Rail Powered, Item No. 20-2085-3, Cab No. NONE
2-Rail, Item No. 20-2093-3S, Cab No. NONE

F-3 B Unit
Lehigh Valley

Fall 1995
September 1995

3-Rail Non-Powered, Item No. 20-2094-3, Cab No. 511
3-Rail Powered, Item No. 20-2086-3, Cab No. 529
2-Rail, Item No. 20-2094-3S, Cab No. 511

F-3 B Unit
Northern Pacific

Fall 1995
July 1995

3-Rail Non-Powered, Item No. 20-2095-3, Cab No. 6506B
3-Rail Powered, Item No. 20-2087-3, Cab No. 6505B
2-Rail, Item No. 20-2095-3S, Cab No. 6506B

F-3 B Unit
Atlantic Coast Line

Fall 1995
July 1995

3-Rail Non-Powered, Item No. 20-2096-3, Cab No. NONE
3-Rail Powered, Item No. 20-2088-3, Cab No. 336-B
2-Rail, Item No. 20-2096-3S, Cab No. NONE

F-3 B Unit
New Haven

Fall 1995
July 1995

3-Rail Non-Powered, Item No. 20-2097-3, Cab No. 1198
3-Rail Powered, Item No. 20-2089-3, Cab No. 1195
2-Rail, Item No. 20-2097-3S, Cab No. 1198

F-3 B Unit
Chesapeake & Ohio

Summer 1996
June 1996

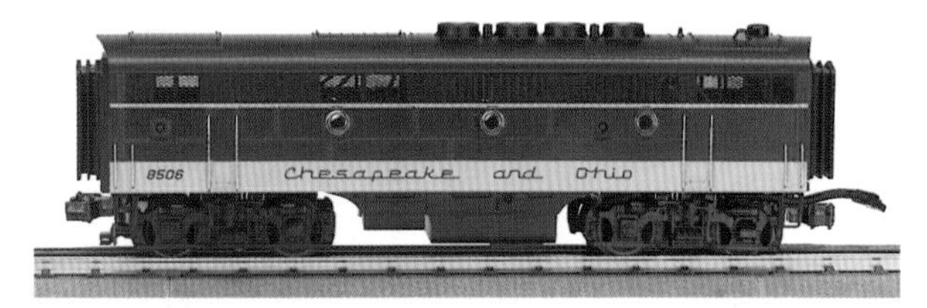

3-Rail Non-Powered, Item No. 20-2125-3, Cab No. 8505
3-Rail Powered, Item No. 20-2125-4, Cab No. 8506
2-Rail, Item No. 20-2125-32, Cab No. 8505

F-3 B Unit
Boston & Maine

Summer 1996
July 1996

3-Rail Non-Powered, Item No. 20-2126-3, Cab No. NONE
3-Rail Powered, Item No. 20-2126-4, Cab No. NONE
2-Rail, Item No. 20-2126-32, Cab No. NONE

F-3 B Unit
Rock Island

Summer 1996
July 1996

3-Rail Non-Powered, Item No. 20-2127-3, Cab No. NONE
3-Rail Powered, Item No. 20-2127-4, Cab No. NONE
2-Rail, Item No. 20-2127-32, Cab No. NONE

F-3 B Unit
Alaska

Summer 1996
July 1996

3-Rail Non-Powered, Item No. 20-2128-3, Cab No. 1517
3-Rail Powered, Item No. 20-2128-4, Cab No. 1503
2-Rail, Item No. 20-2128-32, Cab No. 1517

F-3 B Unit
Santa Fe

Spring 1997
June 1999

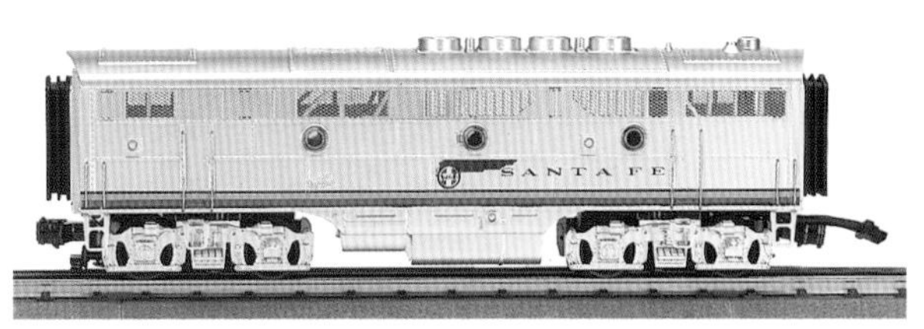

3-Rail Non-Powered, Item No. 20-2151-3, Cab No. NONE
3-Rail Powered, Item No. 20-2151-4, Cab No. NONE

F-3 B Unit
Louisville & Nashville

Spring 1997
July 1997

3-Rail Non-Powered, Item No. 20-2152-3, Cab No. 700B
3-Rail Powered, Item No. 20-2152-4, Cab No. 701

F-3 B Unit
New York Central

2000 Volume 1
May 2000

3-Rail, Item No. 20-2176-3, Cab No. 3600

F-3 B Unit
Southern

2000 Volume 1
May 2000

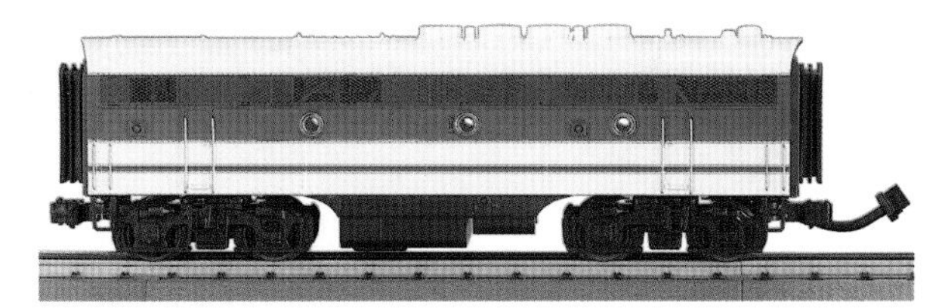

3-Rail, Item No. 20-2177-3, Cab No. NONE

F-3 B Unit
Southern Pacific

2000 Volume 1
May 2000

3-Rail, Item No. 20-2199-3, Cab No. 8081

F-3 B Unit
Reading

2000 Volume 1
May 2000

3-Rail, Item No. 20-2198-3, Cab No. NONE

F-3 B Unit
Canadian Pacific

Uncataloged Item
June 2000

3-Rail, Item No. 20-80002b (2000 DAP), Cab No. 2373

F-3 B Unit
Pennsylvania

1998 Volume 2
December 1998

3-Rail Non-Powered, Item No. 20-2062-3, Cab No. NONE
3-Rail Powered, Item No. 20-2054-3, Cab No. 9505B
2-Rail, Item No. 20-2062-3S, Cab No. NONE

F-3 B Unit
Electro Motive Division

1998 Volume 2
April 1998

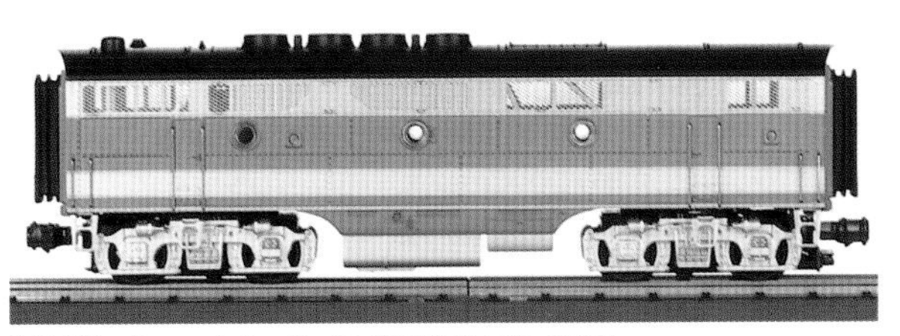

3-Rail Non-Powered, Item No. 20-2098-3, Cab No. NONE
3-Rail Powered, Item No. 20-2090-3, Cab No. NONE
2-Rail, Item No. 20-2098-3S, Cab No. NONE

F40PH Diesel Engine
METRA

Spring 1997
July 1997

3-Rail with Proto-Sound®, Item No. 20-2149-1, Cab Nos. 104, 135, 136
2-Rail, Item No. 20-2149-2, Cab Nos. 104, 135, 136

F40PH Diesel Engine
Caltrain

Spring 1997
July 1997

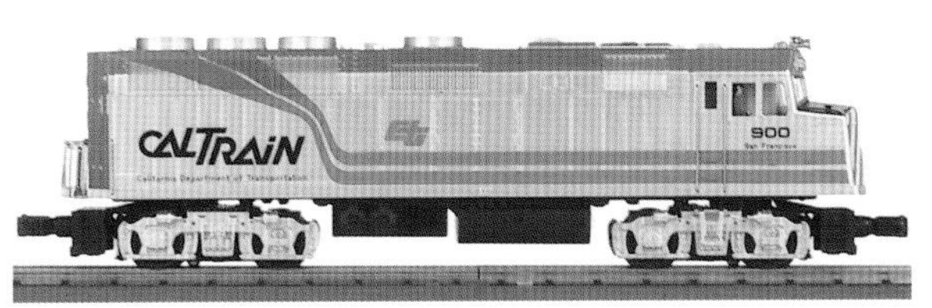

3-Rail with Proto-Sound®, Item No. 20-2150-1, Cab Nos. 900, 902, 904
2-Rail, Item No. 20-2150-2, Cab Nos. 900, 902, 904

F40PH Diesel Engine
Amtrak

Spring 1997
July 1997

3-Rail with Proto-Sound®, Item No. 20-2147-1, Cab Nos. 300, 305, 297
2-Rail, Item No. 20-2147-2, Cab Nos. 300, 305, 297

F40PH Diesel Engine
Massachusetts Bay

Spring 1997
July 1997

3-Rail with Proto-Sound®, Item No. 20-2148-1, Cab Nos. 1000, 1017, 1059
2-Rail, Item No. 20-2148-2, Cab Nos. 1000, 1017, 1059

F59PH Diesel Engine
Amtrak

1999 Volume 3
February 2000

3-Rail with Proto-Sound®, Item No. 20-2213-1, Cab Nos. 451, 454, 458

FA-2 ABA Diesel Engine Set
New Haven

2000 Volume 2
November 2000

3-Rail with Proto-Sound® 2.0, Item No. 20-2238-1, Cab Nos. 0409, 468, 0422

FA-2 ABA Diesel Engine Set
Baltimore & Ohio

2000 Volume 2
November 2000

3-Rail with Proto-Sound® 2.0, Item No. 20-2239-1, Cab Nos. 833A, 833X, 835A

FA-2 ABA Diesel Engine Set
Great Northern

2000 Volume 2
November 2000

3-Rail with Proto-Sound® 2.0, Item No. 20-2240-1, Cab Nos. 278A, 278B, 279A

FA-2 ABA Diesel Engine Set
Lehigh Valley

2000 Volume 2
November 2000

3-Rail with Proto-Sound® 2.0, Item No. 20-2241-1, Cab Nos. 580, 583, 586

FA-2 ABA Diesel Engine Set
Canadian National

2000 Volume 2
November 2000

3-Rail with Proto-Sound® 2.0, Item No. 20-2243-1, Cab Nos. 6706, 6710, 6809

FM H10-44 Diesel Engine
Pennsylvania

Fall 1995
May 1995

3-Rail with Electronic Horn, Item No. 20-2075-0, Cab Nos. 5984, 5985, 5986
3-Rail with Proto-Sound®, Item No. 20-2075-1, Cab Nos. 5984, 5985, 5986
2-Rail, Item No. 20-2075-2, Cab Nos. 5984, 5985, 5986

FM H10-44 Diesel Engine
Frisco

Fall 1995
May 1995

3-Rail with Electronic Horn, Item No. 20-2076-0, Cab Nos. 276, 277, 278
3-Rail with Proto-Sound®, Item No. 20-2076-1, Cab Nos. 276, 277, 278
2-Rail, Item No. 20-2076-2, Cab Nos. 276, 277, 278

FM H10-44 Diesel Engine
Santa Fe

Fall 1995
May 1995

3-Rail with Electronic Horn, Item No. 20-2077-0, Cab Nos. 500, 501, 502
3-Rail with Proto-Sound®, Item No. 20-2077-1, Cab Nos. 500, 501, 502
2-Rail, Item No. 20-2077-2, Cab Nos. 500, 501, 502

FM H10-44 Diesel Engine
Chicago NorthWestern

Fall 1995
May 1995

3-Rail with Electronic Horn, Item No. 20-2078-0, Cab Nos. 1053, 1054, 1055
3-Rail with Proto-Sound®, Item No. 20-2078-1, Cab Nos. 1053, 1054, 1055
2-Rail, Item No. 20-2078-2, Cab Nos. 1053, 1054, 1055

FM H10-44 Diesel Engine
New York Central

Fall 1995
May 1995

3-Rail with Electronic Horn, Item No. 20-2079-0, Cab Nos. 9107, 9108, 9109
3-Rail with Proto-Sound®, Item No. 20-2079-1, Cab Nos. 9107, 9108, 9109
2-Rail, Item No. 20-2079-2, Cab Nos. 9107, 9108, 9109

FM H10-44 Diesel Engine
Milwaukee Road

Fall 1995
May 1995

3-Rail with Electronic Horn, Item No. 20-2080-0, Cab Nos. 762, 763, 764
3-Rail with Proto-Sound®, Item No. 20-2080-1, Cab Nos. 762, 763, 764
2-Rail, Item No. 20-2080-2, Cab Nos. 762, 763, 764

FM H10-44 Diesel Engine
Southern Pacific

Fall 1995
May 1995

3-Rail with Electronic Horn, Item No. 20-2081-0, Cab Nos. 1486, 1487, 1488
3-Rail with Proto-Sound®, Item No. 20-2081-1, Cab Nos. 1486, 1487, 1488
2-Rail, Item No. 20-2081-2, Cab Nos. 1486, 1487, 1488

FM H10-44 Diesel Engine
Union Pacific

Fall 1995
May 1995

3-Rail with Electronic Horn, Item No. 20-2082-0, Cab Nos. 1302, 1303, 1304
3-Rail with Proto-Sound®, Item No. 20-2082-1, Cab Nos. 1302, 1303, 1304
2-Rail, Item No. 20-2082-2, Cab Nos. 1302, 1303, 1304

FM Trainmaster Diesel Engine
New Jersey Central

Spring 1996
May 1996

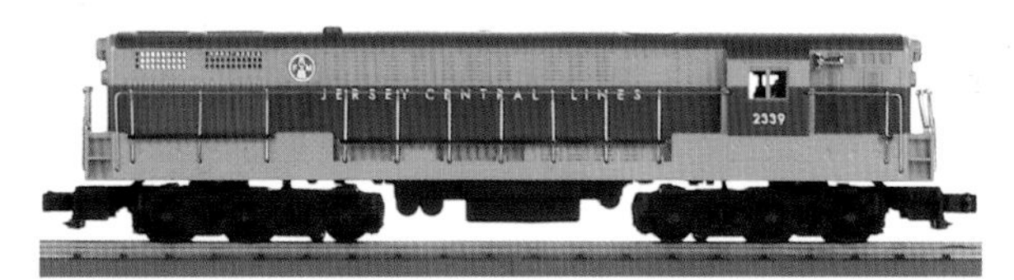

3-Rail with Electronic Horn, Item No. 20-2120-0, Cab Nos. 2341, 2348, 2339
3-Rail with Proto-Sound®, Item No. 20-2120-1, Cab Nos. 2341, 2348, 2339
3-Rail with Proto-Sound®, Item No. 20-2201-1, Cab Nos. 2401, 2404, 2413

FM Trainmaster Diesel Engine
Southern

Spring 1996
May 1996

3-Rail with Electronic Horn, Item No. 20-2121-0, Cab Nos. 2341, 2348, 2339
3-Rail with Proto-Sound®, Item No. 20-2121-1, Cab Nos. 2341, 2348, 2339

FM Trainmaster Diesel Engine
Denver & Rio Grande

Spring 1996
May 1996

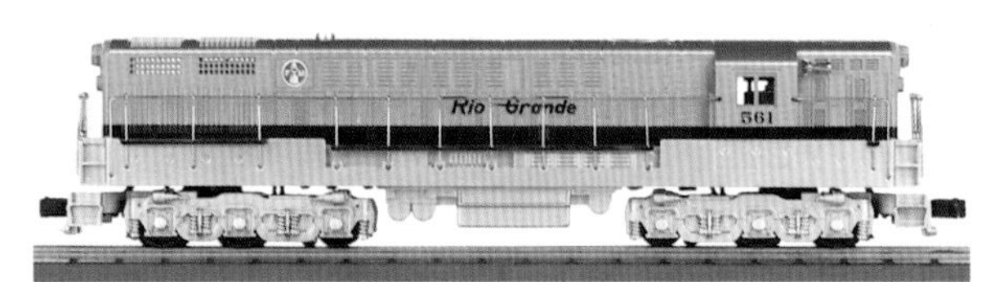

3-Rail with Electronic Horn, Item No. 20-2122-0, Cab Nos. 557, 561, 565
3-Rail with Proto-Sound®, Item No. 20-2122-1, Cab Nos. 557, 561, 565

FM Trainmaster Diesel Engine
Santa Fe

Spring 1996
May 1996

3-Rail with Electronic Horn, Item No. 20-2123-0, Cab Nos. 2580, 2573, 2572
3-Rail with Proto-Sound®, Item No. 20-2123-1, Cab Nos. 2580, 2573, 2572

FM Trainmaster Diesel Engine
Canadian Pacific

1998 Volume 2
November 1998

3-Rail with Proto-Sound®, Item No. 20-2182-1, Cab Nos. 8902, 8905, 8906

FM Trainmaster Diesel Engine
Fairbanks Morse Demo

1998 Volume 2
November 1998

3-Rail with Proto-Sound®, Item No. 20-2183-1, Cab Nos. TM-1, TM-2, TM-4

FM Trainmaster Diesel Engine
Milwaukee Road

1999 Volume 2
August 1999

3-Rail with Proto-Sound®, Item No. 20-2202-1, Cab Nos. 550, 551, 552

FM Trainmaster Diesel Engine
Virginian

2000 Volume 2
July 2000

3-Rail with Proto-Sound® 2.0, Item No. 20-2231-1, Cab No. 2331

FM Trainmaster Diesel Engine
Virginian

2000 Volume 2
July 2000

3-Rail with Proto-Sound® 2.0, Item No. 20-2232-1, Cab Nos. 54, 58, 74

FM Trainmaster Diesel Engine
Southern Pacific

2000 Volume 2
July 2000

3-Rail with Proto-Sound® 2.0, Item No. 20-2240-1, Cab Nos. 4807, 4811, 4813

FM Trainmaster Diesel Engine
Lackawanna

Uncataloged Item
September 1999

3-Rail with Proto-Sound®, Item No. 20-80001d (1999 DAP), Cab No. 2321

FP-45 Diesel Engine
Electro Motive Division

Spring 1997
April 1997

3-Rail with Proto-Sound®, Item No. 20-2146-1, Cab Nos. 268, 218, 169
2-Rail, Item No. 20-2146-2, Cab Nos. 268, 218, 169

FP-45 Diesel Engine
Susquehanna

Spring 1997
July 1997

3-Rail with Proto-Sound®, Item No. 20-2143-1, Cab Nos. 3636, 3406, 3408
2-Rail, Item No. 20-2143-2, Cab Nos. 3636, 3406, 3408

FP-45 Diesel Engine
Burlington Northern

Spring 1997
April 1997

3-Rail with Proto-Sound®, Item No. 20-2144-1, Cab Nos. 6622, 6615, 6619
2-Rail, Item No. 20-2144-2, Cab Nos. 6622, 6615, 6619

FP-45 Diesel Engine
Santa Fe

Spring 1997
April 1997

3-Rail with Proto-Sound®, Item No. 20-2145-1, Cab Nos. 5940, 5942, 5945
2-Rail, Item No. 20-2145-2, Cab Nos. 5940, 5942, 5945

Gas Turbine Diesel Engine
Union Pacific

Spring 1996
June 1996

3-Rail with Proto-Sound®, Item No. 20-2124-1, Cab Nos. 5, 5B
2-Rail, Item No. 20-2124-2, Cab Nos. 5, 5B

Genesis Diesel Engine
Amtrak

1998 Volume 3
February 1999

3-Rail with Proto-Sound®, Item No. 20-2189-1, Cab Nos. 9, 23, 42

Genesis Diesel Engine
Amtrak

2000 Volume 2
July 2000

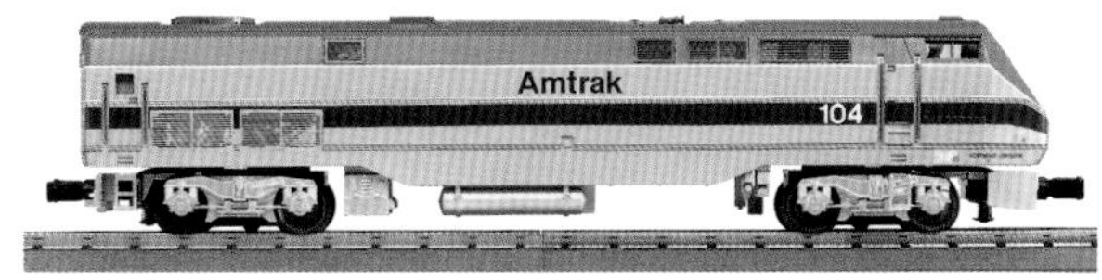

3-Rail with Proto-Sound® 2.0, Item No. 20-2229-1, Cab Nos. 104, 107, 110

Genesis Diesel Engine
Amtrak

2000 Volume 2
July 2000

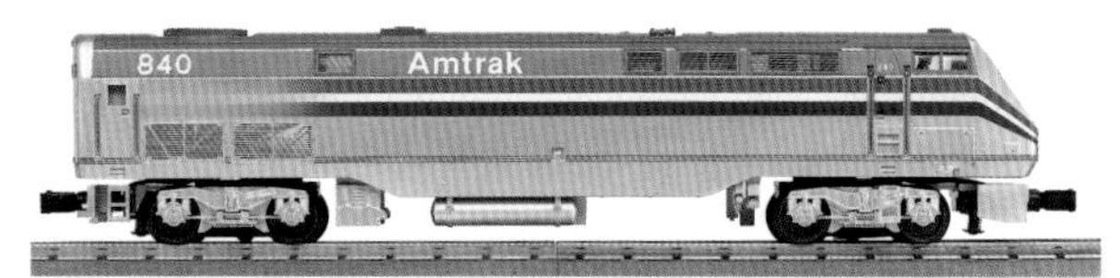

3-Rail with Proto-Sound® 2.0, Item No. 20-2230-1, Cab Nos. 801, 824, 840

GG-1 Electric Engine
Pennsylvania

Spring 1997
April 1997

3-Rail with Proto-Sound®, Item No. 20-5501-1, Cab No. 4876

GG-1 Electric Engine
Pennsylvania

1999 Volume 1
March 1999

3-Rail with Proto-Sound®, Item No. 20-5503-1, Cab No. 4872

GP-20 Diesel Engine
Atlantic Coast Line

Fall/Winter 1996
February 1997

3-Rail with Proto-Sound®, Item No. 20-2139-1, Cab Nos. 1025, 1027, 1029
2-Rail, Item No. 20-2139-2, Cab Nos. 1025, 1027, 1029

GP-20 Diesel Engine
Western Pacific

Fall/Winter 1996
February 1997

3-Rail with Proto-Sound®, Item No. 20-2141-1, Cab Nos. 2001, 2004, 2007
2-Rail, Item No. 20-2141-2, Cab Nos. 2001, 2004, 2007

Genesis Diesel Engine
United States Postal Service

2000 Volume 2
July 2000

3-Rail with Proto-Sound® 2.0, Item No. 20-2240-1, Cab No. 100

GG-1 Electric Engine
Conrail

Spring 1997
April 1997

3-Rail with Proto-Sound®, Item No. 20-5502-1, Cab No. 4800

GG-1 Electric Engine
Pennsylvania

1999 Volume 1
March 1999

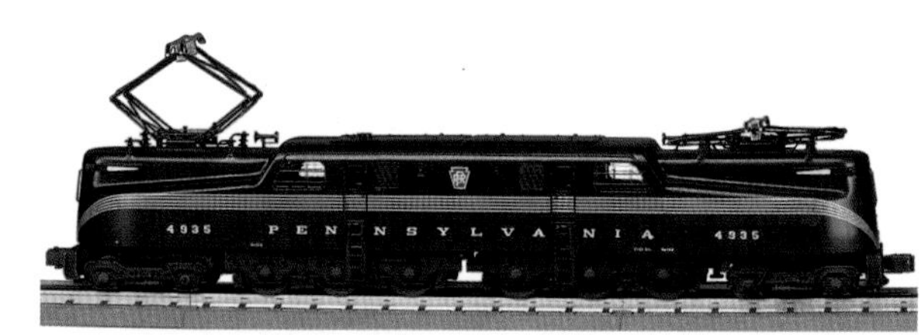

3-Rail with Proto-Sound®, Item No. 20-5504-1, Cab No. 4935

GP-20 Diesel Engine
Burlington Northern

Fall/Winter 1996
February 1997

3-Rail with Proto-Sound®, Item No. 20-2140-1, Cab Nos. 2049, 2052, 2055
2-Rail, Item No. 20-2140-2, Cab Nos. 2049, 2052, 2055

GP-20 Diesel Engine
Electro Motive Division

Fall/Winter 1996
February 1997

3-Rail with Proto-Sound®, Item No. 20-2142-1, Cab Nos. 5625, 5627, 5628
2-Rail, Item No. 20-2142-2, Cab Nos. 5625, 5627, 5628

GP-30 Diesel Engine
CSX

15th Anniversary
May 1995

3-Rail with Electronic Horn, Item No. 20-2066-0, Cab Nos. 4200, 4201, 4202
3-Rail with Proto-Sound®, Item No. 20-2066-1, Cab Nos. 4200, 4201, 4202
2-Rail, Item No. 20-2066-2, Cab Nos. 4200, 4201, 4202

GP-30 Diesel Engine
Burlington Northern

15th Anniversary
May 1995

3-Rail with Electronic Horn, Item No. 20-2067-0, Cab Nos. 2242, 2243, 2244
3-Rail with Proto-Sound®, Item No. 20-2067-1, Cab Nos. 2242, 2243, 2244
2-Rail, Item No. 20-2067-2, Cab Nos. 2242, 2243, 2244

GP-30 Diesel Engine
Rio Grande

15th Anniversary
May 1995

3-Rail with Electronic Horn, Item No. 20-2068-0, Cab Nos. 3007, 3008, 3009
3-Rail with Proto-Sound®, Item No. 20-2068-1, Cab Nos. 3007, 3008, 3009
2-Rail, Item No. 20-2068-2, Cab Nos. 3007, 3008, 3009

GP-30 Diesel Engine
Union Pacific

15th Anniversary
May 1995

3-Rail with Electronic Horn, Item No. 20-2069-0, Cab Nos. 803, 804, 805
3-Rail with Proto-Sound®, Item No. 20-2069-1, Cab Nos. 803, 804, 805
2-Rail, Item No. 20-2069-2, Cab Nos. 803, 804, 805

GP-30 Diesel Engine
Canadian Pacific

15th Anniversary
May 1995

3-Rail with Electronic Horn, Item No. 20-2070-0, Cab Nos. 8200, 8201, 8202
3-Rail with Proto-Sound®, Item No. 20-2070-1, Cab Nos. 8200, 8201, 8202
2-Rail, Item No. 20-2070-2, Cab Nos. 8200, 8201, 8202

GP-30 Diesel Engine
Pennsylvania

15th Anniversary
May 1995

3-Rail with Electronic Horn, Item No. 20-2071-0, Cab Nos. 2231, 2232, 2233
3-Rail with Proto-Sound®, Item No. 20-2071-1, Cab Nos. 2231, 2232, 2233
2-Rail, Item No. 20-2071-2, Cab Nos. 2231, 2232, 2233

GP-30 Diesel Engine
Santa Fe

15th Anniversary
May 1995

3-Rail with Electronic Horn, Item No. 20-2072-0, Cab Nos. 2718, 2719, 2720
3-Rail with Proto-Sound®, Item No. 20-2072-1, Cab Nos. 2718, 2719, 2720
2-Rail, Item No. 20-2072-2, Cab Nos. 2718, 2719, 2720

GP-30 Diesel Engine
Reading

15th Anniversary
May 1995

3-Rail with Electronic Horn, Item No. 20-2073-0, Cab Nos. 5511, 5512, 5513
3-Rail with Proto-Sound®, Item No. 20-2073-1, Cab Nos. 5511, 5512, 5513
2-Rail, Item No. 20-2073-2, Cab Nos. 5511, 5512, 5513

GP-30 Diesel Engine
Clear

Uncataloged Item
January 1995

3-Rail with Proto-Sound®, Item No. 20-2074-1, Cab No. NONE

GP-60M Diesel Engine
Santa Fe

1998 Volume 2
October 1998

3-Rail with Proto-Sound®, Item No. 20-2180-1, Cab Nos. 102, 131, 157

GP-60M Diesel Engine
Maersk

1998 Volume 2
October 1998

3-Rail with Proto-Sound®, Item No. 20-2181-1, Cab Nos. 146, 147, 148

GP-7 Diesel Engine
Pennsylvania

1999 Volume 3
December 1999

3-Rail with Proto-Sound®, Item No. 20-2210-1, Cab Nos. 5865, 5872, 5880

GP-7 Diesel Engine
Boston & Maine

1999 Volume 3
December 1999

3-Rail with Proto-Sound®, Item No. 20-2211-1, Cab Nos. 1555, 1558, 1563

GP-7 Diesel Engine
Great Northern

1999 Volume 3
December 1999

3-Rail with Proto-Sound®, Item No. 20-2212-1, Cab Nos. 620, 602, 600

GP-9 Diesel Engine
New York Central

Fall 1994
August 1994

3-Rail with Electronic Horn, Item No. 20-2033-0, Cab Nos. 5974, 5976, 5978
3-Rail with Proto-Sound®, Item No. 20-2033-1, Cab Nos. 5974, 5976, 5978
2-Rail, Item No. 20-2033-2, Cab Nos. 5974, 5976, 5978

GP-9 Diesel Engine
Baltimore & Ohio

Fall 1994
August 1994

3-Rail with Electronic Horn, Item No. 20-2034-0, Cab Nos. 3415, 3420, 3425
3-Rail with Proto-Sound®, Item No. 20-2034-1, Cab Nos. 3415, 3420, 3425
2-Rail, Item No. 20-2034-2, Cab Nos. 3415, 3420, 3425

GP-9 Diesel Engine
Chicago NorthWestern

Fall 1994
August 1994

3-Rail with Electronic Horn, Item No. 20-2035-0, Cab Nos. 1716, 1718, 1720
3-Rail with Proto-Sound®, Item No. 20-2035-1, Cab Nos. 1716, 1718, 1720
2-Rail, Item No. 20-2035-2, Cab Nos. 1716, 1718, 1720

GP-9 Diesel Engine
Santa Fe

Fall 1994
August 1994

3-Rail with Electronic Horn, Item No. 20-2036-0, Cab Nos. 710, 715, 720
3-Rail with Proto-Sound®, Item No. 20-2036-1, Cab Nos. 710, 715, 720
2-Rail, Item No. 20-2036-2, Cab Nos. 710, 715, 720

GP-9 Diesel Engine
Pennsylvania

Fall 1994
August 1994

3-Rail with Electronic Horn, Item No. 20-2037-0, Cab Nos. 7000, 7001, 7002
3-Rail with Proto-Sound®, Item No. 20-2037-1, Cab Nos. 7000, 7001, 7002
2-Rail, Item No. 20-2037-2, Cab Nos. 7000, 7001, 7002

GP-9 Diesel Engine
Union Pacific

Fall 1994
August 1994

3-Rail with Electronic Horn, Item No. 20-2038-0, Cab Nos. 130, 132, 134
3-Rail with Proto-Sound®, Item No. 20-2038-1, Cab Nos. 130, 132, 134
2-Rail, Item No. 20-2038-2, Cab Nos. 130, 132, 134

GP-9 Diesel Engine
Southern

Fall 1994
August 1994

3-Rail with Electronic Horn, Item No. 20-2039-0, Cab Nos. 6245, 6246, 6247
3-Rail with Proto-Sound®, Item No. 20-2039-1, Cab Nos. 6245, 6246, 6247
2-Rail, Item No. 20-2039-2, Cab Nos. 6245, 6246, 6247

GP-9 Diesel Engine
Southern Pacific

Fall 1994
August 1994

3-Rail with Electronic Horn, Item No. 20-2040-0, Cab Nos. 5600, 5601, 5602
3-Rail with Proto-Sound®, Item No. 20-2040-1, Cab Nos. 5600, 5601, 5602
2-Rail, Item No. 20-2040-2, Cab Nos. 5600, 5601, 5602

GP-9 Diesel Engine
Erie-Lackawanna

1998 Volume 1
April 1998

3-Rail with Proto-Sound®, Item No. 20-2173-1, Cab Nos. 1260, 1263, 1265

GP-9 Diesel Engine
Texas & Pacific

1998 Volume 1
April 1998

3-Rail with Proto-Sound®, Item No. 20-2174-1, Cab Nos. 1137, 1141, 1143

GP-9 Diesel Engine
Western Maryland

1998 Volume 1
April 1998

3-Rail with Proto-Sound®, Item No. 20-2175-1, Cab Nos. 35, 37, 43

GP-9 Diesel Engine
Lehigh Valley

1999 Volume 3
December 1999

3-Rail with Proto-Sound®, Item No. 20-2209-1, Cab Nos. 300, 301, 306

GP-9 Diesel Engine
Clear

Uncataloged Item
April 1994

3-Rail with Proto-Sound®, Item No. 20-2049-1, Cab No. NONE

GP38-2 Diesel Engine
Southern Pacific

1997 Volume 1
November 1997

3-Rail with Proto-Sound®, Item No. 20-2156-1, Cab Nos. 4800, 4806, 4844
2-Rail, Item No. 20-2156-2, Cab Nos. 4800, 4806, 4844

GP38-2 Diesel Engine
Conrail

1997 Volume 1
November 1997

3-Rail with Proto-Sound®, Item No. 20-2157-1, Cab Nos. 8047, 8265, 8076
2-Rail, Item No. 20-2157-2, Cab Nos. 8047, 8265, 8076

GP38-2 Diesel Engine
Gulf Mobile & Ohio

1997 Volume 1
November 1997

3-Rail with Proto-Sound®, Item No. 20-2158-1, Cab Nos. 740, 754, 749
2-Rail, Item No. 20-2158-2, Cab Nos. 740, 754, 749

GP38-2 Diesel Engine
Union Pacific

1998 Volume 3
December 1998

3-Rail with Proto-Sound®, Item No. 20-2188-1, Cab Nos. 2048, 2028, 1987

GP38-2 Diesel Engine
BNSF

1998 Volume 3
December 1998

3-Rail with Proto-Sound®, Item No. 20-2187-1, Cab Nos. 2099, 2094, 2081

GP38-2 Diesel Engine
Chessie

1998 Volume 3
December 1998

3-Rail with Proto-Sound®, Item No. 20-2186-1, Cab Nos. 3874, 3890, 3899

GP38-2 Diesel Engine
Long Island

2000 Volume 1
March 2000

3-Rail with Proto-Sound®, Item No. 20-2226-1, Cab Nos. 256, 269, 277

GP38-2 Diesel Engine
Bangor & Aroostook

2000 Volume 1
March 2000

3-Rail with Proto-Sound®, Item No. 20-2227-1, Cab Nos. 81, 83, 87

GP38-2 Diesel Engine
Canadian National

2000 Volume 1
March 2000

3-Rail with Proto-Sound®, Item No. 20-2228-1, Cab No. 4711

M-1 Steam Turbine Electric Engine
Chesapeake & Ohio

2000 Volume 1
June 2000

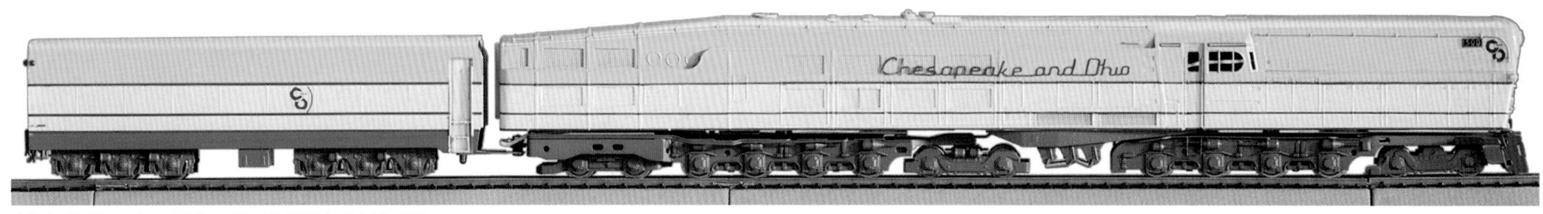

3-Rail with Proto-Sound®, Item No. 20-3042-1, Cab No. 500
2-Rail, Item No. 20-3042-2, Cab No. 500

P2 Box Cab Electric
New York Central

1999 Volume 3
November 1999

3-Rail with Proto-Sound®, Item No. 20-5507-1, Cab Nos. 223, 226, 229

P5a Modified Electric
Pennsylvania

2000 Volume 2
September 2000

3-Rail with Proto-Sound® 2.0, Item No. 20-5510-1, Cab No. 4777
2-Rail, Item No. 20-5510-2, Cab No. 4777

RS-27 Diesel Engine
Green Bay Route

1997 Volume 2
January 1998

3-Rail with Proto-Sound®, Item No. 20-2165-1, Cab Nos. 2404, 2405, 2406
2-Rail, Item No. 20-2165-2, Cab Nos. 2404, 2405, 2406

RS-27 Diesel Engine
Alco Demo

1997 Volume 2
January 1998

3-Rail with Proto-Sound®, Item No. 20-2167-1, Cab Nos. 640-1, 640-3, 640-5
2-Rail, Item No. 20-2167-2, Cab Nos. 640-1, 640-3, 640-5

RS-27 Diesel Engine
Penn Central

1997 Volume 2
January 1998

3-Rail with Proto-Sound®, Item No. 20-2166-1, Cab Nos. 2404, 2405, 2506
2-Rail, Item No. 20-2166-2, Cab Nos. 2404, 2405, 2506

SD-80 Diesel Engine
Conrail

1998 Volume 3
May 1999

3-Rail with Proto-Sound®, Item No. 20-2190-1, Cab Nos. 4125, 4100, 4120

SD-9 Diesel Engine
Pennsylvania

Spring 1996
December 1995

3-Rail with Electronic Horn, Item No. 20-2109-0, Cab Nos. 7600, 7624, 7618
3-Rail with Proto-Sound®, Item No. 20-2109-1, Cab Nos. 7600, 7624, 7618
2-Rail, Item No. 20-2109-2, Cab Nos. 7600, 7624, 7618

SD-9 Diesel Engine
Chessie

Spring 1996
December 1995

3-Rail with Electronic Horn, Item No. 20-2108-0, Cab Nos. 7600, 7624, 7618
3-Rail with Proto-Sound®, Item No. 20-2108-1, Cab Nos. 7600, 7624, 7618
2-Rail, Item No. 20-2108-2, Cab Nos. 7600, 7624, 7618

SD-9 Diesel Engine
Nickel Plate Road

Spring 1996
December 1995

3-Rail with Electronic Horn, Item No. 20-2110-0, Cab Nos. 341, 342, 344
3-Rail with Proto-Sound®, Item No. 20-2110-1, Cab Nos. 341, 342, 344
2-Rail, Item No. 20-2110-2, Cab Nos. 341, 342, 344

SD-9 Diesel Engine
Burlington Route

Spring 1996
December 1995

3-Rail with Electronic Horn, Item No. 20-2111-0, Cab Nos. 325, 355, 374
3-Rail with Proto-Sound®, Item No. 20-2111-1, Cab Nos. 325, 355, 374
2-Rail, Item No. 20-2111-2, Cab Nos. 325, 355, 374

SD-9 Diesel Engine
Southern Pacific

Spring 1996
December 1995

3-Rail with Electronic Horn, Item No. 20-2112-0, Cab Nos. 5360, 5365, 5370
3-Rail with Proto-Sound®, Item No. 20-2112-1, Cab Nos. 5360, 5365, 5370
2-Rail, Item No. 20-2112-2, Cab Nos. 5360, 5365, 5370

SD-9 Diesel Engine
Denver & Rio Grande

Spring 1996
December 1995

3-Rail with Electronic Horn, Item No. 20-2113-0, Cab Nos. 5305, 5310, 5314
3-Rail with Proto-Sound®, Item No. 20-2113-1, Cab Nos. 5305, 5310, 5314
2-Rail, Item No. 20-2113-2, Cab Nos. 5305, 5310, 5314

SD-90 Diesel Engine
Electro Motive Division

1998 Volume 2
May 1999

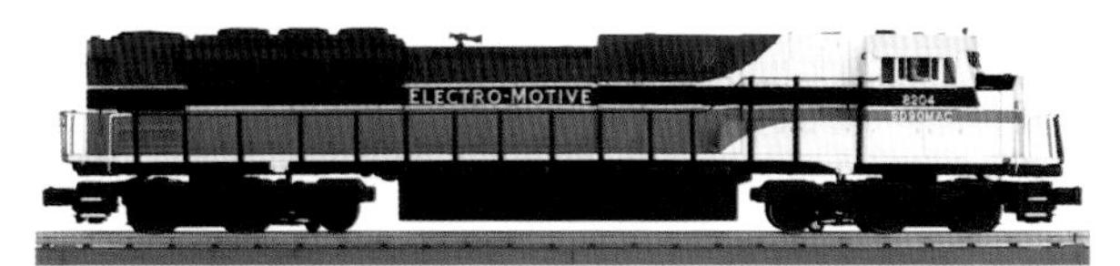

3-Rail with Proto-Sound®, Item No. 20-2184-1, Cab Nos. 8204, 8205, 8504

SD-40-2 Diesel Engine
Canadian National

1997 Volume 2
January 1998

3-Rail with Proto-Sound®, Item No. 20-2161-1, Cab Nos. 5930, 6000, 6009
2-Rail, Item No. 20-2161-2, Cab Nos. 5930, 6000, 6009

SD-40-2 Diesel Engine
Norfolk Southern

1997 Volume 2
January 1998

3-Rail with Proto-Sound®, Item No. 20-2163-1, Cab Nos. 6081, 6094, 6125
2-Rail, Item No. 20-2163-2, Cab Nos. 6081, 6094, 6125

SD40-2 Diesel Engine
Burlington Northern

2000 Volume 1
June 2000

3-Rail with Proto-Sound®, Item No. 20-2217-1, Cab Nos. 6734, 6806, 6928

SD45 Diesel Engine
Pennsylvania

Winter 1995
October 1995

3-Rail with Electronic Horn, Item No. 20-2100-0, Cab Nos. 6145, 6146, 6147
3-Rail with Proto-Sound®, Item No. 20-2100-1, Cab Nos. 6145, 6146, 6147
2-Rail, Item No. 20-2100-2, Cab Nos. 6145, 6146, 6147

SD-90 Diesel Engine
Union Pacific

1998 Volume 3
May 1999

3-Rail with Proto-Sound®, Item No. 20-2191-1, Cab Nos. 8200, 8205, 8207

SD-40-2 Diesel Engine
Illinois Central

1997 Volume 2
January 1998

3-Rail with Proto-Sound®, Item No. 20-2164-1, Cab Nos. 6061, 6030, 6160
2-Rail, Item No. 20-2164-2, Cab Nos. 6061, 6030, 6160

SD-40-2 Diesel Engine
Southern Pacific

1997 Volume 2
January 1998

3-Rail with Proto-Sound®, Item No. 20-2162-1, Cab Nos. 7399, 7342, 7300
2-Rail, Item No. 20-2162-2, Cab Nos. 7399, 7342, 7300

SD40-2 Diesel Engine
Chessie

2000 Volume 1
June 2000

3-Rail with Proto-Sound®, Item No. 20-2216-1, Cab Nos. 7532, 7557, 7580

SD45 Diesel Engine
Reading

Winter 1995
October 1995

3-Rail with Electronic Horn, Item No. 20-2101-0, Cab Nos. 7600, 7601, 7602
3-Rail with Proto-Sound®, Item No. 20-2101-1, Cab Nos. 7600, 7601, 7602
2-Rail, Item No. 20-2101-2, Cab Nos. 7600, 7601, 7602

SD45 Diesel Engine
Seaboard

Winter 1995
October 1995

3-Rail with Electronic Horn, Item No. 20-2102-0, Cab Nos. 8907, 8908, 8909
3-Rail with Proto-Sound®, Item No. 20-2102-1, Cab Nos. 8907, 8908, 8909
2-Rail, Item No. 20-2102-2, Cab Nos. 8907, 8908, 8909

SD45 Diesel Engine
Conrail

Winter 1995
October 1995

3-Rail with Electronic Horn, Item No. 20-2103-0, Cab Nos. 6097, 6098, 6099
3-Rail with Proto-Sound®, Item No. 20-2103-1, Cab Nos. 6097, 6098, 6099
2-Rail, Item No. 20-2103-2, Cab Nos. 6097, 6098, 6099

SD45 Diesel Engine
Great Northern

Winter 1995
October 1995

3-Rail with Electronic Horn, Item No. 20-2104-0, Cab Nos. 400, 401, 402
3-Rail with Proto-Sound®, Item No. 20-2104-1, Cab Nos. 400, 401, 402
2-Rail, Item No. 20-2104-2, Cab Nos. 400, 401, 402

SD45 Diesel Engine
Santa Fe

Winter 1995
October 1995

3-Rail with Electronic Horn, Item No. 20-2105-0, Cab Nos. 5393, 5394, 5395
3-Rail with Proto-Sound®, Item No. 20-2105-1, Cab Nos. 5393, 5394, 5395
2-Rail, Item No. 20-2105-2, Cab Nos. 5393, 5394, 5395

SD45 Diesel Engine
Union Pacific

Winter 1995
October 1995

3-Rail with Electronic Horn, Item No. 20-2106-0, Cab Nos. 50, 55, 60
3-Rail with Proto-Sound®, Item No. 20-2106-1, Cab Nos. 50, 55, 60
2-Rail, Item No. 20-2106-2, Cab Nos. 50, 55, 60

SD45 Diesel Engine
Electro Motive Division

Winter 1995
October 1995

3-Rail with Electronic Horn, Item No. 20-2107-0, Cab Nos. 4351, 4352, 4353
3-Rail with Proto-Sound®, Item No. 20-2107-1, Cab Nos. 4351, 4352, 4353
2-Rail, Item No. 20-2107-2, Cab Nos. 4351, 4352, 4353

SD60 Diesel Engine
CSX

Spring 1996
March 1996

3-Rail with Electronic Horn, Item No. 20-2114-0, Cab Nos. 8700, 8703, 8706
3-Rail with Proto-Sound®, Item No. 20-2114-1, Cab Nos. 8700, 8703, 8706
2-Rail, Item No. 20-2114-2, Cab Nos. 8700, 8703, 8706

SD60 Diesel Engine
Norfolk Southern

Spring 1996
March 1996

3-Rail with Electronic Horn, Item No. 20-2115-0, Cab Nos. 6697, 6694, 6700
3-Rail with Proto-Sound®, Item No. 20-2115-1, Cab Nos. 6697, 6694, 6700
2-Rail, Item No. 20-2115-2, Cab Nos. 6697, 6694, 6700

SD60 Diesel Engine
Burlington Northern

Spring 1996
March 1996

3-Rail with Electronic Horn, Item No. 20-2116-0, Cab Nos. 8300, 8301, 8302
3-Rail with Proto-Sound®, Item No. 20-2116-1, Cab Nos. 8300, 8301, 8302
2-Rail, Item No. 20-2116-2, Cab Nos. 8300, 8301, 8302

SD60 Diesel Engine
Chicago NorthWestern

Spring 1996
March 1996

3-Rail with Electronic Horn, Item No. 20-2117-0, Cab Nos. 8029, 8032, 8035
3-Rail with Proto-Sound®, Item No. 20-2117-1, Cab Nos. 8029, 8032, 8035
2-Rail, Item No. 20-2117-2, Cab Nos. 8029, 8032, 8035

SD60 Diesel Engine
Conrail

Spring 1996
March 1996

3-Rail with Electronic Horn, Item No. 20-2118-0, Cab Nos. 6865, 6858, 6867
3-Rail with Proto-Sound®, Item No. 20-2118-1, Cab Nos. 6865, 6858, 6867
2-Rail, Item No. 20-2118-2, Cab Nos. 6865, 6858, 6867

SD60M Diesel Engine
Union Pacific

Fall 1994
November 1994

3-Rail with Electronic Horn, Item No. 20-2041-0, Cab Nos. 6316, 6317, 6318
3-Rail with Proto-Sound®, Item No. 20-2041-1, Cab Nos. 6316, 6317, 6318
2-Rail, Item No. 20-2041-2, Cab Nos. 6316, 6317, 6318

SD60M Diesel Engine
Conrail

Fall 1994
November 1994

3-Rail with Electronic Horn, Item No. 20-2043-0, Cab Nos. 5500, 5501, 5502
3-Rail with Proto-Sound®, Item No. 20-2043-1, Cab Nos. 5500, 5501, 5502
2-Rail, Item No. 20-2043-2, Cab Nos. 5500, 5501, 5502

SD60M Diesel Engine
Burlington Northern

Fall 1994
November 1994

3-Rail with Electronic Horn, Item No. 20-2045-0, Cab Nos. 9291, 9294, 9295
3-Rail with Proto-Sound®, Item No. 20-2045-1, Cab Nos. 9291, 9294, 9295
2-Rail, Item No. 20-2045-2, Cab Nos. 9291, 9294, 9295

SD60M Diesel Engine
Chicago NorthWestern

Fall 1994
November 1994

3-Rail with Electronic Horn, Item No. 20-2047-0, Cab Nos. 8060, 8061, 8062
3-Rail with Proto-Sound®, Item No. 20-2047-1, Cab Nos. 8060, 8061, 8062
2-Rail, Item No. 20-2047-2, Cab Nos. 8060, 8061, 8062

SD60 Diesel Engine
Electro Motive Division

Spring 1996
March 1996

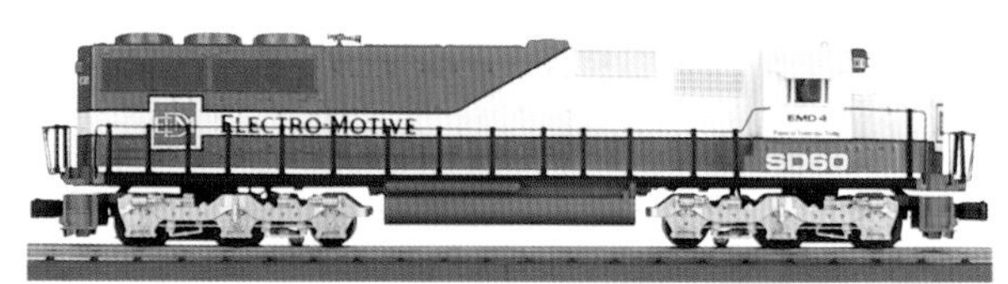

3-Rail with Electronic Horn, Item No. 20-2119-0, Cab Nos. EMD-1, EMD-2, EMD-4
3-Rail with Proto-Sound®, Item No. 20-2119-1, Cab Nos. EMD-1, EMD-2, EMD-4
2-Rail, Item No. 20-2119-2, Cab Nos. EMD-1, EMD-2, EMD-4

SD60M Diesel Engine
Norfolk Southern

Fall 1994
November 1994

3-Rail with Electronic Horn, Item No. 20-2042-0, Cab Nos. 6800, 6801, 6802
3-Rail with Proto-Sound®, Item No. 20-2042-1, Cab Nos. 6800, 6801, 6802
2-Rail, Item No. 20-2042-2, Cab Nos. 6800, 6801, 6802

SD60M Diesel Engine
Soo Line

Fall 1994
November 1994

3-Rail with Electronic Horn, Item No. 20-2044-0, Cab Nos. 6060, 6061, 6062
3-Rail with Proto-Sound®, Item No. 20-2044-1, Cab Nos. 6060, 6061, 6062
2-Rail, Item No. 20-2044-2, Cab Nos. 6060, 6061, 6062

SD60M Diesel Engine
CSX

Fall 1994
November 1994

3-Rail with Electronic Horn, Item No. 20-2046-0, Cab Nos. 8710, 8711, 8712
3-Rail with Proto-Sound®, Item No. 20-2046-1, Cab Nos. 8710, 8711, 8712
2-Rail, Item No. 20-2046-2, Cab Nos. 8710, 8711, 8712

SD60M Diesel Engine
CP Rail

Fall 1994
November 1994

3-Rail with Electronic Horn, Item No. 20-2048-0, Cab Nos. 9025, 9026, 9027
3-Rail with Proto-Sound®, Item No. 20-2048-1, Cab Nos. 9025, 9026, 9027
2-Rail, Item No. 20-2048-2, Cab Nos. 9025, 9026, 9027

SD70 MAC Diesel Engine
BNSF

1997 Volume 1
October 1997

3-Rail with Proto-Sound®, Item No. 20-2154-1, Cab Nos. 9720, 9966, 9400
2-Rail, Item No. 20-2154-2, Cab Nos. 9720, 9966, 9400

SD70 MAC Diesel Engine
Canadian National

1997 Volume 1
October 1997

3-Rail with Proto-Sound®, Item No. 20-2155-1, Cab Nos. 5605, 5600, 5625
2-Rail, Item No. 20-215-2, Cab Nos. 5605, 5600, 5625

SD70 MAC Diesel Engine
BNSF

2000 Volume 1
May 2000

3-Rail with Proto-Sound®, Item No. 20-2215-1, Cab No. 9849

SD70 MAC Diesel Engine
BNSF

2000 Volume 1
May 2000

3-Rail with Proto-Sound®, Item No. 20-2221-1, Cab No. 9647

SD70 MAC Diesel Engine
CSX

2000 Volume 1
May 2000

3-Rail with Proto-Sound®, Item No. 20-2224-1, Cab Nos. 700, 709, 716

U.P. Veranda Turbine
Union Pacific

1998 Volume 2
August 1998

3-Rail with Proto-Sound®, Item No. 20-2185-1, Cab Nos. 61, 75
2-Rail, Item No. 20-2185-2, Cab Nos. 61, 75

PREMIER LINE
Rolling Stock

The M.T.H. Premier Line features an impressive variety of O Scale rolling stock. In fact, at press time, M.T.H. has produced thirty-nine different kinds of freight cars, and counting. The selection covers a range of revenue and non-revenue equipment and includes such unusual pieces as the Westinghouse Schnabel car, a scale depressed-center flat car, and a snow plow. For realistic variety in O Scale rolling stock, one need look no farther than M.T.H. Premier freight cars feature precision-molded ABS plastic bodies mounted atop die-cast, sprung trucks* with operating metal couplers. Each truck features needle-point axles and fast-angle metal wheels for a smooth-rolling, quiet ride. And M.T.H.'s designers are not content to rest on their laurels; they are always seeking new ways to add more detail to the rolling stock. Recent improvements include the addition of interior details and separate metal handrails to cabooses for even further realism.

*Most cars have this feature.

100 Ton Hopper Car
Canada
Item No. 20-97400, Car No. 110060

1997 Volume 2
August 1998

100 Ton Hopper Car
North American
Item No. 20-97401, Car No. 45500

1997 Volume 2
August 1998

100 Ton Hopper Car
Lehigh Valley
Item No. 20-97409, Car No. 50339

1999 Volume 1
March 1999

100 Ton Hopper Car
Burlington
Item No. 20-97410, Car No. 3223

1999 Volume 1
March 1999

100 Ton Hopper Car
Santa Fe
Item No. 20-97421, Car No. 301411

2000 Volume 2
October 2000

100 Ton Hopper Car
Chessie
Item No. 20-97420, Car No. 606171

2000 Volume 2
October 2000

2-Bay Offset Hopper Car
Frisco
Item No. 20-97415, Car No. 90491

1999 Volume 2
October 1999

2-Bay Offset Hopper Car
Chesapeake & Ohio
Item No. 20-97416, Car No. 300027

1999 Volume 2
October 1999

20K Gallon 4-Compartment Tank Car
Burlington Northern
Item No. 20-96010, Car No. 12688

1999 Volume 2
July 1999

20K Gallon 4-Compartment Tank Car
ETCX
Item No. 20-96011, Car No. 4004

1999 Volume 2
July 1999

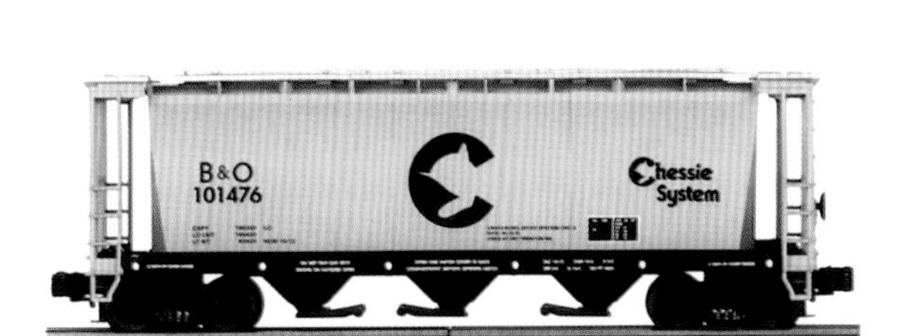

3-Bay Cylindrical Hopper Car
Chessie
Item No. 20-97405, Car No. 101476

1998 Volume 3
December 1998

3-Bay Cylindrical Hopper Car
Santa Fe
Item No. 20-97406, Car No. 314952

1998 Volume 3
December 1999

3-Bay Cylindrical Hopper Car
Union Pacific
Item No. 20-97417, Car No. 21244

1999 Volume 3
January 2000

3-Bay Cylindrical Hopper Car
Canada
Item No. 20-97418, Car No. 110060

1999 Volume 3
January 2000

3-Car Slag Car Set
Item No. 20-90011

2000 Volume 1
May 2000

33K Gallon Tank Car
Suburban Propane
Item No. 20-96006, Car No. 1357

1998 Volume 3
April 1999

33K Gallon Tank Car
Pyrofax Gas
Item No. 20-96007, Car No. 16086

1998 Volume 3
April 1999

33K Gallon Tank Car
Royster
Item No. 20-96012, Car No. 18876

1999 Volume 1
April 1999

33K Gallon Tank Car
Union Texas
Item No. 20-96013, Car No. 933019

1999 Volume 1
April 1999

4-Bay Hopper Car
Western Maryland
Item No. 20-97402, Car No. 90000

1998 Volume 1
August 1998

4-Bay Hopper Car
Union Pacific
Item No. 20-97403, Car No. 37216

1998 Volume 1
November 1997

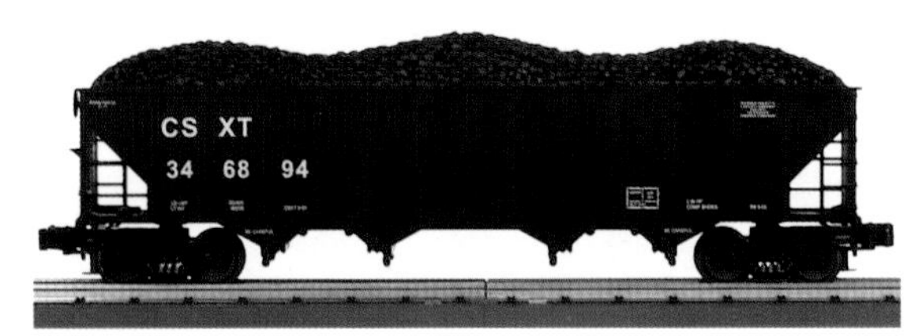

4-Bay Hopper Car
CSX
Item No. 20-97407, Car No. 346894

1998 Volume 3
December 1998

4-Bay Hopper Car
Norfolk & Western
Item No. 20-97408, Car No. 346894

1998 Volume 3
February 1999

50' Box Car
Union Pacific
Item No. 20-93021, Car No. 507406

1999 Volume 2
August 1999

50' Box Car
Nickel Plate Road
Item No. 20-93022, Car No. 22492

1999 Volume 2
August 1999

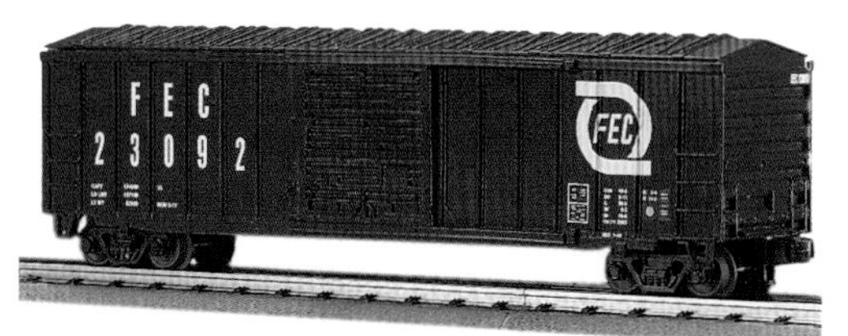

50' Box Car
Florida East Coast
Item No. 20-93035, Car No. 23092

2000 Volume 1
April 2000

50' Box Car
Boston & Maine
Item No. 20-93036, Car No. 969

2000 Volume 1
April 2000

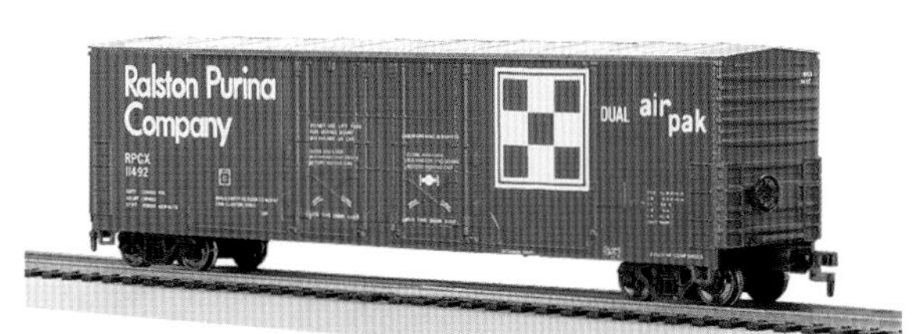

50' Dbl. Door Plugged Boxcar
Ralston Purina
Item No. 20-93025, Car No. 11492

1999 Volume 3
March 2000

50' Dbl. Door Plugged Boxcar
Boston & Maine
Item No. 20-93026, Car No. 111

1999 Volume 3
March 2000

50' Dbl. Door Plugged Boxcar
Southern Pacific
Item No. 20-93032, Car No. 693349

2000 Volume 1
March 2000

50' Dbl. Door Plugged Boxcar
Norfolk & Western
Item No. 20-93033, Car No. 56572

2000 Volume 1
March 2000

50' Dbl. Door Plugged Boxcar
Union Pacific
Item No. 20-93034, Car No. 169461

2000 Volume 1
March 2000

50' Waffle Box Car
Boston & Maine
Item No. 20-93028, Car No. 105

2000 Volume 1
July 2000

50' Waffle Box Car
Seaboard
Item No. 20-93029, Car No. 24125

2000 Volume 1
July 2000

75' Depressed Flat Car
Union Pacific
Item No. 20-98106, Car No. 50006

1998 Volume 2
July 1999

75' Depressed Flat Car
Nickel Plate Road
Item No. 20-98109, Car No. 3022

1999 Volume 3
February 2000

8000 Gallon Tank Car
Norfolk Southern
Item No. 20-9600, Car No. 67845

Spring 1997
June 1997

8000 Gallon Tank Car
Conrail
Item No. 20-9601, Car No. 2315

Spring 1997
June 1997

8000 Gallon Tank Car
Vulcan
Item No. 20-96002, Car No. 1203

1997 Volume 2
January 1998

8000 Gallon Tank Car
CSX
Item No. 20-96003, Car No. 63826

1997 Volume 2
December 1997

8000 Gallon Tank Car
National Starch
Item No. 20-96004, Car No. 76910

1998 Volume 2
August 1998

8000 Gallon Tank Car
Ethyl Corp
Item No. 20-96005, Car No. 6039

1998 Volume 2
August 1998

8000 Gallon Tank Car
Kodak®
Item No. 20-96014, Car No. 93496

1999 Volume 1
Cancelled

8000 Gallon Tank Car
Geigy
Item No. 20-96015 Car No. 88383

1999 Volume 1
January 1999

8000 Gallon Tank Car
G.T.S. - Big Mo
Item No. 20-96018, Car No. 16142

Uncataloged Item
April 1999

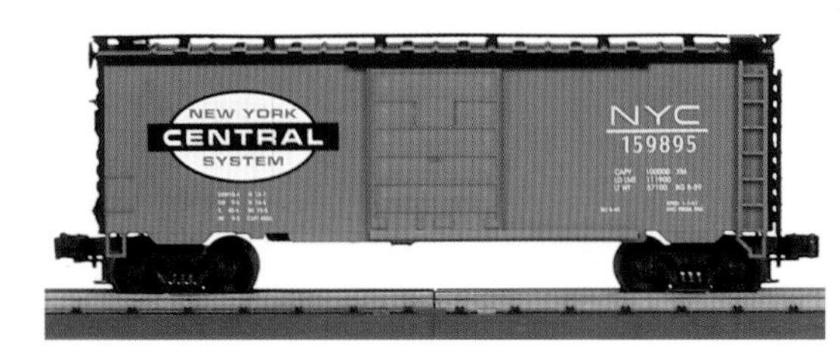

Box Car
New York Central
Item No. 20-9300 Car No. 159895

Summer 1996
November 1996

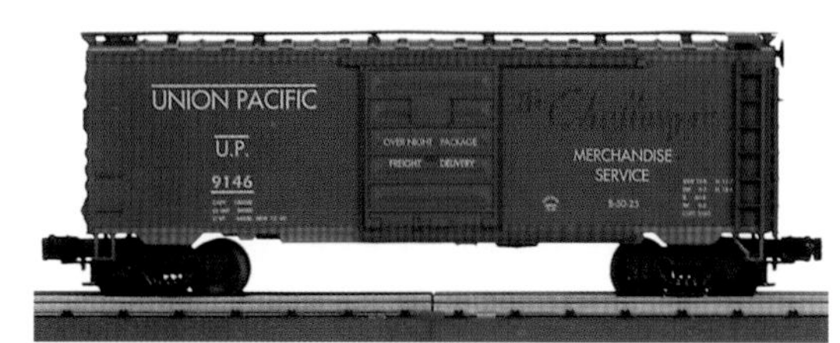

Box Car
Union Pacific
Item No. 20-9301, Car No. 9146

Summer 1996
November 1996

Box Car
Santa Fe
Item No. 20-9303, Car No. 31440

Summer 1996
November 1996

Box Car
Pennsylvania
Item No. 20-9302, Car No. 24086

Fall/Winter 1996
November 1996

Box Car
Southern
Item No. 20-9304, Car No. 550555

Spring 1997
June 1997

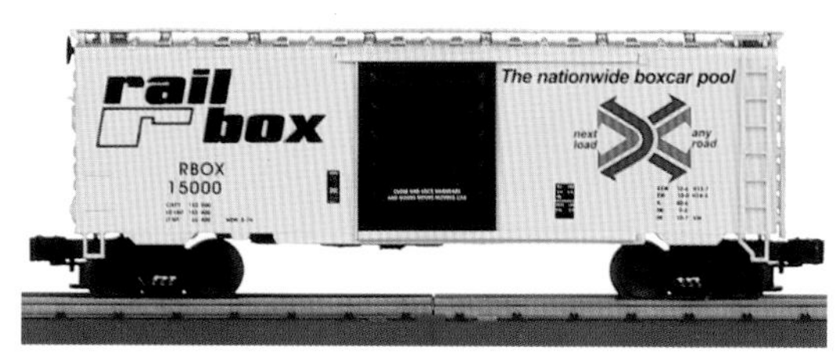

Box Car
Railbox
Item No. 20-9305, Car No. 15000

Spring 1997
June 1997

Box Car
Canadian National
Item No. 20-93006, Car No. 481746

1997 Volume 2
December 1997

Box Car
Illinois Central
Item No. 20-93007, Car No. 12191

1997 Volume 2
January 1998

Box Car
Missouri Pacific
Item No. 20-93008, Car No. 120112

1998 Volume 1
May 1998

Box Car
Western Maryland
Item No. 20-93009, Car No. 27209

1998 Volume 1
February 1998

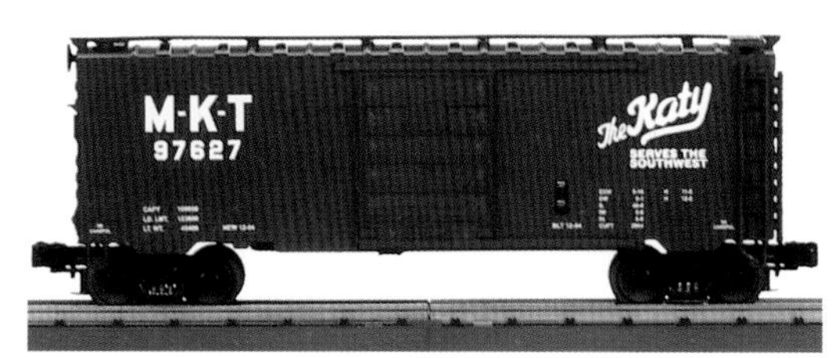

Box Car
Katy
Item No. 20-93010, Car No. 97627

1998 Volume 3
November 1998

Box Car
CCA
Item No. 20-93011, Car No. 20

1998 Volume 3
February 1999

Box Car
Great Northern
Item No. 20-93014 Car No. 20237

1999 Volume 1
May 1999

Box Car
New Haven
Item No. 20-93015, Car No. 22114

1999 Volume 1
May 1999

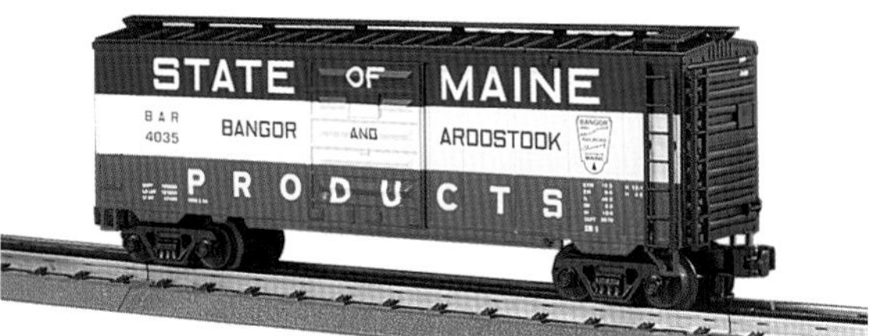

Box Car
State of Maine
Item No. 20-93018, Car No. 4035

1999 Volume 2
December 1999

Box Car
Susquehanna
Item No. 20-93019, Car No. 508

1999 Volume 2
December 1999

Box Car
New York Central
Item No. 20-93037, Car No. 4519

2000 Volume 1
August 2000

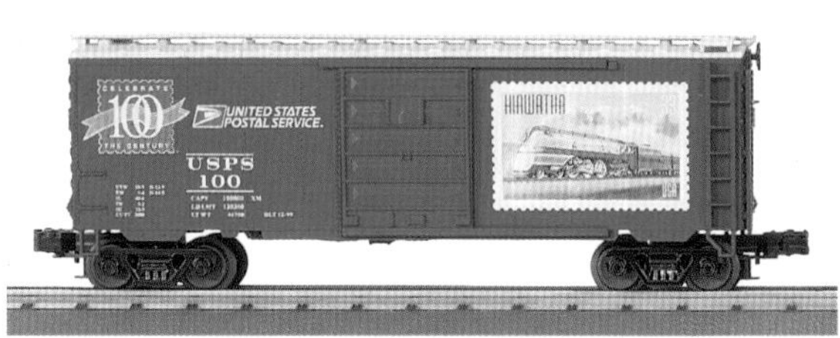

Box Car
USPS #1
Item No. 20-93039, Car No. 100

2000 Volume 2
August 2000

Box Car
USPS #2
Item No. 20-93040, Car No. 5445

2000 Volume 2
August 2000

Box Car
USPS #3
Item No. 20-93041, Car No. 4449

2000 Volume 2
August 2000

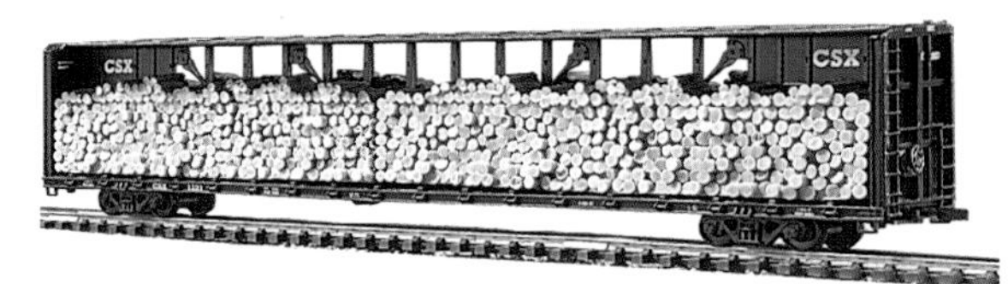

Center Beam Flat Car
CSX
Item No. 20-98211, Car No. 1221

1998 Volume 3
May 1999

Center Beam Flat Car
Union Pacific
Item No. 20-98212, Car No. 2362

1998 Volume 3
May 1999

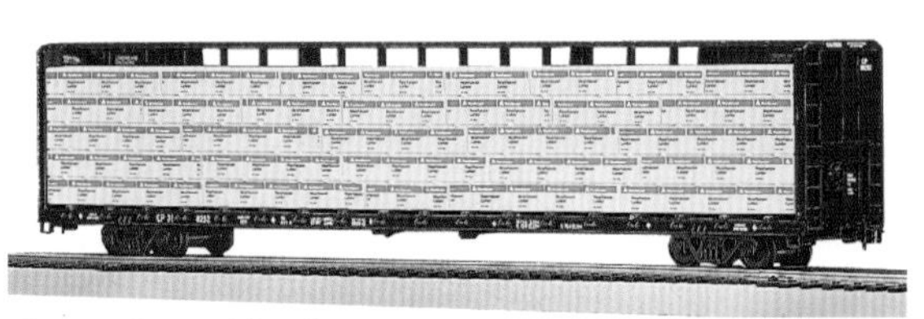

Center Beam Flat Car
CP Rail
Item No. 20-98229, Car No. 8252

1999 Volume 3 7
February 2000

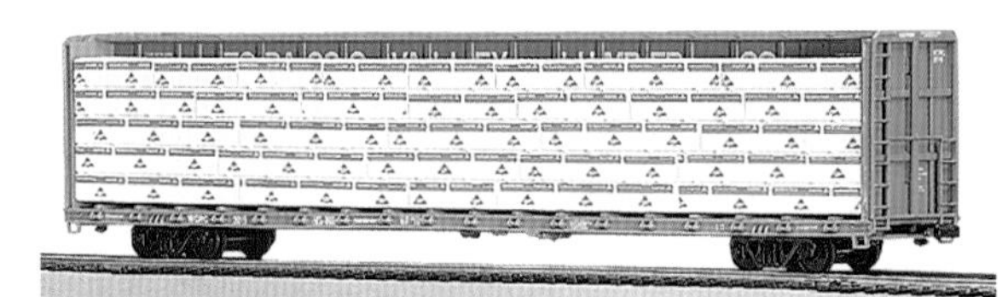

Center Beam Flat Car
Tobacco Valley Lumber
Item No. 20-98230, Car No. 2106

1999 Volume 3
February 2000

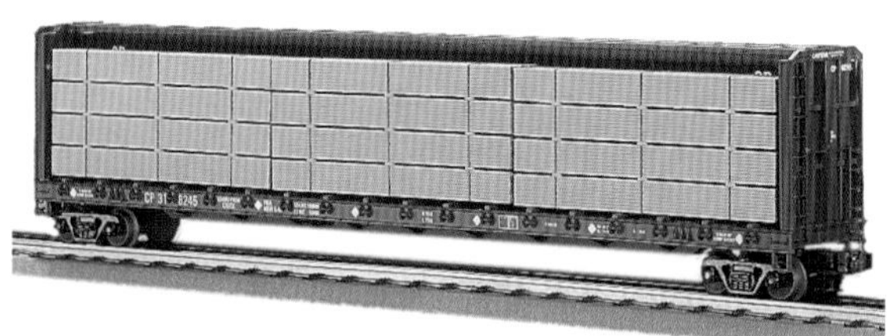

Center Beam Flat Car
CP Rail
Item No. 20-98234, Car No. CP 31 8245

2000 Volume 1
July 2000

Coalporter Hopper Car
CSX
Item No. 20-9700, Car No. 390596

Spring 1997
October 1997

Coalporter Hopper Car
Burlington Northern
Item No. 20-9701, Car No. 534203

Spring 1997
October 1997

Coalporter Hopper Car
BNSF
Item No. 20-97002, Car No. 668225

1997 Volume 2
March 1998

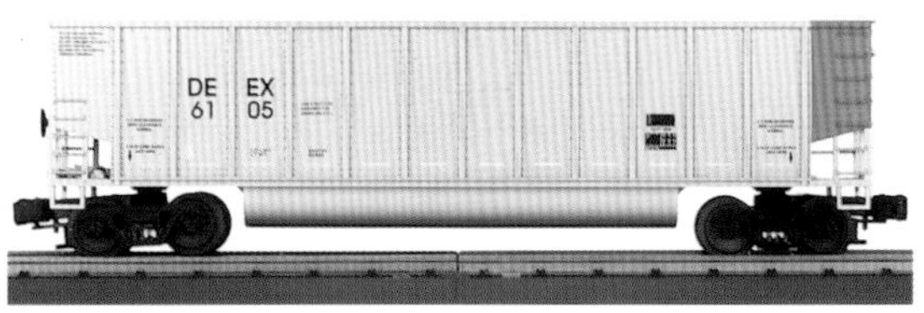

Coalporter Hopper Car
Detroit Edison
Item No. 20-97003, Car No. 6105

1997 Volume 2
February 1998

Coalporter Hopper Car
CSX
Item No. 20-97419, Car No. 392920

2000 Volume 2
November 2000

Coil Car
Norfolk Southern
Item No. 20-98203, Car No. 167000

1998 Volume 1
October 1998

Coil Car
Union Pacific
Item No. 20-98204, Car No. 229606

1998 Volume 1
October 1998

Coil Car
New Haven
Item No. 20-98213, Car No. 62004

1999 Volume 1
March 1999

Coil Car
Southern Pacific
Item No. 20-98214, Car No. 595632

1999 Volume 1
March 1999

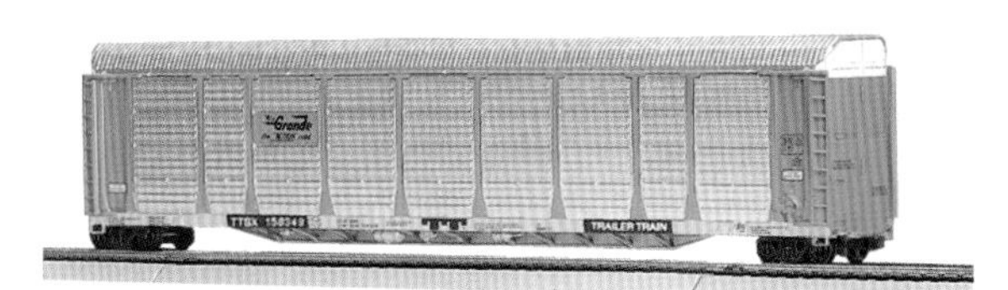

Corrugated Auto Carrier
Denver Rio Grande Western
Item No. 20-98231, Car No. 158349

1999 Volume 3
April 2000

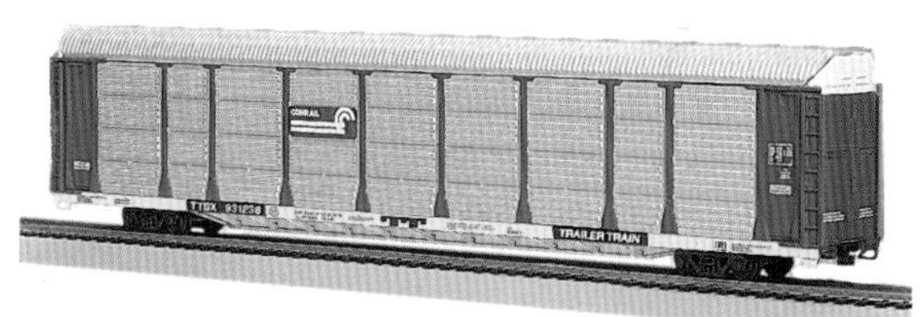

Corrugated Auto Carrier
Conrail
Item No. 20-98241, Car No. 931230

2000 Volume 1
May 2000

Double Door 50' Box Car
Union Pacific
Item No. 20-93012, Car No. 161244

1998 Volume 3
April 1999

Double Door 50' Box Car
Louisville & Nashville
Item No. 20-93013, Car No. 41030

1998 Volume 3
April 1999

Double Door 50' Box Car
Pennsylvania
Item No. 20-93016, Car No. 45643

1999 Volume 1
April 1999

Double Door 50' Box Car
Delaware & Hudson
Item No. 20-93017, Car No. 25002

1999 Volume 1
April 1999

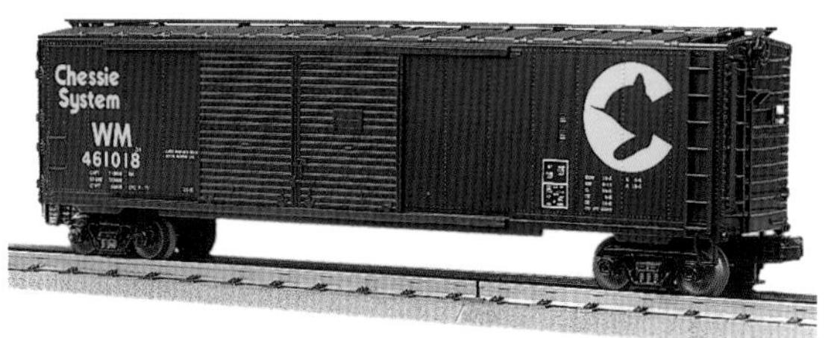

Double Door 50' Box Car
Chessie
Item No. 20-93031, Car No. 461018

2000 Volume 1
February 2000

Extended Vision Caboose
Union Pacific
Item No. 20-9100, Car No. 25214

Summer 1996
January 1997

Extended Vision Caboose
Pennsylvania
Item No. 20-9101, Car No. 477531

Summer 1996
December 1996

Extended Vision Caboose
Norfolk & Western
Item No. 20-9103, Car No. 562624

Fall/Winter 1996
February 1997

Extended Vision Caboose
Chesapeake & Ohio
Item No. 20-9102, Car No. 3289

Fall/Winter 1996
January 1997

Extended Vision Caboose
Chessie System
Item No. 20-9104, Car No. 903192

Spring 1997
April 1997

Extended Vision Caboose
Santa Fe
Item No. 20-9105, Car No. 562624

Spring 1997
April 1997

Extended Vision Caboose
Electro Motive Division
Item No. 20-91006, Car No. 15062

1997 Volume 2
February 1998

Extended Vision Caboose
Canadian National
Item No. 20-91007, Car No. 79575

1997 Volume 2
January 1998

Extended Vision Caboose
Southern
Item No. 20-91009, Car No. 252

1998 Volume 1
May 1998

Extended Vision Caboose
Southern Pacific
Item No. 20-91008, Car No. 324

1998 Volume 1
May 1998

Extended Vision Caboose
Santa Fe
Item No. 20-91010, Car No. 999539

1998 Volume 2
October 1998

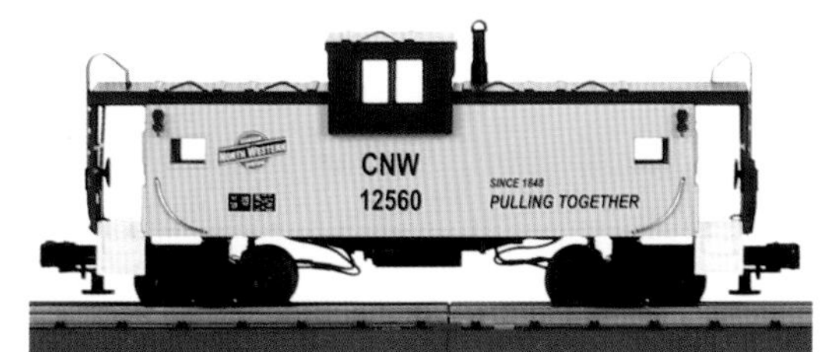

Extended Vision Caboose
Chicago NorthWestern
Item No. 20-91011, Car No. 12560

1998 Volume 2
September 1998

Extended Vision Caboose
Conrail
Item No. 20-91012, Car No. 22000

1998 Volume 2
September 1998

Extended Vision Caboose
Union Pacific
Item No. 20-91013, Car No. 25461

1998 Volume 2
June 1998

Extended Vision Caboose
Lehigh Valley
Item No. 20-91020, Car No. 95016

1999 Volume 3
February 2000

Extended Vision Caboose
New Haven
Item No. 20-91021, Car No. C-649

1999 Volume 3
February 2000

Extended Vision Caboose
Burlington
Item No. 20-91023, Car No. 13635

2000 Volume 1
May 2000

Extended Vision Caboose
Denver Rio Grande Western
Item No. 20-91024, Car No. 01500

2000 Volume 1
May 2000

Extended Vision Caboose
Union Pacific
Item No. 20-80001c (1999 DAP), Car No. 25724

Uncataloged Item
July 1999

Extended Vision Caboose
Santa Fe
3-Rail, Item No. 20-80002c, Cab No. 0010

Uncataloged Item
June 2000

Flat Car
West Virginia Pulp & Paper Co.
Item No. 20-98101 with Log Load, Car No. 153

1997 Volume 1
March 1998

Flat Car
Western Maryland
Item No. 20-98102 with Log Load, Car No. 2317

1997 Volume 1
March 1998

Flat Car
Northern Pacific
Item No. 20-98105 with (2) 20' Trailers, Car No. 66152

1998 Volume 1
January 1999

Flat Car
Pennsylvania
Item No. 20-98104 with (2) 20' Trailers, Car No. 469677

1998 Volume 1
January 1999

Flat Car
Union Pacific
Item No. 20-98107 with (2) 20' Trailers, Car No. 57256

1999 Volume 1
March 1999

Flat Car
Delaware & Hudson
Item No. 20-98108 with (2) 20' Trailers, Car No. 16144

1999 Volume 1
March 1999

Flat Car
Baltimore & Ohio
Item No. 20-98110, with (2) 20' Trailers, Car No. 9126

1999 Volume 3
January 2000

Flat Car
Santa Fe
Item No. 20-98111, with (2) 20' Trailers, Car No. 93537

1999 Volume 3
January 2000

Flat Car
MTH Transport
Item No. 20-98114 with (2) Die-Cast Fire Trucks, Car No. 2000

2000 Volume 1
January 2000

Flat Car
Baltimore & Ohio
Item No. 20-98115, with (1) 40' Trailer, Car No.9132

2000 Volume 2
August 2000

Flat Car
Norfolk Southern
Item No. 20-98116, with (1) 40' Trailer, Car No. 60368

2000 Volume 2
August 2000

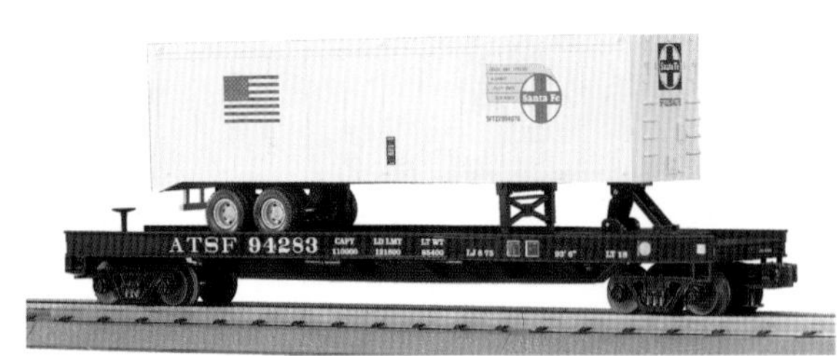

Flat Car
Santa Fe
Item No. 20-98117 with (1) 40' Trailer, Car No. 94283

2000 Volume 2
November 2000

Flat Car
Chicago NorthWestern
Item No. 20-98118 with (1) 40' Trailer, Car No. 44237

2000 Volume 2
November 2000

Flat Car - w/Bulkheads
Great Northern
Item No. 20-98113, Car No. 60418

2000 Volume 1
August 2000

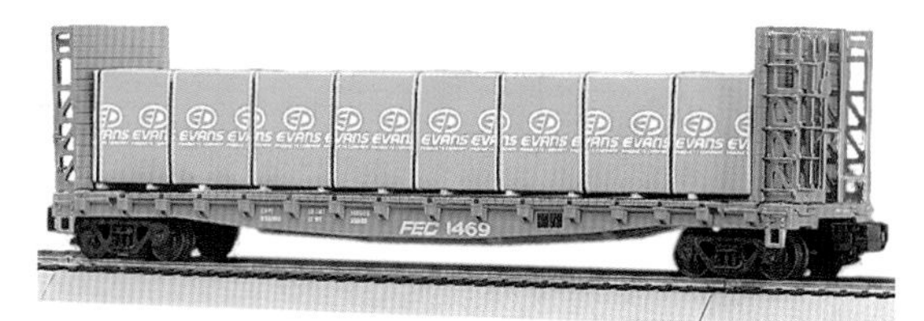

Flat Car - w/Bulkheads
Florida East Coast
Item No. 20-98112, Car No. 1469

2000 Volume 1
August 2000

Gondola Car - Scale Length
Pennsylvania
Item No. 20-98001, Car No. 385405

1997 Volume 1
March 1998

Gondola Car - Scale Length
Union Pacific
Item No. 20-98002, Car No. 30294

1997 Volume 1
March 1998

Gondola Car - Scale Length
Southern
Item No. 20-98004, Car No. 60750

1998 Volume 1
June 1998

Gondola Car - Scale Length
Southern Pacific
Item No. 20-98003 with Junk Load, Car No. 339288

1998 Volume 1
June 1998

Gondola Car - Scale Length
Chicago NorthWestern
Item No. 20-98005 with Junk Load, Car No. 340511

1998 Volume 3
November 1998

Gondola Car - Scale Length
Seaboard
Item No. 20-98006 with Junk Load, Car No. 6950

1998 Volume 3
November 1998

Gondola Car - Scale Length
Delaware & Hudson
Item No. 20-98007 with Junk Load, Car No. 15468

1999 Volume 1
April 1999

Gondola Car - Scale Length
Lehigh Valley
Item No. 20-98008 with Junk Load, Car No. 34679

1999 Volume 1
April 1999

Hot Metal Car
Silver
Item No. 20-98202, Car No. 49

1997 Volume 1
November 1998

Hot Metal Car
Black
Item No. 20-98201, Car No. 52

1997 Volume 1
November 1998

Hot Metal Car
CSX
Item No. 20-98209, Car No. 2

1998 Volume 3
December 1998

Hot Metal Car
Pennsylvania
Item No. 20-98210, Car No. 5

1998 Volume 3
December 1998

Husky Stack Car
Burlington Northern
Item No. 20-9502, Car No. 60009

Fall/Winter 1996
August 1997

Husky Stack Car
Trailer Train
Item No. 20-9501, Car No. 427208

Fall/Winter 1996
August 1997

Husky Stack Car
Southern Pacific
Item No. 20-95003, Car No. 2415

1997 Volume 2
February 1998

Husky Stack Car
Hanjin
Item No. 20-95004, Car No. 56148

1997 Volume 2
February 1998

Husky Stack Car
BNSF
Item No. 20-95005, Car No. 60100

1998 Volume 1
August 1998

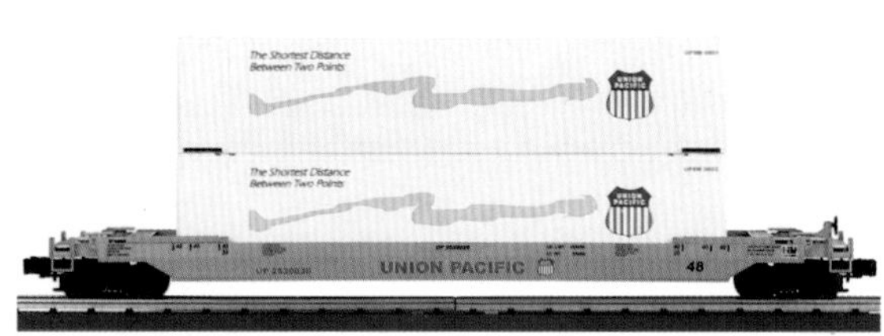

Husky Stack Car
Union Pacific
Item No. 20-95007, Car No. 2520028

1998 Volume 3
October 1998

Husky Stack Car
Maersk
Item No. 20-95006, Car No. 100052

1998 Volume 3
October 1998

Jordan Spreader
Union Pacific
Item No. 20-98205, Car No. 903143

1998 Volume 2
July 1999

Jordan Spreader
Pennsylvania
Item No. 20-98206, Car No. 497928

1998 Volume 2
June 1999

Jordan Spreader
Baltimore & Ohio
Item No. 20-98225, Car No. B 29

1999 Volume 3
February 2000

Jordan Spreader
Denver & Rio Grande
Item No. 20-98226, Car No. AX-41

1999 Volume 3
February 2000

Jordan Spreader
Delaware & Hudson
Item No. 20-98242, Car No. 35054

2000 Volume 2
October 2000

Jordan Spreader
Santa Fe
Item No. 20-98243, Car No. 199232

2000 Volume 2
October 2000

Mail Box Car
Amtrak
Item No. 20-93027, Car No. 1546

1999 Volume 3
May 2000

N-8 Caboose
Pennsylvania
Item No. 20-91014, Car No. 47806

1999 Volume 1
June 1999

O Scale Crane Car
Lehigh Valley
Item No. 20-98221, Car No. 86553

1999 Volume 2
June 2000

O Scale Crane Car
Great Northern
Item No. 20-98222, Car No. 165502

1999 Volume 2
June 2000

O Scale Crane Car
Santa Fe
Item No. 20-98237, Car No. 199796

2000 Volume 1
July 2000

O Scale Crane Car
Chicago NorthWestern
Item No. 20-98238, Car No.6359

2000 Volume 1
July 2000

O Scale Crane Tender
Lehigh Valley
Item No. 20-98223, Car No. 93156

1999 Volume 2
November 1999

O Scale Crane Tender
Great Northern
Item No. 20-98224, Car No. X-2507

1999 Volume 2
November 1999

O Scale Crane Tender
Santa Fe
Item No. 20-98239, Car No. 131400

2000 Volume 1
April 2000

O Scale Crane Tender
Chicago NorthWestern
Item No. 20-98240

2000 Volume 1
April 2000

O Scale Die-Cast Test Car
Union Pacific
Item No. 20-98215, Car No. 03154

1999 Volume 1
March 1999

O Scale Die-Cast Test Car
Pennsylvania
Item No. 20-98216, Car No. 490398

1999 Volume 1
March 1999

Ps-2 Hopper Car
Union Pacific
Item No. 20-97101 Car No. 19395

1997 Volume 1
September 1997

Ps-2 Hopper Car
Chessie
Item No. 20-97102, Car No. 631123

1997 Volume 1
September 1997

Ps-2 Hopper Car
Illinois Central
Item No. 20-97104, Car No. 700311

1997 Volume 2
May 1998

Ps-2 Hopper Car
Burlington
Item No. 20-97105, Car No. 189312

1997 Volume 2
June 1998

Ps-2 Hopper Car
Pennsylvania
Item No. 20-97106, Car No. 257128

1997 Volume 2
May 1998

Ps-2 Hopper Car
Rock Island
Item No. 20-97103, Car No. 500700

1997 Volume 2
June 1998

Ps-2 Hopper Car
Atlantic Coast Line
Item No. 20-97107, Car No. 89134

1998 Volume 3
November 1998

Ps-2 Hopper Car
New York Central
Item No. 20-97108, Car No. 87615

1998 Volume 3
December 1998

Ps-2 Hopper Car
Milwaukee Road
Item No. 20-97109, Car No. 52495

1999 Volume 1
December 1998

Ps-2 Hopper Car
Nickel Plate Road
Item No. 20-97110, Car No. 99290

1999 Volume 2
July 1999

Ps-2 Hopper Car
Great Northern
Item No. 20-97111, Car No. 71436

1999 Volume 2
July 1999

Rapid Discharge Car
Florida East Coast
Item No. 20-98217 Car No. 13001

1999 Volume 2
January 2000

Rapid Discharge Car
Atlantic Coast Line
Item No. 20-98218, Car No. 500000

1999 Volume 2
January 2000

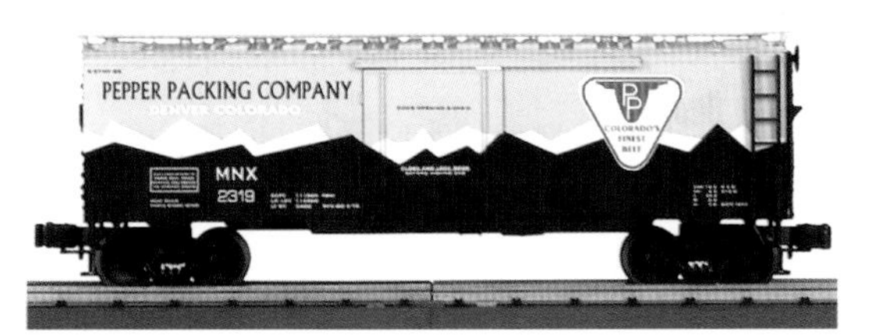

Reefer Car
Pepper Packing
Item No. 20-9400, Car No. 2319

Summer 1996
March 1997

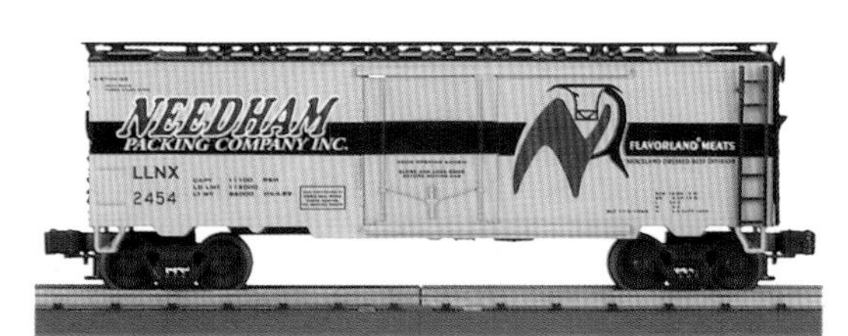

Reefer Car
Needham Packing
Item No. 20-9401, Car No. 2454

Summer 1996
December 1996

Reefer Car
National Packing
Item No. 20-9402, Car No. 2421

Fall/Winter 1996
December 1996

Reefer Car
Chicago NorthWestern
Item No. 20-9403, Car No. 70193

Fall/Winter 1996
March 1997

Reefer Car
Burlington Northern
Item No. 20-9404, Car No. 71049

Spring 1997
July 1997

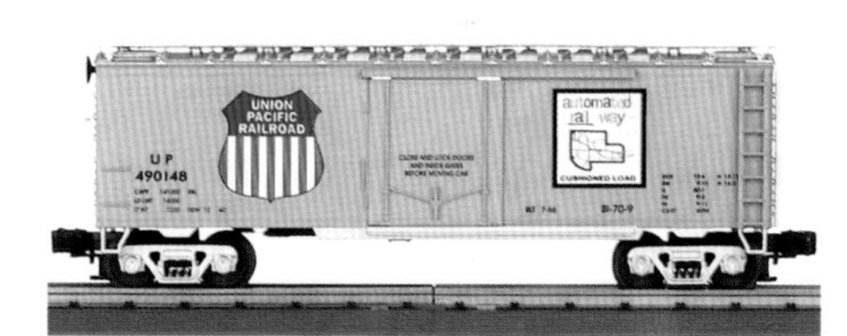

Reefer Car
Union Pacific
Item No. 20-9405, Car No. 490148

Spring 1997
June 1997

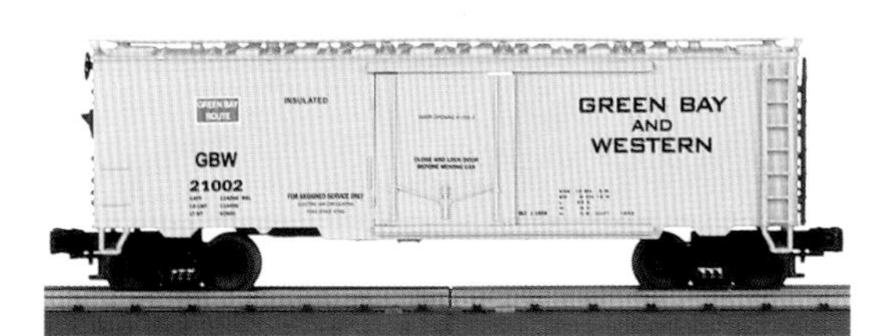

Reefer Car
Green Bay Route
Item No. 20-94006, Car No. 21002

1997 Volume 2
December 1997

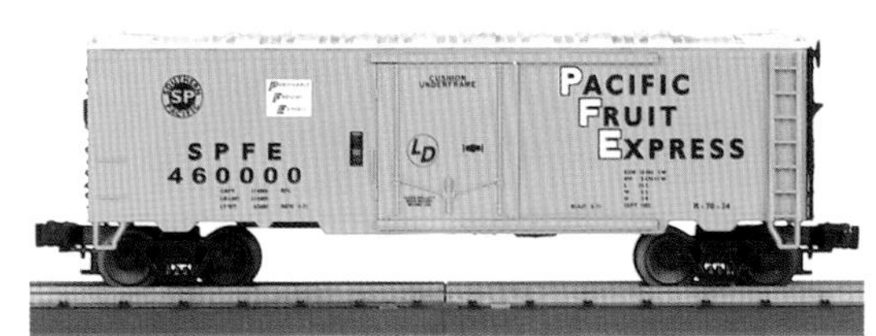

Reefer Car
Southern Pacific
Item No. 20-94007, Car No. 460000

1997 Volume 2
January 1998

Reefer Car
Pennsylvania
Item No. 20-94009, Car No. 19247

1998 Volume 1
February 1998

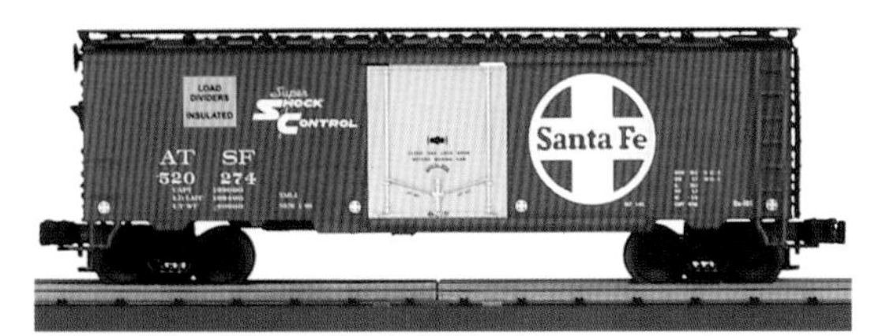

Reefer Car
Santa Fe
Item No. 20-94008, Car No. 520274

1998 Volume 1
February 1998

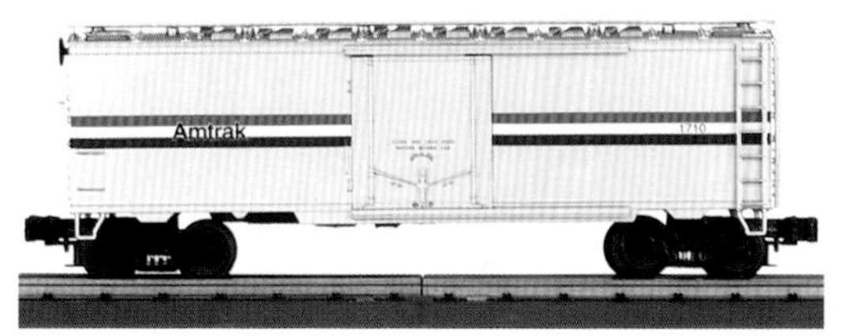

Reefer Car
Amtrak
Item No. 20-94010, Car No. 1710

1998 Volume 3
November 1998

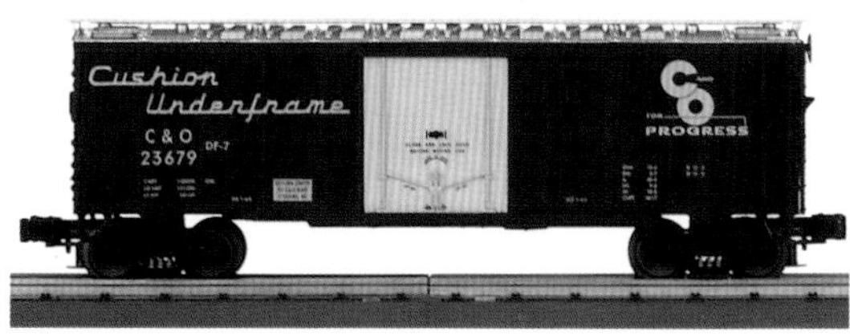

Reefer Car
Chesapeake & Ohio
Item No. 20-94011, Car No. 23679

1998 Volume 3
December 1998

Reefer Car
New Haven
Item No. 20-94012, Car No. 45087

1999 Volume 2
August 1999

Reefer Car
Florida East Coast
Item No. 20-94013, Car No. 602

1999 Volume 2
August 1999
$39.9

Reefer Car
Chesapeake & Ohio
Item No. 20-94014, Car No. 23161

2000 Volume 1
February 2000

Reefer Car
Nestle
Item No. 20-94015, Car No. 8209

2000 Volume 1
February 2000

Snow Plow
Pennsylvania
Item No. 20-98208, Car No. 497788

1998 Volume 3
May 1999

Snow Plow
Union Pacific
Item No. 20-98207, Car No. 900005

1998 Volume 3
May 1999

Snow Plow
New York Central
Item No. 20-98219, Car No. X663

1999 Volume 2
December 1999

Snow Plow
Conrail
Item No. 20-98220, Car No. 64522

1999 Volume 2
December 1999

Snow Plow
Chicago NorthWestern
Item No. 20-98227, Car No. 6419

1999 Volume 3
February 2000

Snow Plow
Canadian National
Item No. 20-98228, Car No. 55283

1999 Volume 3
February 2000

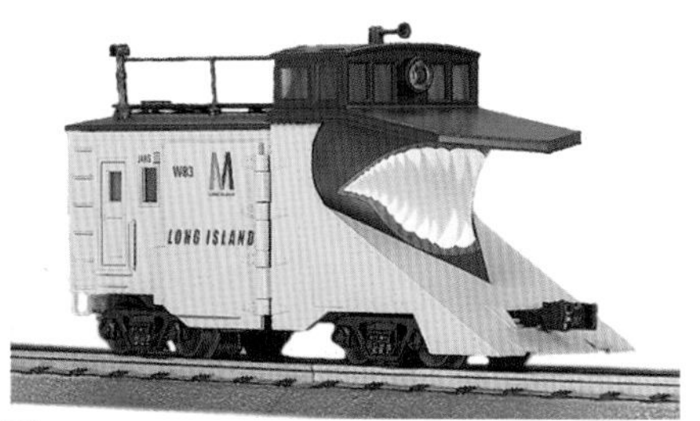

Snow Plow
Long Island
Item No. 20-98235, Car No. W83

2000 Volume 1
April 2000

Snow Plow
Duluth, Missabe & Iron Range
Item No. 20-98236, Car No. W100

2000 Volume 1
April 2000

Snow Plow
Lehigh Valley
Item No. 20-98244, Car No. 96111

2000 Volume 1
November 2000

Snow Plow
Northern Pacific
Item No. 20-98245, Car No. 35

2000 Volume 1
November 2000

Steel Caboose
Duluth Missabe & Iron Range
Item No. 20-91015, Car No. 143

1999 Volume 1
March 1999

Steel Caboose
Great Northern
Item No. 20-91016, Car No. 222

1999 Volume 1
March 1999

Steel Caboose
Norfolk & Western
Item No. 20-91017, Car No. 562748

1999 Volume 2
October 1999

Steel Caboose
Santa Fe
Item No. 20-91018, Car No. 999600

1999 Volume 2
October 1999

Steel Caboose
Union Pacific
Item No. 20-91022, Car No. 25214

2000 Volume 1
April 2000

Steel Caboose
Southern
Item No. 20-91025, Car No. 252

2000 Volume 1
May 2000

Steel Caboose
Burlington Northern
Item No. 20-91026, Car No. 11462

2000 Volume 1
May 2000

Steel Caboose
Norfolk & Western
Item No. 20-91027, Car No. 562720

2000 Volume 1
January 2000

Steel Sided Stock Car
Southern
Item No. 20-94501, Car No. 45778

1999 Volume 3
December 1999

Steel Sided Stock Car
Union Pacific
Item No. 20-94502, Car No. 47456D

1999 Volume 3
December 1999

Steel Sided Stock Car
Pennsylvania
Item No. 20-94503, Car No. 130554

1999 Volume 3
December 1999

Tank Car
Burlington Northern
Item No. 20-9200, Car No. 12686

Summer 1996
January 1997

Tank Car
Denver & Rio Grande
Item No. 20-9201, Car No. 10009

Summer 1996
January 1997

Tank Car
New York Central
Item No. 20-9202 Car No. 1750

Fall/Winter 1996
January 1997

Tank Car
Chicago NorthWestern
Item No. 20-9203, Car No. 3478

Fall/Winter 1996
January 1997

Tank Car
Pennsylvania
Item No. 20-9204, Car No. 6789

Spring 1997
April 1997

Tank Car
Union Pacific
Item No. 20-9205, Car No. 67890

Spring 1997
April 1997

Tank Car
Southern Pacific
Item No. 20-92006, Car No. 34890

1997 Volume 2
December 1997

Tank Car
Chessie
Item No. 20-92007, Car No. 8209

1997 Volume 2
January 1998

Tank Car
G.A.T.X.
Item No. 20-92008, Car No. 44587

1998 Volume 1
May 1998

Tank Car
Southern
Item No. 20-92009, Car No. 995006

1998 Volume 1
May 1998

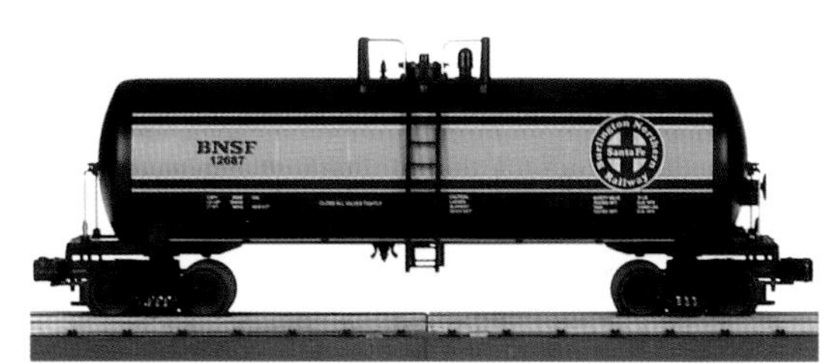

Tank Car
BNSF
Item No. 20-92010, Car No. 12687

1998 Volume 2
August 1998

Tank Car
Airco
Item No. 20-92011, Car No. 3008

1998 Volume 2
September 1998

Tank Car
Hooker
Item No. 20-96008, Car No. 5867

1998 Volume 3
December 1998

Tank Car
Seaboard
Item No. 20-96009, Car No. 67890

1998 Volume 3
November 1998

Tank Car
Santa Fe
Item No. 20-96016, Car No. X-222

1999 Volume 1
May 1999

Tank Car
Great Northern
Item No. 20-96017, Car No. 76488

1999 Volume 1
May 1999

Tank Car
Domino Sugar
Item No. 20-92012, Car No. 1791

2000 Volume 1
February 2000

Tank Car
Engelhard Chemical
Item No. 20-92013, Car No. 1006

2000 Volume 1
February 2000

Tank Car
McDonald's
Item No. 20-96021, Car No. 78390

2000 Volume 2
October 2000

Tank Car
NASA
Item No. 20-96020, Car No. 003

2000 Volume 2
October 2000

Tank Car
BNSF
Item No. 20-92014, Car No.911 R

2000 Volume 2
October 2000

Westinghouse Schnabel
Westinghouse
Item No. 20-98232

2000 Volume 1
April 2000

Wood Chip Hopper Car
Northern Pacific
Item No. 20-97502, Car No. 119743

1998 Volume 1
July 1998

Wood Chip Hopper Car
Southern
Item No. 20-97501, Car No. 139750

1998 Volume 1
July 1998

Wood Chip Hopper Car
Santa Fe
Item No. 20-97503, Car No. 16573

1999 Volume 1
May 1999

Wood Chip Hopper Car
Southern Pacific
Item No. 20-97504, Car No. 355333

1999 Volume 1
May 1999

PREMIER LINE
PASSENGER SETS

M.T.H. offers top-of-the-line passenger cars in a variety of forms. The company's first passenger cars were aluminum cars, made of extruded aluminum in the old-fashioned way. These beautiful cars remain popular today with model railroaders who are nostalgic for the trains of their youth. As O Gaugers began to demand more detail and more realism in their cars, M.T.H. responded by adding the sturdy ABS plastic passenger cars with detailed interiors and overhead lighting to their product line. Through the years, M.T.H. has continued its commitment to providing model railroaders with a rich variety of choices by adding more passenger car types to the Premier line. They now make nineteen distinct kinds of Premier passenger cars, including the basics like Madison cars and smooth- and ribbed-sided streamlined cars as well as more unusual pieces such as Bi-level cars and Superliners. Most M.T.H. Premier passenger cars feature fast-angle metal wheels and needle-point axles for a smooth, quiet ride.

2-Car 60' Aluminum Coach
Canadian Pacific

Uncataloged Item
August 2000

Item No. 20-80002g (2000 D.A.P.), Car Names, Blair Manor, Craig Manor

2-Car 60' Sleeper/Diner Aluminum
Denver & Rio Grande

Fall/Winter 1996
January 1997

Item No. 20-6102, Car Names, Glenwood Springs, Shavano Peak

2-Car 60' Sleeper/Diner Aluminum
Baltimore & Ohio

Fall/Winter 1996
January 1997

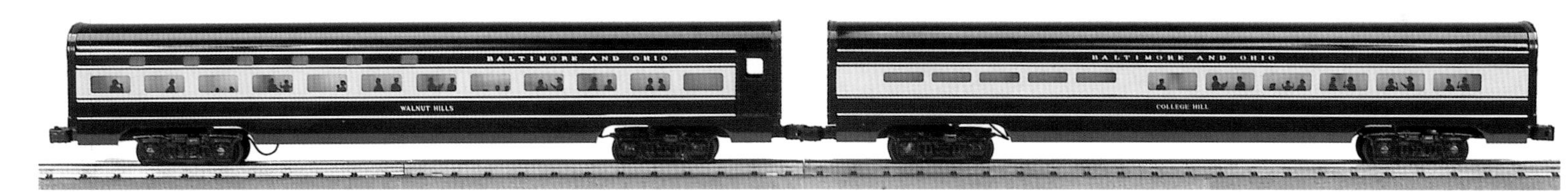

Item No. 20-6108, Car Names, Walnut Hills, College Hill

2-Car 60' Sleeper/Diner Aluminum
New York Central

Fall/Winter 1996
January 1997

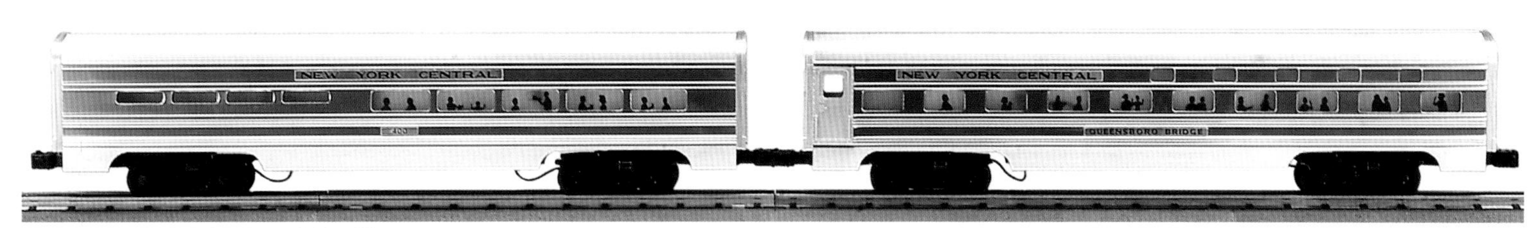

Item No. 20-6113, Car Nos. Queensboro Bridge, 400

2-Car 60' Sleeper/Diner Aluminum
Norfolk & Western

Fall/Winter 1996
January 1997

Item No. 20-6114, Car Names Duke University, Powhatan Arrow

2-Car 60' Sleeper/Diner Aluminum
Santa Fe

Fall/Winter 1996
January 1997

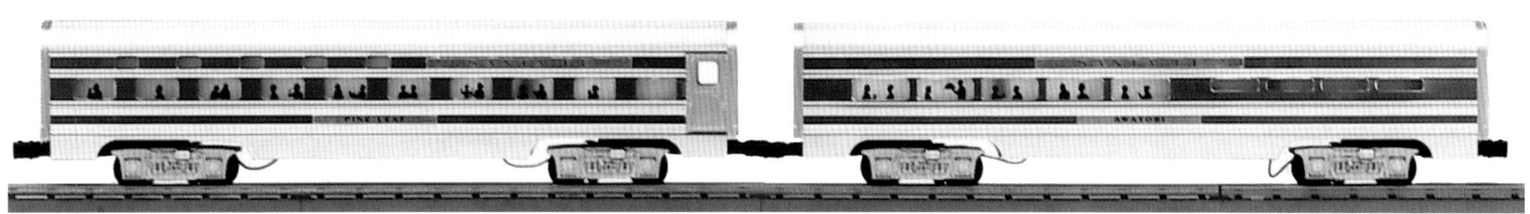

Item No. 20-6116, Car Names Awatobi, Pine Leaf

2-Car 60' Sleeper/Diner Aluminum
Pennsylvania

Fall/Winter 1996
January 1997

Item No. 20-6117, Car Nos. Chartiers Creek, 4020

2-Car 60' Sleeper/Diner Aluminum
Santa Fe

Fall/Winter 1996
December 1996

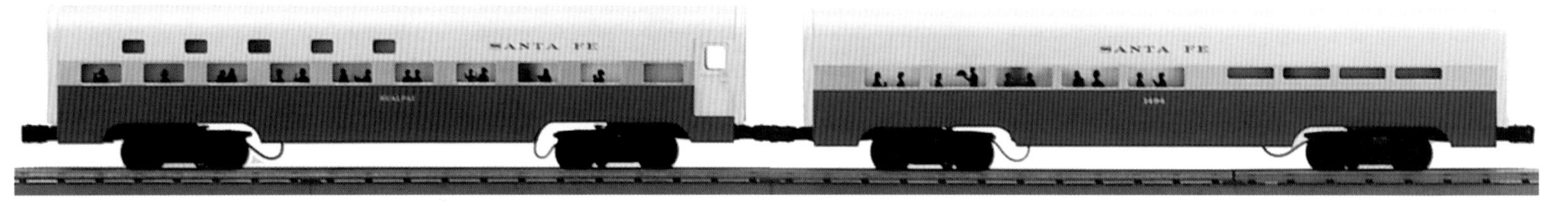

Item No. 20-6118, Car Nos. Hualpai, 1494

2-Car 60' Sleeper/Diner Aluminum
Union Pacific

Fall/Winter 1996
December 1996

Item No. 20-6119, Car Nos. National Command, Mission Dolores

2-Car 60' Sleeper/Diner Aluminum
Louisville & Nashville

1997 Volume 1
October 1997

Item No. 20-6120, Car Names Dixie Journey, Alabama Pine

2-Car 60' Sleeper/Diner Aluminum
Santa Fe

1997 Volume 1
October 1997

Item No. 20-6121, Car Nos. Polacca, 1475
Item No. 20-6122, Car Nos. Laguna, 1505

2-Car 70' ABS Sleeper/Diner Ribbed
Rock Island

1998 Volume 1
November 1998

Item No. 20-6612, Car Names La Costa, El Comedore

2-Car 70' ABS Sleeper/Diner Ribbed
Seaboard

1998 Volume 1
November 1998

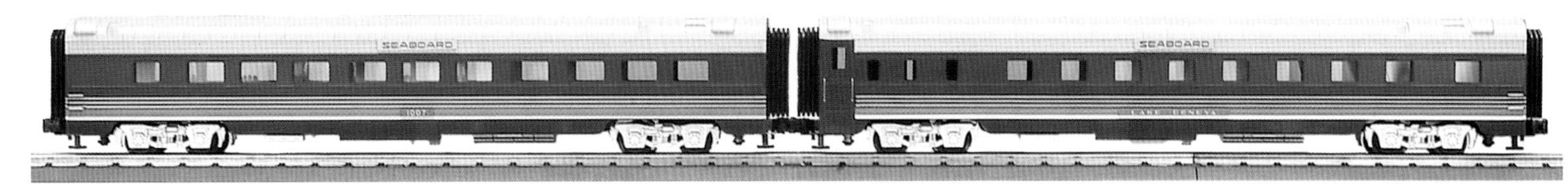

Item No. 20-6615, Car Nos. Lake Geneva, 1007

2-Car 70' ABS Sleeper/Diner Ribbed
Nickel Plate Road

1999 Volume 2
September 1999

Item No. 20-6626, Car Nos. City of Erie, 129

2-Car 70' ABS Sleeper/Diner Ribbed
Lehigh Valley

1999 Volume 2
September 1999

Item No. 20-6627, Car Nos. 1623, 1012

2-Car 70' ABS Sleeper/Diner Ribbed
Texas Special

1999 Volume 2
September 1999

Item No. 20-6628, Car Nos. 1455 George G. Vest, 1100 Sam Houston

2-Car 70' ABS Sleeper/Diner Ribbed
Southern Pacific

1999 Volume 2
September 1999

Item No. 20-6629, Car Nos. 3002, 10201

2-Car 70' ABS Sleeper/Diner Ribbed
New Haven

1999 Volume 2
September 1999

Item No. 20-6625, Car Names Bunker Hill, Shippan Point

2-Car 70' ABS Sleeper/Diner Ribbed
Pennsylvania

1999 Volume 2
September 1999

Item No. 20-6630, Car Nos. 115, 7132 Henry Knox

2-Car 70' ABS Sleeper/Diner Ribbed
California Zephyr

2000 Volume 2
July 2000

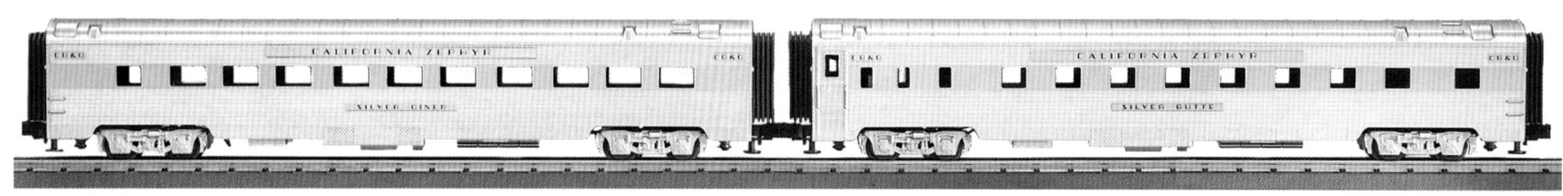

Item No. 20-6645, Car Names Silver Butte, Silver Diner

2-Car 70' ABS Sleeper/Diner Ribbed
Wabash

2000 Volume 2
July 2000

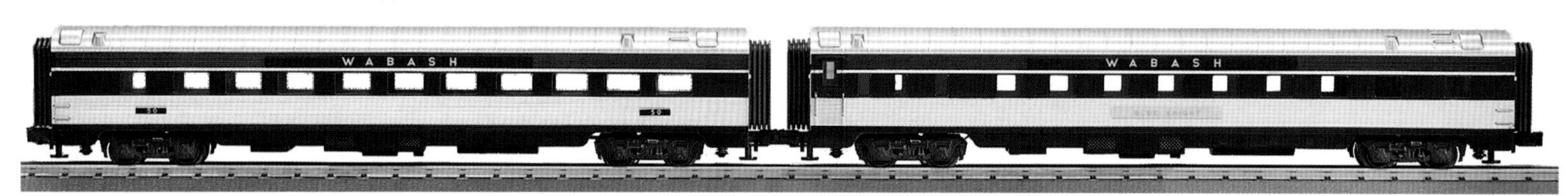

Item No. 20-6646, Car Names Blue Knight, Blue Buffet

2-Car 70' ABS Sleeper/Diner Ribbed
Canadian Pacific

2000 Volume 2
July 2000

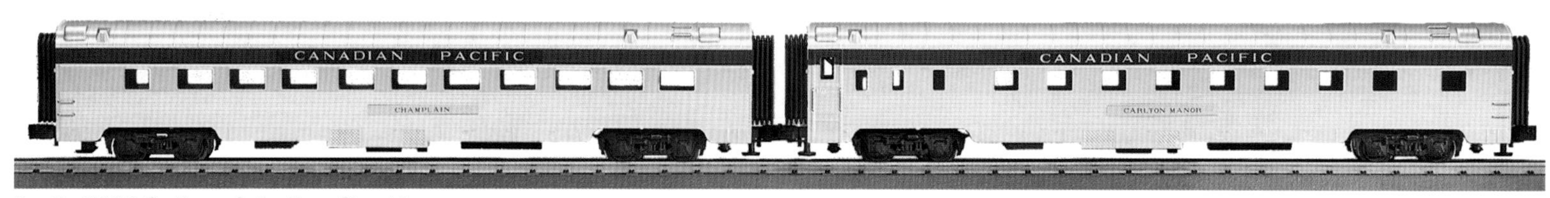

Item No. 20-6647, Car Names Carlton Manor, Champlain

2-Car 70' ABS Sleeper/Diner Ribbed
Santa Fe

2000 Volume 2
July 2000

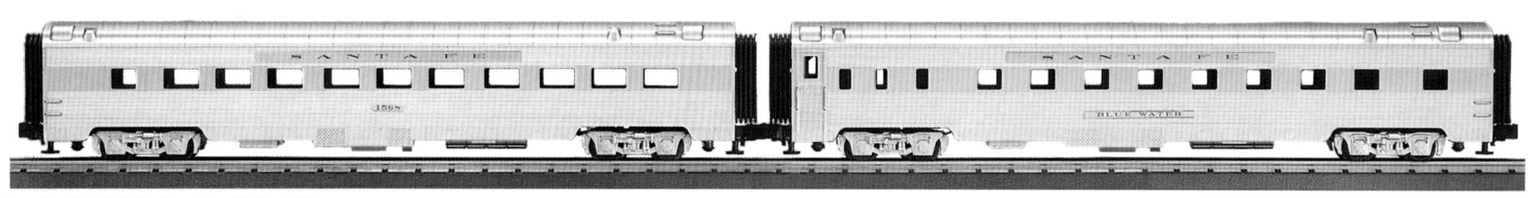

Item No. 20-6643, Car Nos. Blue Water, 1568

2-Car 70' ABS Sleeper/Diner Ribbed
Amtrak

2000 Volume 2
July 2000

Item No. 20-6648, Car Nos. 2097, 8550

2-Car 70' ABS Sleeper/Diner Ribbed
Chessie

2000 Volume 2
July 2000

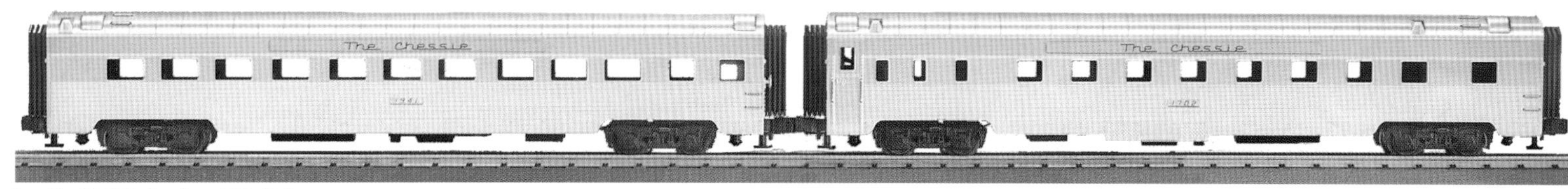

Item No. 20-6649, Car Nos. 1702, 1941

2-Car 70' ABS Sleeper/Diner Ribbed
Florida East Coast

2000 Volume 2
July 2000

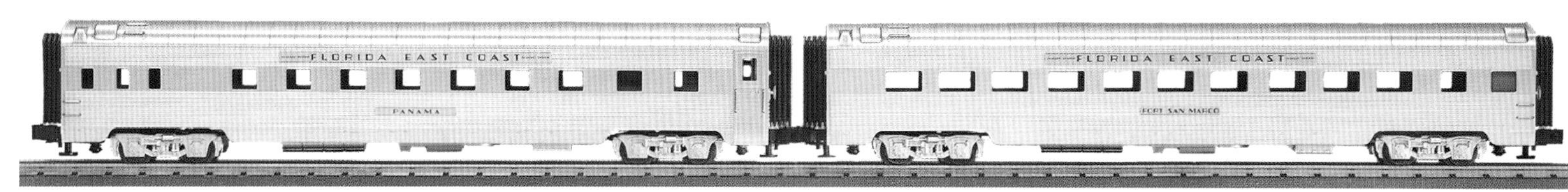

Item No. 20-6650, Car Names Panama, Fort San Marco

2-Car 70' ABS Sleeper/Diner Smooth
Norfolk & Western

1998 Volume 1
November 1998

Item No. 20-6614, Car Nos. Duke University, 491

2-Car 70' ABS Sleeper/Diner Smooth
Southern

1998 Volume 3
April 1999

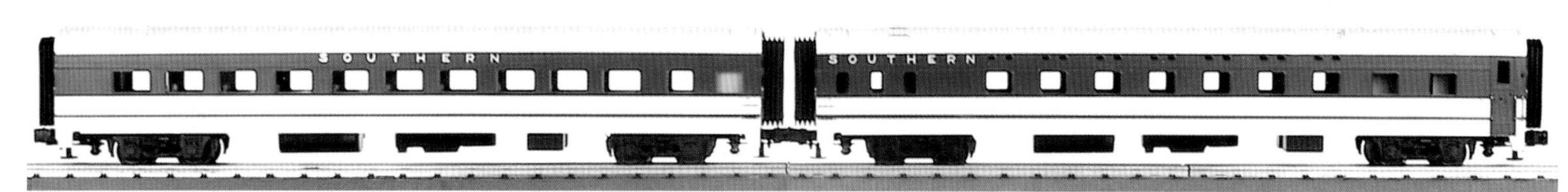

Item No. 20-6617, Car Nos. 2014 Shenandoah River, 3312

2-Car 70' ABS Sleeper/Diner Smooth
Alaska

1998 Volume 3
April 1999

Item No. 20-6618, Car Nos. 173, 208

2-Car 70' ABS Sleeper/Diner Smooth
New York Central

1998 Volume 3
December 1998

Item No. 20-6616, Car Nos. Queensboro Bridge, 406

2-Car 70' ABS Sleeper/Diner Smooth
Southern Pacific

1998 Volume 3
April 1999

Item No. 20-6623, Car Nos. Mount Hood 600, Lake Pepin 156

2-Car 70' ABS Sleeper/Diner Smooth
Chicago NorthWestern

1999 Volume 3
February 2000

Item No. 20-6636, Car Nos. 6154, 6148

2-Car 70' ABS Sleeper/Diner Smooth
Pere Marquette

1999 Volume 3
February 2000

Item No. 20-6633, Car Nos. 35, 11

2-Car 70' ABS Sleeper/Diner Smooth
Kansas City Southern

1999 Volume 3
February 2000

Item No. 20-6635, Car Nos. Tolmak, 56

2-Car 70' ABS Sleeper/Diner Smooth
Electro Motive Division

1999 Volume 3
February 2000

Item No. 20-6634, Car Names Sierra Mountains, Cascade Summit

2-Car 70' ABS Sleeper/Diner Smooth
Union Pacific

1999 Volume 3
February 2000

Item No. 20-6638, Car Names Wyoming, City of Los Angeles
Item No. 20-6653, Car Names Omaha, Overland

2-Car 70' ABS Sleeper/Diner Smooth
New York Central

2000 Volume 2
October 2000

Item No. 20-6654, Car Nos. Imperial Court, 681

2-Car 70' ABS Sleeper/Diner Smooth
Illinois Central

2000 Volume 2
October 2000

Item No. 20-6661, Car Nos. City of New Orleans, 4106 Jackson Square

2-Car 70' ABS Sleeper/Diner Smooth
Milwaukee Road

2000 Volume 2
October 2000

Item No. 20-6652, Car Nos. 19 Madison River, 184 River Grove

2-Car 70' ABS Sleeper/Diner Smooth
Erie

2000 Volume 2
October 2000

Item No. 20-6660, Car Names Pride of Youngstown, Amish Pride

2-Car 70' ABS Sleeper/Diner Smooth
Great Northern

2000 Volume 2
October 2000

Item No. 20-6651, Car Nos. 1373 Santiam Pass, 1240 Crossley Lake

2-Car 70' ABS Sleeper/Diner Smooth
Pennsylvania

2000 Volume 2
October 2000

Item No. 20-6657, Car Nos. 8303 Conemaugh Rapids, 4520

2-Car 70' Aluminum Sleeper/Diner Painted
Atlantic Coast Line

Summer 1996
June 1996

Item No. 20-6600, Car Names Winter Haven, Columbia

2-Car 70' Aluminum Sleeper/Diner Painted
Chesapeake & Ohio

Summer 1996
June 1996

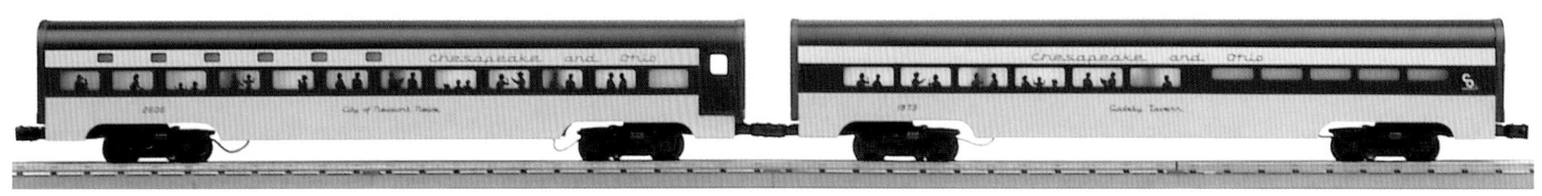

Item No. 20-6602, Car Names City of Newport News, Gadsby Tavern

2-Car 70' Aluminum Sleeper/Diner Painted
Union Pacific

Summer 1996
June 1996

Item No. 20-6606, Car Nos. Ocean Sunset, 4001

2-Car 70' Aluminum Sleeper/Diner Painted
Pennsylvania

Spring 1997
May 1997

Item No. 20-6607, Car Names Omaha, Overland

2-Car 70' Aluminum Sleeper/Diner Painted
Amtrak

Spring 1997
May 1997

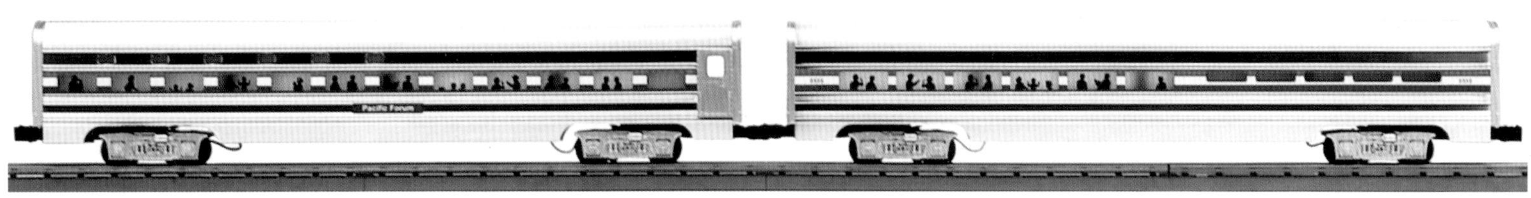

Item No. 20-6608, Car Nos. Pacific Forum , 8555

2-Car 70' Aluminum Sleeper/Diner Painted
Union Pacific

Spring 1997
May 1997

Item No. 20-6610, Car Nos. Pacific Bridge, 5007

2-Car 70' Aluminum Sleeper/Diner Painted
Baltimore & Ohio

Spring 1997
May 1997

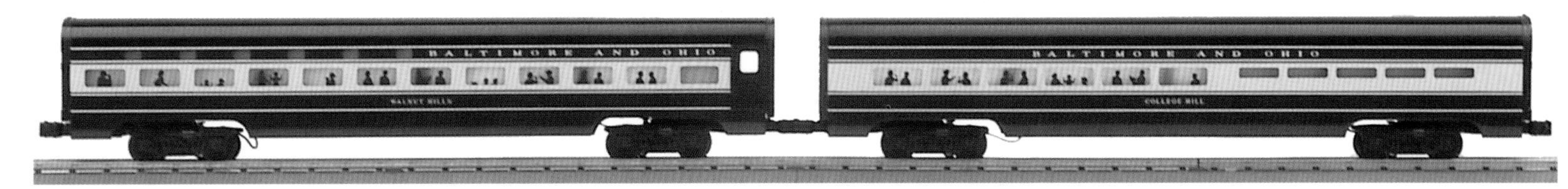

Item No. 20-6611 Car Names Walnut Hills, College Hill
Item No. 20-6613, Car Nos. Park Spur, 1078

2-Car 70' Aluminum Sleeper/Diner Plated
Atlantic Coast Line

Summer 1996
June 1996

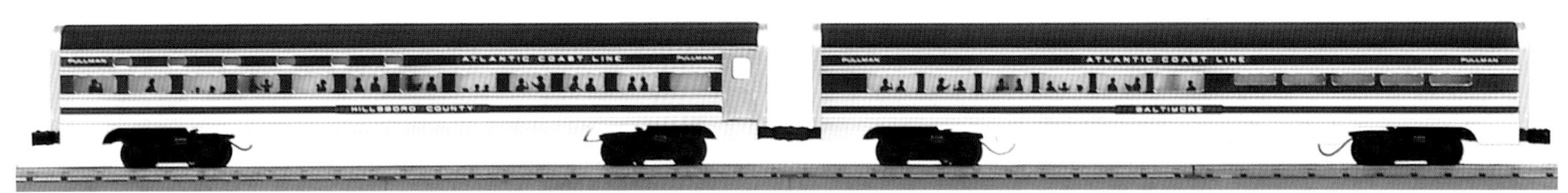

Item No. 20-6601, Car Names Hillsboro County, Baltimore

2-Car 70' Aluminum Sleeper/Diner Plated
Southern

Summer 1996
June 1996

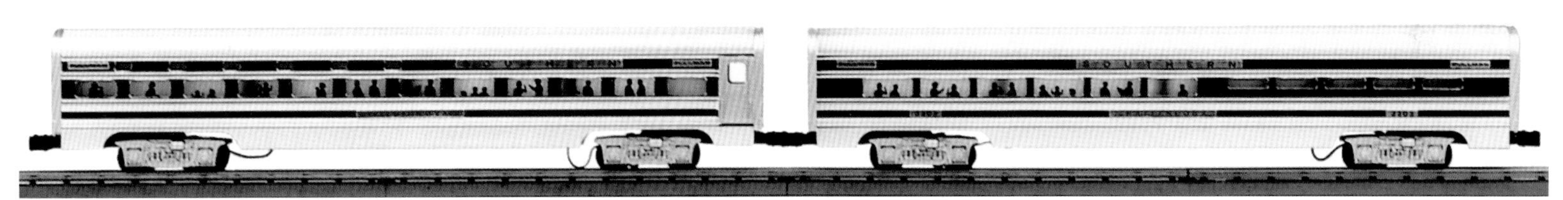

Item No. 20-6603, Car Nos. Shenandoah River, 3312

2-Car 70' Aluminum Sleeper/Diner Plated
New York Central

Summer 1996
June 1996

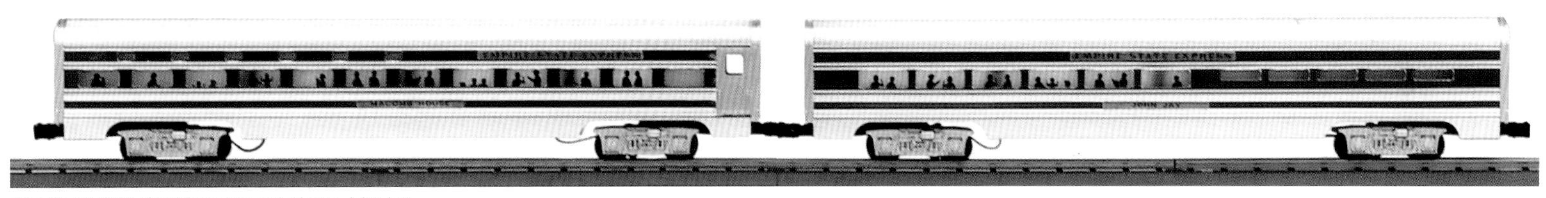

Item No. 20-6604, Car Names Macomb House, John Jay

2-Car 70' Aluminum Sleeper/Diner Plated
California Zephyr

Summer 1996
June 1996

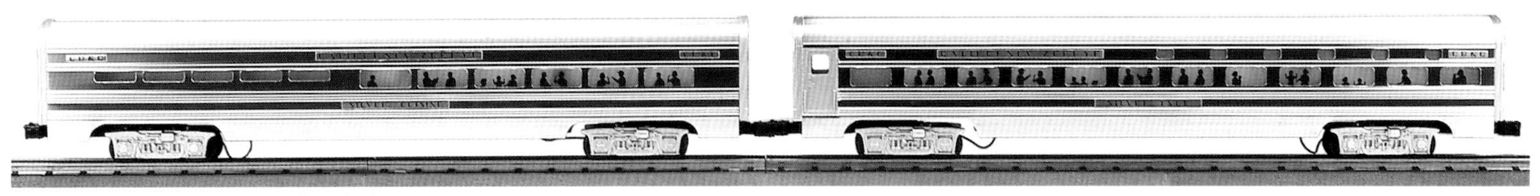

Item No. 20-6605, Car Names Silver Isle, Silver Cuisine

2-Car 70' Madison Combine/Diner
Pennsylvania

Winter 1995
November 1995

Item No. 20-4106, Car Nos. 4406, 6550

2-Car 70' Madison Combine/Diner
Santa Fe

Winter 1995
November 1995

Item No. 20-4107, Car Nos. 1464, 2938

2-Car 70' Madison Combine/Diner
Southern

Winter 1995
November 1995

Item No. 20-4108, Car Names Dining Car, William Moultrie

2-Car 70' Madison Combine/Diner
Texas & Pacific

Winter 1995
November 1995

Item No. 20-4109, Car Nos. 1011, 510

2-Car 70' Madison Combine/Diner
Lehigh Valley

Winter 1995
May 1997

Item No. 20-4110, Car Nos. Not Available

2-Car 70' Madison Combine/Diner
Northern Pacific

Spring 1997
May 1997

Item No. 20-4114, Car Nos. Not Available

2-Car 70' Madison Combine/Diner
Pennsylvania

Spring 1997
May 1997

Item No. 20-4118, Car Nos. Not Available
Item No. 20-4125, Car Nos. 5153, 4484

2-Car 70' Madison Combine/Diner
New York Central

Spring 1997
May 1997

Item No. 20-4119, Car Nos. 405, 4814

2-Car 70' Madison Combine/Diner
Pullman

Spring 1997
May 1997

Item No. 20-4120, Car Nos. 6438, National

2-Car 70' Madison Combine/Diner
New York Central

1999 Volume 3
January 2000

Item No. 20-4126, Car Nos. 219, 391

2-Car 70' Madison Combine/Diner
Boston & Maine

1999 Volume 3
January 2000

Item No. 20-4127, Car Nos. 3608, 84 Mountaineer

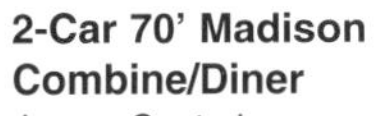

2-Car 70' Madison Combine/Diner
Jersey Central

1999 Volume 3
January 2000

Item No. 20-4121, Car Names Halley, Giacobini

2-Car 70' Madison Combine/Diner
Norfolk & Western

1999 Volume 3
January 2000

Item No. 20-4124, Car Nos. 615, 1014

2-Car 70' Madison Combine/Diner
New York Central

1999 Volume 3
January 2000

Item No. 20-4122, Car Nos. 411, 392

2-Car 70' Madison Combine/Diner
Union Pacific

2000 Volume 1
July 2000

Item No. 20-4131, Car Nos. 3619, 202

2-Car 70' Madison Combine/Diner
Chesapeake & Ohio

2000 Volume 1
July 2000

Item No. 20-4128, Car Nos. 458, 968

2-Car 70' Madison Combine/Diner
Chicago NorthWestern

2000 Volume 1
July 2000

Item No. 20-4130, Car Nos. 7460, The President

2-Car 70' Madison Combine/Diner
Pennsylvania

2000 Volume 2
September 2000

Item No. 20-4132, Car Nos. 4420, 4931

2-Car 70' Madison Combine/Diner
Pullman

2000 Volume 2
September 2000

Item No. 20-4133, Car Nos. 460, 965 Gadsby's Tavern

2-Car 70' Madison Combine/Diner
Nickel Plate Road

2000 Volume 2
September 2000

Item No. 20-4134, Car Nos. 131, 882

2-Car 70' Madison Combine/Diner
Lehigh Valley

2000 Volume 2
September 2000

Item No. 20-4135, Car Nos. 1021, 1028

2-Car 70' Madison Combine/Diner
Southern

2000 Volume 2
September 2000

Item No. 20-4136, Car Nos. 658, 4141

2-Car 70' Madison Combine/Diner
New York Central

2000 Volume 2
September 2000

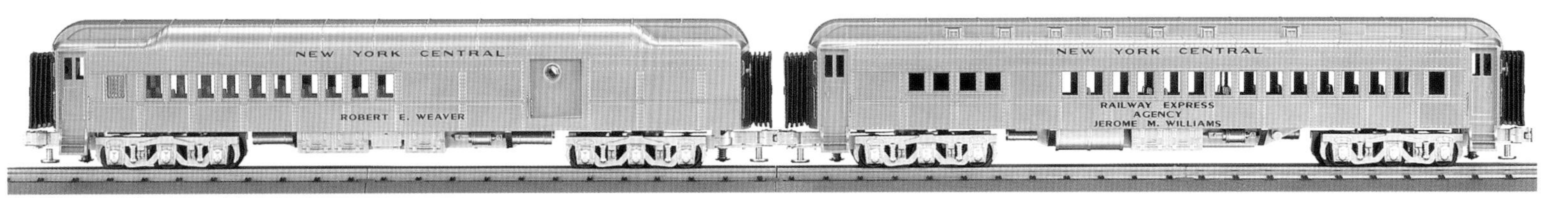

Item No. 20-4129, Car Names Jerome M. Williams, Robert E. Weaver

2-Car Amfleet
Amtrak

2000 Volume 2
September 2000

Item No. 20-6655, Car Nos. 44023, 44019

2-Car Amfleet
Amtrak

2000 Volume 2
September 2000

Item No. 20-6656, Car Nos. 21253, 21200

2-Car SuperLiner Sleeper/Diner
Amtrak

1999 Volume 3
April 2000

Item No. 20-6539, Car Nos. 32009, 38065

2-Car SuperLiner Sleeper/Diner
Amtrak

1999 Volume 3
April 2000

Item No. 20-6541, Car Nos. 38061, 32088 Maryland

4-Car 60' Aluminum
Santa Fe

Spring 1996
March 1996

Item No. 20-6016, Car Nos. 3436, Taos Valley, Regal Pass, Denehosto

4-Car 60' Aluminum
Santa Fe

Fall/Winter 1996
September 1996

Item No. 20-6018, Car Nos. REA 3435, 3151, 500, Denehosto

4-Car 60' Aluminum
Louisville & Nashville

Spring 1997
August 1997

Item No. 20-6020, Car Nos. Not Available

4-Car 60' Aluminum
Santa Fe

Spring 1997
August 1997

Item No. 20-6021, Car Nos. Not Available

4-Car 60' Aluminum
Canadian Pacific

Uncataloged Item
August 1999

Item No. 20-80001b2, Car Names Banff Park (Observation), Skyline 500 (Vista Domes)

4-Car 60' Aluminum Ribbed
Baltimore & Ohio

2000 Volume 2
July 2000

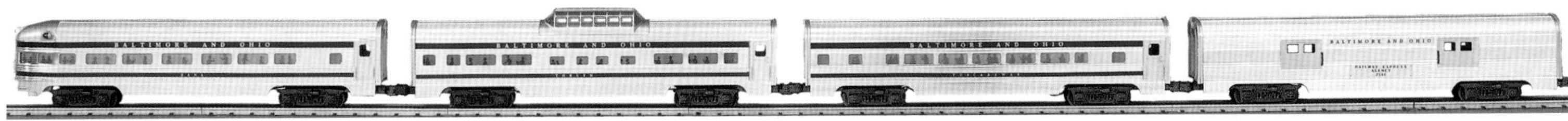

Item No. 20-6022, Car Nos. 2540, Tuscanaway, Thrush, Dana

4-Car 60' Aluminum Ribbed
Santa Fe

2000 Volume 2
July 2000

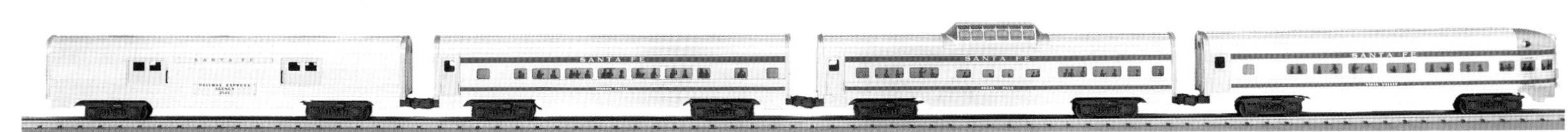

Item No. 20-6023, Car Nos. 2540, Indian Falls, Regal Pass, Vista Valley

4-Car Amfleet Passenger
Caltrain

1998 Volume 1
July 1998

Item No. 20-6521, Car Nos. 520, 523, 527, 304

4-Car Amfleet Passenger
Amtrak

1998 Volume 1
July 1998

Item No. 20-6519, Car Nos. 44103, 43007, 44212, 44002
Item No. 20-6555, Car Nos. 44007, 44123, 44200, 43037

4-Car Amfleet Passenger
Metra

1998 Volume 1
July 1998

Item No. 20-6520 Car Nos. 625, 630, 632, 597

4-Car Amfleet Passenger
Amtrak

1999 Volume 2
October 1999

Item No. 20-6531, Car Nos. 21628, 21265, 44677, 20977

4-Car Amfleet Passenger
Septa

1999 Volume 2
October 1999

Item No. 20-6532, Car Nos. 2502, 2503, 2507, 2802

4-Car Amfleet
Amtrak

2000 Volume 2
July 2000

Item No. 20-6556, Car Nos. 21625, 21255, 21266, 20971

4-Car Scale Bi-Level
Chicago NorthWestern

2000 Volume 2
October 2000

Item No. 20-6558, Car Nos. 152, 228, 700, 705

4-Car Scale Bi-Level
METRA

2000 Volume 2
October 2000

Item No. 20-6559, Car Nos. 7650, 7653, 7659, 7664

4-Car Scale SuperLiner
Amtrak

1998 Volume 3
February 1999

Item No. 20-6524, Car Nos. 34138, 34123, 34104, Lounge-Cafe 33040

4-Car Scale SuperLiner
Amtrak

1999 Volume 3
March 2000

Item No. 20-6537 Car Nos. 34123, 34126, 34110, 33046

5-Car 60' Aluminum
Baltimore & Ohio

15th Anniversary
March 1995

Item No. 20-6008, Car Nos. REA 1300, Indian Hills, Winton Place, Eden Park, Pebbles Corner

5-Car 60' Aluminum
Norfolk & Western

Spring 1996
May 1996

Item No. 20-6014, Car Nos. Not Available

5-Car 70' ABS Ribbed
Rock Island

1997 Volume 2
November 1998

Item No. 20-6512, Car Nos. REA 820, Valle Verde, Valle Vista, Valle Mar, La Mirada

5-Car 70' ABS Ribbed
Baltimore & Ohio

1997 Volume 2
November 1998

Item No. 20-6513, Car Nos. REA 1303, 3568, 3582, 3552, Palm Islands

5-Car 70' ABS Ribbed
Norfolk & Western

1997 Volume 2
November 1998

Item No. 20-6514, Car Nos. REA, 502, 512, 534, 581

5-Car 70' ABS Ribbed
Seaboard

1997 Volume 2
November 1998

Item No. 20-6515, Car Nos. REA 182, Glen Spruce, Oconomowoc, Glen Gary, Waldameer

5-Car 70' ABS Ribbed
Nickel Plate Road

1999 Volume 1
March 1999

Item No. 20-6526, Car Nos. 329, 103, 107, 108, City of Cleveland

5-Car 70' ABS Ribbed
Lehigh Valley

1999 Volume 1
June 1999

Item No. 20-6527, Car Nos. 1224, 1510, 1512, 1519, 1551

5-Car 70' ABS Ribbed
Missouri Pacific

1999 Volume 1
June 1999

Item No. 20-6528, Car Nos. 1000 Anson B. Jones, 1300 Mirabeau B. Lamar, 1650 Sterling Price, 1603 Glendale, 1400 Stephen F. Austin

5-Car 70' ABS Ribbed
Southern Pacific

1999 Volume 1
June 1999

Item No. 20-6529, Car Nos. 6604, 2492, 2488, 2486, 2954

5-Car 70' ABS Ribbed
Pennsylvania

1999 Volume 1
June 1999

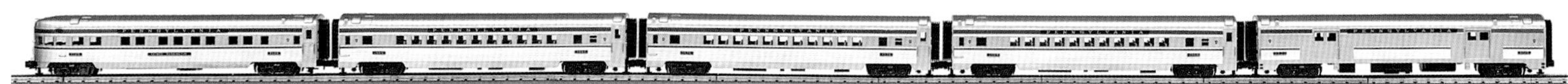

Item No. 20-6530, Car Nos. 9229, 1569, 1576, 1585, 7128 George Washington

5-Car 70' ABS Ribbed
Santa Fe

2000 Volume 1
July 2000

Item No. 20-6543, Car Nos. 1997, 3035, 3041, 3067, 404.

5-Car 70' ABS Ribbed
Cal Zephyr

2000 Volume 1
July 2000

Item No. 20-6545, Car Nos. 903 Silver Bear, 252 Silver Roundup, 4721 Silver Saddle, 4720 Silver Rifle, 375 Silver Horizon

5-Car 70' ABS Ribbed
Wabash

2000 Volume 1
July 2000

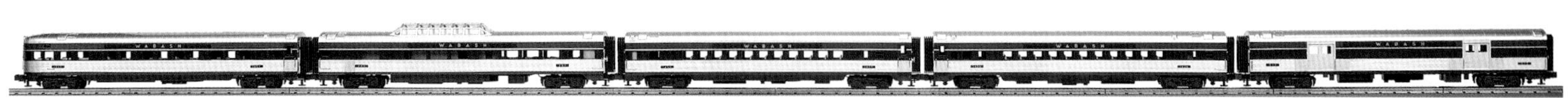

Item No. 20-6546, Car Nos. 375 Blue Pouch, 1425 Blue Silk, 1426 Blue Velvet, 202 Blue Cloud, 1600 Blue Vista

5-Car 70' ABS Ribbed
Canadian Pacific

2000 Volume 1
July 2000

Item No. 20-6547, Car Nos.3017, 110, 111, 515 Skyline, Sibley Park

5-Car 70' ABS Ribbed
Amtrak

2000 Volume 1
July 2000

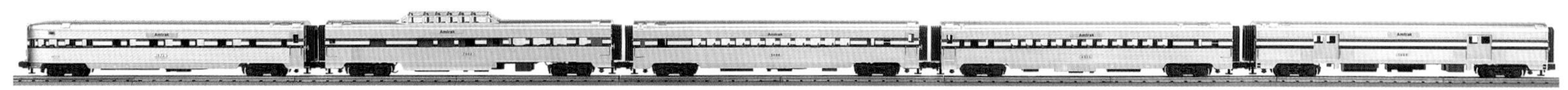

Item No. 20-6548, Car Nos. 1203, 4012, 5698, 7000, 1832

5-Car 70' ABS Ribbed
Chessie

2000 Volume 1
July 2000

Item No. 20-6549, Car Nos. 1402, 1501, 1606, 1850, 1875

5-Car 70' ABS Ribbed
Florida East Coast

2000 Volume 1
July 2000

Item No. 20-6550, Car Nos. 501, Eau Gallie, Delray Beach, Jacksonville, Bay Biscayne

5-Car 70' ABS Smooth
Kansas City Southern

1999 Volume 3
January 2000

Item No. 20-6535, Car Nos. 23, 270, 275, 279, Arthur E. Stillwell

5-Car 70' ABS Smooth
Electro Motive Division

1999 Volume 3
January 2000

Item No. 20-6534, Car Names Colorado River, Tehachapi Mountains, San Joaquin Valley, Pecos River, Promontory

5-Car 70' ABS Smooth
Pere Marquette

1999 Volume 3
January 2000

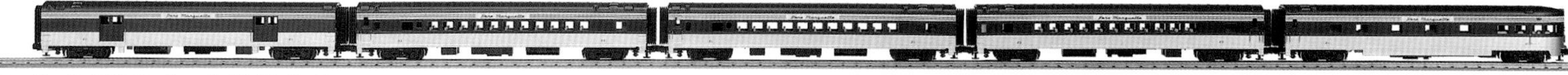

Item No. 20-6533, Car Nos. 61, 31, 33, 23, 21

5-Car 70' ABS Smooth
Chicago NorthWestern

1999 Volume 3
January 2000

Item No. 20-6536, Car Nos. 6130, 6161, 6133, 6145, 6159

5-Car 70' ABS Smooth
Union Pacific

1999 Volume 3
January 2000

Item No. 20-6538, Car Names Pony Express, City of Salina, Challenger, City of San Francisco, Sun Valley

5-Car 70' ABS Smooth
Great Northern

2000 Volume 1
November 2000

Item No. 20-6551, Car Nos. 203, 1213, 1209, 1321, 1190 Chateau Coulee

5-Car 70' ABS Smooth
Milwaukee Road

2000 Volume 1
November 2000

Item No. 20-6552, Car Nos. Not Available

5-Car 70' ABS Smooth
Union Pacific

2000 Volume 2
August 2000

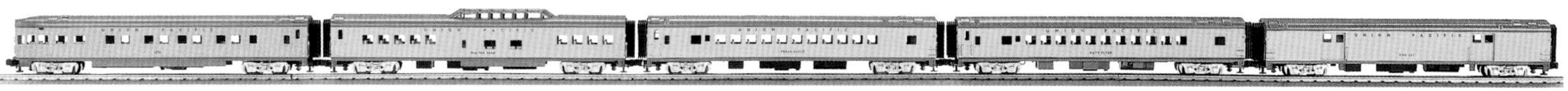

Item No. 20-6553, Car Nos. PWR 207, Katy Flyer, Texas Eagle, Walter Dean, 1576

5-Car 70' ABS Smooth
New York Central

2000 Volume 2
August 2000

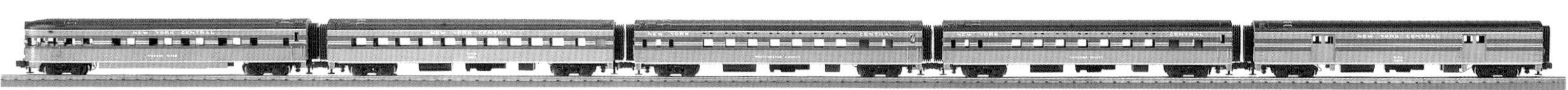

Item No. 20-6554, Car Nos. 9165, Cascade Valley, City Of Toledo, 680, Manhattan Island

5-Car 70' ABS Smooth
Erie

2000 Volume 2
August 2000

Item No. 20-6560, Car Nos. REA 624, 1973, 1966, 1967, Rapid Falls

5-Car 70' ABS Smooth
Illinois Central

2000 Volume 2
August 2000

Item No. 20-6561, Car Nos. 1800, 2610 Chartres, 2611 Calcasieu, Southern Cloud, 3305 Mardi Gras

5-Car 70' ABS Smooth
Pennsylvania

2000 Volume 2
August 2000

Item No. 20-6557, Car Nos. 6695, 4100, 4126, 4158, 7150 Skyline View

5-Car 70' ABS Smooth Painted
Alaska

1998 Volume 1
March 1999

Item No. 20-6518, Car Nos. 100, 201, 202, 501, 503

5-Car 70' ABS Smooth Painted
New York Central

1998 Volume 1
March 1999

Item No. 20-6516, Car Nos. 5018, 2666, 2646, 2642, 10633 Hickory Creek

5-Car 70' ABS Smooth Painted
Southern

1998 Volume 1
April 1999

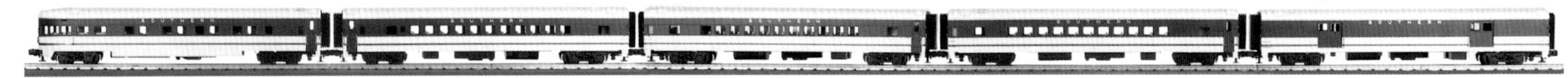

Item No. 20-6517, Car Nos. Not Available

5-Car 70' ABS Smooth Painted
Southern Pacific

1998 Volume 3
March 1999

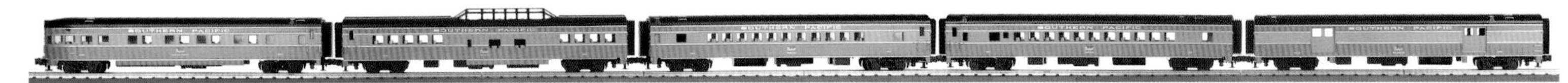

Item No. 20-6523, Car Nos. Tuolumne 510, Mendocino 544, Red River 568, Miln Gillespie 3300, Appekunny 1290

5-Car 70' Aluminum Plated
Atlantic Coast Line

Spring 1996
March 1996

Item No. 20-6501, Car Nos. REA 150, Ashley River, North Hampton County, Edisto Island, 252

5-Car 70' Aluminum Plated
Southern

Spring 1996
March 1996

Item No. 20-6503, Car Nos. Decatur 1750, Huntsville 806, Buntyn 807, Charlottesville 812, Washington 1150

5-Car 70' Aluminum Plated
New York Central

Spring 1996
March 1996

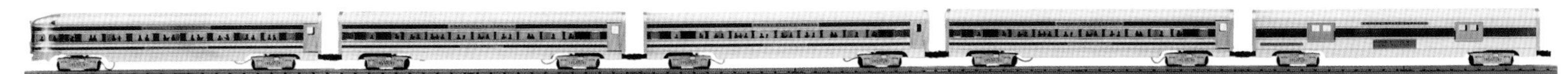

Item No. 20-6504, Car Names U.S. Mail RPO Alonzo B. Cornell, Hamilton Fish, William H. Seward, Silas Wright, Franklin D. Roosevelt
Item No. 20-6509, Car Nos. Not Available

5-Car 70' Aluminum Plated
California Zephyr

Spring 1996
March 1996

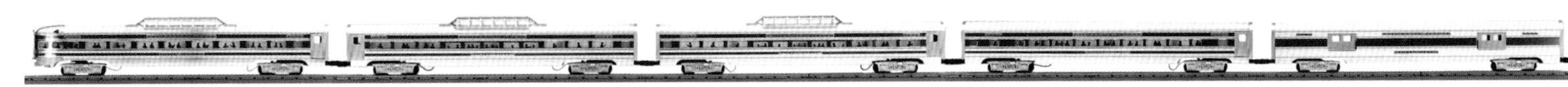

Item No. 20-6505, Car Nos. Silver Bear, Silver Larch, Silver Ranch, Silver Rifle, Silver Solarium

5-Car 70' Aluminum Painted
Amtrak

Spring 1997
March 1997

Item No. 20-6508, Car Nos.1000, 4010, 9400, 9401, 9300 Silver View

5-Car 70' Aluminum Smooth Painted
Atlantic Coast Line

Spring 1996
March 1996

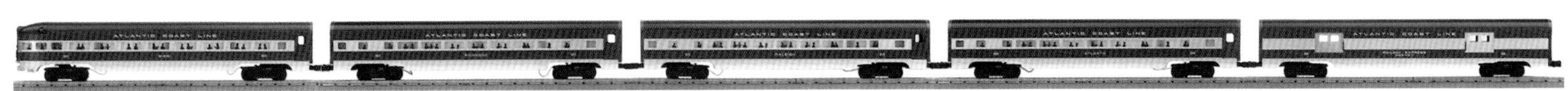

Item No. 20-6500, Car Nos. REA 100, 208 Atlanta, 213 Raleigh, 227 Richmond, 257 Miami

5-Car 70' Aluminum Smooth Painted
Chesapeake & Ohio

Spring 1996
March 1996

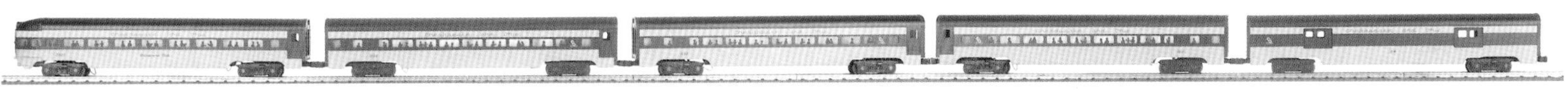

Item No. 20-6502, Car Nos. 314, 1611, 1632, 1658, 2507 Wolverine Club

5-Car 70' Aluminum Smooth Painted
Union Pacific

Spring 1996
March 1996

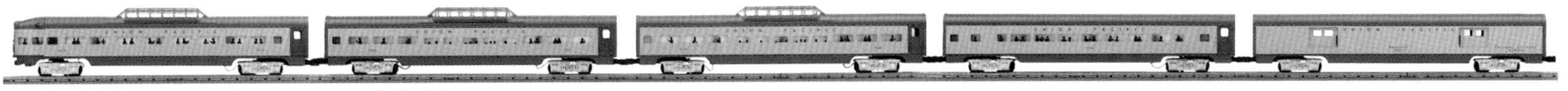

Item No. 20-6506, Car Nos. REA 9501, 5425, 7000, 7002, 9002
Item No. 20-6510, Car Nos. 6300, 5508, 7009, 7005, 9000

5-Car 70' Aluminum Smooth Painted
Pennsylvania

Spring 1997
March 1997

Item No. 20-6507, Car Names Cordelia, Massillon Inn, Imperial Bower, Little Miami Rapids, Tower View

5-Car 70' Aluminum Smooth Painted
Baltimore & Ohio

Spring 1997
April 1997

Item No. 20-6511, Car Nos. 1301, Hyde Park, Norwood, Oakley, Fountain Square

5-Car 70' Madison
Delaware & Hudson

15th Anniversary
December 1994

Item No. 20-4002, Car Nos. 264, 265, 266, 267, 522

5-Car 70' Madison
Pennsylvania

15th Anniversary
November 1995

Item No. 20-4006, Car Nos. 5753, 3486, 3774, 4363, 6905
Item No. 20-4018, Car Nos. 9231, McKendree 4019, Fradel 4020, Fairbanks 4021, Quaker City 7507
Item No. 20-4023, Car Nos. 6063, 1680 Lake Merritt, 3831 Villa Royal, 3833 Caleb Strong, Quaker City
Item No. 20-4025, Car Nos. 6064, Elk's Club 7034, Courageous 7001, Trimount 7033, Williamsport 7053
Item No. 20-4032, Car Nos. 6042, 1640, 1647, 1659, Pittsburgher

5-Car 70' Madison
Santa Fe

15th Anniversary
November 1995

Item No. 20-4007, Car Nos. Not Available

5-Car 70' Madison
Texas & Pacific

15th Anniversary
November 1995

Item No. 20-4009, Car Nos. 910, 1302, 1303, 1307, 1314

5-Car 70' Madison
Lehigh Valley

15th Anniversary
November 1995

Item No. 20-4010, Car Nos. Not Available

5-Car 70' Madison
Chesapeake & Ohio

Winter 1995
November 1995

Item No. 20-4013, Car Nos. 271, 870, 878, 891

5-Car 70' Madison
Milwaukee Road

Winter 1995
November 1995

Item No. 20-4015, Car Nos. Not Available

5-Car 70' Madison
Frisco/Texas Special

Winter 1995
November 1995

Item No. 20-4016, Car Nos. 120, 700, 730, 760, 791

5-Car 70' Madison
New York Central

Fall/Winter 1996
November 1996

Item No. 20-4019, Car Nos. 7469, 853, 2241, 1170
Item No. 20-4022, Car Nos. 5045, 2523, 2525, 2522, 1015

5-Car 70' Madison
Pullman

Fall/Winter 1996
November 1996

Item No. 20-4020, Car Nos. Not Available
Item No. 20-4033, Car Nos. 4109, Hot Springs, Emerald Creek, Night Fern, Tioga Valley

5-Car 70' Madison
Jersey Central

1998 Volume 2
March 1999

Item No. 20-4021, Car Names DeVico, Holmes, Winnecke, Tuttle, Bernard

5-Car 70' Madison
Norfolk & Western

1998 Volume 2
March 1999

Item No. 20-4024, Car Nos. 330, 510, 512, 513, 582

5-Car 70' Madison
New York Central

1999 Volume 3
December 1999

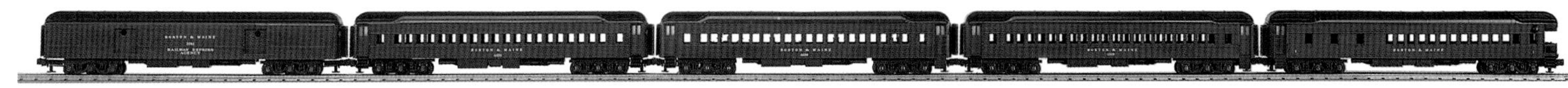

Item No. 20-4026, Car Nos. 9152, 1991, 1996, 1997, Seneca Valley

5-Car 70' Madison
Boston & Maine

1999 Volume 3
December 1999

Item No. 20-4027, Car Nos. 3292, 1329, 4555, 4558, 1

5-Car 70' Madison
Chesapeake & Ohio

1999 Volume 3
December 1999

Item No. 20-4028, Car Nos. 307, 861, 858, 872, 15

5-Car 70' Madison
New York Central

2000 Volume 1
May 2000

Item No. 20-4029, Car Nos. 2000, Harry C. Ives, Louis Marx, J. Lionel Cowen, A.C. Gilbert

5-Car 70' Madison
Union Pacific

2000 Volume 1
May 2000

Item No. 20-4031, Car Nos. 1750, 410, 416, 412, 202

5-Car 70' Madison
Chicago NorthWestern

2000 Volume 1
May 2000

Item No. 20-4030, Car Nos. 5728, 3880, 3411, 3415, Partland Club

5-Car 70' Madison
Nickel Plate Road

2000 Volume 2
August 2000

Item No. 20-4034, Car Nos. 329, 63, 65, 66, 2

5-Car 70' Madison
Lehigh Valley

2000 Volume 2
August 2000

Item No. 20-4035, Car Nos. 1224, 901, 912, 915, 1326

5-Car 70' Madison
Southern

2000 Volume 2
August 2000

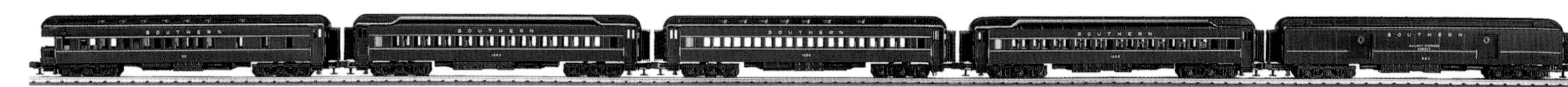

Item No. 20-4036, Car Nos. 523, 1063, 1050, 1052, 22

70' ABS Full Length Vista Dome Ribbed
Rock Island

1999 Volume 1
June 1999

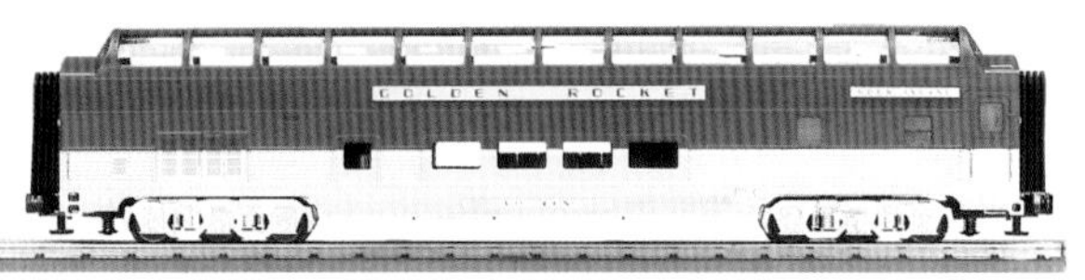

Item No. 20-6712, Car Name Big Ben

70' ABS Full Length Vista Dome Ribbed
Missouri Pacific

1999 Volume 1
June 1999

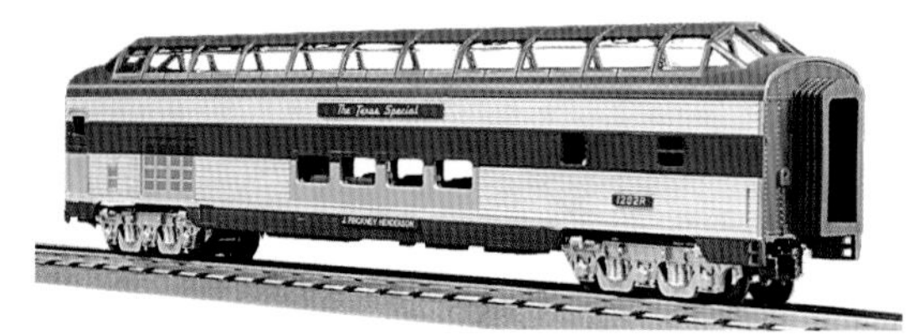

Item No. 20-6729, Car No. 1202R J. Pickney Henderson

70' ABS Full Length Vista Dome Ribbed
Southern Pacific

1999 Volume 1
June 1999

Item No. 20-6717, Car No. 3605

70' ABS Full Length Vista Dome Ribbed
Florida East Coast

2000 Volume 2
August 2000

Item No. 20-6750, Car Name Key Largo

70' ABS Full Length Vista Dome Ribbed
Wabash

2000 Volume 2
August 2000

Item No. 20-6746, Car Name Blue Star

70' ABS Full Length Vista Dome Ribbed
Canadian Pacific

2000 Volume 2 - Premier
August 2000

Item No. 20-6747, Car No. Skyline 517

70' ABS Full Length Vista Dome Ribbed
Santa Fe

2000 Volume 2
August 2000

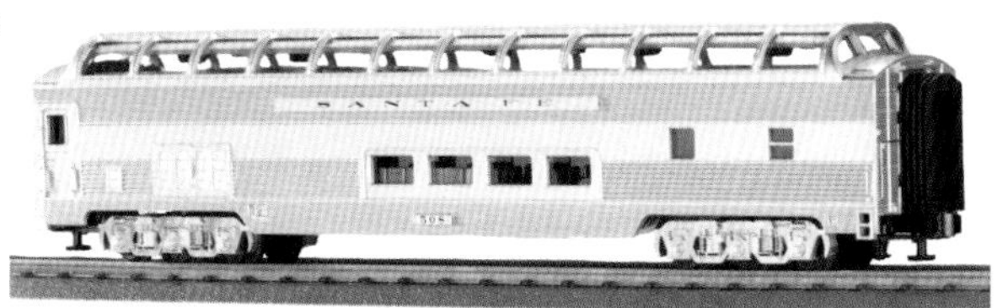
Item No. 20-6743, Car No. 508

70' ABS Full Length Vista Dome Ribbed
Amtrak

2000 Volume 2 - Premier
August 2000
$59.95

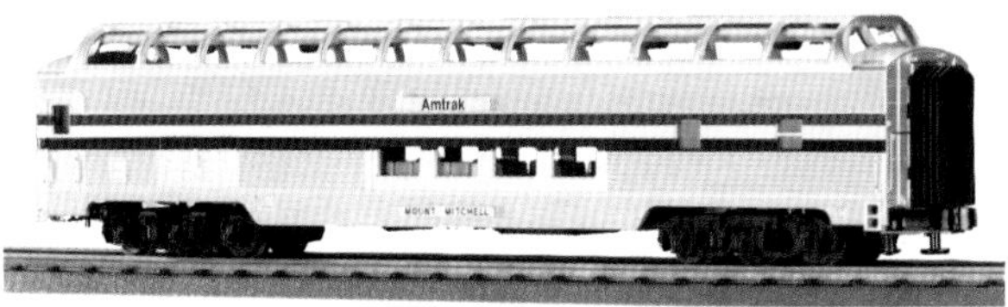

Item No. 20-6737, Car No. 9302

70' ABS Full Length Vista Dome Ribbed
Chessie

2000 Volume 2
August 2000

Item No. 20-6749, Car No. 1852

70' ABS Full Length Vista Dome Ribbed
California Zephyr

2000 Volume 2 - Premier
August 2000
$59.95

Item No. 20-6745, Car No. 12

70' ABS Full Length Vista Dome Smooth
Alaska

1999 Volume 2
November 1999

Item No. 20-6718 Car No. 506

70' ABS Full Length Vista Dome Smooth
Southern Pacific

1999 Volume 2 - Berkshire
November 1999
$59.95

Item No. 20-6719, Car No. 3606

70' ABS Full Length Vista Dome Smooth
Kansas City Southern

2000 Volume 1
March 2000

Item No. 20-6735, Car Name Kaysee

70' ABS Full Length Vista Dome Smooth
Electro Motive Division

2000 Volume 1 - Premier
March 2000
$59.95

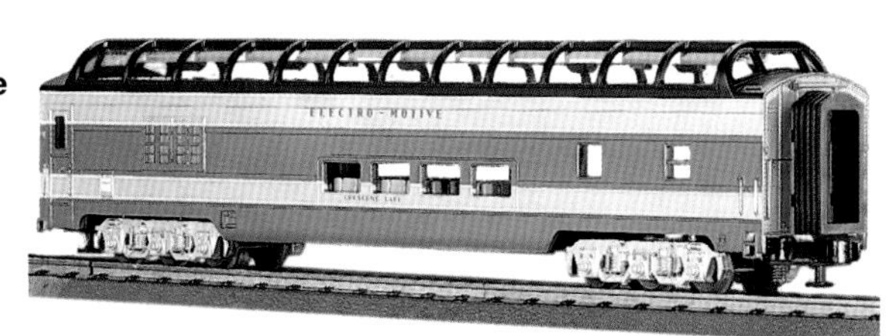
Item No. 20-6734, Car Name Crescent Lake

70' ABS Full Length Vista Dome Smooth
Union Pacific

2000 Volume 1
March 2000

Item No. 20-6738, Car Name City of Denver

70' ABS Full Length Vista Dome Smooth
Milwaukee Road

2000 Volume 1 - Premier
September 2000

Item No. 20-6752, Car Name Super Dome

70' ABS Full Length Vista Dome Smooth
Union Pacific

2000 Volume 1
September 2000

Item No. 20-6753, Car No. 55

70' ABS Full Length Vista Dome Smooth
Illinois Central

2000 Volume 1
November 2000

Item No. 20-6761, Car Name Delta View

70' ABS Full Length Vista Dome Smooth
Erie

2000 Volume 1
September 2000

Item No. 20-6760, Car Name American Vista

70' ABS Full Length Vista Dome Smooth
Great Northern

2000 Volume 2
September 2000

Item No. 20-6751, Car No. 1394 Prairie View

70' ABS Passenger Coach Ribbed
New Haven

1999 Volume 1
April 1999

Item No. 20-6525, Car No. 8701

SuperLiner Transition Sleeper Car
Amtrak

1999 Volume 3
April 2000

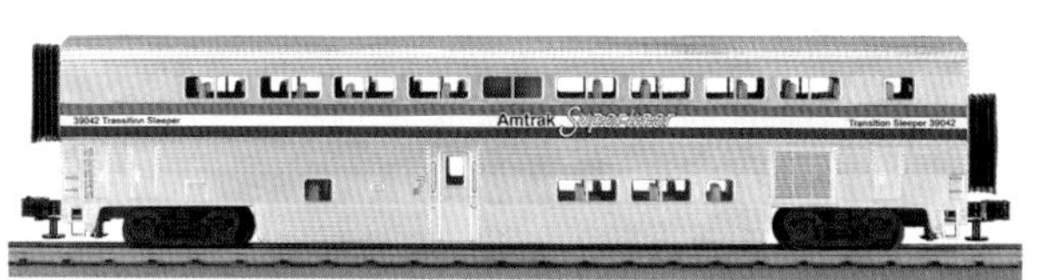

Item No. 20-6540, Car No. 39042

SuperLiner Transitional Sleeper Car
Amtrak

1999 Volume 3
April 2000

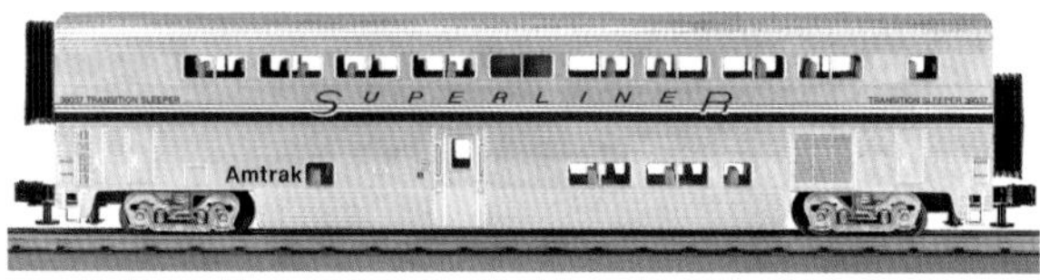

Item No. 20-6542, Car No. 39037

2-Car 60' Sleeper/Diner Aluminum *(photo not available)*
California Zephyr
Item No. 20-6104, Car Names, Silver Aspen, Silver Banquet

Fall/Winter 1996
January 1997

2-Car 60' Sleeper/Diner Aluminum *(photo not available)*
Baltimore & Ohio
Item No. 20-6112, Car Names, Monocacy, 1078

Fall/Winter 1996
January 1997

2-Car 70' Madison Combine/Diner *(photo not available)*
Baltimore & Ohio
Item No. 20-4101, Car No. Not Available

Winter 1995
November 1995

2-Car 60' Sleeper/Diner Aluminum *(photo not available)*
Florida East Coast
Item No. 20-6105, Car Names, Salvador, Fort Matanza

Fall/Winter 1996
January 1997

2-Car 70' Aluminum Sleeper/Diner - Plated *(photo not available)*
New York Central
Item No. 20-6609, Car Name Pringle House

Spring 1997
May 1997

2-Car 70' Madison Combine/Diner *(photo not available)*
Denver & Rio Grande
Item No. 20-4102, Car No. Not Available

Winter 1995
November 1995

2-Car 70' Madison Combine/Diner *(photo not available)*
New York Central
Item No. 20-4105, Car Nos. Not Available

Winter 1995
November 1995

4-Car 60' Aluminum *(photo not available)*
Pennsylvania
Item No. 20-6017, Car Nos. REA 9171, Colonial Flags, Colonial Arms, Alexander Johnston Cassatt

Fall/Winter 1996
September 1996

4-Car Amfleet Passenger *(photo not available)*
Mass Bay
Item No. 20-6522, Car Nos. 1003, 1005, 1010, 2007

1998 Volume 1
July 1998

5-Car 60' Aluminum *(photo not available)*
Union Pacific
Item No. 20-6001, Car Nos. U.S. Mail 5701, National Shores, National Border, Star Dust, Ogallala

15th Anniversary
March 1995

5-Car 60' Aluminum *(photo not available)*
Rio Grande
Item No. 20-6002, Car Nos. REA 1019, Utah, Mount Massive, California, Kansas

15th Anniversary
March 1995

5-Car 60' Aluminum *(photo not available)*
Pennsylvania
Item No. 20-6003, Car Nos. REA 9171, Colonial Houses 7152, Colonial Flags 7150, Colonial Arms 7151, Alexander Johnston Cassatt 8424

15th Anniversary
March 1995

5-Car 60' Aluminum *(photo not available)*
California Zephyr
Item No. 20-6004, Car Nos. REA Silver Buffalo, Silver Dollar, Silver Palace, Silver Club, Silver Penthouse

15th Anniversary
February 1995

5-Car 60' Aluminum *(photo not available)*
Florida East Coast
Item No. 20-6005, Car Nos. REA 501, Eau Gallie, Delroy Beach, South Bay, Hobe Sound

15th Anniversary
March 1995

5-Car 60' Aluminum *(photo not available)*
Delaware & Hudson
Item No. 20-6006, Car Nos. REA 56, Essex County 206, Lake George 204, Bluff Point 36, Night Harbor 200

15th Anniversary
March 1995

5-Car 60' Aluminum *(photo not available)*
Pennsylvania
Item No. 20-6007, Car Nos. REA 9325, Johns Hopkins, Matthias W. Baldwin, Casimir Pulaski, General Lafayette

15th Anniversary
February 1995

5-Car 60' Aluminum *(photo not available)*
ATSF
Item No. 20-6009, Car Nos. REA 3451, Tuba, Polacca, 503, Vista Cavern

15th Anniversary
February 1995

5-Car 60' Aluminum *(photo not available)*
New York Central
Item No. 20-6010, Car Nos. 9100, Ashtabula County, Elkhart County, Dutchess County, Sandy Creek 10634

15th Anniversary
March 1995

5-Car 60' Aluminum *(photo not available)*
Canadian Pacific
Item No. 20-6011, Car Nos. REA 3008, Wolfe Manor, Dawson Manor, Christie Manor, Waterton Park

15th Anniversary
February 1995

5-Car 60' Aluminum *(photo not available)*
Baltimore & Ohio
Item No. 20-6012, Car Nos. REA 1302, Mahoning, Cacapon, High Dome, Washington

15th Anniversary
April 1995

5-Car 60' Aluminum *(photo not available)*
New York Central
Item No. 20-6013, Car Nos. Not Available

Spring 1996
May 1998

5-Car 60' Aluminum *(photo not available)*
Union Pacific
Item No. 20-6015, Car Nos. Not Available
Item No. 20-6019, Car Nos. Not Available

Spring 1996
May 1996

5-Car 70' Madison *(photo not available)*
Baltimore & Ohio
Item No. 20-4001, Car Nos. Not Available

Winter 1994
December 1994

5-Car 70' Madison *(photo not available)*
Denver & Rio Grande
Item No. 20-4003, Car Nos. Not Available

15th Anniversary
December 1994

5-Car 70' Madison *(photo not available)*
Norfolk & Western
Item No. 20-4004, Car Nos. 330 , 513 , 610 , 512 , 582.

15th Anniversary
December 1994

5-Car 70' Madison *(photo not available)*
New York Central
Item No. 20-4005, Car Nos. Not Available

15th Anniversary
November 1995

5-Car 70' Madison *(photo not available)*
Southern
Item No. 20-4008, Car Nos. 6200, Robert F. Hoke, Henry W. Grady, William Rufus King, Joel Chandler Harris

15th Anniversary
November 1995

5-Car 70' Madison *(photo not available)*
Union Pacific
Item No. 20-4011, Car Nos. Not Available

15th Anniversary
December 1994

5-Car 70' Madison *(photo not available)*
Central of New Jersey
Item No. 20-4012, Car Nos. Not Available

15th Anniversary
November 1995

5-Car 70' Madison *(photo not available)*
Northern Pacific
Item No. 20-4014, Car Nos. Not Available

Winter 1995
November 1995

PREMIER LINE
Specialty Sets

M.T.H. Premier specialty sets are designed to make it easy for O Scale railroaders to assemble long, authentic consists. Among the specialty sets M.T.H. has promoted are a series of six-car freight sets in a variety of roadnames and the popular merger series freight sets. The merger series sets cover the many mergers that America's railroads have been involved in over the years, making available entire family trees and cars from rarely modeled roads. Other sets have featured six identical hoppers or other cars, each numbered differently, so model railroaders can display realistic trains with ease. The wide variety of specialty sets M.T.H. makes available means there is something for everyone. And the freight cars in these sets are of the same durable and detailed construction customers have come to expect from M.T.H. rolling stock.

3-Car Flat Car Set
West Virginia Pulp & Paper Co.

1997 Volume 1
June 1998

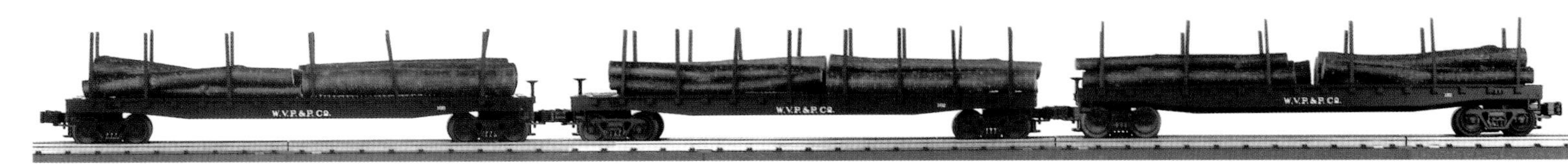

Item No. 20-98103, Car Nos. 162, 169, 176

3-Car Weed Sprayer Set
Union Pacific

2000 Volume 2
November 2000

Item No. 20-2251-1, Cab Car No. 903168, Tankcar Nos. 903097, 903096

4-Bay Hopper 6 Car Set
Union Pacific

1998 Volume 2
August 1998

Item No. 20-97404, Car Nos. 37186, 37275, 37290, 37346, 37415, 37463
Item No. 20-97059, Car Nos. 37451, 37219, 37238, 37222, 37349, 37478
Item No. 20-97060, Car Nos. 37238, 37349, 37451, 37519, 37611, 37714

4-Bay Hopper 6 Car Set
Norfolk & Western

1999 Volume 2
October 1999

Item No. 20-97057, Car Nos. 107701, 107707, 107713, 107719, 107725, 107732
Item No. 20-97061, Car Nos.10357, 10369, 10379, 10391, 10415, 10422
Item No. 20-97062, Car Nos. 11439, 11440, 11450, 11454, 11465, 11510

4-Bay Hopper 6 Car Set
Santa Fe

1999 Volume 2
December 1999

Item No. 20-97058, Car Nos. 81820, 81825, 81830, 81841, 81856, 81870

4-Bay Hopper 6 Car Set
Virginian

2000 Volume 2
September 2000

Item No. 20-97063, Car Nos. 5675, 5680, 5683, 5691, 5694, 5697

5-Car Spline Car Set
T.T.A.X.

1997 Volume 1
May 1998

Item No. 20-95035, Car No.TTAX 79876

5-Car Spline Car Set
Conrail

1998 Volume 2
April 1998

Item No. 20-95036, Car No. TTAX 78359

6-Car Flat Car Set
Hillcrest Lumber Co.

2000 Volume 2
July 2000

Item No. 20-98119, Car Nos. 1, 2, 3, 4, 5, 6
Item No. 20-98120, Car Nos. 7, 8, 9, 10, 11, 12

6-Car Freight Set
Reading

1999 Volume 2
July 1999

Item No. 20-90001, Car No. Steel Caboose 92894, Tank Car 90946, Flat Car with 20' Trailers 9475, Gondola with Junk Load 38709, 4-Bay Hopper with Coal Load 41653, Box Car 110000

6-Car Freight Set
Nickel Plate Road

1999 Volume 2
October 1999

Item No. 20-90002, Car Nos. Bay Window Caboose 714, Tank Car 3842, Flat Car with 20' Trailers 2004, Gondola with Junk Load 44622, 4-Bay Hopper with Coal Load 79559, Box Car 13157

6-Car Freight Set
Pennsylvania

1999 Volume 2
October 1999

Item No. 20-90003, Car Nos. N-8 Caboose 478134, Tank Car 1021, 4-Bay Hopper with Coal Load 673467, Gondola with Junk Load 366103, 50' Box Car 47136, Flat Car with 20' Trailers 470590

6-Car Freight Set
Pennsylvania

1999 Volume 3
March 2000

Item No. 20-90005, Car Nos. N-8 Caboose 478067, Box Car 498736, Crane Car 490904, Flat Car with Freight Trucks 491063, Gondola with Junk Load 620893, Madison Coach (Yellow)

6-Car Freight Set
Great Northern

1999 Volume 3
March 2000

Item No. 20-90006, Car Nos. Steel Caboose X-66, 50' Box Car 36871, Tank Car 100013, Flat Car with 20' Trailers 60207, 3-Bay Cylindrical Hopper 171863, Stock Car 55924

6-Car Freight Set
Conrail

2000 Volume 1
April 2000

Item No.20-90009, Car Nos. Steel Caboose 19662, 50' Double Door Box Car 266878, 4-Bay Hopper with Coal Load 496843, Gondola 585517 with Junk Load, Flat Car with 20' Trailers 718905, PS2 Hopper 876409

6-Car Freight Set
BNSF

2000 Volume 1
February 2000

Item No. 20-90010 Car Nos. Extended Vision Caboose 136118, PS2 Hopper 909085, Gondola with Junk Load 519337, 4-Bay Hopper with Coal Load 263415, Flatcar with 20' Trailers 60114, 50' Double Door Box Car 71414

6-Car Freight Set
Chessie

2000 Volume 1
June 2000

Item No.20-90012 Car Nos. Extended Vision Caboose 3143, Crane Tender 1641, Crane Car 940000, Coil Car with Cover 306910, 4-Bay Hopper with Coal Load 192006, 4-Compartment Tank Car 192903

6-Car Freight Set
Santa Fe

2000 Volume 1
July 2000

Item No. 20-90013, Car Nos. Steel Caboose 999600, 50' Box Car 15776, PS2 Hopper 82297, Coil Car with Cover 91971, Flatcar with 20' Trailers 290543, Tank Car 98501

6-Car Freight Set
Burlington Northern

2000 Volume 1
May 2000

Item No. 20-90014 Car Nos: Extended Vision Caboose 170, 50' Double Door Box Car 376513, 2 Bay Offset Hopper with Coal Load 516147, Flat Car with 20' Trailers 961050, Center I Beam Flat Car 624216, 20K 4-Compartment Tank Car FT21

6-Car Freight Set
Chesapeake & Ohio

2000 Volume 1
April 2000

Item No. 20-90015, Car Nos. Steel Caboose 903328, PS2 Hopper 2230, Gondola with Junk Load 31709, 2 Bay Offset Hopper with Coal Load 58546, Flat Car with 20' Trailers 81315, Box Car 15153

6-Car Freight Set
Chicago NorthWestern

2000 Volume 1
February 2000

Item No. 20-90016, Car Nos. Bay Window Caboose 11190, 50' Box Car 154960, 4-Bay Hopper with Coal Load 471788, Flat Car with 20' Trailers 44237, 3-Bay Cylindrical Hopper 460937, Stock Car 14536

6-Car Freight Set
New York Central

2000 Volume 1
April 2000

Item No. 20-90017, Car Nos. Steel Caboose 18096, Reefer Car 2507, 100 Ton Hopper 885900, Flat Car with 20' Trailers 499388, Tank Car 71071, 50' Double Door Box Car 46190

6-Car Freight Set
Pennsylvania

2000 Volume 1
July 2000

Item No. 20-90018, Car Nos: N5c Caboose 477926, Cylindrical Hopper 260018, Reefer Car 91904, Coil Car with Cover 387031, PS2 Hopper 257128, Double Door Box Plugged Box Car 112116

6-Car Freight Set
CSX

2000 Volume 1
May 2000

Item No.20-90019, Car Nos. Extended Vision Caboose 900242, Gondola with Junk Load 705665, Flat Car with 40' Trailer 400780, Coil Car with Cover 498100, 4-Bay Hopper with Coal Load 3509, Double Door 50' Box Car 500762

6-Car Freight Set
New Haven

2000 Volume 1
March 2000

Item No.20-90020, Car Nos. Steel Caboose, Ps-2 Hopper, Gondola with Junk Load 81072, Crane Car D-100, Box Car 36501, 2 Bay Offset Hopper 81023

6-Car Freight Set
Union Pacific

2000 Volume 2
November 2000

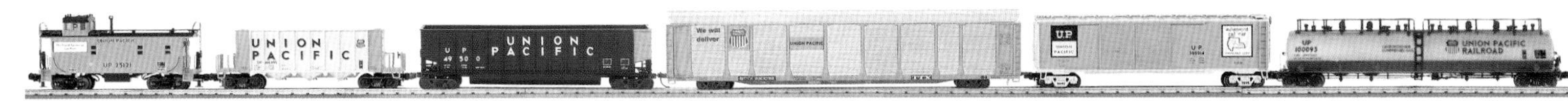

Item No. 20-90022, Car Nos. Steel Caboose Car 25121, Rapid Discharge Hopper Car 106995, Coalporter Hopper Car 49500, Enclosed Auto Carrier Car 930032, 50' Double Door Box Car 300014, 20K Gal. Tank Car 100093

6-Car Freight Set
Union Pacific

2000 Volume 2
November 2000

Item No. 20-90023, Car Nos. 50' Box Car 492161, Tank Car 69713, 100 T Hopper Car 21247, Flat Car with 20' Trailers 57246, Ps-2 Hopper Car 19396, 4-Bay Hopper with Coal Load 37361

6-Car Freight Set
Baltimore & Ohio

2000 Volume 2
October 2000

Item No. 20-90026, Car Nos. Bay Window Caboose C2858, 4-Bay Hopper with Coal Load 125558, Flat with 20' Trailers 9208, Gondola with Junk Load 351198, Tank Car 341512, Box Car 467085

6-Car Freight Set
New Haven

2000 Volume 2
January 2000

Item No. 20-90027, Car Nos. Steel Caboose C-667, Stock Car 23702, Flat w/Bulkheads 19111, Tank Car 30101, 3-Bay Cylindrical Hopper 16018, Box Car 40602

6-Car Freight Set
Great Northern

2000 Volume 2
September 2000

Item No. 20-90028, Car Nos. Extended Vision Caboose X-106, Coil Car with Cover 85139, 4-Bay Cylindrical Hopper 171000, Reefer Car 70598, Gondola with Cover 73818, 50' 2-Door Plugged Box Car 19174

6-Car Freight Set
Canadian National

2000 Volume 2
October 2000

Item No. 20-90029, Car Nos. Extended Vision Caboose 79269, 3-Bay Cylindrical Hopper 386425, Tank Car 26330, Flat Car with Logs 681019, Box Car 535099, Reefer Car 212106

6-Car Freight Set
Lehigh Valley

2000 Volume 2
November 2000

Item No. 20-90030, Car Nos. Steel Caboose 95003, 4-Bay Hopper with Coal Load 25438, 3-Bay Cylindrical Hopper 51102,, Flat Car with 40' Trailer 10038, Gondola with Junk Load 33059, 50' Box Car 8671

6-Car Ore Car Set
DMIR

1999 Volume 1
May 1999

Item No. 20-97505, Car Nos. 30167, 30207, 30222, 30351, 30414, 30475
Item No. 20-97506, Car Nos. 30506, 30626, 30698, 30712, 30819, 30912
Item No. 20-97507, Car Nos. 30277, 30357, 30438, 30520, 30524, 30665

Boxed Set #2 Dash-9 Unit Train
BNSF

1998 Volume 1
August 1998

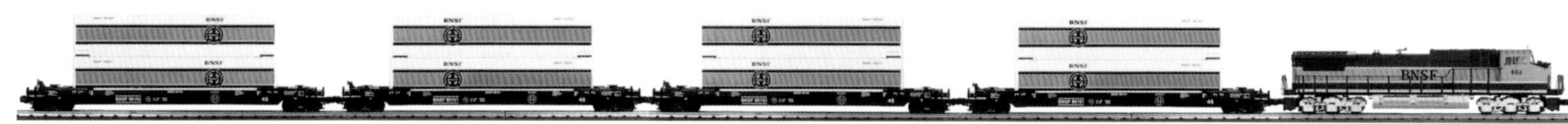

3-Rail with Proto-Sound®, Item No. 20-2179, Engine Cab No. 964, Husky Stacks 60101, 60102, 60103, 60104

El Capitan Boxed Set
Santa Fe

Spring 1997
August 1997

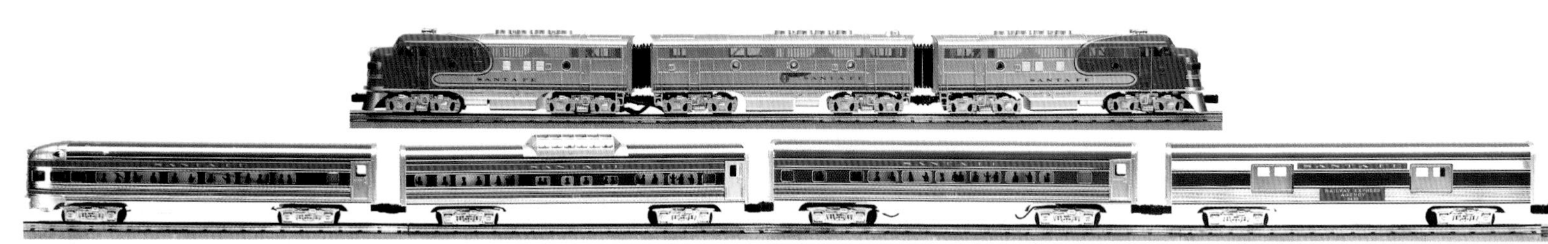

Item No. 20-2153-1, Engine Nos. 18, 19, Car Nos. 500, 3430, 3103, Coconino

EP-5 Electric Engine Boxed Set
New Haven

1999 Volume 1
March 1999

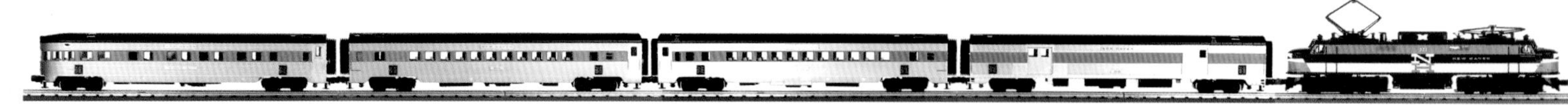

Item No. 20-2197-1, Engine 371, Car Nos. 5581, 8648, 8696, Bunker Hill

Merger Series Freight Car Set
BNSF

1999 Volume 3
March 2000

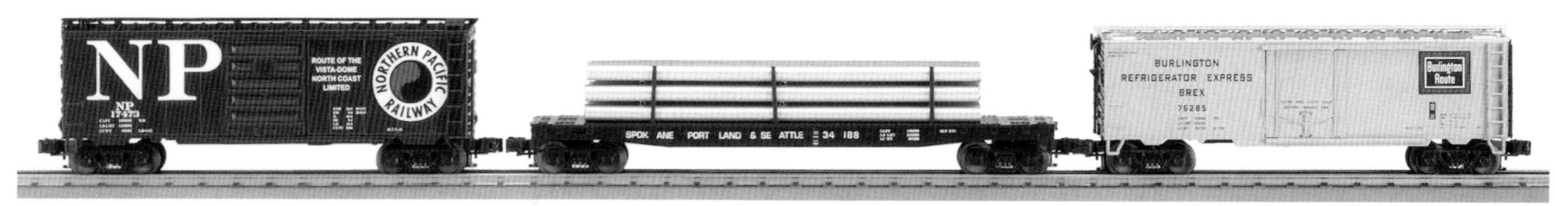

Item No. 20-90007, Car Nos. Northern Pacific Boxcar 17473, Spokane, Portland & Seattle Flat Car with Logs 34188, Burlington Route Reefer Car 76285

Merger Series Freight Car Set
BNSF

2000 Volume 1
March 2000

Item No.20-90021, Car Nos. Colorado & Southern Stock Car 7064, Frisco 2-Bay Offset Hopper 90438, Great Northern 4-Bay Hopper with Coal Load 70458

Merger Series Freight Car Set
BNSF

2000 Volume 2
August 2000

Item No. 20-90025, Car Nos. TP&W Box Car 607, ATSF Tank Car 100271, BN 3-Bay Cylindrical Hopper 445030

Merger Series Freight Car Set
Union Pacific

2000 Volume 2
August 2000

Item No. 20-90008, Car Nos. St. Louis Gateway Route 2-Bay Hopper Car 1196, Corn Belt Route Steel Sided Stock Car 823, Moffat Tunnel Route 4-Bay Hopper Car with Coal Load 34806

PREMIER LINE
Accessories

Premier line accessories provide the final touches necessary to bring realism to any layout: coal and junk loads for hoppers and gondolas and container sets closely modeled on the prototypes. ScaleTrax™ is a revolutionary track system M.T.H. designed to be as close to scale dimensions as possible. Before ScaleTrax, O Gauge three-rail track systems had maintained very similar profiles to the standard that Lionel set decades before. ScaleTrax has a profile much lower than previous three-rail track systems so it approaches closer to actual scale than any have before. O Gauge modelers will no longer have to accept the "tubular" track look that mars an otherwise accurate layout. With the trends showing O scale operators building more scale layouts, this track allows for a level of authenticity three-rail operators have never experienced before.

20' Container Set
20' Container Set

2000 Volume 2
August 2000

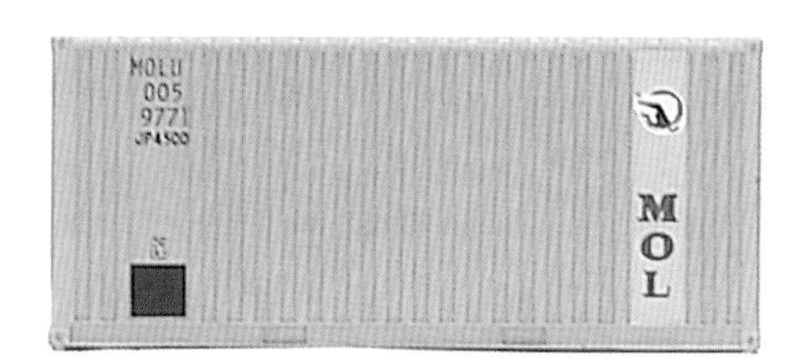

Item No. 20-95037 Mitsui, "K" Line, CP Ships

20' Container Set
20' Container Set

2000 Volume 2
August 2000

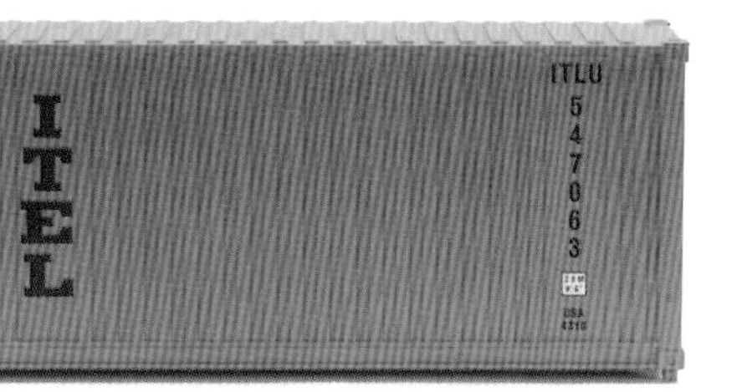

Item No. 20-95041, ITEL, FlexiVan, Evergreen

40' Container Set
40' Container Set

2000 Volume 1
December 1999

Item No. 20-95038, Maersk, Hyundai, Rio Grande

40' Container Set
40' Container Set

2000 Volume 2
August 2000

Item No. 20-95042, Schneider, Hanjin, Santa Fe

48' Container Set
48' Container Set

2000 Volume 1
December 1999

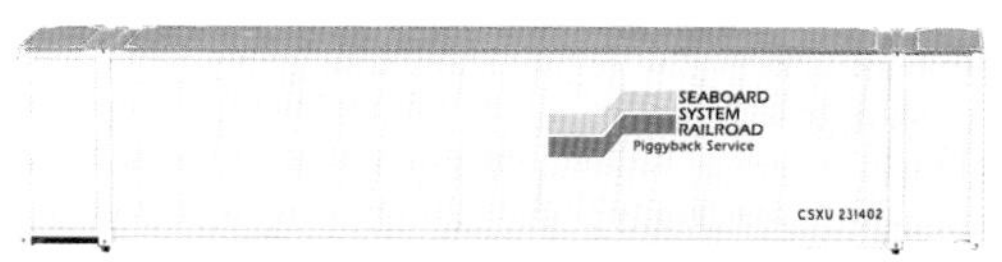

Item No. 20-95039 Seaboard, Transamerica, Burlington Northern

48' Container Set
48' Container Set

2000 Volume 2
August 2000

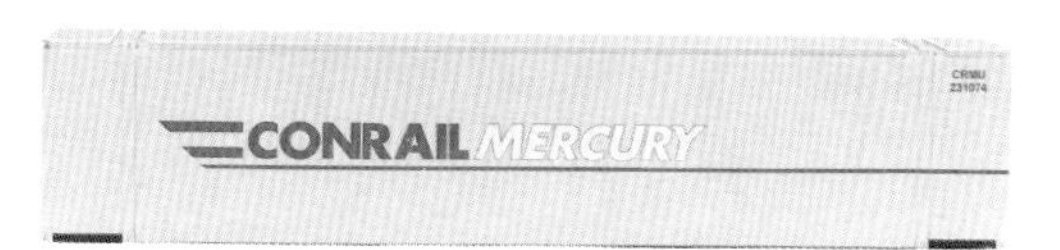

Item No. 20-95043, Conrail, Burlington Northern, KBS

Tank Container Set
Tank Container Set

2000 Volume 1
December 1999

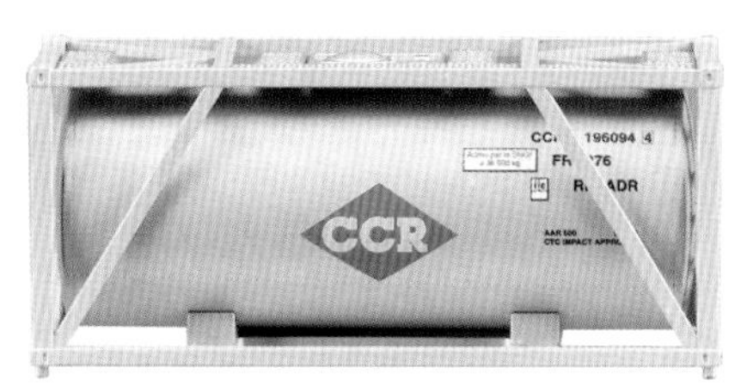

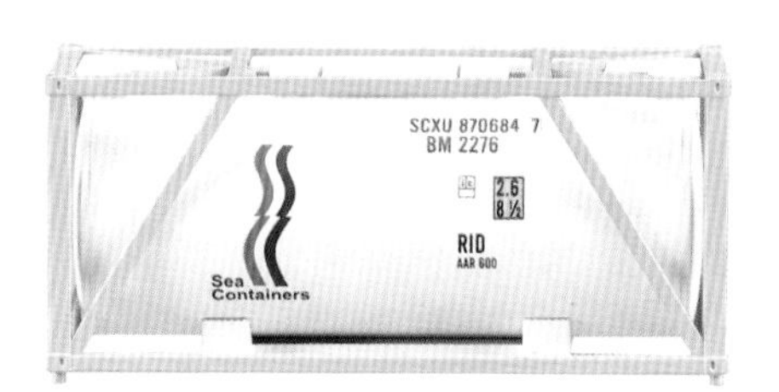

Item No. 20-95040, CCR, Stolt, Sea Container

Tank Container Set
Tank Container Set

2000 Volume 2
August 2000

Item No. 20-95044, Seaco, VanHool, Transamerica

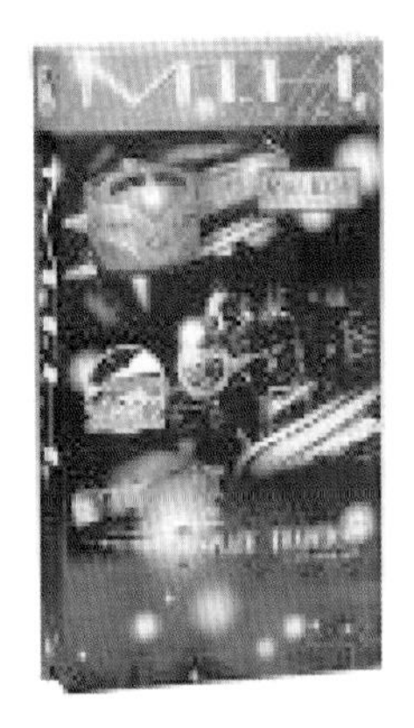

M.T.H. Video History

Item No. 60-1320

Junk Load
Premier

1998 Volume 3
November 1998

Item No. 20-30001

DCS Accessory Interface Unit (AIU)

2000 Volume 2 - Premier
October 2000

Item No. 50-1004

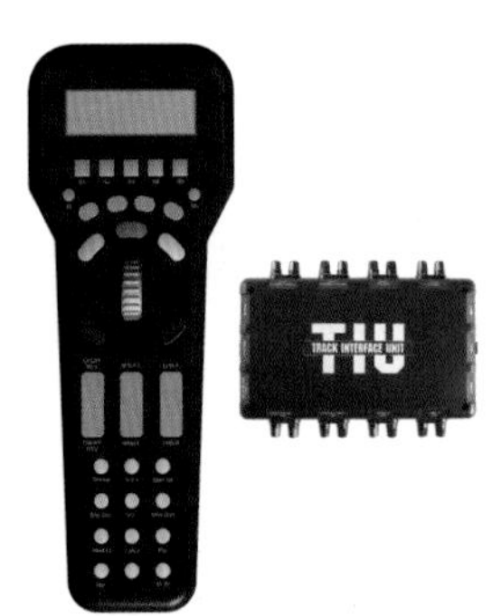

DCS Remote Control Set

2000 Volume 2
October 2000

Item No. 50-1001, Includes (1) DCS Remote Controller and (1) TIU

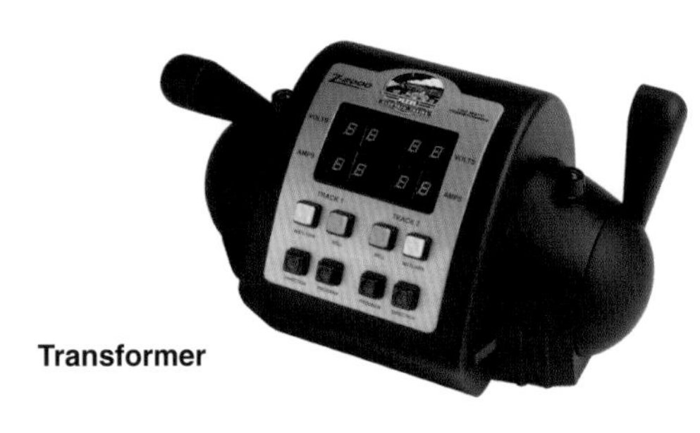

Transformer

Winter 1995
Cancelled

Item No. 20-Z2000, Changed to Z-4000

Z-4000 Remote Commander System

1999 Volume 3
April 2000

Item No. 40-4001, Featuring (1) Z-4000 Remote Controller and (1) Z-4000 Remote Control Receiver

Z-4000 Transformer

1998 Volume 1
November 1998

Item No. 40-4000

DCS Remote Control

2000 Volume 2
October 2000

Item No. 50-1002

DCS Track Interface Unit (TIU)

2000 Volume 2
October 2000

Item No. 50-1003

Z-4000 Remote Commander Receiver

1999 Volume 3
April 2000

Item No. 40-4002

Z-4000 Remote Commander Handheld

1999 Volume 3
April 2000

Item No. 40-4003

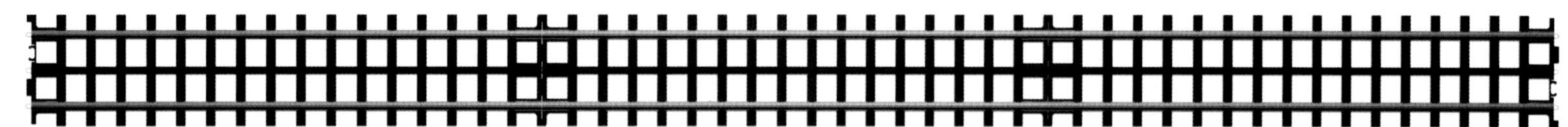

ScaleTrax™ - 1.75" Track Section
Item No. 45-1011

1999 Volume 3
June 2000

ScaleTrax™ - 10" Straight Track Section
Item No. 45-1001

1999 Volume 2
April 2000

ScaleTrax™ - 15" Uncoupling Track Section
Item No. 45-1035

2000 Volume 1
November 2000

ScaleTrax™ - 22.5° Crossover Track
Item No. 45-1015

1999 Volume 3
September 2000

ScaleTrax™ - 30" Flex Track Section
Item No. 45-1049

1999 Volume 2
July 2000

ScaleTrax™ - 30" Straight Track Section
Item No. 45-1019

1999 Volume 2
July 2000

ScaleTrax™ - 4.25" Track Section
Item No. 45-1012

1999 Volume 3
June 2000

ScaleTrax™ - 45° Crossover Track
Item No. 45-1006

1999 Volume 3
September 2000

ScaleTrax™ - 5.0" Track Section
Item No. 45-1013

1999 Volume 3
June 2000

ScaleTrax™ - 5.5" Track Section
Item No. 45-1014

1999 Volume 3
June 2000

ScaleTrax™ - 90° Crossover Track
Item No. 45-1005

1999 Volume 3
October 2000

ScaleTrax™ - Lock-On
Item No. 45-1033

2000 Volume 2
May 2000

ScaleTrax™ - O-31 Curved Track Section
Item No. 45-1002

1999 Volume 3
July 2000

ScaleTrax™ - O-31 Switch (LH)
Item No. 45-1003

1999 Volume 3
July 2000

ScaleTrax™ - O-31 Switch (RH)
Item No. 45-1004

1999 Volume 3
July 2000

ScaleTrax™ - O-54 Curved Track Section
Item No. 45-1007

1999 Volume 3
September 2000

ScaleTrax™ - O-54 Switch (LH)
Item No. 45-1008

1999 Volume 3
October 2000

ScaleTrax™ - O-54 Switch (RH)
Item No. 45-1009

1999 Volume 3
October 2000

ScaleTrax™ - O-72 Curved Track Section
Item No. 45-1010

1999 Volume 2
April 2000

ScaleTrax™ - O-72 Switch (LH)
Item No. 45-1021

1999 Volume 2
June 2000

ScaleTrax™ - O-72 Switch (RH)
Item No. 45-1020

1999 Volume 2
June 2000

ScaleTrax™ - O-80 Curved Track Section
Item No. 45-1034

2000 Volume 1
September 2000

RAILKING LINE

781

RAILKING LINE
INTRODUCTION

M.T.H.'s RailKing® line was introduced in 1995 as a lower-priced alternative to Premier line products. The product line includes steam, diesel, and electric locomotives, freight and passenger cars, Ready-To-Run starter sets, RealTrax track system, accessories, and less expensive electronic equipment such as the Z-500 and -750 transformers and the IR Remote Control System. RailKing items are generally somewhat smaller than ¼" scale - often referred to as "traditionally sized" - so that they can operate on O-31 or even O-27 circles of track. However, RailKing models of small prototypes, such as the 0-8-0 switcher, the PCC car, and the Brill semi-convertible, are made to scale. RailKing products are made for the entry- or mid-level hobbyist who enjoys trains but does not require the precise accuracy of the Premier line or who wishes to spend less money on the models.

RailKing locomotives and powered units are offered in three-rail versions only, and almost all are offered with or without Proto-Sound®. Beginning with the 2000 volume 2 catalog, RailKing products offer a choice between Loco-Sound™ or Proto-Sound® 2.0 with Digital Command System.

RailKing products have a "30-" prefix to distinguish them from Premier items. The suffixes work as follows:
30-1118-0 electronic horn or whistle/beginning with 2000 volume two, Loco-Sound
30-1118-1 Proto-Sound/beginning with 2000 volume two, Proto-Sound 2.0 with DCS
30-1118-3 Calf or B unit

RailKing Ready-To-Run sets are the most complete on the O Gauge market. Buyers get everything they need to get up and running in a single purchase: a sturdy locomotive and set of freight or passenger cars, a powerful transformer, a circle or oval of easy-to-use RealTrax™ snap together track, among other equipment. And unlike many starter sets, Ready-To-Run sets are available with full digital sound systems.

The models in this section are arranged by item type (i.e. F-3 AA sets are all together), then by item name and catalog introductory date. The delivery date is also included. You can also see the indexes, which are organized in the same order as the book's pictures. The indexes also include information on operation (i.e. O-31, O-72, etc.). The item page layouts provide complete information on each item: item type, roadname, the first catalog the item was offered in, the date the item was delivered, item number, and equipment available.

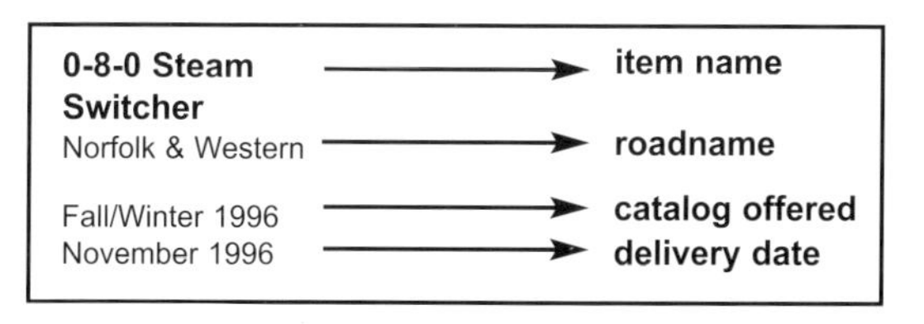

RAILKING LINE
Steam Locomotives

RailKing steam engines are designed to give hobbyists solid, well-crafted steam engines like those they remember from childhood. All RailKing steamers have die-cast boilers/cabs, drivers, frames, and trucks, and most tenders also have die-cast shells, floors, and trucks. Most RailKing steamers are available with optional sound systems, which give them added realism and make them more fun to run. They also boast flywheel-equipped motors, operating smoke units, and many other features that make them an excellent value. Both frames of RailKing articulated locomotives are pivoted, to allow operation on O-31 track. Most short-frame steamers will run on O-27 track. This makes RailKing steam engines the ideal option for people without large layouts. As this book goes to press, RailKing customers have had thirty-four different steam engines and two auxiliary tenders to choose from. M.T.H. believes that everyone who enjoys model railroading should be able to afford a high quality, powerful steam engine, and RailKing makes that dream a reality.

0-8-0 Steam Switcher
Norfolk & Western

Fall/Winter 1996
November 1996

3-Rail with Electronic Whistle, Item No. 30-1111-0, Cab No. 244
3-Rail with Proto-Sound®, Item No. 30-1111-1, Cab No. 244

0-8-0 Steam Switcher
Chicago NorthWestern

Fall/Winter 1996
November 1996

3-Rail with Electronic Whistle, Item No. 30-1112-0, Cab No. 65
3-Rail with Proto-Sound®, Item No. 30-1112-1, Cab No. 65

0-8-0 Steam Switcher
New York Central

1997 Volume 2
December 1997

3-Rail with Electronic Whistle, Item No. 30-1123-0, Cab No. 415
3-Rail with Proto-Sound®, Item No. 30-1123-1, Cab No. 415

0-8-0 Steam Switcher
Northern Pacific

1997 Volume 2
December 1997

3-Rail with Electronic Whistle, Item No. 30-1124-0, Cab No. 1189
3-Rail with Proto-Sound®, Item No. 30-1124-1, Cab No. 1189

2-6-0 Steam Engine
Santa Fe

1998 Volume 2
October 1998

3-Rail with Electronic Whistle, Item No. 30-1136-0, Cab No. 605
3-Rail with Proto-Sound®, Item No. 30-1136-1, Cab No. 605

2-6-0 Steam Engine
Baltimore & Ohio

1998 Volume 2
October 1998

3-Rail with Electronic Whistle, Item No. 30-1137-0, Cab No. 946
3-Rail with Proto-Sound®, Item No. 30-1137-1, Cab No. 946

2-6-0 Steam Engine
Pennsylvania

1999 Volume 2
September 1999

3-Rail with Electronic Whistle, Item No. 30-1148-0, Cab No. 1014
3-Rail with Proto-Sound®, Item No. 30-1148-1, Cab No. 1014

2-6-0 Steam Engine
Union Pacific

1999 Volume 2
September 1999

3-Rail with Electronic Whistle, Item No. 30-1150-0, Cab No. 5646
3-Rail with Proto-Sound®, Item No. 30-1150-1, Cab No. 5646

2-6-6-6 Allegheny Steam Engine
Chesapeake & Ohio

Spring 1997
June 1997

3-Rail with Electronic Whistle, Item No. 30-1116-0, Cab No. 1604
3-Rail with Proto-Sound®, Item No. 30-1116-1, Cab No. 1604

2-8-0 Steam Engine
Pennsylvania

2000 Volume 1
July 2000

3-Rail with Electronic Whistle, Item No. 30-1159-0, Cab No. 9915
3-Rail with Proto-Sound®, Item No. 30-1159-1, Cab No. 9915

2-8-2 L-1 Mikado
Steam Engine
Pennsylvania

2000 Volume 2
November 2000

3-Rail with Proto-Sound® 2.0, Item No. 30-1164-1, Cab No. 1627
3-Rail with Loco-Sound™, Item No. 30-1164-0, Cab No. 1627

2-8-4 Berkshire
Steam Engine
Nickel Plate Road

Summer 1996
October 1996

3-Rail with Electronic Whistle, Item No. 30-1109-0, Cab No. 759

2-8-4 Berkshire
Steam Engine
Erie

Summer 1996
October 1996

3-Rail with Electronic Whistle, Item No. 30-1110-0, Cab No. 3389

2-8-4 Berkshire
Steam Engine
Chesapeake & Ohio

1998 Volume 1
April 1998

3-Rail with Electronic Whistle, Item No. 30-1128-0, Cab No. 2744
3-Rail with Proto-Sound®, Item No. 30-1128-1, Cab No. 2744

2-8-8-2 USRA
Steam Engine
Pennsylvania

2000 Volume 1
May 2000

3-Rail with Electronic Whistle, Item No. 30-1156-0, Cab No. 373
3-Rail with Proto-Sound®, Item No. 30-1156-1, Cab No. 373

2-8-8-2 USRA Steam Engine
Northern Pacific

2000 Volume 1
May 2000

3-Rail with Electronic Whistle, Item No. 30-1157-0, Cab No. 4502
3-Rail with Proto-Sound®, Item No. 30-1157-1, Cab No. 4502

2-8-8-2 Y6b Steam Engine
Norfolk & Western

2000 Volume 2
November 2000

3-Rail with Proto-Sound® 2.0, Item No. 30-1163-1, Cab No. 2195
3-Rail with Loco-Sound™, Item No. 30-1163-0, Cab No. 2195

4-4-0 General Steam Engine
W.A.R.R.-General

1997 Volume 1
December 1997

3-Rail with Electronic Whistle, Item No. 30-1120-0, Cab No. 3
3-Rail with Proto-Sound®, Item No. 30-1120-1, Cab No. 3

4-4-0 General Steam Engine
W.A.R.R. Texas

1998 Volume 2
October 1998

3-Rail with Electronic Whistle, Item No. 30-1135-0, Cab No. 49
3-Rail with Proto-Sound®, Item No. 30-1135-1, Cab No. 49

4-4-0 General Steam Engine
Wild Wild West - Wanderer

1999 Volume 3
November 1999

3-Rail with Electronic Whistle, Item No. 30-1155-0, Cab No. 5
3-Rail with Proto-Sound®, Item No. 30-1155-1, Cab No. 5

4-6-0 Camelback Steam Engine
Reading

1999 Volume 1
June 1999

3-Rail with Electronic Whistle, Item No. 30-1142-0, Cab No. 650
3-Rail with Proto-Sound®, Item No. 30-1142-1, Cab No. 650

4-6-0 Camelback Steam Engine
Jersey Central

1999 Volume 1
June 1999

3-Rail with Electronic Whistle, Item No. 30-1141-0, Cab No. 631
3-Rail with Proto-Sound®, Item No. 30-1141-1, Cab No. 631

4-6-0 Steam Engine
Denver & Rio Grande

1999 Volume 3
June 2000

3-Rail with Electronic Whistle, Item No. 30-1153-0, Cab No. 1331
3-Rail with Proto-Sound®, Item No. 30-1153-1, Cab No. 1331

4-6-0 Steam Engine
Chesapeake & Ohio

1999 Volume 3
June 2000

3-Rail with Electronic Whistle, Item No. 30-1154-0, Cab No. 784
3-Rail with Proto-Sound®, Item No. 30-1154-1, Cab No. 784

4-6-0 Steam Engine
New York Central

2000 Volume 1
June 2000

3-Rail with Electronic Whistle, Item No. 30-1158-0, Cab No. 1244
3-Rail with Proto-Sound®, Item No. 30-1158-1, Cab No. 1244

4-6-0 Ten Wheeler Steam Engine
Denver & Rio Grande

2000 Volume 1
June 2000

3-Rail with Electronic Whistle, Item No. 30-1160-0, Cab No. 781
3-Rail with Proto-Sound®, Item No. 30-1160-1, Cab No. 781

4-6-2 Crusader Steam Engine
Reading

1999 Volume 3
January 2000

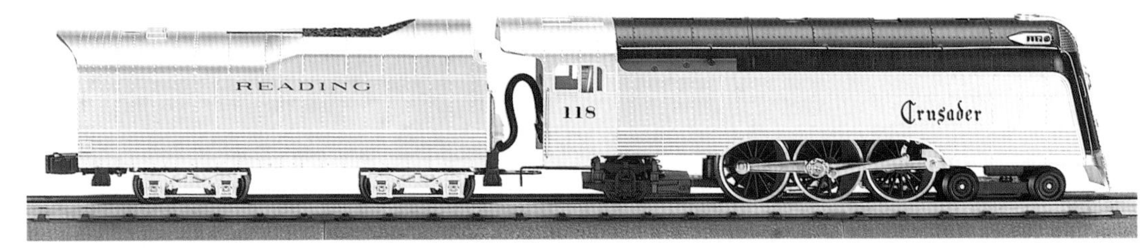

3-Rail with Electronic Whistle, Item No. 30-1152-0, Cab No. 118
3-Rail with Proto-Sound®, Item No. 30-1152-1, Cab No. 118

4-6-2 Forty-Niner Steam Engine
Union Pacific

1998 Volume 3
November 1998

3-Rail with Electronic Whistle, Item No. 30-1139-0, Cab No. 2906
3-Rail with Proto-Sound®, Item No. 30-1139-1, Cab No. 2906

4-6-2 K-4s Pacific Steam Engine
Pennsylvania

Spring 1997
July 1997

3-Rail with Electronic Whistle, Item No. 30-1115-0, Cab No. 1361
3-Rail with Proto-Sound®, Item No. 30-1115-1, Cab No. 1361

4-6-2 K-4s Pacific Steam Engine
Pennsylvania

1998 Volume 3
October 1998

3-Rail with Electronic Whistle, Item No. 30-1138-0, Cab No. 5446
3-Rail with Proto-Sound®, Item No. 30-1138-1, Cab No. 5446
3-Rail with Proto-Sound® 2.0, Item No. 30-1162-1, Cab No. 3761
3-Rail with Loco-Sound™, Item No. 30-1162-0, Cab No. 3761

4-6-2 Pacific
Steam Engine
Denver & Rio Grande

1997 Volume 1
September 1997

3-Rail with Proto-Sound®, Item No. 30-1122-1, Cab No. 809

4-6-2 PS-4
Steam Engine
Southern Crescent

1997 Volume 2
January 1998

3-Rail with Electronic Whistle, Item No. 30-1125-0, Cab No. 1396
3-Rail with Proto-Sound®, Item No. 30-1125-1, Cab No. 1396

4-6-2 Torpedo
Steam Engine
Pennsylvania

1997 Volume 1
June 1997

3-Rail with Electronic Whistle, Item No. 30-1118-0, Cab No. 3768
3-Rail with Proto-Sound®, Item No. 30-1118-1, Cab No. 3768

4-6-4 Commodore Hudson
Steam Engine
New York Central

1998 Volume 2
July 1998

3-Rail with Electronic Whistle, Item No. 30-1133-0, Cab No. 5344
3-Rail with Proto-Sound®, Item No. 30-1133-1, Cab No. 5344

4-6-4 Dreyfuss
Steam Engine
New York Central

Fall/Winter 1996
January 1997

3-Rail with Electronic Whistle, Item No. 30-1113-0, Cab No. 5445
3-Rail with Proto-Sound®, Item No. 30-1113-1, Cab No. 5445

4-6-4 Empire State Express Steam Engine
New York Central

1999 Volume 1
May 1999

3-Rail with Electronic Whistle, Item No. 30-1143-0, Cab No. 5426
3-Rail with Proto-Sound®, Item No. 30-1143-1, Cab No. 5426

4-6-4 Hiawatha Hudson Steamer
Milwaukee Road

1998 Volume 1
June 1998

3-Rail with Electronic Whistle, Item No. 30-1127-0, Cab No. 100
3-Rail with Proto-Sound®, Item No. 30-1127-1, Cab No. 100

4-6-4 Hudson Steam Engine
New York Central

Spring 1996
November 1997

3-Rail with Electronic Whistle, Item No. 30-1103-0, Cab No. 5344
3-Rail with Electronic Whistle, Item No. 30-1121-0, Cab No. 5405
3-Rail with Proto-Sound®, Item No. 30-1121-1, Cab No. 5405
3-Rail with Proto-Sound®, Item No. 30-1146-1, Cab No. 5412

4-6-4 Hudson Steam Engine
Union Pacific

Spring 1996
January 1996

3-Rail with Electronic Whistle, Item No. 30-1104-0, Cab No. 3225

4-6-4 Streamlined Hudson Steam Engine
Wabash

1999 Volume 2
July 1999

3-Rail with Electronic Whistle, Item No. 30-1147-0, Cab No. 702
3-Rail with Proto-Sound®, Item No. 30-1147-1, Cab No. 702

4-6-4 Streamlined Hudson Steam Engine
Chesapeake & Ohio

2000 Volume 1
April 2000

3-Rail with Electronic Whistle, Item No. 30-1161-0, Cab No. 491
3-Rail with Proto-Sound®, Item No. 30-1161-1, Cab No. 491

4-6-6-4 Challenger Steam Engine
Union Pacific

Summer 1996
August 1996

3-Rail with Electronic Whistle, Item No. 30-1107-0, Cab No. 3982

4-6-6-4 Challenger Steam Engine
Union Pacific

Summer 1996
August 1996

3-Rail with Electronic Whistle, Item No. 30-1108-0, Cab No. 3985

4-8-2 L-3 Mohawk Steam Engine
New York Central

Fall 1995
September 1995

3-Rail with Electronic Whistle, Item No. 30-1101-0, Cab No. 3000
3-Rail with Proto-Sound® 2.0, Item No. 30-1165-1, Cab No. 3024
3-Rail with Loco-Sound™, Item No. 30-1165-0, Cab No. 3024

4-8-2 L-3 Mohawk Steam Engine
Santa Fe

Fall 1995
September 1995

3-Rail with Electronic Whistle, Item No. 30-1102-0, Cab No. 3700

4-8-2 L-3 Mohawk Steam Engine
Texas & Pacific

Spring 1997
March 1997

3-Rail with Electronic Whistle, Item No. 30-1114-0, Cab No. 907
3-Rail with Proto-Sound®, Item No. 30-1114-1, Cab No. 907

4-8-2 L-3 Mohawk Steam Engine
New York Ontario & Western

2000 Volume 2
August 2000

3-Rail with Proto-Sound® 2.0, Item No. 30-1166-1, Cab No. 458
3-Rail with Loco-Sound™, Item No. 30-1166-0, Cab No. 458

4-8-4 FEF Northern Steam Engine
Union Pacific

1999 Volume 3
February 2000

3-Rail with Electronic Whistle, Item No. 30-1151-0, Cab No. 838
3-Rail with Proto-Sound®, Item No. 30-1151-1, Cab No. 838

4-8-4 GS-4 Northern Steam Engine
Southern Pacific

1997 Volume 1
August 1997

3-Rail with Electronic Whistle, Item No. 30-1119-0, Cab No. 4449
3-Rail with Proto-Sound®, Item No. 30-1119-1, Cab No. 4449

4-8-4 Gs-4 Northern Steam Engine
Nabisco

Uncataloged Item
August 1997

3-Rail with Electronic Whistle, Item No. 30-1131-0, Cab No. 1998

4-8-4 "J" Northern Steam Engine
Norfolk & Western

Spring 1996
May 1996

3-Rail with Electronic Whistle, Item No. 30-1105-0, Cab No. 611

4-8-4 "J" Northern Steam Engine
Santa Fe

Spring 1996
May 1996

3-Rail with Electronic Whistle, Item No. 30-1106-0, Cab No. 3760

4-8-4 Northern Steam Engine
Santa Fe

1998 Volume 3
March 1999

3-Rail with Electronic Whistle, Item No. 30-1140-0, Cab No. 2926
3-Rail with Proto-Sound®, Item No. 30-1140-1, Cab No. 2926

4-8-8-2 Cab-Forward Steam Engine
Southern Pacific

1999 Volume 1
May 1999

3-Rail with Electronic Whistle, Item No. 30-1144-0, Cab No. 4294
3-Rail with Proto-Sound®, Item No. 30-1144-1, Cab No. 4294

4-8-8-4 Big Boy Steam Engine
Union Pacific

1998 Volume 1
May 1998

3-Rail with Electronic Whistle, Item No. 30-1129-0, Cab No. 4020
3-Rail with Proto-Sound®, Item No. 30-1129-1, Cab No. 4020

6-8-6 Baby Turbine Steam Engine
Pennsylvania

2000 Volume 2
August 2000

3-Rail with Proto-Sound® 2.0, Item No. 30-1167-1, Cab No. 6200
3-Rail with Loco-Sound™, Item No. 30-1167-0, Cab No. 6200
3-Rail with Proto-Sound®, Item No. 20-80002i (2000 DAP), Cab No. 6200

6-8-6 S-2 Turbine Steam Engine
Pennsylvania

1999 Volume 2
May 2000

3-Rail with Electronic Whistle, Item No. 30-1149-0, Cab No. 6200
3-Rail with Proto-Sound®, Item No. 30-1149-1, Cab No. 6200

Auxiliary Fuel Tender
Norfolk & Western

Spring 1997
August 1997

3-Rail, Item No. 30-1117, Cab No. NONE

Auxiliary Fuel Tender
Southern Pacific Daylight

1997 Volume 2
January 1998

3-Rail, Item No. 30-1126, Cab No. NONE

Auxiliary Water Tender II
Union Pacific

1998 Volume 1
July 1998

3-Rail, Item No. 30-1130, Cab No. 2

RAILKING LINE
Diesel and Electric Locomotives

Variety is the hallmark of RailKing products, and the huge selection of diesel and electric locomotives amply demonstrates why. The thirty-two different diesel/electric RailKing locomotives M.T.H. has produced as this book goes to press covers a range including traditional favorites such as F-3s and E-8s but also PCC electric street cars, Doodlebug diesel engines, and the Galloping Goose. Most RailKing diesel and electric engines have sturdy injection-molded ABS plastic bodies and two flywheel-equipped motors. This means they can handle heavy loads and long trains with ease. And like RailKing steamers, almost all RailKing diesels and electrics are available with sound system options. The digital systems such as Proto-Sound®, Loco-Sound™ and Proto-Sound® 2.0 include realistic diesel roar and electric motor sounds, as well as bells and horns. No matter what a person's model railroading interest, RailKing diesel/electric engines can provide something that pleases.

Alco PA AA Diesel Set
Delaware & Hudson

1998 Volume 1
July 1998

3-Rail with Electronic Horn, Item No. 30-2125-0, Cab Nos. 17, 19
3-Rail with Proto-Sound®, Item No. 30-2125-1, Cab Nos. 17, 19

Alco PA AA Diesel Set
Denver & Rio Grande

1998 Volume 1
July 1998

3-Rail with Electronic Horn, Item No. 30-2126-0, Cab Nos. 6003, 6011
3-Rail with Proto-Sound®, Item No. 30-2126-1, Cab Nos. 6003, 6011

Alco PA AA Diesel Set
Santa Fe

1999 Volume 2
October 1999

3-Rail with Electronic Horn, Item No. 30-2150-0, Cab Nos. 64, 69
3-Rail with Proto-Sound®, Item No. 30-2150-1, Cab Nos. 64, 69

Alco PA AA Diesel Set
Southern

1999 Volume 2
October 1999

3-Rail with Electronic Horn, Item No. 30-2151-0, Cab Nos. 6902, 6903
3-Rail with Proto-Sound®, Item No. 30-2151-1, Cab Nos. 6902, 6903

Alco PA AA Diesel Set
Lehigh Valley

2000 Volume 2
October 2000

3-Rail with Proto-Sound® 2.0, Item No. 30-2196-1, Cab Nos. 603, 605
3-Rail with Loco-Sound™, Item No. 30-2196-0, Cab Nos. 603, 605

Alco PA AA Diesel Set
Southern Pacific

2000 Volume 2
October 2000

3-Rail with Proto-Sound® 2.0, Item Nos. 30-2195-1, Cab Nos. 6016, 6014
3-Rail with Loco-Sound™, Item Nos. 30-2195-0, Cab Nos. 6016, 6014

Alco PA ABA Diesel Set
TCA 1999 Convention

Uncataloged Item
September 1999

3-Rail with Proto-Sound®, Item No. 30-2172-1, Cab No. 4599

Alco PA B Unit
Delaware & Hudson

1998 Volume 1
July 1997

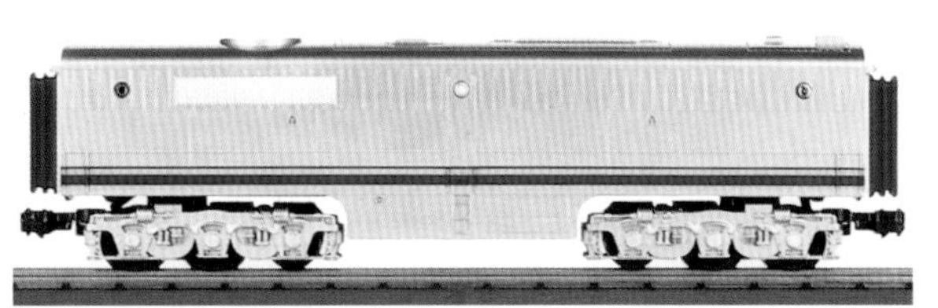

3-Rail, Item No. 30-2127, Cab No. 20

Alco PA B Unit
Denver & Rio Grande

1998 Volume 1
July 1998

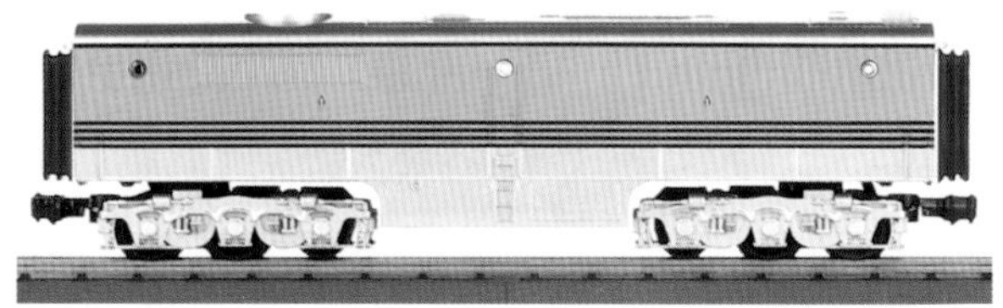

3-Rail, Item No. 30-2128, Cab No. NONE

Alco PA B Unit
Santa Fe

1999 Volume 2
October 1999

3-Rail, Item No. 30-2150-3, Cab No. NONE

Alco PA B Unit
Southern

1999 Volume 2
October 1999

3-Rail, Item No. 30-2151-3, Cab No. NONE

Alco PA B Unit
Southern Pacific

2000 Volume 2
October 2000

3-Rail, Item No. 30-2195-3, Cab No. 5914

Alco PA B Unit
Lehigh Valley

2000 Volume 2
October 2000

3-Rail, Item No. 30-2196-3, Cab No. NONE

Brill Semi-Convertible Trolley
Allentown

2000 Volume 1
March 2000

3-Rail, Item No. 30-2512-0, Cab No. 212
3-Rail with Proto-Sound®, Item No. 30-2512-1, Cab No. 212

Dash-8 Diesel Engine
Norfolk Southern

1997 Volume 1
November 1997

3-Rail with Electronic Horn, Item No. 30-2114-0, Cab No. 8763
3-Rail with Proto-Sound®, Item No. 30-2114-1, Cab No. 8763

Dash-8 Diesel Engine
Santa Fe

1997 Volume 1
November 1997

3-Rail with Electronic Horn, Item No. 30-2115-0, Cab No. 7745
3-Rail with Proto-Sound®, Item No. 30-2115-1, Cab No. 7745

Dash-8 Diesel Engine
Amtrak

Summer 1996
August 1996

3-Rail with Electronic Horn, Item No. 30-2003-0, Cab No. 500

Dash-8 Diesel Engine
Santa Fe

Summer 1996
August 1996

3-Rail with Electronic Horn, Item No. 30-2004-0, Cab No. 560

Dash-8 Diesel Engine
BNSF

1998 Volume 2
September 1998

3-Rail with Electronic Horn, Item No. 30-2129-0, Cab No. 740
3-Rail with Proto-Sound®, Item No. 30-2129-1, Cab No. 740

Dash-8 Diesel Engine
Conrail

1998 Volume 2
September 1998

3-Rail with Electronic Horn, Item No. 30-2136-0, Cab No. 6062
3-Rail with Proto-Sound®, Item No. 30-2136-1, Cab No. 6062

Dash-8 Diesel Engine
Chicago NorthWestern

1999 Volume 2
September 1999

3-Rail with Electronic Horn, Item No. 30-2155-0, Cab No. 8651
3-Rail with Proto-Sound®, Item No. 30-2155-1, Cab No. 8651

Doodlebug Diesel Engine
Baltimore & Ohio

1998 Volume 2
November 1998

3-Rail with Electronic Horn, Item No. 30-2134-0, Cab No. 6005
3-Rail with Proto-Sound®, Item No. 30-2134-1, Cab No. 6005

Doodlebug Diesel Engine
Santa Fe

1998 Volume 2
November 1998

3-Rail with Electronic Horn, Item No. 30-2135-0, Cab No. M.131
3-Rail with Proto-Sound®, Item No. 30-2135-1, Cab No. M.131

Doodlebug Diesel Engine
Chicago NorthWestern

1999 Volume 2
October 1999

3-Rail with Electronic Horn, Item No. 30-2159-0, Cab No. 9923
3-Rail with Proto-Sound®, Item No. 30-2159-1, Cab No. 9923

Doodlebug Diesel Engine
Pennsylvania

1999 Volume 2
October 1999

3-Rail with Electronic Horn, Item No. 30-2158-0, Cab No. 4666
3-Rail with Proto-Sound®, Item No. 30-2158-1, Cab No. 4666

Doodlebug Diesel Engine
Boston & Maine

2000 Volume 2
August 2000

3-Rail with Proto-Sound® 2.0, Item No. 30-2190-1, Cab No. 181
3-Rail with Loco-Sound™, Item No. 30-2190-0, Cab No. 181

Doodlebug Diesel Engine
Union Pacific

2000 Volume 2
August 2000

3-Rail with Proto-Sound® 2.0, Item No. 30-2191-1, Cab No. M-32
3-Rail with Loco-Sound™, Item No. 30-2191-0, Cab No. M-32

Doodlebug Non-Powered Diesel Engine
Baltimore & Ohio

2000 Volume 1
February 2000

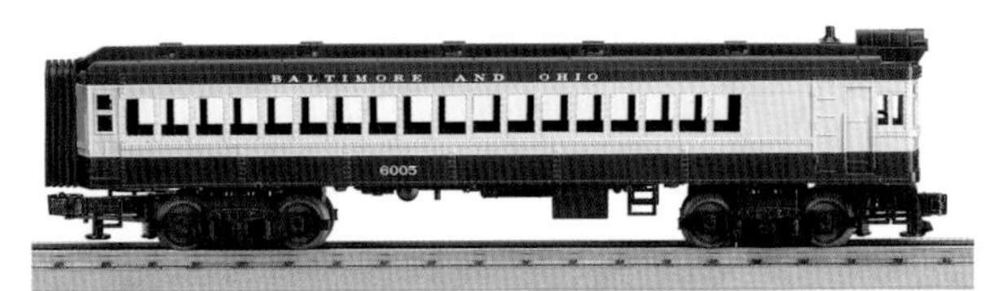

3-Rail, Item No. 30-2134-3, Cab No. 6015

Doodlebug Non-Powered Diesel Engine
Santa Fe

2000 Volume 1
February 2000

3-Rail, Item No. 30-2135-3, Cab No. M.132

Doodlebug Non-Powered Diesel Engine
Pennsylvania

2000 Volume 1
February 2000

3-Rail, Item No. 30-2158-3, Cab No. 4667

Doodlebug Non-Powered Diesel Engine
Chicago NorthWestern

2000 Volume 1
February 2000

3-Rail, Item No. 30-2159-3, Cab No. 9924

E-8 AA Diesel Engine Set
New York Central

1999 Volume 1
May 1999

3-Rail with Electronic Horn, Item Nos. 30-2140-0, Cab Nos. 4045, 4084
3-Rail with Proto-Sound®, Item Nos. 30-2140-1, Cab Nos. 4045, 4084

E-8 AA Diesel Engine Set
Southern Pacific

1999 Volume 1
May 1999

3-Rail with Electronic Horn, Item No. 30-2141-0, Cab Nos. 6018, 6048
3-Rail with Proto-Sound®, Item No. 30-2141-1, Cab Nos. 6018, 6048

E-8 AA Diesel Engine Set
Union Pacific

2000 Volume 1
June 2000

3-Rail with Electronic Horn, Item Nos. 30-2180-0, Cab Nos. 927A, 928A
3-Rail with Proto-Sound®, Item Nos. 30-2180-1, Cab Nos. 927A, 928A

E-8 AA Diesel Engine Set
Seaboard

2000 Volume 1
June 2000

3-Rail with Electronic Horn, Item Nos. 30-2181-0, Cab Nos. 3053, 3054
3-Rail with Proto-Sound®, Item Nos. 30-2181-1, Cab Nos. 3053, 3054

E-8 AA Diesel Engine Set
Rock Island

2000 Volume 1
June 2000

3-Rail with Electronic Horn, Item Nos. 30-2187-0, Cab Nos. 643, 646
3-Rail with Proto-Sound®, Item Nos. 30-2187-1, Cab Nos. 643, 646

E-8 B-Unit Diesel Engine
New York Central - Lightning

1999 Volume 1
May 1999

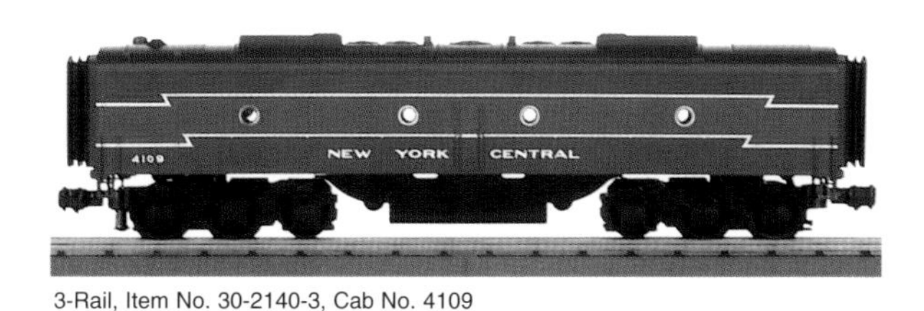

3-Rail, Item No. 30-2140-3, Cab No. 4109

E-8 B-Unit Diesel Engine
Southern Pacific

1999 Volume 1
May 1999

3-Rail, Item No. 30-2141-3, Cab No. 6002-B

E-8 B-Unit Diesel Engine
Union Pacific

2000 Volume 1
June 2000

3-Rail, Item No. 30-2180-3, Cab No. 927B

E-8 B-Unit Diesel Engine
Seaboard

2000 Volume 1
June 2000

3-Rail, Item No. 30-2181-3, Cab No. 3106

E-8 B-Unit Diesel Engine
Rock Island

2000 Volume 1
June 2000

3-Rail, Item No. 30-2187-3, Cab No. NONE

EP-5 Electric Engine
New Haven

1999 Volume 3
March 2000

3-Rail with Electronic Horn, Item No. 30-2170-0, Cab No. 377
3-Rail with Proto-Sound®, Item No. 30-2170-1, Cab No. 377

EP-5 Electric Engine
Great Northern

1999 Volume 3
March 2000

3-Rail with Electronic Horn, Item No. 30-2171-0, Cab No. 2356
3-Rail with Proto-Sound®, Item No. 30-2171-1, Cab No. 2356

F-3 A Unit - Non-Powered
Chessie

1997 Volume 2
November 1997

3-Rail, Item No. 30-2119, Cab No. 4321

F-3 A Unit - Non-Powered
Santa Fe

1998 Volume 2
November 1998

3-Rail, Item No. 30-2137, Cab No. 17

F-3 AA Diesel Set
Union Pacific

Summer 1996
March 1996

3-Rail with Electronic Horn, Item No. 30-2002-0, Cab Nos. 900, 901

F-3 AA Diesel Set
Western Pacific

Spring 1997
February 1997

3-Rail with Electronic Horn, Item No. 30-2008-0, Cab Nos. 301, 302
3-Rail with Proto-Sound®, Item No. 30-2008-1, Cab Nos. 301, 302

F-3 AA Diesel Set
New York Central

1998 Volume 1
March 1998

3-Rail with Electronic Horn, Item No. 30-2001-0, Cab Nos. 1606, 1607

F-3 AA Diesel Set
Florida East Coast

1998 Volume 1
February 1997

3-Rail with Electronic Horn, Item No. 30-2007-0, Cab Nos. 503, 504
3-Rail with Proto-Sound®, Item No. 30-2007-1, Cab Nos. 503, 504

F-3 AA Diesel Set
Pennsylvania

1998 Volume 2
September 1998

3-Rail with Electronic Horn, Item No. 30-2130-0, Cab Nos. 9505, 9507
3-Rail with Proto-Sound®, Item No. 30-2130-1, Cab Nos. 9505, 9507

F-3 AA Diesel Set
Santa Fe

1998 Volume 2
September 1998

3-Rail with Electronic Horn, Item No. 30-2131-0, Cab Nos. 16, 17
3-Rail with Proto-Sound®, Item No. 30-2131-1, Cab Nos. 16, 17

F-3 AA Diesel Set
Electro Motive Division

1999 Volume 1
June 1999

3-Rail with Electronic Horn, Item No. 30-2142-0, Cab Nos. 291, 292
3-Rail with Proto-Sound®, Item No. 30-2142-1, Cab Nos. 291, 292

F-3 AA Diesel Set
Baltimore & Ohio

1999 Volume 1
June 1999

3-Rail with Electronic Horn, Item No. 30-2143-0, Cab Nos. 951, 956
3-Rail with Proto-Sound®, Item No. 30-2143-1, Cab Nos. 951, 956

F-3 AA Diesel Set
Denver & Rio Grande

2000 Volume 1
July 2000

3-Rail with Electronic Horn, Item No. 30-2184-0, Cab Nos. 5623, 5624
3-Rail with Proto-Sound®, Item No. 30-2184-1, Cab Nos. 5623, 5624

F-3 AA Diesel Set
Chesapeake & Ohio

2000 Volume 1
July 2000

3-Rail with Electronic Horn, Item No. 30-2185-0, Cab Nos. 8006, 8007
3-Rail with Proto-Sound®, Item No. 30-2185-1, Cab Nos. 8006, 8007

F-3 B Unit
New York Central

Spring 1997
May 1997

3-Rail, Item No. 30-2010-3, Cab No. 2404

F-3 B Unit
Union Pacific

Spring 1997
May 1997

3-Rail, Item No. 30-2011-3, Cab No. 905

F-3 B Unit
Florida East Coast

Spring 1997
May 1997

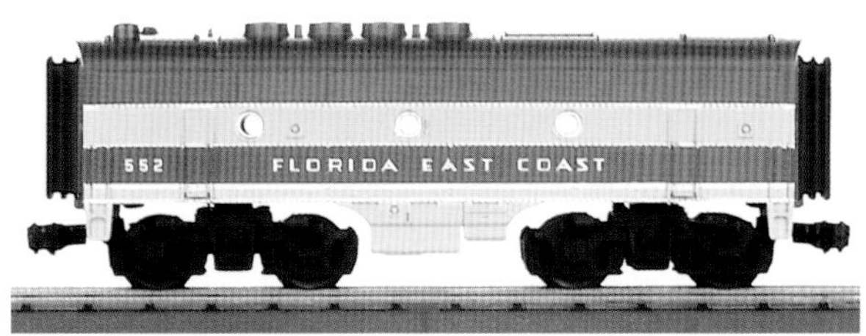

3-Rail, Item No. 30-2012-3, Cab No. 552

F-3 B Unit
Western Pacific

Spring 1997
May 1997

3-Rail, Item No. 30-2013-3, Cab No. NONE

F-3 B Unit
Pennsylvania

1998 Volume 2
November 1998

3-Rail, Item No. 30-2132, Cab No. NONE

F-3 B Unit
Santa Fe

1998 Volume 2
November 1998

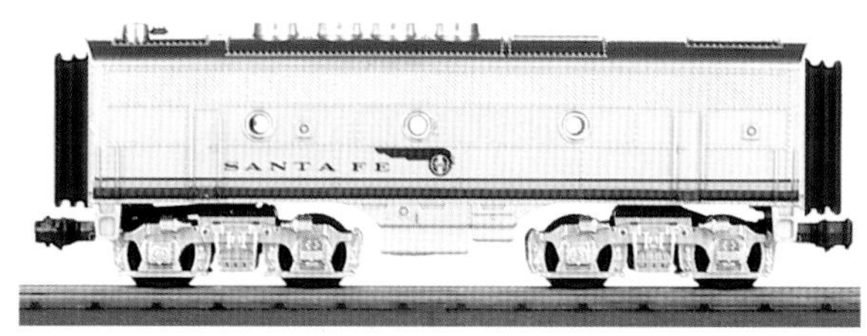

3-Rail, Item No. 30-2133, Cab No. NONE

F-3 B Unit
Electro Motive Division

1999 Volume 1
June 1999

3-Rail, Item No. 30-2142-3, Cab No. NONE

F-3 B Unit
Baltimore & Ohio

1999 Volume 1
June 1999

3-Rail, Item No. 30-2143-3, Cab No. NONE

F-3 B Unit
Denver & Rio Grande

2000 Volume 1
July 2000

3-Rail, Item No. 30-2184-3, Cab No. NONE

F-3 B Unit
Chesapeake & Ohio

2000 Volume 1
July 2000

3-Rail, Item No. 30-2185-3, Cab No. 8503

F40PH Diesel Engine
Caltrain

2000 Volume 2
September 2000

3-Rail with Proto-Sound® 2.0, Item No. 30-2199-1, Cab No. 901
3-Rail with Loco-Sound™, Item No. 30-2199-0, Cab No. 901

FA-2 AA Diesel Set
Pennsylvania

2000 Volume 1
April 2000

3-Rail with Electronic Horn, Item No. 30-2173-0, Cab Nos. 9618, 9619
3-Rail with Proto-Sound®, Item No. 30-2173-1, Cab Nos. 9618, 9619

FA-2 AA Diesel Set
Baltimore & Ohio

2000 Volume 1
April 2000

3-Rail with Electronic Horn, Item No. 30-2174-0, Cab Nos. 4003, 4004
3-Rail with Proto-Sound®, Item No. 30-2174-1, Cab Nos. 4003, 4004

FA-2 B Unit
Pennsylvania

2000 Volume 1
April 2000

3-Rail, Item No. 30-2173-3, Cab No. 9618B

FA-2 B Unit
Baltimore & Ohio

2000 Volume 1
April 2000

3-Rail, Item No. 30-2174-3, Cab No. 9618B

Galloping Goose Diesel
Rio Grande Southern

1999 Volume 2
September 1999

3-Rail with Electronic Horn, Item No. 30-2154-0, Cab No. 5
3-Rail with Proto-Sound®, Item No. 30-2154-1, Cab No. 5

Galloping Goose Diesel
Denver & Rio Grande

2000 Volume 2
August 2000

3-Rail with Proto-Sound®, Item No. 30-2203-1, Cab No. 6

Gas Turbine Diesel Engine
Union Pacific

Spring 1997
May 1997

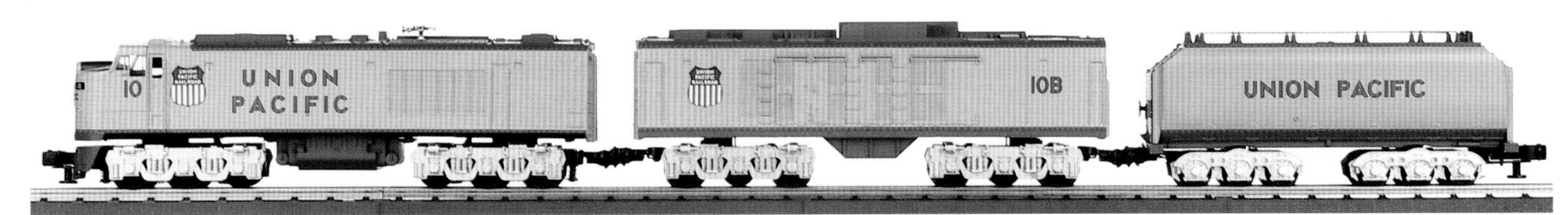

3-Rail with Electronic Horn, Item No. 30-2009-0, Cab Nos. 10, 10B
3-Rail with Proto-Sound®, Item No. 30-2009-1, Cab Nos. 10, 10B

Genesis Diesel
Amtrak

1999 Volume 2
August 1999

3-Rail with Electronic Horn, Item No. 30-2160-0, Cab No. 805
3-Rail with Proto-Sound®, Item No. 30-2160-1, Cab No. 805

GG-1 Electric Engine
Pennsylvania

Fall 1995
April 1995

3-Rail with Electronic Horn, Item No. 30-5100-0, Cab No. 4811

GG-1 Electric Engine
Pennsylvania

Fall 1995
April 1995

3-Rail with Electronic Horn, Item No. 30-2501-0, Cab No. 4929
3-Rail with Electronic Horn, Item No. 30-2507-0, Cab No. 4916
3-Rail with Electronic Horn, Item No. 30-5101-0, Cab No. 4876

GG-1 Electric Engine
Pennsylvania

Fall 1995
April 1995

3-Rail with Electronic Horn, Item No. 30-5102-0, Cab No. 4829

GG-1 Electric Engine
Pennsylvania

Fall 1995
April 1995

3-Rail with Electronic Horn, Item No. 30-5103-0, Cab No. 4899

GG-1 Electric Engine
Pennsylvania

Fall 1995
April 1995

3-Rail with Electronic Horn, Item No. 30-5104-0, Cab No. 4872

GG-1 Electric Engine
Pennsylvania

Fall 1995
April 1995

3-Rail with Electronic Horn, Item No. 30-2500-0, Cab No. 4935
3-Rail with Electronic Horn, Item No. 30-2506-0, Cab No. 4824
3-Rail with Electronic Horn, Item No. 30-5105-0, Cab No. 4935

GG-1 Electric Engine
Amtrak

Summer 1996
August 1996

3-Rail with Electronic Horn, Item No. 30-2502-0, Cab No. 926

GG-1 Electric Engine
Pennsylvania

2000 Volume 1
September 2000

3-Rail with Electronic Horn, Item No. 30-2514-0, Cab No. 2000

GG-1 Electric Engine
Pennsylvania

2000 Volume 2
August 2000

3-Rail with Proto-Sound® 2.0, Item No. 30-2515-1, Cab No. 4812
3-Rail with Loco-Sound™, Item No. 30-2515-0, Cab No. 4812

GG-1 Electric Engine
Conrail

2000 Volume 2
August 2000

3-Rail with Proto-Sound® 2.0, Item No. 30-2516-1, Cab No. 4859
3-Rail with Loco-Sound™, Item No. 30-2516-0, Cab No. 4859

GG-1 Electric Engine
Penn Central

2000 Volume 2
August 2000

3-Rail with Proto-Sound® 2.0, Item No. 30-2517-1, Cab No. 4915
3-Rail with Loco-Sound™, Item No. 30-2517-0, Cab No. 4915

GG-1 Electric Engine
Pennsylvania

Uncataloged Item
August 2000

3-Rail with Proto-Sound® 2.0, Item No. 20-80002e (2000 DAP), Cab No. 2340

NW-2 Switcher Diesel Engine
Union Pacific

1998 Volume 3
November 1998

3-Rail with Electronic Horn, Item No. 30-2138-0, Cab No. D.S.1050
3-Rail with Proto-Sound®, Item No. 30-2138-1, Cab No. D.S.1050

NW-2 Switcher Diesel Engine
Chicago NorthWestern

1998 Volume 3
November 1998

3-Rail with Electronic Horn, Item No. 30-2139-0, Cab No. 1017
3-Rail with Proto-Sound®, Item No. 30-2139-1, Cab No. 1017

NW-2 Switcher Diesel Engine
Santa Fe

1999 Volume 2
November 1999

3-Rail with Electronic Horn, Item No. 30-2156-0, Cab No. 2419
3-Rail with Proto-Sound®, Item No. 30-2156-1, Cab No. 2419

NW-2 Switcher Diesel Engine
Southern

1999 Volume 2
November 1999

3-Rail with Electronic Horn, Item No. 30-2157-0, Cab No. 1039
3-Rail with Proto-Sound®, Item No. 30-2157-1, Cab No. 1039

NW-2 Switcher Diesel Engine Calf
Chicago NorthWestern

1999 Volume 1
March 1999

3-Rail, Item No. 30-2139-3, Cab No. 1105

NW-2 Switcher
Diesel Engine Calf
Union Pacific

1999 Volume 1
March 1999

3-Rail, Item No. 30-2138-3, Cab No. D.S.1050B

NW-2 Switcher
Diesel Engine Calf
Santa Fe

1999 Volume 3
April 2000

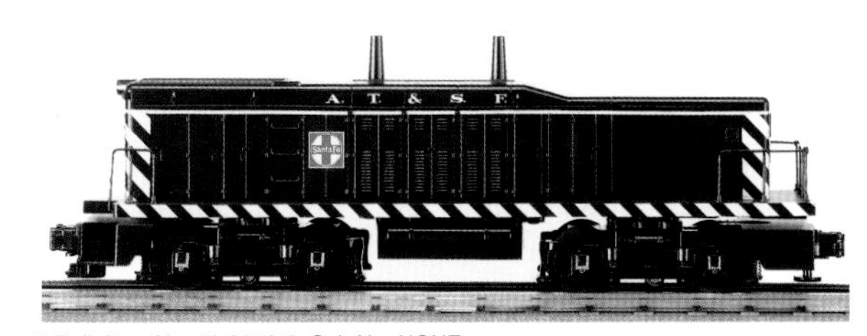

3-Rail, Item No. 30-2156-3, Cab No. NONE

NW-2 Switcher
Diesel Engine Calf
Southern

1999 Volume 3
April 2000

3-Rail, Item No. 30-2157-3, Cab No. 1039

PCC Electric Street Car
SEPTA

Fall/Winter 1996
March 1997

3-Rail with Electronic Horn, Item No. 30-2503, Cab No. 2165

PCC Electric Street Car
San Francisco

1997 Volume 1
January 1998

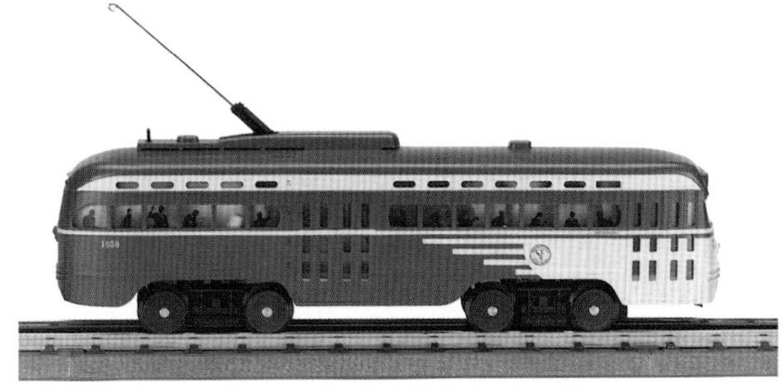

3-Rail with Electronic Horn, Item No. 30-2504-0, Cab No. 1050
3-Rail with Proto-Sound®, Item No. 30-2504-1, Cab No. 1050

PCC Electric Street Car
Pittsburgh

1998 Volume 2
January 1999

3-Rail with Electronic Horn, Item No. 30-2505-0, Cab No. 1734
3-Rail with Proto-Sound®, Item No. 30-2505-1, Cab No. 1734

PCC Electric Street Car
Washington

1999 Volume 3
November 1999

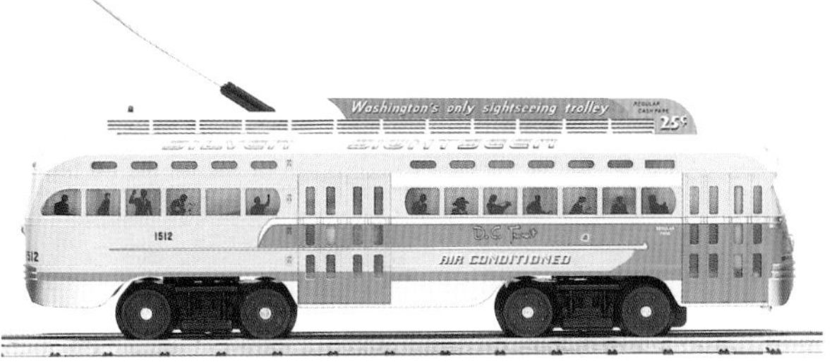

3-Rail with Electronic Horn, Item No. 30-2510-0, Cab No. 1512
3-Rail with Proto-Sound®, Item No. 30-2510-1, Cab No. 1512

PCC Electric Street Car
Pacific Electric

2000 Volume 1
March 2000

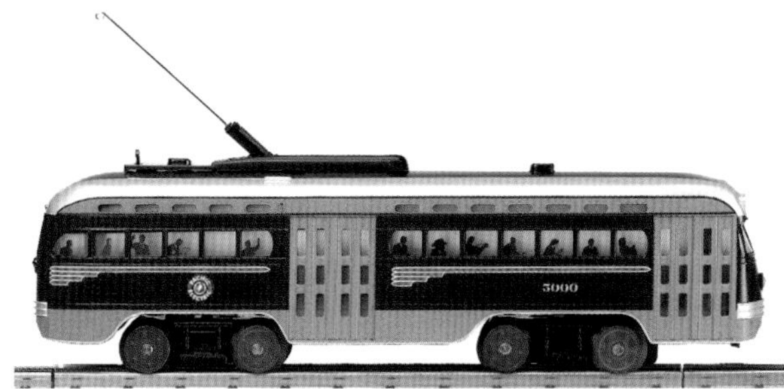

3-Rail with Electronic Horn, Item No. 30-2513-0, Cab No. 5000
3-Rail with Proto-Sound®, Item No. 30-2513-1, Cab No. 5000

PCC Electric Street Car
Chicago

2000 Volume 2
September 2000

3-Rail with Proto-Sound® 2.0, Item No. 30-2521-1, Cab No. 4015
3-Rail with Loco-Sound™, Item No. 30-2521-0, Cab No. 4015

PCC Electric Street Car
2000 DAP

Uncataloged Item
March 2000

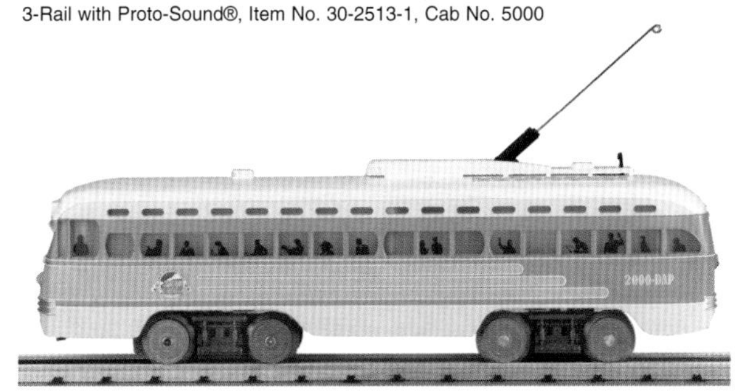

3-Rail with Proto-Sound®, Item No. 20-80002h (2000 DAP), Cab No. 2000

RDC Budd Car Set
Santa Fe

1999 Volume 1
June 1999

Caption3-Rail with Electronic Horn, Item No. 30-2145-0, Cab Nos. 191, 192
3-Rail with Proto-Sound®, Item No. 30-2145-1, Cab Nos. 191, 192

RDC Budd Car Set
Baltimore & Ohio

1999 Volume 1
June 1999

3-Rail with Electronic Horn, Item No. 30-2144-0, Cab Nos. 9920, 9932
3-Rail with Proto-Sound®, Item No. 30-2144-1, Cab Nos. 9920, 9932

RDC Budd Car Set
New York Central

2000 Volume 1
July 2000

3-Rail with Electronic Horn, Item No. 30-2182-0, Cab Nos. 465, 497
3-Rail with Proto-Sound®, Item No. 30-2182-1, Cab Nos. 465, 497

RDC Budd Car Set
Canadian Pacific

2000 Volume 1
July 2000

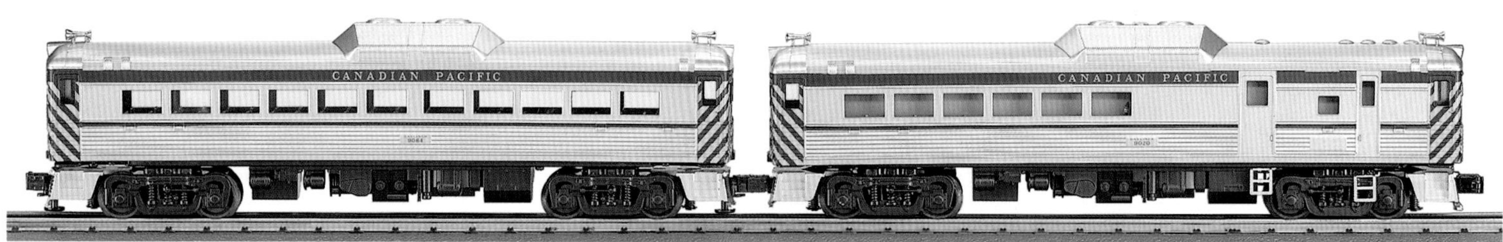

3-Rail with Electronic Horn, Item No. 30-2183-0, Cab Nos. 9064, 9020
3-Rail with Proto-Sound®, Item No. 30-2183-1, Cab Nos. 9064, 9020

Rectifier Electric
New Haven

2000 Volume 2
November 2000

3-Rail with Proto-Sound® 2.0, Item No. 30-2518-1, Cab No. 305
3-Rail with Loco-Sound™, Item No. 30-2518-0, Cab No. 305

Rectifier Electric
Virginian

2000 Volume 2
November 2000

3-Rail with Proto-Sound® 2.0, Item No. 30-2519-1, Cab No. 135
3-Rail with Loco-Sound™, Item No. 30-2519-0, Cab No. 135

RS-3 Diesel Engine
Rock Island

2000 Volume 2
August 2000

3-Rail with Proto-Sound® 2.0, Item No. 30-2202-1, Cab No. 493
3-Rail with Loco-Sound™, Item No. 30-2202-0, Cab No. 493

RS-3 Diesel Engine
Union Pacific

2000 Volume 2
August 2000

3-Rail with Proto-Sound® 2.0, Item No. 30-2200-1, Cab No. 1291
3-Rail with Loco-Sound™, Item No. 30-2200-0, Cab No. 1291

RS-3 Diesel Engine
Pennsylvania

2000 Volume 2
August 2000

3-Rail with Proto-Sound® 2.0, Item No. 30-2201-1, Cab No. 8469
3-Rail with Loco-Sound™, Item No. 30-2201-0, Cab No. 8469

SD-45 Diesel Engine
Union Pacific

1999 Volume 2
August 1999

3-Rail with Electronic Horn, Item No. 30-2152-0, Cab No. 3644
3-Rail with Proto-Sound®, Item No. 30-2152-1, Cab No. 3644

SD-45 Diesel Engine
Pennsylvania

1999 Volume 2
August 1999

3-Rail with Electronic Horn, Item No. 30-2153-0, Cab No. 6176
3-Rail with Proto-Sound®, Item No. 30-2153-1, Cab No. 6176

SD-45 Diesel Engine
Electro Motive Division

2000 Volume 2
August 2000

3-Rail with Proto-Sound® 2.0, Item No. 30-2193-1, Cab No. 4354
3-Rail with Loco-Sound™, Item No. 30-2193-0, Cab No. 4354

SD-45 Diesel Engine
Conrail

2000 Volume 2
August 2000

3-Rail with Proto-Sound® 2.0, Item No. 30-2194-1, Cab No. 6080
3-Rail with Loco-Sound™, Item No. 30-2194-0, Cab No. 6080

SD-60 Diesel Engine
Conrail

Fall/Winter 1996
November 1996

3-Rail with Electronic Horn, Item No. 30-2005-0, Cab No. 6867
3-Rail with Proto-Sound®, Item No. 30-2005-1, Cab No. 6867

SD-60 Diesel Engine
Chicago NorthWestern

Fall/Winter 1996
November 1996

3-Rail with Electronic Horn, Item No. 30-2006-0, Cab No. 8032
3-Rail with Proto-Sound®, Item No. 30-2006-1, Cab No. 8032

SD-60M Diesel Engine
CSX

1997 Volume 1
August 1997

3-Rail with Electronic Horn, Item No. 30-2116-0, Cab No. 8715
3-Rail with Proto-Sound®, Item No. 30-2116-1, Cab No. 8715

SD-60M Diesel Engine
Union Pacific

1997 Volume 1
August 1997

3-Rail with Electronic Horn, Item No. 30-2117-0, Cab No. 6365
3-Rail with Proto-Sound®, Item No. 30-2117-1, Cab No. 6365

SD-90 MAC Diesel Engine
Conrail

1998 Volume 1
March 1998

3-Rail with Electronic Horn, Item No. 30-2120-0, Cab No. 4128
3-Rail with Proto-Sound®, Item No. 30-2120-1, Cab No. 4128

SD-90 MAC Diesel Engine
Santa Fe

1998 Volume 1
March 1998

3-Rail with Electronic Horn, Item No. 30-2121-0, Cab No. 8300
3-Rail with Proto-Sound®, Item No. 30-2121-1, Cab No. 8300

SW-1500 Switcher Diesel Engine
NASA

2000 Volume 2
October 2000

3-Rail with Proto-Sound® 2.0, Item No. 30-2188-1, Cab No. 1
3-Rail with Loco-Sound™, Item No. 30-2188-0, Cab No. 1

SW-1500 Switcher Diesel Engine
Reading

2000 Volume 2
October 2000

3-Rail with Proto-Sound® 2.0, Item No. 30-2189-1, Cab No. 2758
3-Rail with Loco-Sound™, Item No. 30-2189-0, Cab No. 2758

SW-8 Switcher Diesel Engine
Atlantic Coast Line

1999 Volume 1
April 1999

3-Rail with Electronic Horn, Item No. 30-2146-0, Cab No. 57
3-Rail with Proto-Sound®, Item No. 30-2146-1, Cab No. 57

SW-8 Switcher Diesel Engine
Erie Lackawanna

1999 Volume 1
April 1999

3-Rail with Electronic Horn, Item No. 30-2147-0, Cab No. 363
3-Rail with Proto-Sound®, Item No. 30-2147-1, Cab No. 363

SW-8 Switcher Diesel Engine
Chicago NorthWestern

1999 Volume 3
August 1999

3-Rail with Electronic Horn, Item No. 30-2165-0, Cab No. 126
3-Rail with Proto-Sound®, Item No. 30-2165-1, Cab No. 126

SW-8 Switcher Diesel Engine
CP Rail

1999 Volume 3
August 1999

3-Rail with Electronic Horn, Item No. 30-2166-0, Cab No. 6706
3-Rail with Proto-Sound®, Item No. 30-2166-1, Cab No. 6706

SW-8 Switcher Diesel Engine
New York Central

2000 Volume 1
May 2000

3-Rail with Electronic Horn, Item No. 30-2176-0, Cab No. 9606
3-Rail with Proto-Sound®, Item No. 30-2176-1, Cab No. 9606

SW-8 Switcher Diesel Engine
Great Northern

2000 Volume 1
May 2000

3-Rail with Electronic Horn, Item No. 30-2177-0, Cab No. 101
3-Rail with Proto-Sound®, Item No. 30-2177-1, Cab No. 101

SW-8 Switcher Diesel Engine
Texas & Pacific

2000 Volume 1
May 2000

3-Rail with Electronic Horn, Item No. 30-2178-0, Cab No. 817
3-Rail with Proto-Sound®, Item No. 30-2178-1, Cab No. 817

SW-9 Switcher Diesel Engine
Western Pacific

1999 Volume 1
April 1999

3-Rail with Electronic Horn, Item No. 30-2148-0, Cab No. 601
3-Rail with Proto-Sound®, Item No. 30-2148-1, Cab No. 601

SW-9 Switcher Diesel Engine
Pennsylvania

1999 Volume 1
April 1999

3-Rail with Electronic Horn, Item No. 30-2149-0, Cab No. 8524
3-Rail with Proto-Sound®, Item No. 30-2149-1, Cab No. 8524

SW-9 Switcher Diesel Engine
Union Pacific

1999 Volume 3 - AEM-7
August 1999
$229.95

3-Rail with Electronic Horn, Item No. 30-2167-0, Cab No. 1834
3-Rail with Proto-Sound®, Item No. 30-2167-1, Cab No. 1834

SW-9 Switcher Diesel Engine
Chesapeake & Ohio

1999 Volume 3
August 1999

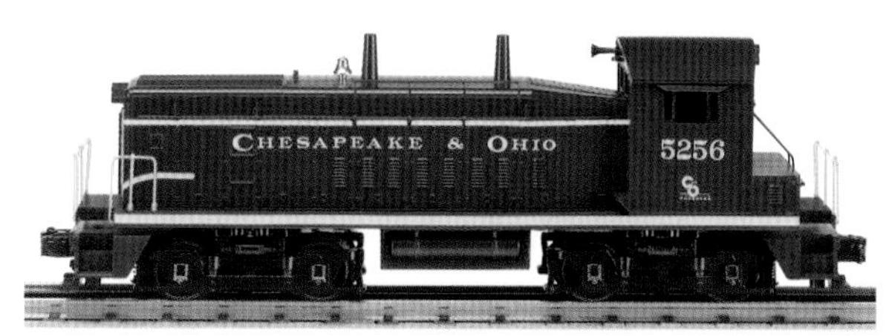

3-Rail with Electronic Horn, Item No. 30-2168-0, Cab No. 5256
3-Rail with Proto-Sound®, Item No. 30-2168-1, Cab No. 5256

SW-9 Switcher Diesel Engine
BNSF

1999 Volume 3
August 1999

3-Rail with Electronic Horn, Item No. 30-2169-0, Cab No. 3505
3-Rail with Proto-Sound®, Item No. 30-2169-1, Cab No. 3505

SW-9 Switcher Diesel Engine
Boston & Maine

2000 Volume 1
May 2000

3-Rail with Electronic Horn, Item No. 30-2179-0, Cab No. 1230
3-Rail with Proto-Sound®, Item No. 30-2179-1, Cab No. 1230

RAILKING LINE
Rolling Stock

RailKing rolling stock continues M.T.H.'s commitment to variety, with fifty-one different kinds of freight and non-revenue cars advertised by the time this book went to press. The RailKing line contains both durable ABS plastic and die-cast metal items, as well as modern and nineteenth-century options. While most RailKing freight cars are not scale models, most are, like the locomotives, faithful representations of the prototypes. But because RailKing is less dedicated to absolute realism than the Premier line, M.T.H. is free to add some fun and unusual pieces, like the searchlight cars. Also among the RailKing selection are several operating freight cars, including a 3-bay hopper with an operating coal load, a dump car with an operating bay, and a flat car with an operating helicopter that actually takes off and flies. These operating cars add enjoyment and authenticity to any O Gauge layout. Combine this enormous variety of cars with the huge range of roadnames offered, and RailKing has something for everyone.

3-Bay Hopper Car with Operating Coal Load
Norfolk & Western
Item No. 30-7525, Car No. 12915

1999 Volume 3
April 2000

3-Bay Hopper Car with Operating Coal Load
Union Pacific
Item No.30-7538, Car No. 37715

2000 Volume 2
November 2000

3-Dome Tank Car
Union Pacific
Item No. 30-7318, Car No. 69713

1999 Volume 2
November 1999

3-Dome Tank Car
Pennsylvania
Item No. 30-7319, Car No. 498748

1999 Volume 2
November 1999

3-Dome Tank Car
Great Northern
Item No. 30-7326, Car No. X-1382

2000 Volume 1
March 2000

3-Dome Tank Car
Conrail
Item No. 30-7321, Car No. 80136

2000 Volume 1
March 2000

34' Box Car - 19th Century
W.A.R.R.
Item No. 30-7439, Car No. 12220X

2000 Volume 1
July 2000

50' Modern Box Car
Lehigh Valley
Item No. 30-7442, Car No. 8208

2000 Volume 1
March 2000

50' Modern Box Car
Union Pacific
Item No. 30-7443, Car No. 160407

2000 Volume 1
March 2000

50' Modern Box Car
State of Maine
Item No.30-7450, Car No. 6005

2000 Volume 2
July 2000

50' Modern Box Car
Pennsylvania
Item No.30-7448, Car No. 117824

2000 Volume 2
July 2000

Airslide Hopper Car
Union Pacific
Item No. 30-7532, Car No. 20434

2000 Volume 1
July 2000

Airslide Hopper Car
Seaboard
Item No. 30-7533, Car No. 7143

2000 Volume 1
July 2000

American Crane Car
Union Pacific
Item No. 30-7931, Car No. 903080

2000 Volume 1
June 2000

American Crane Car
Pennsylvania
Item No. 30-7932, Car No. 85384

2000 Volume 1
June 2000

Auto Carrier Flat Car
MTH Auto Transport
Item No. 30-7628 with (2) 1955 Coupes and (2) 1949 Coupes , Car No. 4952

1998 Volume 2
December 1998

Auto Carrier Flat Car
MTH Auto Transportation
Item No. 30-7638 with (2) 1967 Pontiac Firebirds and (2) 1970 Chevy Novas, Car No. 6770

1999 Volume 2
January 2000

Auto Carrier Flat Car
MTH Auto Transportation
Item No. 30-7656 with (4) 1957 Chevys , Car No. 6779

1999 Volume 3
January 2000

Auto Carrier Flat Car
MTH Auto Transport
Item No. 30-7666 with (2) 1967 Camaros and (2) 1967 Shelby Mustangs, Car No. 6767

2000 Volume 1
June 2000

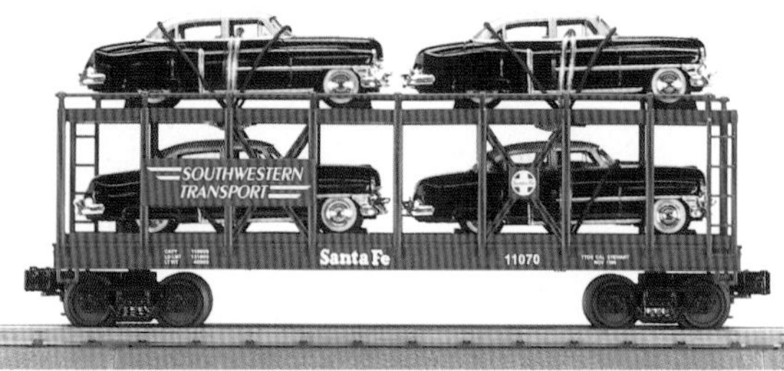

Auto Carrier Flat Car
TTOS
Item No. 30-7659 with (4) 1952 Cadillacs

Uncataloged Item
September 1999

Bay Window Caboose
Norfolk Southern
Item No. 30-7711, Car No. 63297

1997 Volume 1
November 1997

Bay Window Caboose
New York Central
Item No. 30-7712, Car No. 21574

1997 Volume 1
December 1997

Bay Window Caboose
Chessie
Item No. 30-7713, Car No. C-3027

1997 Volume 1
November 1997

Bay Window Caboose
Santa Fe
Item No. 30-7716, Car No. 999131

1998 Volume 1
May 1998

Bay Window Caboose
Conrail
Item No. 30-7717 Car No. 21694

1998 Volume 1
May 1998

Bay Window Caboose
BNSF
Item No. 30-7718, Car No. 12112

1998 Volume 2
October 1998

Bay Window Caboose
Fairbanks Morse Demo
Item No. 30-7719, Car No. 11015

1998 Volume 2
October 1998

Bay Window Caboose
NASA
Item No.30-7735, Car No. C13

2000 Volume 2
August 2000

Bobber Caboose
Baltimore & Ohio
Item No. 30-7728, Car No. C1145

2000 Volume 1
June 2000

Bobber Caboose
Union Pacific
Item No. 30-7729, Car No. 2117

2000 Volume 1
June 2000

Box Car
Pennsylvania
Item No. 30-7400, Car No. 47011

Fall 1995
June 1995

Box Car
New York Central
Item No. 30-7401, Car No. 180190
Item No. 50-7903, Car No. 180190, with ProtoFreight Sound Module
Item No. 50-7909, Car No. 180190, with ProtoFreight Sound Module

Fall 1995
June 1995

Box Car
Union Pacific
Item No. 30-7402, Car No. 150231
Item No. 30-7907, Car No. 150231, with ProtoFreight Sound Module

Fall 1995
June 1995

Box Car
Santa Fe
Item No. 30-7403 Car No. 20860
Item No. 30-7908, Car No. 20860, with ProtoFreight Sound Module

Fall 1995
June 1995

Box Car
Illinois Central
Item No. 30-7404, Car No. 22094
Item No. 50-7902, Car No. 22094, with ProtoFreight Sound Module

Fall 1995
June 1995

Box Car
Union Pacific - Map
Item No. 30-7405, Car No. 168043

Summer 1996
November 1996

Box Car
Santa Fe
Item No. 30-7406, Car no. 37625

Summer 1996
January 1997

Box Car
New York Central
Item No. 30-7407, Car No. 174020

Summer 1996
January 1997

Box Car
Pennsylvania
Item No. 30-7408, Car No. 28051
Item No. 30-7906, Car No. 28051, with ProtoFreight Sound Module

Summer 1996
March 1997

Box Car
Railbox
Item No. 30-7409, Car No. 15507

Summer 1996
October 1997

Box Car
'96 Christmas
Item No. 30-7410, Car No. 122596

Fall/Winter 1996
December 1996

Box Car
Chesapeake & Ohio
Item No. 30-7411, Car No. 18499

Spring 1997
June 1997

Box Car
Union Pacific
Item No. 30-7412, Car No. 126167

Spring 1997
June 1997

Box Car
Texas & Pacific
Item No. 30-7413, Car No. 41200

1997 Volume 1
August 1997

Box Car
New York Central
Item No. 30-7414, Car No. 4503

1997 Volume 1
July 1997

Box Car
'97 Christmas
Item No. 30-7318, Car No. 1997

1997 Volume 2
November 1997

Box Car
Union Pacific
Item No. 30-7420, Car No. 4031

1998 Volume 2
June 1998

Box Car
Amtrak
Item No. 30-7421, Car No. 1670

1998 Volume 2
June 1998

Box Car
Arrow Stapler
Item No. 30-7422, Car No. 12509

1998 Volume 2
June 1998

Box Car
MTHRRC 1998
Item No. 30-7423, Car No. NONE

1998 Volume 2
August 1998

Box Car
'98 Christmas
Item No. 30-7426, Car No. 1998

1998 Volume 3
September 1998

Box Car
Atlantic Coast Line
Item No. 30-7427, Car No. 24183

1999 Volume 1
April 1999

Box Car
Erie Lackawanna
Item No. 30-7428, Car No. 55205

1999 Volume 1
April 1999

Box Car
Santa Fe
Item No. 30-7431, Car No. 142472

1999 Volume 2
October 1999

Box Car
'99 Christmas Car
Item No. 30-7434, Car No. 1999

1999 Volume 3
October 1999

Box Car
Pennsylvania
Item No. 30-7437, Car No. 28667

1999 Volume 3
January 2000

Box Car
Reading
Item No. 30-7438, Car No. 110020

1999 Volume 3
January 2000

Box Car
Southern Pacific
Item No. 30-7441, Cab No. 92268

2000 Volume 1
January 2000

Box Car
New York Central
Item No. 30-7440, Car No. 164203

2000 Volume 1
January 2000

Box Car
Western Pacific
Item No. 30-7444, Car No. 20807

2000 Volume 1
February 2000

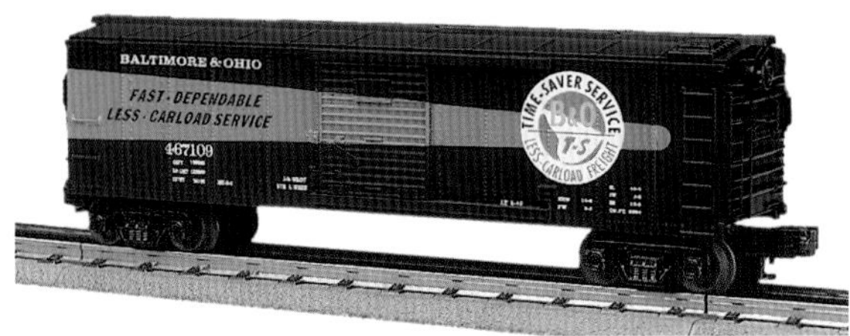

Box Car
Baltimore & Ohio
Item No. 30-7445, Car No. 467109

2000 Volume 1
February 2000

Box Car
Pennsylvania
Item No. 30-7446, Car No. 28649

2000 Volume 1
August 2000

Box Car
Oreo
Item No. 30-7415, Car No. 031797

Uncataloged Item
August 1997

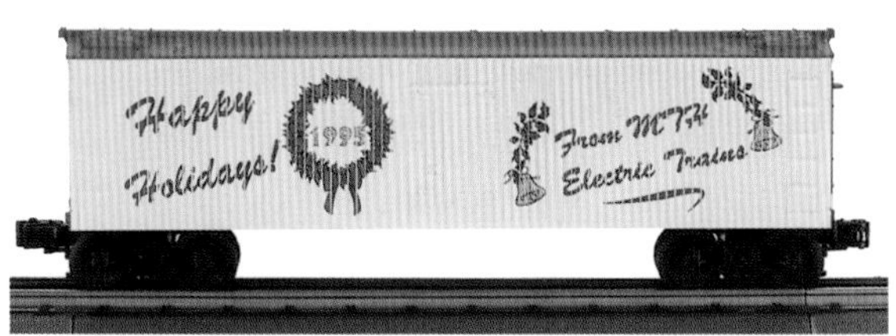

Box Car
'95 Christmas
Item No. 30-7415, Car No. NONE

Uncataloged Item
December 1995

Box Car
I Love Toy Trains® Limited Edition
Item No. 30-7499, Car No. 1999

Uncataloged Item
August 1999

Box Car
G.T.S. - Big Mo
Item No. 30-7425, Car No. 16314

Uncataloged Item
April 1998

Box Car
1999 D.A.P. Christmas
Item No. 20-80001e, Car No. 1999

Uncataloged Item
December 1999

Box Car
2000 D.A.P. Christmas
Item No. 20-80002d, Car No. NONE

Uncataloged Item
June 1999

Bunk Car
Conrail
Item No. 30-7920, Car No. 38941

1999 Volume 1
January 1999

Bunk Car
Amtrak
Item No. 30-7216, Car No. 21136

1999 Volume 2
September 1999

Crane Car
Northern Pacific
Item No. 30-7911, Car No. 10970

1997 Volume 2
January 1999

Crane Car
New York Central
Item No. 30-7910, Car No. X-27

1997 Volume 2
January 1999

Crane Car
Chessie
Item No. 30-7916 Car No. 900029

1998 Volume 3
March 1999

Crane Car
Conrail
Item No. 30-7917, Car No. X47

1998 Volume 3
February 1999

Crane Car
Amtrak
Item No. 30-7918, Car No. 11070

1999 Volume 1
June 1999

Crane Car
Nickel Plate Road
Item No. 30-7919, Car No. X50009

1999 Volume 1
June 1999

Crane Car
MTHRRC-1999
Item No. 30-7928, Car No. NONE

1999 Volume 2
October 1999

Crane Car
Jersey Central
Item No.30-7935, Car No. 6

2000 Volume 2
October 2000

Crane Tender Car
New York Central
Item No. 30-7912, Car No. X-27

Spring 1996
November 1998

Crane Tender Car
Northern Pacific
Item No. 30-7913, Car No. 10970

Spring 1996
November 1998

Crane Tender Car
MTHRRC 2000
Item No.30-7939, Car No. NONE

2000 Volume 2
June 2000

Dep. Center Flat Car
MTH Farm Equipment Co.
Item No. 30-7611 with Ertl® New Holland Tractor , Car No. 22893

1997 Volume 1
November 1997

Dep. Center Flat Car
MTH Construction Co.
Item No. 30-7618 with Ertl® Bulldozer, Car No. 19982

1998 Volume 1
June 1998

Dep. Center Flat Car
MTH Farm Equipment Co.
Item No. 30-7622 with Ertl® New Holland Tractor , Car No. 21136

1998 Volume 2
December 1998

Depressed Center Flat Car
MTH Construction Co.
Item No. 30-7612 with Transformer, Car No. 1990

1999 Volume 2
October 1999

Die-Cast Box Car
Pennsylvania
Item No. 30-8401, Car No. 100800

1999 Volume 3
June 2000

Die-Cast Box Car
Western Pacific
Item No. 30-8402, Car No. 1953

1999 Volume 3
June 2000

Die-Cast Depressed Center Flat Car
Santa Fe
Item No. 30-8301 with Transformer, Car No. 90000

1999 Volume 3
June 2000

Die-Cast Depressed Center Flat Car
Illinois Central
Item No. 30-8302 with Transformer, Car No. 60575

1999 Volume 3
June 2000

Die-Cast Flat Car
Milwaukee Road
Item No. 30-8303 with (2) Ertl® 1932 Panel Trucks , Car No. 64391

1999 Volume 3
June 2000

Die-Cast Flat Car
Chesapeake & Ohio
Item No. 30-8304 with (2) Ertl® 1932 Panel Trucks, Car No. 80410

1999 Volume 3
June 2000

Die-Cast Gondola Car
Union Pacific
Item No. 30-8201 with Junk Load, Car No. 30275

1999 Volume 3
June 2000

Die-Cast Gondola Car
Boston & Maine
Item No. 30-8202 with Junk Load, Car No. 9738

1999 Volume 3
June 2000

Die-Cast Hopper Car
Baltimore & Ohio
Item No. 30-8001 with Coal Load, Car No. 532000

1999 Volume 3
June 2000

Die-Cast Hopper Car
Lehigh Valley
Item No. 30-8002 with Coal Load, Car No. 25471

1999 Volume 3
June 2000

Die-Cast Reefer Car
Erie Lackawanna
Item No. 30-8601, Cab No. 62203

2000 Volume 1
July 2000

Die-Cast Reefer Car
Santa Fe
Item No. 30-8602, Cab No. 33111

2000 Volume 1
July 2000

Die-Cast Searchlight Car
Northern Pacific
Item No.30-8306, Car No. 62601

2000 Volume 2
October 2000

Die-Cast Searchlight Car
New York Central
Item No.30-8305, Car No. 498991

2000 Volume 2
October 2000

Die-Cast Stock Car
Chesapeake & Ohio
Item No.30-8701, Car No. 95237

2000 Volume 2
August 2000

Die-Cast Stock Car
Union Pacific
Item No.30-8702, Car No. 42400

2000 Volume 2
August 2000

Die-Cast Tank Car
Shell
Item No. 30-8101, Car No. S.E.P.X. 8124

1999 Volume 3
June 2000

Die-Cast Tank Car
Denver & Rio Grande
Item No. 30-8102, Car No. 10016

1999 Volume 3
June 2000

Die-Cast Woodsided Caboose
New York Central
Item No. 30-8501, Car No. 19400

1999 Volume 3
June 2000

Die-Cast Woodsided Caboose
Chesapeake & Ohio
Item No. 30-8502, Car No. 90382

1999 Volume 3
June 2000

Dump Car with Operating Bay
Northern Pacific
Item No. 30-7924, Car No. R3119

1999 Volume 2
January 2000

Dump Car with Operating Bay
CSX
Item No. 30-7925, Car No. 705665

1999 Volume 2
January 2000

Dump Car with Operating Bay
Conrail
Item No.30-7934, Car No. 53516

2000 Volume 2
August 2000

Dump Car with Operating Bay
New York Central
Item No.30-7941, Car No. X29225

2000 Volume 2
August 2000

Flat Car
Pennsylvania
Item No. 30-7600, Car No. 468115

Fall 1995
August 1995

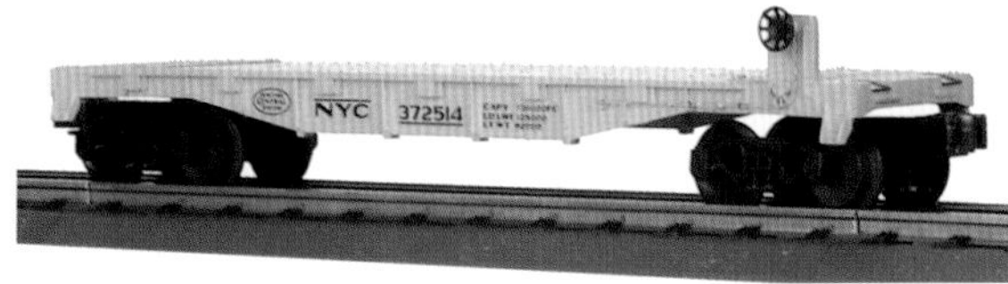

Flat Car
New York Central
Item No. 30-7601, Car No. 372514

Fall 1995
August 1995

Flat Car
Union Pacific
Item No. 30-7602, Car No. 56935

Fall 1995
August 1995

Flat Car
Trailer Train
Item No. 30-7604, Car No. 24071

Fall 1995
August 1995

Flat Car
Nickel Plate Road
Item No. 30-7605, Car No. 67534

Fall/Winter 1996
November 1996

Flat Car
MTH Construction Co.
Item No. 30-7606 with Ertl® Backhoe, Car No. 19961

Fall/Winter 1996
November 1996

Flat Car
MTH Classic Auto Transport
Item No. 30-7607 with (2) Ertl® 1952 Cadillacs , Car No. 1952

Fall/Winter 1996
November 1996

Flat Car
New York Central
Item No. 30-7608 with 40' Trailer, Car No. 499706

1997 Volume 1
September 1997

Flat Car
Norfolk Southern
Item No. 30-7609 with 40' Trailer, Car No. 60372

1997 Volume 1
November 1997

Flat Car
MTH Classic Auto Transport
Item No. 30-7610 with (2) Ertl® 1957 Chevys, Car No. 1957

1997 Volume 1
July 1997

Flat Car
MTH Classic Auto Transport
Item No. 30-7613 with (2) Ertl® 1957 T-Birds, Car No. 1957

1997 Volume 2
December 1997

Flat Car
MTH Construction Co.
Item No. 30-7614 with Ertl® Dump Truck, Car No. 19971

1997 Volume 2
December 1997

Flat Car
MTH Classic Auto Transport
Item No. 30-7617 with (2) Ertl® 1964 Mustangs, Car No. 1964

1998 Volume 1
January 1998

Flat Car
MTH Service Center
Item No. 30-7615 with (2) Ertl® 1955 Tow Trucks, Car No. 1955

1998 Volume 1
January 1999

Flat Car
MTH Construction Co.
Item No. 30-7619 with Ertl® Front End Loader, Car No. 19984

1998 Volume 1
May 1998

Flat Car
MTH Construction Co.
Item No. 30-7616 with Ertl® Earth Mover, Car No. 19952

1998 Volume 1
January 1998

Flat Car
MTH Transportation Co.
Item No. 30-7621 with Airplane, Car No. 1959

1998 Volume 2
December 1998

Flat Car
MTH Classic Auto Transport
Item No. 30-7623 with (2) Ertl® Fire Cars, Car No. 1949

1998 Volume 2
July 1998

Flat Car
MTH Classic Auto Transport
Item No. 30-7624 with (2) Ertl® 1964 Corvettes , Car No. 1964

1998 Volume 2
November 1998

Flat Car
MTH Classic Auto Transport
Item No. 30-7625 with (2) Ertl® 1959 Taxis, Car No. 1959

1998 Volume 2
November 1998

Flat Car
Pennsylvania
Item No. 30-7626 with 40' Trailer, Car No. 474399

1998 Volume 2
April 1998

Flat Car
Florida East Coast
Item No. 30-7627 with 40' Trailer, Car No. 64273

1998 Volume 2
December 1998

Flat Car
MTH Construction Co.
Item No. 30-7620 with Ertl® Road Grader, Car No. 19983

1998 Volume 2
May 1998

Flat Car
MTH Transportation Company
Item No. 30-7629 with Ertl® Fire Truck, Car No. 1979

1998 Volume 2
June 1998

Flat Car
Union Pacific
Item No. 30-7632 with 40' Trailer, Car No. 53007

1999 Volume 1
April 1999

Flat Car
MTH Classic Auto Transport
Item No. 30-7634 with (2) Ertl® 1969 Camaros, Car No. 1969

1999 Volume 1
April 1999

Flat Car
Baltimore & Ohio
Item No. 30-7633 with 40' Trailer, Car No. 9129

1999 Volume 1
April 1999

Flat Car
Union 76
Item No. 30-7640 with (2) Ertl® 1955 Tow Trucks, Car No. 1955

1999 Volume 2
October 1999

Flat Car
MTH Transportation Co.
Item No. 30-7639 with (2) Ertl® 1967 GTO's, Car No. 1968

1999 Volume 2
October 1999

Flat Car
MTH Farm Equipment Co.
Item No. 30-7642 with (2) Ertl® Farm Tractors, Car No. 1998

1999 Volume 2
August 1999

Flat Car
MTH Transportation Co.
Item No. 30-7647 with (2) Ertl® 1950 Panel Vans, Car No. 1950

1999 Volume 3
February 2000

Flat Car
MTH Classic Auto Transport
Item No. 30-7660 with (2) Ertl® 1965 Ford Cobras, Car No. 1965

2000 Volume 1
May 2000

Flat Car
MTH Classic Auto Transport
Item No. 30-7661 with (2) Ertl® 1970 Novas, Car No. 1970

2000 Volume 1
May 2000

Flat Car
MTH Classic Auto Transport
Item No. 30-7662 with (2) Ertl® 1940 Woody Wagons, Car No. 1940

2000 Volume 1
May 2000

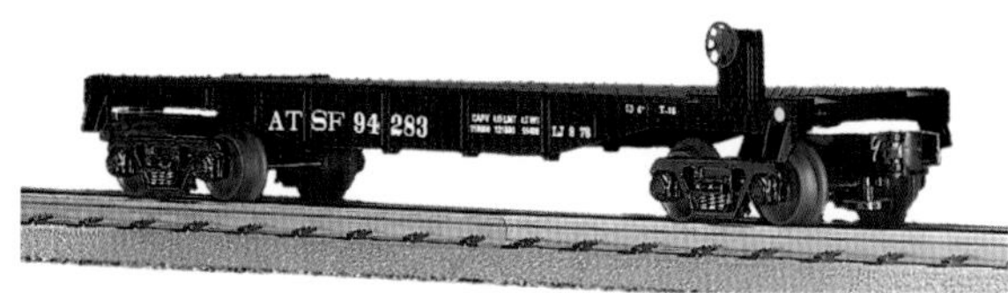

Flat Car
Santa Fe
Item No. 30-7664, Car No. 94283

2000 Volume 1
February 2000

Flat Car
Pennsylvania
Item No. 30-7665, Car No. 474396

2000 Volume 1
February 2000

Flat Car
MTH Maintenance Of Way
Item No. 30-7668 with Axle Sets, Car No. 2000

2000 Volume 2
August 2000

Flat Car
MTH Maintenance Of Way
Item No.30-7669 with Freight Car Trucks, Car No. 1998

2000 Volume 2
August 2000

Flat Car
MTH Classic Auto Transport
Item No. 30-7670 with (2) Ertl® 1967 Camaros, Car No. 1967

2000 Volume 2
October 2000

Flat Car
MTH Classic Auto Transport
Item No. 30-7671 with (2) Ertl® 1930 Half-Ton Panel Vans, Car No. 1930

2000 Volume 2
October 2000

Flat Car
MTH Transportation Co.
Item No. 30-7672 with Airplane, Car No. 1961

2000 Volume 2
October 2000

Flat Car - 19th Century
W.A.R.R.
Item No. 30-7635 with Cannon, Car No. 1862

1999 Volume 1
May 1999

Flat Car - w/Bulkheads
Southern Pacific
Item No. 30-7636, Car No. SP 564800

1999 Volume 1
June 1999

Flat Car - w/Bulkheads
Erie Lackawanna
Item No. 30-7637, Car No. 7000

1999 Volume 1
June 1999

Flat Car with Operating Helicopter
MTH Transportation Co.
Item No. 30-7658, Car No. 1970

1999 Volume 3
January 2000

Flat Car with Operating Helicopter
NASA
Item No. 30-7940, Car No. 141403

2000 Volume 2
September 2000

Flat Car with Operating Helicopter
Red Cross
Item No. 30-7942, Car No. 105004

2000 Volume 2
December 2000

Flat Car with Operating Logs
Western Maryland
Item No. 30-7648, Car No. 380

1999 Volume 3
March 2000

Flat Car with Operating Logs
Northern Pacific
Item No. 30-7649, Car No. 120317

1999 Volume 3
March 2000

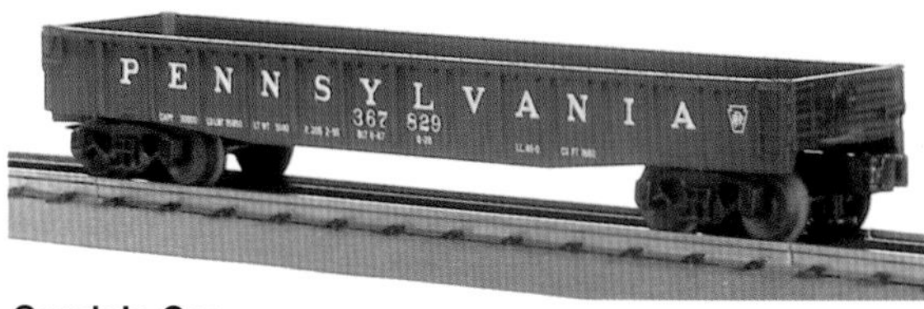

Gondola Car
Pennsylvania
Item No. 30-7200, Car No. 367829

Fall 1995
May 1995

Gondola Car
Milwaukee Road
Item No. 30-7204 with Crates, Car No. 93077

Winter 1995
May 1995

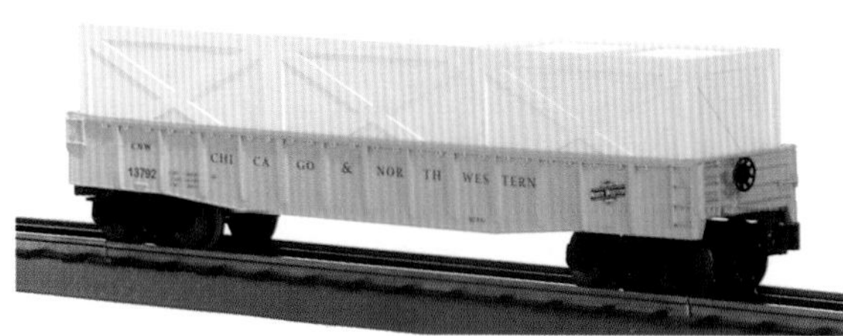

Gondola Car
Chicago NorthWestern
Item No. 30-7205 with Crates, Car No. 13792

Fall/Winter 1996
November 1996

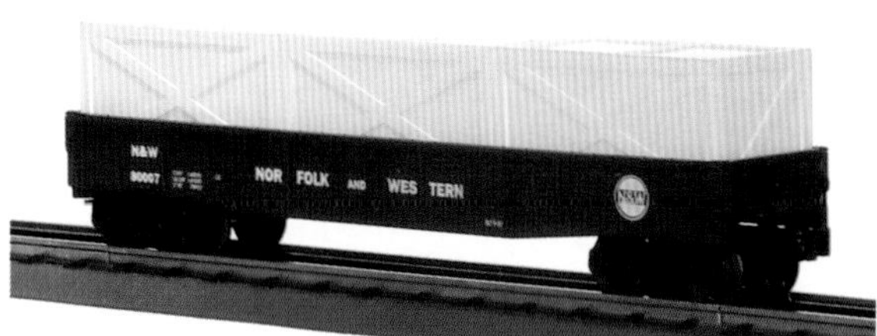

Gondola Car
Norfolk & Western
Item No. 30-7206 with Crates, Car No. 80007

Fall/Winter 1996
December 1996

Gondola Car
Conrail
Item No. 30-7207 with Crates, Car No. 604768

Fall/Winter 1996
November 1996

Gondola Car
Union Pacific
Item No. 30-7208 with Crates, Car No. 65239

1997 Volume 1
June 1997

Gondola Car
Pennsylvania
Item No. 30-7209 with Crates, Car No. 367829

1997 Volume 1
July 1997

Gondola Car
CSX
Item No. 30-7211 with Crates, Car No. 11671

1997 Volume 2
November 1997

Gondola Car
Northern Pacific
Item No. 30-7210 with Crates, Car No. 50161

1997 Volume 2
December 1997

Gondola Car
Pennsylvania
Item No. 30-7212 with Crates, Car No. 376901

1997 Volume 2
November 1997

Gondola Car
Baltimore & Ohio
Item No. 30-7213, Car No. XM890

1998 Volume 2
September 1998

Gondola Car
Chesapeake & Ohio
Item No. 30-7214, Car No. 31722

1998 Volume 2
July 1998

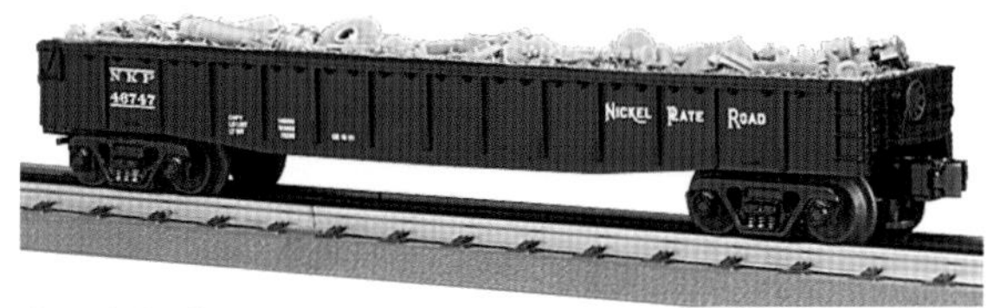

Gondola Car
Nickel Plate Road
Item No. 30-7215, Car No. 46747

1999 Volume 2
September 1999

Gondola Car - 19th Century
W.A.R.R.
Item No. 30-7216, Car No. NONE

2000 Volume 1
July 2000

Hopper Car
Pennsylvania
Item No. 30-7500, Car No. 675347

Fall 1995
June 1995

Hopper Car
New York Central
Item No. 30-7501, Car No. 868001

Fall 1995
June 1995

Hopper Car
Union Pacific
Item No. 30-7502, Car No. 91084

Fall 1995
June 1995

Hopper Car
Santa Fe
Item No. 30-7503, Car No. 181764

Fall 1995
June 1995

Hopper Car
C B & Q
Item No. 30-7504, Car No. 190359

Fall 1995
June 1995

Hopper Car
Nickel Plate Road
Item No. 30-7505, Car No. 30160

Fall/Winter 1996
November 1996

Hopper Car
Norfolk & Western
Item No. 30-7506, Car No. 131248

Fall/Winter 1996
December 1996

Hopper Car
Chesapeake & Ohio
Item No. 30-7507, Car No. 69576

Fall/Winter 1996
November 1996

Hopper Car
Pennsylvania
Item No. 30-7508, Car No. 192164

Spring 1997
June 1997

Hopper Car
Union Pacific
Item No. 30-7509, Car No. 12727

Spring 1997
June 1997

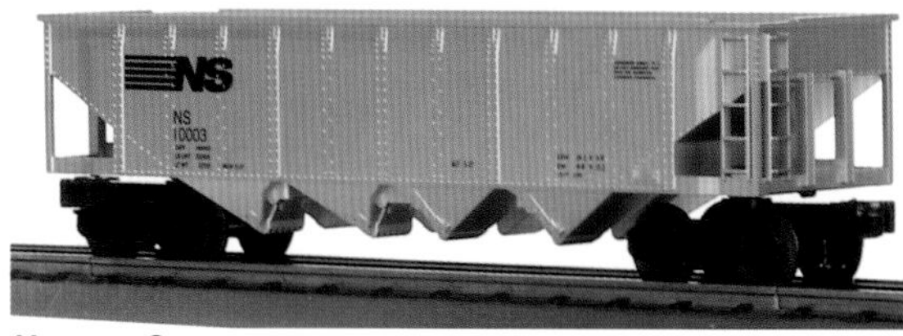

Hopper Car
Norfolk Southern
Item No. 30-7510, Car No. 10003

1997 Volume 1
May 1997

Hopper Car
Chicago NorthWestern
Item No. 30-7511, Car No. 67655

1997 Volume 2
May 1997

Hopper Car
Chessie
Item No. 30-7514, Car No. 82701

1997 Volume 2
September 1997

Hopper Car
Northern Pacific
Item No. 30-7512, Car No. 70245

1997 Volume 2
October 1997

Hopper Car
New York Central
Item No. 30-7513, Car No. 904420

1997 Volume 2
November 1997

Hopper Car
Norfolk & Western
Item No. 30-7515, Car No. 30771

1998 Volume 2
September 1998

Hopper Car
Western Maryland
Item No. 30-7516, Car No. 90005

1998 Volume 2
September 1998

Hopper Car
New York Central
Item No. 30-7517, Car No.

1998 Volume 2
April 1998

Hopper Car
Erie Lackawanna
Item No. 30-7523, Car No. 33249

1999 Volume 2
October 1999

Hopper Car
Southern
Item No. 30-7524, Car No. 73464

1999 Volume 2
October 1999

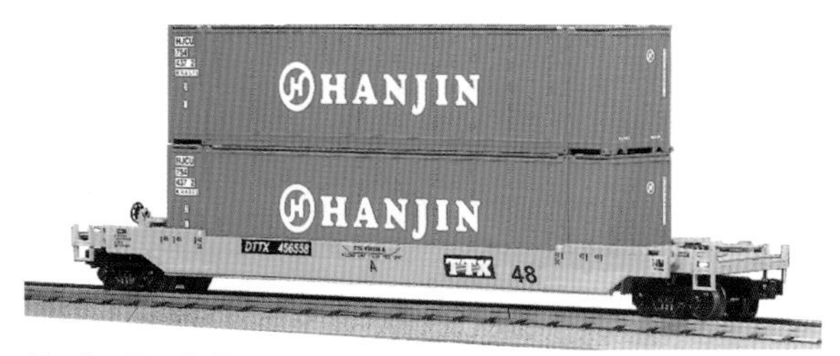

Husky Stack Car
Hanjin
Item No. 30-7643, Car No. 48

1999 Volume 2
November 1999

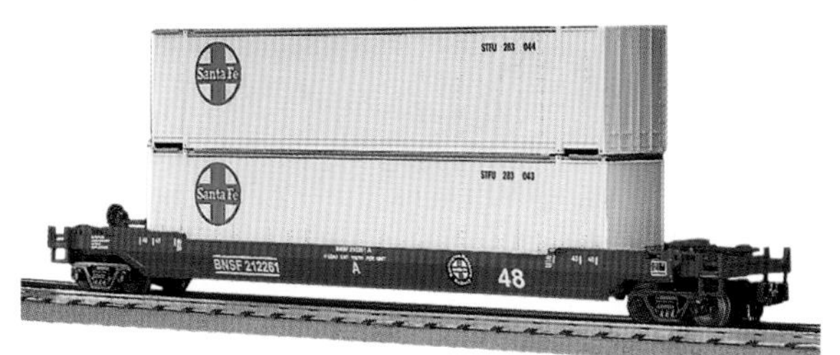

Husky Stack Car
Santa Fe
Item No. 30-7644, Car No. N/A

1999 Volume 2
November 1999

Modern Tank Car
New York Central
Item No. 30-7322, Car No. 16000

2000 Volume 1
July 2000

Modern Tank Car
Santa Fe
Item No. 30-7323, Car No. 98506

2000 Volume 1
July 2000

N5c Caboose
Pennsylvania
Item No. 30-7730, Car No. 477879

2000 Volume 1
January 2000

Operating Hand Car
Black
Item No. 30-2508, Car No. NONE

1999 Volume 1
April 1999

Operating Hand Car
Tuscan
Item No. 30-2509, Car No. NONE

1999 Volume 2
April 1999

Operating Hand Car
Santa
Item No. 30-2511, Car No. NONE

1999 Volume 3
September 1999

Operating Hand Car
Yellow
Item No.30-2520, Car No. NONE

2000 Volume 2
July 1999

Ore Car
Baltimore & Ohio
Item No. 30-7518, Car No. 6453

1998 Volume 3
April 1999

Ore Car
Chicago NorthWestern
Item No. 30-7519, Car No. 55378

1998 Volume 3
April 1999

Ore Car
Pennsylvania
Item No. 30-7522, Car No. 15886

1999 Volume 2
September 1999

Ore Car
Union Pacific
Item No. 30-7527, Car No. 27001

1999 Volume 3
January 2000

Ore Car
Great Northern
Item No. 30-7529, Car No. 92607

2000 Volume 1
January 2000

Ore Car
Jersey Central
Item No. 30-7528, Car No. 60949

2000 Volume 1
January 2000

Ps-2 Discharge Hopper Car
Conrail
Item No.30-7534, Car No. 884173

2000 Volume 2
October 2000

Ps-2 Discharge Hopper Car
Pennsylvania
Item No.30-7537, Car No. 257912

2000 Volume 2
October 2000

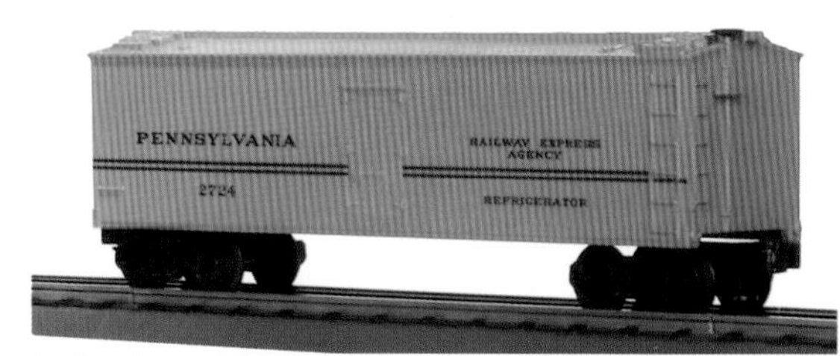

Reefer Car
Pennsylvania
Item No. 30-7800, Car No. 2724

Fall 1995
August 1995

Reefer Car
New York Central
Item No. 30-7801, Car No. 6078

Fall 1995
August 1995

Reefer Car
Union Pacific
Item No. 30-7802, Car No. 78676
Item No. 50-7912, Car No. 78676, with ProtoFreight Sound Module

Fall 1995
August 1995

Reefer Car
Santa Fe
Item No. 30-7803, Car No. 13448
Item No. 50-7913, Car No. 13448, with Proto-Freight Sound Module

Fall 1995
August 1995

Reefer Car
Railway Express
Item No. 30-7804, Car No. R.E.X. 6435
Item No. 50-7914, Car No. R.E.X. 6435, with ProtoFreight Sound Module

Fall 1995
August 1995

Reefer Car
Burlington
Item No. 30-7806, Car No. 75285

Fall/Winter 1996
January 1997

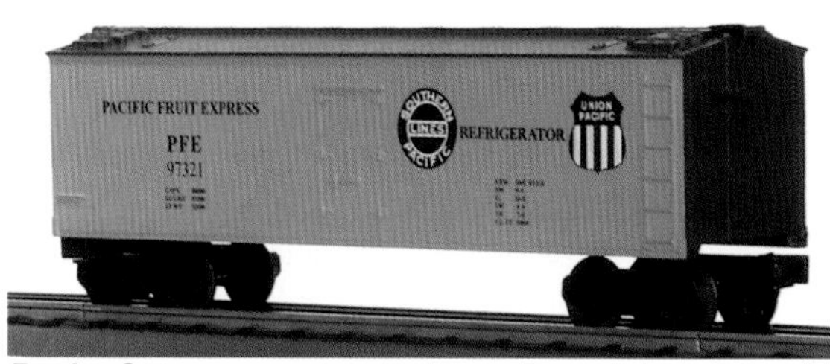

Reefer Car
Union Pacific
Item No. 30-7807, Car No. 97231

Fall/Winter 1996
January 1997

Reefer Car
Santa Fe
Item No. 30-7808, Car No. 1899

Fall/Winter 1996
January 1997

Reefer Car
Pennsylvania
Item No. 30-7809, Car No. 97101

Fall/Winter 1996
January 1997

Reefer Car
Railway Express Agency
Item No. 30-7810, Car No. 6113

Fall/Winter 1996
January 1997

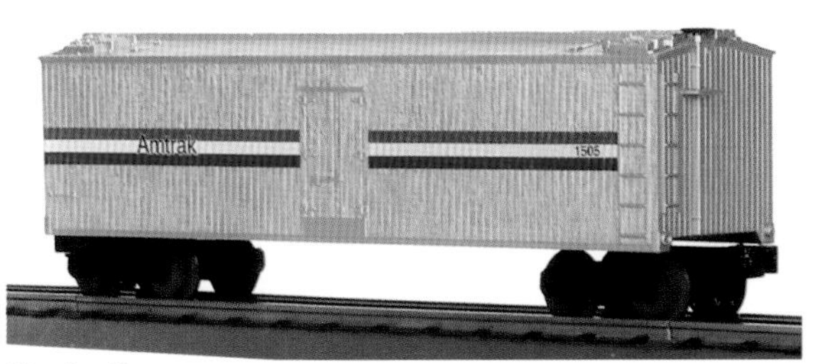

Reefer Car
Amtrak
Item No. 30-7811, Car No. 1505

1997 Volume 1
June 1998

Reefer Car
Florida East Coast
Item No. 30-7812, Car No. 21019

1997 Volume 1
June 1997

Reefer Car
Union Pacific
Item No. 30-7813, Car No. 73800

1998 Volume 2
July 1998

Reefer Car
Santa Fe
Item No. 30-7814, Car No. 37715

1998 Volume 2
September 1998

Reefer Car
Needham Packing
Item No. 30-7815, Car No. 2374

2000 Volume 2
October 2000

Reefer Car
Pepper Packing
Item No. 30-7816, Car No. 2319

2000 Volume 2
October 2000

Rotary Snow Plow
Denver & Rio Grande
Item No. 30-2123, Car No. OM

1998 Volume 1
March 1998

Rotary Snow Plow
Pennsylvania
Item No. 30-2124, Car No. 497788

1998 Volume 1
July 1999

Rotary Snow Plow
Chicago NorthWestern
Item No. 30-7921, Car No. 263000

1999 Volume 1
May 1999

Rotary Snow Plow
Canadian National
Item No. 30-7922, Car No. CN 79814

1999 Volume 1
May 1999

Rotary Snow Plow
Great Northern
Item No. 30-7929, Car No. X-1512

2000 Volume 1
January 2000

Rotary Snow Plow
Southern Pacific
Item No. 30-7930, Car No. MW 221

2000 Volume 1
January 2000

Rounded Roof Box Car
Great Northern
Item No. 30-7419, Car No. 27751

1998 Volume 1
June 1998

Rounded Roof Box Car
Pennsylvania
Item No. 30-7418, Car No. 76642

1998 Volume 1
July 1998

Rounded Roof Box Car
Baltimore & Ohio
Item No. 30-7429, Car No. 385186

1999 Volume 1
March 1999

Rounded Roof Box Car
Union Pacific
Item No. 30-7430, Car No. 9367

1999 Volume 1
March 1999

Rounded Roof Box Car
New York Central
Item No.30-7447, Car No. 200495

2000 Volume 2
September 2000

Rounded Roof Box Car
Seaboard
Item No.30-7449, Car No. 19268

2000 Volume 2
September 2000

Searchlight Car
Conrail
Item No. 30-7926, Car No. CR 766155

1999 Volume 2
September 1999

Searchlight Car
Amtrak
Item No. 30-7927, Car No. 16000

1999 Volume 2
September 1999

Searchlight Car
Southern Pacific
Item No.30-7938, Car No. 500514

2000 Volume 2
October 2000

Searchlight Car
Chessie
Item No. 30-7933, Car No. 80996

2000 Volume 2
October 2000

Searchlight Car
Pennsylvania
Item No. 30-7937, Car No. 470275

2000 Volume 2
October 2000

Searchlight Car
New York Central
Item No. 30-7936, Car No. 498996

2000 Volume 2
October 2000

Steel Caboose
Chicago NorthWestern
Item No. 30-7727, Car No. 10801

1999 Volume 3
February 2000

Steel Caboose
Southern Pacific
Item No. 30-7731, Car No. 10101

2000 Volume 1
May 2000

Steel Caboose
Western Maryland
Item No. 30-7732, Car No. 1802

2000 Volume 1
May 2000

Steel Caboose
Reading
Item No. 30-7733, Car No. 92878

2000 Volume 1
May 2000

Steel Caboose
Southern Pacific
Item No. 30-7737, Car No. 1123

2000 Volume 2
August 2000

Steel Caboose
Chicago NorthWestern
Item No. 30-7734, Car No. 11125

2000 Volume 2
August 2000

Stock Car
Pennsylvania
Item No. 30-7100, Car No. 128749

Fall 1995
June 1995

Stock Car
New York Central
Item No. 30-7101, Car No. 27641
Item No. 50-7904, Car No. 27641, with Proto-Freight Sound Module

Fall 1995
June 1995

Stock Car
Union Pacific
Item No. 30-7102, Car No. 47729
Item No. 50-7901, Car No. 47729, with Proto-Freight Sound Module

Fall 1995
May 1995

Stock Car
Atlantic Coast Line
Item No. 30-7104 Car No. 140297
Item No. 50-7900, Car No. 140297, with ProtoFreight Sound Module

Fall 1995
May 1995

Stock Car
Pennsylvania
Item No. 30-7105, Car No. 128079

Summer 1996
November 1996

Stock Car
Nickel Plate Road
Item No. 30-7106, Car No. 67534

Summer 1996
November 1996

Stock Car
Union Pacific
Item No. 30-7107, Car No. 48216

Summer 1996
November 1996

Stock Car
Santa Fe
Item No. 30-7108, Car No. 26425

Summer 1996
November 1996

Stock Car
Chicago NorthWestern
Item No. 30-7109, Car No. 15033

Summer 1996
December 1996

Stock Car
Santa Fe
Item No. 30-7103, Car No. 128016
Item No. 30-7905, Car No. 128016, with ProtoFreight Sound Module

Fall/Winter 1996
May 1995

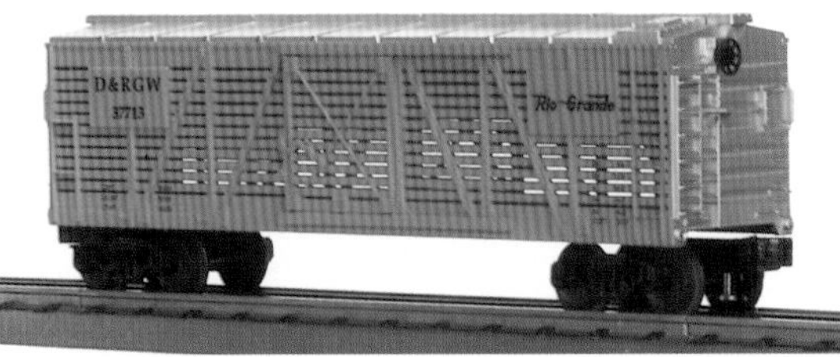

Stock Car
Denver & Rio Grande
Item No. 30-7110, Car No. 37713

1997 Volume 1
June 1997

Stock Car
Erie
Item No. 30-7111, Car No. 56634

1997 Volume 1
June 1997

Stock Car
New York Central
Item No. 30-7112, Car No. 74105

1998 Volume 2
July 1998

Stock Car
Chesapeake & Ohio
Item No. 30-7113, Car No. 95237

1998 Volume 2
October 1998

Stock Car - 19th Century
W.A.R.R.
Item No. 30-7114, Car No. 1270

1999 Volume 1
May 1999

Tank Car
Pennsylvania
Item No. 30-7300, Car No. 498639

Fall 1995
July 1995

Tank Car
New York Central
Item No. 30-7301, Car No. 4725

Fall 1995
June 1995

Tank Car
Union Pacific
Item No. 30-7302, Car No. 70084

Fall 1995
June 1995

Tank Car
Santa Fe
Item No. 30-7303, Car No. 101125

Fall 1995
May 1996

Tank Car
Baltimore & Ohio
Item No. 30-7304, Car No. X416

Fall 1995
June 1995

Tank Car
Conrail
Item No. 30-7305, Car No. 5010

Fall/Winter 1996
November 1996

Tank Car
Santa Fe
Item No. 30-7306, Car No. 100943

Fall/Winter 1996
December 1996

Tank Car
Chicago NorthWestern
Item No. 30-7307, Car No. 32308

Fall/Winter 1996
November 1996

Tank Car
Chesapeake & Ohio
Item No. 30-7308, Car No. 4123

Spring 1997
May 1997

Tank Car
Union Pacific
Item No. 30-7309, Car No. 69012

Spring 1997
May 1997

Tank Car
New York Central
Item No. 30-7310, Car No. 5791

1997 Volume 1
May 1997

Tank Car
Sinclair
Item No. 30-7311, Car No. 9131

1997 Volume 1
December 1997

Tank Car
Norfolk Southern
Item No. 30-7312, Car No. 10238

1997 Volume 2
November 1997

Tank Car
Southern Pacific
Item No. 30-7313, Car No. 52578, Car No. 52578

1997 Volume 2
February 1998

Tank Car
Esso
Item No. 30-7314, Car No. 91863

1998 Volume 2
August 1998

Tank Car
Denver & Rio Grande
Item No. 30-7315, Car No. 10009

1998 Volume 2
June 1998

Tank Car
Texaco
Item No. 30-7316, Car No. 878991

1999 Volume 1
June 1999

Tank Car
Pennsylvania
Item No. 30-7317, Car No. 500001

1999 Volume 1
June 1999

Tank Car
Baker's Chocolate
Item No. 30-7324, Car No. GATX 31057

2000 Volume 1
February 2000

Tank Car
Corn Industrial
Item No. 30-7325, Car No. CCL x3014

2000 Volume 1
February 2000

Tank Car
McDonald's
Item No. 30-7327, Car No. 78391

2000 Volume 2
August 2000

Wooden Tank Car - 19th Century
W.A.R.R.
Item No. 30-7320, Car No. 516

2000 Volume 1
May 2000

Woodsided Caboose
New York Central
Item No. 30-7701, Car No. 18205

Fall 1995
December 1995

Woodsided Caboose
Union Pacific
Item No. 30-7702, Car No. 3821

Fall 1995
August 1995

Woodsided Caboose
Santa Fe
Item No. 30-7703, Car No. 1997

Fall 1995
December 1995

Woodsided Caboose
Nickel Plate Road
Item No. 30-7705, Car No. 1115

Fall/Winter 1996
November 1996

Woodsided Caboose
Erie
Item No. 30-7706, Car No. 04942

Fall/Winter 1996
November 1996

Woodsided Caboose
Chicago NorthWestern
Item No. 30-7707, Car No. 12560

Fall/Winter 1996
January 1997

Woodsided Caboose
Conrail
Item No. 30-7708, Car No. CR22000

Fall/Winter 1996
December 1996

Woodsided Caboose
Chesapeake & Ohio
Item No. 30-7709, Car No. 90912

Spring 1997
June 1997

Woodsided Caboose
Union Pacific
Item No. 30-7710, Car No. 25602

Spring 1997
June 1997

Woodsided Caboose
Texas & Pacific
Item No. 30-7714, Car No. 2569

1997 Volume 1
June 1997

Woodsided Caboose
Pennsylvania RR
Item No. 30-7715, Car No. 980824

1997 Volume 1
June 1997

Woodsided Caboose
Pennsylvania
Item No. 30-7700, Car No. 477618

1997 Volume 2
August 1995

Woodsided Caboose
Santa Fe
Item No. 30-7720, Car No. 1612

1998 Volume 2
September 1998

Woodsided Caboose
New York Central
Item No. 30-7721, Car No. 19654

1998 Volume 2
July 1998

Woodsided Caboose
Pennsylvania
Item No. 30-7722, Car No. 981801

1999 Volume 1
March 1999

Woodsided Caboose
Baltimore & Ohio
Item No. 30-7723 Car No. C1678

1999 Volume 1
March 1999

Woodsided Caboose
Norfolk & Western
Item No. 30-7736, Car No. 518364

2000 Volume 2
December 2000

Woodsided Caboose - 19th Century
W.A.R.R.
Item No. 30-7724, Car No. 58

1999 Volume 1
May 1999

Work Caboose
Northern Pacific
Item No. 30-7725, Car No. 1537

1999 Volume 2
August 1999

Work Caboose
New York Central
Item No. 30-7726, Car No. 18087

1999 Volume 2
August 1999

Box Car *(photo not available)*
Chessie
Item No. 30-7417, Car No. 26621

1997 Volume 2
December 1997

Gondola Car *(photo not available)*
New York Central
Item No. 30-7201, Car No. N/A

Winter 1995
May 1995

Gondola Car *(photo not available)*
Santa Fe
Item No. 30-7203, Car No. N/A

Winter 1995
May 1995

Flat Car *(photo not available)*
Santa Fe
Item No. 30-7603, Car No. N/A

Fall 1995
August 1995

Gondola Car *(photo not available)*
Union Pacific
Item No. 30-7202, Car No. 65230

Winter 1995
May 1995

Searchlight Car *(photo not available)*
New York Central
Item No. 30-7914, Car No. N/A

Spring 1996
June 2000

Woodsided Caboose *(photo not available)*
Norfolk & Western
Item No. 30-7704, Car No. N/A

Fall 1995
December 1995

Searchlight Car *(photo not available)*
Union Pacific
Item No. 30-7915, Car No. N/A

1998 Volume 2
June 2000

RAILKING LINE
Passenger Sets

M.T.H. RailKing passenger cars are designed with the space-conscious model railroader in mind. At press time, there are twenty-two distinct kinds of RailKing passenger cars, many of which run on O-27 track. Thanks to the art that M.T.H. designers say goes into every RailKing piece, these non-scale reproductions of long passenger cars maintain an air of accuracy, including interior and undercarriage details on ABS plastic models. RailKing passenger cars include such eternal favorites as the streamlined cars and Madison cars, as well as superliners, subway car add-ons for the subway sets sold in the diesel/electric part of the catalog, and Overton cars to accompany nineteenth-century steamers. M.T.H. also makes a RailKing version of the nostalgic and ever-popular aluminum cars. RailKing passenger cars come in initial four-car sets, followed by single and two-car add-on pieces, so that model railroaders can build long, realistic consists.

2-Car 60’ Streamlined ABS Sleeper/Diner Smooth Sided
Union Pacific

2000 Volume 2
September 2000

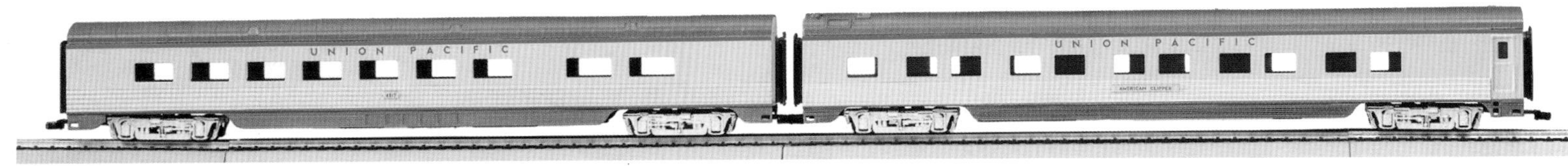

Item No. 30-6722, Car Nos. American Clipper, 4817

2-Car 60’ Streamlined ABS Sleeper/Diner Smooth Sided
Seaboard

2000 Volume 2
September 2000

Item No. 30-6720, Car Nos. Sebring, 1008

2-Car 60’ Streamlined ABS Sleeper/Diner Smooth Sided
Pennsylvania

2000 Volume 2
September 2000

Item No. 30-6717, Car Nos. 4502, Cascade Echo

2-Car 60’ Streamlined ABS Sleeper/Diner Smooth Sided
Santa Fe

2000 Volume 2
September 2000

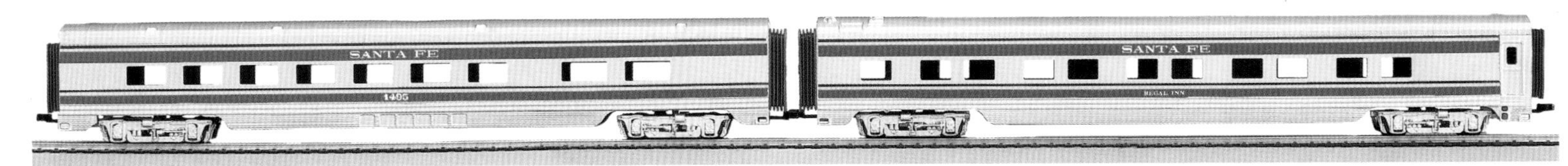

Item No. 30-6719, Car Nos. 1495, Regal Inn

2-Car 60’ Streamlined ABS Sleeper/Diner Smooth Sided
Rock Island

2000 Volume 2
September 2000

Item No. 30-6710, Car Names Golden Goblet, Golden Crest

2-Car O-27 Madison Combo/Diner
Pennsylvania

1997 Volume 2
January 1998

Item No. 30-6204, Car Nos. 4910, 4484

2-Car O-27 Madison Combo/Diner
Texas & Pacific

1997 Volume 2
April 1998

Item No. 30-6224, Car Nos. 800, 1015

2-Car O-27 Madison Combo/Diner
Denver &Rio Grande

1997 Volume 2
February 1998

Item No. 30-6234, Car Nos. 633, 804 Pikes Peak

2-Car O-27 Madison Combo/Diner
New York Central

1997 Volume 2
January 1998

Item No. 30-6214, Car Names. New York, Albany

2-Car O-27 Madison Combo/Diner
Southern

1998 Volume 2
July 1998

Item No. 30-6241, Car Nos. William Moultrie, 3159

2-Car O-27 Madison Combo/Diner
Nickel Plate Road

1998 Volume 2
June 1998

Item No. 30-6245, Car Nos. 830, 126

2-Car O-27 Madison Combo/Diner
Chesapeake & Ohio

1998 Volume 2
June 1998

Item No. 30-6249, Car Nos. 50, 10

2-Car O-27 Madison Combo/Diner
Union Pacific

1998 Volume 2
June 1998

Item No. 30-6253, Car Nos. 5616, 3633

2-Car O-27 Madison Combo/Diner
Jersey Central

2000 Volume 1
December 1999

Item No. 30-6267, Car Nos. 212, 1014

2-Car O-27 Madison Combo/Diner
Reading

2000 Volume 1
December 1999

Item No. 30-6268, Car Nos. 593, 1186

2-Car O-27 Madison Combo/Diner
Baltimore & Ohio

2000 Volume 2
January 2000

Item No. 30-6269, Car Nos. 3667, 3669

2-Car O-27 Madison Combo/Diner
New York Central

1998 Volume 3
April 1999

Item No. 30-6257, Car Nos. 8987, 574

2-Car O-27 Madison Combo/Diner
Wabash

1999 Volume 3
February 2000

Item No. 30-6263, Car Nos. 454, 649

2-Car O-27 Streamlined Combo/Diner
Santa Fe

1997 Volume 2
December 1997

Item No. 30-6014, Car Nos. 3481, 1503

2-Car O-27 Streamlined Combo/Diner
New York Central

1997 Volume 2
February 1998

Item No. 30-6024, Car Nos. 450, 290

2-Car O-27 Streamlined Combo/Diner
Amtrak

1997 Volume 2
February 1998

Item No. 30-6004, Car Names. New Haven, Boston

2-Car O-27 Streamlined Combo/Diner
Union Pacific

1997 Volume 2
December 1997

Item No. 30-6034, Car Nos. 5007, 6005

2-Car O-27 Streamlined Combo/Diner
California Zephyr

1998 Volume 1
January 1998

Item No. 30-6054, Car Nos. 196, 800

2-Car O-27 Streamlined Combo/Diner
Florida East Coast

1998 Volume 1
April 1998

Item No. 30-6044, Car Nos. 1901, 4128

2-Car O-27 Streamlined Combo/Diner
New York Central

1998 Volume 1
January 1998

Item No. 30-6083, Car Nos. 290, 450

2-Car O-27 Streamlined Combo/Diner
Pennsylvania

1998 Volume 1
January 1998

Item No. 30-6073, Car Nos. 6365, 1155

2-Car O-27 Streamlined Combo/Diner
Southern Pacific

1998 Volume 1
December 1997

Item No. 30-6063, Car Nos. 6099, 10214

2-Car O-27 Streamlined Combo/Diner
Milwaukee Road

1998 Volume 2
February 1999

Item No. 30-6091, Car Nos. 1220, 170

2-Car O-27 Streamlined Combo/Diner
Denver & Rio Grande

1998 Volume 2
December 1998

Item No. 30-6095, Car Nos. 738, 1280

2-Car O-27 Streamlined Combo/Diner
Delaware & Hudson

1998 Volume 2
January 1998

Item No. 30-6099, Car Nos. 43, 54

2-Car O-27 Streamlined Combo/Diner
Santa Fe

1998 Volume 3
February 1999

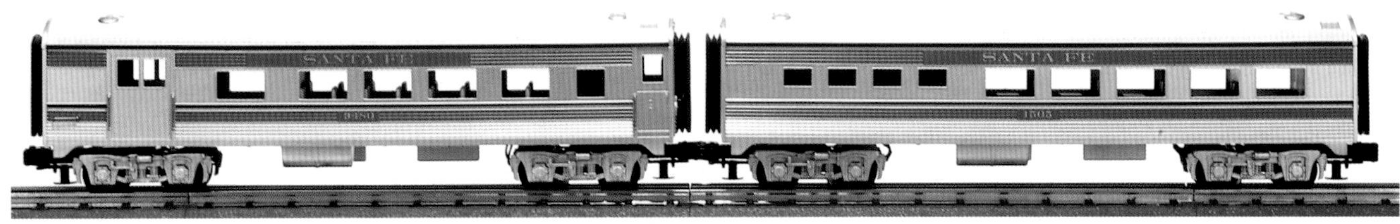

Item No. 30-6105, Car Nos. 3480, 1505

2-Car O-27 Streamlined Combo/Diner
Pennsylvania

1998 Volume 3
December 1999

Item No. 30-6106, Car Nos. 4507, 5109

2-Car O-27 Streamlined Combo/Diner
Union Pacific

1999 Volume 1
January 1999

Item No. 30-6108, Car Nos. 5010, 5601

2-Car O-27 Streamlined Combo/Diner
Southern Pacific

1999 Volume 3
January 2000

Item No. 30-6064 Car Nos. 6098, 10213

2-Car O-27 Streamlined Combo/Diner
New York Central

1999 Volume 3
January 2000

Item No. 30-6084, Car Nos. 281, 440

2-Car O-27 Streamlined Combo/Diner
New York Central - Empire

1999 Volume 3
January 2000

Item No. 30-6126, Car Nos. 33, 687

2-Car O-27 Streamlined Combo/Diner
Baltimore & Ohio

1999 Volume 3
January 2000

Item No. 30-6127, Car Nos. 1429, 1036

2-Car O-27 Streamlined Combo/Diner
Electro Motive Division

1999 Volume 3
January 2000

Item No. 30-6128, Car Nos. 1011, 904

2-Car O-27 Streamlined Combo/Diner
Santa Fe

1999 Volume 3
January 2000

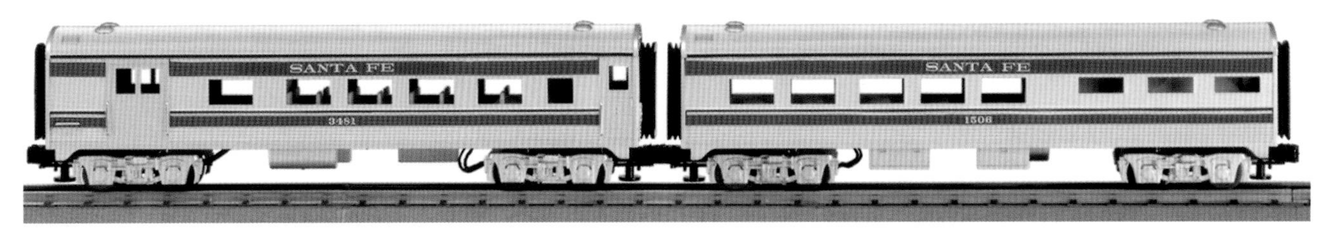

Item No. 30-6129, Car Nos. 3481, 1506

2-Car O-27 Streamlined Combo/Diner
Southern

1999 Volume 3
January 2000

Item No. 30-6130, Car Nos. 727, 3309

2-Car O-27 Streamlined Combo/Diner
New Haven

2000 Volume 1
July 2000

Item No. 30-6137, Car Nos. 905, 200

2-Car O-27 Streamlined Combo/Diner
Reading

2000 Volume 1
July 2000

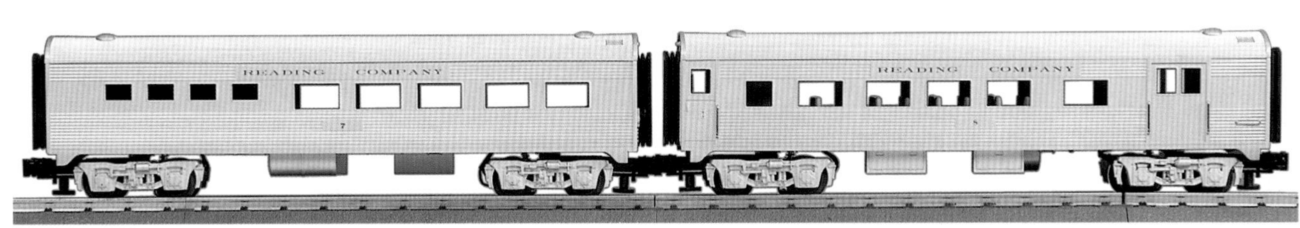

Item No. 30-6138, Car Nos. 8, 7

2-Car O-27 Streamlined Combo/Diner
Denver & Rio Grande

2000 Volume 2
September 2000

Item No. 30-6150, Car Nos. 1231, 1116

2-Car O-27 Streamlined Combo/Diner
Chesapeake & Ohio

2000 Volume 2
September 2000

Item No. 30-6148, Car Nos. 1403, 1903

2-Car O-27 SuperLiner Sleeper/Diner
Amtrak

1998 Volume 3
November 1998

Item No. 30-6501, Car Nos. 32023, 38041

2-Car Subway Add-On Non Powered
New York Transit

1999 Volume 2
September 1999

Item No. 30-2161, Car Nos. 4550, 4551

2-Car Subway Add-On Non Powered
New York Transit

1999 Volume 2
September 1999

Item No. 30-2163, Car Nos. 4824, 4825

3-Car Overton Coach
Western & Atlantic

1997 Volume 1
April 1998

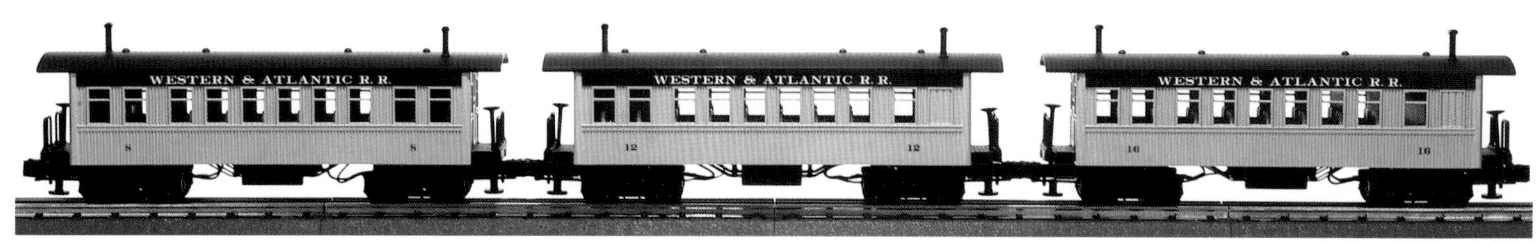

Item No. 30-6400, Car Nos. 8, 12, 16

3-Car Overton Coach
Wanderer

2000 Volume 1
December 1999

Item No. 30-6405, Car Nos. 1999, 1968, 1965

3-Car Overton Coach
Denver & Rio Grande

2000 Volume 1
December 1999

Item No. 30-6406, Car Nos. 256, 410, 350

4-Car 60' Aluminum
Pennsylvania

2000 Volume 1
August 2000

Item No. 30-6707, Car Nos. 134, 1216, 1214, 821

4-Car 60' Aluminum
Pennsylvania

Uncataloged Item
July 2000

Item No. 20-80002f (2000 DAP), Car Names Betsy Ross, William Penn, Molly Pitcher, Alexander Hamilton

4-Car 60' Streamlined ABS Smooth Sided
Union Pacific

2000 Volume 1
June 2000

Item No. 30-6701, Car Nos. 6334, 514, 7008, 1576

4-Car 60' Streamlined ABS Smooth Sided
Seaboard

2000 Volume 1
July 2000

Item No. 30-6703, Car Nos. 185, Glen Gary, Sunshine, Lake Geneva

4-Car 60' Streamlined ABS Smooth Sided
Santa Fe

2000 Volume 1
April 2000

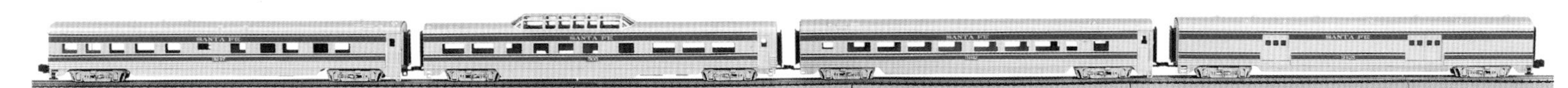

Item No. 30-6705, Car Nos. 3425, 3162, 505, 3247

4-Car 60' Streamlined ABS Smooth Sided
Rock Island

2000 Volume 1
April 2000

Item No. 30-6708, Car Names 820, La Palma, La Quinta, La Mirada

4-Car 60' Streamlined ABS Smooth Sided
Pennsylvania

2000 Volume 2
January 2001

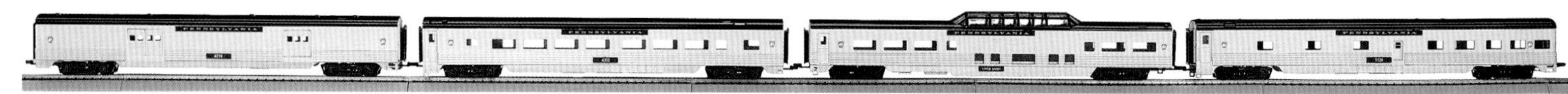

Item No. 30-6715, Car Nos. 4019, 4008, Upper Darby, 1126

4-Car 60' Streamlined ABS Smooth Sided
Southern Pacific

2000 Volume 2
October 2000

Item No. 30-6724, Car Nos. 6601, 2357, 2485, 2950

4-Car 60' Streamlined ABS Smooth Sided
Lehigh Valley

2000 Volume 2
October 2000

Item No. 30-6711, Car Nos. 1200, 1511, 1016, 353

4-Car O-27 Madison
Denver & Rio Grande

1997 Volume 1
November 1997

Item No. 30-6230, Car Nos. 711, 1021, 1013, Granite Canyon

4-Car O-27 Madison
Southern

1997 Volume 2
May 1998

Item No. 30-6240, Car Nos. 0200 Railway Express Agency, Robert F. Hoke, Henry W. Grady, Joel Chandler Harris

4-Car O-27 Madison
Chesapeake & Ohio

1998 Volume 1
May 1998

Item No. 30-6248 Car Nos. 60, 1626, 1649, 1803 Elk Lake

4-Car O-27 Madison
Nickel Plate Road

1998 Volume 1
May 1998

Item No. 30-6244, Car Nos. 349, 101, 107, 130

4-Car O-27 Madison
Union Pacific

1998 Volume 1
July 1998

Item No. 30-6252, Car Nos. 1735, 418, 405, 1548

4-Car O-27 Madison
New York Central

1998 Volume 2
December 1998

Item No. 30-6256, Car Nos. 8986, Park Trail, Wappingers Falls, Maumee River

4-Car O-27 Madison
Pennsylvania

1998 Volume 3
December 1998

Item No. 30-6250, Car Nos. 9055, 1032, 1048, 180

4-Car O-27 Madison
Jersey Central

1999 Volume 1
June 1999

Item No. 30-6258, Car Nos. 918, 210

4-Car O-27 Madison
Reading

1999 Volume 1
June 1999

Item No. 30-6260, Car Nos. 1715, 1505, 1507, 10

4-Car O-27 Madison
Wabash

1999 Volume 2
July 1999

Item No. 30-6262, Car Nos. 1222, 1227, 336, 6

4-Car O-27 Madison
New York Central

1999 Volume 3
December 1999

Item No. 30-6264, Car Nos. 3311, 143, 1017, 745

4-Car O-27 Madison
Baltimore & Ohio

2000 Volume 1
January 2000

Item No. 30-6265, Car Nos. 658, 3661, 3663, 901

4-Car O-27 Madison
Pennsylvania

2000 Volume 2
November 2000

Item No. 30-6236, Car Nos. 9056, 1033, 1049, 120

4-Car O-27 Madison
Southern Pacific

1997 Volume 1
May 1997

Item No. 30-6060, Car Nos. 6092, 2430, 10281, 10282

4-Car O-27 Madison
Pennsylvania

1997 Volume 1
August 1997

Item No. 30-6070, Car Nos. 6368, 4008, 2036, 1126

4-Car O-27 Madison
New York Central

1997 Volume 1
November 1997

Item No. 30-6080, Car Nos. 5018, 2942, 2580, 10634

4-Car O-27 Streamlined
Pennsylvania

1998 Volume 2
December 1998

Item No. 30-6104, Car Nos. 5248, 4518, 2673, 1123

4-Car O-27 Streamlined
Union Pacific

1998 Volume 3
December 1998

Item No. 30-6107, Car Nos. 103, 102, 101, 100

4-Car O-27 Streamlined
Southern Pacific

1999 Volume 1
March 1999

Item No. 30-6109, Car Nos. 6625, 2483, 3603, 2951

4-Car O-27 Streamlined
New York Central

1999 Volume 1
March 1999

Item No. 30-6110, Car Nos. 9150, 3123, 2582, 1063

4-Car O-27 Streamlined
Baltimore & Ohio

1999 Volume 1
April 1999

Item No. 30-6111, Car Nos. 662, 3567, 5551, 7512

4-Car O-27 Streamlined
EMD Demonstrator

1999 Volume 1
April 1999

Item No. 30-6112, Car Nos. 9612, 1021, 2743, 5646

4-Car O-27 Streamlined
New York Central

1999 Volume 1
March 1999

Item No. 30-6113, Car Nos. 5002, 2933, 3030, 50

4-Car O-27 Streamlined
Southern

1999 Volume 2
November 1999

Item No. 30-6123, Car Nos. 1702, 837, 3787, 951

4-Car O-27 Streamlined
Santa Fe

1999 Volume 2
November 1999

Item No. 30-6120, Car Nos. 3482, 3161, 502, 3199

4-Car O-27 Streamlined
New Haven

1999 Volume 3
March 2000

Item No. 30-6131, Car Nos. 5578, 8677, 8645, 475

4-Car O-27 Streamlined
Reading

1999 Volume 3
March 2000

Item No. 30-6133 Car Nos. 5022, 2933, 3030, 50

4-Car O-27 Streamlined
Denver & Rio Grande

2000 Volume 1
July 2000

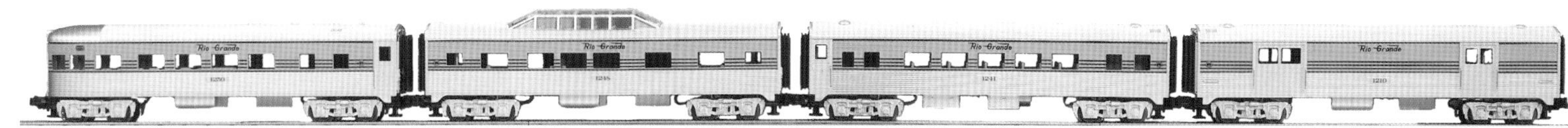

Item No. 30-6139, Car Nos. 1211, 1242, 1249, 1251

4-Car O-27 Streamlined
Chesapeake & Ohio

2000 Volume 1
July 2000

Item No. 30-6141, Car Nos. 247, 1652, 1875, 29

4-Car O-27 Streamlined
Delaware & Hudson

1998 Volume 1
July 1998

Item No. 30-6098, Car Nos. 39, 53, 23, 42

4-Car O-27 Streamlined
Denver & Rio Grande

1998 Volume 1
September 1998

Item No. 30-6094, Car Nos. 1210, 1241, 1248, 1250

4-Car O-27 Streamlined
Milwaukee Road

1998 Volume 1
August 1998

Item No. 30-6090, Car Nos. 1331, 437, 450, Miller

4-Car O-27 Streamlined
New York Central

1999 Volume 3
March 2000

Item No. 30-6135, Car Nos. 9152, 10510, 10511, 10633

4-Car O-27 SuperLiner
Amtrak

1999 Volume 2
September 1999

Item No. 30-6500, Car Nos. 34022, 34022, 33010, 34022

4-Car Overton Coach
Western & Atlantic

1998 Volume 2
April 1998

Item No. 30-6404, Car Nos. 20, 22, 24, 28

60' Streamlined ABS Coach Car
Union Pacific

2000 Volume 1
June 2000

Item No. 30-6702, Car No. 591

60' Streamlined ABS Coach Car
Santa Fe

2000 Volume 1
April 2000

Item No. 30-6706, Car No. 3158

60' Streamlined ABS Coach Car
Pennsylvania

2000 Volume 2
January 2001

Item No. 30-6716, Car No. 4000

60' Streamlined ABS Coach Car
Lehigh Valley

2000 Volume 2
October 2000

Item No. 30-6712, Car No. 1513

60' Streamlined ABS Full-Length Vista Dome Car
Seaboard

2000 Volume 2
October 2000

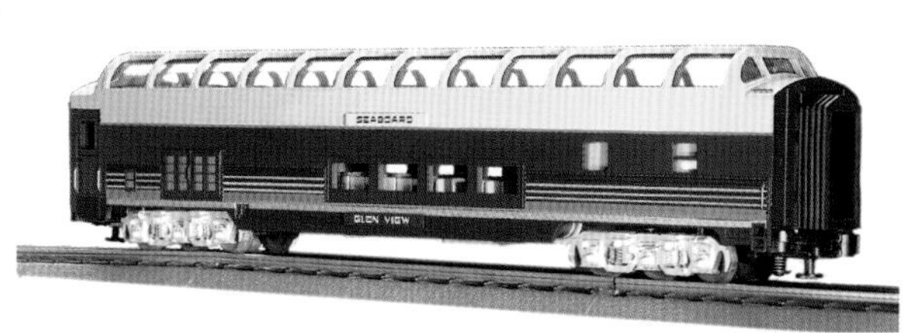

Item No. 30-6721, Car Name Glen View

60' Streamlined ABS Full-Length Vista Dome Car
Rock Island

2000 Volume 2
October 2000

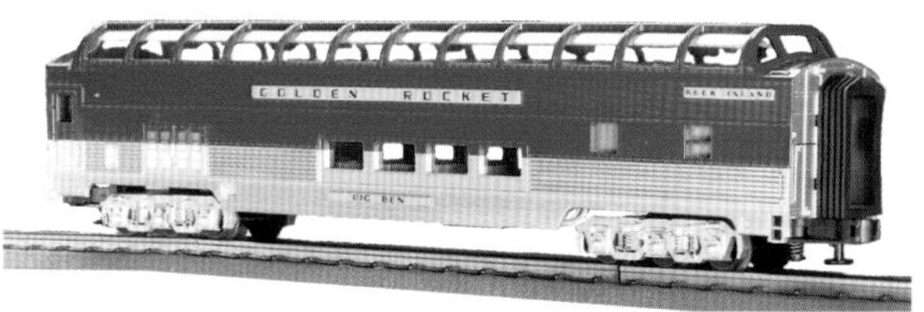

Item No. 30-6729, Car Name Big Ben

60' Streamlined ABS Coach Car
Seaboard

2000 Volume 1
July 2000

Item No. 30-6704, Car Name Glen Spruce

60' Streamlined ABS Coach Car
Rock Island

2000 Volume 1
April 2000

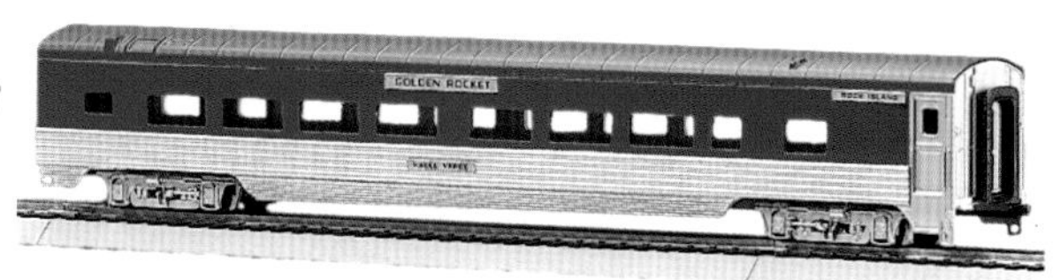

Item No. 30-6709, Car Name Valle Verde

60' Streamlined ABS Coach Car
Southern Pacific

2000 Volume 2
October 2000

Item No. 30-6727, Car No. 2356

60' Streamlined ABS Full-Length Vista Dome Car
Union Pacific

2000 Volume 2
October 2000

Item No. 30-6723, Car Name City of Portland

60' Streamlined ABS Full-Length Vista Dome Car
Santa Fe

2000 Volume 2
October 2000

Item No. 30-6728, Car No. 508

O-27 Madison Baggage Car
Pennsylvania

Spring 1997
September 1997

Item No. 30-6200, Car No. 5753

O-27 Madison Baggage Car
New York Central

Spring 1997
September 1997

Item No. 30-6210, Car Name Utica

O-27 Madison Coach Car
Pennsylvania

Spring 1997
September 1997

Item No. 30-6201, Car No. 3466

O-27 Madison Coach Car
New York Central

Spring 1997
September 1997

Item No. 30-6211, Car Name Rochester

O-27 Madison Coach Car
Texas & Pacific

Spring 1997
October 1997

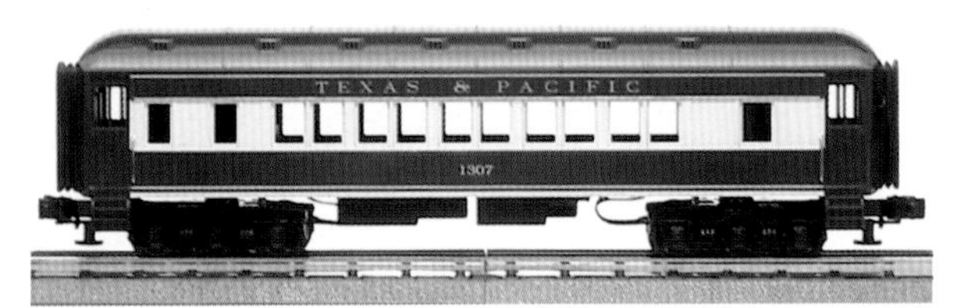

Item No. 30-6221, Car No. 1302

O-27 Madison Coach Car
Denver & Rio Grande

1997 Volume 1
November 1997

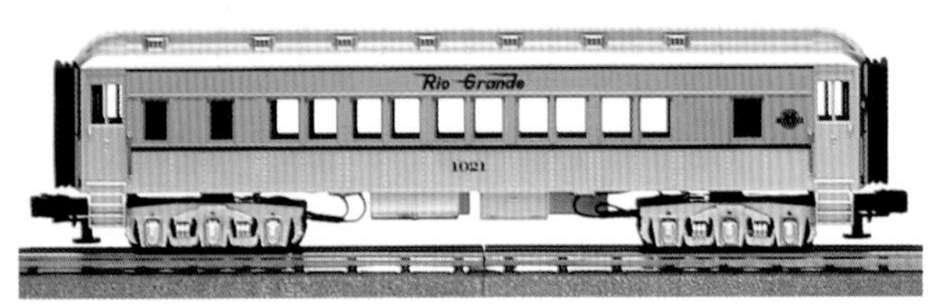

Item No. 30-6231, Car No. 1021

O-27 Madison Coach Car
Pennsylvania

2000 Volume 2
November 2000

Item No. 30-6237, Car No. 1034

O-27 Madison Baggage Car
Texas & Pacific

Spring 1997
October 1997

Item No. 30-6220, Car No. 910

O-27 Madison Coach Car
Pennsylvania

Spring 1997
September 1997

Item No. 30-6202, Car No. 4363

O-27 Madison Coach Car
New York Central

Spring 1997
September 1997

Item No. 30-6212, Car Name Syracuse

O-27 Madison Coach Car
Texas & Pacific

Spring 1997
October 1997

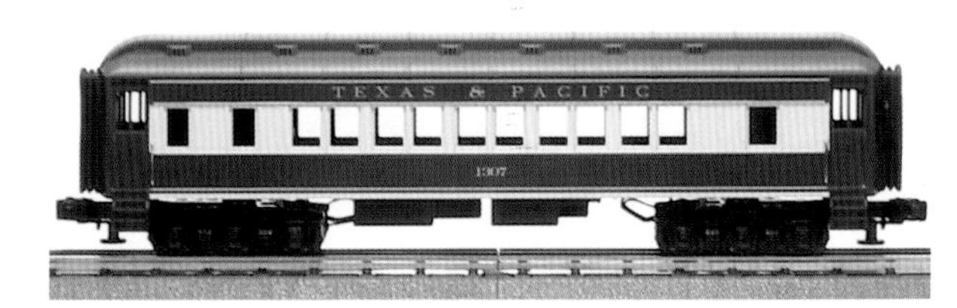

Item No. 30-6222, Car No. 1307

O-27 Madison Coach Car
Baltimore & Ohio

2000 Volume 1
January 2000

Item No. 30-6266, Car No. 365

O-27 Madison Observation Car
Pennsylvania

Spring 1997
September 1997

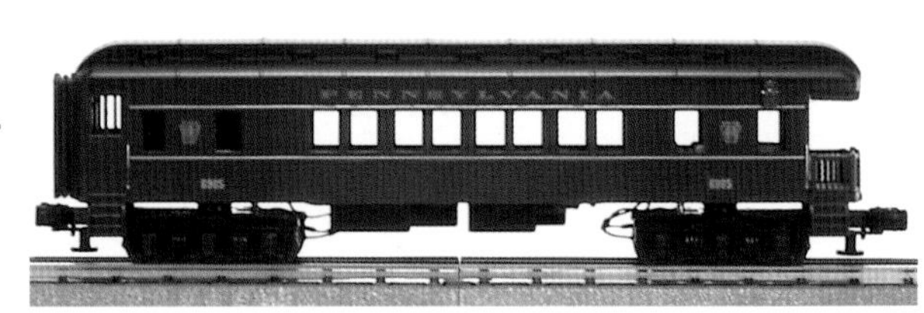

Item No. 30-6203, Car No. 6905

O-27 Madison Observation Car
New York Central

Spring 1997
September 1997

Item No. 30-6213, Car Name Buffalo

O-27 Streamlined Baggage Car
Amtrak

Fall/Winter 1996
March 1997

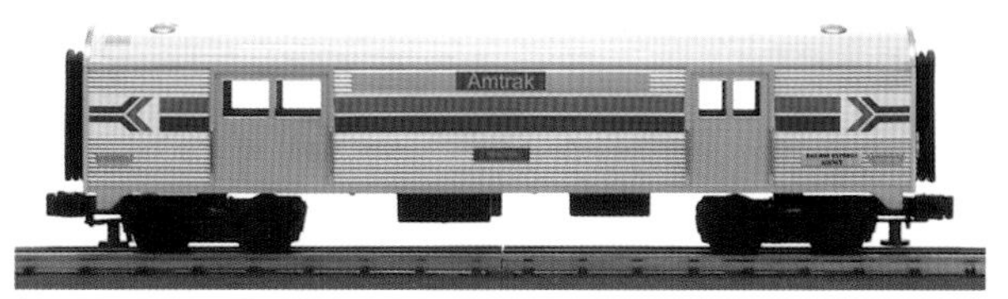

Item No. 30-6000, Car Name New York

O-27 Streamlined Baggage Car
New York Central

Spring 1997
April 1997

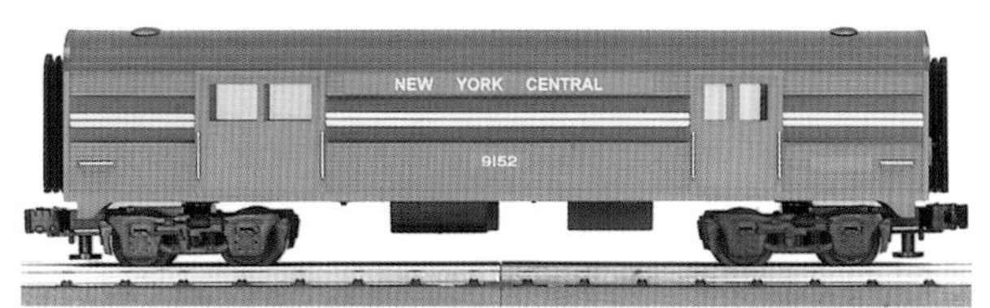

Item No. 30-6020, Car No. 9152

O-27 Streamlined Baggage Car
Florida East Coast

Spring 1997
March 1997

Item No. 30-6040, Car No. 443

O-27 Streamlined Coach Car
Amtrak

Fall/Winter 1996
March 1997

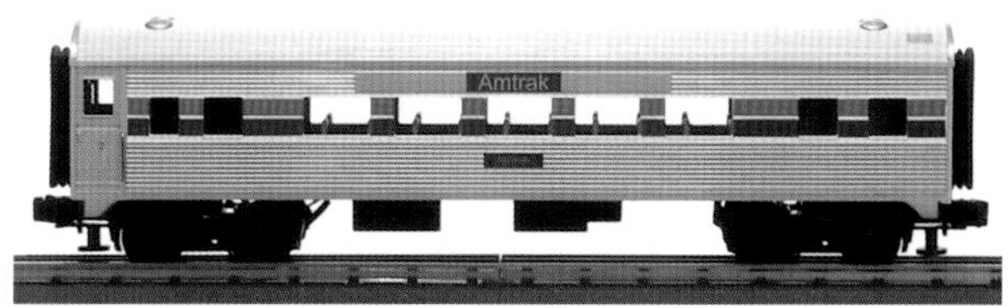

Item No. 30-6001, Car Name Baltimore

O-27 Streamlined Coach Car
New York Central

Spring 1997
April 1997

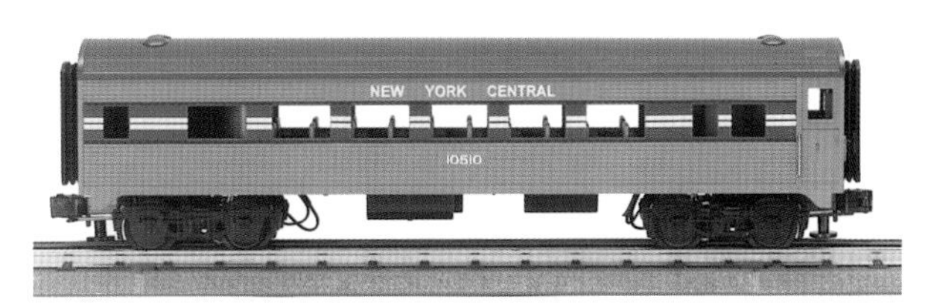

Item No. 30-6021, Car No. 10510

O-27 Madison Observation Car
Texas & Pacific

Spring 1997
October 1997

Item No. 30-6223, Car No. 1314

O-27 Streamlined Baggage Car
Santa Fe

Fall/Winter 1996
March 1997

Item No. 30-6010, Car No. 3480

O-27 Streamlined Baggage Car
Union Pacific

Spring 1997
May 1997

Item No. 30-6030, Car No. 6327

O-27 Streamlined Baggage Car
California Zephyr

Spring 1997
March 1997

Item No. 30-6050, Car No. 900

O-27 Streamlined Coach Car
Santa Fe

Fall/Winter 1996
March 1997

Item No. 30-6011, Car No. 3163

O-27 Streamlined Coach Car
Union Pacific

Spring 1997
May 1997

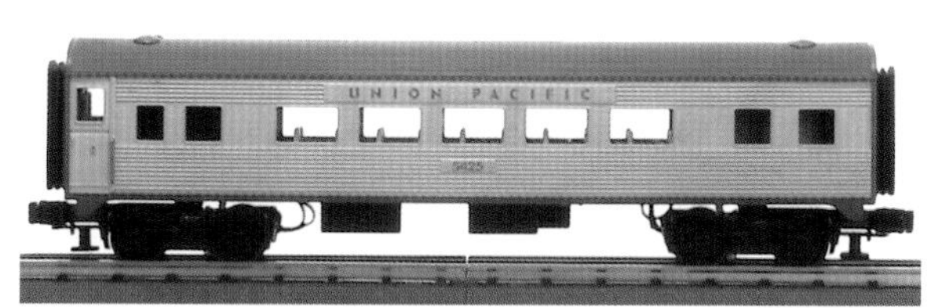

Item No. 30-6031, Car No. 5425

O-27 Streamlined Coach Car
Florida East Coast

Spring 1997
May 1997

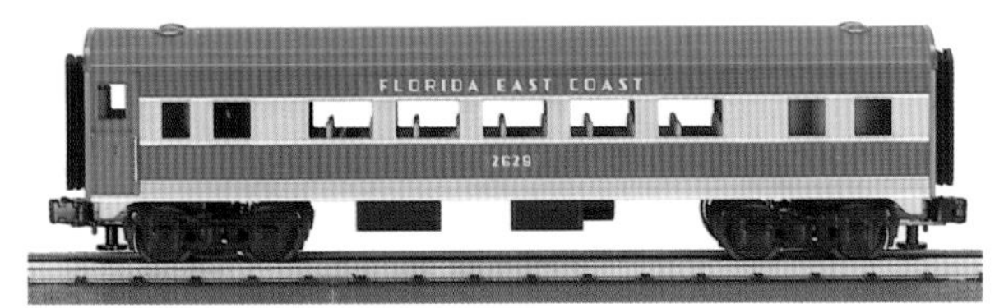

Item No. 30-6041, Car No. 2629

O-27 Streamlined Coach Car
New York Central

1997 Volume 1
December 1997

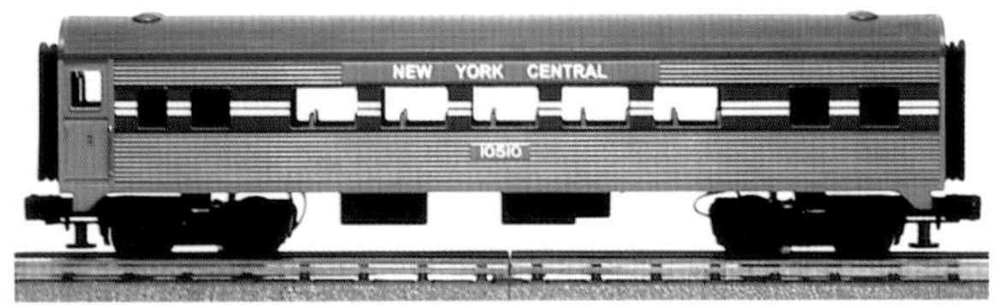

Item No. 30-6081, Car No. 10510

O-27 Streamlined Coach Car
Southern Pacific

1999 Volume 1
March 1999

Item No. 30-6114, Car No. 2486

O-27 Streamlined Coach Car
New York Central

1999 Volume 1
April 1999

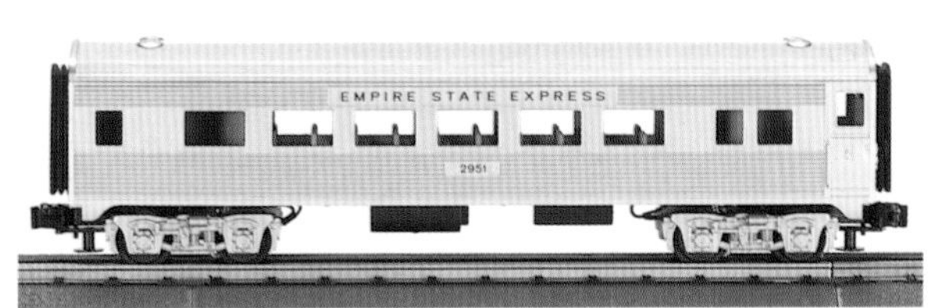

Item No. 30-6119, Car No. 2951

O-27 Streamlined Coach Car
Electro Motive Division

1999 Volume 1
April 1999

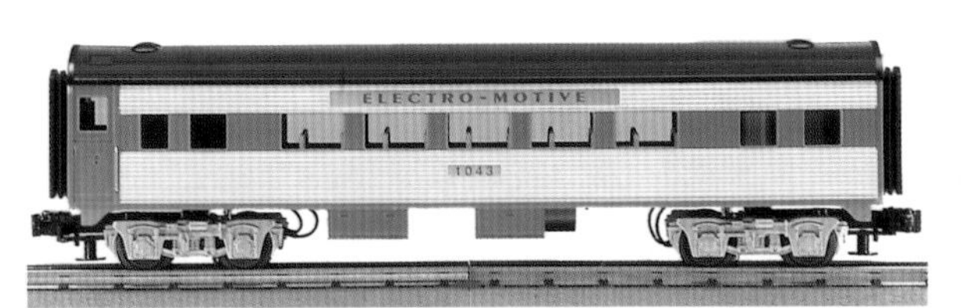

Item No. 30-6117, Car No. 1043

O-27 Streamlined Coach Car
New Haven

1999 Volume 3
March 2000

Item No. 30-6132, Car No. 8677

O-27 Streamlined Coach Car
California Zephyr

Spring 1997
March 1997

Item No. 30-6051, Car No. 4707

O-27 Streamlined Coach Car
Santa Fe

1998 Volume 2
April 1998

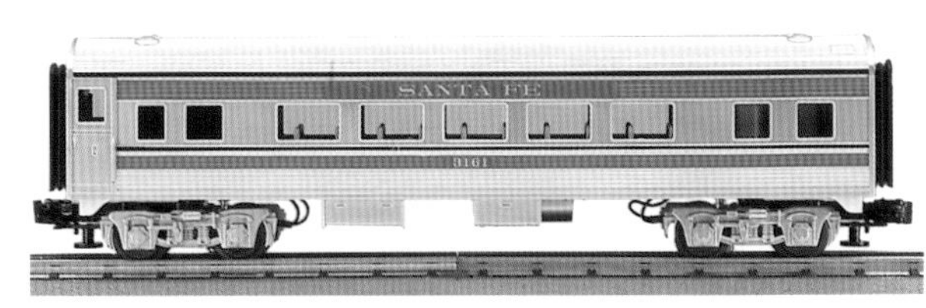

Item No. 30-6102, Car No. 3161

O-27 Streamlined Coach Car
New York Central

1999 Volume 1
March 1999

Item No. 30-6115, Car No. 2666

O-27 Streamlined Coach Car
Baltimore & Ohio

1999 Volume 1
April 1999

Item No. 30-6116, Car No. 3568

O-27 Streamlined Coach Car
Southern

1999 Volume 2
November 1999

Item No. 30-6124, Car No. 837

O-27 Streamlined Coach Car
Reading

1999 Volume 3
March 2000

Item No. 30-6134, Car No. 2951

O-27 Streamlined Coach Car
Denver & Rio Grande

2000 Volume 1
July 2000

Item No. 30-6140, Car No. 1243

O-27 Streamlined Full-Length Vista Dome Car
Southern Pacific

2000 Volume 1
June 2000

Item No. 30-6065, Car No. 3606

O-27 Streamlined Full-Length Vista Dome Car
Santa Fe

2000 Volume 1
June 2000

Item No. 30-6145, Car No. 500

O-27 Streamlined Full-Length Vista Dome Car
New Haven

2000 Volume 1
June 2000

Item No. 30-6144, Car No. 435

O-27 Streamlined Full-Length Vista Dome Car
Chesapeake & Ohio

2000 Volume 2
October 2000

Item No. 30-6149, Car No. 1876

O-27 Streamlined Observation Car
Santa Fe

Fall/Winter 1996
March 1997

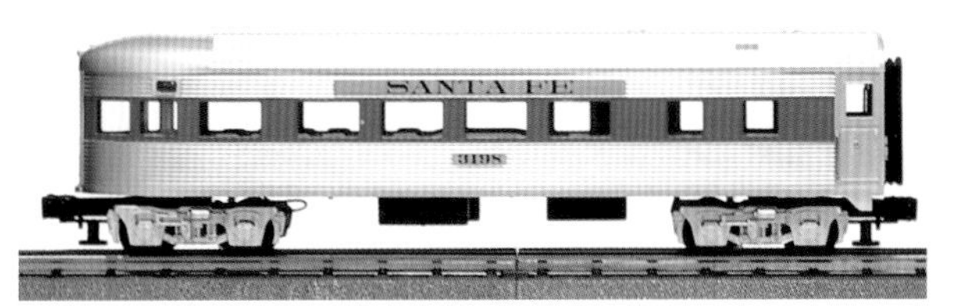

Item No. 30-6013, Car No. 3198

O-27 Streamlined Coach Car
Chesapeake & Ohio

2000 Volume 1
July 2000

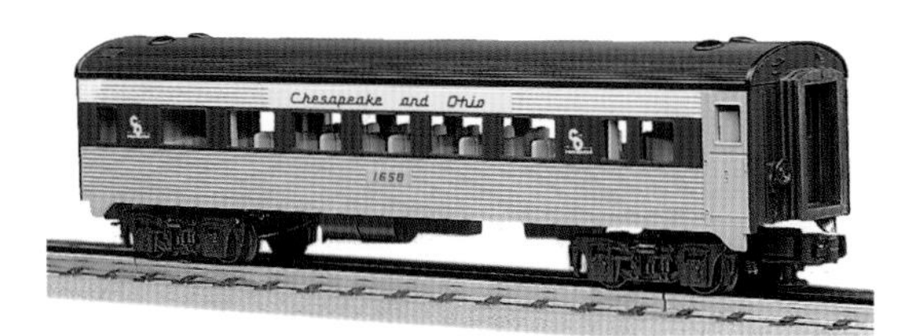

Item No. 30-6142, Car No. 1658

O-27 Streamlined Full-Length Vista Dome Car
Milwaukee Road

2000 Volume 1
June 2000

Item No. 30-6092, Car No. 50

O-27 Streamlined Full-Length Vista Dome Car
Electro Motive Division

2000 Volume 1
June 2000

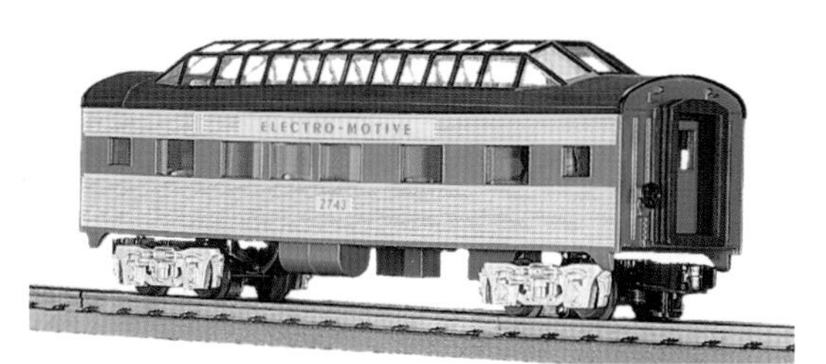

Item No. 30-6143, Car No. 2743

O-27 Streamlined Full-Length Vista Dome Car
Denver & Rio Grande

2000 Volume 2
October 2000

Item No. 30-6151, Car Name Vista Grande

O-27 Streamlined Observation Car
Amtrak

Fall/Winter 1996
March 1997

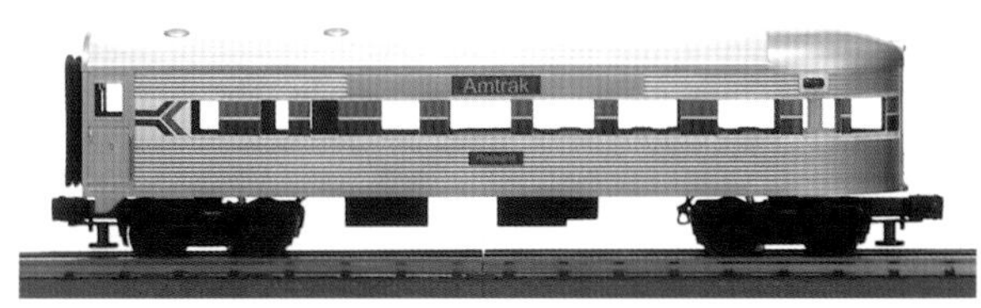

Item No. 30-6003, Car Name Philadelphia

O-27 Streamlined Observation Car
New York Central

Spring 1997
April 1997

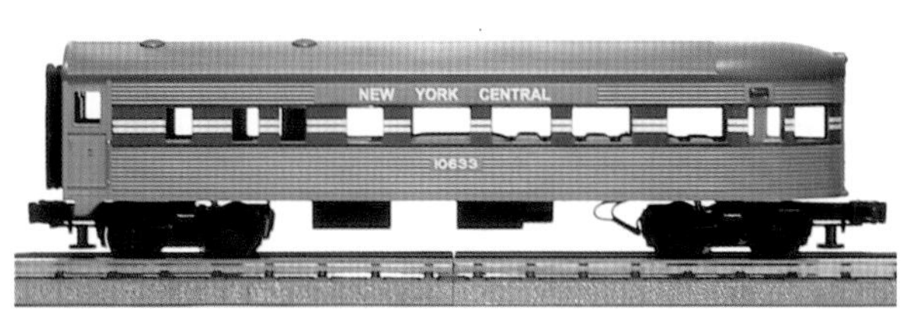

Item No. 30-6023, Car No. 10633

O-27 Streamlined Observation Car
Union Pacific

Spring 1997
May 1997

Item No. 30-6033, Car No. 9356

O-27 Streamlined Observation Car
Florida East Coast

Spring 1997
May 1997

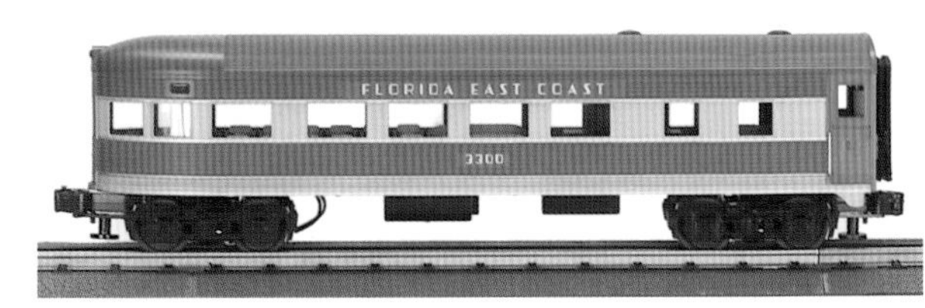

Item No. 30-6043, Car No. 3300

O-27 Streamlined Observation Car
California Zephyr

Spring 1997
March 1997

Item No. 30-6053, Car No. 302

O-27 Streamlined Observation Car
Reading

2000 Volume 1
December 1999

Item No. 30-6136, Car No. 6

O-27 Streamlined Vista Dome Car
Amtrak

Fall/Winter 1996
March 1997

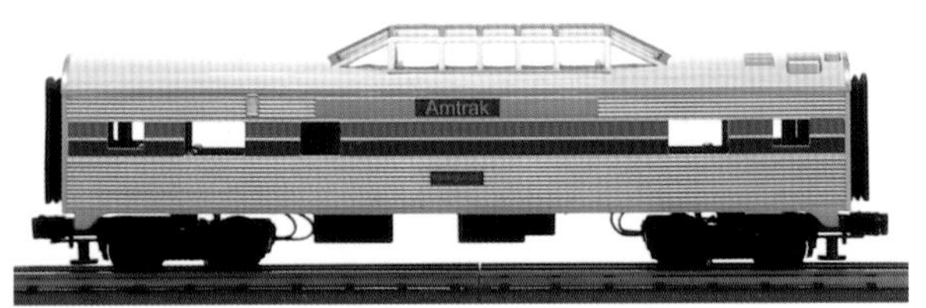

Item No. 30-6002, Car Name Washington D.C.

O-27 Streamlined Vista Dome Car
Santa Fe

Fall/Winter 1996
March 1997

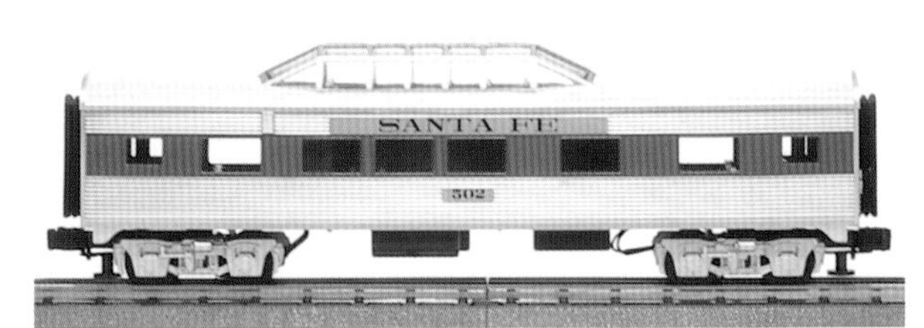

Item No. 30-6012, Car No. 502

O-27 Streamlined Vista Dome Car
New York Central

Spring 1997
April 1997

Item No. 30-6022, Car No. 10590

O-27 Streamlined Vista Dome Car
Union Pacific

Spring 1997
May 1997

Item No. 30-6032, Car No. 8001

O-27 Streamlined Vista Dome Car
Florida East Coast

Spring 1997
May 1997

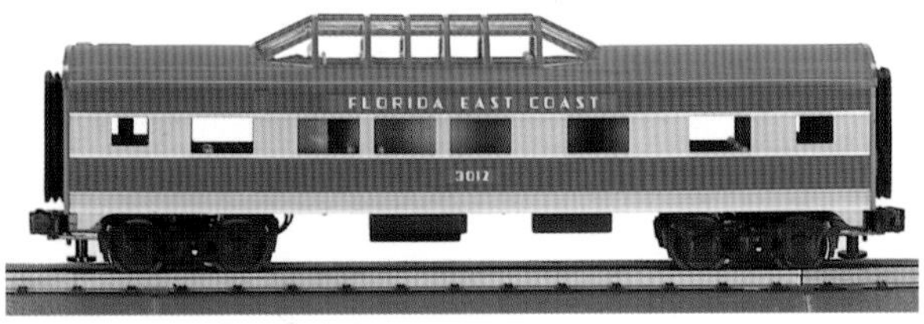

Item No. 30-6042, Car No. 3012

O-27 Streamlined Vista Dome Car
California Zephyr

Spring 1997
March 1997

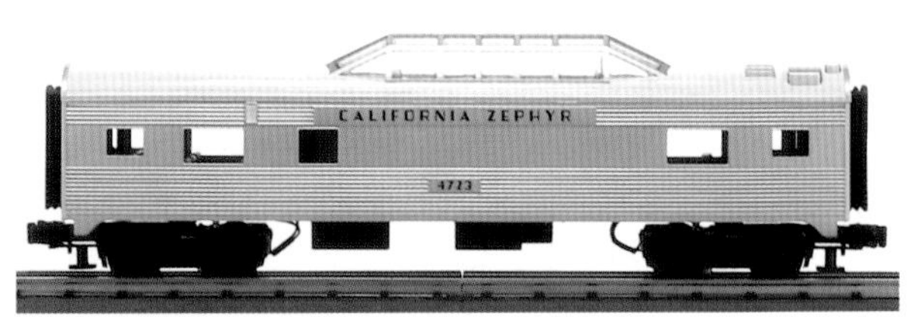

Item No. 30-6052, Car No. 4723

O-27 Streamlined Vista Dome Car
New York Central

1997 Volume 1
October 1997

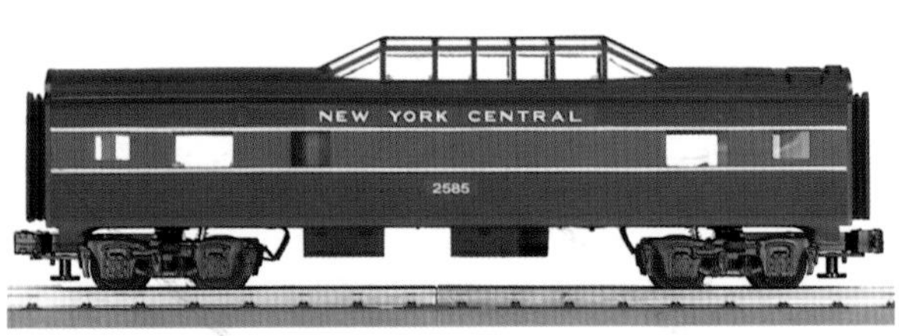

Item No. 30-6082, Car No. 2585

O-27 Streamlined Vista Dome Car
Southern Pacific

1999 Volume 1
March 1999

Item No. 30-6118, Car No. 3660

O-27 Streamlined Vista Dome Car
Santa Fe

1999 Volume 2
November 1999

Item No. 30-6121, Car No. 502

SuperLiner Transitional Sleeper Car\Diner Cars
Amtrak

1999 Volume 3
January 2000

Item No. 30-6503, Car Nos. 38026, 32013

O-27 Streamlined Coach Car *(photo not available)*
Southern Pacific
Item No. 30-6061

1997 Volume 1
September 1997

O-27 Streamlined Coach Car *(photo not available)*
Pennsylvania
Item No. 30-6071, Car No. 4005

1997 Volume 1
August 1997

O-27 Streamlined Vista Dome Car *(photo not available)*
Southern Pacific
Item No. 30-6062

1997 Volume 1
September 1997

O-27 Streamlined Vista Dome Car *(photo not available)*
Pennsylvania
Item No. 30-6072, Car No. 2032

1997 Volume 1
August 1997

4-Car O-27 Streamlined *(photo not available)*
Santa Fe
Item No. 30-6103

1998 Volume 2
April 1998

RAILKING LINE
Ready-To-Run / Specialty Sets

The highest profile RailKing specialty sets are the Ready-To-Run™ starter sets. Since M.T.H. made its first train set, (without track and transformer) in 1995, Ready-To-Run sets have grown to become the most complete sets and best value in O Gauge railroading. They now include a loop of M.T.H.'s RealTrax™ snap-together track with lock-on, a powerful transformer, a RailWare interactive CD Rom with track layout software and other information helpful to beginning model railroaders, and, beginning with the 2000 volume two catalog, a wireless infrared remote control. They are also unique in offering complete sound systems in a starter set. M.T.H. also makes other kinds of RailKing specialty sets, including 6-car freight sets and operating sets like the 4-car subway set and the hand car set. There are also complete train sets, like the Amtrak diesel set, that contain an engine and matching cars but not the remainder of the Ready-To-Run package. These sets make it easy for an established model railroader who has no need for additional track or another transformer to buy a whole train at once. All RailKing specialty sets are of the same quality construction as other RailKing items.

4-Bay Hopper 6 Car Set
Union Pacific

1999 Volume 2
May 1999

Item No. 30-7521, Car Nos. 38277, 38397, 38430, 38438, 38454, 38465

4-Bay Hopper 6 Car Set
Chesapeake & Ohio

1999 Volume 2
November 1999

Item No. 30-7520, Car Nos. 72194, 72135, 72126, 71909, 71800, 71504

4-Bay Hopper 6 Car Set
Pennsylvania

2000 Volume 1
December 1999

Item No. 30-7530, Car Nos. 137761, 137763, 137769, 137775, 137779, 137782

4-Bay Hopper 6 Car Set
Northern Pacific

2000 Volume 1
May 2000

Item No. 30-7531, Car Nos. 73484, 73475, 73472, 73470, 73468, 73450

4-Bay Hopper 6 Car Set
Norfolk & Western

2000 Volume 2
December 2000

Item No. 30-7535, Car Nos. 131082, 131094, 131103, 13117, 131121, 131126
Item No. 30-7536, Car Nos. 131129, 131133, 131135, 131140, 131142, 131146

6-Car Freight Set
Jersey Central

1999 Volume 2
June 1999

Item No. 30-7003, Car Nos. Bay Window Caboose 91515, Gondola with Junk Load 90170, Crane Car 6, Crane Tender 92615, Rounded Roof Box Car 22861, Tank Car 92511

6-Car Freight Set
Wabash

1999 Volume 2
September 1999

Item No. 30-7001, Car Nos. Woodsided Caboose 2624, Flat Car with Trailer 25536, Gondola with Junk Load 11615, Crane Car 0137, Crane Tender 01014, Box Car 60800

6-Car Freight Set
Southern

1999 Volume 2
November 1999

Item No. 30-7002, Car Nos. Steel Caboose X-253, Depressed Flat Car with Transformer 50052, Searchlight Car 50011, 3-Dome Tank Car 995006, Stock Car 45778, Box Car 45581

6-Car Freight Set
Union Pacific

1999 Volume 3
July 2000

Item No. 30-7005, Car Nos. Steel Caboose 25506, PS2 Discharge Hopper 11136, 33g Tank Car 75224, Modern Reefer Car 41950, Husky Stack Car 2520031, 4-Bay Cylindrical Hopper 25744

6-Car Freight Set
Great Northern

1999 Volume 3
April 2000

Item No. 30-7006, Car Nos. Steel Caboose X-108, 4-Bay Hopper with Coal Load 70458, Gondola with Junk Load 72839, Crane Car X-1724, Crane Tender X-2507, Box Car 6341

6-Car Freight Set
Pennsylvania

2000 Volume 1
June 2000

Item No. 30-7007, Car Nos. N5c Caboose 477846, Tank Car 102097, Auto Carrier with Corvettes 30063, Gondola with Junk Load 376901, Stock Car 131253, Bulkhead Flat Car 469808

6-Car Freight Set
Louisville & Nashville

2000 Volume 1
June 2000

Item No. 30-7008, Car Nos. Steel Caboose 1067, Gondola with Junk Load 56943, Crane Car 40029, Rounded Roof Box Car 97892, 3-Dome Tank Car 20963, Flat Car with Trailer 476508

6-Car Freight Set
CP Rail

2000 Volume 1
April 2000

Item No. 30-7009, Car Nos. Steel Caboose 434162, Gondola with Junk Load 340222, Flat Car with Trucks 412569, Crane Car 414475, Madison Diner 412668, Bunk Car 412667

6-Car Freight Set
Baltimore & Ohio

2000 Volume 1
May 2000

Item No. 30-7010, Car Nos. Woodsided Caboose C1684, Flat Car with Trailer 9130, 4-Bay Hopper with Coal Load 433554, Searchlight Car 9935, Tank Car X-417, Box Car 270446

6-Car Freight Set
Conrail

2000 Volume 2
November 2000

Item No. 30-7011, Car Nos. Bay Window Caboose 21280, 3-Dome Tank Car 5011, Searchlight Car 766156, 4-Bay Hopper with Coal Load 196600, Gondola with Junk Load 510475, Box Car 231663

6-Car Freight Set
Pennsylvania

2000 Volume 2
October 2000

Item No. 30-7016, Car Nos. Woodsided Caboose 982014, 3-Dome Tank Car 498752, Flat Car with Trailer 469980, Flat Car with Fire Truck 1979, 4-Bay Hopper with Coal Load 744433, 50' Modern Box Car 569356

6-Car Freight Set
Reading

2000 Volume 2
August 2000

Item No. 30-7017, Car Nos. Steel Caboose 92911, 4-Bay Hopper with Coal Load 86178, Tank Car 90980, Flat Car with Trailer 9475, Gondola with Junk Load 96316, Box Car 118237

6-Car Freight Set
New Haven

2000 Volume 2
September 2000

Item No. 30-7013, Car Nos. Steel Caboose C-649, Depressed Flat Car with Transformer 17100, 4-Bay Hopper with Coal Load 81008, Covered Gondola 61072, Flat Car with Trailer 17369, 50' Modern Box Car 36438

6-Car Freight Set
Electro Motive Division

2000 Volume 2
October 2000

Item No. 30-7012, Car Nos. Steel Caboose SD45, Depressed Flat Car with Transformer EMDX106, 4-Bay Hopper with Coal Load 33556, Flat Car with Trailer SD912, Auto Carrier with '57 Chevys 10199, Box Car 20677

6-Car Freight Set
Virginian

2000 Volume 2
November 2000

Item No. 30-7018, Car Nos. Woodsided Caboose 327, Crane Car X-243, Crane Tender 90076, Searchlight Car X-11408, Flat Car with Trailer 10634, Box Car 63143

6-Car Freight Set
New York Ontario & Western

2000 Volume 2
November 2000

Item No. 30-7015, Car Nos. Woodsided Caboose 8343, Tank Car PPGX1080, 4-Bay Hopper with Coal Load 919, 2-Bay Offset Hopper WDLX101, Gondola with Junk Load No number, Box Car 5003

6-Car Freight Set
New York Central

2000 Volume 2
December 2000

Item No. 30-7014, Car Nos. Bay Window Caboose 21693, 4-Bay Hopper with Coal Load 862543, Flat Car with Trailer 50609, 3-Dome Tank Car X103001, Stock Car 27303, Box Car 92102

0-4-0 R-T-R Train Set
Baltimore & Ohio

1999 Volume 2
September 1999

3-Rail with Electronic Whistle, Item No. 30-4026-0, Car Nos. Caboose SF-45, Box Car 466038, Gondola with Junk Load 897, Engine No. 97

0-4-0 R-T-R Train Set
Jersey Central

2000 Volume 2
October 2000

3-Rail with Mechanical Whistle, Item No. 30-4035-0, Car Nos. Woodsided Caboose 91309, Hopper Car 61261, Box Car 20551, Engine No. 840

2-6-0 R-T-R Train Set
Baltimore & Ohio

1998 Volume 2
January 1998

3-Rail with Electronic Whistle, Item No. 30-4020-0, Car Nos. Caboose SF-43, Box Car 466032, Gondola with Junk Load XM890, Engine No. 946
3-Rail with Proto-Sound®, Item No. 30-4020-1, Car Nos. See above

2-6-0 R-T-R Train Set
Santa Fe

1998 Volume 2
December 1998

3-Rail with Electronic Whistle, Item No. 30-4017-0, Car Nos. Caboose 1604, Tank Car 91270, Reefer 37625, Engine No. 605
3-Rail with Proto-Sound®, Item No. 30-4017-1, Car Nos. See above

2-8-0 R-T-R Train Set
Pennsylvania

1999 Volume 2
August 1999

3-Rail with Electronic Whistle, Item No. 30-4023-0, Car Nos. Caboose 477899, Box Car 28647, 4-Bay Hopper with Coal Load 189453, Engine No. 9915
3-Rail with Proto-Sound®, Item No. 30-4023-1, Car Nos. See above

2-8-0 R-T-R Train Set
Christmas 2000

2000 Volume 2
October 2000

3-Rail with Proto-Sound® 2.0, Item No. 30-4033-1, Car Nos. Caboose No number, Gondola MTH2000, Box Car 122500, Engine No. 1225
3-Rail with Loco-Sound™, Item No. 30-4033-0, Car Nos. See Above

4-6-2 Pacific Passenger Train Set
Denver & Rio Grande

1997 Volume 1
November 1997

3-Rail with Electronic Horn, Item No. 30-1035, Engine No. 809 Car Nos. 711 Baggage, 1013 Coach, 1011 Coach, Granite Canyon Observation

4-6-4 Hudson R-T-R Train Set
New York Central

1997 Volume 2
December 1997

3-Rail with Electronic Whistle, Item No. 30-1025-0, Engine No. 5405 Car Nos. Box Car 4503, Tank Car 5791, Flat Car with Trailer 499706, Caboose 21574

4-8-4 GS-4 Steam Passenger R-T-R Train Set
Southern Pacific

2000 Volume 2
October 2000

3-Rail with Proto-Sound® 2.0, Item No. 30-4039-1, Car Nos. Observation Car 2952, Vista Dome 2462, Baggage Car 6600, Engine No. 4449
3-Rail with Loco-Sound™, Item No. 30-4039-0, Car Nos. See above

4-8-4 J Steam Passenger R-T-R Train Set
Norfolk & Western

2000 Volume 2
October 2000

3-Rail with Proto-Sound® 2.0, Item No. 30-4036-1, Car Nos. Observation Car 582, Vista Dome 1612, Baggage Car 1425, Engine No. 612
3-Rail with Loco-Sound™, Item No. 30-4036-0, Car Nos. See above

6-8-6 Turbine Steam Passenger R-T-R Train Set
Pennsylvania

2000 Volume 2
October 2000

3-Rail with Proto-Sound® 2.0, Item No. 30-4038-1, Car Nos. Observation Car 1120, Vista Dome 209, Baggage Car 9230, Engine No. 6200
3-Rail with Loco-Sound™, Item No. 30-4038-0, Car Nos. See above

6-8-6 Turbine Steam R-T-R Train Set
Pennsylvania

2000 Volume 2
October 2000

3-Rail with Proto-Sound® 2.0, Item No. 30-4037-1, Car Nos. Caboose 477954, Box Car 567427, Tank Car 498748, Engine No. 6200
3-Rail with Loco-Sound™, Item No. 30-4037-0, Car Nos. See above

Diesel R-T-R Construction Train Set
Chessie

1997 Volume 2
November 1997

3-Rail with Electronic Horn, Item No. 30-4016-0, Engine No. 4320 Car Nos. Flat Car with Loader 22897, Hopper Car with Coal Load 82701, Caboose 3027
3-Rail with Proto-Sound®, Item No. 30-4016-1, Car Nos. See above

Diesel R-T-R Work Train Set
Conrail

1998 Volume 2
April 1998

3-Rail with Electronic Horn, Item No. 30-4019-0, Engine No. 6260 Car Nos. Gondola 604768, Crane Tender 60368, Engineering Car 52578, Work Caboose 43023
3-Rail with Proto-Sound®, Item No. 30-4019-1, Car Nos. See above

Diesel R-T-R Work Train Set
Amtrak

1999 Volume 2
August 1999

3-Rail with Electronic Horn, Item No. 30-4024-0, Car Nos. Work Caboose 92268, Crane Tender 81973, Gondola 13237, Engineering Car 81479, Engine No. 500
3-Rail with Proto-Sound®, Item No. 30-4024-1, Car Nos. See above

F-3 R-T-R Passenger Train Set
Santa Fe

1998 Volume 2
December 1998

3-Rail with Electronic Horn, Item No. 30-4021-0, Car Nos. 3199 Observation, 502 Vista Dome, 3482 Baggage, Engine No. 16
3-Rail with Proto-Sound®, Item No. 30-4021-1, Car Nos. See above
3-Rail with Proto-Sound® 2.0, Item No. 30-4043-1, Car Nos. See above
3-Rail with Loco-Sound™, Item No. 30-4043-0, Car Nos. See above

F40PH R-T-R Passenger Train Set
Amtrak

1999 Volume 2
July 1999

3-Rail with Electronic Horn, Item No. 30-4025-0, Engine No. 300, Car Nos. 44277 Coach, 44080 Coach, 48152 Club/Dinette
3-Rail with Proto-Sound®, Item No. 30-4025-1, Car Nos. See above

F40PH R-T-R Train Set
CSX

2000 Volume 2
September 2000

3-Rail with Proto-Sound® 2.0, Item No. 30-4034-1, Car Nos. Caboose 903880 , Tank Car 993368, Box Car 129770, Engine No. 9993
3-Rail with Loco-Sound™, Item No. 30-4034-0, Car Nos. See above

F40PH R-T-R Train Set
McDonald's

2000 Volume 2
September 2000

3-Rail with Proto-Sound® 2.0, Item No. 30-4042-1, Car Nos. Caboose MCD 3255, Flat Car with Trailer 1955, Box Car MCD 2000, Engine No. 414
3-Rail with Loco-Sound™, Item No. 30-4042-0, Car Nos. See above

Genesis R-T-R Train Set
Amtrak

1998 Volume 2
December 1998

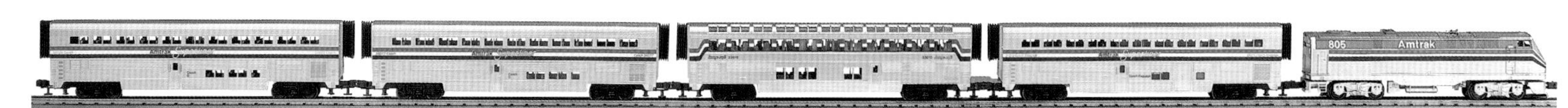

3-Rail with Electronic Horn, Item No. 30-4018-0, Car Nos. Coach 34077, Coach 34022, Coach Baggage 31019, Lounge/Cafe 33010 , Engine No. 805
3-Rail with Proto-Sound®, Item No. 30-4018-1, Car Nos. See above

Operating Hand Car Train Set
Tuscan

2000 Volume 2
May 2000

3-Rail, Item No. 30-4044-0

Operating Hand Car Train Set
Santa

2000 Volume 2
May 2000

3-Rail, Item No. 30-4045-0

Sears R-T-R O Gauge Toy Train Set
Pennsylvania

Uncataloged Item
August 1998

3-Rail with Electronic Whistle, Item No. 30-4031-0, Car Nos. Caboose 479815, Box Car 30989, Tank Car 102097, Engine No. 1014

Sears R-T-R O Gauge Toy Train Set
New York Central

Uncataloged Item
September 1998

3-Rail with Electronic Whistle, Item No. 30-4022-0, Car Nos. Engine 2743, Box Car, Flat Car, Caboose 19702

Trolley R-T-R Train Set
Baltimore Transit Company

1999 Volume 2
September 1999

3-Rail, Item No. 30-4027-0, Car No. 414

Trolley R-T-R Train Set
Christmas

1999 Volume 2
September 1999

3-Rail, Item No. 30-4027-0 Car Name MTH

Trolley R-T-R Train Set
Christmas

2000 Volume 2
August 2000

3-Rail, Item No. 30-4040-0, Car No. 2000

Trolley R-T-R Train Set
New York Transit

2000 Volume 2
August 2000

3-Rail, Item No. 30-4041-0, Car No. 6688

4-Car Modern Subway Set
Chicago Transit

2000 Volume 1
May 2000

3-Rail with Electronic Horn, Item No. 30-2175-0, Car Nos. MTH 3201, 3202, 3225, 3226
3-Rail with Proto-Sound®, Item No. 30-2175-1, Cab Nos. See above

4-Car Subway Set
New York Transit

1998 Volume 1
November 1997

3-Rail with Electronic Horn, Item No. 30-2122-0, Car Nos. 4698, 4699, 4714, 4715
3-Rail with Proto-Sound®, Item No. 30-2122-1, Car Nos. See above

4-Car Subway Set
New York Transit

1999 Volume 2
October 1999

3-Rail with Electronic Horn, Item No. 30-4062-0, Car Nos.4824, 4825, 4904, 4905
3-Rail with Proto-Sound®, Item No. 30-4062-1, Car Nos.See above

4-Car R21 Subway Set
New York Transit

2000 Volume 2
November 2000

3-Rail with Proto-Sound® 2.0, Item No. 30-2198-1, Cab Nos. 7090, 7092, 7110, 7111
3-Rail with Loco-Sound™, Item No. 30-2198-0, Cab Nos. 7090, 7092, 7110, 7111

Berkshire Freight Set
Erie

Summer 1996
December 1996

3-Rail with Electronic Whistle, Item No. 30-Set-025, Car Nos. Caboose 04942, Box Car 174020, Stock Car 140297, Reefer Car 2724, Engine No. 3389

Dash-8 Diesel Passenger Train Set
Amtrak

1999 Volume 3
October 1999

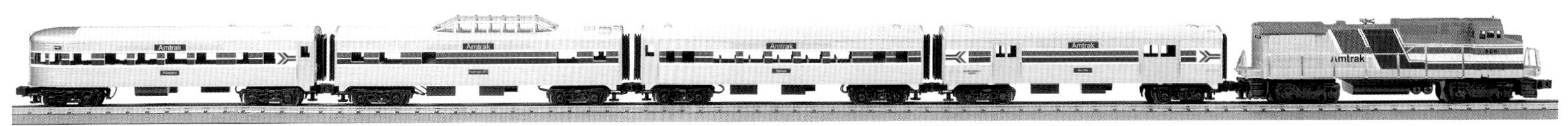

3-Rail with Proto-Sound®, Item No. 30-2164-1, Car Nos. Observation Philadelphia, Vista Dome Washington D.C., Coach Baltimore, Baggage New York, Engine No. 517

F-3 Freight Set
Union Pacific

Spring 1996
March 1996

3-Rail with Electronic Horn, Item No. 30-Set-020, U.P. F-3 Engine No. 900, 901, Car Nos. Reefer Car 7802, Gondola 7202, Tank Car 7302, Caboose 7702

FM Trainmaster Freight Set
Santa Fe

Spring 1996
May 1996

3-Rail with Electronic Horn, Item No. 30-Set-021, S.F. FM Trainmaster Engine No. 2576, Car Nos. Stock Car 128016, Box Car 20860, Hopper Car 181764, Caboose 1997

GG-1 Freight Set
Pennsylvania

Summer 1996
November 1996

3-Rail with Electronic Horn, Item No. 30-Set-022, PRR (Tuscan) GG-1 Engine No. 4913, Car Nos. Box Car 47011, Reefer Car 2724, Tank Car 498639, Caboose 477618

GG-1 Freight Set
Pennsylvania

Summer 1996
November 1996

3-Rail with Electronic Horn, Item No. 30-Set-023, PRR (Green) GG-1 Engine No. 5105, Car Nos. Stock Car 128749, PRR Reefer Car 2724, Tank Car 498639, Caboose 477618

Pioneer Zephyr Diesel Passenger Set
Burlington

2000 Volume 1
March 2000

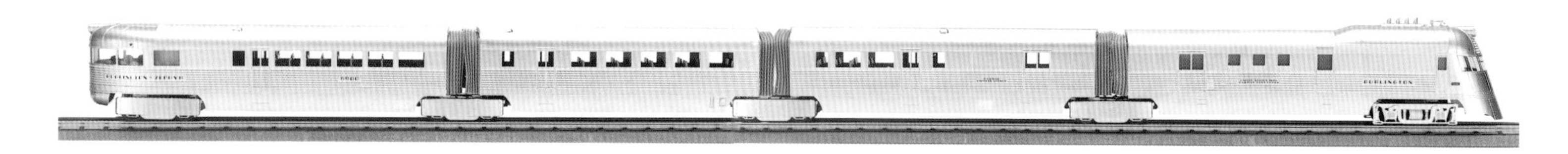

3-Rail with Electronic Horn, Item No. 30-2186-0, Engine No. 9900
3-Rail with Proto-Sound®, Item No. 30-2186-1, Engine No. 9900

0-8-0 Steam Engine Coal Train Set *(photo not available)*
Norfolk & Western
Item No. 30-Set-026, Engine No. 244 Car Nos. 131248

Fall/Winter 1996
November 1996

0-8-0 Steam Engine Freight Set *(photo not available)*
Chicago NorthWestern
Item No. 30-Set-027, Engine No. 65 Car Nos. Stock Car 15033, Gondola Car 13792, Tank Car 32308, Caboose 12560

Fall/Winter 1996
December 1996

Hudson Freight Set *(photo not available)*
New York Central
3-Rail with Electronic Whistle, Item No. 30-Set-017, Engine No. 5344 Car Nos. Reefer Car 6078, Gondola Car 762453, Tank Car 4725, Caboose 18205

Spring 1996
January 1996

Hudson Freight Set *(photo not available)*
Union Pacific
3-Rail with Electronic Whistle, Item No. 30-Set-018, Engine No. 3225 Car Nos. Reefer Car 78676, Tank Car 70084, Gondola Car 65230, Caboose 3821

Spring 1996
January 1996

F-3 Freight Set *(photo not available)*
New York Central
3-Rail with Electronic Horn, Item No. 30-Set-019, Engine Nos. 1606-1607 Car Nos. Reefer Car 6078, Gondola Car 762453, Tank Car 4725, Caboose 18205

Spring 1996
March 1996

Berkshire Freight Set *(photo not available)*
Nickel Plate Road
3-Rail with Electronic Whistle, Item No. 30-Set-024, Engine No. 759 Car Nos. Stock Car 67534, Flat Car 67534, Hopper 30160, Caboose 1115

Summer 1996
November 1996

Unit Train R-T-R Diesel Train Set *(photo not available)*
Norfolk Southern
3-Rail with Electronic Horn, Item No. 30-1015, Engine No. 8763 Car Nos. 60368

1997 Volume 1
November 1997

SD-60 Freight Set *(photo not available)*
Chicago NorthWestern
3-Rail with Electronic Horn, Item No. 30-Set-029, Engine No. 8032 Car Nos. Stock Car 15033, Gondola Car 13792, Tank Car 32308, Caboose 12560

Fall/Winter 1996
December 1996

SD-60 Freight Set *(photo not available)*
Conrail
3-Rail with Electronic Horn, Item No. 30-Set-028, Engine No. 6867 Car Nos. Flatcar with Backhoe 19961, Gondola Car 604768, Tank Car 5010, Caboose CR22000

Fall/Winter 1996
November 1996

RAILKING LINE
Accessories

RailKing accessories offer a variety that makes it unnecessary for a model railroader to look anywhere else for all the genuine touches that bring a layout to life. These accessories include everything from operating railroad signals to road signs and street lamps and even tiny passengers to ride in the passenger cars. M.T.H. makes buildings, too, including several kinds of houses, a bank, a water tower, stores and even a vintage McDonald's restaurant. Among the most popular of the operating accessories are buildings that operate. The first of these were the operating gas station and firehouse, produced in 1997, and followed by the car wash and the drive-in diner. And, of course, even with all these accessories, no layout would be complete without the true railroading touches, such as the dispatch board, a coaling tower, operating passenger and freight platforms, and an engine shed. Other small touches, such as bags of coal, junk loads and ProtoSmoke fluid complete the picture. RailKing accessories come in three different classifications: O Scale, Traditional, and Miscellaneous. Among them, they offer everything a model railroader could want. RailKing RealTrax™ is the easiest-to-use O Gauge track system on the market. It snaps together in minutes, with no need for pins that are easy to lose. Plus it contains its own roadbed, which means it works anywhere, even on carpet, without leaving an oily mess behind like most track systems. It's ideal for the model railroader who doesn't have a permanent layout in a dedicated space.

#151 Operating Semaphore
Green/Silver
Item No. 30-1035A

Summer 1996
January 1997

#151 Operating Semaphore
Green Base
Item No. 30-1075

1998 Volume 1
September 1998

#152 Operating Crossing Gate
Red/Aluminum
Item No. 30-11008

1999 Volume 2
January 1999

#153 Operating Block Signal
Black/Silver
Item No. 30-1034

Summer 1996
January 1997

#153 Operating Block Signal
Black/Silver
Item No. 30-1076

1997 Volume 1
September 1998

#154 Highway Flashing Signal
Black/Silver
Item No. 30-1074

1997 Volume 1
September 1998

#193 Industrial Water Tower
Black/Red/White
Item No. 30-9029

1999 Volume 3
September 1999

#262 Crossing Gate/Signal
Black
Item No. 30-1073

1997 Volume 1
January 1998

#334 Dispatch Board
Cream
Item No. 30-9022

1999 Volume 3
November 1999

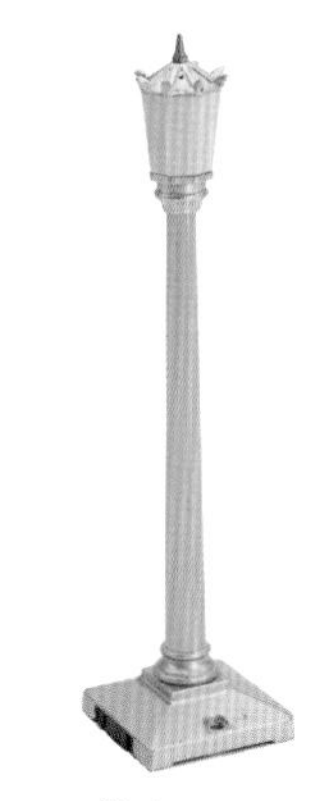

#35 Street Lamp Set
Aluminum
Item No. 30-1059

Spring 1997
June 1997

#35 Street Lamp Set
Gray
Item No. 30-1058

Spring 1997
June 1997

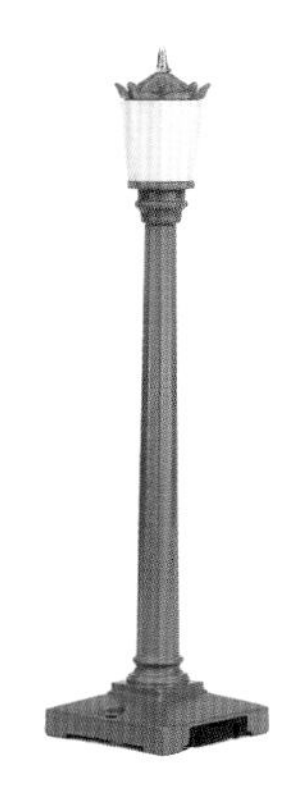

#35 Street Lamp Set
Pea Green
Item No. 30-1099

1998 Volume 2
May 1998

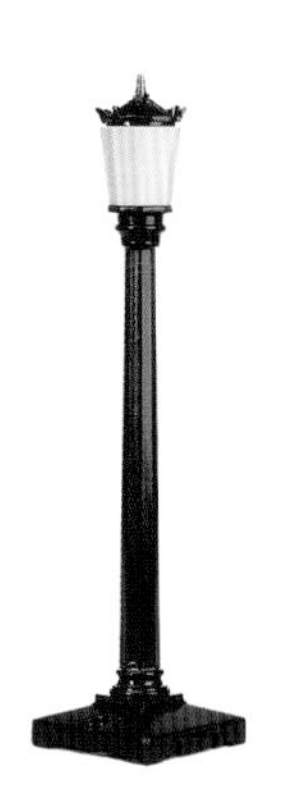

#35 Street Lamp Set
Red
Item No. 30-11001

1998 Volume 2
May 1998

#395 Floodlight Tower
Yellow/Black
Item No. 30-9025

1999 Volume 3
September 1999

#455 Oil Derrick
Green/Red Base
Item No. 30-9027

1999 Volume 3
November 1999

#46 Crossing Gate and Signal
Green/Cream
Item No. 30-11017

2000 Volume 1
June 2000

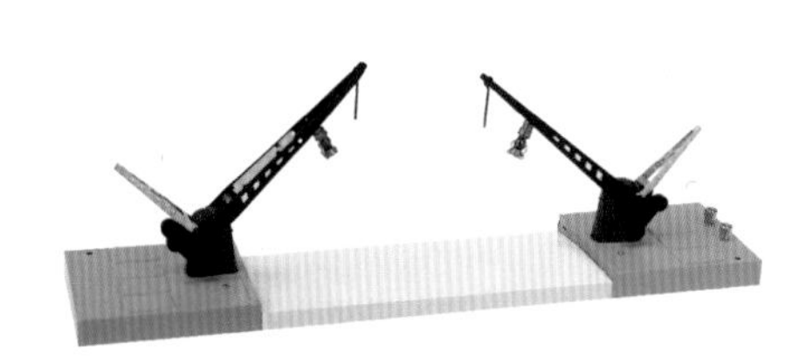

#47 Crossing Gate and Signal
Green/Cream
Item No. 30-1080

1997 Volume 2
July 1997

#54 Street Lamp Set
Maroon
Item No. 30-1019

Spring 1996
August 1996

#54 Street Lamp Set
Green
Item No. 30-1020

Spring 1996
September 1996

#54 Street Lamp Set
State Car Brown
Item No. 30-1066

1997 Volume 1
November 1996

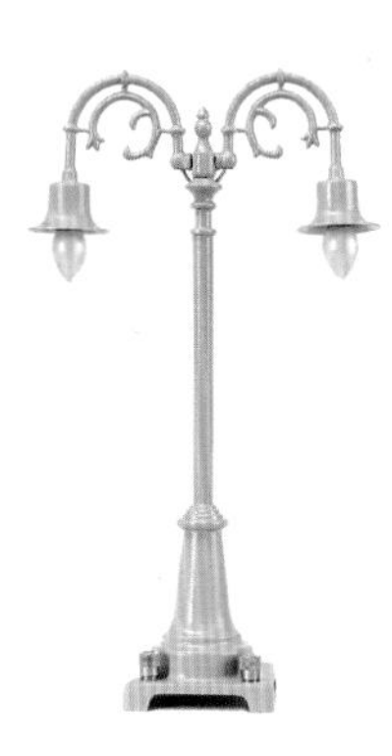

#54 Street Lamp Set
Cream
Item No. 30-1096

1998 Volume 2
May 1998

#56 Gas Lamp Set
Green
Item No. 30-1026

Summer 1996
August 1996

#56 Gas Lamp Set
Maroon
Item No. 30-1027

Summer 1996
August 1996

#56 Gas Lamp Set
Copper
Item No. 30-1069

1997 Volume 1
December 1997

#56 Gas Lamp Set
Black
Item No. 30-1098

1998 Volume 2
May 1998

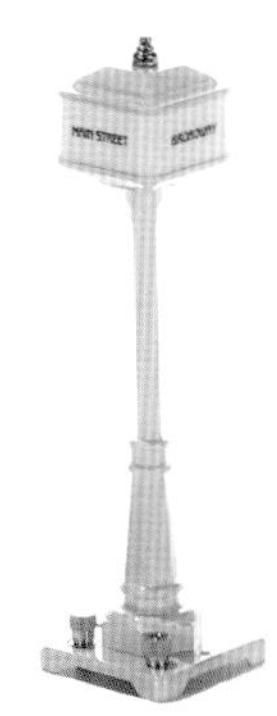

#57 Corner Lamp Set
Yellow
Item No. 30-1028

Summer 1996
August 1998

#57 Corner Lamp Set
Orange
Item No. 30-1029

Summer 1996
August 1996

#57 Corner Lamp Set
Gray
Item No. 30-1068

1997 Volume 1
December 1997

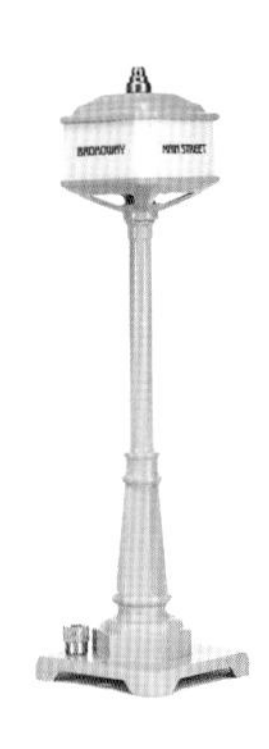

#57 Corner Lamp Set
Cream
Item No. 30-1097

1998 Volume 2
May 1998

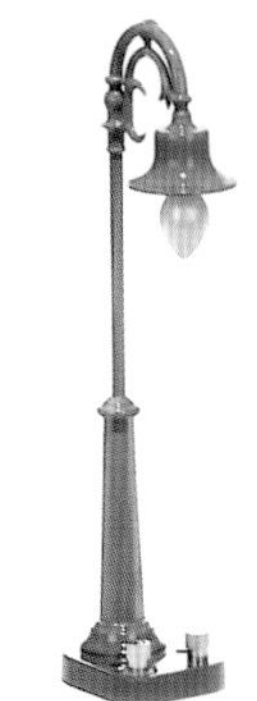

#58 Lamp Set - Single Arc
Pea Green
Item No. 30-1057

Spring 1997
June 1997

#58 Lamp Set - Single Arc
Maroon
Item No. 30-1090

1998 Volume 2
May 1998

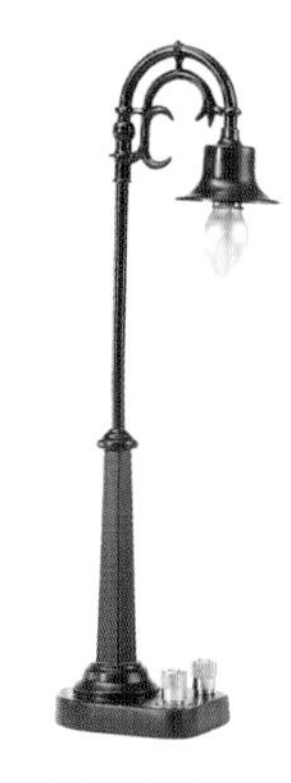

#58 Lamp Set - Single Arc
Dark Green
Item No. 30-11002

1998 Volume 2
May 1998

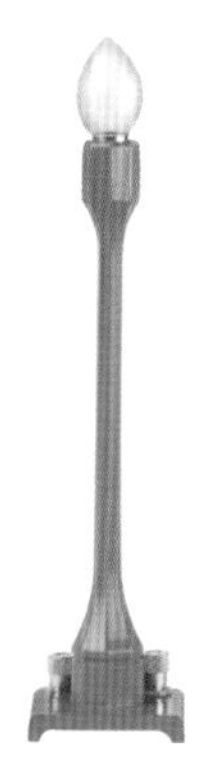

#580-1 Teardrop Lamp Set
Green
Item No. 30-1070

1997 Volume 1
October 1997

#580-1 Teardrop Lamp Set
Silver
Item No. 30-1078A

1997 Volume 2
July 1997

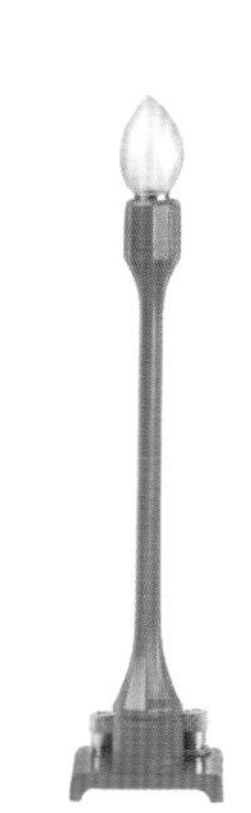

#580-1 Teardrop Lamp Set
Pea Green
Item No. 30-1079A

1998 Volume 1
July 1997

#580-2 Teardrop Lamp Set
Green
Item No. 30-1071

1997 Volume 1
July 1997

#580-2 Teardrop Lamp Set
Pea Green
Item No. 30-1080A

1997 Volume 2
July 1997

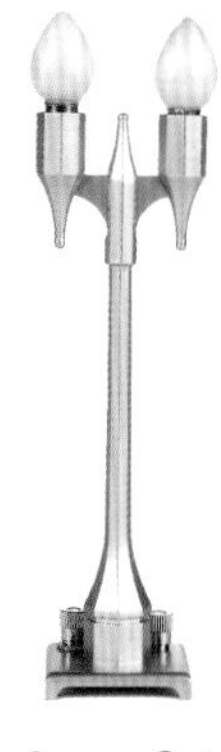

#580-2 Teardrop Lamp Set
Silver
Item No. 30-1082A

1997 Volume 2
July 1997

#580-2 Teardrop Lamp Set
Maroon
Item No. 30-1081A

1997 Volume 2
July 1997

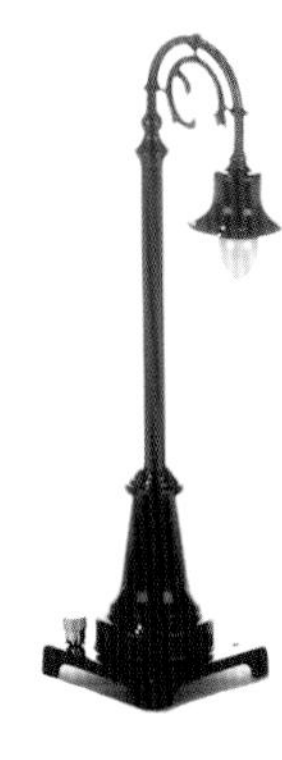

#59 Gooseneck Lamp Set
Maroon
Item No. 30-1030

Summer 1996
September 1996

#59 Gooseneck Lamp Set
Green
Item No. 30-1031

Summer 1996
September 1996

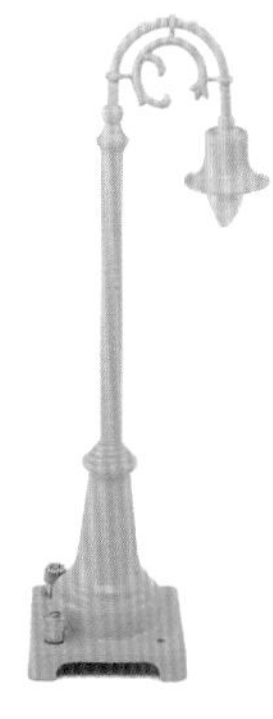

#59 Gooseneck Lamp Set
Cream
Item No. 30-1067

1997 Volume 1
November 1997

#64 Highway Lamp Set
Green
Item No. 30-1032

Summer 1996
January 1997

#64 Highway Lamp Set
Maroon
Item No. 30-1033

Summer 1996
December 1996

#64 Highway Lamp Set
Dark Green
Item No. 30-1065

1997 Volume 1
November 1997

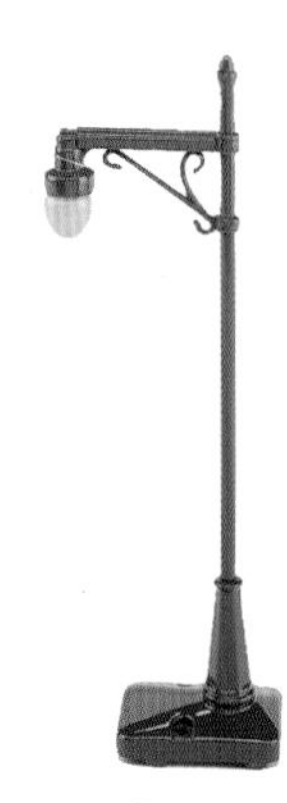

#64 Highway Lamp Set
Silver
Item No. 30-1095

1998 Volume 2
May 1998

#64 Highway Lamp Set
Black
Item No. 30-11003

1998 Volume 2
May 1998

#69 Operating Warning Bell
Red/Silver
Item No. 30-1036

Summer 1996
June 1997

#69 Operating Warning Bell
Maroon
Item No. 30-1077

1997 Volume 1
December 1997

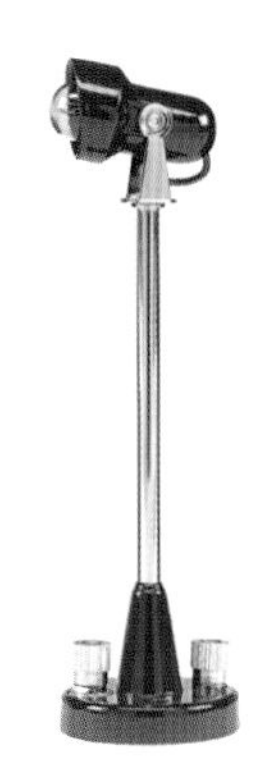

#70 Yard Lamp Set
Black
Item No. 30-1060

Spring 1997
July 1998

Coaling Tower
Cream/Orange
Item No. 30-9043

2000 Volume 2
September 2000

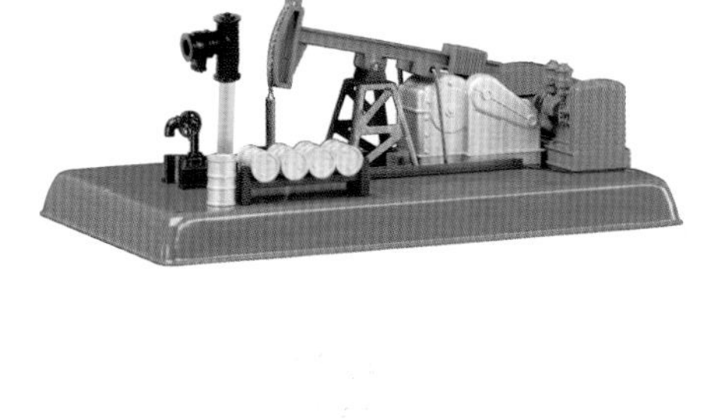

Oil Pumping Station
Green/Blue/Gray
Item No. 30-9028

1999 Volume 3
November 1999

Operating Street Clock
Red
Item No. 30-1061

Spring 1997
November 1997

Operating Street Clock
Teal
Item No. 30-1072

1997 Volume 1
October 1997

Operating Street Clock
Blue
Item No. 30-1085

1998 Volume 1
February 1998

Operating Street Clock
Dark Green
Item No. 30-1094

1998 Volume 2
May 1998

Radar Tower
Gray/Black
Item No. 30-9032

2000 Volume 1
June 2000

Rotary Beacon
Red/Gray
Item No. 30-9033

2000 Volume 1
June 2000

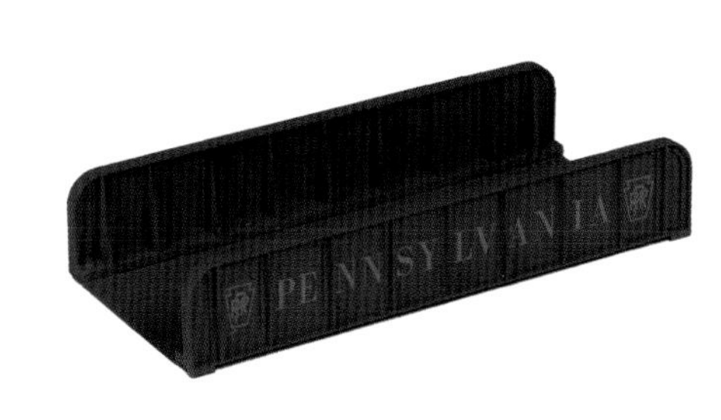

314 Girder Bridge
Black
Item No. 30-12001

2000 Volume 2
April 2000

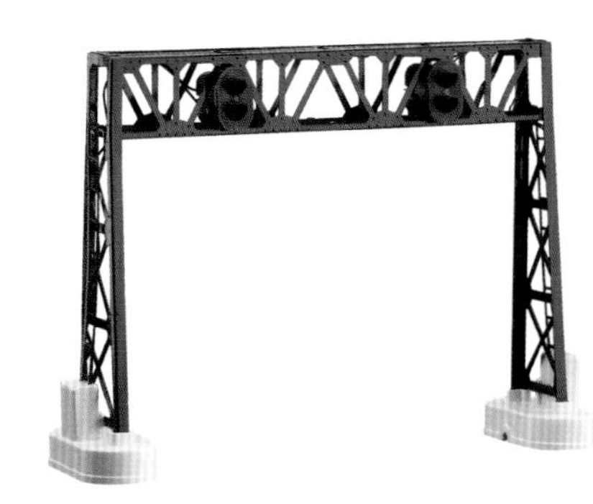

#450 Signal Bridge
Black/Cream Base
Item No. 30-9026

1999 Volume 3
October 1999

“O” Lamp Set - Hexagonal
Black
Item No. 30-1062

Spring 1997
June 1997

“O” Lamp Set - Round
Black
Item No. 30-1078

1997 Volume 2
November 1997

“O” Lamp Set - Square
Black
Item No. 30-1079

1997 Volume 2
November 1997

“O” Operating Crossing Flashers with Sound
Silver/Black
Item No. 30-11014

1999 Volume 3
October 1999

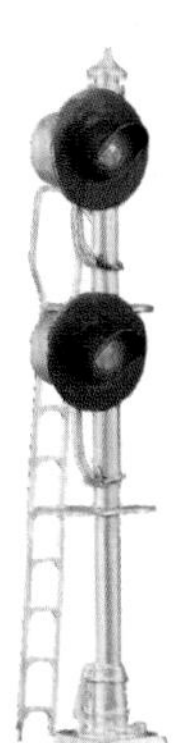

O Scale 1 Over 1 Signal
Silver/Black
Item No. 30-11025

2000 Volume 2
August 2000

O Scale 3 Over 3 Vertical Signal
Silver/Black
Item No. 30-11024

2000 Volume 2
August 2000

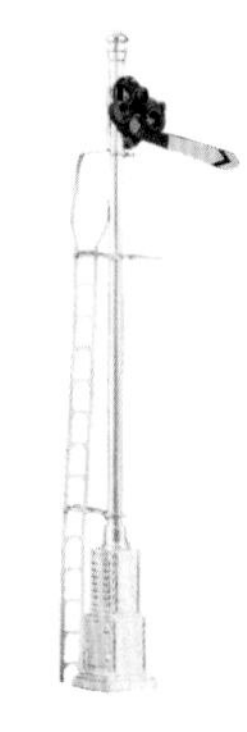

O Scale 3-Position Semaphore
Silver/Black
Item No. 30-11023

2000 Volume 2
September 2000

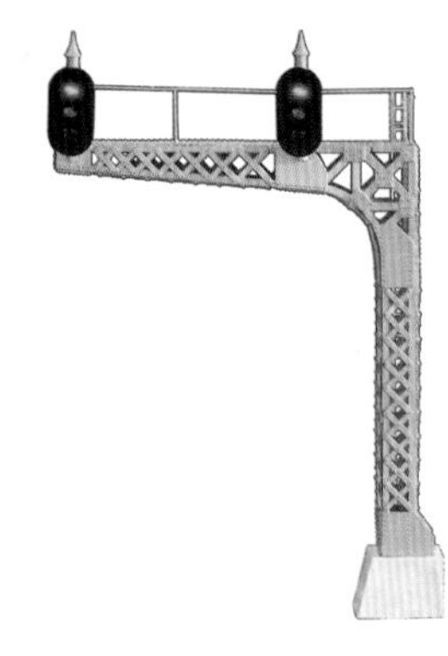

O Scale Cantilevered Signal Bridge
Silver/Cream
Item No. 30-11009

1999 Volume 2
August 1999

O Scale Flashing Barricades
White/Orange
Item No. 30-11021

2000 Volume 2
August 2000

“O” Scale Modern Operating Crossing Signal
Silver/Black
Item No. 30-11006

1998 Volume 3
January 1999

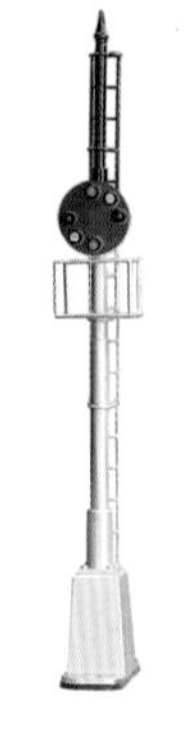

“O” Scale Operating Block Signal
Silver/Black
Item No. 30-11005

1998 Volume 3
January 1999

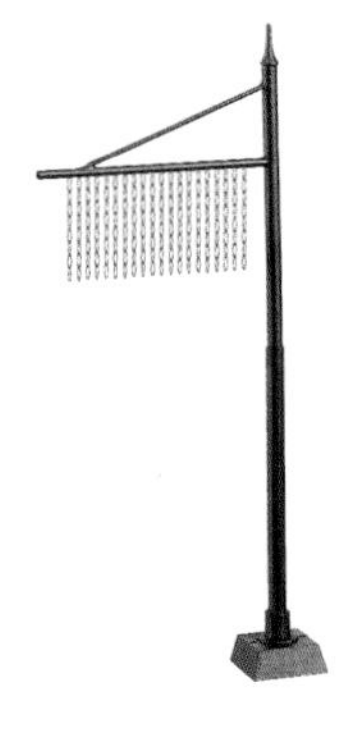

O Scale Tell Tale
Brown
Item No. 30-11026

2000 Volume 2
March 2000

O Scale Vertical Signal lamps
Black
Item No. 30-11009A

2000 Volume 1
November 1999

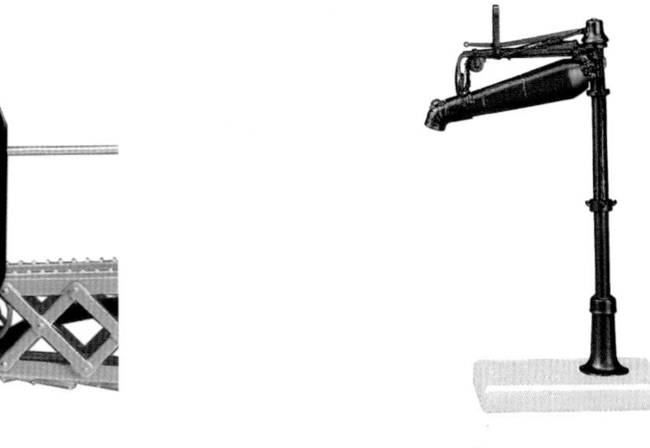

O Scale Water Column
Black/White
Item No. 30-11007

1999 Volume 1
January 1999

O-Scale 7 Light Block Signal
Black
Item No. 30-11013

1999 Volume 3
September 1999

O-Scale Dwarf Signal
Black
Item No. 30-11011

1999 Volume 3
October 1999

O-Scale Operating Crossing Gate Signal
Silver
Item No. 30-11012

1999 Volume 3
October 1999

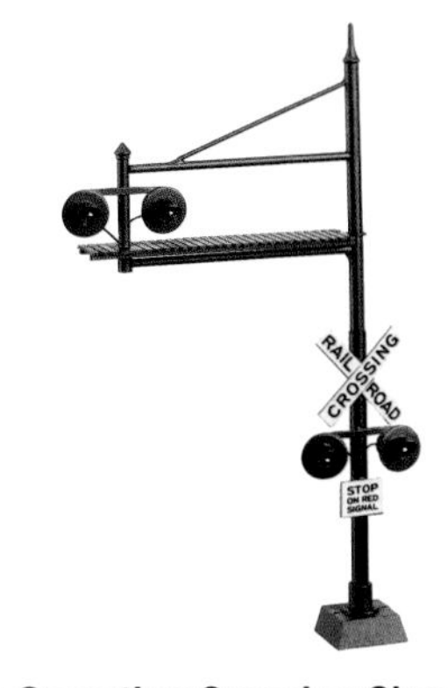

O-Scale Operating Crossing Signal
Black
Item No. 30-11010

1999 Volume 3
September 1999

Operating Banjo Signal
Black
Item No. 30-1093

1998 Volume 2
May 1998

Road Sign Set

Item No. 30-1087

1998 Volume 2
May 1998

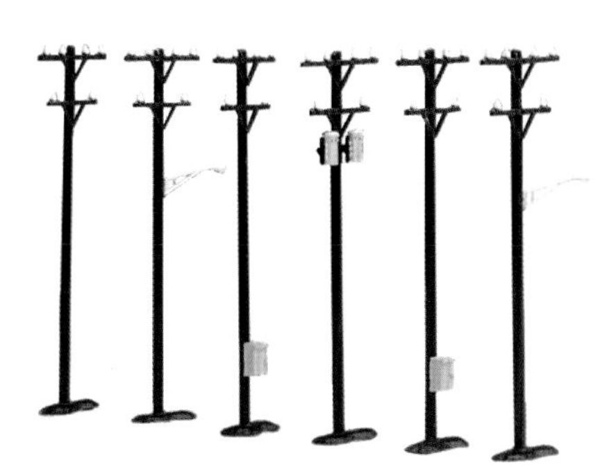

Telephone Pole Set

Item No. 30-1088

1998 Volume 2
May 1998

Traffic Light Set - Double Lamp
Silver
Item No. 30-1089-2

1998 Volume 2
May 1998

Traffic Light Set - Single Lamp
Silver
Item No. 30-1089-1

1998 Volume 2
May 1998

12-Piece Figure Set #1

Item No. 30-11016

2000 Volume 1
February 2000

Bag Of Coal

Item No. 30-50005

1999 Volume 3
December 1999

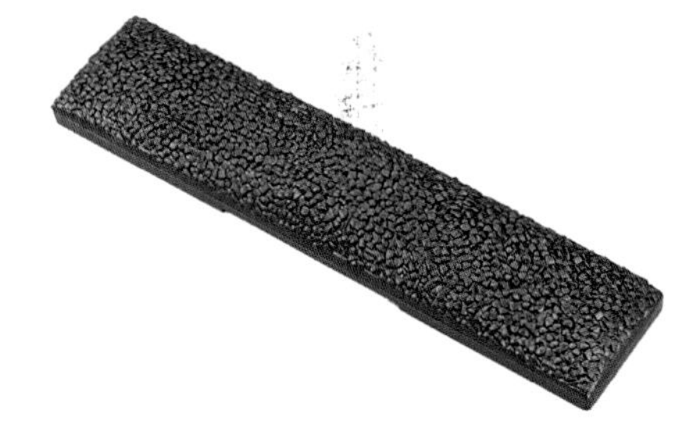

Coal Load

Item No. 30-50001

1998 Volume 3
November 1998

Die-Cast Fuel Truck
Sinclair
Item No. 30-1086, Never Produced

1998 Volume 1
CANCELLED

Die-Cast Trailer
Big Mo
Item No. 30-50004

1999 Volume 3
February 2000

Fence Set
White
Item No. 30-50002

1998 Volume 3
November 1998

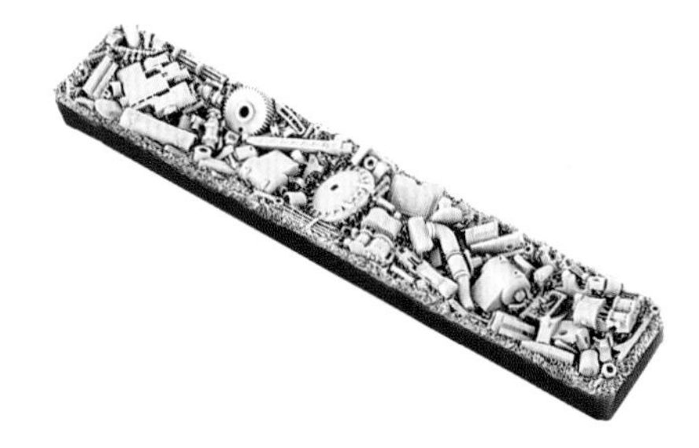

Junk Load

Item No. 30-50003

1998 Volume 3
November 1998

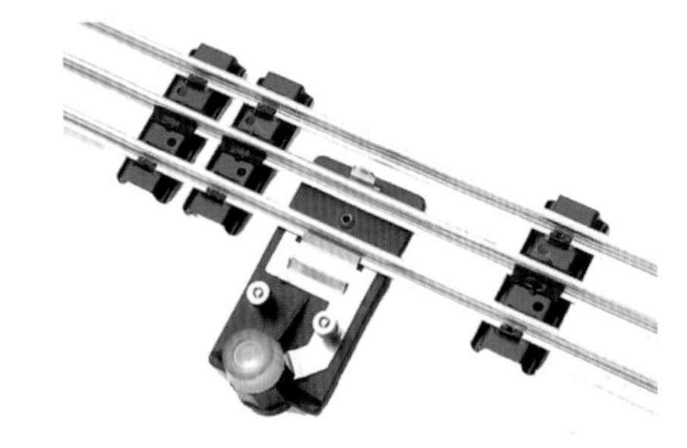

Lighted Lock-on

Item No. 10-1021

Spring 1996
July 1998

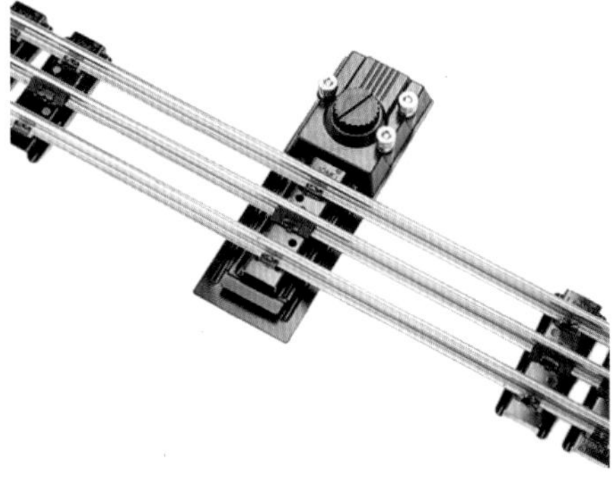

O Gauge Track Activation Device (TAD)

Item No. 10-1037

Summer 1996
October 1997

Operating Flag
American
Item No. 30-9103

1997 Volume 2
August 1997

ProtoSmoke Fluid
7oz Bottle
Item No. 60-1045

1997 Volume 2
December 1998

RailKing IR Remote Control
Black
Item No. 50-1011

2000 Volume 2
August 2000

RailKing IR Remote Control System

Item No. 50-1012

2000 Volume 2
August 2000

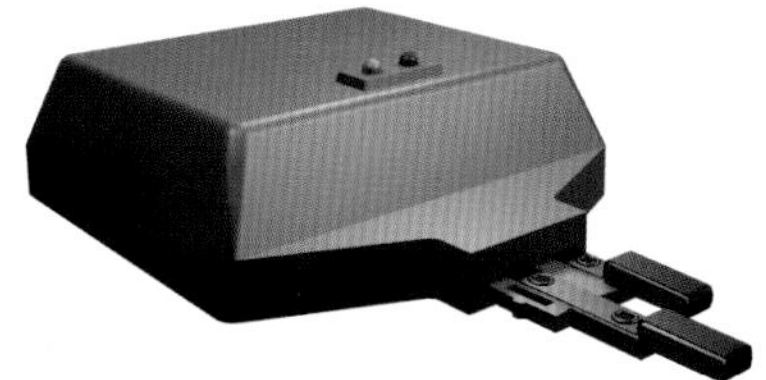

RailKing Remote Lock-On
Gray
Item No. 50-1013

2000 Volume 2
August 2000

Z-500 Transformer

Item No. 40-500

2000 Volume 2
May 2000

Z-750 Transformer

Item No. 40-750

1998 Volume 1
March 1998

#4 Country House
Grey/Yellow/Grey
Item No. 30-9001

Fall/Winter 1996
January 1997

#4 Country House
Blue
Item No. 30-9008

1997 Volume 2
October 1997

#4 Country House
Yellow/White/Brown
Item No. 30-9016

1999 Volume 2
September 1999

4-Story Building
Red/Gray/White
Item No. 30-9013

1998 Volume 2
April 1998

#5 Country Church
White/Grey/Grey
Item No. 30-9002

Fall/Winter 1996
January 1997

#6 Farm House
White/Red/Grey
Item No. 30-9003,

Spring 1997
January 1997

#6 Farm House
Yellow
Item No. 30-9007

1997 Volume 2
November 1997

#6 Farm House
Red/White
Item No. 30-9015

1999 Volume 2
September 1999

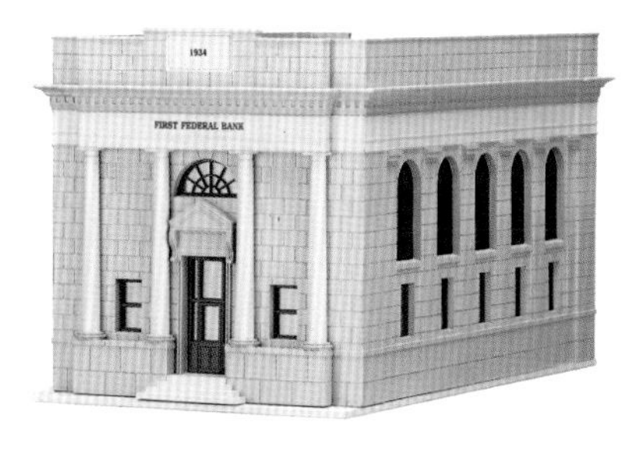

Corner Bank
Gray/Brown
Item No. 30-9017

1999 Volume 3
November 1999

Corner Building
Drug Store
Item No. 30-9012

1998 Volume 1
November 1997

Engine Shed
Red/Gray
Item No. 30-9030

2000 Volume 1
June 2000

Hardware Store
Red/Gray/White
Item No. 30-9018

1999 Volume 2
August 1999

Hi-tension Tower Set
Silver
Item No. 30-1056

Spring 1997
October 1999

Hobby Shop
RailTown Train Shop
Item No. 30-9004

1997 Volume 1
December 1997

O Scale Water Tower
Yellow/Brown
Item No. 30-11028

2000 Volume 2
August 2000

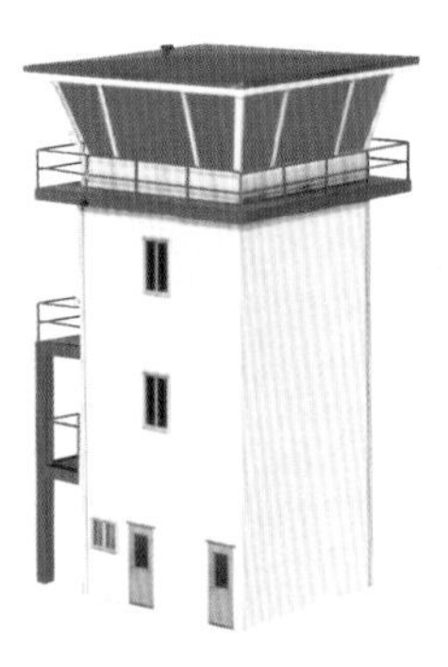

O Scale Yard Master Tower
Yellow/Green
Item No. 30-11027

2000 Volume 2
August 2000

Oil Refinery
Sinclair
Item Not Produced

1998 Volume 1
CANCELLED

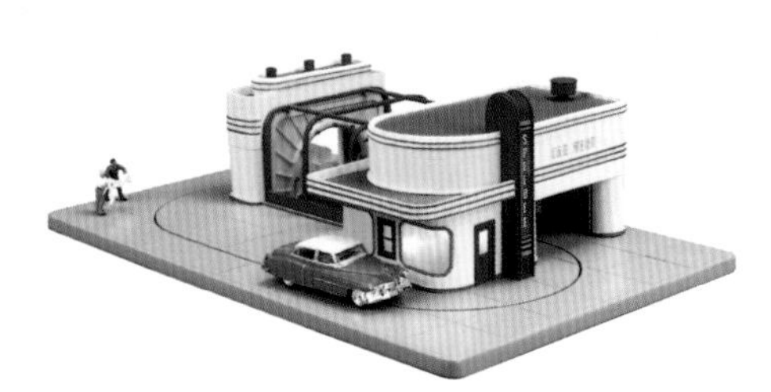

Operating Car Wash
Speedy Car Wash
Item No. 30-9104

1998 Volume 1
March 1998

Operating Drive-In Diner
Mel's Drive-In
Item No. 30-9105

1998 Volume 2
April 1998

Operating Firehouse
Red/Gray
Item No. 30-9102

1997 Volume 2
August 1997

Operating Firehouse
Gray/Brown
Item No. 30-9112

2000 Volume 2
July 2000

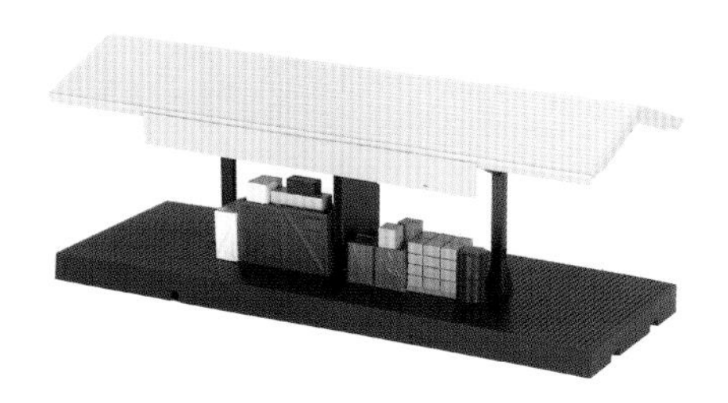

Operating Freight Platform
Gray/Brown
3-Rail, Item No. 30-9111

2000 Volume 2
May 2000

Operating Gas Station
Sinclair
Item No. 30-9101

1997 Volume 1
April 1998

Operating Gas Station
Esso
Item No. 30-9106

1998 Volume 2
December 1998

Operating Gas Station
Union 76
Item No. 30-9109

1999 Volume 2
January 2000

Operating Gas Station
Citgo
3-Rail, Item No. 30-9113

2000 Volume 2
October 2000

Operating Transfer Dock
Brick/Gray/Brown
Item No. 30-9110

2000 Volume 1
July 2000

Original McDonald's Restaurant
McDonald's
3-Rail, Item No. 30-9034

2000 Volume 2
September 2000

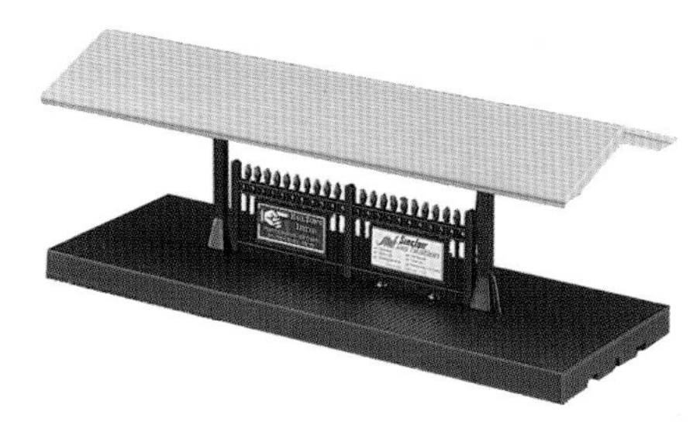

Passenger Station Platform
Gray/Brown
Item No. 30-9006

1997 Volume 2
July 1998

Passenger Station Platform - Operating
Gray/Brown
Item No. 30-9107

1999 Volume 1
April 1999

Passenger Station with dual Platforms
Orange
Item No. 30-9005

1997 Volume 2
February 1998

Passenger Station with dual Platforms
Red
Item No. 30-9014

1998 Volume 2
April 1998

RailKing Hell Gate Bridge
Red/White
Item No. 30-9020

1999 Volume 2
November 1999

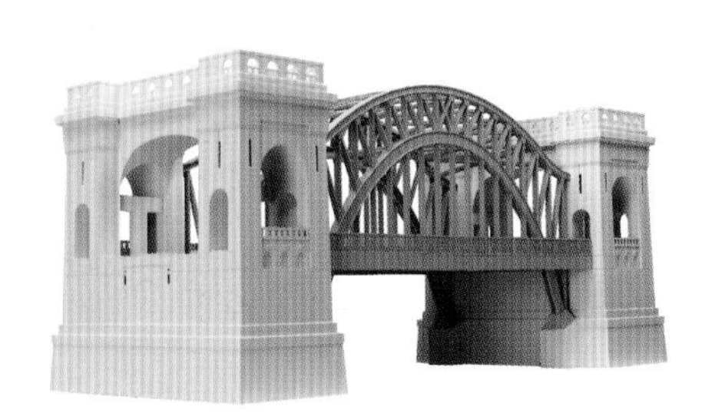

RailKing Hell Gate Bridge
Cream/Green
Item No. 30-9021

1999 Volume 2
November 1999

Row House #1
Yellow/Green
Item No. 30-9023

1999 Volume 3
November 1999

Row House #2
Gray/Red
Item No. 30-9024

1999 Volume 3
November 1999

Switch Tower
CSX Gray
Item No. 30-9011

1998 Volume 1
November 1997

Switch Tower
Pennsylvania
Item No. 30-9031

2000 Volume 1
May 2000

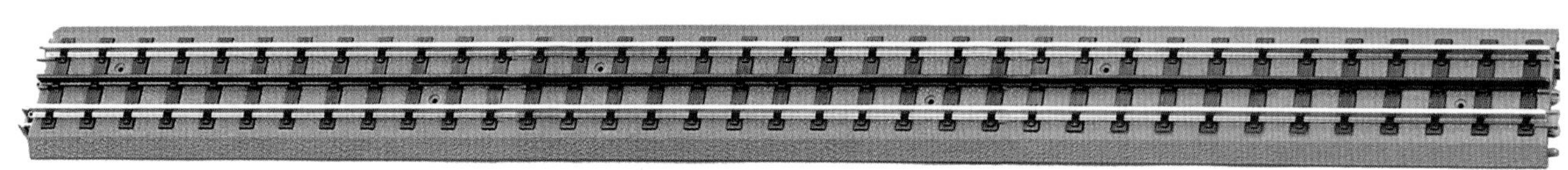

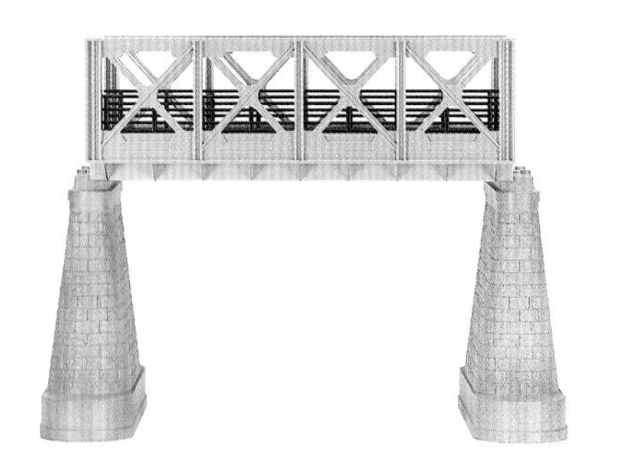

O Bridge Girder
Silver
Item No. 40-1014

1998 Volume 2
December 1998

O Bridge Girder
Rust
Item No. 40-1032

1999 Volume 3
July 1999

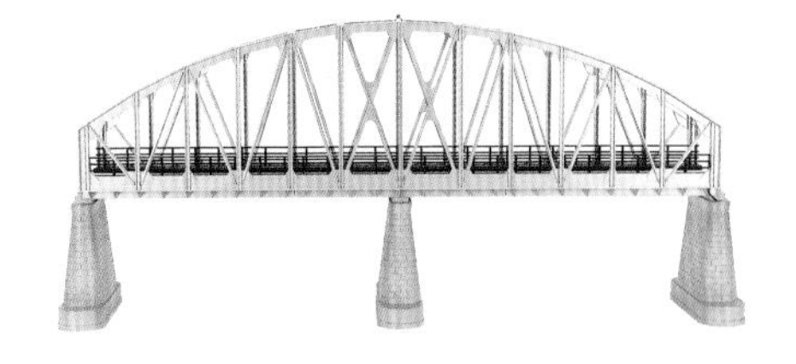

O Steel Arch Bridge
Silver
Item No. 40-1013

1998 Volume 2
December 1998

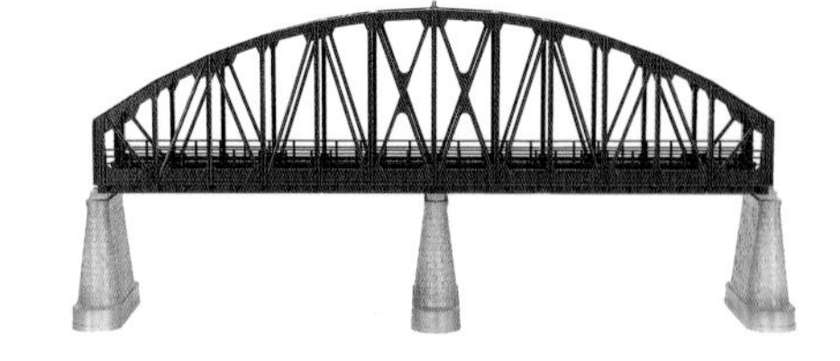

O Steel Arch Bridge
Rust
Item No. 40-1031

1999 Volume 3
December 1998

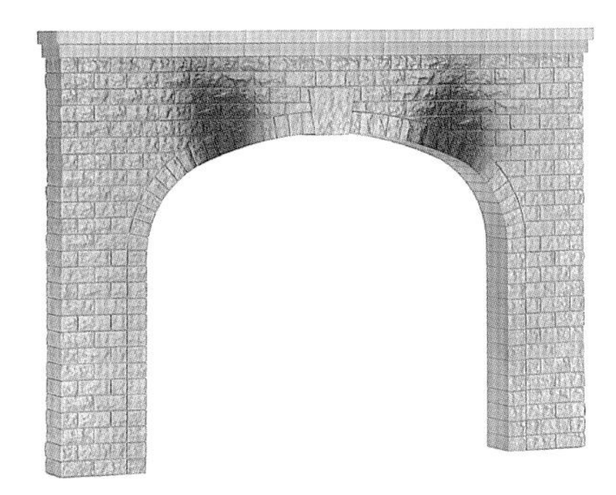

Tunnel Portal - Double
3-Rail, Item No. 40-9015

1998 Volume 2
November 1998

Tunnel Portal - Single
3-Rail, Item No. 40-9014

1998 Volume 2
November 1998

RealTrax - 10" Insulated Straight Section Set
3-Rail, Item No. 40-1029

1999 Volume 2
May 1999

RealTrax - 3.5" Track Section
3-Rail, Item No. 40-1018

1998 Volume 3
July 1998

RealTrax - 4-Piece Add-On Catenary System
3-Rail, Item No. 40-1036

2000 Volume 2
December 2000

RealTrax - 10" Straight Section
3-Rail, Item No. 40-1001

1997 Volume 1
September 1998

RealTrax - 30" Straight Track Section
3-Rail, Item No. 40-1019

1999 Volume 3
April 1999

RealTrax - 4.25" Track Section
3-Rail, Item No. 40-1017

1998 Volume 3
July 1998

RealTrax - 45° Crossover Track
3-Rail, Item No. 40-1007

1999 Volume 3
July 1999

RealTrax - 5.0" Track Section
3-Rail, Item No. 40-1016

1998 Volume 3
July 1998

RealTrax - 5.5" Track Section
3-Rail, Item No. 40-1012

1998 Volume 2
November 1998

RealTrax - 8-Piece Catenary System
3-Rail, Item No. 40-1035

2000 Volume 2
December 2000

RealTrax - 90° Crossover
3-Rail, Item No. 40-1006

1998 Volume 1
August 1998

RealTrax - Adapter Track Section
3-Rail, Item No. 40-1011

1998 Volume 2
September 1998

RealTrax - Figure 8 Layout Builder
3-Rail, Item No. 40-1025

1999 Volume 2
June 1999

RealTrax - Left Hand Track Siding Layout Builder
3-Rail, Item No. 40-1026

1999 Volume 2
July 1999

RealTrax - Lighted Bumper
3-Rail, Item No. 40-1024

1999 Volume 2
June 1999

RealTrax - Lighted Lockon
3-Rail, Item No. 40-1003

1998 Volume 1
March 1998

RealTrax - O-31 Curved Section

3-Rail, Item No. 40-1002

1997 Volume 1
September 1998

RealTrax - O-31 Half Curve
3-Rail, Item No. 40-1022

1998 Volume 3
September 1998

RealTrax - O-31 Switch (L)
3-Rail, Item No. 40-1005

1998 Volume 2
November 1998

RealTrax - O-31 Switch (R)
3-Rail, Item No. 40-1004

1998 Volume 2
November 1998

RealTrax - O-42 Curved Section
3-Rail, Item No. 40-1042

1999 Volume 2
February 2000

RealTrax - O-42 Switch (L)
3-Rail, Item No. 40-1044

1999 Volume 2
March 2000

RealTrax - O-42 Switch (R)
3-Rail, Item No. 40-1043

1999 Volume 2
March 2000

RealTrax - O-54 Curved Track Section
3-Rail, Item No. 40-1054

2000 Volume 2
September 2000

RealTrax - O-54 Half Curve Track
3-Rail, Item No. 40-1057-2

2000 Volume 2
September 2000

RealTrax - O-54 Switch (L)
3-Rail, Item No. 40-1056

2000 Volume 2
October 2000

RealTrax - O-54 Switch (R)
3-Rail, Item No. 40-1055

2000 Volume 2
September 2000

RealTrax- O-72 Curved Section
3-Rail, Item No. 40-1010

1998 Volume 2
December 1998

RealTrax - O-72 Switch (L)
3-Rail, Item No. 40-1021

1998 Volume 3
October 1998

RealTrax - O-72 Switch (R)
3-Rail, Item No. 40-1020

1998 Volume 3
October 1998

RealTrax - Right Hand Track Siding Layout Builder
3-Rail, Item No. 40-1027

1999 Volume 2
July 1999

RealTrax - Track Activation Device (I.T.A.D.)
3-Rail, Item No. 40-1028

1999 Volume 2
June 1999

RealTrax Track Layout Software
Item No. 60-1322

1999 Volume 2
April 1999

RealTrax - Uncoupling Section
3-Rail, Item No. 40-1008

1998 Volume 2
September 1998

RealTrax Wire Harness
3-Rail, Item No. 40-1015

1998 Volume 2
August 1998

UNCATALOGED ITEMS

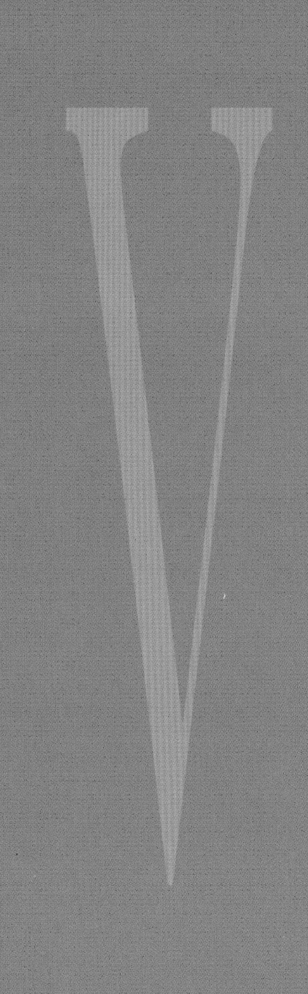

UNCATALOGED ITEMS

M.T.H. has produced a number of items that were never cataloged but were offered to dealers or customers. TCA and TTOS convention cars are among the best known of these. The company has also released two Dealer Appreciation Packages, in 1999 and 2000. These are designed to thank the M.T.H. dealers for their support and to show appreciation for strong relationships that are very important to M.T.H.'s success. Pennsylvania and New York Central Ready-To-Run™ sets that were developed specifically to be sold in Sears stores rather than through the dealer network also fall into this category. Uncataloged items range from Ready-To-Run sets to freight cars and passenger car sets, to Premier steam and diesel locomotives. Each item is made with the same care and attention to detail that model railroaders admire in M.T.H. products.

PREMIER DIESEL LOCOMOTIVES

F-3 AA Diesel Set
Canadian Pacific

1999 D.A.P Brochure
August 1999

3-Rail with Proto-Sound®, Item No. 20-80001b1, Cab No. 2373

F-3 ABA Diesel Set
Santa Fe - Clear Body

2000 D.A.P. Brochure
June 2000

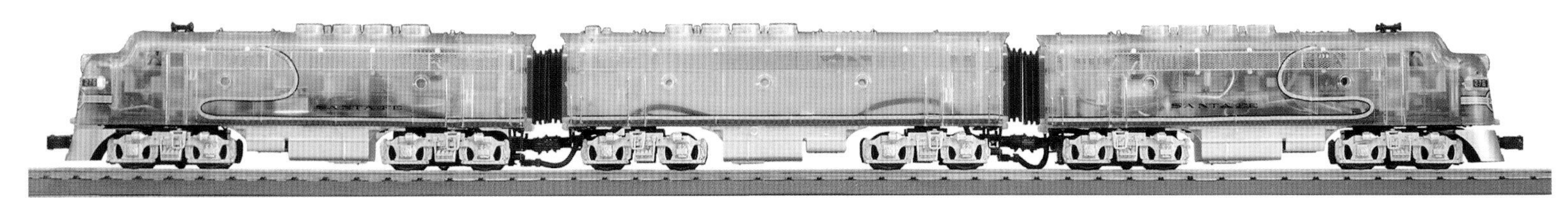
3-Rail with Proto-Sound® 2.0, Item No. 20-80002a, Cab No. 2334 (A Units), NONE (B Unit)

F-3 B Unit
Canadian Pacific

2000 D.A.P. Brochure
June 2000

3-Rail, Item No. 20-80002b, Cab No. 2373

FM Trainmaster Diesel Engine
Lackawanna

1999 D.A.P. Brochure
September 1999

3-Rail with Proto-Sound®, Item No. 20-80001d, Cab No. 2321

GP-30 Diesel Engine
Clear

January 1995

3-Rail with Proto-Sound®, Item No. 20-2074-1, Cab No. NONE

GP-9 Diesel Engine
Clear

April 1994

3-Rail With Proto-Sound®, Item No. 20-2049-1, Cab No. NONE

PREMIER PASSENGER CARS

2-Car 60' Aluminum Coach Passenger Set
Canadian Pacific

2000 D.A.P. Brochure
August 2000

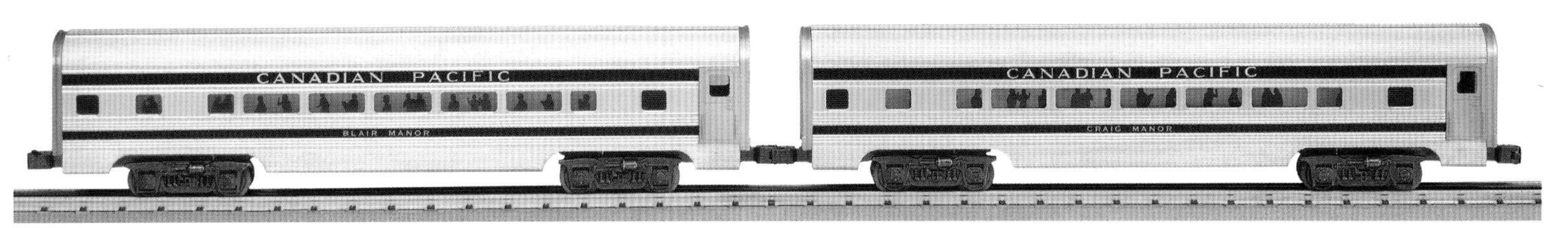

3-Rail, Item No. 20-80002g, Car Names Blair Manor, Craig Manor

4-Car 60' Aluminum Passenger Set
Canadian Pacific

1999 D.A.P. Brochure
August 1999

3-Rail, Item No. 20-80001b2, Car Nos. Banff Park (Observation), Skyline 500 (Vista Domes)

PREMIER ROLLING STOCK

8000 Gallon Tank Car
G.T.S. - Big Mo

April 1999

Item No. 20-96018, Car No. 16142

Extended Vision Caboose
Union Pacific

1999 D.A.P. Brochure
July 1999

Item No. 20-80001c, Car No. 25724

Extended Vision Caboose
Santa Fe

2000 D.A.P. Brochure
June 2000

3-Rail, Item No. 20-80002c, Car No. 0010

PREMIER STEAM LOCOMOTIVES

4-8-8-4 Big Boy Steam Engine
Union Pacific

1999 D.A.P. Brochure
July 1999

3-Rail with Proto-Sound®, Item No. 20-80001a, Cab No. 4018

RAILKING DIESEL / ELECTRIC LOCOMOTIVES

Alco PA ABA Diesel Set
TCA 1999 Convention

September 1999

3-Rail With Proto-Sound®, Item No. 30-2172-1, Cab No. 4599

GG-1 Electric Engine
Pennsylvania

2000 D.A.P. Brochure
August 2000

3-Rail with Proto-Sound® 2.0, Item No. 20-80002e, Cab No. 2340

PCC Electric Street Car With Proto-sound®
2000 D.A.P.

2000 D.A.P. Brochure
March 2000

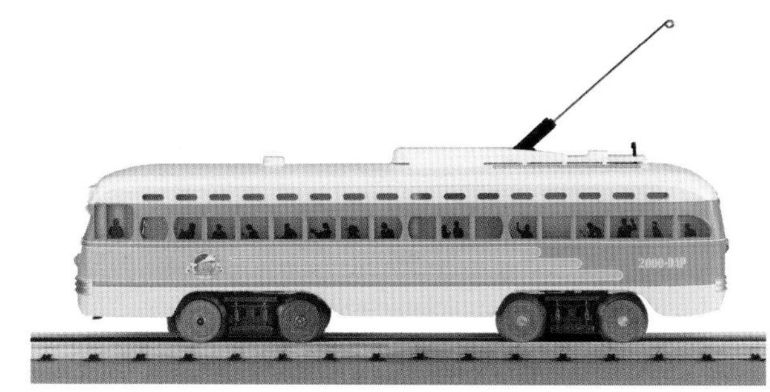
3-Rail with Proto-Sound®, Item No. 20-80002h (2000 DAP), Cab No. 2000

RAILKING PASSENGER CARS

4-Car 60' Aluminum Passenger Set
Pennsylvania

2000 D.A.P. Brochure
July 2000

3-Rail, Item No. 20-80002f, Car Names Betsy Ross, William Penn, Molly Pitcher, Alexander Hamilton

RAILKING RTR / SPECIALTY SETS

Sears R-T-R O Gauge Toy Train Set
Pennsylvania

August 1999

3-Rail With Electronic Whistle, Item No. 30-4031-0, Car Nos. Woodsided Caboose 479815, Box Car 30989, Tank Car 102097, Engine No.1014

Sears R-T-R O Gauge Toy Train Set
New York Central

September 1998

3-Rail With Electronic Whistle, Item No. 30-4022-0, Car Nos. Engine No.2743, Box Car 60368, Flat Car 19983, Woodsided Caboose 19702

RAILKING ROLLING STOCK

Auto Carrier Flat Car
TTOS

September 1999

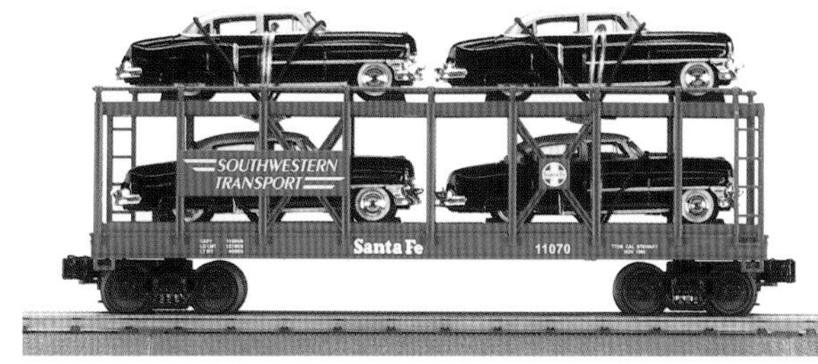

Item No. 30-7659 with (4) 1952 Cadillacs.

Box Car
Oreo

August 1997

Item No. 30-7415, Car No. 031797

Box Car
'95 Christmas

August 1997

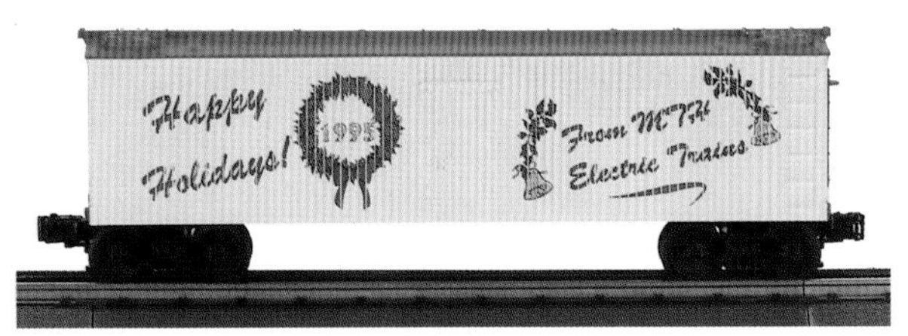

Item No. 30-7415

Box Car
I Love Toy Trains®
Limited Edition

August 1999

Item No. 30-7499, Car No. 1999

Box Car
G.T.S. - Big Mo

April 1998

Item No. 30-7425, Car No.16314

Box Car
1999 D.A.P. Christmas

1999 D.A.P. Brochure
December 1999

Item No. 20-80001e, Car No. 1999

Box Car
2000 D.A.P. Christmas

2000 D.A.P.
June 1999

Item No. 20-80002d, Cab No. NONE

Flat Car
1990 Christmas

December 1990

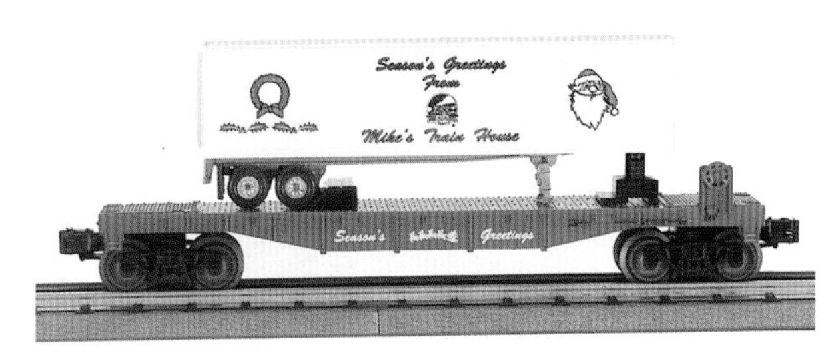

Item No. none, Car No. 1990

RAILKING STEAM LOCOMOTIVES

4-8-4 Gs-4 Northern Steam Engine
Nabisco

August 1997

3-Rail with Electronic Whistle, Item No. 30-1131-0, Cab No. 1998

TINPLATE ACCESSORIES

Show Case Mr. Atomic

April 1994

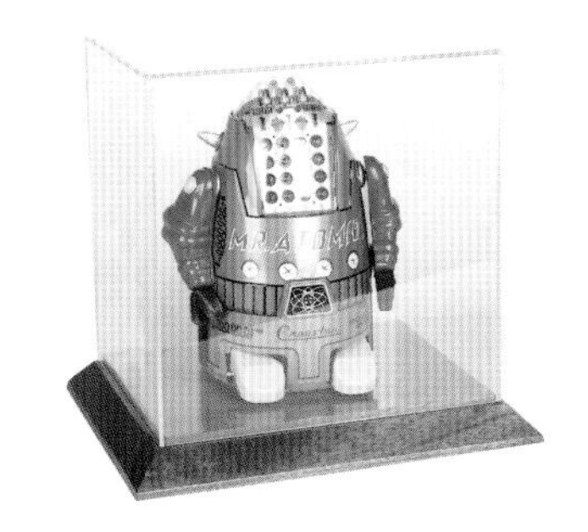

Item No. 10-1011

TINPLATE ROLLING STOCK

200 Series Std. Gauge Caboose
Train Collector's Association

June 1999

Item No. 10-2001, Car No.1999

APPENDICES

MTH
N.Y.C
NEW YORK CENTRAL
M.T.H.

Appendix A:

PROTO-SOUND® HISTORY
1990 - 1993

During the three years between 1990 and 1993, sound systems existed only on the wish lists of M.T.H. model railroaders. Neither the Weaver Gold Edition locomotives that M.T.H. produced nor the first M.T.H. Premier Line locomotive, the GE Dash 8-40, had sound systems installed by the manufacturer.

However, the QSI®-produced DCRU® electronic reverse units in the Weaver Gold Edition locomotives were designed to accept a retrofitted QSI sound system, which could be plugged into the existing DCRU printed circuit board. This could be done by the dealer, the purchaser, or even at M.T.H. headquarters. The retrofit involved attaching a speaker to the floor of the locomotive or tender over the sound escape holes already provided, mounting the back-up battery wherever possible, plugging in the add-on printed circuit board, and connecting wiring as necessary.

1993-2000

By the time 1993 arrived, M.T.H. realized that customer demand for sound systems must be met. There were so many requests for sound systems to be added to the Dash 8-40 that M.T.H. included a built-in, custom designed QSI® sound system in their next locomotive, the Challenger steamer. This was the advent of the well-known Proto-Sound system, which was prominently featured in M.T.H.'s Spring 1994 catalog.

The original version of Proto-Sound was a simplified version of QSI's QS-1 system, and it had no automatic disconnect circuit for the back-up battery. The battery had to be turned on and off by means of a slide switch mounted on the locomotive or tender floor. The switch is normally set in the off position, to reduce battery drain, and turned on when operating the locomotive. If the switch is accidentally left in the on position when power to the locomotive is turned off, there will be two blasts of the horn or whistle to remind the operator to set the switch to off. This first version of Proto-Sound, installed in the Challenger and 4-6-2 steamers, and in ALCO PA, C 30-7, and GP-9 diesels, provided only two remote-control features. They were Sound Volume (feature 6), and Chuff Threshold/Chuff Rate Adjustment (feature 27).

In 1994, the second version of Proto-Sound, installed in the SD-60M and F-3 (first run) diesels and the Y-6B and Y-3 steamers, retained the use of the back-up battery switch, but provided additional sound features. These features included Remote Bell Control (feature 20), Cab Chatter, Horn or Whistle Operation in neutral (feature 25), Diesel Start-up and Shutdown, and Pop-off/Blowdown-Injector Sounds for steamers.

In the fall of 1994 M.T.H. offered model railroaders who had the original Proto-Sound version a chance to upgrade their systems. M.T.H. devised a replacement software chip that could be installed into the existing system to upgrade the capabilities to include those features provided in the second version of Proto-Sound.

Before long, M.T.H. introduced a third version of Proto-Sound. This enhanced system eliminated the external back-up battery switch, incorporating automatic disconnect and charging capability instead. The program features remained the same as those in the second version, except for the addition of a Coil Coupler On/Off capability (feature 10). This third adaptation of Proto-Sound was first installed in the GP-30, H 10-44, and F-3 (second run) diesels.

The fourth Proto-Sound version was essentially the same as version three, except for the addition of a Default System Reset capability (feature 18). This adaptation was built into diesels beginning with the SD-45, and into steamers beginning with the AT & SF 4-8-4.

The term Proto-Sound® is a registered trademark of M.T.H. Electric Trains, and refers to a series of sound generating and control systems used in M.T.H. locomotives and aftermarket sound packages. The original Proto-Sound® systems were designed by QS Industries, Inc., of Beaverton, Oregon. The Proto-Sound® system should not be confused with Proto-Sound 2.0, which was developed by M.T.H.'s own Research and Development team. They are completely different systems.

The next Proto-Sound upgrade retained all previous features and sounds, and added braking sounds and passenger/freight announcements. In the meantime, with each new and enhanced version of Proto-Sound, computer memory capacity was also increased to permit storage of the increased program bits required. Eventually, Proto-Sound systems were modified to enable the Lockout of Locomotive Reversing (feature 40) and Control of Squeaking Brake Sound (feature 45).

A specific Proto-Sound feature identified as X, is accessed by turning the track voltage on and off "X" number of times. The locomotive will then acknowledge the instruction with a coded reply. M.T.H.'s Z-4000 transformer allows simpler, easier selection of features. Complete, detailed instructions on how to select every feature is contained in each locomotive's operating instructions and in the Z-4000 operating instructions.

Beginning with the 2000 Volume Two catalog, the earlier QSI-designed Proto-Sound was replaced by Proto-Sound 2.0, which was created by M.T.H.'s own Research and Development Department, headed by Dave Krebiehl, in Michigan. Proto-Sound 2.0 retains all of the capability of original Proto-Sound, but with improved sound quality and many additional features.

This new sound and control system is compatible with any transformer capable of operating the original Proto-Sound equipment. To use it, operators need a DCS (Digital Command System) handheld Remote Control and a DCS Track Interface Unit (TIU). An optional Accessory Interface Unit (AIU) is used to remotely control accessories and track switches.

The possible different levels of operation of new Proto-Sound 2.0 locomotives and related equipment configurations are explained below:

- ***Proto-Sound 2.0-equipped engine and a compatible transformer***
  Conventional Mode Functions, including the richer-sounding new locomotive sounds (such as chuffing or diesel roar, bells

By 1999, Proto-Sound systems included the following program features:

Feature 6: Select 100%, 50%, 25%, or 0% diesel or steam noise level. Bell, whistle, or horn volume levels are not affected.

Feature 10: Disabling Proto-Coupler operation. A two-ding response from the locomotive indicates that uncoupling is disabled.

Feature 18: Resets all program features to the original factory settings. A warbled bell sound acknowledges the instruction.

Feature 20: Allows bell operation using a separate bell button controller.

Feature 23: Selects cab chatter sounds. One ding from the locomotive indicates that cab chatter is activated; two dings means that cab chatter is turned off.

Feature 25: Enables horn operation in neutral. One ding indicates that the horn is disabled in neutral. Two dings means the horn can be sounded in neutral.

Feature 27: Enables setting the chuff threshold speed and chuff rate for steam locomotives.

Feature 28: Enables or disables freight yard or passenger station effects. One ding indicates that these sounds are enabled. Two dings mean the sound feature is disabled.

Feature 40: Enables the lockout of the locomotive reverse capability, which is useful when operating locomotives in pairs.

Feature 45: Enables or disables squeaking brake sounds. One ding indicates that sounds are activated by the bell button. Two dings mean that brake sounds are set for full-time operation. Three dings mean that brake sounds are turned off.

and whistles or horns), Proto-Effects (such as cab chatter and station announcements), basic locomotive speed control (but not in 1 scale mph increments), and locomotive direction.

- ***Proto-Sound 2.0-equipped engine, a compatible transformer, and the DCS Remote Control System (which includes the DCS remote handheld and the Track Interface Unit (TIU)***

The Features listed above, plus:

DCS Command Mode operation of locomotives, including individual control of up to 50 different locomotives (when you use additional TIUs) on the same track at the same time, enhanced Proto-Speed Control (operate locomotives in 1 scale mph increments), independent volume control of bell, horn or whistle, engine sounds, and the Proto-Effects set, turn lights on and off, Proto-Doppler, Proto-Dispatch, Proto-Cast, and many, many more.

The ability to download additional sound effects from the M.T.H. website.

- ***Proto-Sound 2.0-equipped engine, a compatible transformer, the DCS Remote Control System, and DCS Accessory Interface Unit (AIU)***

The Features listed above, plus:

Remote Control over Layout Accessories - Requires no modification to accessories.

Remote Control over Track Blocks and Track Switches-Requires no modification to tracks and track switches.

Proto-Sound 2.0 was designed to be completely compatible with previous M.T.H. engines, with other manufacturers' engines in conventional mode, and even with Lionel's® Trainmaster® command control system (as long as the operator has a Lionel Command Base connected to the DCS system). It is possible to run a Proto-Sound 2.0 and a Lionel Trainmaster engine in command mode on the same track at the same time with a conventional mode locomotive. Proto-Sound 2.0 engines can, of course, also be run in conventional mode by operators who prefer not to invest in the new DCS Remote equipment or who simply prefer conventional mode.

Any of the M.T.H. remote controls (the DCS Remote, the Z-4000 Remote, or the RailKing Remote) can be used to access conventional features, though only the DCS Remote will control command features. A single DCS remote can control command mode and conventional mode locomotives at the same time. As this book goes to press, there are no firm plans to market an upgrade package for earlier locomotives.

Prior to the RailKing products advertised in the 2000 Volume Two catalogs, non Proto-Sound powered units provided only a whistle or horn sound, activated by the whistle controller on a transformer. Beginning with the 2000 Volume Two catalog, most RailKing powered units are available with a choice of Loco-Sound™ or Proto-Sound 2.0, both of which are new technologies for the year 2000.

Loco-Sound is a major upgrade of the modest sound capability previously offered with non Proto-Sound units. Loco-Sound-equipped items all have digitally stored background steam, diesel, or electric motor sounds that vary with speed, whistle or horn, and bell sounds. Sound fidelity is much improved over earlier production. Whistle or horn and bell sounds can still be put into action as before, by means of a conventional transformer with whistle controller and an auxiliary bell button, or from any M.T.H. transformer or remote control. When used with the Remote Lock-On the Loco-Sound system also allows use of the Proto-Cast and Proto-Dispatch features. A description of these features follows in subsequent pages.

Loco-Sound also includes locomotive speed control, which functions as a cruise control mechanism. As long as all loads are within power supply capacity, the train will maintain a constant speed up and down grades and around curves, consistent with the power capability of the transformer used. The speed of Loco-Sound-equipped locomotives can be controlled from the transformer, but can also be remotely boosted or retarded by using the rocker switch on an M.T.H. remote.

ADDITIONAL M.T.H. SYSTEM FEATURES

ProtoSmoke®

ProtoSmoke, which refers to the built-in smoke generating components found in all Premier and RailKing steam locomotives and in many diesels, is another registered M.T.H. trademark. The SD-9 and SD-60 diesels in the Spring 1996 catalog were the first diesels to incorporate ProtoSmoke. Because of space limitations inside the shell some diesels are unable to include smoking capability. Some early steam locomotives used a pumping device to generate smoke, and this caused the smoke to puff in spurts. However, later ProtoSmoke locomotives produced until the spring of 2000 emit continuous smoke. Beginning with the 2000 Volume Two catalog, those Proto-Sound 2.0 locomotives with ProtoSmoke produce smoke that can be varied, puff, or be turned off remotely.

Proto-Coupler®

The Proto-Coupler system, which is another registered trademark, provides operators with the ability to operate a locomotive's automatic couplers anywhere on the track. The feature was first included on the Premier Challenger Steamer and appeared somewhat later on Premier diesel locomotives. Beginning with the 2000 Volume Two catalog, locomotives are equipped with a newer version of Proto-Coupler, which operates at a lower voltage than before.

Proto-Effects™

Proto-Effects refers to train sounds other than bells, whistle or horn, chuffing, diesel or electric noise. It originally included cab chatter, passenger station sounds, freight yard sounds, and squeaking brakes. Proto-Effects now has been expanded in Proto-Sound 2.0 to include coupler release noise, coupler slack sounds, wheel clickety-clacks, train wreck sounds, and more.

Proto-Speed Control™

This new Proto-Sound 2.0 feature monitors a locomotive's motor revolutions, continuously correcting motor voltage to maintain constant locomotive speed. When active, this system will permit only slight changes in speed when ascending or descending grades or rounding curves. Proto-Speed Control also enhances train performance at very slow speeds. The system can be overridden when double-heading with non-Proto-Sound or earlier Proto-Sound locomotives.

Proto-Doppler™

Proto-Doppler takes its name from the Doppler Effect, named for the scientist who first defined the phenomenon. As it is explained, the Doppler Effect occurs when a noisy object approaches a listener, and it generates sound with a frequency or pitch greater than when motionless. Similarly, such an object, when moving away from someone who is listening, generates noise frequencies lower than those when at rest. Thus a train or ambulance exhibits an apparent drop in noise or siren frequency as it passes anyone hearing the sound. Proto-Sound 2.0 enables the train operator to create the Doppler effect with his/her model railroad.

Proto-Dispatch™

Using the Proto-Dispatch feature, the operator can substitute his/her own 'cab chatter' or station announcements for the pre-recorded Cab Chatter or Station Announcements provided by Proto-Sound 2.0 when a DCS TIU is used. This feature is also available with Loco-Sound, when a RailKing IR Remote Lock-On is used. A small microphone is built into the DCS Remote Control, and the Proto-Sound 2.0 operator simply presses a button on the control and speaks into the microphone to play his or her own voice through the engine in real time. The operator must provide his or her own inexpensive microphone to use this feature with Loco-Sound and the RailKing Remote Lock-On.

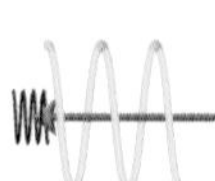

Proto-Cast™

Proto-Cast is the Proto-Sound 2.0 and Loco-Sound feature that enables an operator to broadcast any recorded message or music through the speaker built into the locomotive. Using the DCS Track Interface Unit with Proto-Sound 2.0 or the RailKing IR Remote Lock-on with Loco-Sound and any outside audio source, an operator can play his or her favorite music, prototype recording, or children's story while the train runs around the track. The audio source must be provided by the operator.

Z-4000® Transformer

The M.T.H. Z-4000 is the most powerful commercial UL-approved transformer available to the model railroading community. After M.T.H.'s competition declared the impossibility of developing such a transformer, Mike Wolf decided to head up the development of the Z-4000 himself. The project was born as the 200-watt Z-2000, but as the research and development team systematically worked through the difficulties associated with such a large transformer, they realized they could make it even more powerful than they had originally planned. The 400-watt, UL-approved Z-4000 was born. It has two large throttle handles, to control two loops of track, LED displays that tell the operator the exact voltage and amperage being used, and control buttons that not only work the bell, whistle or horn, and change the direction, but also allow easy programming of Proto-Sound features.

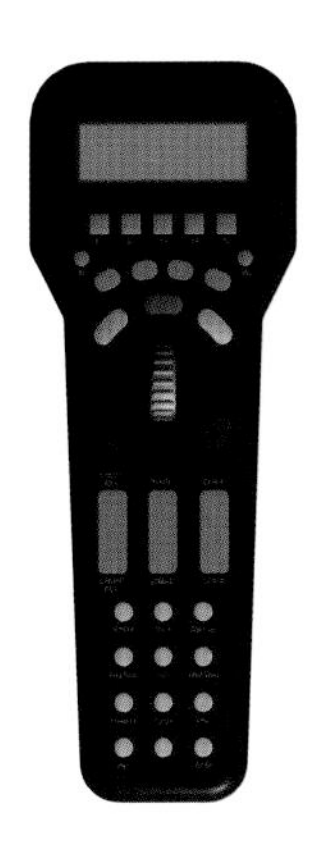

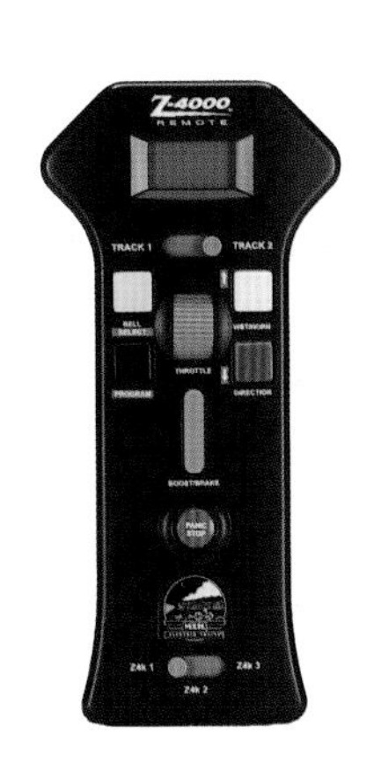

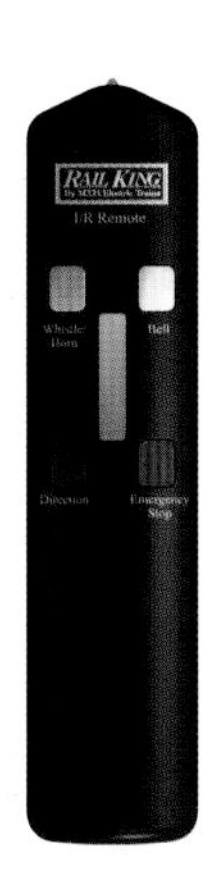

Remote Controls

The DCS Remote Control, when used with the Track Interface Unit, allows the operator to control command and conventional mode engines at the same time. It individually identifies and controls up to fifty locomotives at a time (when sufficient TIUs are used), which gives the operator more freedom than ever to operate a layout realistically. The DCS remote can operate from a range of fifty feet or more, offering the ultimate in operator mobility. It is scheduled to arrive in late 2000.

The Z-4000 handheld remote control and receiver arrived in spring, 2000. The remote system uses 900Mhz technology to allow users remote control of trains from up to thirty feet away, and each handheld remote unit will control up to three Z-4000 transformers (with one receiver for each transformer). The remote also allows users easy access to all of their conventional operation and Proto-Sound features along with the freedom to wander around the room to view and enjoy layouts from different perspectives. It even provides brake and boost buttons that allow one-touch momentary control of train speed without re-setting track voltage.

The RailKing Remote Control, scheduled to arrive in fall, 2000, essentially replaces the control boxes that accompany M.T.H.'s Z-500™ or Z-750® transformers by remotely regulating the power output of the "bricks." The operator simply aims the Remote at the Remote Lock-On and presses the desired button on the remote. This remote allows operator access to all conventional mode Proto-Sound features. The RailKing remote, which is similar to a TV remote control, operates at a distance of up to fifteen feet.

Appendix B:

COMMAND CONTROL

Communicating with Passengers on the M.T.H. Line

Mike Wolf has always been cognizant of the importance of staying in touch with dealers and customers. Knowing that effective communication and entrepreneurial success go hand-in-hand, M.T.H. has always sought out the most current and useful vehicles for communication.

M.T.H. Electric Trains uses a variety of modern promotional techniques and devices to reach a wider audience of potential new O and Standard Gauge owners and operators, and to improve communications with dealers and customers. The following are some examples of M.T.H.'s efforts to implement key marketing strategies as well as to take advantage of the latest technology.

Big Mo was identified as "the world's largest traveling train layout " by the Guinness Book of Records 1989 edition. This traveling train layout is used as a public relations and advertising tool, and it was the brainchild of a train collector and promoter named Harry Turner from Cochranton, Pennsylvania. It was used for several years by Lionel Trains to endorse the sale of their products.

When Lionel decided to stop using Big Mo, M.T.H. seized the opportunity to gain more company recognition. M.T.H. quickly con-

The "Big Mo" dream layout inside the customized trailer includes:

- *400 feet of track running 7 - 11 classic O Gauge trains through scenes presenting all four seasons of the year;*
- *custom animation such as men chopping trees and sawing logs, children playing on swings and teeter totters, and ice skaters gliding across ponds;*
- *interactive components with control buttons located where visitors can reach them to operate parts of the display;*
- *digital stereo sound recordings of train operations that are very realistic; and*
- *fiber-optics overhead scenery depicting twinkling stars, meteor showers, and a space shuttle.*

M.T.H. frequently updates the display with new products and makes other changes, like rotating some of the favorite M.T.H. products.

tacted Harry Turner and negotiated a contract with him to use Big Mo to advertise the company's model railroad products. Once an agreement was established, some changes were made in the appearance of this gigantic road vehicle and its valuable cargo. The trailer was repainted RailKing orange, the train display inside was modified, and relevant components of it were replaced with M.T.H. products. All of the changes were made by Mr. Turner with the approval of M.T.H. Then Big Mo became an M.T.H. vehicle used to display and promote the high quality and affordability of M.T.H. model railroad products.

Big Mo has logged thousands of miles traveling coast-to-coast, appearing at all kinds of events like hobby shows, festivals, state and local fairs, railroad museums, as well as at home, boat, and auto shows. Big Mo has also been featured in hundreds of newspapers, on local television news, on CNN, Nickelodeon, PBS, and CNTV. Big Mo has even made an appearance on national television in Russia. The schedule for this huge train layout on wheels is jointly determined by M.T.H. and Harry Turner. Big Mo's calendar is routinely published on the M.T.H. web site and in The CrossingGate®, the M.T.H. Club Newsletter.

Videotapes featuring different aspects of the company and demonstrations of M.T.H. products are an extremely valuable marketing tool. Because toy train products are animated, M.T.H. sees video tapes as an excellent way to advertise their interactive nature. In fact, the M.T.H. web site (www.mth-railking.com) includes video clips, as does the interactive CD ROM that M.T.H. has available.

M.T.H. worked with professional videographers to produce several 30-minute color videotapes, which are designed to introduce model railroad enthusiasts to the M.T.H. line. The videos spotlight M.T.H. products including RailKing, Premier, and Tinplate Traditions, as well as the Proto-Sound 2.0 with DCS sound and command system, and they emphasize performance features. In some instances, the videos include comparisons to competitor's products while confirming the quality and value of the M.T.H. line.

As part of the effort to implement the company's strategic marketing plan, more than 100,000 of these videotapes have been given away free of charge over the last 5 years. M.T.H. believes that these videos help to capture the magic of M.T.H. Electric Trains, while showing that this hobby is much more than just a set of tracks with some electric trains running on them.

M.T.H. views these videos as one of its most successful marketing tools because they provide quick and easy access to many potential customers. Furthermore, when a video is given to one person, chances are that many more people will eventually see it also. Frequently, when one recipient receives a video, he or she usually watches it several times, and then passes it on to others.

The ***M.T.H. Web Site*** (www.mth-railking.com), which was originally designed and maintained by an outside internet firm, became the sole in-house responsibility of M.T.H. in 1998. The web site is designed to offer a multitude of products and services to both longtime, die-hard model railroaders, as well as to those who are just beginning to develop an interest in the hobby. Visitors to the site can access information about the M.T.H. Railroaders Club, browse through the catalogs, shop in the M.T.H. Online Store, get updates on the latest technological innovations like the Proto-Sound 2.0 System, and explore the M.T.H. Dealer/Product Locator Service database. In addition, the web site has an interactive component which allows visitors to view special M.T.H. products by clicking on various controls in a simulated train engine.

The M.T.H. web site also publishes a free electronic newsletter. The newsletter was first generated in October 1999, and it is designed to stimulate the interests of model railroaders and railfans. It is also a means to introduce those who might be new to the hobby to some of the M.T.H. products. The content of the electronic newsletter is purposefully general in nature so as not to compete or conflict with the other M.T.H. newsletter publications: the CrossingGate club newslet-

ter and the M.T.H. Express dealer newsletter. All issues of the electronic newsletter to-date are accessible at the M.T.H. web site.

M.T.H. is enormously proud of the company's outstanding web site, which is far superior to those of the competition. The professional and significantly experienced full-time web staff strive to continuously improve, update, and create new features to provide the best available source for fun and information relating to the hobby. The M.T.H. web site is frequently updated so that the information provided is current and useful. The M.T.H. web site routinely experiences a heavy volume of traffic. For example, on any given day there may be as many as 3,000 visitors to the site.

Newsletters give M.T.H. direct access to their dealers and their most devoted customers. The CrossingGate, the M.T.H. Railroaders Club Newsletter, is published six times a year. This slick four-color professional publication is filled with important and entertaining information for all M.T.H. Railroaders Club Members. It includes product spotlights, insider reports, shipping schedules, service updates, M.T.H. Employee Profiles, letters from M.T.H. Club members, train trivia, and an FYI (For Your Information/Focus on Your Interests) feature section on railroad history.

The writers of The CrossingGate conduct considerable research to substantiate the content, and they routinely identify their sources. In addition, The CrossingGate staff constantly works to move the publication to the next level of professionalism to provide readers with as much useful information as possible.

The black-and white dealer newsletter, the M.T.H. Express, is distributed to 800 Authorized M.T.H. Train Merchants monthly. The M.T.H. Express contains vital information about M.T.H.'s newest technological developments, service updates for dealers, product focus data, shipping schedules, and a dealer information exchange column. The M.T.H. Express also provides information on marketing and sales techniques.

Licensing Agreements are a valuable way to pique consumer interest and to reach new customers. M.T.H. has participated in a number of these arrangements, as both licensor and licensee. M.T.H. has a continuing interest in making connections between the all-American hobby of model railroading and other familiar names on the American landscape. To that end, they have made licensing agreements with several well-known brand names and introduced their images to model railroading layouts. Among the companies with whom they have had licensing agreements are Warner Brothers, McDonald's, Nabisco, the United States Postal Service, Union 76, Maytag, Caterpillar, the Metropolitan Transit Authority of New York, and others.

The M.T.H. products that have resulted from these agreements range from models of movie trains (the 4-4-0 Wanderer from the 1999 feature film, Wild Wild West), to realistic gas stations with real company names on them, to models of freight cars and locomotives, such as the U.S. Postal Service's "Celebrate the Century Express."

Licensing popular brand names has become more common within M.T.H.'s product line over the past few years.

In 1998 M.T.H. developed an agreement with Sears to allow them (Sears) to sell a Ready-To-Run starter set especially developed for the Sears market during the holidays, in a designated number of stores across the country. The sales of the sets were successful so the agreement was renewed for another holiday season in 1999.

Comparison advertising has been a staple in M.T.H.'s marketing techniques. There was a time when comparing competitor's products to your own to gain an advantage with the consumer was not acceptable in the complex world of advertising. Even today, ads making direct comparisons between products made by competing firms are often thought to be controversial, even confrontational. However, M.T.H.'s management believes that advertising that demonstrates how much better and/or less expensive the M.T.H.

Exclusive production of train sets for retailing giant Sears began in 1988.

product is when compared with competitor's, is a direct and honest way to address customers. The stated claims made in this type of M.T.H. ad are true and substantiated, and if presented well they can be a significant stimulant to M.T.H.'s sales.

In 1996 M.T.H. began placing comparison ads in major 3-rail train and hobby magazines. M.T.H. runs feature ads in such publications as Model Retailer, O Gauge Railroading, Hobby Merchandiser, and Classic Toy Trains. All claims and comparisons in these ads are carefully researched with diligent product testing. Furthermore, every statement, real or implied, is reviewed point by point by experienced legal counsel before publication.

A somewhat controversial but highly effective ad campaign was typical of M.T.H.'s aggressive marketing style.

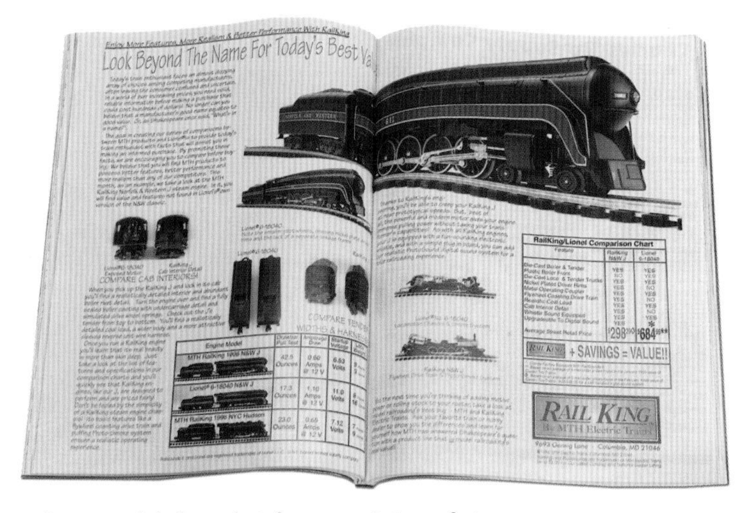

Ads frequently compared similar products from competing manufacturers.

Appearances on television are always a tremendous way to advertise, and as the years go by, M.T.H. is seeking more opportunities for this type of exposure.

M.T.H.'s most recent experience in this area was on the CBS morning television broadcast, The Early Show, on February 18, 2000, when Mike Wolf appeared in an interview Bryant Gumble conducted with quarterback Dan Marino of the Miami Dolphins. The interview

The Dan Marino Foundation is just one of the many organizations that receive support from M.T.H..

focused on the Celebrity Golf Tournament held in Florida each year to benefit the Dan Marino Foundation. Mike competed in the Tournament, and the interview segment included his presentation of a $200,000 check from M.T.H. Electric Trains® to Dan Marino for the Foundation.

M.T.H. has been represented on national television in a few other spots. For example, in 1998 M.T.H. trains played a role in an episode of the CBS television show Touched By An Angel. The producers of the show contacted M.T.H. and requested that they provide the trains and a display for a presentation, which focused on a handicapped young man who was a model train hobbyist. Throughout the segment, M.T.H. model trains ran on the layout and M.T.H. packaging was clearly visible.

In the spring of 1998, a New York publicity firm contacted Mike Wolf to arrange an interview with him at one of the big York Train Meets. The interview with Mike was part of a show on how the hobby of toy trains has thrived even though it no longer has the national exposure it used to enjoy. The Financial News Division of CNN produced this show.

Interactive Kiosks have been used by M.T.H. for several years. These kiosks are actually touch-screen devices which display video clips and photographs of M.T.H. products. Originally they were created as a point-of-sale vehicle for customers to direct order M.T.H products featured in the kiosk display. In addition, they included an M.T.H. Dealer Locator feature.

Located in high traffic areas, interactive, multi-media kiosks help spread the word about M.T.H.

The kiosks now also demonstrate the excitement of model railroading. M.T.H. installs these portable kiosks in several shopping malls and at other events throughout the winter holiday season, and they are usually set up with an M.T.H. train layout.

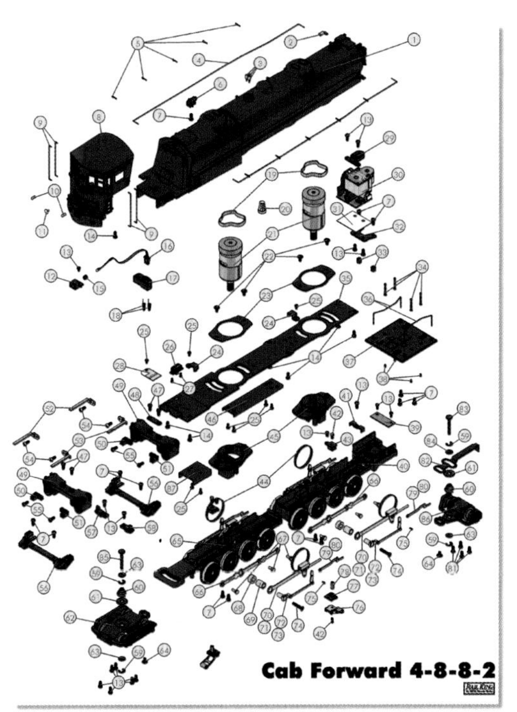

Improved/Enhanced Illustration of Parts Information, which is based on actual engineering drawings, has been developed for model railroaders using M.T.H. products. These illustrations are found in the parts catalogs as well as the M.T.H. web site. An in-house full-time staff of graphic specialists produces these detailed views of M.T.H. products. Each illustration is presented in such a way as to make it easy to understand how a particular item is put together and how it operates.

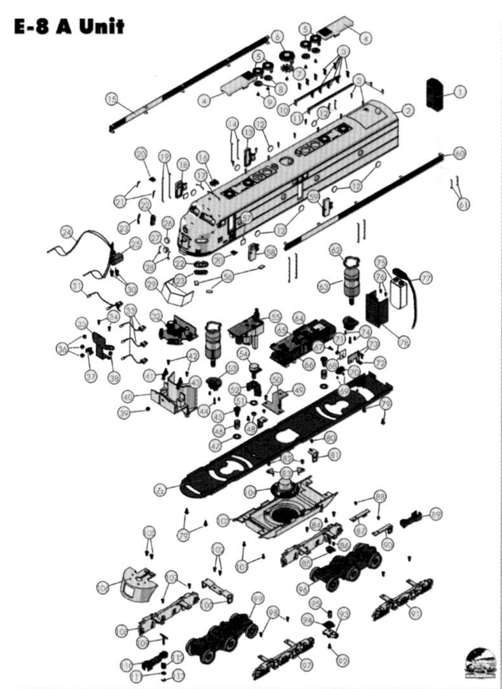

Appendix C:

PAPER

The following section presents the primary promotional materials M.T.H. has produced over the last twenty years. The captions for these catalogs, flyers, and brochures give the dates they were published and the products or product lines they promote. M.T.H. has always handled the planning, design, writing, and layout of all its promotional materials in-house. The M.T.H. photography lab is equipped with state-of-the-art digital equipment, and the art department includes people skilled in photography, exploded views, layout, and design. M.T.H.'s own marketing personnel, writers, and artists collaborate to plan and produce promotional materials that present their high-quality products in the best light.

MTH Tinplate Brochure
381/408 Brochure
Printed 1983

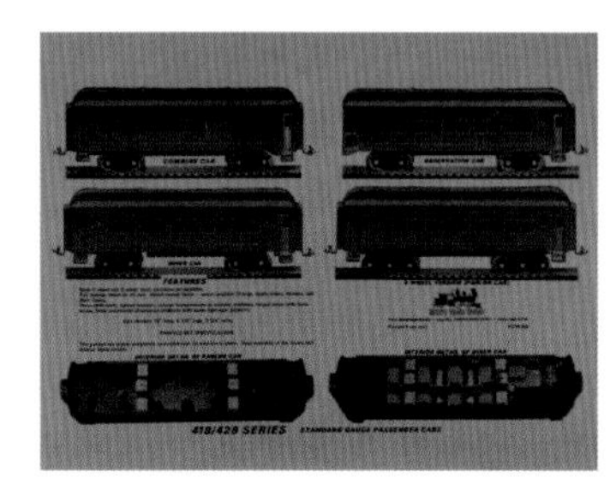

MTH Tinplate Brochure
418 Brochure
Printed 1984

MTH Tinplate Brochure
200 Series Freight Brochure No. 1
Printed 1985

MTH Tinplate Brochure
200 Series Freight Brochure No. 2
Printed 1986

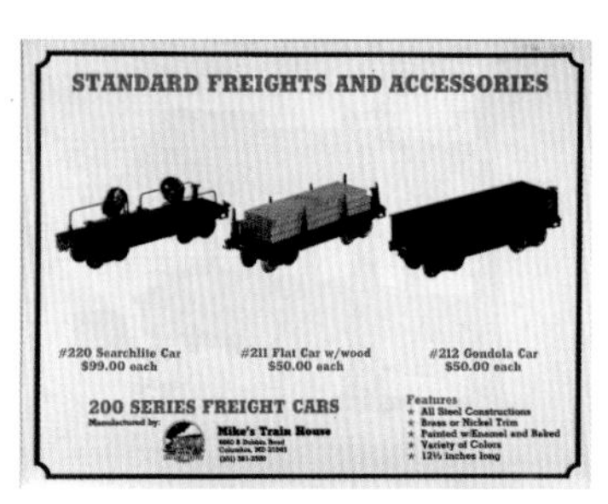

MTH Tinplate Brochure
200 Series Freight Brochure No. 3
Printed 1986

MTH Tinplate Brochure
400E Brochure
Printed 1985

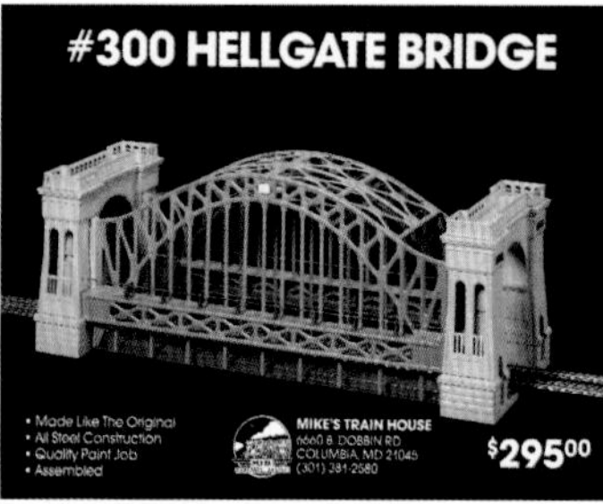

MTH Tinplate Brochure
Hell gate Bridge Brochure
Printed 1987

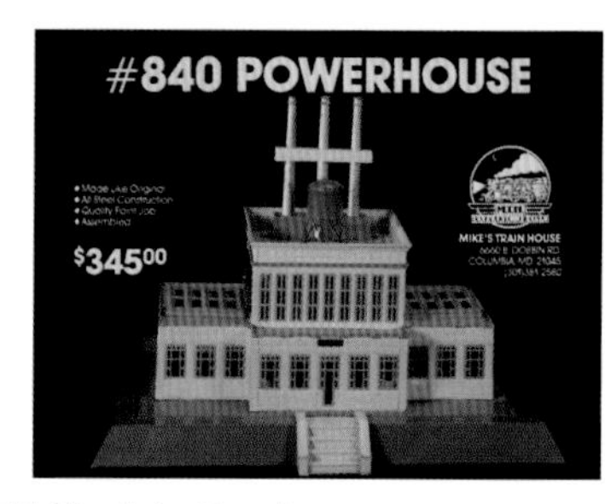

MTH Tinplate Brochure
840 Powerhouse Brochure
Printed 1986

MTH Tinplate Brochure
Blue Comet Passenger Set Brochure
Printed 1986

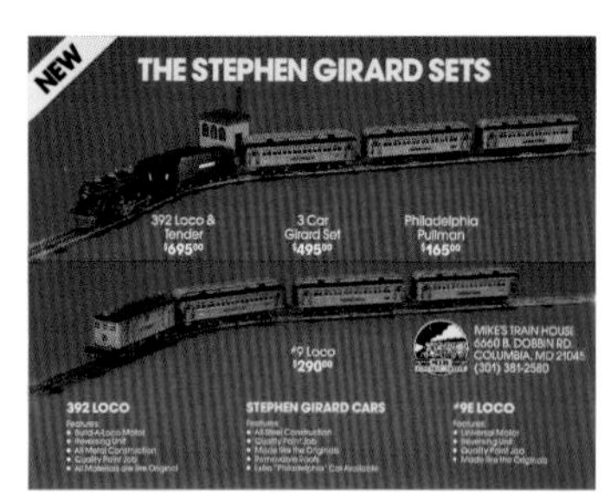

MTH Tinplate Brochure
Girard Passenger Set Brochure
Printed 1987

MTH Tinplate Brochure
Spring 1987 Tinplate Catalog
Printed 1987

MTH Tinplate Brochure
Accessories Brochure
Printed 1987

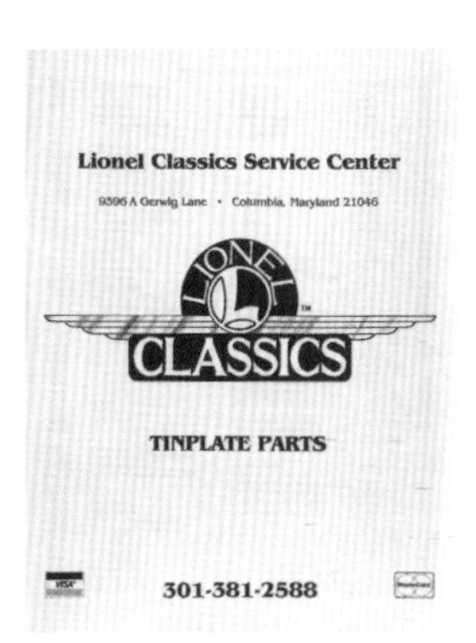

MTH Tinplate Parts Catalog
Lionel Classics Tinplate Parts Catalog 1
Printed 1988

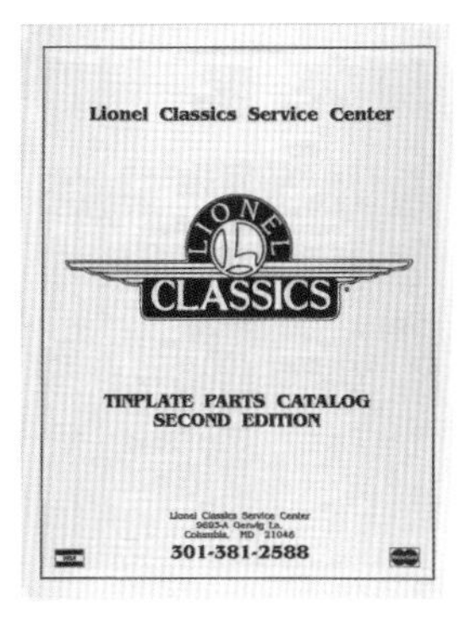

MTH Tinplate Parts Catalog
Lionel Classics Tinplate Parts Catalog 2
Printed 1991

Brochure
Tinplate Toy Brochure 1
Printed 1993

Brochure
Tinplate Toy Brochure 2
Printed 1992

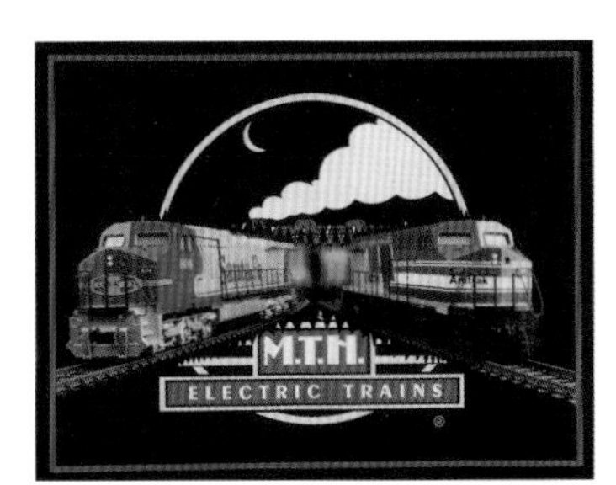

Catalog
Fall 1993 Catalog - Dash 8 Cover
Printed Fall 1993

Catalog
Spring 1994 Catalog - Challenger Cover
Printed Spring 1994

Catalog
Fall 1994 Catalog - Southern Ps-4 Cover
Printed Summer 1994

Catalog
Winter 1994 Catalog - F-3 Diesel Cover
Printed Fall 1994

Catalog
15th Anniversary Catalog - N&W Y6b Cover
Printed Winter 1994/95

Catalog
Fall 1995 Catalog - Santa Fe 4-8-4 Cover
Printed Summer 1995

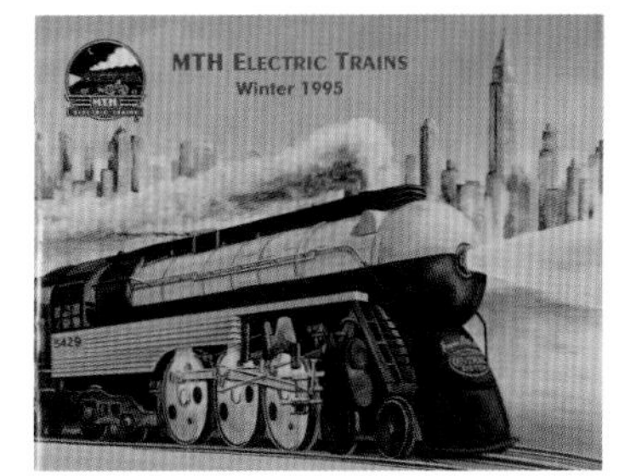

Catalog
Winter 1995 Catalog - NYC Empire Cover
Printed Fall 1995

Catalog
Spring 1996 Catalog - C&O Allegheny Cover
Printed Winter 1995/96

Catalog
Summer 1996 Catalog - PRR K4 Cover
Printed Spring 1996

Catalog
Fall/Winter 1996 Catalog - NYC J-1e Cover
Printed Summer 1996

Catalog
Spring 1997 Catalog - Big Boy Cover
Printed Fall 1996

Catalog
1997 Vol. 1 Catalog - WVPP Shay Cover
Printed Winter 1996/97

Catalog
1997 Vol. 2 Catalog - N&W J Cover
Printed Spring 1997

Catalog
1998 Vol. 1 Catalog - BNSF Cover
Printed Summer 1997

Catalog
1998 Vol. 2 Catalog - Blue Comet Cover
Printed Winter 1997/98

RTR Train Set Brochure
1998 RTR Train Set Brochure
Printed Spring 1998

Catalog
1998 Vol. 3 Catalog - SP Daylight Cover
Printed Spring 1998

Mini-Catalog
1998 Mini-Catalog
Printed Summer 1998

Catalog
1999 Vol. 1 Catalog - Camelback Cover
Printed Summer 1998

Catalog
1999 Vol. 2 Catalog - Berkshire Cover
Printed Winter 1998/99

D.A.P. Brocbure
1999 D.A.P. Brochure
Printed Winter 1998/99

RTR Train Set Brochure
1999 RTR Train Set Brochure
Printed Spring 1999

Catalog
1999 Vol. 3 Catalog - AEM 7 Cover
Printed Spring 1999

Mini-Catalog
1999 Mini-Catalog
Printed Summer 1999

Catalog
2000 Vol. 1 Catalog - Premier Gold Cover
Printed Summer 1999

Catalog
2000 Vol. 1 Catalog - RailKing Silver Cover
Printed Summer 1999

Catalog
2000 Vol. 2 Catalog - Premier Gold Cover
Printed Winter 1999/2000

Catalog
2000 Vol. 2 Catalog - RailKing Silver Cover
Printed Winter 1999/2000

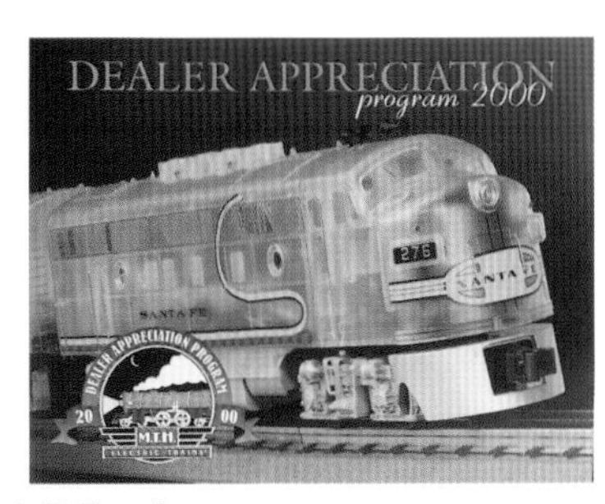

D.A.P. Brochure
2000 D.A.P. Brochure
Printed Winter 1999/2000

RTR Train Set Brochure
2000 RTR Train Set Brochure
Printed Winter 1999/2000

Index

M.T.H. ELECTRIC TRAINS®
M.T.H. Electric Trains
H ELECTRIC TRAINS
SPRING 1987 CATALOG
Spring 1997
MTH Electric Trains
Winter 1995
H ELECTRIC TRAINS
1998 VOLUME III
1999 VOL III
Amtrak
450
2320
964
BNSF

TINPLATE TRADITIONS Accessories

ITEM DESCRIPTION	ROADNAME	ITEM NO.	PAGE
Std. Gauge Track - Reg. Straight		10-1038	78
Std. Gauge Track - Wide Radius Curve		10-1041	78
Std. Gauge Track - Wide Radius Straight		10-1040	78

MTH TINPLATE Steam Engine

ITEM DESCRIPTION	ROADNAME	ITEM NO.	PAGE
#260 O Gauge Locomotive	Black / Green	NONE	79
#260 O Gauge Locomotive	Black / Black	NONE	79
#260 O Gauge Locomotive	Black / Green	NONE	79
#260 O Gauge Locomotive	Black / Black	NONE	79
#260 O Gauge Locomotive	Gunmetal	NONE	79
#263 O Gauge Locomotive	Gunmetal	NONE	79
#263 O Gauge Locomotive	Black	NONE	80
#263 O Gauge Locomotive	TwoTone Blue	NONE	80
#385 Standard Gauge Locomotive	Black w/Brass Trim	NONE	79
#385 Standard Gauge Locomotive	Black w/Nickel Trim	NONE	80
#385 Standard Gauge Locomotive	Gunmetal w/Brass Trim	NONE	80
#385 Standard Gauge Locomotive	Gunmetal w/Nickel Trim	NONE	80
#385 Standard Gauge Locomotive	Crackle Black w/Nickel Trim	NONE	80
#392 Standard Gauge Locomotive	Black w/Brass Trim	NONE	80
#392 Standard Gauge Locomotive	Black w/Nickel Trim	NONE	80
#392 Standard Gauge Locomotive	Gunmetal w/Brass Trim	NONE	80
#392 Standard Gauge Locomotive	Gunmetal w/Nickel Trim	NONE	80
#392 Standard Gauge Locomotive	TwoTone Blue w/Brass Trim	NONE	80
#392 Standard Gauge Locomotive	TwoTone Blue w/Nickel Trim	NONE	80
#392 Standard Gauge Locomotive	Crackle Black w/Brass Trim	NONE	80
#392 Standard Gauge Locomotive	Crackle Black w/Nickel Trim	NONE	80
#400 E Standard Gauge Locomotive	TwoTone Blue w/Nickel Trim	NONE	80
#400 E Standard Gauge Locomotive	TwoTone Blue w/Brass Trim	NONE	80
#400 E Standard Gauge Locomotive	Black w/Brass Trim	NONE	80
#400 E Standard Gauge Locomotive	Grey w/Nickel Trim	NONE	80
#400 E Standard Gauge Locomotive	Gunmetal w/Brass Trim	NONE	80
#400 E Standard Gauge Locomotive	Crackle Black w/Brass Trim	NONE	80
#400 E Standard Gauge Locomotive	TwoTone Brown w/Brass Trim	NONE	80
#400 E Standard Gauge Locomotive	State Green w/Brass Trim	NONE	80
#400 E Standard Gauge Locomotive	Black w/Nickel Trim	NONE	80
#400 E Std. Gauge Locomotive Kit	Kit, no motor	NONE	80

MTH TRADITIONS Diesel/Electric Engine

ITEM DESCRIPTION	ROADNAME	ITEM NO.	PAGE
#381 Std. Gauge Locomotive	State Green	NONE	80
#408 Std. Gauge Locomotive	Two-Tone Brown	NONE	81
#408 Std. Gauge Locomotive	Apple Green	NONE	81
#408 Std. Gauge Locomotive	Dark Green	NONE	81
#408 Std. Gauge Locomotive	Mojave	NONE	81
#9E Std. Gauge Locomotive	Gunmetal Gray/Nickel Trim	NONE	81
#9E Std. Gauge Locomotive	Two-Tone Green/Brass Trim	NONE	81
#9E Std. Gauge Locomotive	Dark Green/Brass Trim	NONE	81
#9E Std. Gauge Locomotive	Orange/Brass Trim	NONE	81
#9E Std. Gauge Locomotive Kit	Undecorated	NONE	81

MTH TRADITIONS Rolling Stock

ITEM DESCRIPTION	ROADNAME	ITEM NO.	PAGE
#211 Flat Car Standard Gauge	Black / Brass	NONE	81
#211 Flat Car Standard Gauge	Black/Nickel	NONE	81
#212 Gondola Standard Gauge	Grey/Brass	NONE	81
#212 Gondola Standard Gauge	Maroon/Brass	NONE	81
#212 Gondola Standard Gauge	Medium Green/Nickel	NONE	81
#212 Gondola Standard Gauge	Dark Green/Brass	NONE	81
#213 Cattle Car Standard Gauge	Cream/Maroon, Nickel	NONE	81
#213 Cattle Car Standard Gauge	Terra Cotta/Green, Brass	NONE	81
#213 Cattle Car Standard Gauge	Terra Cotta/Maroon, Brass	NONE	81
#213 Cattle Car Standard Gauge	Mojave/Maroon, Brass	NONE	81
#213 Cattle Car Standard Gauge	Dark Blue/Gold - TCA	NONE	81
#214 Box Car Standard Gauge	Cream/Orange, Brass	NONE	81
#214 Box Car Standard Gauge	Terra Cotta, Dark Green, Brass	NONE	81
#214 Box Car Standard Gauge	Yellow/Brown, Nickel	NONE	81
#214 Box Car Standard Gauge	Yellow/Brown, Brass	NONE	81
#214 R Refrig. Car Standard Gauge	Ivory/Peacock, Brass	NONE	81
#214 R Refrig. Car Standard Gauge	White/Light Blue, Nickel	NONE	81
#214 R Refrig. Car Standard Gauge	Red/Cream - TCA	NONE	82
#215 Tank Car Standard Gauge	Pea Green/Brass	NONE	82

MTH TRADITIONS Rolling Stock

ITEM DESCRIPTION	ROADNAME	ITEM NO.	PAGE
#215 Tank Car Standard Gauge	Ivory Brass	NONE	82
#215 Tank Car Standard Gauge	Aluminum/Nickel	NONE	82
#215 Tank Car Standard Gauge	Aluminum/Brass	NONE	82
#215 Tank Car Standard Gauge	Orange/Brass	NONE	82
#216 Hopper Standard Gauge	Dark Green/Brass	NONE	82
#216 Hopper Standard Gauge	Dark Green / Nickel	NONE	82
#216 Hopper Standard Gauge	Red/Brass	NONE	82
#216 Hopper Standard Gauge	Red/Nickel	NONE	82
#217 Caboose Standard Gauge	Orange/Maroon, Green	NONE	82
#217 Caboose Standard Gauge	Red/Peacock, Brass	NONE	82
#217 Caboose Standard Gauge	Red/Red, Nickel	NONE	82
#217 Caboose Standard Gauge	Pea Green/Red, Brass	NONE	82
#218 Dump Car Standard Gauge	Mojave/Brass	NONE	82
#218 Dump Car Standard Gauge	Mojave/Nickel	NONE	82
#218 Dump Car Standard Gauge	Dark Green/Brass	NONE	82
#218 Dump Car Standard Gauge	Dark Green/Nickel	NONE	82
#219 Crane Car Standard Gauge	Peacock/Brass	NONE	82
#219 Crane Car Standard Gauge	White/Brass	NONE	82
#219 Crane Car Standard Gauge	Yellow/Nickel	NONE	82
#219 Crane Car Standard Gauge	Cream/Nickel	NONE	82
#219 Crane Car Standard Gauge	Ivory/Nickel	NONE	82
#220 Searchlight Car Standard Gauge	Terra Cotta/Brass	NONE	82
#220 Searchlight Car Standard Gauge	Green/Nickel	NONE	82

MTH TRADITIONS Passenger Sets

ITEM DESCRIPTION	ROADNAME	ITEM NO.	PAGE
#1766 Ives Std. Gauge 3-Car	Terra Cotta/Maroon	NONE	79
#1766 Ives Std. Gauge 3-Car	Terra Cotta	NONE	82
#1766 Ives Std. Gauge 4-Car	Red/Maroon	NONE	83
#1766 Ives Std. Gauge 4-Car	Terra Cotta/Maroon	NONE	83
#1766 Ives/Lionel Std. Gauge Coach	Red/Maroon	NONE	83
#1766 Ives/Lionel Std. Gauge Coach	Terra Cotta/Maroon	NONE	83
3-Car Standard Gauge Blue Comet	Light Two-Tone Blue	NONE	83
3-Car Standard Gauge Blue Comet	Dark Two-Tone Blue	NONE	83
4-Car Std. Gauge 418 Set w/4-Wheel Trucks	Orange	NONE	83
4-Car Std. Gauge 418 Set w/4-Wheel Trucks	Dark Green	NONE	83
4-Car Std. Gauge 418 Set w/4-Wheel Trucks	Apple Green	NONE	83
4-Car Std. Gauge 418 Set w/4-Wheel Trucks	Mojave	NONE	83
4-Car Std. Gauge 418 Set w/4-Wheel Trucks	Two-Tone Brown	NONE	83
4-Car Std. Gauge 418 Set w/4-Wheel Trucks	State Green	NONE	83
4-Car Std. Gauge 418 Set w/6-Wheel Trucks	Orange	NONE	83
4-Car Std. Gauge 418 Set w/6-Wheel Trucks	Dark Green	NONE	83
4-Car Std. Gauge 418 Set w/6-Wheel Trucks	Apple Green	NONE	83
4-Car Std. Gauge 418 Set w/6-Wheel Trucks	Mojave	NONE	83
4-Car Std. Gauge 418 Set w/6-Wheel Trucks	Two-Tone Brown	NONE	83
4-Car Std. Gauge 418 Set w/6-Wheel Trucks	State Green	NONE	83
#423 Halley Pullman Standard Gauge	Dark Two-Tone Blue	NONE	83
#423 Halley Pullman Standard Gauge	Light Two-Tone Blue	NONE	83
#427 Philadelphia Stephen Girard Standard Gauge Car	Two-Tone Green/Brass	NONE	83
#427 Philadelphia Stephen Girard Standard Gauge Car	Two-Tone Green/Nickel	NONE	83
#427 Philadelphia Stephen Girard Standard Gauge Car	Two-Tone Blue/Brass	NONE	83
#427 Philadelphia Stephen Girard Standard Gauge Car	Two-Tone Blue/Nickel	NONE	83
600 Series O Gauge 4-Car	Terra Cotta/Maroon	NONE	83
600 Series O Gauge 4-Car	Lt. Red/Aluminum	NONE	83
600 Series O Gauge 4-Car	State Green	NONE	83
600 Series O Gauge 4-Car	Two-Tone Blue	NONE	84
#616 Pullman Extra Coach	Terra Cotta/Maroon	NONE	84
#616 Pullman Extra Coach	Red/Aluminum	NONE	84
#616 Pullman Extra Coach	Two-Tone Green	NONE	84
#616 Pullman Extra Coach	Two-Tone Blue	NONE	84
Stephen Girard Standard Gauge 3-Car	Two-Tone Green/Brass	NONE	84
Stephen Girard Standard Gauge 3-Car	Two-Tone Green/Nickel	NONE	84
Stephen Girard Standard Gauge 3-Car	Two-Tone Blue/Nickel	NONE	84
Stephen Girard Standard Gauge 3-Car	Two-Tone Blue/Brass	NONE	84

MTH TRADITIONS Accessories

ITEM DESCRIPTION	ROADNAME	ITEM NO.	PAGE
#155 Freight Shed	Yellow/Maroon	NONE	84
#155 Freight Shed	White/Grey	NONE	84
#163 Freight Cart Set	Red/Blue/Green	NONE	79
#163 Freight Cart Set	Red/Green/Orange	NONE	84
#200 Turntable	Green	NONE	84

MTH TRADITIONS Accessories

PREMIER Steam Engine

PREMIER Steam Engine

PREMIER Diesel/Electric Engine

PREMIER DIESEL/ELECTRIC ENGINE

ITEM DESCRIPTION	ROADNAME	ITEM NO.	TURN RAD.	PAGE
Dash-8 Diesel Engine	Burlington	20-2003-0, 20-2003-1 20-2003-2	O-31	106
Dash-8 Diesel Engine	Conrail	20-2004-0, 20-2004-1 20-2004-2	O-31	106
Dash-8 Diesel Engine	Chicago NorthWestern	20-2005-0, 20-2005-1 20-2005-2	O-31	106
Dash-8 Diesel Engine	CSX	20-2006-0, 20-2006-1 20-2006-2	O-31	106
Dash-8 Diesel Engine	Amtrak	20-2007-0, 20-2007-1 20-2007-2	O-31	106
Dash-8 Diesel Engine	Santa Fe	20-2008-0, 20-2008-1 20-2008-2	O-31	106
Dash-8 Diesel Engine	Amtrak	20-2171-1	O-31	106
Dash-9 Diesel Engine	Chicago Northwestern	20-2159-1, 20-2159-2	O-31	107
Dash-9 Diesel Engine	G.E. Demonstrator	20-2160-1, 20-2160-2	O-31	107
Dash-9 Diesel Engine (WC)	BNSF	20-2172-1, 20-2172-2	O-31	107
DC-3 Rail Inspection Car	Union Pacific	20-2242-1	O-72	107
DD40AX Diesel Engine	Union Pacific	20-2178-1	O-72	107
DL-109 Diesel Engine	Milwaukee Road	20-2222-1	O-42	107
DL-109 Diesel Engine w/Proto-Sound	Santa Fe	20-2223-1	O-42	107
DL-110 Powered B Unit Diesel Engine	Santa Fe	20-2223-3	O-42	107
DL-110 Powered B Unit Diesel Engine	Milwaukee Road	20-2222-3	O-42	107
E-2 Bi-Polar Electric	Milwaukee Road	20-5511-1, 20-5511-2	O-72	108
E-33 Rectifier Electric	New Haven	20-5508-1	O-31	108
E-33 Rectifier Electric	Conrail	20-5509-1	O-31	108
E-8 ABA Diesel Engine Set	Seaboard	20-2168-1	O-31	108
E-8 ABA Diesel Engine Set	Rock Island	20-2169-1	O-31	108
E-8 ABA Diesel Engine Set	Baltimore & Ohio	20-2170-1	O-31	108
E-8 ABA Diesel Engine Set	Pere Marquette	20-2205-1	O-31	109
E-8 ABA Diesel Engine Set	Electro Motive Division	20-2206-1	O-31	109
E-8 ABA Diesel Engine Set	Kansas City Southern	20-2207-1	O-31	109
E-8 ABA Diesel Engine Set	Union Pacific	20-2208-1	O-31	109
E-8 ABA Diesel Engine Set	Santa Fe	20-2234-1	O-31	109
E-8 ABA Diesel Engine Set	Illinois Central	20-2235-1	O-31	110
E-8 ABA Diesel Engine Set	Erie	20-2236-1	O-31	110
E-8 ABA Diesel Engine Set	Chicago NorthWestern	20-2237-1	O-31	110
EP-5 Electric Engine	New Haven	20-2195-1	O-31	110
EP-5 Electric Engine	Great Northern	20-2196-1	O-31	110
F-3 AA Diesel Set	Baltimore & Ohio	20-2050-0, 20-2050-1 20-2050-2	O-31	110
F-3 AA Diesel Set	Denver & Rio Grande	20-2051-0, 20-2051-1 20-2051-2	O-31	111
F-3 AA Diesel Set	Florida East Coast	20-2052-0, 20-2052-1 20-2052-2	O-31	111
F-3 AA Diesel Set	Jersey Central	20-2053-0, 20-2053-1 20-2053-2	O-31	111
F-3 AA Diesel Set	Pennsylvania	20-2054-0, 20-2054-1 20-2054-2	O-31	111
F-3 AA Diesel Set	Union Pacific	20-2055-0, 20-2055-1 20-2055-2	O-31	111
F-3 AA Diesel Set	Western Pacific	20-2056-0, 20-2056-1 20-2056-2	O-31	112
F-3 AA Diesel Set	Canadian Pacific	20-2057-0, 20-2057-1 20-2057-2	O-31	112
F-3 AA Diesel Set	Western Maryland	20-2083-0, 20-2083-1 20-2083-2	O-31	112
F-3 AA Diesel Set	Texas Special	20-2084-0, 20-2084-1 20-2084-2	O-31	112
F-3 AA Diesel Set	Burlington	20-2085-0, 20-2085-1 20-2085-2	O-31	112
F-3 AA Diesel Set	Lehigh Valley	20-2086-0, 20-2086-1 20-2086-2	O-31	113
F-3 AA Diesel Set	Northern Pacific	20-2087-0, 20-2087-1 20-2087-2	O-31	113
F-3 AA Diesel Set	Atlantic Coast Line	20-2088-0, 20-2088-1 20-2088-2	O-31	113
F-3 AA Diesel Set	New Haven	20-2089-0, 20-2089-1 20-2089-2	O-31	113
F-3 AA Diesel Set	Electro Motive Division	20-2090-0, 20-2090-1 20-2090-2	O-31	113
F-3 AA Diesel Set	Chesapeake & Ohio	20-2125-0, 20-2125-1 20-2125-2	O-31	114
F-3 AA Diesel Set	Boston & Maine	20-2126-0, 20-2126-1 20-2126-2	O-31	114
F-3 AA Diesel Set	Rock Island	20-2127-0, 20-2127-1 20-2127-2	O-31	114
F-3 AA Diesel Set	Alaska	20-2128-0, 20-2128-1 20-2128-2	O-31	114
F-3 AA Diesel Set	Santa Fe	20-2151-1	O-31	114

PREMIER DIESEL/ELECTRIC ENGINE

ITEM DESCRIPTION	ROADNAME	ITEM NO.	TURN RAD.	PAGE
F-3 AA Diesel Set	Louisville & Nashville	20-2152-1	O-31	115
F-3 AA Diesel Set	Canadian Pacific	20-80001b1	O-31	115
F-3 ABA Diesel Set	New York Central	20-2176-1	O-31	115
F-3 ABA Diesel Set	Southern	20-2177-1	O-31	115
F-3 ABA Diesel Set	Reading	20-2198-1	O-31	115
F-3 ABA Diesel Set	Southern Pacific	20-2199-1	O-31	116
F-3 ABA Diesel Set	Santa Fe	20-2219-1	O-31	116
F-3 ABA Diesel Set	Pennsylvania	20-2218-1	O-31	116
F-3 ABA Diesel Set	Great Northern	20-2220-1	O-31	116
F-3 ABA Diesel Set	Santa Fe - Clear Body	20-80002a	O-31	116
F-3 B Unit	Baltimore & Ohio	20-2058-3, 20-2050-3 20-2058-2	O-31	117
F-3 B Unit	Denver & Rio Grande	20-2059-3, 20-2051-3 20-2059-2	O-31	117
F-3 B Unit	Florida East Coast	20-2060-3, 20-2052-3 20-2060-3S	O-31	117
F-3 B Unit	Jersey Central	20-2061-3, 20-2053-3 20-2061-3S	O-31	117
F-3 B Unit	Union Pacific	20-2063-3, 20-2055-3 20-2063-3S	O-31	117
F-3 B Unit	Western Pacific	20-2064-3, 20-2056-3 20-2064-3S	O-31	117
F-3 B Unit	Canadian Pacific	20-2065-3, 20-2057-3 20-2065-3S	O-31	117
F-3 B Unit	Western Maryland	20-2091-3, 20-2083-3 20-2091-3S	O-31	117
F-3 B Unit	Texas Special	20-2092-3, 20-2084-3 20-2092-3S	O-31	117
F-3 B Unit	Burlington	20-2093-3, 20-2085-3 20-2093-3S	O-31	117
F-3 B Unit	Lehigh Valley	20-2094-3, 20-2086-3 20-2094-3S	O-31	118
F-3 B Unit	Northern Pacific	20-2095-3, 20-2087-3 20-2095-3S	O-31	118
F-3 B Unit	Atlantic Coast Line	20-2096-3, 20-2088-3 20-2096-3S	O-31	118
F-3 B Unit	New Haven	20-2097-3, 20-2089-3 20-2097-3S	O-31	118
F-3 B Unit	Chesapeake & Ohio	20-2125-3, 20-2125-4 20-2125-32	O-31	118
F-3 B Unit	Boston & Maine	20-2126-3, 20-2126-4 20-2126-32	O-31	118
F-3 B Unit	Rock Island	20-2127-3, 20-2127-4 20-2127-32	O-31	118
F-3 B Unit	Alaska	20-2028-3, 20-2128-4 20-2128-32	O-31	118
F-3 B Unit	Santa Fe	20-2151-3, 20-2151-4	O-31	118
F-3 B Unit	Louisville & Nashville	20-2152-3, 20-2152-4	O-31	118
F-3 B Unit	New York Central	20-2176-3	O-31	119
F-3 B Unit	Southern	20-2177-3	O-31	119
F-3 B Unit	Southern Pacific	20-2199-3	O-31	119
F-3 B Unit	Reading	20-2198-3	O-31	119
F-3 B Unit	Canadian Pacific	20-80002b	O-31	119
F-3 B-Unit	Pennsylvania	20-2062-3, 20-2054-3 20-2062-3S	O-31	119
F-3 B-Unit	Electro Motive Division	20-2098-3, 20-2090-3 20-2098-3S	O-31	119
F40PH Diesel Engine	METRA	20-2149-1, 20-2149-2	O-31	119
F40PH Diesel Engine	CALTRAN	20-2150-1, 20-2150-2	O-31	119
F40PH Diesel Engine	Amtrak	20-2147-1, 20-2147-2	O-31	119
F40PH Diesel Engine	Massachusetts Bay	20-2148-1, 20-2148-2	O-31	120
F59PH Diesel Engine	Amtrak	20-2213-1	O-31	120
FA-2 ABA Diesel Engine Set	New Haven	20-2238-1	O-31	120
FA-2 ABA Diesel Engine Set	Baltimore & Ohio	20-2239-1	O-31	120
FA-2 ABA Diesel Engine Set	Great Northern	20-2240-1	O-31	120
FA-2 ABA Diesel Engine Set	Lehigh Valley	20-2241-1	O-31	120
FA-2 ABA Diesel Engine Set	Canadian National	20-2243-1	O-31	121
FM H10-44 Diesel Engine	Pennsylvania	20-2075-0, 20-2075-1 20-2075-2	O-27	121
FM H10-44 Diesel Engine	Frisco	20-2076-0, 20-2076-1 20-2076-2	O-27	121
FM H10-44 Diesel Engine	Santa Fe	20-2077-0, 20-2077-1 20-2077-2	O-27	121
FM H10-44 Diesel Engine	Chicago Northwestern	20-2078-0, 20-2078-1 20-2078-2	O-27	121
FM H10-44 Diesel Engine	New York Central	20-2079-0, 20-2079-1 20-2079-2	O-27	121
FM H10-44 Diesel Engine	Milwaukee Road	20-2080-0, 20-2080-1 20-2080-2	O-27	121

PREMIER DIESEL/ELECTRIC ENGINE

PREMIER DIESEL/ELECTRIC ENGINE

PREMIER Diesel/Electric Engine

ITEM DESCRIPTION	ROADNAME	ITEM NO.	TURN RAD.	PAGE
SD60M Diesel Engine	Soo Line	20-2044-0, 20-2044-1 20-2044-2	O-31	132
SD60M Diesel Engine	Burlington Northern	20-2045-0, 20-2045-1 20-2045-2	O-31	132
SD60M Diesel Engine	CSX	20-2046-0, 20-2046-1 20-2046-2	O-31	132
SD60M Diesel Engine	Chicago NorthWestern	20-2047-0, 20-2047-1 20-2047-2	O-31	132
SD60M Diesel Engine	CP Rail	20-2048-0, 20-2048-1 20-2048-2	O-31	132
SD70 MAC Diesel Engine	BNSF	20-2154-1, 20-2154-2	O-31	133
SD70 MAC Diesel Engine	Canadian National	20-2155-1, 20-215-2	O-31	133
SD70 MAC Diesel Engine	BNSF	20-2215-1	O-31	133
SD70 MAC Diesel Engine	BNSF	20-2221-1	O-31	133
SD70 MAC Diesel Engine	CSX	20-2224-1	O-31	133
U.P. Veranda Turbine	Union Pacific	20-2185-1, 20-2185-2	O-72	133

PREMIER Rolling Stock

ITEM DESCRIPTION	ROADNAME	ITEM NO.	TURN RAD.	PAGE
100 Ton Hopper Car	Canada	20-97400	O-31	135
100 Ton Hopper Car	North American	20-97401	O-31	135
100 Ton Hopper Car	Lehigh Valley	20-97409	O-31	135
100 Ton Hopper Car	Burlington	20-97410	O-31	135
100 Ton Hopper Car	Santa Fe	20-97421	O-31	135
100 Ton Hopper Car	Chessie	20-97420	O-31	135
2-Bay Offset Hopper Car	Frisco	20-97415	O-31	135
2-Bay Offset Hopper Car	Chesapeake & Ohio	20-97416	O-31	135
20K Gallon 4-Compartment Tank Car	Burlington Northern	20-96010	O-31	135
20K Gallon 4-Compartment Tank Car	ETCX	20-96011	O-31	135
3-Bay Cylindrical Hopper Car	Chessie	20-97405	O-31	135
3-Bay Cylindrical Hopper Car	Santa Fe	20-97406	O-31	135
3-Bay Cylindrical Hopper Car	Union Pacific	20-97417	O-31	136
3-Bay Cylindrical Hopper Car	Canada	20-97418	O-31	136
3-Car Slag Car Set	None	20-90011	O-31	136
33K Gallon Tank Car	Suburban Propane	20-96006	O-31	136
33K Gallon Tank Car	Pyrofax Gas	20-96007	O-31	136
33K Gallon Tank Car	Royster	20-96012	O-31	136
33K Gallon Tank Car	Union Texas	20-96013	O-31	136
4-Bay Hopper Car	Western Maryland	20-97402	O-31	136
4-Bay Hopper Car	Union Pacific	20-97403	O-31	136
4-Bay Hopper Car	CSX	20-97407	O-31	136
4-Bay Hopper Car	Norfolk & Western	20-97408	O-31	136
50' Box Car	Union Pacific	20-93021	O-31	136
50' Box Car	Nickel Plate Road	20-93022	O-31	137
50' Box Car	Florida East Coast	20-93035	O-31	137
50' Box Car	Boston & Maine	20-93036	O-31	137
50' Dbl. Door Plugged Boxcar	Ralston Purina	20-93025	O-31	137
50' Dbl. Door Plugged Boxcar	Boston & Maine	20-93026	O-31	137
50' Dbl. Door Plugged Boxcar	Southern Pacific	20-93032	O-31	137
50' Dbl. Door Plugged Boxcar	Norfolk & Western	20-93033	O-31	137
50' Dbl. Door Plugged Boxcar	Union Pacific	20-93034	O-31	137
50' Waffle Box Car	Boston & Maine	20-93028	O-31	137
50' Waffle Box Car	Seaboard	20-93029	O-31	137
75' Depressed Flat Car	Union Pacific	20-98106	O-54	137
75' Depressed Flat Car	Nickel Plate Road	20-98109	O-54	137
8000 Gallon Tank Car	Norfolk Southern	20-9600	O-27	138
8000 Gallon Tank Car	Conrail	20-9601	O-27	138
8000 Gallon Tank Car	Vulcan	20-96002	O-27	138
8000 Gallon Tank Car	CSX	20-96003	O-27	138
8000 Gallon Tank Car	National Starch	20-96004	O-27	138
8000 Gallon Tank Car	Ethyl Corp	20-96005	O-27	138
8000 Gallon Tank Car	Kodak®	20-96014	O-27	138
8000 Gallon Tank Car	Geigy	20-96015	O-27	138
8000 Gallon Tank Car	G.T.S. - Big Mo	20-96018	O-27	138
Box Car	New York Central	20-9300	O-31	138
Box Car	Union Pacific	20-9301	O-31	138
Box Car	Santa Fe	20-9303	O-31	138
Box Car	Pennsylvania	20-9302	O-31	139
Box Car	Southern	20-9304	O-31	139
Box Car	Railbox	20-9305	O-31	139
Box Car	Canadian National	20-93006	O-31	139
Box Car	Illinois Central	20-93007	O-31	139
Box Car	Missouri Pacific	20-93008	O-31	139
Box Car	Western Maryland	20-93009	O-31	139

PREMIER Rolling Stock

ITEM DESCRIPTION	ROADNAME	ITEM NO.	TURN RAD.	PAGE
Box Car	Katy	20-93010	O-31	139
Box Car	CCA	20-93011	O-31	139
Box Car	Great Northern	20-93014	O-31	139
Box Car	New Haven	20-93015	O-31	139
Box Car	State of Maine	20-93018	O-31	139
Box Car	Susquehanna	20-93019	O-31	140
Box Car	New York Central	20-93037	O-31	140
Box Car	USPS #1	20-93039	O-31	140
Box Car	USPS #2	20-93040	O-31	140
Box Car	USPS #3	20-93041	O-31	140
Center Beam Flat Car	CSX	20-98211	O-54	140
Center Beam Flat Car	Union Pacific	20-98212	O-54	140
Center Beam Flat Car	CP Rail	20-98229	O-54	140
Center Beam Flat Car	Tobacco Valley Lumber	20-98230	O-54	140
Center Beam Flat Car	CP Rail	20-98234	O-54	140
Coalporter Hopper Car	CSX	20-9700	O-31	140
Coalporter Hopper Car	Burlington Northern	20-9701	O-31	140
Coalporter Hopper Car	BNSF	20-97002	O-31	141
Coalporter Hopper Car	Detroit Edison	20-97003	O-31	141
Coalporter Hopper Car	CSX	20-97419	O-31	141
Coil Car	Norfolk Southern	20-98203	O-31	141
Coil Car	Union Pacific	20-98204	O-31	141
Coil Car	New Haven	20-98213	O-31	141
Coil Car	Southern Pacific	20-98214	O-31	141
Corrugated Auto Carrier	Denver Rio Grande Western	20-98231	O-54	141
Corrugated Auto Carrier	Conrail	20-98241	O-54	141
Double Door 50' Box Car	Union Pacific	20-93012	O-31	141
Double Door 50' Box Car	Louisville & Nashville	20-93013	O-31	141
Double Door 50' Box Car	Pennsylvania	20-93016	O-31	141
Double Door 50' Box Car	Delaware & Hudson	20-93017	O-31	142
Double Door 50' Box Car	Chessie	20-93031	O-31	142
Extended Vision Caboose	Union Pacific	20-9100	O-27	142
Extended Vision Caboose	Pennsylvania	20-9101	O-27	142
Extended Vision Caboose	Norfolk & Western	20-9103	O-27	142
Extended Vision Caboose	Chesapeake & Ohio	20-9102	O-27	142
Extended Vision Caboose	Chessie System	20-9104	O-27	142
Extended Vision Caboose	Santa Fe	20-9105	O-27	142
Extended Vision Caboose	Electro Motive Division	20-91006	O-27	142
Extended Vision Caboose	Canadian National	20-91007	O-27	142
Extended Vision Caboose	Southern	20-91009	O-27	142
Extended Vision Caboose	Southern Pacific	20-91008	O-27	142
Extended Vision Caboose	Santa Fe	20-91010	O-27	143
Extended Vision Caboose	Chicago Northwestern	20-91011	O-27	143
Extended Vision Caboose	Conrail	20-91012	O-27	143
Extended Vision Caboose	Union Pacific	20-91013	O-27	143
Extended Vision Caboose	Lehigh Valley	20-91020	O-27	143
Extended Vision Caboose	New Haven	20-91021	O-27	143
Extended Vision Caboose	Burlington	20-91023	O-27	143
Extended Vision Caboose	Denver Rio Grande Western	20-91024	O-27	143
Extended Vision Caboose	Union Pacific	20-80001c	O-27	143
Extended Vision Caboose	Santa Fe	20-80002c	O-27	143
Flat Car	West Virginia Pulp & Paper Co.	20-98101	O-31	143
Flat Car	Western Maryland	20-98102	O-31	143
Flat Car	Northern Pacific	20-98105	O-31	144
Flat Car	Pennsylvania	20-98104	O-31	144
Flat Car	Union Pacific	20-98107	O-31	144
Flat Car	Delaware & Hudson	20-98108	O-31	144
Flat Car	Baltimore & Ohio	20-98110	O-31	144
Flat Car	Santa Fe	20-98111	O-31	144
Flat Car	MTH Transport	20-98114	O-31	144
Flat Car	Baltimore & Ohio	20-98115	O-31	144
Flat Car	Norfolk Southern	20-98116	O-31	144
Flat Car	Santa Fe	20-98117	O-31	144
Flat Car	Chicago NorthWestern	20-98118	O-31	144
Flat Car - w/Bulkheads	Great Northern	20-98113	O-31	144
Flat Car - w/Bulkheads	Florida East Coast	20-98112	O-31	145
Gondola Car - Scale Length	Pennsylvania	20-98001	O-31	145
Gondola Car - Scale Length	Union Pacific	20-98002	O-31	145
Gondola Car - Scale Length	Southern	20-98004	O-31	145
Gondola Car - Scale Length	Southern Pacific	20-98003	O-31	145
Gondola Car - Scale Length	Chicago Northwestern	20-98005	O-31	145
Gondola Car - Scale Length	Seaboard	20-98006	O-31	145
Gondola Car - Scale Length	Delaware & Hudson	20-98007	O-31	145
Gondola Car - Scale Length	Lehigh Valley	20-98008	O-31	145

PREMIER Passenger Sets

ITEM DESCRIPTION	ROADNAME	ITEM NO.	TURN RAD.	PAGE
2-Car 70' ABS Slpr/Diner - Smooth	Union Pacific	20-6638	O-42	162
2-Car 70' ABS Slpr/Diner - Smooth	Union Pacific	20-6653	O-42	162
2-Car 70' ABS Slpr/Diner - Smooth	New York Central	20-6654	O-42	163
2-Car 70' ABS Slpr/Diner - Smooth	Illinois Central	20-6661	O-42	163
2-Car 70' ABS Slpr/Diner - Smooth	Milwaukee Road	20-6652	O-42	163
2-Car 70' ABS Slpr/Diner - Smooth	Erie	20-6660	O-42	163
2-Car 70' ABS Slpr/Diner - Smooth	Great Northern	20-6651	O-42	163
2-Car 70' ABS Slpr/Diner - Smooth	Pennsylvania	20-6657	O-42	163
2-Car 70' Aluminum Slp/Din Set - Painted	Atlantic Coast Line	20-6600	O-42	164
2-Car 70' Aluminum Slp/Din Set - Painted	Chesapeake & Ohio	20-6602	O-42	164
2-Car 70' Aluminum Slp/Din Set - Painted	Union Pacific	20-6606	O-42	164
2-Car 70' Aluminum Slp/Din Set - Painted	Pennsylvania	20-6607	O-42	164
2-Car 70' Aluminum Slp/Din Set - Painted	Amtrak	20-6608	O-42	164
2-Car 70' Aluminum Slp/Din Set - Painted	Union Pacific	20-6610	O-42	164
2-Car 70' Aluminum Slp/Din Set - Painted	Baltimore & Ohio	20-6611	O-42	165
2-Car 70' Aluminum Slp/Din Set - Painted	Baltimore & Ohio	20-6613	O-42	165
2-Car 70' Aluminum Slp/Din Set - Plated	Atlantic Coast Line	20-6601	O-42	165
2-Car 70' Aluminum Slp/Din Set - Plated	Southern	20-6603	O-42	165
2-Car 70' Aluminum Slp/Din Set - Plated	New York Central	20-6604	O-42	165
2-Car 70' Aluminum Slp/Din Set - Plated	California Zephyr	20-6605	O-42	165
2-Car 70' Aluminum Slp/Din Set - Plated	New York Central	20-6609	O-42	182
2-Car 70' Madison Comb/Din	Baltimore & Ohio	20-4101	O-42	182
2-Car 70' Madison Comb/Din	Denver & Rio Grande	20-4102	O-42	182
2-Car 70' Madison Comb/Din	New York Central	20-4105	O-42	183
2-Car 70' Madison Comb/Din	Pennsylvania	20-4106	O-42	165
2-Car 70' Madison Comb/Din	Santa Fe	20-4107	O-42	166
2-Car 70' Madison Comb/Din	Southern	20-4108	O-42	166
2-Car 70' Madison Comb/Din	Texas & Pacific	20-4109	O-42	166
2-Car 70' Madison Comb/Din	Lehigh Valley	20-4110	O-42	166
2-Car 70' Madison Comb/Din	Northern Pacific	20-4114	O-42	166
2-Car 70' Madison Comb/Din	Pennsylvania	20-4118	O-42	166
2-Car 70' Madison Comb/Din	New York Central	20-4119	O-42	167
2-Car 70' Madison Comb/Din	Pullman	20-4120	O-42	167
2-Car 70' Madison Comb/Din	Pennsylvania	20-4125	O-42	166
2-Car 70' Madison Comb/Din	New York Central	20-4126	O-42	167
2-Car 70' Madison Comb/Din	Boston & Maine	20-4127	O-42	167
2-Car 70' Madison Comb/Din	Jersey Central	20-4121	O-42	167
2-Car 70' Madison Comb/Din	Norfolk & Western	20-4124	O-42	167
2-Car 70' Madison Comb/Din	New York Central	20-4122	O-42	168
2-Car 70' Madison Comb/Din	Union Pacific	20-4131	O-42	168
2-Car 70' Madison Comb/Din	Chesapeake & Ohio	20-4128	O-42	168
2-Car 70' Madison Comb/Din	Chicago NorthWestern	20-4130	O-42	168
2-Car 70' Madison Comb/Din	Pennsylvania	20-4132	O-42	168
2-Car 70' Madison Comb/Din	Pullman	20-4133	O-42	168
2-Car 70' Madison Comb/Din	Nickel Plate Road	20-4134	O-42	169
2-Car 70' Madison Comb/Din	Lehigh Valley	20-4135	O-42	169
2-Car 70' Madison Comb/Din	Southern	20-4136	O-42	169
2-Car 70' Madison Comb/Din	Millennium	20-4129	O-42	169
2-Car Amfleet	Amtrak	20-6655	O-42	169
2-Car Amfleet	Amtrak	20-6656	O-42	169
2-Car SuperLiner Slpr/Diner Set	Amtrak	20-6539	O-42	170
2-Car SuperLiner Slpr/Diner Set	Amtrak	20-6541	O-42	170
4-Car 60' Aluminum	Santa Fe Plated	20-6016	O-31	170
4-Car 60' Aluminum	Pennsylvania	20-6017	O-31	183
4-Car 60' Aluminum	Santa Fe	20-6018	O-31	170
4-Car 60' Aluminum	Louisville & Nashville	20-6020	O-31	170
4-Car 60' Aluminum	Santa Fe	20-6021	O-31	170
4-Car 60' Aluminum	Canadian Pacific	20-80001b2	O-31	170
4-Car 60' Aluminum - Ribbed	Baltimore & Ohio	20-6022	O-31	171
4-Car 60' Aluminum - Ribbed	Santa Fe	20-6023	O-31	171
4-Car Amfleet	Amtrak	20-6519	O-42	171
4-Car Amfleet	Cal Train	20-6521	O-42	171
4-Car Amfleet	Mass Bay	20-6522	O-42	183
4-Car Amfleet	Metra	20-6520	O-42	171
4-Car Amfleet	Amtrak	20-6531	O-42	171
4-Car Amfleet	Septa	20-6532	O-42	171
4-Car Amfleet	Amtrak	20-6555	O-42	171
4-Car Amfleet	Amtrak	20-6556	O-42	171
4-Car Scale Bi-Level	Chicago NorthWestern	20-6558	O-42	172
4-Car Scale Bi-Level	METRA	20-6559	O-42	172
4-Car Scale SuperLiner Set	Amtrak	20-6524	O-42	172
4-Car Scale SuperLiner Set	Amtrak	20-6537	O-42	172
5-Car 60' Aluminum	Union Pacific	20-6001	O-31	183
5-Car 60' Aluminum	Rio Grande	20-6002	O-31	183

PREMIER Passenger Sets

ITEM DESCRIPTION	ROADNAME	ITEM NO.	TURN RAD.	PAGE
5-Car 60' Aluminum	Pennsylvania	20-6003	O-31	183
5-Car 60' Aluminum	California Zephyr	20-6004	O-31	183
5-Car 60' Aluminum	Florida East Coast	20-6005	O-31	183
5-Car 60' Aluminum	Delaware & Hudson	20-6006	O-31	183
5-Car 60' Aluminum	Pennsylvania	20-6007	O-31	183
5-Car 60' Aluminum	Baltimore & Ohio	20-6008	O-31	172
5-Car 60' Aluminum	Santa Fe	20-6009	O-31	183
5-Car 60' Aluminum	New York Central	20-6010	O-31	183
5-Car 60' Aluminum	Canadian Pacific	20-6011	O-31	183
5-Car 60' Aluminum	Baltimore & Ohio	20-6012	O-31	183
5-Car 60' Aluminum	New York Central	20-6013	O-31	183
5-Car 60' Aluminum	Norfolk & Western	20-6014	O-31	172
5-Car 60' Aluminum	Union Pacific	20-6015	O-31	183
5-Car 60' Aluminum	Union Pacific	20-6019	O-31	183
5-Car 70' ABS - Ribbed	Rock Island	20-6512	O-42	172
5-Car 70' ABS - Ribbed	Baltimore & Ohio	20-6513	O-42	172
5-Car 70' ABS - Ribbed	Norfolk & Western	20-6514	O-42	173
5-Car 70' ABS - Ribbed	Seaboard	20-6515	O-42	173
5-Car 70' ABS - Ribbed	Nickel Plate Road	20-6526	O-42	173
5-Car 70' ABS - Ribbed	Lehigh Valley	20-6527	O-42	173
5-Car 70' ABS - Ribbed	MoPac Katy	20-6528	O-42	173
5-Car 70' ABS - Ribbed	Southern Pacific	20-6529	O-42	173
5-Car 70' ABS - Ribbed	Pennsylvania	20-6530	O-42	173
5-Car 70' ABS - Ribbed	Santa Fe	20-6543	O-42	173
5-Car 70' ABS - Ribbed	Cal Zephyr	20-6545	O-42	174
5-Car 70' ABS - Ribbed	Wabash	20-6546	O-42	174
5-Car 70' ABS - Ribbed	Canadian Pacific	20-6547	O-42	174
5-Car 70' ABS - Ribbed	Amtrak	20-6548	O-42	174
5-Car 70' ABS - Ribbed	Chessie	20-6549	O-42	174
5-Car 70' ABS - Ribbed	Florida East Coast	20-6550	O-42	174
5-Car 70' ABS - Smooth	Kansas City Southern	20-6535	O-42	174
5-Car 70' ABS - Smooth	Electro Motive Division	20-6534	O-42	174
5-Car 70' ABS - Smooth	Pere Marquette	20-6533	O-42	175
5-Car 70' ABS - Smooth	Chicago Northwestern	20-6536	O-42	175
5-Car 70' ABS - Smooth	Union Pacific	20-6538	O-42	175
5-Car 70' ABS - Smooth	Great Northern	20-6551	O-42	175
5-Car 70' ABS - Smooth	Milwaukee Road	20-6552	O-42	175
5-Car 70' ABS - Smooth	Union Pacific	20-6553	O-42	175
5-Car 70' ABS - Smooth	New York Central	20-6554	O-42	175
5-Car 70' ABS - Smooth	Erie	20-6560	O-42	175
5-Car 70' ABS - Smooth	Illinois Central	20-6561	O-42	176
5-Car 70' ABS - Smooth	Pennsylvania	20-6557	O-42	176
5-Car 70' ABS - Smooth Painted	Alaska	20-6518	O-42	176
5-Car 70' ABS - Smooth Painted	New York Central	20-6516	O-42	176
5-Car 70' ABS - Smooth Painted	Southern	20-6517	O-42	176
5-Car 70' ABS - Smooth Painted	Southern Pacific	20-6523	O-42	176
5-Car 70' Aluminum - Painted	Amtrak	20-6508	O-42	177
5-Car 70' Aluminum - Plated	Atlantic Coast Line	20-6501	O-42	176
5-Car 70' Aluminum - Plated	Southern	20-6503	O-42	176
5-Car 70' Aluminum - Plated	New York Central	20-6504	O-42	177
5-Car 70' Aluminum - Plated	California Zephyr	20-6505	O-42	177
5-Car 70' Aluminum - Plated	New York Central	20-6509	O-42	177
5-Car 70' Aluminum - Smooth Painted	Atlantic Coast Line	20-6500	O-42	177
5-Car 70' Aluminum - Smooth Painted	Chesapeake & Ohio	20-6502	O-42	177
5-Car 70' Aluminum - Smooth Painted	Union Pacific	20-6506	O-42	177
5-Car 70' Aluminum - Smooth Painted	Pennsylvania	20-6507	O-42	177
5-Car 70' Aluminum - Smooth Painted	Union Pacific	20-6510	O-42	177
5-Car 70' Aluminum - Smooth Painted	Baltimore & Ohio	20-6511	O-42	177
5-Car 70' Madison	Baltimore & Ohio	20-4001	O-42	183
5-Car 70' Madison	Delaware & Hudson	20-4002	O-42	178
5-Car 70' Madison	Denver & Rio Grande	20-4003	O-42	183
5-Car 70' Madison	Norfolk & Western	20-4004	O-42	183
5-Car 70' Madison	New York Central	20-4005	O-42	183
5-Car 70' Madison	Pennsylvania	20-4006	O-42	178
5-Car 70' Madison	Santa Fe	20-4007	O-42	178
5-Car 70' Madison	Southern	20-4008	O-42	183
5-Car 70' Madison	Texas & Pacific	20-4009	O-42	178
5-Car 70' Madison	Lehigh Valley	20-4010	O-42	178
5-Car 70' Madison	Union Pacific	20-4011	O-42	183
5-Car 70' Madison	Jersey Central	20-4012	O-42	183
5-Car 70' Madison	Chesapeake & Ohio	20-4013	O-42	178
5-Car 70' Madison	Northern Pacific	20-4014	O-42	183
5-Car 70' Madison	Milwaukee Road	20-4015	O-42	178
5-Car 70' Madison	Frisco/Texas Special	20-4016	O-42	178

PREMIER Passenger Sets

PREMIER Specialty Sets

PREMIER Specialty Sets

PREMIER Accessories

PREMIER ScaleTrax

RAILKING Steam

RAILKING Steam Engine

ITEM DESCRIPTION	ROADNAME	ITEM NO.	TURN RAD.	PAGE
2-6-0 Steam Engine	Santa Fe	30-1136-0, 30-1136-1	O-27	201
2-6-0 Steam Engine	Baltimore & Ohio	30-1137-0, 30-1137-1	O-27	202
2-6-0 Steam Engine	Pennsylvania	30-1148-0, 30-1148-1	O-27	202
2-6-0 Steam Engine	Union Pacific	30-1150-0, 30-1150-1	O-27	202
2-6-6-6 Allegheny Steam Engine	Chesapeake & Ohio	30-1116-0, 30-1116-1	O-31	202
2-8-0 Steam Engine	Pennsylvania	30-1159-0, 30-1159-1	O-27	202
2-8-2 L-1 Mikado Steam Engine	Pennsylvania	30-1164-1, 30-1164-0	O-31	203
2-8-4 Berkshire Steam Engine	Nickel Plate Road	30-1109-0	O-31	203
2-8-4 Berkshire Steam Engine	Erie	30-1110-0	O-31	203
2-8-4 Berkshire Steam Engine	Chesapeake & Ohio	30-1128-0, 30-1128-1	O-31	203
2-8-8-2 USRA Steam Engine	Pennsylvania	30-1156-0, 30-1156-1	O-31	203
2-8-8-2 USRA Steam Engine	Northern Pacific	30-1157-0, 30-1157-1	O-31	204
2-8-8-2 Y6b Steam Engine	Norfolk & Western	30-1163-1, 30-1163-0	O-31	204
4-4-0 General Steam Engine	W.A.R.R.	30-1120-0, 30-1120-1	O-27	204
4-4-0 General Steam Engine	W.A.R.R.	30-1135-0, 30-1135-1	O-27	204
4-4-0 General Steam Engine	Wild Wild West - Wanderer	30-1155-0, 30-1155-1	O-27	204
4-6-0 Camelback Steam Engine	Reading	30-1142-0, 30-1142-1	O-27	205
4-6-0 Camelback Steam Engine	Jersey Central	30-1141-0, 30-1141-1	O-27	205
4-6-0 Steam Engine	Denver Rio Grande	30-1153-0, 30-1153-1	O-27	205
4-6-0 Steam Engine	Chesapeake & Ohio	30-1154-0, 30-1154-1	O-27	205
4-6-0 Steam Engine	New York Central	30-1158-0, 30-1158-1	O-27	205
4-6-0 Ten Wheeler Steam Engine	Denver Rio Grande	30-1160-0, 30-1160-1	O-27	206
4-6-2 Crusader Steam Engine	Reading	30-1152-0, 30-1152-1	O-31	206
4-6-2 Forty-Niner Steam Engine	Union Pacific	30-1139-0, 30-1139-1	O-27	206
4-6-2 K-4s Pacific Steam Engine	Pennsylvania	30-1115-0, 30-1115-1	O-27	206
4-6-2 K-4s Pacific Steam Engine	Pennsylvania	30-1138-0, 30-1138-1 30-1162-1, 30-1162-0	O-27	206
4-6-2 Pacific Steam Engine	Denver & Rio Grande	30-1122-1	O-27	207
4-6-2 PS-4 Steam Engine	Southern	30-1125-0, 30-1125-1	O-27	207
4-6-2 Torpedo Steam Engine	Pennsylvania	30-1118-0, 30-1118-1	O-31	207
4-6-4 Commodore Hudson Steam Engine	New York Central	30-1133-0, 30-1133-1	O-27	207
4-6-4 Dreyfuss Steam Engine	New York Central	30-1113-0, 30-1113-1	O-27	207
4-6-4 Empire State Express Steam Engine	New York Central	30-1143-0, 30-1143-1	O-31	208
4-6-4 Hiawatha Hudson Steamer	Milwaukee Road	30-1127-0, 30-1127-1	O-27	208
4-6-4 Hudson Steam Engine	New York Central	30-1103-0, 30-1121-0 30-1121-1, 30-1146-1	O-31	208
4-6-4 Hudson Steam Engine	Union Pacific	30-1104-0	O-31	208
4-6-4 Streamlined Hudson Steam Engine	Wabash	30-1147-0, 30-1147-1	O-27	208
4-6-4 Streamlined Hudson Steam Engine	Chesapeake & Ohio	30-1161-0, 30-1161-1	O-31	209
4-6-6-4 Challenger Steam Engine	Union Pacific	30-1107-0	O-31	209
4-6-6-4 Challenger Steam Engine	Union Pacific	30-1108-0	O-31	209
4-8-2 L-3 Mohawk Steam Engine	New York Central	30-1101-0, 30-1165-1 30-1165-0	O-31	209
4-8-2 L-3 Mohawk Steam Engine	Santa Fe	30-1102-0	O-31	209
4-8-2 L-3 Mohawk Steam Engine	Texas & Pacific	30-1114-0, 30-1114-1	O-31	210
4-8-2 L-3 Mohawk Steam Engine	New York Ontario & Western	30-1166-1, 30-1166-0	O-31	210
4-8-4 FEF Northern Steam Engine	Union Pacific	30-1151-0, 30-1151-1	O-31	210
4-8-4 GS-4 Northern Steam Engine	Southern Pacific	30-1119-0, 30-1119-1	O-31	210
4-8-4 Gs-4 Northern Steam Engine	Nabisco	30-1131-0	O-31	210
4-8-4 "J" Northern Steam Engine	Norfolk & Western	30-1105-0	O-31	211
4-8-4 "J" Northern Steam Engine	Santa Fe	30-1106-0	O-31	211
4-8-4 Northern Steam Engine	Santa Fe	30-1140-0, 30-1140-1	O-31	211
4-8-8-2 Cab-Forward Steam Engine	Southern Pacific	30-1144-0, 30-1144-1	O-31	211
4-8-8-4 Big Boy Steam Engine	Union Pacific	30-1129-0, 30-1129-1	O-31	211
6-8-6 Baby Turbine Steam Engine	Pennsylvania	30-1167-1, 30-1167-0 20-80002i	O-27	212
6-8-6 S-2 Turbine Steam Engine	Pennsylvania	30-1149-0, 30-1149-1	O-31	212
Auxiliary Fuel Tender	Norfolk & Western	30-1117	O-27	212
Auxiliary Fuel Tender	Southern Pacific	30-1126	O-27	212
Auxiliary Water Tender II	Union Pacific	30-1130	O-27	212

RAILKING Diesel/Electric Engine

ITEM DESCRIPTION	ROADNAME	ITEM NO.	TURN RAD.	PAGE
Alco PA AA Diesel Set	Delaware & Hudson	30-2125-0, 30-2125-1	O-31	215
Alco PA AA Diesel Set	Denver Rio Grande	30-2126-0, 30-2126-1	O-31	215
Alco PA AA Diesel Set	Santa Fe	30-2150-0, 30-2150-1	O-31	215
Alco PA AA Diesel Set	Southern	30-2151-0, 30-2151-1	O-31	215
Alco PA AA Diesel Set	Lehigh Valley	30-2196-1, 30-2196-0	O-31	215
Alco PA AA Diesel Set	Southern Pacific	30-2195-1, 30-2195-0	O-31	216
Alco PA ABA Diesel Set	TCA 1999 Convention	30-2172-1	O-31	216
Alco PA B Unit	Delaware & Hudson	30-2127	O-31	216
Alco PA B Unit	Denver Rio Grande	30-2128	O-31	216
Alco PA B Unit	Santa Fe	30-2150-3	O-31	216
Alco PA B Unit	Southern	30-2151-3	O-31	216

RAILKING Diesel/Electric Engine

ITEM DESCRIPTION	ROADNAME	ITEM NO.	TURN RAD.	PAGE
Alco PA B Unit	Southern Pacific	30-2195-3	O-31	216
Alco PA B Unit	Lehigh Valley	30-2196-3	O-31	216
Brill Semi-Convertible Trolley	Allentown	30-2512-0, 30-2512-1	O-27	217
Dash-8 Diesel Engine	Norfolk Southern	30-2114-0, 30-2114-1	O-27	217
Dash-8 Diesel Engine	Santa Fe	30-2115-0, 30-2115-1	O-27	217
Dash-8 Diesel Engine	Amtrak	30-2003-0	O-27	217
Dash-8 Diesel Engine	Santa Fe	30-2004-0	O-27	217
Dash-8 Diesel Engine	BNSF	30-2129-0, 30-2129-1	O-27	217
Dash-8 Diesel Engine	Conrail	30-2136-0, 30-2136-1	O-27	217
Dash-8 Diesel Engine	Chicago Northwestern	30-2155-0, 30-2155-1	O-27	217
Doodlebug Diesel Engine	Baltimore & Ohio	30-2134-0, 30-2134-1	O-31	217
Doodlebug Diesel Engine	Santa Fe	30-2135-0, 30-2135-1	O-31	217
Doodlebug Diesel Engine	Chicago Northwestern	30-2159-0, 30-2159-1	O-31	218
Doodlebug Diesel Engine	Pennsylvania	30-2158-0, 30-2158-1	O-31	218
Doodlebug Diesel Engine	Boston & Maine	30-2190-1, 30-2190-0	O-31	218
Doodlebug Diesel Engine	Union Pacific	30-2191-1, 30-2191-0	O-31	218
Doodlebug Non-Powered Diesel Engine	Baltimore & Ohio	30-2134-3	O-31	218
Doodlebug Non-Powered Diesel Engine	Santa Fe	30-2135-3	O-31	218
Doodlebug Non-Powered Diesel Engine	Pennsylvania	30-2158-3	O-31	218
Doodlebug Non-Powered Diesel Engine	Chicago NorthWestern	30-2159-3	O-31	218
E-8 AA Diesel Engine Set	New York Central	30-2140-0, 30-2140-1	O-31	218
E-8 AA Diesel Engine Set	Southern Pacific	30-2141-0, 30-2141-1	O-31	219
E-8 AA Diesel Engine Set	Union Pacific	30-2180-0, 30-2180-1	O-31	219
E-8 AA Diesel Engine Set	Seaboard	30-2181-0, 30-2181-1	O-31	219
E-8 AA Diesel Engine Set	Rock Island	30-2187-0, 30-2187-1	O-31	219
E-8 B-Unit Diesel Engine	New York Central	30-2140-3	O-31	219
E-8 B-Unit Diesel Engine	Southern Pacific	30-2141-3	O-31	219
E-8 B-Unit Diesel Engine	Union Pacific	30-2180-3	O-31	220
E-8 B-Unit Diesel Engine	Seaboard	30-2181-3	O-31	220
E-8 B-Unit Diesel Engine	Rock Island	30-2187-3	O-31	220
EP-5 Electric Engine	New Haven	30-2170-0, 30-2170-1	O-27	220
EP-5 Electric Engine	Great Northern	30-2171-0, 30-2171-1	O-27	220
F-3 A Unit - Non-Powered	Chessie	30-2119	O-27	220
F-3 A Unit - Non-Powered	Santa Fe	30-2137	O-27	220
F-3 AA Diesel Set	Union Pacific	30-2002-0	O-27	220
F-3 AA Diesel Set	Western Pacific	30-2008-0, 30-2008-1	O-27	221
F-3 AA Diesel Set	New York Central	30-2001-0	O-27	221
F-3 AA Diesel Set	Florida East Coast	30-2007-0, 30-2007-1	O-27	221
F-3 AA Diesel Set	Pennsylvania	30-2130-0, 30-2130-1	O-27	221
F-3 AA Diesel Set	Santa Fe	30-2131-0, 30-2131-1	O-27	221
F-3 AA Diesel Set	Electro Motive Division	30-2142-0, 30-2142-1	O-27	222
F-3 AA Diesel Set	Baltimore & Ohio	30-2143-0, 30-2143-1	O-27	222
F-3 AA Diesel Set	Denver Rio Grande	30-2184-0, 30-2184-1	O-27	222
F-3 AA Diesel Set	Chesapeake & Ohio	30-2185-0, 30-2185-1	O-27	222
F-3 B Unit	New York Central	30-2010-3	O-27	222
F-3 B Unit	Union Pacific	30-2011-3	O-27	222
F-3 B Unit	Florida East Coast	30-2012-3	O-27	223
F-3 B Unit	Western Pacific	30-2013-3	O-27	223
F-3 B Unit	Pennsylvania	30-2132	O-27	223
F-3 B Unit	Santa Fe	30-2133	O-27	223
F-3 B Unit	Electro Motive Division	30-2142-3	O-27	223
F-3 B Unit	Baltimore & Ohio	30-2143-3	O-27	223
F-3 B Unit	Denver Rio Grande	30-2184-3	O-27	223
F-3 B Unit	Chesapeake & Ohio	30-2185-3	O-27	223
F40PH Diesel Engine	CalTrain	30-2199-1, 30-2199-0	O-27	223
FA-2 AA Diesel Set	Pennsylvania	30-2173-0, 30-2173-1	O-27	224
FA-2 AA Diesel Set	Baltimore & Ohio	30-2174-0, 30-2174-1	O-27	224
FA-2 B Unit	Pennsylvania	30-2173-3	O-27	224
FA-2 B Unit	Baltimore & Ohio	30-2174-3	O-27	224
Galloping Goose Diesel	Denver Rio Grande	30-2154-0, 30-2154-1	O-27	224
Galloping Goose Diesel	Denver Rio Grande	30-2203-1	O-27	224
Gas Turbine Engine	Union Pacific	30-2009-0, 30-2009-1	O-27	225
Genesis Diesel	Amtrak	30-2160-0, 30-2160-1	O-27	225
GG-1 Electric Engine	Pennsylvania	30-5100-0	O-27	225
GG-1 Electric Engine	Pennsylvania	30-2501-0, 30-2507-0 30-5101-0	O-27	225
GG-1 Electric Engine	Pennsylvania	30-5102-0	O-27	225
GG-1 Electric Engine	Pennsylvania	30-5103-0	O-27	225
GG-1 Electric Engine	Pennsylvania	30-5104-0	O-27	225
GG-1 Electric Engine	Pennsylvania	30-2500-0, 30-2506-0 30-5105-0	O-27	225
GG-1 Electric Engine	Amtrak	30-2502-0	O-27	225
GG-1 Electric Engine	Pennsylvania	30-2514-0	O-27	226
GG-1 Electric Engine	Pennsylvania	30-2515-1, 30-2515-	O-27	226

RAILKING DIESEL/ELECTRIC ENGINE

RAILKING ROLLING STOCK

RAILKING ROLLING STOCK

RAILKING ROLLING STOCK

ITEM DESCRIPTION	ROADNAME	ITEM NO.	TURN RAD.	PAGE
Die-Cast Box Car	Pennsylvania	30-8401	O-27	240
Die-Cast Box Car	Western Pacific	30-8402	O-27	240
Die-Cast Dep. Center Flat Car	Santa Fe	30-8301	O-31	240
Die-Cast Dep. Center Flat Car	Illinois Central	30-8302	O-31	240
Die-Cast Flat Car	Milwaukee Road	30-8303	O-27	240
Die-Cast Flat Car	Chesapeake & Ohio	30-8304	O-27	240
Die-Cast Gondola Car	Union Pacific	30-8201	O-27	240
Die-Cast Gondola Car	Boston & Maine	30-8202	O-27	240
Die-Cast Hopper Car	Baltimore & Ohio	30-8001	O-27	240
Die-Cast Hopper Car	Lehigh Valley	30-8002	O-27	240
Die-Cast Reefer Car	Erie Lackawanna	30-8601	O-27	240
Die-Cast Reefer Car	Santa Fe	30-8602	O-27	241
Die-Cast Searchlight Car	Northern Pacific	30-8306	O-31	241
Die-Cast Searchlight Car	New York Central	30-8305	O-31	241
Die-Cast Stock Car	Chesapeake & Ohio	30-8701	O-27	241
Die-Cast Stock Car	Union Pacific	30-8702	O-27	241
Die-Cast Tank Car	Shell	30-8101	O-27	241
Die-Cast Tank Car	Denver Rio Grande	30-8102	O-27	241
Die-Cast Woodsided Caboose	New York Central	30-8501	O-27	241
Die-Cast Woodsided Caboose	Chesapeake & Ohio	30-8502	O-27	241
Dump Car w/Operating Bay	Northern Pacific	30-7924	O-27	241
Dump Car w/Operating Bay	CSX	30-7925	O-27	241
Dump Car w/Operating Bay	Conrail	30-7934	O-27	241
Dump Car w/Operating Bay	New York Central	30-7941	O-27	242
Flat Car	Pennsylvania	30-7600	O-27	242
Flat Car	New York Central	30-7601	O-27	242
Flat Car	Union Pacific	30-7602	O-27	242
Flat Car	Santa Fe	30-7603	O-27	258
Flat Car	Trailer Train	30-7604	O-27	242
Flat Car	Nickel Plate Road	30-7605	O-27	242
Flat Car	MTH Construction Co.	30-7606	O-27	242
Flat Car	MTH Classic Auto Transport	30-7607	O-27	242
Flat Car	New York Central	30-7608	O-27	242
Flat Car	Norfolk Southern	30-7609	O-27	242
Flat Car	MTH Classic Auto Transport	30-7610	O-27	242
Flat Car	MTH Classic Auto Transport	30-7613	O-27	242
Flat Car	MTH Construction Co.	30-7614	O-27	243
Flat Car	MTH Classic Auto Transport	30-7617	O-27	243
Flat Car	MTH Service Center	30-7615	O-27	243
Flat Car	MTH Construction Co.	30-7619	O-27	243
Flat Car	MTH Construction Co.	30-7616	O-27	243
Flat Car	MTH Transportation Co.	30-7621	O-27	243
Flat Car	MTH Classic Auto Transport	30-7623	O-27	243
Flat Car	MTH Classic Auto Transport	30-7624	O-27	243
Flat Car	MTH Classic Auto Transport	30-7625	O-27	243
Flat Car	Pennsylvania	30-7626	O-27	243
Flat Car	Florida East Coast	30-7627	O-27	243
Flat Car	MTH Construction Co.	30-7620	O-27	243
Flat Car	MTH Transportation Company	30-7629	O-27	244
Flat Car	Union Pacific	30-7632	O-27	244
Flat Car	MTH Classic Auto Transport	30-7634	O-27	244
Flat Car	Baltimore & Ohio	30-7633	O-27	244
Flat Car	Union 76	30-7640	O-27	244
Flat Car	MTH Transportation Co.	30-7639	O-27	244
Flat Car	MTH Farm Equipment Co.	30-7642	O-27	244
Flat Car	MTH Transportation Co.	30-7647	O-27	244
Flat Car	MTH Classic Auto Transport	30-7660	O-27	244
Flat Car	MTH Classic Auto Transport	30-7661	O-27	244
Flat Car	MTH Classic Auto Transport	30-7662	O-27	244
Flat Car	Santa Fe	30-7664	O-27	244
Flat Car	Pennsylvania	30-7665	O-27	245
Flat Car	MTH Maintenance Of Way	30-7668	O-27	245
Flat Car	MTH Maintenance Of Way	30-7669	O-27	245
Flat Car	MTH Classic Auto Transport	30-7670	O-27	245
Flat Car	MTH Classic Auto Transport	30-7671	O-27	245
Flat Car	MTH Transportation Co.	30-7672	O-27	245
Flat Car - 19th Century	W.A.R.R.	30-7635	O-27	245
Flat Car - w/Bulkheads	Southern Pacific	30-7636	O-27	245
Flat Car - w/Bulkheads	Erie Lackawanna	30-7637	O-27	245
Flat Car w/Operating Helicopter	MTH Transportation Co.	30-7658	O-27	245
Flat Car w/Operating Helicopter	NASA	30-7940	O-27	245
Flat Car w/Operating Helicopter	Red Cross	30-7942	O-27	245
Flat Car w/Operating Logs	Western Maryland	30-7648	O-27	246

RAILKING ROLLING STOCK

ITEM DESCRIPTION	ROADNAME	ITEM NO.	TURN RAD.	PAGE
Flat Car w/Operating Logs	Northern Pacific	30-7649	O-27	246
Gondola Car	Pennsylvania	30-7200	O-27	246
Gondola Car	New York Central	30-7201	O-27	258
Gondola Car	Union Pacific	30-7202	O-27	258
Gondola Car	Santa Fe	30-7203	O-27	258
Gondola Car	Milwaukee Road	30-7204	O-27	246
Gondola Car	Chicago Northwestern	30-7205	O-27	246
Gondola Car	Norfolk & Western	30-7206	O-27	246
Gondola Car	Conrail	30-7207	O-27	246
Gondola Car	Union Pacific	30-7208	O-27	246
Gondola Car	Pennsylvania	30-7209	O-27	246
Gondola Car	CSX	30-7211	O-27	246
Gondola Car	Northern Pacific	30-7210	O-27	246
Gondola Car	Pennsylvania	30-7212	O-27	246
Gondola Car	Baltimore & Ohio	30-7213	O-27	247
Gondola Car	Chesapeake & Ohio	30-7214	O-27	247
Gondola Car	Nickel Plate Road	30-7215	O-27	247
Gondola Car - 19th Century	W.A.R.R.	30-7216	O-27	247
Hopper Car	Pennsylvania	30-7500	O-27	247
Hopper Car	New York Central	30-7501	O-27	247
Hopper Car	Union Pacific	30-7502	O-27	247
Hopper Car	Santa Fe	30-7503	O-27	247
Hopper Car	C B & Q	30-7504	O-27	247
Hopper Car	Nickel Plate Road	30-7505	O-27	247
Hopper Car	Norfolk & Western	30-7506	O-27	247
Hopper Car	Chesapeake & Ohio	30-7507	O-27	247
Hopper Car	Pennsylvania	30-7508	O-27	248
Hopper Car	Union Pacific	30-7509	O-27	248
Hopper Car	Norfolk & Southern	30-7510	O-27	248
Hopper Car	Chicago Northwestern	30-7511	O-27	248
Hopper Car	Chessie	30-7514	O-27	248
Hopper Car	Northern Pacific	30-7512	O-27	248
Hopper Car	New York Central	30-7513	O-27	248
Hopper Car	Norfolk & Western	30-7515	O-27	248
Hopper Car	Western Maryland	30-7516	O-27	248
Hopper Car	New York Central	30-7517	O-27	248
Hopper Car	Erie Lackawanna	30-7523	O-27	248
Hopper Car	Southern	30-7524	O-27	248
Husky Stack Car	Hanjin	30-7643	O-27	249
Husky Stack Car	Santa Fe	30-7644	O-27	249
Modern Tank Car	New York Central	30-7322	O-27	249
Modern Tank Car	Santa Fe	30-7323	O-27	249
N5c Caboose	Pennsylvania	30-7730	O-27	249
Operating Hand Car	Black	30-2508	O-27	249
Operating Hand Car	Tuscan	30-2509	O-27	249
Operating Hand Car	Santa	30-2511	O-27	249
Operating Hand Car	Yellow	30-2520	O-27	249
Ore Car	Baltimore & Ohio	30-7518	O-27	249
Ore Car	Chicago Northwestern	30-7519	O-27	249
Ore Car	Pennsylvania	30-7522	O-27	249
Ore Car	Union Pacific	30-7527	O-27	250
Ore Car	Great Northern	30-7529	O-27	250
Ore Car	Jersey Central	30-7528	O-27	250
Ps-2 Discharge Hopper Car	Conrail	30-7534	O-27	250
Ps-2 Discharge Hopper Car	Pennsylvania	30-7537	O-27	250
Reefer Car	Pennsylvania	30-7800	O-27	250
Reefer Car	New York Central	30-7801	O-27	250
Reefer Car	Union Pacific	30-7802	O-27	250
Reefer Car with Proto-Freight	Union Pacific	50-7912	O-27	250
Reefer Car	Santa Fe	30-7803	O-27	250
Reefer Car with Proto-Freight	Santa Fe	50-7913	O-27	250
Reefer Car	Railway Express	30-7804	O-27	250
Reefer Car with Proto-Freight	Railway Express	50-7914	O-27	250
Reefer Car	Burlington	30-7806	O-27	250
Reefer Car	Union Pacific	30-7807	O-27	250
Reefer Car	Santa Fe	30-7808	O-27	251
Reefer Car	Pennsylvania	30-7809	O-27	251
Reefer Car	Railway Express Agency	30-7810	O-27	251
Reefer Car	Amtrak	30-7811	O-27	251
Reefer Car	Florida East Coast	30-7812	O-27	251
Reefer Car	Union Pacific	30-7813	O-27	251
Reefer Car	Santa Fe	30-7814	O-27	251
Reefer Car	Needham Packing	30-7815	O-27	251

RAILKING Rolling Stock

RAILKING Rolling Stock

RAILKING Passenger Sets

RAILKING Passenger Sets

ITEM DESCRIPTION	ROADNAME	ITEM NO.	TURN RAD.	PAGE
4-Car 60' Streamlined ABS - Smooth Sided	Rock Island	30-6708	O-31	270
4-Car 60' Streamlined ABS - Smooth Sided	Pennsylvania	30-6715	O-31	270
4-Car 60' Streamlined ABS - Smooth Sided	Southern Pacific	30-6724	O-31	270
4-Car 60' Streamlined ABS - Smooth Sided	Lehigh Valley	30-6711	O-31	270
4-Car O-27 Madison	Denver Rio Grande	30-6230	O-27	270
4-Car O-27 Madison	Southern	30-6240	O-27	270
4-Car O-27 Madison	Chesapeake & Ohio	30-6248	O-27	270
4-Car O-27 Madison	Nickel Plate	30-6244	O-27	270
4-Car O-27 Madison	Union Pacific	30-6252	O-27	271
4-Car O-27 Madison	New York Central	30-6256	O-27	271
4-Car O-27 Madison	Pennsylvania	30-6250	O-27	271
4-Car O-27 Madison	Jersey Central	30-6258	O-27	271
4-Car O-27 Madison	Reading	30-6260	O-27	271
4-Car O-27 Madison	Wabash	30-6262	O-27	271
4-Car O-27 Madison	New York Central	30-6264	O-27	271
4-Car O-27 Madison	Baltimore & Ohio	30-6265	O-27	271
4-Car O-27 Madison	Pennsylvania	30-6236	O-27	272
4-Car O-27 Streamlined	Southern Pacific	30-6060	O-27	272
4-Car O-27 Streamlined	Pennsylvania	30-6070	O-27	272
4-Car O-27 Streamlined	New York Central	30-6080	O-27	272
4-Car O-27 Streamlined	Santa Fe	30-6103	O-27	281
4-Car O-27 Streamlined	Pennsylvania	30-6104	O-27	272
4-Car O-27 Streamlined	Union Pacific	30-6107	O-27	272
4-Car O-27 Streamlined	Southern Pacific	30-6109	O-27	272
4-Car O-27 Streamlined	New York Central	30-6110	O-27	272
4-Car O-27 Streamlined	Baltimore & Ohio	30-6111	O-27	273
4-Car O-27 Streamlined	EMD Demonstrator	30-6112	O-27	273
4-Car O-27 Streamlined	New York Central	30-6113	O-27	273
4-Car O-27 Streamlined	Southern	30-6123	O-27	273
4-Car O-27 Streamlined	Santa Fe	30-6120	O-27	273
4-Car O-27 Streamlined	New Haven	30-6131	O-27	273
4-Car O-27 Streamlined	Reading	30-6133	O-27	273
4-Car O-27 Streamlined	Denver Rio Grande	30-6139	O-27	273
4-Car O-27 Streamlined	Chesapeake & Ohio	30-6141	O-27	274
4-Car O-27 Streamlined	Delaware & Hudson	30-6098	O-27	274
4-Car O-27 Streamlined	Denver Rio Grande	30-6094	O-27	274
4-Car O-27 Streamlined	Milwaukee Road	30-6090	O-27	274
4-Car O-27 Streamlined	New York Central	30-6135	O-27	274
4-Car O-27 SuperLiner Set	Amtrak	30-6500	O-31	274
4-Car Overton Passenger Coach Set	Texas	30-6404	O-27	274
60' Streamlined ABS Coach Car	Union Pacific	30-6702	O-31	275
60' Streamlined ABS Coach Car	Seaboard	30-6704	O-31	275
60' Streamlined ABS Coach Car	Santa Fe	30-6706	O-31	275
60' Streamlined ABS Coach Car	Rock Island	30-6709	O-31	275
60' Streamlined ABS Coach Car	Pennsylvania	30-6716	O-31	275
60' Streamlined ABS Coach Car	Southern Pacific	30-6727	O-31	275
60' Streamlined ABS Coach Car	Lehigh Valley	30-6712	O-31	275
60' Streamlined ABS Full-Length Vista Dome	Union Pacific	30-6723	O-31	275
60' Streamlined ABS Full-Length Vista Dome	Seaboard	30-6721	O-31	275
60' Streamlined ABS Full-Length Vista Dome	Santa Fe	30-6728	O-31	275
60' Streamlined ABS Full-Length Vista Dome	Rock Island	30-6729	O-31	275
O-27 Madison Baggage Car	Pennsylvania	30-6200	O-27	275
O-27 Madison Baggage Car	New York Central	30-6210	O-27	276
O-27 Madison Baggage Car	Texas & Pacific	30-6220	O-27	276
O-27 Madison Coach Car	Pennsylvania	30-6201	O-27	276
O-27 Madison Coach Car	Pennsylvania	30-6202	O-27	276
O-27 Madison Coach Car	New York Central	30-6211	O-27	276
O-27 Madison Coach Car	New York Central	30-6212	O-27	276
O-27 Madison Coach Car	Texas & Pacific	30-6221	O-27	276
O-27 Madison Coach Car	Texas & Pacific	30-6222	O-27	276
O-27 Madison Coach Car	Denver Rio Grande	30-6231	O-27	276
O-27 Madison Coach Car	Baltimore & Ohio	30-6266	O-27	276
O-27 Madison Coach Car	Pennsylvania	30-6237	O-27	276
O-27 Madison Observation Car	Pennsylvania	30-6203	O-27	276
O-27 Madison Observation Car	New York Central	30-6213	O-27	277
O-27 Madison Observation Car	Texas & Pacific	30-6223	O-27	277
O-27 Streamlined Baggage Car	Amtrak	30-6000	O-27	277
O-27 Streamlined Baggage Car	Santa Fe	30-6010	O-27	277
O-27 Streamlined Baggage Car	New York Central	30-6020	O-27	277
O-27 Streamlined Baggage Car	Union Pacific	30-6030	O-27	277
O-27 Streamlined Baggage Car	Florida East Coast	30-6040	O-27	277
O-27 Streamlined Baggage Car	California Zephyr	30-6050	O-27	277
O-27 Streamlined Coach Car	Amtrak	30-6001	O-27	277

RAILKING Passenger Sets

ITEM DESCRIPTION	ROADNAME	ITEM NO.	TURN RAD.	PAGE
O-27 Streamlined Coach Car	Santa Fe	30-6011	O-27	277
O-27 Streamlined Coach Car	New York Central	30-6021	O-27	277
O-27 Streamlined Coach Car	Union Pacific	30-6031	O-27	277
O-27 Streamlined Coach Car	Florida East Coast	30-6041	O-27	278
O-27 Streamlined Coach Car	California Zephyr	30-6051	O-27	278
O-27 Streamlined Coach Car	Southern Pacific	30-6061	O-27	281
O-27 Streamlined Coach Car	Pennsylvania	30-6071	O-27	281
O-27 Streamlined Coach Car	New York Central	30-6081	O-27	278
O-27 Streamlined Coach Car	Santa Fe	30-6102	O-27	278
O-27 Streamlined Coach Car	Southern Pacific	30-6114	O-27	278
O-27 Streamlined Coach Car	New York Central	30-6115	O-27	278
O-27 Streamlined Coach Car	New York Central	30-6119	O-27	278
O-27 Streamlined Coach Car	Baltimore & Ohio	30-6116	O-27	278
O-27 Streamlined Coach Car	Electro Motive Division	30-6117	O-27	278
O-27 Streamlined Coach Car	Southern	30-6124	O-27	278
O-27 Streamlined Coach Car	New Haven	30-6132	O-27	278
O-27 Streamlined Coach Car	Reading	30-6134	O-27	278
O-27 Streamlined Coach Car	Denver Rio Grande	30-6140	O-27	279
O-27 Streamlined Coach Car	Chesapeake & Ohio	30-6142	O-27	279
O-27 Streamlined Full-Length Vista Dome Car	Southern Pacific	30-6065	O-27	279
O-27 Streamlined Full-Length Vista Dome Car	Milwaukee Road	30-6092	O-27	279
O-27 Streamlined Full-Length Vista Dome Car	Santa Fe	30-6145	O-27	279
O-27 Streamlined Full-Length Vista Dome Car	Electro Motive Division	30-6143	O-27	279
O-27 Streamlined Full-Length Vista Dome Car	New Haven	30-6144	O-27	279
O-27 Streamlined Full-Length Vista Dome Car	Denver Rio Grande	30-6151	O-27	279
O-27 Streamlined Full-Length Vista Dome Car	Chesapeake & Ohio	30-6149	O-27	279
O-27 Streamlined Observation Car	Amtrak	30-6003	O-27	279
O-27 Streamlined Observation Car	Santa Fe	30-6013	O-27	279
O-27 Streamlined Observation Car	New York Central	30-6023	O-27	279
O-27 Streamlined Observation Car	Union Pacific	30-6033	O-27	280
O-27 Streamlined Observation Car	Florida East Coast	30-6043	O-27	280
O-27 Streamlined Observation Car	California Zephyr	30-6053	O-27	280
O-27 Streamlined Observation Car	Reading	30-6136	O-27	280
O-27 Streamlined Vista Dome Car	Amtrak	30-6002	O-27	280
O-27 Streamlined Vista Dome Car	Santa Fe	30-6012	O-27	280
O-27 Streamlined Vista Dome Car	New York Central	30-6022	O-27	280
O-27 Streamlined Vista Dome Car	Union Pacific	30-6032	O-27	280
O-27 Streamlined Vista Dome Car	Florida East Coast	30-6042	O-27	280
O-27 Streamlined Vista Dome Car	California Zephyr	30-6052	O-27	280
O-27 Streamlined Vista Dome Car	Southern Pacific	30-6062	O-27	281
O-27 Streamlined Vista Dome Car	Pennsylvania	30-6072	O-27	281
O-27 Streamlined Vista Dome Car	New York Central	30-6082	O-27	280
O-27 Streamlined Vista Dome Car	Southern Pacific	30-6118	O-27	280
O-27 Streamlined Vista Dome Car	Santa Fe	30-6121	O-27	281
SuperLiner Transitional Sleeper Car	Amtrak	30-6503	O-31	281

RAILKING Ready-to-Run / Specialty Sets

ITEM DESCRIPTION	ROADNAME	ITEM NO.	TURN RAD.	PAGE
0-4-0 R-T-R Train Set	Baltimore & Ohio	30-4026-0		286
0-4-0 R-T-R Train Set	Jersey Central	30-4035-0		286
0-8-0 Steam Engine Coal Train Set	Norfolk & Western	30-Set-026		292
0-8-0 Steam Engine Freight Set	Chicago Northwestern	30-Set-027		292
2-6-0 R-T-R Train Set	Baltimore & Ohio	30-4020-0, 30-4020-1		287
2-6-0 R-T-R Train Set	Santa Fe	30-4017-0, 30-4017-1		287
2-8-0 R-T-R Train Set	Pennsylvania	30-4023-0, 30-4023-1		287
2-8-0 R-T-R Train Set	Christmas 2000	30-4033-1, 30-4033-0		287
4-6-2 Pacific Passenger Train Set	Denver Rio Grande	30-1035		287
4-6-4 Hudson R-T-R Train Set	New York Central	30-1025-0		287
4-8-4 GS-4 Steam Passenger R-T-R Train Set	Southern Pacific	30-4039-1, 30-4039-0		288
4-8-4 J Steam Passenger R-T-R Train Set	Norfolk & Western	30-4036-1, 30-4036-0		288
4-Bay Hopper 6 Car Set	Union Pacific	30-7521		283
4-Bay Hopper 6 Car Set	Chesapeake & Ohio	30-7520		283
4-Bay Hopper 6 Car Set	Pennsylvania	30-7530		283
4-Bay Hopper 6 Car Set	Northern Pacific	30-7531		283
4-Bay Hopper 6 Car Set	Norfolk & Western	30-7535		283
4-Bay Hopper 6 Car Set	Norfolk & Western	30-7536		283
4-Car Modern Subway Set	Chicago Transit	30-2175-0, 30-2175-1		290
4-Car Subway Set	New York Transit	30-2122-0, 30-2122-1		291
4-Car Subway Set	New York Transit	30-4062-0, 30-4062-1		291
R21 4-Car Subway Set	New York Transit	30-2198-1, 30-2198-0	O-27	291
6-8-6 Turbine Steam Passenger R-T-R Train Set	Pennsylvania	30-4038-1, 30-4038-0		288
6-8-6 Turbine Steam R-T-R Train Set	Pennsylvania	30-4037-1, 30-4037-0		288

RAILKING Ready-to-Run / Specialty Sets

ITEM DESCRIPTION	ROADNAME	ITEM NO.	PAGE
6-Car Freight Set	Jersey Central	30-7003	283
6-Car Freight Set	Wabash	30-7001	284
6-Car Freight Set	Southern	30-7002	284
6-Car Freight Set	Union Pacific	30-7005	284
6-Car Freight Set	Great Northern	30-7006	284
6-Car Freight Set	Pennsylvania	30-7007	284
6-Car Freight Set	Louisville & Nashville	30-7008	284
6-Car Freight Set	CP Rail	30-7009	285
6-Car Freight Set	Baltimore & Ohio	30-7010	285
6-Car Freight Set	Conrail	30-7011	285
6-Car Freight Set	Pennsylvania	30-7016	285
6-Car Freight Set	Reading	30-7017	285
6-Car Freight Set	New Haven	30-7013	285
6-Car Freight Set	Electro Motive Division	30-7012,	286
6-Car Freight Set	Virginian	30-7018	286
6-Car Freight Set	New York Ontario & Western	30-7015	286
6-Car Freight Set	New York Central	30-7014	286
Berkshire Freight Set	Nickel Plate Road	30-Set-024	293
Berkshire Freight Set	Erie	30-Set-025	291
Dash-8 Diesel Passenger Train Set	Amtrak	30-2164-1	291
Diesel R-T-R Construction Train Set	Chessie	30-1016-0, 30-1016-1	288
Diesel R-T-R Work Train Set	Conrail	30-4019-0, 30-4019-1	288
Diesel R-T-R Work Train Set	Amtrak	30-4024-0, 30-4024-1	289
F-3 Freight Set	New York Central	30-Set-019	293
F-3 Freight Set	Union Pacific	30-Set-020	291
F-3 R-T-R Passenger Train Set	Santa Fe	30-4021-0, 30-4021-1 30-4043-1, 30-4043-0	289
F40PH R-T-R Passenger Train Set	Amtrak	30-4025-0, 30-4025-1	289
F40PH R-T-R Train Set	CSX	30-4034-1, 30-4034-0	289
F40PH R-T-R Train Set	McDonalds	30-4042-1, 30-4042-0	289
FM Trainmaster Freight Set	Santa Fe	30-Set-021	292
Genesis R-T-R Train Set	Amtrak	30-4018-0, 30-4018-1	289
GG-1 Freight Set	Pennsylvania	30-Set-022	292
GG-1 Freight Set	Pennsylvania	30-Set-023	292
Hudson Freight Set	New York Central	30-Set-017	292
Hudson Freight Set	Union Pacific	30-Set-018	292
Operating Hand Car Train Set	Tuscan	30-4044-0	290
Operating Hand Car Train Set	Santa	30-4045-0	290
Pioneer Zephyr Diesel Passenger Set	Burlington	30-2186-0, 30-2186-1	292
SD-60 Freight Set	Chicago Northwestern	30-Set-029	293
SD-60 Freight Set	Conrail	30-Set-028	293
Sears R-T-R O Gauge Toy Train Set	Pennsylvania	30-4031-0	290
Sears R-T-R O Gauge Toy Train Set	New York Central	30-4022-0.	290
Trolley R-T-R Train Set	Baltimore & Ohio	30-4027-0	290
Trolley R-T-R Train Set	Christmas	30-4027-0	290
Trolley R-T-R Train Set	Christmas	30-4040-0	290
Trolley R-T-R Train Set	New York Transit	30-4041-0	290
Unit Train R-T-R Diesel Train Set	Norfolk Southern	30-1015	293

RAILKING Traditional Accessories

ITEM DESCRIPTION	ROADNAME	ITEM NO.	PAGE
#151 Operating Semaphore	Black / Silver	30-1035A	295
#151 Operating Semaphore	Green Base	30-1075	295
#152 Operating Crossing Gate	Red/Aluminum	30-11008	295
#153 Operating Block Signal	Green / Silver	30-1034	295
#153 Operating Block Signal	Black / Silver	30-1076	295
#154 Highway Flashing Signal	Black / Silver	30-1074	295
#193 Industrial Water Tower	Black / Red & White	30-9029	295
#262 Crossing Gate/Signal	Black	30-1073	295
#334 Dispatch Board	Cream	30-9022	295
#35 Street Lamp Set	Aluminum	30-1059	295
#35 Street Lamp Set	Gray	30-1058	295
#35 Street Lamp Set	Pea Green	30-1099	295
#35 Street Lamp Set	Red	30-11001	296
#395 Floodlight Tower	Yellow / Black	30-9025	296
#455 Oil Derrick	Green / Red Base	30-9027	296
#46 Crossing Gate and Signal	Green / Cream	30-11017	296
#47 Crossing Gate and Signal	Green / Cream	30-1080	296
#54 Street Lamp Set	Maroon	30-1019	296
#54 Street Lamp Set	Green	30-1020	296
#54 Street Lamp Set	State Car Brown	30-1066	296
#54 Street Lamp Set	Cream	30-1096	296
#56 Gas Lamp Set	Green	30-1026	296
#56 Gas Lamp Set	Maroon	30-1027	296
#56 Gas Lamp Set	Copper	30-1069	296
#56 Gas Lamp Set	Black	30-1098	297
#57 Corner Lamp Set	Yellow	30-1028	297
#57 Corner Lamp Set	Orange	30-1029	297
#57 Corner Lamp Set	Gray	30-1068	297
#57 Corner Lamp Set	Cream	30-1097	297
#58 Lamp Set - Single Arc	Pea Green	30-1057	297
#58 Lamp Set - Single Arc	Maroon	30-1090	297
#58 Lamp Set - Single Arc	Dark Green	30-11002	297
#580-1 Teardrop Lamp Set	Green	30-1070	297
#580-1 Teardrop Lamp Set	Silver	30-1078A	297
#580-1 Teardrop Lamp Set	Pea Green	30-1079A	297
#580-2 Teardrop Lamp Set	Green	30-1071	297
#580-2 Teardrop Lamp Set	Pea Green	30-1080A	298
#580-2 Teardrop Lamp Set	Silver	30-1082A	298
#580-2 Teardrop Lamp Set	Maroon	30-1081A	298
#59 Gooseneck Lamp Set	Maroon	30-1030	298
#59 Gooseneck Lamp Set	Green	30-1031	298
#59 Gooseneck Lamp Set	Cream	30-1067	298
#64 Highway Lamp Set	Green	30-1032	298
#64 Highway Lamp Set	Maroon	30-1033	298
#64 Highway Lamp Set	Dark Green	30-1065	298
#64 Highway Lamp Set	Silver	30-1095	298
#64 Highway Lamp Set	Black	30-11003	298
#69 Operating Warning Bell	Red / Silver	30-1036	298
#69 Operating Warning Bell	Maroon	30-1077	299
#70 Yard Lamp Set	Black	30-1060	299
Coaling Tower	Cream / Orange	30-9043	299
Oil Pumping Station	Green / Blue / Gray	30-9028	299
Operating Street Clock	Red	30-1061	299
Operating Street Clock	Teal	30-1072	299
Operating Street Clock	Blue	30-1085	299
Operating Street Clock	Dark Green	30-1094	299
Radar Tower	Gray / Black	30-9032	299
Rotary Beacon	Red / Gray	30-9033	299
314 Girder Bridge	Black	30-12001	299
#450 Signal Bridge	Black / Cream Base	30-9026	299

RAILKING O Scale Accessories

ITEM DESCRIPTION	ROADNAME	ITEM NO.	PAGE
"O" Lamp Set - Hexagonal	Black	30-1062	300
"O" Lamp Set - Round	Black	30-1078	300
"O" Lamp Set - Square	Black	30-1079	300
"O" Operating Crossing Flasher w/Sound	Silver / Black	30-11014	300
O Scale 1 Over 1 Signal	Silver / Black	30-11025	300
O Scale 3 Over 3 Vertical Signal	Silver / Black	30-11024	300
O Scale 3-Position Semaphore	Silver / Black	30-11023	300
O Scale Cantilevered Signal Bridge	Silver / Cream	30-11009	300
O Scale Flashing Barricades	White / Orange	30-11021	300
"O" Scale Modern Operating Crossing Signal	Silver / Black	30-11006	300
"O" Scale Operating Block Signal	Silver / Black	30-11005	300
O Scale Tell Tale	Brown	30-11026	300
O Scale Vertical Signal lamps	Black	30-11009A	301
O Scale Water Column	Black / White	30-11007	301
O-Scale 7 Light Block Signal	Black	30-11013	301
O-Scale Dwarf Signal	Black	30-11011	301
O-Scale Operating Crossing Gate Signal	Silver	30-11012	301
O-Scale Operating Crossing Signal	Black	30-11010	301
Operating Banjo Signal	Black	30-1093	301
Road Sign Set		30-1087	301
Telephone Pole Set		30-1088	301
Traffic Light Set - Double Lamp	Silver	30-1089-2	301
Traffic Light Set - Single Lamp	Silver	30-1089-1	301

RAILKING Miscellaneous Accessories

ITEM DESCRIPTION	ROADNAME	ITEM NO.	PAGE
12-Piece Figure Set #1		30-11016	301
Bag Of Coal		30-50005	302
Coal Load		30-50001	302
Die-Cast Fuel Truck	Sinclair	30-1086, Never Prod.	302
Die-Cast Trailer	Big Mo	30-50004	302

RAILKING Miscellaneous Accessories

ITEM DESCRIPTION	ROADNAME	ITEM NO.	PAGE
Fence Set	White	30-50002	302
Junk Load		30-50003	302
Lighted Lock-on		10-1021	302
O Ga. Track Activation Device (TAD)		10-1037	302
Operating Flag	American	30-9103	302
ProtoSmoke Fluid	7oz Bottle	60-1045	302
RailKing IR Remote Control	Black	50-1011	302
RailKing IR Remote Control System		50-1012	302
RailKing Remote Lock-On	Gray	50-1013	303
Z-500 Transformer		40-500	303
Z-750 Transformer		40-750	303

RAILKING Railtown Buildings

ITEM DESCRIPTION	ROADNAME	ITEM NO.	PAGE
#4 Country House	Grey/Yellow/Grey	30-9001	303
#4 Country House	Blue	30-9008	303
#4 Country House	Yellow / White / Brown	30-9016	303
4-Story Building	Red / Gray / White	30-9013	303
#5 Country Church	White/Grey/Grey	30-9002	303
#6 Farm House	White/Red/Grey	30-9003	303
#6 Farm House	Yellow	30-9007	303
#6 Farm House	Red / White	30-9015	303
Corner Bank	Gray / Brown	30-9017	303
Corner Building	Drug Store	30-9012	304
Engine Shed	Red / Gray	30-9030	304
Hardware Store	Red / Gray / White	30-9018	304
Hi-tension Tower Set	Silver	30-1056	304
Hobby Shop	RailTown Train Shop	30-9004	304
O Scale Water Tower	Yellow / Brown	30-11028	304
O Scale Yard Master Tower	Yellow / Green	30-11027	304
Oil Refinery	Sinclair	Item Not Produced	304
Operating Car Wash	Speedy Car Wash	30-9104	304
Operating Drive-In Diner	Mel's Drive-In	30-9105	304
Operating Firehouse	Red / Gray	30-9102	304
Operating Firehouse	Gray / Brown	30-9112	304
Operating Freight Platform	Gray / Brown	30-9111	305
Operating Gas Station	Sinclair	30-9101	305
Operating Gas Station	Esso	30-9106	305
Operating Gas Station	Union 76	30-9109	305
Operating Gas Station	Citgo	30-9113	305
Operating Transfer Dock	Brick / Gray / Brown	30-9110	305
Original McDonalds Restaurant	McDonald's	30-9034	305
Passenger Station Platform	Gray / Brown	30-9006	305
Passenger Station Platform - Operating	Gray / Brown	30-9107	305
Passenger Station w/dual Platforms	Orange	30-9005	305
Passenger Station w/dual Platforms	Red	30-9014	305
RailKing Hell Gate Bridge	Red & Gray	30-9020	305
RailKing Hell Gate Bridge	Cream & Green	30-9021	306
Row House #1	Yellow / Green	30-9023	306
Row House #2	Gray / Red	30-9024	306
Switch Tower	CSX Gray	30-9011	306
Switch Tower	Pennsylvania	30-9031	306

RAILKING RealTrax

ITEM DESCRIPTION	ROADNAME	ITEM NO.	PAGE
O Bridge Girder	Silver	40-1014	306
O Bridge Girder	Rust	40-1032	306
O Steel Arch Bridge	Silver	40-1013	306
O Steel Arch Bridge	Rust	40-1031	306
RealTrax - 10" Insulated Straight Section Set		40-1029	307
RealTrax - 10" Straight Section		40-1001	307
RealTrax - 3.5" Track Section		40-1018	307
RealTrax - 30" Straight Track Section		40-1019	307
RealTrax - 4-Piece Add-On Catenary System		40-1036	307
RealTrax - 4.25" Track Section		40-1017	307
RealTrax - 45* Crossover Track		40-1007	307
RealTrax - 5.0" Track Section		40-1016	307
RealTrax - 5.5" Track Section		40-1012	307
RealTrax - 8-Piece Catenary System		40-1035	307
RealTrax - 90* Crossover		40-1006	307
RealTrax - Adapter Track Section		40-1011	307
RealTrax - Figure 8 Layout Builder		40-1025	307

RAILKING RealTrax

ITEM DESCRIPTION	ROADNAME	ITEM NO.	TURN RAD.	PAGE
RealTrax - O-31 Half Curve		40-1022		307
RealTrax - O-31 Switch (L)		40-1005		307
RealTrax - O-31 Switch (R)		40-1004		307
RealTrax - O-42 Curved Section		40-1042		307
RealTrax - O-42 Switch (L)		40-1044		307
RealTrax - O-42 Switch (R)		40-1043		307
RealTrax - O-54 Curved Track Section		40-1054		307
RealTrax - O-54 Half Curve Track		40-1057-2		307
RealTrax - O-54 Switch (L)		40-1056		307
RealTrax - O-54 Switch (R)		40-1055		307
RealTrax- O-72 Curved Section		40-1010		307
RealTrax - O-72 Switch (L)		40-1021		307
RealTrax - O-72 Switch (R)		40-1020		307
RealTrax - Right Hand Track Siding Layout Builder		40-1027		307
RealTrax - Track Activation Device (I.T.A.D.)		40-1028		307
RealTrax Track Layout Software		60-1322		307
RealTrax - Uncoupling Section		40-1008		307
RealTrax Wire Harness		40-1015		307
Tunnel Portal - Double		40-9015		307
Tunnel Porthole - Single		40-9014		307

RAILKING Uncatalogued Items

ITEM DESCRIPTION	ROADNAME	ITEM NO.	TURN RAD.	PAGE
Show Case Mr. Atomic		10-1011		315
Alco PA ABA Diesel Set	TCA 1999 Convention	30-2172-1	O-31	312
F-3 AA Diesel Set	Canadian Pacific	20-80001b1	O-31	311
F-3 ABA Diesel Set	Santa Fe - Clear Body	20-80002a	O-31	311
F-3 B Unit	Canadian Pacific	20-80002b	O-31	311
FM Trainmaster Diesel Engine	Lackawanna	20-80001d	O-31	311
GG-1 Electric Engine	Pennsylvania	20-80002e	O-27	313
GP-30 Diesel Engine	Clear	20-2074-1	O-31	311
GP-9 Diesel Engine	Clear	20-2049-1	O-31	311
PCC Electric Street Car With Proto-Sound	2000 DAP	20-80002h	O-27	313
2-Car 60' Aluminum Coach Passenger Set	Canadian Pacific	20-80002g	O-31	311
4-Car 60' Aluminum Passenger Set	Canadian Pacific	20-80001b2	O-31	312
4-Car 60' Aluminum Passenger Set	Pennsylvania	20-80002f	O-31	313
Sears R-T-R O Gauge Toy Train Set	Pennsylvania	30-4031-0	O-31	313
Sears R-T-R O Gauge Toy Train Set	New York Central	30-4022-0	O-31	313
200 Series Std. Gauge Caboose	Train Collector's Association	10-2001	N/A	315
8000 Gallon Tank Car	G.T.S. - Big Mo	20-96018	O-27	312
Auto Carrier Flat Car	TTOS	30-7659	O-27	313
Box Car	Oreo	30-7415	O-27	313
Box Car	'95 Christmas	30-7415	O-27	314
Box Car	I Love Toy Trains - Limited Edition	30-7499	O-27	314
Box Car	G.T.S. - Big Mo	30-7425	O-27	314
Box Car	1999 D.A.P. Christmas	20-80001e	O-27	314
Box Car	2000 D.A.P. Christmas	20-80002d	O-27	314
Extended Vision Caboose	Union Pacific	20-80001c	O-27	312
Extended Vision Caboose	Santa Fe	20-80002c	O-27	312
4-8-4 Gs-4 Northern Steam Engine	Nabisco	30-1131-0	O-31	314
4-8-8-4 Big Boy Steam Engine	Union Pacific	20-80001a	O-72	312

Printed in Hong Kong